The Shakespeare Promptbooks

University of Illinois Press, Urbana and London, 1965

The Shakespeare Promptbooks

A Descriptive Catalogue

CHARLES H. SHATTUCK

Preface and Acknowledgments

The terminal date of this catalogue of Shakespeare promptbooks is the year 1961. But this is not the real end of it. The Festival Theatres of the three Stratfords, whose books I have accounted for, have already added four seasons, and presumably they will march on to the millennium, accumulating more (and ever more illuminating) records of their productions. A fourth Stratford in New Zealand has been rumored. The newly established National Theatre in England, New York's Shakespeare in the Park, and many another festival theatre yet to be created or to be professionalized, besides independent productions in usual frequency, will swell the records of the future.

Nor is the catalogue final for the theatre of the more remote past. Although I have combed the well-known depositories of theatrical *ana* and canvassed by mail several hundred libraries, museums, and historical societies where older promptbooks *might* be stored, undoubtedly I have missed a good many. Some now in private hands will eventually drift into public collections. Some now buried unrecognized in the general shelves of library stacks, or even taken for junk and scheduled for the dustbin, may become known for what they are and be moved to prouder places.

In order that the record can be brought nearer to completeness, the editors of *Theatre Notebook,* the organ of the Society for Theatre Research, have generously agreed to print supplemental lists from time to time. If the discoverers of new-old material will communicate their findings to me, I shall assemble these lists, with full acknowledgment to the contributors. Here too can be corrected the grosser errors I have committed, as users of the catalogue point them out to me.

This cooperative gesture by the Society for Theatre Research is not my only reason for gratitude to the officers and members of that organization, for they have assisted in many ways to make my project known while it was in process and to direct me toward sources of material in England. The American Society for Theatre Research and Conference 3 (Restoration and Eighteenth-Century Theatre Research) of the Modern Language Association have also afforded me opportunity in their bulletins and at their annual conferences to advertise my needs.

I am grateful to nearly three hundred librarians and curators throughout America, the British Isles, Australia, and New Zealand, who have responded to inquiry about their institutional holdings; but there is room here to speak only of those who, having found material for me, have generously sent along detailed information or made the material accessible. These include John Alden of the Boston Public Library, Phyllis Ball of the University of Arizona, Anne Bolton of the Old Vic Theatre, Clara Mae Brown of the Joint University Libraries

of Nashville, Mrs. Cavanna of the Edwin Forrest Home, Flora Colton
and William Miller of the University of Pennsylvania, Mary Isabel
Fry and the staff of the Henry E. Huntington Library, Freda Gaye of
the British Theatre Museum, Margaret Hackett of the Boston Athenaeum, John Hayes of the Festival Theatre at Stratford, Ontario,
Martin Holmes of the London Museum, James Kingsley of the Uni-
versity of Minnesota, Marion P. Linton of the National Library of
Scotland, Raymond Mander and Joe Mitchenson, June Moll of the
University of Texas, Waveney R. N. Payne and the staff of the Bir-
mingham Shakespeare Memorial Library, Robert Quinsey of the University of Nebraska, May Davenport Seymour of the Museum of the
City of New York, Alan Suddon of the Toronto Public Library, and
Edwin Wolf of the Library Company of Philadelphia. At the Theatre
Collection of the New York Public Library George Freedley and his
staff, at the Enthoven Collection George Nash and his staff, at The
Players Louis Rachow and the late Patrick Carroll have been partic-
ularly hospitable and helpful during my protracted tours of study in
those places. Alma De Jordy, Clarissa Lewis, Isabelle Grant, and Helen
Welch of my own University's Library have been patient with demands
for more books, more film-strips to work with. Mrs. Herbert McAneny
of Princeton has found and described for me several documents not
available during my visits there. Eileen Robinson of the Royal Shakespeare Theatre Library not only provided generous working accom-
modations during a month's visit in 1962 but has reported new ac-
quisitions and answered many queries since then. Helen Willard of
the Harvard Theatre Collection has gone far beyond the call of duty
to put the Harvard books and the whole working apparatus of the
collection at my disposal. To Dorothy Mason of the Folger my indebt-
edness can hardly be reckoned—except to say that she has encouraged
this project from its inception, helped to define the method and from
time to time criticized the results, invented the excellent numbering
system of the great Folger collection of promptbooks, and spent many
weeks of working days putting that collection in its present fine order
so that I could proceed with it.

  Friends and professional fellow workers who have contributed ad-
vice, information, and encouragement include Muriel St. Clare Byrne,
G. B. Harrison, Hubert Heffner, Barnard Hewitt, Philip Highfill,
Lucyle Hook, Laurence Irving, James McManaway, A. M. Nagler,
A. H. Scouten, and J. Wesley Swanson. Paul Cooper of the Pratt Institute and Frederick Hunter of the University of Texas have reported
the facts about two important books that would not otherwise have
been available. David MacArthur of Milwaukee Downer has supplied

the chronology of Winthrop Ames's productions. Sybil Rosenfeld, from her knowledge of eighteenth-century actors and scene painters, has dated and localized several hitherto unidentifiable promptbooks of that era. My colleague G. Blakemore Evans, deeply versed in the mysteries of the oldest promptbooks, has steadily afforded me his counsel and the raw materials of his own research. Alan S. Downer and Arthur Colby Sprague have kept my courage up by friendly assurances that the catalogue would be worth doing, and have given to an early draft of the first fourth of it a severe and most helpful reading. Elizabeth Dulany, assistant editor at the University Press, has prevented innumerable errors and inconsistencies from going into print. Last and above all I am grateful to my wife, whose judgment, skill, and hard labor at note-taking made the gathering of materials possible in the allotted time. To all these helpers my thanks. The mistakes are my own.

The work has been sustained by a Folger Fellowship in the summer of 1961, a sabbatical leave from the University of Illinois and a Guggenheim Fellowship through 1961-62, and several grants for purchase of tools and materials by the Graduate College Research Board of the University of Illinois.

CHARLES H. SHATTUCK
University of Illinois
Urbana, Illinois
June 1, 1964

Contents

Introduction

The purpose of this catalogue of promptbooks is to promote new studies in the history of staged Shakespeare. When this history can be written entire, it will touch upon nearly everything that matters in the English-speaking theatre. For through all the centuries that our theatre has been professionally conscious of itself, the plays of Shakespeare have given the body its spine; and whatever fashions in dramatic form, production method, and social or esthetic intention have come and gone, the plays of Shakespeare have been keyed to those fashions. It does not matter very much, practically, whether the original author of the plays was Francis Bacon or Edward de Vere; it has often mattered greatly that the "effective" authors have been the Nahum Tates and Colley Cibbers and modern film scenarists who actually rewrote the plays, the multitude of Johnsons and Coleridges and Dr. Joneses who have told us what they "mean," and all the Garricks and Guthries whose stage imagery has spread upon the plays the form and pressure of their separate generations.

There is no end to the vitality of "Shakespeare." Like the mythic John Barleycorn of Burns's ballad, he has always given us good whiskey. In every theatrical season "they took a plough and ploughed him down, put clods upon his head," but under the cheerful spring showers he rose again.

> The sultry suns of Summer came
> And he grew thick and strong;
> His head weel arm'd wi' pointed spears,
> That no one should him wrong.

Came the autumn, "they've taen a weapon, long and sharp, and cut him by the knee"; they carted him, beat him, hung him up for the wind to blow through him, drowned him in a pit, macerated him, roasted him, crushed him between stones.

> And they hae taen his very heart's blood
> And drank it round and round;
> And still the more and more they drank,
> Their joy did more abound.

No matter how barbarously Shakespeare-Barleycorn is murdered, he springs to new life, ripens to new sacrifice however peculiar. As cultural historians we are most fortunate in this Shakespearean susceptibility to fluctuant taste, style, and idea; for by the uses and abuses of Shakespeare in the theatre every period of our culture has made itself known and got itself recorded in terms understandable (even if laughable), remembrable (even if contemptible) to the periods that follow. What the theatre did with *The Conquest of Granada*, *Pizarro*, *Richelieu*, or *Death of a Salesman* is interesting to specialists, but we all have a stake in what Betterton, Kemble, Irving, Barrymore, Gielgud did with *Hamlet*. The memory of these master producers or mis-producers is pertinent to our interest in the play that lives on our own stages and hereafter.

The whole history has yet to be written, and probably we need much more spadework, bit-and-piece work, before it *can* be written. Forty-five years ago the late Professor Odell made a brave first go at it in *Shakespeare from Betterton to Irving,* a book to which we are immensely indebted. By now, of course, Odell's work is sorely inadequate. He wrote of the London theatre only, without reference to the theatre of America or of the English provinces. Half a century has passed since the close of his record. His evaluations of the theatre nearest to him—his adulation of Irving and Beerbohm Tree, his distaste for such new men as Barker and Craig—are absurd. Everyone who has got beneath the surface of his older history is aware of errors of fact and queer lapses of judgment which must be corrected. This is not to speak ill of a pioneering hero, but rather to reproach ourselves that forty-five years later we can do little better than be grateful that Odell's book has lately come back into print.

Meanwhile much excellent work has gone into partial studies contributory to the whole history and into the perfecting of tools to work with. One thinks offhand of the many fine histories of special periods—by Alwin Thaler, Ernest Bradlee Watson, James Lynch, George Rowell, Allardyce Nicoll; of such theatrical biographies as Hillebrand's *Kean,* Baker's *Kemble,* Laurence Irving's *Irving;* of Bertram Joseph's *The Tragic Actor.* More immediate to the subject are G. Blakemore Evans' *Shakespearean Prompt-Books,* which are providing us facsimiles of the important marked copies of the plays used in the theatres of the seventeenth century; James McManaway's studies of various prompt-books of the early eighteenth century; George Winchester Stone's many essays on Garrick's handling of Shakespeare and Kalman Burnim's book which treats Garrick as a stage director; Charles Beecher Hogan's *Shakespeare in the Theatre, 1701-1800;* the gigantic redoing of Genest called *The London Stage;* Odell's *Annals of the New York Stage;* the Kemp and Trewin history of the theatre at Stratford-upon-Avon; A. C. Sprague's several studies, including his record of traditional stage business in *Shakespeare and the Actors* and his recent *Shakespeare's Histories;* Marvin Rosenberg's *The Masks of Othello;* Muriel St. Clare Byrne's classic essay on Shakespeare production in the twentieth century and J. C. Trewin's recent book on the same subject. None of these (and the list is as incomplete as it is haphazard) was available when Odell wrote.

In working over the documents of this catalogue I am convinced that we can do with many further contributory studies before we are quite ready to rewrite Odell and discard him. We ought to know a great deal more about what actually happened and what those happenings meant in dozens of significant productions of Shakespeare's plays: the text, the scenery, the dresses, the blocking and movement, the acting, the audience—the ideas that went in and the results that came out—together with a thorough regathering and reinterpreting of the published reports of the critics. For such studies, promptbooks and related primary documents from behind the scenes can bring us countless vivid illuminations which Odell knew nothing about.

The work to be done is not easy. Promptbooks are tricky, secretive, stubborn informants. They chatter and exclaim about what we hardly need to know: that certain characters are being readied by the callboy to make their entrances; that the scene is about to change or the curtain to drop; that the orchestra is about to play at the act-end. They fall blackly silent just when we most hope to be told where the actor stood or how he looked or what he did. Rarely do they give us a hint of voice or temper or histrionic manner. They tell lies, as anybody knows who ever produced a play and failed to write into the book his own last-minute revisions or the happy inspirations that come to the actors midway in a run of performances. I have been taught a lesson in discretion in these matters by one of the finest Shakespeare directors of our time, who assured me that she would rather see her own books burned than be judged in travesty by their misleading contents. Even if the actor's movement is recorded, she protests, the motive for it is not, and the movement without the motive is an absurdity. One can only respect the integrity of the protest, and promise oneself never to conclude anything about the work of the artists, even the unharmable dead ones, without the utmost conscientious and sympathetic effort to perceive the whole truth. A promptbook is indeed a Rosetta stone to the uninitiate, and those of us who are teachers should be wary of loosing upon promptbooks any but our best-trained and most theatre-wise students, except in the way of laboratory exercise. In the measure that we bring knowledge and understanding to these documents, they may give back more knowledge to us. I think no one can read Kalman Burnim's chapter on Garrick's production of *Macbeth* without acquiring valuable insights into that play in that day at Drury Lane Theatre; and one reason is that Mr. Burnim had a promptbook of Garrick's period into which he could organize his knowledge of Garrick's way of working. That particular promptbook is, comparatively speaking, a rather thinly marked one. In later generations, as the actors and prompters learned to keep fuller records, the opportunities abound for replacing vaguely general impressions with vivid, specific ones—sometimes with true ones.

Another kind of lie that promptbooks tell, or perhaps in all innocence suggest, has to do with origin or authority. It is never safe to deal with any given promptbook in isolation, for the very bit of stage business or scenic arrangement which appears most novel or significant may in fact be older than the promptbook writer's grandfather. The working of "tradition" is more likely to be detected in books of, say, pre-1920 vintage, before the age of the modern director, whose price is gauged by the originality of his inventions. Yet even today one can purchase from Samuel French copies of the plays marginally annotated with stage business, in several of which I have noticed gobbets of business which were practiced in Augustin Daly's theatre. Daly himself got it, or much of it, by way of his old stage manager, John Moore, from such long-dead producers as William Burton, Mme. Vestris, and William Charles Macready. Daly is sometimes credited or blamed for introducing certain non-Shakespearean drinking songs into *Twelfth Night;* but these songs had been heard in every performance of *Twelfth Night* at least back to the days of John Philip Kemble.

Henry Irving had a compilation of the traditional business in *Macbeth* made for him by Percy Fitzgerald; Fred Williams made one of *Hamlet* for E. H. Sothern. Winthrop Ames, though one of the "new men," systematically investigated the stage history of any play before launching into his own production of it. Robert Mantell's promptbooks of *Julius Caesar* and *The Merchant of Venice* are derived from Edwin Booth's. Charles Hanford's *Cymbeline* is a replica of Viola Allen's. One cannot evaluate Henrietta Crosman's *As You Like It* of 1901 without reference to Julia Arthur's 1898 book, of which it is largely a copy: one wonders how much of it was original with Miss Arthur. When Beerbohm Tree was first preparing *The Merry Wives* in 1889 he hired Edward Hastings, the oldest prompter in England, to coach him in the Falstaff business as George Bartley played it in 1840; Bartley had first played Falstaff, following who knows how much "tradition," as early as 1815. John McCullough's *King Lear* book is literally a Charles Kean book modified by erasure and writing over. Macready's promptbooks were widely copied, and, as I have shown elsewhere, Charles Kean's celebrated New York production of *King John* was essentially a pilfering of Macready's London production. Macready himself in his early years, as did everyone in the first decades of the nineteenth century, took text and basic stage arrangements of the standard plays from the authority of John Philip Kemble. In this catalogue I have called attention to some of the major borrowings and symbiotic relationships, but am certain that I have missed a great many more.

The word "promptbook" in the title of this catalogue is to be interpreted rather loosely. I have described all the *marked copies* of Shakespeare used in English-language, professional theatre productions from the 1620's to 1961—all, that is, that are held in public collections and in the production departments of the late Old Vic and the Festival Theatres at the three Stratfords. "Marked copies" include many varieties of document. A promptbook proper is the book actually used by prompters or stage managers in conducting performances, and although some promptbooks contain "everything," many of them are rather barren, showing little beyond the working essentials of cuts, calls, and cues for effects. Somewhat more interesting is a "final or souvenir promptbook," which is a perfected copy of the promptbook of a famous production, often handsomely written and decorated, sometimes profuse in detail, made up as a record or keepsake or as the model for future *re*production. A "memorial book" is still more fruitful, being a book written up during or after a production by an interested participant or observer who wants to preserve his own account of the scenery, the stage business, the histrionics, etc. "Stage managers' workbooks," "rehearsal promptbooks," and directors' "preparation copies" are likely to contain much more productional data, albeit in scrambled, chaotic form, than appears in the tidied-up promptbook proper. "Studybooks," "rehearsal copies," and "partbooks" are the working documents of the individual actor, sometimes little marked and of no more than fetishistic interest, sometimes scored and annotated in detail, with the personality of the actor implicit in every note.

I have not listed books now in private hands, since presumably they are not available for general inspection. Occasionally, although a book is housed in a public collection the rights to use or reproduce it are reserved: I have entered books of this sort with a note on the ownership.[1]

I have not included books of the modern nonprofessional theatre for the obvious reason of space; but I have included the few amateur or private theatre books that are old enough or curious enough to have been prized by collectors: the Douai manuscripts of the 1690's,

---

[1] A special warning about the Beerbohm Tree Books: Tree's entire theatre library, Shakespearean and non-Shakespearean, has recently been deposited in the Enthoven Collection at the Victoria and Albert, but at present none of it can be reproduced without special permission of the Executors of the Tree Estate.

Lumley Skeffington's schoolboy *Cymbeline* of 1785, a Cambridge University *Henry IV* of the 1850's which derived from Charles Kean's, a school *King Lear* from 1913 in which Lear's daughters became Lear's sons, etc. The very few foreign-language books that have turned up (including some excellent German ones) I have listed with "other books" at the end of each section. Although I have made no effort to *find* extra-textual productional material—scene designs, costume designs, music scores, stage managers' work-sheets, etc.—when these have come to hand as part and parcel of promptbook collections I have listed them. The user of the catalogue would presumably rather know than not know that these items exist, and will understand that this part of the record is accidental and fragmentary.

The documents for each play are entered in chronological order (except the group at the end of each section called "other books," which are mostly books without interesting marking, of association value only). The documents are numbered serially and they are indexed not by pages but by document number: AYL, 28; PER, 5; TN, 17. Each document is described in four "lines." The following explanations and cautions about the descriptive system should be examined with some care.

Line 1. Here are given: a) the actor, director, prompter, or stage manager with whom I have associated the book; b) the city and theatre, or sometimes only the country, where the book was first or significantly used; c) the date or approximate date of first or significant use. It rarely happens that all three of these items appear upon the book itself. Sometimes none of them appear. Sometimes ambiguous or misleading notations have led to former ascriptions or datings which I have altered. In short, more often than not one or two or all of the items of the first line are derived from secondary sources of information: biographies, histories, annals, playbills, or journals of the day. To have documented all these items would be otiose. The user of the catalogue is warned that they may be fallible.

An example or two may be instructive. Consider number 12 of *Henry IV,* part 1. Unquestionably it is James H. Hackett's, being part of his set of books in the Enthoven Collection. Written upon it—but I think by a modern annotator (here a quick curse upon those meddlers who write their own notes or helpful hints upon the *pages* of promptbooks)—is a dating at the Haymarket Theatre as of May 15, 1833. Perhaps Hackett did use the book then and there. Inside it, however, and unquestionably in an "old" hand, is the date *1828.* I prefer then to assign the book to the New York Park Theatre as of May 15, 1828, the occasion of Hackett's first performance of this play. For a more complicated problem, consider number 19 of *King John*. This handsome promptbook, owned by the Newberry Library, is inscribed "The Private Property of the T.R.D.L.," and it is endorsed "H. Scharf/ Novr. 1844." In November of 1844 Henry Scharf was, I believe, a member of Samuel Phelps's company at Sadler's Wells, and Phelps had produced *King John* a month or two earlier. Thus the book might have been entered under Scharf's name, or, since Scharf was neither then or at any later time responsible for an independent production of the play, under Phelps's name. But those words "The Private Property of the T.R.D.L." make plain that the book is simply a transcription of Macready's Drury Lane book of two years earlier, and I have chosen to enter it along with Macready's. Phelps's own book, incidentally, although also a transcription of Macready's, is entered under Phelps's name because he used it and modified it for his own known and datable productions. The point here for the user of this catalogue is that he should not ask at the Newberry for "Macready's" *King John,* for it is not likely that the book is recognized as Macready's in the Newberry catalogue.

Line 2. Here are given the library or collection where the book is to be found, and, if catalogued, the call number. As an aid to librarians and a safeguard against error, inquiries ought to carry not only the call number but enough descriptive details of the book to make identification easy and certain.

Line 3. Here are given details of the physical makeup of the document—not, obviously, such as would gratify a scientific bibliographer, but merely enough to rough out an image of the book so that it can be recognized. Since most of these documents are "home-made" objects, their variations of form are extremely numerous.

The first important item is the physical and editorial nature of the text. *Manuscript* promptbooks are generally rare and are no longer in use. Sir Edward Dering's *Henry IV,* which is perhaps the oldest promptbook in the catalogue, is a manuscript; Edwin Booth used manuscript promptbooks as late as 1875. *Typescript* promptbooks are, of course, modern and are more common in America than in England. The earliest I have noticed are Edwin Booth's in the late 1870's. Sothern and Marlowe used typescripts almost exclusively from the beginning of their collaboration in 1904. *Mimeographed* promptbooks begin to be seen in the late 1940's and are increasingly common, especially in the American theatre.

The usual form in which the text is given is, of course, some sort of *printed book.* A very few marked copies of early but uncertain provenience are made upon original Quartos; the "Padua" promptbooks (e.g., MAC, 1), which probably date from the 1630's or 1640's, are in an unbroken First Folio; the Dublin Smock Alley promptbooks of the 1670's and 1680's, though long since divided and bound separately, were originally in an unbroken Third Folio. Garrick seems regularly to have used separate editions of the plays, either in complete texts or in "acting editions" such as those derived from Betterton.

The acting edition, cut for performance, became regularized and popular in the profession with Bell's *Shakespeare*, which appeared in 1773 and was widely used for promptbook-making for two or three decades. Kemble's acting editions of the separate plays in his own repertoire were printed and reprinted in the 1790's and down to about 1815, and they generally displaced Bell for professional uses. After the turn of the century "standard" acting editions proliferated: Mrs. Inchbald's about 1808, Oxberry's by 1820, Cumberland's about 1830 and after, Hinds English Stage in the later 1830's, Thomas Hailes Lacy's from the 1840's to about 1864; in America, the Dramatic Repository about 1810 to 1815, Oxberry's in a Boston reprinting in 1822, the Modern Standard Drama in the 1840's, which became French's Standard Drama in the 1850's, Spencer's Boston Theatre in the 1850's. All these standard acting editions were widely used. In the 1850's Charles Kean revived the Kemble practice of publishing his own versions of the plays as he staged them, and after him Charles Calvert, Henry Irving, and others followed suit; in America Edwin Booth published one series with Henry Hinton as editor in the 1860's and the more important Prompt-Book edition with William Winter as editor in the 1870's and after. In the 1880's and down to the 1920's, many individual actors—Mary Anderson, Richard Mansfield, Beerbohm Tree, Viola Allen, Julia Marlowe, E. H. Sothern, etc.—occasionally brought out an acting edition of a single play. But as the fashion in production became increasingly individual, even idiosyncratic, few of these actors' editions, except perhaps the Booth-Winter Prompt-Book, were much used except by their "authors."

Meanwhile, beginning about with Macready in the late 1830's and after, Phelps in the 1840's and after, and others of the "restorers," the usual practice was to eschew the acting editions with their petrified "errors" and to work from a "true text," using sheets from one or another well-printed, good paper, multi-volume complete *Works*. Many such editions came out in the first half of the nineteenth century, and since promptbooks made from them rarely include title pages, I have not usually been able to identify the exact publishing auspices—points to be settled by further research. About the beginning of the twentieth century the beautifully printed little Temple edition came into particular stage favor in England, followed by the New Temple edition in the 1930's. The Eversley edition, the National Classics, and by now the Penguin and other inexpensive modern texts have also been popular. In promptbooks where the text pages stand free and whole, I have given the *page size* in inches, and have regarded this measurement as the fundamental one, rather than the outside measurement, since bindings are variable and alterable. The page size does not, to be sure, mean much where we seek a clue to identity of edition, for sometimes the pages are cropped to less than "normal" size, and sometimes they are quite untrimmed, as if taken from the printer's shop directly to the theatre workrooms before binding.

The next point regularly noticed is that of *interleaves*. The makers of the earliest promptbooks using printed text marked them upon the text, between the lines, and along the margins. About the 1780's the practice arose of inserting blank sheets between the text sheets to provide more room for the prompter's markings. Interleaving was extremely common throughout the nineteenth century, and occasionally, even with typescript or mimeographed texts, it is still used. If the interleaves are larger than the printed sheets, thus enlarging the whole book, their size is also given in inches. Watermark dates in the interleaves are recorded if those dates are later than the date of publication of the text. As a substitute for interleaving, from Charles Kean's time (the 1850's) on, copies of the actor's own edition were sometimes printed on recto only, so that the left-hand pages were left blank for actors' and prompters' notations. I have sometimes, but not consistently, noted this phenomenon with the phrase "proof sheets of" such-and-such an edition.

Beginning about the end of the nineteenth century arose the further, and by now very common, substitute for interleaves of pasting the printed text sheets onto the large pages (the right-hand pages usually) of a ledger or workbook. This provides very wide margins and a wholly blank left-hand page for the most elaborate systems of annotation. For books of this kind the fundamental measurement given is not that of the text sheet but that of the workbook sheet.

The binding is described only to show the material of which it is made—paper, paper boards, cloth boards, leather, etc.—and the color or colors. The term "half" means what is sometimes called "three-quarters": "half brown leather" means "spine and corner-tips of brown leather." I regret not to have distinguished between "original" binding and "library" binding. And here I must protest against the misplaced piety of librarians and curators who damage the integrity and sometimes obscure the identity of promptbooks by dressing them up in sturdy buckram boards or elegant showcase gilt-and-tooled leather. One knows where he stands when he handles a Covent Garden book of 1810 bound in full calf with its distinctive theatre-library symbols stamped on the spine, just as John Kemble left it; or one of John Moore's foul books wrapped in tattered paper pasted over with scraps of old playbills. Who would dream of replacing (and destroying) the original boards of a 1623 Folio? (but the promptbook First Folio at Padua has been "handsomely" rebound within the last decade!) Boxing, not rebinding, is the proper way to care for old promptbooks. Their very filth is part of their history.

External titles and other identifications printed or handwritten on cover or spine ("on," "down," or "up" the spine) are usually indicated and are given in full if of special interest.

Line 4. Describing the contents of a promptbook is something like describing a bowl of soup, and an adequate description would be co-extensive with the contents. But in a catalogue one can report only the barest essentials according to a system or formula more or less consistently adhered to. The items of the formula I have tried to follow occur (when they do occur) in the following order. *The kind of book.* Each document is designated as a "promptbook," "studybook," "preparation copy," etc., according to its contents. Most modern books— those, that is, since about 1920—may be assumed to be promptbooks unless otherwise stated. *The actors, the designers.* The modern books— this being the "age of the director"—are with few exceptions entered under the name of the director (in England until recently called "producer"). Yet this is also still the "age of the actor," and partly too the "age of the designer," and one is more likely to remember a Coriolanus as Olivier's, an Othello as Robeson's, or a "show" as Motley's or Moiseiwitsch's, than remember the production by its director's name. I have therefore regularly given for the modern books the names of a few of the principal players and of the designers. *Identifying data.* For older books of questionable provenience there may be given notes on the handwriting, dating, or signs of authorship or original ownership. *Cuts, alterations, restorations.* All texts are "cut," of course, or some-how tinkered with for acting, however urgently the producer claims fullness of text and faithfulness to the original. The fact of "cuts" is noted when the cuts are plainly and conspicuously marked. When the words "cuts on full text" occur, the user of the catalogue may anticipate that a proper and complete Shakespeare text has been used and the cuts are therefore instantly discernible; if an acting edition has been used, or a Shakespeare text scissored and pasted, or if the text is in manuscript or typescript, he will understand that a heavy labor of collation is in store for him.

Scenic indications. This catchall term indicates that all or some of the scenic units have been described or specified. In the oldest books this will mean no more than the appearance of such words as "Towne" or "Castle"; in late eighteenth- or in nineteenth-century books it may mean only reference to stock units—"Carvers Garden," "Gothic Hall," "Wood and Cut Wood"; in books preparatory to new productions the scenery may be described in suggestive or even fulsome detail. *Scene designs, sketches, groundplans.* Only Charles Kean's books regularly contain full watercolors of the scenery. Old prompters often scribbled rough sketches or drew neat ones to remind themselves of the arrangement of properties and scenic units. The scientifically plotted groundplan is not common until near the end of the nineteenth century. *Grooves.* In eighteenth- and nineteenth-century books of the "wing-and-shutter" theatre, the numbers of the grooves in which the flats stood are often given at the heads of scenes.

Calls. Every efficient promptbook down through the nineteenth century shows neat lists of the characters to be summoned, together with their hand properties, a page or two before their entrance. Occasionally the callbook, into which these were transcribed for use of the prompter's assistant or callboy, has been preserved.

Stage business. The amount of stage business to be found in these documents varies immensely according to era and type of book. The oldest promptbooks typically show nothing beyond entrances and exits, and even these are usually unlocalized. By the end of the eighteenth century entrances and exits are regularly marked as to side of the stage; and certain major or significant movements—"Pistol crosses the stage behind Falstaff," "Benedick leads her forward by the hand"—are recorded. With the growth of more elaborately scenic productions involving crowd scenes, from perhaps the 1830's onward, the written directions become increasingly meaningful in terms both of "picture" and "motive": "The Nobles, &c, have broke into various groups, by the end of his speech, and appear to be remarking on the proposal, and its effect on the Kings." The intention of these directions, however, is mainly to govern and manipulate the crowds and secondary characters as part of the supporting background. The central characters were in the hands of accomplished actors who supplied their own histrionics and did not need to be told their "business," at least not by the prompter.

By the end of the nineteenth century there appear many books which attempt to capture in explicit statement the whole picture, rationale, and psychology of the production, with the business of the central characters, too, written out in full. In some of these the sentimentality and melodrama is pretty amusing—self-consciously noble Brutuses, rose-dropping Juliets, apron-twisting, coy, kiss-throwing Rosalinds hang their hearts up in their promptbooks for us latter-day daws to peck at. About the turn of the century, too, incidental local-color effects—street musicians, flirtatious sailors lounging along wharves, old crones telling fortunes beside wishing wells, maids a-spinning, children bobbing for apples, ambulating monks doling out their *benedicites*—proliferate oppressively, teaching us of the double drive inherent in the theatre of the time: toward the cinema, which would discard language entirely and tell the whole story in pictures; toward the new art of theatre, which would clear the stage of such irrelevant detail and try once more to "get back to Shakespeare."

In promptbooks of our own day, put together "for the record" by stage managers and their crews, the ideal appears to be to set down in the most economical (almost telegraphic) form every minutia of the blocking, but with no reference whatever to the "meaning" of what goes on. Modern promptbooks often appear in pairs: the full record for the archives; the "working" promptbook actually used for running the show, stripped down to barest essentials of text, calls, and cues for effects.

To suggest the amount or interestingness of stage business in the documents, I have used the words "little," "some," "considerable," "much," and "copious." My usage is loose and impressionistic, however, and it varies according to era. The "much" stage business of Kemble's *King Lear*, remarkable for its time, is not comparable to the muchness of a fully developed book a century later.

Maps. This term, following after "stage business," signifies those patterns of dots and lines (and sometimes little sketches) showing the positions of actors relative to each other or to furniture in the stage space.

Cues for effects. In this phrase, economy of space has been peculiarly defeating, for I have lumped together all the markings for lights, music and sound, operation of traps, slotes, and other machines, scene change, and curtains. To have recorded all of these, and the symbols by which they were effected, would be impractical.

Further notes. I have mentioned the presence of *timings;* of *working papers* (free sheets containing cast lists, rehearsal schedules, property

plots, light plots, business and lines for extras, dressing room assignments, touring schedules, etc.); of *playbills, programs, reviews,* and
other insertions; of *ownership* later than the original. For those documents which have been written up by modern investigators or published in facsimile, I have given bibliographical reference. Cross-refer-
ences are given between documents which are significantly related.

Symbols and Abbreviations in the Older Promptbooks

The investigator whose experience with promptbooks is limited to those of the modern theatre may, upon looking into the older books, be somewhat puzzled by various markings which once were a lingua franca among prompters and stage managers but have long since passed out of use. The following notes, though neither exhaustive nor definitive, may dispel doubts.

Lengths. In several books marked by John Philip Kemble and occasionally in books of later managers (HAM, 11; TEM, 3; WT, 5), one finds alongside the names of "Persons Represented" numerals ranging from a fraction to as high as 15 or 20. These signify the sizes of the roles in terms of "lengths"—i.e., manuscript sheets of speeches and cues. In practice these sheets were of varying sizes, but the standard which Kemble probably measured by was the traditional one of 42 lines. George Frederick Cooke put down the role of Hamlet as 26 lengths (HAM, 7). William Creswick noted in his *King Lear* book (KL, 92) that Kent was, including cues, "6 lengths + 32 lines."

Property manuscripts. At the front of a promptbook or at the heads of acts there often appear production lists—costumes, properties, scenic units (especially wings and shutters with their groove numbers), processions, supernumeraries, etc.—which are self-explanatory. Among these, somewhat cryptically, are lists of "papers required." In the older theatre it was the prompter's duty to see that all letters, scrolls, treaties, bills, challenges, etc. were in good order for every performance. If a letter was to be read aloud, it had to be legibly written out, for the actor was not expected to have memorized it (MAC, 80); if a paper was only to be delivered it could be blank. Common abbreviations are *Lre* (letter); *Pap* (paper); *W, W^n, Wrt, Wrot, W^t* (written); *B, Blk* (blank). One of Charles Kean's touring notebooks (HAM, 22) contains the text of several stage messages for prompters to transcribe.

Stage carpet. At the head of most of Kemble's promptbooks is the call for "Green Cloth," and this is variously expressed in other books as "Green Cloth down," "Stage Cloth," "Green Baize down," "Green Baize Carpet." The earliest stage carpets were small squares of green baize laid out only late in the play for tragic heroes and heroines to spread themselves and their gorgeous costumes upon at death. Thus, in the Garrick *Macbeth* book (MAC, 8), the words "Stage Cloth on" do not appear until the beginning of the fifth act; in a Boston *Othello* book of the 1820's (OTH, 13), "Green cloth down next act" is written at the end of Act IV. But in the better-equipped theatres of the nineteenth century, unless the stage floor was to be broken up with trap work, a cloth covering (usually green) became an expectable feature of the decor. Charles Kean's early *Hamlet* book (HAM, 20) calls for "Green Cloth laid" at the beginning, but just before the play scene someone must also "See Carpet laid all over Stage to float lights," and after it "See Carpet taken up now." Kean was perhaps the first to incorporate the stage cloth into the overall scene design by painting patterns on it: in the first act of his *King John* the cloth exhibited a huge design of the royal arms of England surmounted by a crucifix (KJ, 39). By the end of the century, in such a production as Viola Allen's *Twelfth Night* (TN, 55), we find not only "ground cloth" but "mosaic cloth," "dark brown cloth," and "tesselated cloth." Beerbohm Tree's floor coverings of "real" grass with pluckable flowers and scampering rabbits carried the art of the stage cloth to the limit.

Call-lists. At the head of each act, under a boldly inscribed number *one*, there is usually a list of all the characters for the first entrance, together with their hand properties if they are to carry any. In some very early (seventeenth-century) books the names of the actors are given instead of the characters' names (CE, 2; MM, 2); and occasionally this happens, thanks to the prompters' informal scribblings, in promptbooks of the nineteenth century and after (AYL, 18; CYM, 15). A character who is to make two or three entrances during the act may be marked 2^{ce} or 3^{ce}; or if he is simply to keep himself available throughout the act he may be marked *Act.* As the act proceeds, further numbered lists are posted some 30 to 50 lines in advance of the entrances. Each act begins a new numbered series, so that the normal Shakespeare promptbook contains five series of calls. (Down through the nineteenth century, with such rare exceptions as Macready's cut-down *Henry V*, George Ellis' one-act *Comedy of Errors,* or the long-popular Garrick reduction of *Taming of the Shrew,* Shakespeare's plays were presented in five acts; Beerbohm Tree popularized the three-act form, chopping the texts about mercilessly to make them fit; the occasional two-part divisioning is a recent development pendent to modern efforts toward fullest possible restoration.) The call-lists were also written upon slips of paper made up into tall narrow booklets, which the callboy carried to summon the actors from the green rooms (AYL, 20; JC, 13). Since the prompter needed only to speak out the number to the callboy, who found the actors, many promptbooks show only numbers where the call-lists ought to be.

The numbering system seems to have been invented in the eighteenth century: the earliest books to use numbered call-lists that I have noticed are John Ward's *Hamlets* of about 1740 (HAM, 3, 4). A peculiarity of many books of the seventeenth and early eighteenth centuries (down through Ward's) is that the exact moment of entrance is marked by a long horizontal line with several vertical slashes, thus:

Groove numbers. Some promptbooks of the eighteenth century and most of those of the nineteenth show at the head of each scene not only a word or two to indicate what sets are to be used (*Old Palace, Carvers Rock, Prison Arch, Wood and Cut Wood*), but also the number or numbers of the grooves in which the wings and shutters (flats) are to stand: *1 G., 3 & 4 Gr., A Set to 7th Gro⁸.*, etc. Sometimes only the numerals appear without the word *Groove* or its abbreviation. (These numerals are not to be confused with those attached to entering characters denoting the order of entrance.) In a few books the exact slot or "cut" in the groove is prescribed, as *1 G. 2C.* in Kemble's *Winter's Tale* (WT, 4, 5); or *sink Gauze waters 3rd Cut 2 Grs* in Charles Kean's *Winter's Tale* (WT, 20). In describing the first scene of Macready's *Macbeth,* George Ellis specified that the shutters, set in the first grooves, do not meet at center as usual but overlap, one being in the *first cut* and one in the *fourth cut,* "so that the 1st Witch can easily pass between" (MAC, 27). Toward the end of the nineteenth century, as the groove system was disappearing, the numerals (or *in 1, in 3,* etc.) continued to be used to indicate the depth of the stage at which drops or set pieces were to be located.

Sides of the stage and points of entrance. From the beginning of the eighteenth century (we do not know precisely when), the sides of the stage were called *prompt side* and *opposite prompt,* and the symbols of entrance and exit were *PS* and *OP.* The geography of these terms is confusing. *PS* at Covent Garden, it is said, meant stage left, but at Drury Lane stage right. Yet Wyatt's groundplan of the Drury Lane of 1812 seems to show the prompter's booth at stage left. (See also MWW, 11.)

The earliest promptbooks that locate entrances and exits mention *doors* as well as sides of the stage, since movement to and from the deep forestage was mainly by way of the two or three doors that flanked the forestage on either side. The Smock Alley *Richard II* of about 1720 (RII, 1) gives *P.D.* (prompt side door), *L:D:O.P.* (lower door opposite prompt), *U:D:P:S:* (upper door prompt side), etc. One of Ward's *Hamlet* books of about 1740 (HAM, 4)) gives *M:D:O:P:* (middle door opposite prompt). West Digges's *Macbeth* of 1757 (MAC, 6) gives *DOP, LDPS,* etc. Thomas Hull's *Cymbeline* of 1767 (CYM, 1) gives *L.D.O.P., M.D.,* and *M.D.P.S.* An *As You Like It* of about 1780 (AYL, 4) gives *Pd* (prompt side door). By the end of the eighteenth century the doors had dwindled to a single one on each side. They persisted in many theatres well into the nineteenth century, but as the forestage shrank and entrances tended more and more to originate in the scenic area behind the proscenium, the use of the doors atrophied. At the head of Act I in many of Kemble's promptbooks is the firm order to "Lock Stage-Doors"; his *Othello* (OTH, 9), a rare exception, calls for "Stage-doors unlocked." Most references to doors in nineteenth-century promptbooks indicate that they are constructions (set pieces) located in the entrances at right or left of the scenic area; or *DF* (a door built into one or the other of the sliding back flats); or *CD* (center door: a set piece at upstage center flanked or framed by the two sliding back flats). Of course, as "built scenery" replaced the wing-and-shutter system, doors could be placed anywhere on the stage, at any angle, and the old location terms fell out of use.

Entrances and exits from behind the proscenium sometimes occurred at the back of the stage, or, in a phrase favored in the eighteenth century, "at the Top" (MAC, 8; RIII, 3). Usually, however, they were made through the spaces between the wings at the sides of the stage, which were sometimes called *W* (wings) as in George Frederick Cooke's *Hamlet* (HAM, 7), but nearly universally called *E* (entrance). The entrances were numbered from the front to the back of the stage: *1E.RH* (first entrance right hand), *2E.L* (second entrance left), *R.3E* (right, third entrance), *U.E.L* or *L.U.E* (upper entrance left), etc. Eventually the *E* dropped out, leaving only *R1, L2,* etc. Whether the entrances as numbered were behind or in front of the correspondingly numbered wings (grooves) is perhaps disputable. Kalman Burnim states categorically that in the eighteenth century "an entrance designated as effected at a wing position was located upstage of the wing itself" (*David Garrick, Director,* p. 207), and he refers to a stage diagram of the 1880's in Richard Southern's *Changeable Scenery* for confirmation from later practice. My impression, gathered from various nineteenth-century promptbooks (AYL, 22; HAM, 30; KJ, 27; KL, 57; MA, 18; RIII, 48), is exactly the opposite. Time and again scenes created by flats in the second grooves show entrances in *R.2E, L.2E*— manifestly impossible unless the second entrance was *downstage* of the second groove.

PS and *OP*, whether they meant left or right, were in common use down to the end of the eighteenth century, but in the first two decades of the nineteenth they generally gave way to the more precise *LH* (left hand) and *RH* (right hand). These new symbols were promoted— perhaps invented—by George Frederick Cooke, who used them in his *Hamlet* book (HAM, 7) as early as 1785. From 1803 on John Philip

Kemble nearly always wrote *LH* and *RH* in his Covent Garden promptbooks, and these books, widely disseminated by transcription, spread the practice into a fashion. The old symbols did not die out at once, of course. One senses the change coming at Drury Lane when an actor there about 1813 writes into his promptbook equations of the old symbols and the new (MWW, 11); but one notices also that the Drury Lane *Othello* (OTH, 12), written somewhat later and used steadily for the next quarter-century, is steadfast in *PS* and *OP*. In the 1840's the Sadler's Wells prompter, Pepper Williams, now and then reverted to the old forms in his promptbook jottings (TEM, 8). The clerkly George Ellis, stage manager at the Princess's in the 1850's, would not let *PS* and *OP* appear in final promptbooks made under his supervision, but he used them freely in his technical notes and rehearsal work-sheets (TEM, 21). They lived on in oral tradition and in the vocabulary of old stagers throughout the nineteenth century. By now they are wholly archaic.

The seemingly needless letter *H* in *LH* and *RH* persisted in some quarters far into the second half of the nineteenth century. The probable reason for this is that the letter *R* not only meant *Right* but also *Ring;* and so long as the prompter's bell was in use to start up the music or bring down the act drop the *H* in *RH* was an insurance against disastrous misreading. George Ellis' beautiful transcriptions of Macready's and Kean's books, made in the 1840's and 1850's, drop the *H*, but Ellis was careful to spell out *RING* in handsome Gothic letters and to box it too, so that no such misreading was possible.

Prompters' signals. In the older theatre, at every scene change within an act the prompter cued the carpenters (stagehands) to thrust on stage in their grooves the wings and shutters of the new scene, or to reveal the new scene by drawing off the wings and shutters of the scene just concluded. These within-the-act changes were instantaneous, and they were executed in full view of the audience, who indeed took especial delight in the magic of it all.

Little time was lost in arranging and manipulating the scenery of the wing-and-shutter system, for "deep scenes" could be prepared while "front scenes" (sometimes referred to as "carpenters' scenes") were being acted. By careful planning, all the scenes of a given act might be set in place during the brief entr'acte ("wait"), while the act drop was down and the orchestra was playing; then be revealed as a series of scenes alternating in the various forward grooves and climaxing in a deep "Set of the entire stage," or a "Set to the 7th grooves." As I have shown elsewhere, the total amount of "non-playing" time in Macready's production of *King John,* which had 15 scenes, was only 18 minutes—something less than is usually consumed in modern intermissions.

The cue for scene change was the shrill of a whistle. At this sound, wrote Aaron Hill in *The Prompter* (1734), "I have seen Houses move, as it were, upon Wings, Cities turned into Forests, and dreary Desarts converted into superb Palaces: I have seen an Audience removed, in a Moment, from *Britain* to *Japan,* and the frozen Mountains of *Zembla* resembling the sunny Vales of *Arabia Felix:* I have seen Heaven and Earth pass away, and Chaos ensue, and from thence a new Creation arise, fair and blooming, as the Poet's Fancy; and all by the powerful magic Influence of this Wonder-working Whistle."

The earliest symbol for "Whistle," dating from Restoration times, was a circle with a dot in it, thus: ⊙ (See Montague Summers, *Essays in Petto,* pp. 103-110). During the eighteenth century several variants appeared, including undotted circles, double dotted circles (MAC, 7), and pairs of circles connected with a horizontal line (MAC, 5). No constant patterns of meaning for these different circle symbols can be established. Sometimes a circle was accompanied by the word "continues," meaning *no* change of scene (TEM, 2). West Digges used the dotted circle to mean "Ring" as well as "Whistle" (MAC, 6). Probably, as Kalman Burnim has suggested (*David Garrick, Director,* p. 205), the circles ultimately became mere eye-catchers to alert the prompter to *some* kind of duty.

The indubitable symbol for "Whistle," which appeared in Garrick's time, was the letter *W,* usually boxed or circled. The *W* was at first used in combination with circle symbols, but by the beginning of the nineteenth century it had entirely displaced them. To recapitulate with examples, the Smock Alley *Othello* (OTH, 2), which was probably entirely marked in the seventeenth century, shows several dotted circles; Ward's *Hamlet* books of about 1740 (HAM, 3, 4) show a few dotted circles; the Beatt and Love *Macbeth* of 1761 (MAC, 7) combines *W* with circles dotted, double-dotted, and undotted; an *As You Like It* and a *Tempest* of about 1780 (AYL, 4; TEM, 2) show *W* combined with dotted and undotted circles.

From the time of John Philip Kemble's Covent Garden books (after 1803), *W* became the only symbol for "Whistle," except that occasionally the word was spelled out (KL, 14, 20; MAC, 16). Eventually the word *Change* began to appear, especially in books written after the mid-century, including some of John Moore's (AYL, 24; R&J, 23); and this is perhaps a sign that the whistle was going out of use. That its shrill sound was felt intrusive in still, mysterious moments is apparent, for example, in many *Hamlet* books: the scene change between Hamlet's exit with the Ghost and the re-entry for their interview was effected by "quiet signal" (HAM, 20, 48, 89). In Charlotte Cushman's *Romeo and Juliet,* after the potion scene, we read "Change Slowly without Whistle" (R&J, 31). In Samuel Phelps's *Macbeth* book of 1860 (MAC, 63) the *W* is often scratched and the word "Flag" written beside it. As the wing-and-shutter scenery gave way to more and more "built" scenery, which needed stagehands to move it, the call appears for *Dark Change,* as in Adelaide Neilson's *Twelfth Night* (TN, 26), Charles Hanford's *Winter's Tale* (WT, 30), Robert Mantell's *Macbeth* (MAC, 111). In earlier times left-over furniture had been tugged off the stage by cords, or if too heavy for that, had been removed by costumed supernumeraries, or even by "Green Coats"—i.e., stage carpenters—without attempt at concealment (KJ, 18, 27).

The use of *flags* as a silent substitute for whistles has been noticed in Phelps's *Macbeth* of 1860. In the 1850's at the Princess's, George Ellis gave flag cues whenever possible. In King Lear he would "Signal white flag down to stop the trumpets"—the trumpeters apparently standing at one of the entrances across the stage (KL, 54). In *The Tempest* he would make "Red flag signal to Bartram, in flies, to light flame, ready," and wave the flag again for the flame to descend (TEM, 22).

Among the prompter's "Implements of Government" in 1734, Aaron Hill took notice of "a little Bell, which hangs over his Arm: by the Tinkling of this Bell, if a Lady in Tragedy be in the Spleen for the Absence of her Lover, or a Hero in the Dumps for the Loss of a Battle, he can conjure up soft Musick to soothe their Distress." The call for music seems, indeed, to have been the *principal* use of the bell in earliest times. This might be music incidental to the action, as the "soft musick" which Hill speaks of; or music for songs, dances, and processions; or trumpet flourishes, rolls of drums, charges, retreats, etc. accompanying military actions. Wind, thunder, knocking, hoofbeats, the crashing of gates, and other sound effects not strictly musical were likewise answerable to the prompter's signal, though he may not always have used his bell to summon them. By the later eighteenth century a nest of triple *x*es (or later, triple musical sharps) was a common eye-catcher to denote "Musick" or "Music in Orchestre" (MV, 3; TEM, 2). By the nineteenth century, the prompters often warned themselves to "call up" trumpets or flutes or violins—i.e., to summon the players to the wings or the back of the stage or the green room so the music would blend into the action with more realistic effect.

The most frequent call for music was for the entr'actes. In seventeenth-century promptbooks, long before the act drop came into service, one finds near the end of an act the words *Act redy* or *Act* (HAM, 1; OTH, 2). At this point the prompter alerted the musicians with a warning bell; then at *Act ends* or *Ring* he rang a second time to make them play. By the 1780's one finds *Act* followed by *Drop Landskip* or *Drop Street* (TEM, 2; MV, 3), by which I take it that at the second bell not only the music played in front of the stage but also a painted act drop fell. In Kemble's books, when use of the act drop had become standardized the symbols for these operations are usually *R* and *Act.* In later books they became more or less regularly *RMB* (ring music bell) to alert the orchestra, and *R* or *RING* to begin the music and bring the curtain down.

The prompter also used his bell to make the curtain rise, but this is entered in the promptbooks only when the rise of the curtain is tied to special pre-curtain effects. It was the fashion with *Hamlet,* especially in America, to start the play with a great gong tolling twelve o'clock, and according to the whim of the producing actor or manager the prompter "rang up" on one stroke or another: Edwin Forrest's prompter made the curtain rise on the sixth stroke; Edwin Booth's and most others' on the seventh or eighth. In plays-within-plays, as in *Midsummer Night's Dream* and *Hamlet,* realism dictated that the curtains of the stage-within-stage should be opened by a prompter's bell (HAM, 85; MND, 12).

There were bells underneath the stage and bells in the flies, these probably being manipulated by cords from the prompter's table. About 1740 John Ward's prompter could "Ring for Trap to be Ready" and "Ring three times for the Ghost to cry under the stage" (HAM, 4, 5). In 1757, Digges's prompter could "Ring to raise trap OP," "Ring to raise Hobs trap," and "Ring for Trap PS" (MAC, 6). The *Tempest* prompter about 1780 could work the B̄ (trap bell). In the nineteenth century the words *Pull* and *Check* prove the use of cords for distant ringings. At the end of the wrestling match in *As You Like It,* the Drury Lane prompter, John Willmott, could "Pull to let go posts"— i.e., signal by bell someone under the stage to release the posts thrust into the stage floor to form the wrestling ring (AYL, 18). The American prompter Asa Cushman could "Check above, when Hecate in, for car to ascend" (MAC, 41). In *The Tempest* at the Princess's, George Ellis could "Pull below, for waters to abate," and "Pull above and below for general change" (TEM, 21). Augustin Daly's *As You Like It* in 1889 (AYL, 59) used bells below to sink scenes, bells above to fly them, and yet other bells to make moving panoramas stop and go.

The following abbreviations involving bells cover most of the exigencies of interpretation: *R* (ring), *RMB, MB, M* (ring music bell), *RWB* (ring warning bell), *RAB, RAD, AD* (ring act bell, or act drop), *WC, WD, WAD* (warn curtain, warn drop, warn act drop), *CB* (curtain bell), *RT, RTB* (ring trap bell), *ST* (sink trap).

Lighting. Promptbook markings for lighting control in the older theatre are comparatively sparse and uncomplicated. One should remember that oil lamps and candles were the only means of lighting throughout the eighteenth century and John Philip Kemble's day. Gas lighting came into the London theatres in 1817, was in general use by about 1830, and prevailed nearly to the end of the century. The limelight (*Limes, Calciums*), although invented as early as 1816, seems not to have been used much in Shakespeare production until the 1840's and 1850's. Electric lighting was introduced about 1880 but did not at once displace gas (Henry Irving carried his own gas equipment when he went on tour). The auditorium was lighted throughout performances, with rare exceptions, until Irving began darkening it about 1881.

The earliest promptbooks say nothing about lighting. The Beatt and Love *Macbeth* of 1767 gives "Stage dark/Lamps down," "Stage light/Lamps up" (MAC, 7), and we glean nothing more instructive than this from other eighteenth-century books. Kemble adds only an occasional cautionary "little" or "half" or "quite" to the directions for darkening. The word *Lamps* was still the only term for the sources of light in Kemble's time, and it persisted to the middle of the century, though gradually giving way to the word *Lights*. Footlights had long been called *Floats* or *Flotes,* we are told, but the words do not appear in promptbooks until after Kemble's time (when, strictly speaking, they had become anachronistic). By the 1840's we find many references to green and blue *Mediums* (of glass at first, later of silk) applied to lights to create night effects. George Ellis' work-sheets from the Princess's in the 1850's refer to *Battens* (overhead strips of gas jets), *Wing Ladders* (strips of gas jets hung vertically behind the wings), and *Limes.* And he reminds us of the danger of so much living flame: as he waved his red flags to signal the hurling about of thunderbolts and fires in *The Tempest* he ordered the placing of "Pails of water & Mops w firemen, R&L, each Act" (TEM, 21, 22). Meanwhile, of course, the extensive use of dioramas, gauzes, transparencies, etc. at the better-equipped metropolitan theatres implies lighting effects of considerable sophistication, even if the promptbook notations remain unsuggestive.

The most exciting instrument of the nineteenth century was, of course, the limelight, and from the 1850's or 1860's on one begins to find wonderfully romantic uses of it. In American books it was usually called the *Calcium*. When Booth's Theatre opened in 1869, Juliet in her balcony was bathed in green light from the battens, but was picked out by a white calcium shining down from the "R Fly" (R&J, 37). The inside of Brutus' tent, in Lawrence Barrett's *Julius Caesar* in the 1870's, was flooded with blue, but the back of the tent was a transparency, through which Caesar's ghost could be seen drifting across the stage from left to right into a beam of green calcium (JC, 33-37). A purple calcium poured over the marriage altar in Margaret Mather's *Romeo and Juliet* in the 1880's (R&J, 51).

"Who gives out?" This query, or the order to "Give out the Play," often occurs at the end of the fourth act in promptbooks of the late eighteenth and early nineteenth centuries. At this point the manager or one of his officers came before the act drop to announce the bill for the following night. This "giving out" is reminiscent of the "Oration" of Molière's theatre, although in England it seems never to have developed into so fixed and elaborate a performance as was expected of the French "Orateur." Nonetheless, when it was a question of a new play, a new production, or a newly featured actor, the moment could be a tense one, necessitating a curtain speech of tact and eloquence.

Timings. In many well-ordered promptbooks the playing time for each act is systematically entered, and the total playing time, with "waits," is given at the end. Sometimes, too, a prompter would scribble the actual clock time of beginnings, endings, and entr'actes on particular evenings. Performances in the older theatre were long, and considering how drastically the texts were cut they would seem by modern standards to have been intolerably slow. Kemble's *Othello,* for instance, was 3:35. Edmund Kean got through it once in 2:08, but that was an evening in 1825 when, as the prompter says, there was "a great Row" in the house over the Kean-Cox affair. Timings for the *Othellos* of Macready, Vandenhoff, and Forrest about 1835 ranged from 3:20 to 3:36. Kemble's *Macbeth, The Merchant of Venice,* and *Romeo and Juliet* were about 3:10; his *Winter's Tale* 3:45. Macready's *Hamlet* was 3:35. Charles Kean's *Winter's Tale* was 3:30, his *Hamlet* 3:40, his *Henry V* 4:05. These are examples of extreme rather than average length, but in our ultimate understanding of Shakespeare in the older theatre they are facts to be reckoned with.

A Register of Libraries and
Collections with Promptbook Holdings

The American Shakespeare Festival Theatre, Stratford, Connecticut
Promptbooks and other production materials of this theatre
have accumulated in the Production Department since the beginning of the theatre in 1955.

Biblioteca Universitaria, Padova, Italy

Bibliothèque de Douai, Douai, France

Birmingham, Shakespeare Memorial Library, Birmingham Public
Library, Ratcliff Place, Birmingham, England

The Boston Athenaeum, The Library, 10½ Beacon Street, Boston 8,
Massachusetts

Boston Public Library, Boston 17, Massachusetts

The British Drama League, 9 Fitzroy Square, London, W. 1, England

The British Museum, Bloomsbury, London, W. C. 1, England

The British Theatre Museum, Leighton House, 12 Holland Park
Road, London, W. 14, England

Brown University Library, Providence, Rhode Island

Connecticut State Library, Hartford, Connecticut

Dartmouth College, Baker Library, Hanover, New Hampshire

The Edwin Forrest Home, 4849 Parkside Avenue, Philadelphia, Pennsylvania
> This is a home for retired actors, not a public library, and ar-
> rangements to visit it should be made in advance. The bulk of
> Forrest's personal library is housed here. It is being catalogued.
> Most of its promptbooks and other manuscript rarities are on
> loan to the Library of the University of Pennsylvania, Rare
> Book Room.

The Enthoven Collection, The Victoria and Albert Museum, Cromwell Road, South Kensington, London, S. W. 7, England
> The late Gabrielle Enthoven's collection is most remarkable for
> its runs of London playbills. Promptbooks include James H.
> Hackett's, some of Poel's. There is a full collection of Charles
> Kean's scene designs. Beerbohm Tree's whole library of prompt-
> books from His Majesty's Theatre is housed here, but rights of
> reproduction are at present reserved by the Tree Estate.

The Essex Institute, Salem, Massachusetts

The Folger Shakespeare Library, Washington 3, D.C.
> A vast collection of promptbooks, Shakespearean and non-
> Shakespearean, mainly pre-1920: most of the Smock Alley books
> and a number of eighteenth-century books, including Garrick's;
> many of Kemble's, of Macready's; nearly all of Phelps's and
> Charles Kean's; many nineteenth-century American books, in-

cluding nearly all of John Moore's (Augustin Daly's), some of George Becks's; a full set of Sothern and Marlowe's; all of Henry Jewett's. Reading privileges are reserved for graduate and postgraduate scholars, and must be arranged for in advance.

The Garrick Club, Garrick Street, London, W. C. 2, England
A fine set of promptbooks of Covent Garden Theatre under John Philip Kemble and Charles Kemble. Admission by prearrangement with The Secretary.

The Harvard Theatre Collection, Harvard College Library, Cambridge 38, Massachusetts
The infinite riches of this theatre collection include a large number of old promptbooks, especially American, originally gathered by Robert Gould Shaw and gradually augmented since his time by William Van Lennep and others. Admission to accredited scholars, who should give advance notice of their visit.

The Henry E. Huntington Library, San Marino 9, California

The Historical and Philosophical Society of Ohio, University of Cincinnati Library Building, Cincinnati 21, Ohio

The Johns Hopkins University, The Tudor and Stuart Club, Baltimore 18, Maryland

Joint University Libraries, Nashville 4, Tennessee

The Library Company of Philadelphia, Broad and Christian Streets, Philadelphia 47, Pennsylvania

The Library of Congress, Manuscripts Division, Washington, D.C.

The Library of Congress, Batchelder Collection, Rare Books Division, Washington, D.C.

The Literary and Philosophical Society, Newcastle-on-Tyne, England

The London Museum, Kensington Palace, London, W. 8, England

The Raymond Mander and Joe Mitchenson Theatre Collection, 5 Venner Road, Sydenham, London, S. E. 26, England

The Missouri Historical Society Library, Jefferson Memorial, St. Louis 12, Missouri
A vast number of old playbooks of the St. Louis theatre managers of the nineteenth century, but very few with interesting markings.

Museum of the City of New York, Fifth Avenue and 103rd Street, New York 29, New York
A number of nineteenth- and twentieth-century books of New York provenience, including especially a good many of Sothern and Marlowe's. Admission to the Theatre Collection of the museum by appointment.

The Newberry Library, 60 West Walton, Chicago, Illinois

The New York Public Library, Theatre Collection, Lincoln Center, 111 Amsterdam Avenue, New York, New York

> A large collection of old promptbooks, especially American but including many English also, many of them originally collected or made by George Becks in the last years of the nineteenth century. The library continues to acquire modern promptbooks.

Old Vic Theatre, Waterloo Road, London, S. E. 1, England

> Production books of the last years of the late Old Vic organization were preserved in the Publicity Department up to 1962, and presumably are still in the building, which now houses the National Theatre. There may be some older books than listed in this catalogue, but pre-war books are said to have been damaged or destroyed by enemy action.

The Players, The Walter Hampden Memorial Library, 16 Gramercy Park, New York 3, New York

> Edwin Booth's promptbooks and records in great quantity, together with a few older books which Booth collected, and some later ones including Sothern and Marlowe's. A research library for accredited scholars.

Princeton University Library, William Seymour Theatre Collection, Princeton, New Jersey

> A large number of playbooks and marked copies used or gathered by William Seymour; the books and papers of George Tyler; other accretions.

Rutgers State University Library, New Brunswick, New Jersey

Shakespeare Centre Library, Stratford-upon-Avon, Warwickshire, England (Shakespeare Birthplace Trust)

> The best collection of nineteenth-century promptbooks in England, many of them from the library of the actor William Creswick (d. 1888). Later acquisitions include some books of Sullivan, Benson, and Asche. Since about 1930 the promptbooks of the Festival Theatre have mostly been preserved, and the file for the last 15 or 20 years is excellent. In 1964 the Royal Shakespeare Theatre Library, which housed these promptbooks, was amalgamated with the library of The Shakespeare Birthplace Trust and moved to The Shakespeare Centre in Henley Street.

Smallhythe: The Ellen Terry Memorial Museum, Smallhythe, near Tenterden, Kent, England

> Miss Terry's own rehearsal copies in considerable number, and a few older books which she collected.

Stratford Shakespearean Festival, Festival Theatre, Stratford, Ontario, Canada

> Promptbooks and other production materials of this theatre, and very full scrapbooks, have been carefully preserved in the Production Department since the beginning of the theatre in 1953.

Toronto Public Library, College and St. George Streets, Toronto 2B, Canada

University of Arizona Library, Tucson, Arizona

> The Thomas Wood Stevens books and papers, including 23 promptbooks of 12 Shakespeare plays. These do not appear in this catalogue, however, since they are mainly of school and community productions.

University of California Library, Los Angeles 24, California

> Small collection of nineteenth-century promptbooks including several of Frederick Warde's. Large collection of John Houseman's.

University of Edinburgh Library, Edinburgh, Scotland

> A small collection of seventeenth-century promptbooks including some of the Smock Alley.

University of Illinois Library, Rare Book Room, Urbana, Illinois

> A set of Hermann Vezin's promptbooks, a few Macready books and costume designs, a few nineteenth-century American promptbooks.

University of Michigan Library, Ann Arbor, Michigan

University of Minnesota Library, Minneapolis 14, Minnesota

University of Nebraska Libraries, Lincoln, Nebraska

> A small but significant collection of London promptbooks, circa 1810-25.

University of North Carolina Library, Tannenbaum Shakespeare Collection, Chapel Hill, North Carolina

University of Pennsylvania Library, The Horace Howard Furness Collection, Philadelphia 4, Pennsylvania

> A few dozen excellent eighteenth- and nineteenth-century promptbooks collected by the editor of the Variorum.

University of Pennsylvania Library, Rare Book Room, Philadelphia 4, Pennsylvania

University of Texas Library, Hoblitzelle Theatre Arts Library, Austin 12, Texas

The Victoria and Albert Museum, Forster Library, Cromwell Road, South Kensington, London, S. W. 7, England

> The originals of several Macready promptbooks.

W. A. Clark Memorial Library, 2205 West Adams Boulevard, Los Angeles 18, California

Yale University, The Beinecke Rare Book Library, New Haven, Connecticut

Yale University, The Elizabethan Club, 459 College Street, New Haven 11, Connecticut

All's Well That Ends Well

1. Anonymous   London, Covent Garden   c.1780

   Folger: All's Well, 3

   [Bell edition, 1773, 4¼ x 6⅞; interleaves; red, yellow, and blue marbled boards and half brown leather; title inked down spine label.]

   Promptbook marked in a neat round hand. Enclosed note suggests Kemble used this book to prepare his edition of 1793, but internal evidence does not confirm this. Cuts, many restorations. Scenic indications (including "Dall's Hall"), properties, calls, little stage business beyond that printed, cues for effects. Belonged to Lewis Mestayer. (Compare AYL, 4; MV, 3; R&J, 4; TEM, 2.)

2. William B. Wood   Philadelphia   c.1804

   New York Public Library: *NCP.P164542

   [Kemble edition, 1793, 5 x 7⅜; black and white marbled boards and blue cloth spine; title inked up spine.]

   Promptbook systematically but sparsely marked, probably not used. Cuts, scene changes, properties, calls, cues for effects.

3. John Philip Kemble   London, Covent Garden   May 24, 1811

   Garrick Club

   [Kemble edition, 1811, 5⅛ x 8¼; interleaves; blue cloth boards and brown leather spine; title gilt up spine.]

   Promptbook lightly marked in Kemble's hand. Little stage business, maps, cues for effects

4. [Kemble]

   Boston Public Library: G.4012.5

   [Two books. Kemble editions, 1793 and 1811, bound together, 4¾ x 8; marbled boards and red leather spine; title gilt on spine.]

   The 1811 copy lightly marked in Kemble's hand as rehearsal book for "Dumain," played by Barrymore. Some stage business.

5. [Kemble]

   Folger: All's Well, 2

   [Kemble edition, 1811, 5½ x 8⅞; red and blue marbled boards and half brown leather; spine label missing.]

   Rehearsal copy checked for Parolles, played by John Fawcett.

6. Harry Edwards   Sydney   1858

   Harvard Theatre Collection: TS.2027.100

   [Davidson issue of Cumberland edition, 3½ x 5¾; blue interleaves, 4 x 6¼; brown marbled boards and green cloth spine.] Promptbook carefully marked for Edwards by Joe J. Downey. Scenic indications, grooves, calls, some stage business, maps and sketches, cues for effects.

7. George Becks

New York Public Library: *NCP.342927

[French issue of Cumberland edition, 4 x 7; interleaves, 4⅜ x 7¼; red cloth boards; title gilt up spine.]

Apparently a transcription of the preceding (Edwards) book. Carefully done in the hand of George Becks.

8. Anonymous   1860's

Harvard Theatre Collection: (Widener, 13484.3.10)

[Pages 327-448 from volume I of a *Works* (pictorial edition, cheap paper), 5 x 8; interleaves; green cloth boards; title inked up spine.]

Promptbook checked for Parolles. Cuts on full text. At the front a complete scene plot with grooves. Some stage business, maps, cues for effects.

9. Augustin Daly   c.1882

Folger: All's Well, 1

[Portions of a text, with many passages in longhand, pasted in a workbook, 6⅞ x 8¼; gray cloth boards.]

Preparation copy, identified in a note by William Winter as the work of Daly.

10. [Daly]   1882

Folger: All's Well, 5, 6

[Shakespeare text pasted in two workbooks, 7⅜ x 9⅛; red marbled boards and red leather spine.]

Preparation copy made for Daly by William Winter in 1882. Cuts and rearrangements, little stage business.

11. F. R. Benson   England   August, 1898

Shakespeare Centre Library: 50.01(1889)

[Memorial Theatre edition, 1889, 4⅞ x 7¼; green cloth boards.]

Cutting of the play made by Benson in 1898, and transcribed into this copy by Mrs. C. E. Flower.

[ACTOR LISTS FOR FOLLOWING BOOKS ARE GIVEN IN THIS ORDER: Helena, Bertram, Countess, Parolles.]

12. W. Bridges-Adams   Stratford-upon-Avon   April 23, 1922

Shakespeare Centre Library: 71.21/1922A

[Favourite Classics edition pasted in a workbook, 6¾ x 9; blue cloth boards and red leather spine.]

Cast includes Maureen Shaw, Maurice Colbourne, Dorothy Green, Baliol Holloway. Cuts, calls, scenic indications, stage business, maps, cues for effects.

13. B. Iden Payne   Stratford-upon-Avon   April 23, 1935

Shakespeare Centre Library: 71.21/1935A, 1935AL

[Two books. Temple edition pasted in a workbook, 7 x 9; purple cloth boards and half black leather.]

Cast includes Jean Shepeard, Raymond Raikes, Catherine Lacey, Roy Emerton. Designed by Lloyd Weninger and Aubrey Hammond. Cuts, much stage business, maps, cues for effects. First book a preparation copy. Second book, somewhat more fully developed, used in performance.

14. Tyrone Guthrie   Stratford, Ontario   July 14, 1953

Festival Theatre, Library

[Temple edition pasted in a workbook, 7¾ x 12⅝; blue cloth boards and green cloth spine.]

Cast includes Irene Worth, Donald Harron, Eleanor Stuart, Douglas Campbell. Designed by Tanya Moiseiwitsch. Calls, much stage business, maps, cast list.

15. Michael Benthall   London, Old Vic   September 15, 1953

Old Vic, Publicity Department

[Temple edition pasted in a workbook, 8 x 10½; black ring binder.]

Cast includes Claire Bloom, John Neville, Fay Compton, Michael Hordern. Designed by Osbert Lancaster. Cuts, stage business, maps, cues for effects. Many production papers: cast, properties, fly plot, call-lists, etc.

16. Noel Willman   Stratford-upon-Avon   April 26, 1955

Shakespeare Centre Library: O.S.71.21/1955A

[Mimeograph, 8 x 13, taken from New Cambridge edition; red cloth spring binder.]

Cast includes Joyce Redman, Michael Denison, Rosalind Atkinson, Keith Michell. Designed by Mariano Andreu. Cuts, stage

business numbered and typed on facing pages, maps on mimeographed groundplans, cues for effects.

17. Tyrone Guthrie   Stratford-upon-Avon   April 21, 1959
    Shakespeare Centre Library: O.S.71.21/1959A
    [New Temple edition pasted in a workbook, 8 x 13; black cloth
    board ring binder; title on spine and cover labels.]
    Cast includes Zoe Caldwell, Edward de Souza, Edith Evans, Cyril
    Luckham. Designed by Tanya Moiseiwitsch. Cuts and additional
    dialogue, copious stage business numbered and entered on fac-
    ing pages, 18 large maps and many small ones, cues for effects.

18. John Houseman   Stratford, Connecticut   August 1, 1959
    Festival Theatre, Production Department
    [Two books. Mimeograph, 8½ x 11; blue cloth board ring binder.]
    Cast includes Nancy Wickwire, John Ragin, Aline Macmahon,
    Richard Waring. Designed by Will Steven Armstrong and
    Dorothy Jeakins. The first book is the director's workbook, with
    copious stage business and a sheaf of rehearsal notes. The second,
    called "Operating Script," has cuts, stage business, maps (some on
    mimeographed groundplans), cues for effects, some production
    papers.

19. [Houseman]
    University of California, Los Angeles: Houseman Box 14
    [Mimeograph, 8½ x 11; black cloth board spring binder.]
    Rough production book. Some stage business and other notes.

20. [Houseman]
    University of California, Los Angeles: Houseman Box 11
    [Mimeograph, 8½ x 11; blue interleaves; blue cloth boards; title
    gilt on cover.]
    Final or souvenir promptbook prepared for John Houseman by
    the Connecticut stage managers. Stage business typed on inter-
    leaves. Full set of production papers at the back.

21. Other books of *All's Well That Ends Well:*
    Boston Public Library: G.4012.5, no. 2, Barrymore.
    Folger: All's Well, 4, John Sefton and Charles Bennett.
    Princeton University, Seymour Collection: AW, 3, B. K. Brown,
    1839.

Antony and Cleopatra

1. David Garrick   London, Drury Lane   January 3, 1759

   Folger: Ant, 3

   [Tonson edition, 1734, 4¼ x 7; red and blue marbled boards and brown leather spine.]

   Cuts and alterations, with a few additions of stage business, done in ink by Edward Capell, in preparation for the acting edition published by the Tonsons on October 23, 1758. Further cuts in pencil.

2. John Philip Kemble   London, Covent Garden   Nov. 15, 1813

   Shakespeare Centre Library: 50.02(1813)

   [Kemble edition, J. Barker, 1813, 5 x 8¼; interleaves; brown leather; title gilt on red spine label, spine stamped "TR/CG/PB/A12."]

   Promptbook marked in Kemble's hand. Calls, some stage business, properties, cues for effects. Names of minor actors written in.

3. [Kemble]

   Folger: S.a.125

   [Manuscript, 7 x 8⅞; brown leather gilt; title gilt on spine.]

   Adaptation of Shakespeare's play (no Dryden included) in 1,931 lines, in Kemble's hand. Scenic indications given in some detail and with historical authorities cited, grooves. George Lamb purchased this book at the Kemble sale in 1821.

4. William Charles Macready

        London, Drury Lane   November 21, 1833

   Folger: S.a.130

   [Manuscript, 7⅜ x 8⅞; brown and green marbled boards and half maroon leather.]

   Adaptation of Shakespeare's play with Dryden materials, in 17 scenes, dated July 13, 1833, entirely in Macready's hand. Used as promptbook. Pencilings on facing pages, probably by John Willmott, the prompter, include calls, maps, sketches, cues for effects.

5. Samuel Phelps   London, Sadler's Wells   October 22, 1849

   Folger: Ant, 8

   [Shakespeare edition, 4 x 6⅜; gray interleaves watermarked 1847; gray cardboard and brown cloth spine; title inked on cover.]

   Promptbook of the restored version of the play, much used, partly in the hand of Williams, the prompter, partly in Phelps's hand.

Heavy cuts, scenic indications, grooves, much stage business, maps and sketches, costume list for Antony, cues for effects.

6. Isabella Glyn   London   c.1855

Folger: Ant, 2

[Pages 343-480 from volume VII of a *Works*, 5⅛ x 8⅛; lavender interleaves watermarked 1854; brown leather, but front cover missing and back detached.]

Reading copy. Miss Glyn, Phelps's Cleopatra in 1849, also gave Shakespearean readings. Her photograph at front. Cuts, no production notes.

7. Charles A. Calvert   Manchester, Prince's   1866

New York Public Library: *NCP.164539

[Calvert edition, 1867, 4⅞ x 7¼; green publisher's wrappers under blue cloth boards; title gilt up spine.]

Preparation copy owned by George Becks and perhaps used for Mrs. Lander's production (see nos. 11-15). Cuts and restorations, much stage business, notes on costumes and effects.

8. Anonymous

Harvard Theatre Collection: (Widener, 13484.6.10)

[Calvert edition, 1867, 4¾ x 7¼; brown marbled boards and cloth spine.]

Promptbook. Some scenic indications, grooves, some stage business, procession list, maps, cues for effects.

9. Anonymous   London, Drury Lane   September 20, 1873

Enthoven Collection: Tree, 199

[Pages from a double-column edition pasted in a workbook, 7 x 9; black glossy cardboard with sketch of Antony and Cleopatra from orange publisher's wrapper pasted on front.]

E. Edmonds, who transcribed this book, calls it "extremely archaic" and says it is taken from the promptbook of Drury Lane (presumably of above date). Wavy lines indicate cuts "for occasional condensation." Much stage business, cues for effects, often verbatim from Phelps's book. Belonged to Beerbohm Tree.

10. Anonymous

University of Pennsylvania, Furness Collection: C59.Shlan

[Pages 343-478 from volume VII of a *Works*, 5⅜ x 8¾; interleaves; crimson cloth boards; title gilt on spine.]

Thoroughly marked promptbook probably taken from the preceding (Drury Lane) book, or from the Phelps book, with which
it is often verbatim. At the tops of pages, names (Charles, Par-
geter, Drake, Henry, etc.) randomly penciled. Does not appear to
have been used for production.

11. Jean Davenport (Mrs. F. W.) Lander
              Brooklyn, Brooklyn Theatre   September 2, 1874
    New York Public Library: *NCP.342921
    [Halliday edition, 1873, 4⅛ x 7⅛, plus bits of other texts and
    manuscript restorations; interleaves, 4¾ x 8; brown cloth boards
    and half maroon leather; title inked on spine label.]
    Promptbook based on the Drury Lane version (Halliday edition)
    of 1873, much amended for Mrs. Lander's American production.
    At the front a list of scenes, and, bound upside down, a version
    of the galley scene for Act III. Calls, some stage business, maps,
    cues for effects.

12. [Lander]
    New York Public Library: *NCP.346654
    [Manuscripts, 7½ x 6¼; black and white marbled boards and
    blue cloth spine.]
    Thirteen manuscript partbooks (none for Cleopatra), made for
    Mrs. Lander's production by W. H. Crompton, Pittsburgh Opera
    House.

13. [Lander]
    New York Public Library: *NCP.342925
    [Pages of an edition pasted in a workbook, 4⅞ x 8; black cloth
    boards; title gilt on spine.]
    Promptbook. The manuscript title page says this version was ar-
    ranged for Mrs. Lander's production. Made up by George Becks.
    Sparse scenic indications, grooves, some stage business, maps, cues
    for effects. Galley scene given as an appendix. (See no. 7.)

14. [Lander]
    Folger: Ant, 1
    [Lacy edition, 1867, 4 x 6⅞; interleaves; black cloth boards and
    black leather spine; title gilt on spine.]
    George Becks's memorial reconstruction of the performances of
    Mrs. Lander and J. H. Taylor in the leading roles; also it is a new
    cutting—"A short cast Version—& regardless of Scenery—the pith

of the play." Colored pictures of various Egyptian scenery. Several reviews of productions. Copious stage business given in great detail.

15. [Lander]

Harvard Theatre Collection: *61.2354

[Lacy edition, 4⅛ x 7¼; interleaves; black cloth boards and black leather spine; title gilt on spine; in box of gray cloth boards and black leather spine; title gilt up spine.]

J. H. Taylor's copy of the preceding book, nearly identical in its record of stage business.

16. Kyrle Bellew   New York, Palmer's   January 8, 1889

Princeton University, Seymour Collection: AC,4

[Bellew edition, 1889, 5⅞ x 8⅞; gray publisher's wrappers.]

Stage manager's workbook. Some cues for effects.

17. Edmund Tearle   England   1890's

Shakespeare Centre Library: 72.902TEA

[Cassell's National Library edition, 1891, pasted in a workbook, 7⅜ x 9; tan boards, much worn and patched; title on cover label.]

Promptbook of Tearle's production. Belonged to F. Owen Chambers, who played Caesar. Much cut and altered. Scenic indications given in detail, elaborate stage business especially for openings and tableaux, cues for effects.

18. Charles B. Hanford   America   c.1900

Folger: Ant, 6

[Temple edition, 1896, pasted in a workbook, 7½ x 9½; gray cloth boards with red corners.]

Promptbook of a touring production. Cuts, alterations, heavy addition of dialogue and songs. Spectacular scenic effects, pantomimes, tableaux. Much stage business.

19. [Hanford]

Folger: Ant, 7

[Temple edition, 1896, pasted in a workbook, 7½ x 9½; gray cloth boards with red corners.]

Studybook of Hanford's wife, Marie Drofnah (Hanford), who played Cleopatra.

20. [Hanford]

Folger: Ant, 4, 5

[Typescripts, 7⅞ x 6⅜; blue paper.]

Two bundles of partbooks: 19 unused; 24 (and 2 music scores) much used, with penciled cuts and notes.

21. Herbert Beerbohm Tree   London, His Majesty's   Nov. 27, 1906
    Enthoven Collection: Tree, 199

    [Pages of a text pasted in a workbook, 8 x 10; glossy black cardboard; title inked on cover label, "Glasgow . . . Technical College" printed on label.]

    Identified on package wrapper as "Mr. Tree's original working copy." The many production notes are provisional.

22. [Tree]

    Enthoven Collection: Tree, 193

    [Proof sheets of Tree edition pasted in a workbook, 7 x 8¾; red marbled boards and green cloth spine.]

    Preparation book containing random stage directions, marked "Mr. Tree's copy."

23. [Tree]

    Enthoven Collection: Tree, 193

    [Wide-margin Temple edition, 1895, 4½ x 7; blue cloth boards; title stamped on cover, gilt up spine.]

    Promptbook used by Edward Broadley, assistant stage manager. Partial cast, cuts, maps, and copious stage directions, all roughly penciled.

24. [Tree]

    Enthoven Collection: Tree, 193

    [Proof sheets of Tree edition pasted in a workbook, 7 x 8¾; red marbled boards and green cloth spine.]

    Rehearsal promptbook, much worn, initialed by Cecil King, the stage manager. Cuts, notes on music, dance, and other effects, and much stage business, all roughly penciled.

25. [Tree]

    Enthoven Collection: Tree, 193

    [Five books. Favourite Classics edition, 1904, 3¾ x 6; publisher's green cloth boards.]

    Rehearsal copies for various characters, with cuts and random notes on scenes and stage business. Three more copies unmarked.

26. [Tree]

Enthoven Collection: Tree, 193

[Proof sheets of Tree edition pasted in a workbook, 10¼ x 11½; blue boards and purple cloth spine; title pasted on cover.]

Rehearsal copy checked for Antony. Copious stage business, maps, groundplans, cues for effects, all roughly penciled.

27. [Tree]

Enthoven Collection: Tree, 193

[Proof sheets of Tree edition pasted in a workbook, 10½ x 11¼; blue boards and blue cloth spine; title pasted on cover.]

Fully developed promptbook, all in ink. Cuts, copious stage business, maps, cues for effects.

28. [Tree]

Enthoven Collection: Tree, 193

[Proof sheets of Tree edition pasted in a workbook, 10½ x 11½; blue boards and blue cloth spine; no title on outside.]

Final promptbook, made up by Edward Broadley, assistant stage manager. Contains all the matter of the preceding book but is executed more systematically. Music cues are entered in red. Calls are slips typed in purple and pasted in. Cast, list of scenes, etc., from the printed program are pasted on the fly.

29. [Tree]

Enthoven Collection: Tree, 193

[Tree edition, 1907, pasted in a workbook, 8 x 9¾; green cloth boards and half tan leather.]

This was to be a final promptbook, but only the first few pages are marked. Printed cast pasted in the front.

30. [Tree]

Enthoven Collection: Tree, 194

[Folder, 20⅞ x 15½, containing papers.]

The folder is a character distribution chart. Many production papers: drawings of the barge, plots of properties, supers, dresses, limes, ladies' business, etc.

31. [Tree]

New York Public Library: *NCP.44x545

[Typescript, 8¼ x 10⅞; blue cloth boards; title gilt on spine.]

Typescript of Tree's acting version, freely arranged in 4 acts and 13 scenes, with Tree's Foreword dated December 27, 1906. On the title page is penciled "produced at the Mansfield Theatre, 10 Nov., 1937." (See no. 41.)

32. E. H. Sothern and Julia Marlowe
             New York, New Theatre   November 8, 1909
New York Public Library: *NCP

[Temple edition, 1896, pasted in a workbook, 7 x 8⅞; red limp leather; title gilt up spine.]

Preparation copy, heavily penciled for cuts, stresses, pronunciations, with notes on stage arrangements and business.

33. [Sothern and Marlowe]
New York Public Library: *NCP.44x220

[Temple edition, 1896, pasted in a workbook, 6¼ x 7⅞; green limp leather; title gilt on red leather cover label.]

Preparation copy of the text only. No markings, but the text has been "improved" over that of preceding book.

34. [Sothern and Marlowe]
Museum of the City of New York: 43.430.621

[Temple edition, 1896, pasted in a workbook, 7¾ x 10; brown marbled boards and brown cloth spine; title pasted on cover.]

Preparation copy, fully marked for stresses, much stage business, cues for effects.

35. [Sothern and Marlowe]
Museum of the City of New York: 43.430.622

[Antony scenes from Temple edition, 1896, pasted in a workbook, 3⅞ x 6½; black rubberized cloth.]

Sothern's partbook for Antony, fully marked for stresses.

36. Winthrop Ames   New York, New Theatre   November 8, 1909
New York Public Library: *NCP+.51624B

[Typescript, 8 x 13; red cloth boards; title gilt on spine.]

The director's text of the New Theatre production, different from that prepared by Sothern and Marlowe (see nos. 32-35). Notes on meaning of words, historical backgrounds, and interpretation. At the back a vast compilation of opinion on the main characters, including descriptions of past performances. A list of 22 English and American productions.

37. [Ames]

New York Public Library: *NCP.38x1111

[Proof copy of Ames edition, 5¼ x 8¾; brown paper under red cloth boards; title gilt up spine.]

The Ames version with printed text, typescript Preface dated November, 1909, and manuscript title page.

38. Oscar Asche and Lily Brayton   Melbourne   December 26, 1912

Shakespeare Centre Library: F.72.902ASC

[Temple edition, 1896, pasted in a workbook, 9½ x 14; heavy tan suede; title gilt on red leather cover and spine labels.]

Souvenir promptbook of the Asche production in Australia in 1912 and South Africa in 1913. Belonged to his wife Lily Brayton (later Mrs. Douglas Chalmers Watson). Much cut and rearranged. Elaborate scenic effects, much stage business. Plots of lights and properties, groundplan for each scene. Large photographs of most of the principals. The original cast is given.

[ACTOR LISTS FOR FOLLOWING BOOKS ARE GIVEN IN THIS ORDER: Antony, Cleopatra, Caesar, Enobarbus.]

39. W. Bridges-Adams   Stratford-upon-Avon   June 29, 1931

Shakespeare Centre Library: 71.21/1931A(2179)

[Temple edition pasted in a workbook, 7 x 9; green boards and red cloth spine; title on cover label.]

The cast includes Gyles Isham, Dorothy Massingham, Eric Maxon, Randle Ayrton. Costumes by Eric Maxon. Cuts, calls, relatively sparse stage business, maps, cues for effects.

40. B. Iden Payne   Stratford-upon-Avon   April 15, 1935

Shakespeare Centre Library: 71.21/1931A(7925)

[New Temple edition pasted in a workbook, 7 x 9; purple cloth boards and half black leather; title on cover label.]

Though identified on the title page as Bridges-Adams' book of 1931, this appears to be Payne's of 1935. Cast includes Roy Emerton, Catherine Lacey, Eric Maxon, Randle Ayrton. Designed by Aubrey Hammond. Unused copy, done in pencil: much stage business, maps. (See no. 42.)

41. Tallulah Bankhead   New York, Mansfield   November 10, 1937

New York Public Library: *NCP.49x168

[Typescript, 8⅛ x 10⅞; green cloth boards; title gilt up spine.]
Cast includes Conway Tearle, Tallulah Bankhead, Conrad Emery,
Thomas Chalmers. Designed by Jo Mielziner. Directed by Regi-
nald Bach. Unmarked copy of the acting version by William
Strunk, which is much altered and partly converted to prose.
(See no. 31.)

42. Robert Atkins   Stratford-upon-Avon   April 23, 1945
    Shakespeare Centre Library: 71.21/1945A
    [Temple edition pasted in a workbook, 7 x 9; purple cloth boards
    and half black leather.]
    Cast includes Antony Eustrel, Claire Luce, David Read, Tristan
    Rawson. Designed by J. Gower Parks. Cuts, calls, much stage busi-
    ness, maps, cues for music. A small red callbook is enclosed. Orig-
    inally used in B. Iden Payne's production in 1935 (see no. 40);
    was erased and reused.

43. Glen Byam Shaw   Stratford-upon-Avon   April 28, 1953
    Shakespeare Centre Library: O.S.71.21/1953A
    [New Temple edition pasted in a workbook, 8 x 13; red cloth
    boards.]
    Cast includes Michael Redgrave, Peggy Ashcroft, Marius Goring,
    Harry Andrews. Designed by Motley. Cuts, calls, much stage busi-
    ness, maps, cues for effects.

44. [Shaw]   London, Prince's, and Continental Tour   Oct. 31, 1953
    Shakespeare Centre Library: O.S.71.21/1953-54
    [New Temple edition pasted in a workbook, 8 x 13; red cloth
    boards.]
    Same production as at Stratford-upon-Avon but as taken on tour.
    Cuts and cues. Stage business entered very sparsely. Light plot
    and curtain call routine.

45. [Shaw]
    Shakespeare Centre Library: O.S.71.21/1953-54
    [New Temple edition pasted in a workbook, 6½ x 8; blue ring
    binder.]
    Another promptbook for the Stratford production on tour, show-
    ing cuts and cues only. Recorded music plot of 49 cues.

46. Robert Helpmann   London, Old Vic   March 5, 1957
    Old Vic, Publicity Department

[New Temple edition pasted in a workbook, 8 x 10½; black ring binder.]

Cast includes Keith Michell, Margaret Whiting, Leon Gluckman, Derek Godfrey. Designed by Loudon Sainthill. Much stage business (roughly entered), maps, cues for effects. Many production papers, for lights, properties, flies, timings, etc.

47. Jack Landau   Stratford, Connecticut   July 31, 1960
Festival Theatre, Production Department

[Two books. Mimeograph, 8½ x 11; interleaves; blue cloth board ring binders.]

Cast includes Robert Ryan, Katharine Hepburn, John Ragin, Donald Davis. Designed by Rouben Ter-Arutunian. The first book has copious stage business typed on interleaves, cues for effects typed on text sheets; production papers include understudies, properties, costumes, wigs, fly and trap cues, curtain calls. The second book, called "Stage Management," is also fully developed, and includes music score.

As You Like It

1. Anonymous   Douai   1695

   Bibliothèque de Douai: MS.7.87

   [Manuscript, folios 32-65 of a volume, $6\frac{3}{4}$ x $8\frac{5}{8}$; parchment.]

   Manuscript version used for amateur staging at Douai. Cuts and alterations, some stage business. Dated March 9, 1695. (See G. Blakemore Evans, *Philological Quarterly,* XLI, 158-172.)

2. Charles Macklin   London, Drury Lane   October 15, 1741

   Folger: S.a.25

   [Manuscript, $5\frac{7}{8}$ x $7\frac{1}{4}$; red and yellow marbled boards and half red leather gilt; title gilt up spine.]

   Macklin's partbook for Touchstone. Few annotations.

3. Anonymous   England   1700's

   Shakespeare Centre Library: 50.03(1734)

   [Tonson edition, 1734, $3\frac{3}{4}$ x $6\frac{7}{8}$; green cloth boards and green leather spine; title gilt up spine.]

   Promptbook perhaps for amateur production. Checked for Orlando. Cuts and a few rough notes. The name of Roben Walker is inked on the title page and the names Neals, Ross, Barnett on the page of Persons Represented.

4. Anonymous   London, Covent Garden   c.1780

   New York Public Library: *NCP.709468

   [Bell edition, 1773, $4\frac{1}{2}$ x $7\frac{3}{8}$; brown cloth boards; title gilt up spine.]

   Promptbook marked in ink in a neat round hand, with penciled corrections. Scenic indications (including "Carver's Gar."), grooves, little stage business, properties, cues for effects. Rosalind is to sing the Cuckoo Song, but provisional note assigns it to Celia. (Compare AW, 1; MV, 3; R&J, 4; TEM, 2.)

5. Anonymous

   Harvard Theatre Collection: (Widener, 13484.11.10)

   [J. Barker edition, 1794, $4\frac{1}{8}$ x $7\frac{1}{4}$; brown marbled boards and brown cloth spine.]

   Promptbook probably of the eighteenth century. Cuts, restorations, some stage business, a map.

6. Anonymous   Aberdeen   January, 1806

   New York Public Library: *NCP.342936

   [Edition printed for Rivington, 1775, 4 x $6\frac{7}{8}$; interleaves; leaves and interleaves tipped to stubs to make a book 5 x 6⅞; black cloth boards; title gilt on spine.]

Sparsely but systematically marked book. Many cuts, calls, cues for effects.

7. John Philip Kemble   London, Covent Garden   March 19, 1811
Smallhythe

[Kemble edition, 1810, 5 x 8⅛; interleaves; brown leather; title gilt up red leather spine label.]

Identified on flyleaf as Kemble's "authentic" copy, and marked in Kemble's hand. Cuts, properties, little stage business, cues for effects. Belonged to Ellen Terry.

8. [Kemble]
Folger: T.a.39

[Manuscript, 7 x 8⅞; brown leather gilt; title gilt up spine.]

Kemble's 12-page partbook for Jaques, in his own hand, 200 lines. Dated Drury Lane, February 14, 1799, and Covent Garden, October 25, 1805, but probably written much later.

9. Charles Kemble   London, Covent Garden   December 10, 1824
Garrick Club

[Kemble edition, 1810, 5¼ x 8¼; interleaves; blue cloth boards and brown leather spine; title gilt up spine.]

Promptbook originally marked with calls and some stage business; later much cut in pencil and augmented with songs and musical effects to become Frederic Reynolds' operatic version.

10. William Charles Macready
                London, Covent Garden   January 11, 1820
Shakespeare Centre Library: 50.03(1815)

[Kemble edition, 1815, 4⅛ x 6⅞; no binding but wrapped in cardboard with typewritten titles.]

Promptbook signed "Wm M'Cready." Probably the book of the younger Macready, though not in his hand. Cuts, calls, cues for effects. Later belonged to Frederick Haywel. (See nos. 17-24.)

11. Anonymous   America   1820's
Harvard Theatre Collection: (Widener, 13484.11.20)

[Two books bound together. Oxberry edition, Boston, 1822, 3¾ x 6¼; first copy interleaved; red cloth boards; title on spine.]

First copy is a neatly written promptbook with cuts, calls, some stage business, maps and sketches, cues for effects. Second copy very lightly marked.

12. John Sefton   New York   1830's
Folger: AYL, 17

[Inchbald edition, $4\frac{1}{8}$ x $6\frac{1}{2}$; brown marbled boards and brown leather spine, broken.]

Promptbook lightly marked. Cuts, some calls, some cues for effects.

13. Anonymous   Sheffield and Doncaster   November, 1834
New York Public Library: *NCP.164456

[Cumberland edition, $3\frac{1}{2}$ x $5\frac{3}{4}$; black cloth boards; title gilt up spine.]

Promptbook neatly written in a flowing hand. Cuts, grooves, sparse stage business, cues for effects. Contains playbills of the Cushmans in Birmingham in 1847, and Henry Farren at the Howard in Boston in 1856. Probably brought to America by Henry Farren.

14. Anonymous   London, Drury Lane   October 18, 1837
London Museum: Sp.822.33

[Kemble edition, 1815, $4\frac{3}{8}$ x $7\frac{3}{8}$; tan paper; title inked on cover.]
A Drury Lane promptbook in several hands. The list of written papers and various other notations in the first act are in a neat hand. Certain timing notes and references to Miss Chorley in 1837 appear to be by the prompter, John Willmott. Cuts and restorations, notes on songs, calls, some stage business, warnings for costume change (including Mr. Wallack's). Probably in use long before 1837.

15. Helen Faucit   London, Covent Garden   April 18, 1839
Folger: AYL, 40

[Kemble edition, $4\frac{1}{8}$ x $7\frac{1}{4}$; brown paper, much worn; title and Miss Faucit's name inked on cover.]

Rehearsal copy checked for Rosalind. Cuts, many light pencilings. Notes of cuts and restorations suggest she used this book during Macready's Drury Lane production of 1842 (see nos. 17-24).

16. Charles Kean   England-America   1840's
Folger: W.a.10

[Notebook, $4\frac{3}{4}$ x $7\frac{3}{4}$, sheets watermarked 1837; brown marbled boards and half brown leather; "Theatrical Costumes" inked on spine label.]

Kean's touring wardrobe list for Jaques is the fifteenth of 16 such lists in this book. (See nos. 21, 31.)

17. William Charles Macready   London, Drury Lane   Oct. 1, 1842
    University of Illinois: x792.9/Sh15as/no.1

    [Pages 103-207 from a volume of *Works,* 4½ x 7; interleaves water-marked 1842; brown marbled boards and half brown leather; title gilt on black spine label.]

    Macready's preparation copy marked in his own hand, signed and dated September 8, 1842, in the front cover. Cuts and alterations, copious stage business, scenic arrangements, entered in ink and augmented in pencil. (See no. 10.)

18. [Macready]
    Folger: AYL, 3

    [Pages 5 to 96 from volume IV of a *Works,* 5⅛ x 8⅛; interleaves, 5½ x 8; white cardboard, grayed and broken; title inked on front.]

    "Original promptbook" of Macready's 1842 production. Professional transcription of all the matter in Macready's preparation copy. Much additional matter penciled by John Willmott, the prompter: cuts, calls, stage business, maps and sketches, list of 74 actors for the wrestling scene, cues for sound and curtains, timings. A few additions by George Ellis, the assistant prompter.

19. [Macready]
    University of Illinois

    [Watercolors, 4⅛ x 6⅝.]

    Eight costume designs for Macready's 1842 production, by Charles Hamilton Smith. (See Charles H. Shattuck, *Mr. Macready Produces "As You Like It."*)

20. [Macready]
    Folger: AYL, 4

    [Pages 103-204 from volume III of a *Works,* 5⅛ x 7½; inter-leaves, 4⅞ x 8; white cardboard and cloth spine, contents not sewn in; title written on cover.]

    A transcription of Macready's perfected 1842 book, done in pencil by George Ellis. Contains a 12-page callbook, 3 x 8, water-marked 1842, written by Ellis and corrected by Willmott; also a slip embossed "Windsor Castle" describing scenery for I, 2.

21. [Macready]

Folger: AYL, 9

[Pages 102-205 from volume III of a *Works*, 5⅜ x 8¾; inter-leaves watermarked 1844, 7½ x 9½; red, tan, and blue marbled boards and half red leather gilt; title and "C.K." gilt on spine, "Prompt Copy/Mr. Charles Kean" gilt on black leather cover label.]

Excellent transcription of Macready's 1842 book made by George Ellis for Charles Kean, dated 1850, used for Windsor Castle pro-duction on January 31, 1851. (See nos. 16, 31.)

22. [Macready]

University of Illinois: x792.9/Sh15as/no.2

[Pages 1-105 from volume III of a *Works*, 5¼ x 8⅛; interleaves watermarked 1848, 1852, 7¾ x 9¾; blue marbled boards and half maroon leather; title gilt on black cover label and spine.]

Transcription of Macready's 1842 book made by George Ellis for Hermann Vezin in the 1850's. Additional alterations and mark-ings by Vezin or others. (See selective facsimile in Charles H. Shattuck, *Mr. Macready Produces "As You Like It."*)

23. [Macready]

Folger: AYL, 5

[Modern Standard Drama, 1848, 4½ x 7⅜; interleaves, 5 x 8; tan paper; title written on cover.]

John Moore's transcription made on an acting edition from one of Ellis' copies of Macready's 1842 book, with restorations entered by hand. Contains cast lists from Manchester, 1844, and the New York Theatre, 1868.

24. [Macready]

New York Public Library: *NCP.285348

[French's Standard Drama, 4¼ x 7½; interleaves, 5 x 8; gray paper under green cloth boards; title gilt on spine.]

Another of John Moore's transcriptions made on an acting edi-tion, his markings derived from the Macready production, with additional jottings by George Becks, to whom it later belonged. Restorations and most of the stage business verbatim from Mac-ready; alterations of scenic arrangements and text. (See nos. 37-38, 58-62.)

25. Edward Loomis Davenport   London, Olympic   1847

Princeton University, Seymour Collection: AYL, 2

[Cumberland edition, 1827, 3¾ x 6; interleaves; paper wrapper.]

Promptbook dated 1840, and said on the cover to have been used in London in 1847. It later belonged to May Davenport, and is checked for Celia. Heavy cuts, a few scenic indications, calls, some music cues.

26. Samuel Phelps   London, Sadler's Wells   November 29, 1847

Folger: AYL, 18

[Pages 103-205 from volume III of a *Works,* 5 x 8¾; interleaves, 4⅜ x 7¼; gray cardboard, broken and very soiled; title and dates (1848 to 1858) inked on cover.]

Phelps's promptbook for a decade, marked by Phelps and Williams, the prompter. Cuts vary from year to year. Few scenic indications, some grooves, calls, stage business, maps and sketches, cues for effects, timings, a penciled cast.

27. [Phelps]

Folger: AYL, 19

[Pages 191-284 from volume III of Knight's Cabinet Edition, 3½ x 5½; interleaves, 4¼ x 7; yellow and blue marbled boards and half brown leather, broken; title gilt on spine.]

Good transcription of Phelps's book, much used at Sadler's Wells, the directions in brown ink in a small neat hand, the cuts and alterations in bright blue ink.

28. Henry Marsh Clifford   England

Folger: AYL, 34

[Kemble edition, 1810, 5 x 8¼; interleaves; dark green cloth boards and half black leather; Clifford's name gilt up spine.]

Promptbook originally marked for calls and cues on an unrestored text; later augmented with stage business, sketches, etc., apparently derived from Phelps's book. The name of Jenny Marston is on the title page; Clifford's name, as of Brighton, is on the back fly.

29. Henry Betty   England

Folger: AYL, 43, 44

[Two books. Pages 191-284 from volume III of Knight's Cabinet Edition, 1847-48, 3⅜ x 5⅛; interleaves; gray boards and green cloth spine.]

Two carefully marked promptbooks, using red ink for scenic indications, grooves, calls, and cues; brown ink for stage business. Directions partly derived from Macready and Phelps.

30. W. E. Burton   New York, Burton's   1848
   Folger: AYL, 24

   [Modern Standard Drama, 4½ x 7½; brown paper and purple spine; title and date on cover.]

   Rough promptbook of Burton's Theatre. Cuts, calls, cues for some effects.

31. Charles Kean   London, Princess's   February 1, 1851
   Folger: AYL, 10

   [Pages 5-96 from volume IV of a *Works*, 4⅞ x 7¾; interleaves watermarked 1858, 6¾ x 8½; tan cloth boards and half brown leather; title gilt on spine, "Mr. Charles Kean/Prompt Copy" gilt on black leather cover label.]

   Final or souvenir promptbook made about 1859 by T. W. Edmonds, the prompter. Cuts, alterations, grooves, some stage business, maps, cues, timings. (See nos. 16, 21.)

32. John A. Ellsler   Philadelphia   1850's
   Folger: AYL, 14

   [Oxberry edition, Boston, 1822, 3⅜ x 5½; tan and red marbled boards and half brown leather, loose and patched.]

   Promptbook checked for Jaques, with rough cuts and calls in a neat hand. "Ellsler" is penciled on front flyleaf. Bookplate of William Murray, Philadelphia Theatre.

33. Robert Jones   Boston, Howard Athenaeum   1852
   New York Public Library: *NCP.342942

   [Modern Standard Drama, 1848, 4¼ x 7½; gray interleaves, 5¾ x 7½; blue cloth boards.]

   Carefully marked but little used promptbook made by the Howard Athenaeum stage manager. Scenic indications, grooves, calls, much stage business, maps and sketches, cues for scene changes and curtains, timings.

34. John B. Wright   Boston   c.1854
   New York Public Library: *NCP.342988

   [Modern Standard Drama, 1848, 4½ x 7½; gray interleaves; card-

board under black and green marbled boards and black cloth
spine.]

A roughly marked but useful promptbook, with scenic indications, grooves, calls, much stage business, maps. (See Melinda
Jones's book, no. 44.)

35. Thomas Barry   Boston, Boston Theatre   1854
Harvard Theatre Collection: uncatalogued

[Two books: Cumberland edition, 3¾ x 6; interleaves, 5 x 7⅞;
gray boards and brown leather spine; title and "6" inked on cover
label.]

Two promptbooks probably made by Charles Melville, an English
prompter, whose collection was brought to Boston by Thomas
Barry in 1854. The fuller of the two was originally marked in
brown ink, later augmented in pencil. Contains at the front a
chart of scenes, wings, grooves, and lights. Cuts, calls, some stage
business, cues for effects.

36. James William Wallack   London, Marylebone   October, 1854
New York Public Library: *NCP.342961

[Pages 191-284 from volume III of Knight's Cabinet Edition, 1847-
48, 3½ x 5⅜; gray interleaves, 4 x 6⅛; black cloth boards; title
gilt on spine.]

Very carefully developed promptbook, which appears to derive
from Phelps's book. Scenic indications, grooves, calls, much stage
business, maps and sketches, cues for effects. This is apparently
the book of the younger J. W. Wallack; later belonged to George
Becks.

37. John Moore   New York   1855-76
Folger: AYL, 23

[Modern Standard Drama, 1848, 4½ x 7½; blue interleaves;
crude cover pasted with programs.]

A vast collection of information made by Moore during decades
of acting and stage-managing the play. Programs and reviews of
many productions (mainly New York) from 1855 to 1876. The
text is cut in red as played by Charlotte Cushman at Burton's in
1857. The Rosalind business derives variously from Helen Faucit,
Ellen Kean, Louisa Nisbett, Charlotte Cushman, Avonia Jones,
Mrs. Scott-Siddons. Elaborate scenic indications, a properties list,
much detailed stage business, maps and sketches, cues for effects

—generally relevant to Daly's production of 1876. (See nos. 23-24, 58-62.)

38. [Moore]   New York
    Folger: T.b.2
    [Notebook, 6⅛ x 10¼; blue boards and black cloth spine.]
    Cues for the band for 48 plays, including *As You Like It*.

39. Kate Reignolds   Boston   1860's
    Harvard Theatre Collection: uncatalogued
    [French's Standard Drama, 4⅝ x 7½; in an envelope.]
    Lightly marked promptbook checked for Celia, with some stage
    business and cues for effects. In the same envelope are 2 copies
    of the French edition printed for the Langtry tour of 1882-83,
    with some penciled cuts. (See no. 52.)

40. F. Harrington   Chicago, McVicker's   1860
    University of Pennsylvania, Furness Collection: C59.Shlas.1848
    [Modern Standard Drama, 1848; interleaves, 5 x 7⅝; green mar-
    bled boards and half black leather.]
    Carefully marked promptbook, nearly identical with Robert
    Jones's book of the Howard Athenaeum (see no. 33). Scenic indica-
    tions, grooves, calls, stage business, maps and sketches, cues for
    effects, timings. At I, 3, "No change for Miss Cushman."

41. Frederick Haywel   England
    Shakespeare Centre Library: O.S.P.50.03(1829)
    [Cumberland edition, 1829, 3½ x 5½; heavy tan paper; title
    inked on cover.]
    Rehearsal copy checked for Orlando, Jaques, and Duke. "With
    Shakespearian Restorations by F. Haywell" (stage name of Fred-
    erick Hawley).

42. John Baldwin Buckstone   London, Haymarket   Sept. 2, 1867
    Harvard Theatre Collection: *61.2355
    [Lacy edition, 4 x 7; interleaves; limp blue cloth boards; title
    gilt on cover; in box of gray cloth boards and red leather spine;
    title gilt up spine.]
    Promptbook neatly marked in black and red for the Haymarket,
    and with penciled additions for later use at Manchester. Cuts,
    calls, very little stage business, maps, cues for effects, timing
    (2:30).

43. Charles Dornton   Birmingham   1870's
    Birmingham, Shakespeare Memorial Library: C53/455744
    [French issue of Lacy edition, 4¼ x 7¼; publisher's wrappers;
    bound with other Shakespeare plays in green cloth boards.]
    Promptbook. Cuts and alterations, cues for effects. "Recd from
    Mr. Potter in lieu of one I lent, Sept. 19th, 1876."

44. Fanny Davenport
                    New York, Fifth Avenue   May 24, Nov. 18, 1876
    Princeton University, Seymour Collection: AYL, 3
    [Oxberry edition, 1822, 4 x 6⅞; interleaves partly of stationery
    of Daly's Theatre; binding and last pages lost.]
    Originally the book of Melinda Jones, Boston, 1853, but marked
    "Fanny Davenport's P. B^k. arranged by Augustin Daly." Checked
    for Rosalind. The original markings for Mrs. Jones are full and
    careful, including scenic indications, stage business, etc., closely
    resembling J. B. Wright's book (see no. 34). Daly has restored cer-
    tain passages by pasting them onto the interleaves made from
    stationery of the Fifth Avenue Theatre. Belonged to William
    Seymour. (See no. 57.)

45. [Davenport]
    Harvard Theatre Collection: (Widener, 13484.12.10)
    [Three books. Cumberland edition, 4 x 6⅜; green publisher's
    wrappers under green cloth boards; title gilt on spine.]
    Three rehearsal copies, "Property of Miss Davenport," for Phebe,
    Oliver (Lackaye), Banished Duke (Sutherland). Cuts, some stage
    business.

46. William Seymour   Boston, Boston Museum   c.1880
    Princeton University, Seymour Collection: AYL, 4
    [Oxberry edition, Boston, 1822, 3¾ x 6⅛; publisher's wrappers
    under limp cloth; "Boston Museum" inked on cover.]
    Roughly marked but much used promptbook, probably of early
    nineteenth-century origin, with cuts, scenic indications, grooves,
    some stage business, cues for effects.

47. [Seymour]
    Princeton University, Seymour Collection: AYL, 6
    [French issue of Cumberland-Duncombe edition, 4 x 6¼; blue
    wrappers.]
    Preparation copy. Early scenes carefully marked for cuts, scenic

indications, grooves, maps. The markings dwindle into pencilings and are probably not finished. A review of Julia Marlowe in Springfield, 1908.

48. [Seymour]

Princeton University, Seymour Collection: AYL, 8

[French's Standard Drama, 4½ x 7½; coarse cloth; title and "Boston Museum 1859" inked on cover.]

Crude promptbook, with property list, cues for effects.

49. Marie Litton   London, Imperial   February 25, 1880

Folger: AYL, 2

[Litton edition, 5⅜ x 8¼; gray publisher's wrappers.]

Marked copy of Miss Litton's acting version. Some penciled stage business.

50. Lester Wallack   New York, Wallack's   September 30, 1880

New York Public Library: *NCP.342956

[French's Standard Drama pasted in a workbook of brown paper, 5½ x 8¼; in blue cloth board case; title gilt on spine.]

Rough but working promptbook, with cuts and restorations, calls, some stage business, maps, cues for effects. A penciled cast includes the English actors Wallack imported for the occasion: Tearle, Pitt, Elton.

51. May Davenport   New York, Fifth Avenue   January 3, 1882

Princeton University, Seymour Collection: AYL, 12

[French's Standard Drama, 4½ x 7⅜; publisher's wrappers.]

Rehearsal copy checked for Celia and Oliver. Cuts and some cues and business. May Davenport was supporting Fanny Davenport's Rosalind in 1881-82.

52. Lily Langtry   New York, Wallack's   November 13, 1882

University of Michigan: PR.2803.A22.A12

[French edition "as played by Mrs. Langtry," 5⅞ x 9; tan publisher's wrapper with her photograph pasted on.]

Spectator's copy. Many notes of stage business, maps, cues for effects, and critical notes.

53. James L. Carhart

Harvard Theatre Collection: (Widener, 13484.13.10)

[Two books. French edition "as played by Mrs. Langtry," 5⅝ x

9⅛; publisher's wrappers with two different photographs of Langtry pasted on, under maroon cloth boards; title gilt up spine.]

Rehearsal copies, the second checked for Adam and Duke. Cuts, some penciled stage business.

54. Helena Modjeska   New York, Booth's   December 11, 1882
Folger: AYL, 15

[French's Standard Drama pasted in a workbook, 6½ x 7½; brown cloth boards and half brown leather; title on cover and spine.]

Carefully made, much used promptbook. Systematic scenic indications, stage business, cues for effects in red ink. At the back a printed scene plot with grooves, and plots for properties, gas, calcium, curtains, supers, ballet. Contains a letter from "Elizabeth" to "Rob" telling how she obtained it from Count Bozenta, who said, "It is the copy Madam always used."

55. [Modjeska]
Folger: AYL, 25

[Modjeska edition, 1883, 4⅜ x 7½; brown and red publisher's wrappers.]

Rehearsal copy. Many pencilings in unidentified hand of stage business, maps, some cues for effects.

56. George Becks   America
New York Public Library: *NCP.342946

[Lacy edition, 4 x 6¾; interleaves; black cloth boards; title gilt on spine.]

Much used promptbook. Some scenic indications, calls, much stage business, maps, cues for effects. Some notes on Modjeska's and Marie Litton's productions. At the front notes on critical interpretations.

57. Fanny Davenport   America   c.1885
Harvard Theatre Collection: TS.3059.500

[French's Standard Drama pasted in a workbook, 6⅞ x 8¼; green marbled boards and red leather spine.]

Carefully developed promptbook. Cuts and restorations, scenic indications given in some detail, stage business especially elaborate for tableaux, maps, cues for effects. A note by A. C. Sprague dates the book after January 1, 1885. (See no. 44.)

58. Augustin Daly   New York, Daly's   December 17, 1889
    Folger: AYL, 16
    [Daly edition, 1890, 5¾ x 9¼; interleaves, 4¾ x 7¾; buff paper
    pasted with printed matter about the play.]
    Printed stage directions largely derived from promptbooks of
    John Moore (see nos. 23-24, 37-38, 59-62). This copy, signed by
    Fred Sherman, is heavily annotated by Moore. Much additional
    stage business and notes on special arrangements in Daly's pro-
    duction.

59. [Daly]
    New York Public Library: *NCP.686456
    [Proof sheets of Daly edition, 1890, 5¾ x 9¼, pasted back to back;
    interleaves; stiffened linen covered with programs, under red
    cloth boards and half red leather; title gilt on spine, "Augustin
    Daly" gilt on red leather cover label.]
    The working promptbook of the 1889 production. Most of the
    stage directions are printed, but there are many additions, some
    by Moore (brown ink), some by another hand (red ink). These
    include stage business, scene change by sink, fly, and moving
    panorama, detailed cues for effects.

60. [Daly]
    Folger: Prints and Engravings
    [Daly edition, 1890, mounted in albums (2 volumes), 12⅜ x 16¾;
    maroon marbled boards and half brown leather gilt; title gilt on
    spines.]
    Souvenir album in 2 volumes. The first volume contains many
    old prints of actors, some eighteenth-century playbills, many
    prints of scenes from the play, 19 watercolor costume designs for
    Daly's production, 52 photographs of actors, and 4 photographs
    of scenes from Daly's production. The second volume contains an
    Introduction to the play by Edward Dowden, a facsimile of the
    1632 Folio text, Stothard's illustrations of the "Seven Ages of
    Man," etc., many portraits of actors of Rosalind and Touchstone,
    pictorial records of Daly's 1876 production with Fanny Daven-
    port, of the Litton, Langtry, Anderson, and other recent produc-
    tions, a silk bill for Daly's fiftieth performance, reviews, 13 pho-
    tographs of Daly's actors, etc.

61. [Daly]
    New York Public Library: 8*T*NCP+

[Daly edition, 1890, mounted in large album, 12¼ x 16⅞; red and blue marbled boards and half blue leather.]

Ada Rehan's souvenir album given her by Daly in 1890, containing many photographs of characters and scenes, reviews, a silk program, old engravings, playbills, etc.

62. [Daly]

Harvard Theatre Collection: (Widener, 13484.12)

[Three books. French's Standard Drama, 4½ x 7¼.]

Rehearsal copies of James Lewis, checked for Touchstone, with bits of stage business; Orlando; Aunt Louisa Eldridge, checked for Audrey.

63. Hallam Bosworth

New York Public Library: *NCP.52x296

[American Academy of Dramatic Arts edition, no. 7, 1903, 5½ x 8; interleaves, 6¼ x 8¼; black cloth boards; title gilt up spine.]

Promptbook done in pencil by Hallam Bosworth, the annotations largely from Daly's production. At the front plots of scenes (with maps), properties, lights, doubles and supers. Scenic indications, vocabulary notes, copious stage business, maps, cues for effects.

64. Julia Marlowe   New York, Fifth Avenue   January 27, 1889

Museum of the City of New York: 43.430.623

[Rolfe edition, 1878, pasted in a workbook, 5½ x 8½; brown limp leather.]

Early preparation copy, partly cut and marked for stresses. A few scenic notes at front. This and the two following books are probably for the 1889 production. (See nos. 83-91.)

65. [Marlowe]

Museum of the City of New York: 43.430.624

[Pages of Rolfe edition tipped between leaves of a workbook, 6 x 8⅝; black cloth boards.]

More fully developed preparation copy. Cuts on full text, much stage business.

66. [Marlowe]

Museum of the City of New York: 43.430.625

[Rolfe edition pasted in a workbook, 7⅞ x 10⅛; blue cloth boards and half blue leather gilt; title printed on cover label.]

Fully developed promptbook, frequently verbatim from preceding book. Cuts, scenic indications, groundplans, much stage business, maps, cues for effects. At the front a cast and plots of properties, arms, scenes.

67. Anonymous   America   1890's

Folger: AYL, 20

[French's Standard Drama, $4\frac{1}{2}$ x $7\frac{1}{2}$; interleaves, $6\frac{5}{8}$ x 8; black and white mottled boards and red leather spine, pictorial endpapers of a bookstore.]

Very carefully developed promptbook of late nineteenth-century American provenience. Scenic prescriptions with maps given in detail. Stage business often very full—and naive in effect. At the end of Act IV, "Marlowe falls on stage in a faint." Does not appear to have been used.

68. Albert Taverner   Toronto   1890's

Toronto Public Library: 822.33/S.13

[French's Standard Drama, $4\frac{3}{8}$ x $7\frac{3}{8}$; interleaves.]

Rehearsal copy checked for several characters. Cuts, calls, scattered notes on stage business and acting manner.

69. Eleanor Barry   San Francisco   January 28, 1893

Folger: AYL, 36

[French's Standard Drama pasted in a workbook, $6\frac{5}{8}$ x $8\frac{1}{4}$; red limp imitation leather; title on cover label.]

Carefully made promptbook, similar to Modjeska's (see no. 54). Scenic indications with maps and sketches, stage business in considerable detail, cues for effects.

70. Robert B. Mantell   Asbury Park   1895

Folger: AYL, 6

[French's Standard Drama, $4\frac{1}{2}$ x $7\frac{1}{4}$; interleaves; blue limp leather; title gilt on cover.]

Crude but much used promptbook with cuts, abbreviated notations of "Bus.," and irregular cues for effects.

71. Blanche Bates   America   c.1898

Museum of the City of New York: 43.98.188

[Pages of Rolfe edition, 1902(?), $4\frac{1}{2}$ x $6\frac{3}{8}$, tipped between leaves of a workbook, $7\frac{1}{4}$ x $9\frac{5}{8}$; brown leather; title gilt on cover.]

Very carefully developed book. Scenic descriptions given in detail with grooves and maps, much stage business, cues for effects. Included are scores for the songs and an elaborate account of the wrestling scene.

72. Julia Arthur   New York, Wallack's   November 28, 1898
Folger: AYL, 7
[French edition pasted in a workbook, 8 x 10½; gray cardboard.]
Very full promptbook. The text much cut and altered. Stage business given in great detail, especially for pantomimic passages that end each act. Cues for effects, timings. At the front are plots of supers, properties, scenes and lines, electrics. Contains two programs for Miss Arthur, one for Mrs. Rousby, one for Adelaide Neilson, and a photograph of Dorothea Baird as Audrey.

73. William Redmond   New York   c.1900
Harvard Theatre Collection: uncatalogued
[French's Standard Drama, 4½ x 7½; interleaves.]
Copiously marked in red ink for production by the Murray Hill Stock Company "where father played." Cuts and restorations, scenic indications, copious stage business, maps, cues for effects. Redmond was a stage director for Augustin Daly.

74. Viola Allen   America   c.1900
Harvard Theatre Collection: uncatalogued
[Popular Education Library edition pasted in a workbook, 7⅞ x 10⅛; red flexible leather; title on cover label.]
Memorial of the actors' business as reconstructed by Frank Andrews, Miss Allen's stage manager, and given to Harvard in 1944. Cuts and restorations, copious stage business through three acts and part of the fourth—thereafter sparse. The writing is vivid though ill-spelled.

75. Henrietta Crosman   New York, Republic   February 27, 1901
Folger: AYL, 38
[Shakespeare text pasted in a workbook, 7½ x 9⅝; black cloth boards and half red leather.]
Very fully developed book. The text much cut and rearranged. Scenic indications with maps, cues for effects. The stage business, given in great detail, is partly copied from Julia Arthur (see no. 72) and partly new. At the front plots of supers, lights. Prompter's warning sheets are pasted at head of each act.

76. F. R. Benson   England   c.1904

    Shakespeare Centre Library: 72.903BEN(4163)

    [Shakespeare text pasted in a workbook, 6½ x 8; black cardboard and black cloth spine; title inked on spine label.]

    Promptbook with text much cut and altered. Considerable stage business, cues for effects.

77. [Benson]

    Shakespeare Centre Library: 72.903BEN(4962)

    [Cassell's National Library edition, 1904, pasted in a workbook, 7¾ x 9⅝; red cloth boards, much damaged; title inked on spine and cover labels.]

    Much used promptbook. Contents similar to preceding book. Stage business with maps, cues for effects. A plot for gas and limes.

78. [Benson]   1904-21

    Shakespeare Centre Library: 72.903BEN(4963)

    [Cassell's National Library edition pasted in a workbook, 8 x 10¼; red cloth boards; title inked on spine label.]

    This book, dated 1904, is thought to have been used down to 1921. The text somewhat restored, the markings similar to preceding books. Contains an actor list and lists of hand props and supers.

79. Winthrop Ames   Boston, Castle Square   June 19, 1904

    New York Public Library: *NCP.40737B

    [Mixture of manuscript and typescript, 8 x 13; green cloth boards; title gilt on spine.]

    Detailed preparation copy for the Castle Square production. Copious stage business and production details, with notes on productions of Augustin Daly and George Alexander. Production revived February 18, 1907.

80. [Ames]

    New York Public Library: *NCP.40739B

    [Typescript, 7¾ x 12¾; green cloth boards; title gilt on spine.]
    Carbon copy of Ames's production book, dated New York, February, 1907. Full record of stage directions, maps, cast, timing, etc. Notes on several past productions, quotations from critics, etc. At the back are plots of scenes, music, properties, costumes, etc.

81. [Ames]

    New York Public Library: *NCP

[Typescript, 7¾ x 6½; brown paper covers, bound together in green cloth boards; title gilt on spine.]

Twenty-one partbooks used at Castle Square. Actors' names are on the covers.

82. Priestly Morrison   New York

New York Public Library: 9-*NCPp.v.5.143137

[French's Standard Drama pasted in a workbook, 7 x 11¼; bound with two books of *Romeo and Juliet* in black cloth boards; title gilt up spine.]

Promptbook made by Morrison, then of the Actors Society. Cast list includes Edna Phillips, Theodore Gamble, George Farren. Stage business is typed in purple on slips pasted at tops of sheets, and is keyed to text by numerals. At the back good maps and plots of scenes, properties, lights.

83. E. H. Sothern and Julia Marlowe

                    London, Waldorf   April 27, 1907

Folger: AYL, 33

[Pages 512-572 of a Shakespeare text, 4¼ x 6¾, pasted in a workbook, 6¾ x 8¼; red limp cover.]

Souvenir record of the Sothern and Marlowe production made by Lark Taylor on May 1 and 2, 1907. Cuts on full text. Much stage business, maps, cues for effects. (See nos. 64-66.)

84. [Sothern and Marlowe]

W. A. Clark Library, Los Angeles

[Acting edition, 4¾ x 7⅛; interleaves; brown cloth boards; title gilt on spine.]

Souvenir record made by Lark Taylor "with cuts—transpositions of scenes." Cast of Ada Rehan in 1900; cast of Sothern and Marlowe. Cuts, copious stage business, groundplans, cues for effects, wrestling routine.

85. [Sothern and Marlowe]

Folger: AYL, 22

[Manuscript, 8½ x 11.]

A 6-page description (of unknown authorship) of Miss Marlowe's production, including stage business and a tabulation of her cuts, dated February 27, 1908. In same hand as and in folder with description of Viola Allen's *Cymbeline* (see CYM, 30).

86. Oscar Asche   London, His Majesty's   October 7, 1907
Shakespeare Centre Library: 72.903ASC

[Asche edition, 1907, pasted in a workbook, 6¾ x 8¾; wrapped in cardboard; title typed on labels.]

Promptbook used by Asche and Lily Brayton in 1907 and also in Australia in 1909-10. The calls, done in red and black decorated lettering, name several actors. Cuts, much stage business including tableaux to end acts, numerous maps, cues for effects.

87. E. H. Sothern and Julia Marlowe
                New York, Academy of Music   March 21, 1910
Folger: AYL, 8

[Typescript, 8 x 10¾ ; brown limp leather.]

The Sothern and Marlowe version compiled and used by Frederick Kaufman, then general stage manager. Text arranged in 4 acts, scenic descriptions, much stage business.

88. [Sothern and Marlowe]
Folger: AYL, 32

[Typescript, 8¾ x 11½; gray paper.]

Retyping of preceding book, unused.

89. [Sothern and Marlowe]
New York Public Library: *NCP.276555B

[Typescript, 8⅜ x 11; brown cloth boards; title gilt on spine.]

Unused carbon. Stage directions underlined in red. Perhaps same version as preceding book, cropped for binding.

90. [Sothern and Marlowe]
The Players: TS.116.A, B

[Two typescripts, 8 x 10½; acts bound separately in blue paper.]

These two copies appear to have been used for rehearsal. Stage directions far from complete. Actors' names penciled in.

91. [Sothern and Marlowe]
The Players: TS.116.C

[Typescript, 8 x 10½; brown limp leather.]

Carbon copy, with stage directions underlined in red; seems to be a later version than preceding books. At the front is a page of music cues and a Dramatis Personae. Scenic indications with maps, stage business, cues for effects. A map in Act II shows names of actors.

92. Maude Adams   Berkeley, Greek Theatre   June 6, 1910

New York Public Library: *NCP.53x300

[Typescript, $7\frac{1}{4}$ x $10\frac{1}{2}$; each act cover in gray paper, bound in black cardboard and black cloth spine; title gilt up spine.]

Unused copy. Minimal stage business. Management of Charles Frohman.

93. Margaret Anglin   New York, Hudson   March 16, 1914

New York Public Library: 8-*NCP.54x218

[See TN, 75.]

At the back of Miss Anglin's copy of *Twelfth Night* are 7 ground-plans for *As You Like It*.

94. Henry Jewett   Boston   January 1, 1915

Folger: AYL, 11

[Roycroft edition, 1903, $7\frac{7}{8}$ x $10\frac{1}{8}$; brown boards and brown leather spine; title gilt on spine.]

Preparation copy, with cuts on full text, much stage business, maps of three scenes.

95. [Jewett]

Folger: AYL, 12

[Typescript, $8\frac{1}{2}$ x 11; gray cardboard and green cloth spine.]

Final promptbook. Stage directions typed in red, with penciled additions. Plots of properties, music, and 3 pages of timings. Programs of 1915 and 1927 enclosed.

96. Lena Ashwell   London   1919-29

Birmingham, Shakespeare Memorial Library: 370.421198

[Temple edition pasted in a workbook, 7 x 9; black cloth boards; title gilt up spine.]

Promptbook of the Lena Ashwell Players. Some stage business, maps, cues for effects. Two sheets of costumes.

[ACTOR LISTS FOR FOLLOWING BOOKS ARE GIVEN IN THIS ORDER: Rosalind, Orlando, Jaques, Touchstone.]

97. W. Bridges-Adams   Stratford-upon-Avon   April 19, 1933

Shakespeare Centre Library: 71.21/1933A

[Temple edition pasted in a workbook, $7\frac{1}{8}$ x 9; purple cloth boards and half black leather; title on spine and cover labels.]

Cast includes Fabia Drake, John Wyse, Stanley Howlett, Laidman

Browne. Unused copy of promptbook, with cuts, calls, much stage business, maps, cues for effects. Program included. A revival of the 1932 production.

98. B. Iden Payne   Stratford-upon-Avon   April 17, 1935
Shakespeare Centre Library: 71.21/1935AS
[New Temple edition pasted in a workbook, 7⅛ x 9; purple cloth boards and half black leather; title on cover and spine labels.]
Cast includes Gwynne Whitby, Ernest Hare, Neil Porter, Raymond Raikes. Designed by Aubrey Hammond. A clean copy, with cuts, calls, considerable stage business, maps, sketch of forest scene, cues for effects.

99. Baliol Holloway   Stratford-upon-Avon   April 4, 1939
Shakespeare Centre Library: 71.21/1942
[Eversley text pasted in a workbook, 7⅛ x 9; purple cloth boards and half black leather; title on cover and spine labels.]
The book was used for at least 3 productions (1939, 1940, 1942), and shows many erasures and corrections. The 1942 cast includes Margaretta Scott, Lee Fox, Baliol Holloway, Jay Laurier. Designed by Baliol Holloway. Cuts, calls, stage business, maps, cues for effects.

100. Robert Atkins   Stratford-upon-Avon   April 14, 1944
Shakespeare Centre Library: 71.21/1944A
[Penguin edition pasted in a workbook, 6⅝ x 8⅞; black cloth boards and red leather spine; title on cover and spine labels.]
Cast includes Helen Cherry, John Byron, George Hayes, Michael Martin-Harvey. The book is said to have been used previously by Atkins at another theatre. At the front is a view of an Elizabethan playhouse by Walter Godfrey. Cuts, calls, stage business, maps, cues for effects.

101. Herbert M. Prentice   Stratford-upon-Avon   May 31, 1946
Shakespeare Centre Library: O.S.71.21/1946A
[Temple edition pasted in a workbook, 6⅞ x 9; purple cloth boards and half black leather; title on cover and spine labels.]
Cast includes Ruth Lodge, Myles Eason, Julian Somers, Hugh Griffith. Designed by Joyce Hammond. Cuts, calls, stage business, maps, cues for effects. The book was formerly used by B. Iden Payne on March 31, 1937, with Joyce Bland, Godfrey Kenton,

Baliol Holloway, Donald Wolfit. Designed by Barbara Heseltine. The old markings are erased.

102. Glen Byam Shaw   Stratford-upon-Avon   April 29, 1952
Shakespeare Centre Library: O.S.71.21/1952A
[New Temple edition pasted in a workbook, 8 x 13; black cardboard spring binder; title on spine label.]
Cast includes Margaret Leighton, Laurence Harvey, Michael Hordern, Michael Bates. Designed by Motley. Cuts, very detailed stage business, many maps, cues for effects.

103. [Shaw]   New Zealand, Australia   1953
Shakespeare Centre Library: O.S.71.21/1953A
[New Temple edition pasted in a workbook, 7⅞ x 12¾; red cardboard and red cloth spine; title on spine label.]
This book, based on the preceding, was used for touring company. Cast includes Barbara Jefford, Keith Michell, Anthony Quayle, Leo McKern. Stage business revised and improved, maps more carefully executed, cues for effects systematized. Loose production sheets included.

104. Robert Helpmann   London, Old Vic   March 1, 1955
Old Vic, Publicity Department
[Temple edition pasted in a workbook, 8 x 10½; black ring binder.]
Cast includes Virginia McKenna, John Neville, Eric Porter, Paul Rogers. Designed by Domenico Gnoli. Cuts, calls, stage business, maps, cues for effects. Many production papers, small red callbook.

105. Glen Byam Shaw   Stratford-upon-Avon   April 2, 1957
Shakespeare Centre Library: O.S.71.21/1957A
[New Temple edition pasted in a workbook, 8 x 12¾; red cloth board spring binder; title on spine label.]
Cast includes Peggy Ashcroft, Richard Johnson, Robert Harris, Patrick Wymark. Designed by Motley. Cuts, calls, much stage business, maps, cues for effects. Extra sheets include plots for rehearsal, properties, wrestling scene, music, and 44 maps.

106. Peter Wood   Stratford, Ontario   June 29, 1959
Festival Theatre, Library

[Two books. Penguin edition pasted in a workbook, 7¾ x 13⅛; blue cloth boards bordered in red; title pasted on cover.]

Cast includes Irene Worth, William Sylvester, William Hutt, Douglas Campbell. Designed by Desmond Heeley. The first book has much stage business, maps, cues for effects, light plot. The second has calls, cues for effects.

107. Wendy Toye   London, Old Vic   September 3, 1959
Old Vic, Publicity Department

[Temple edition pasted in a workbook, 8 x 10½; black ring binder.]

Cast includes Barbara Jefford, John Justin, Donald Houston, Alec McCowen. Designed by Malcolm Pride. Cuts, calls, much stage business, maps, cues for effects. Many production papers: props, groundplans, etc.

108. Word Baker   Stratford, Connecticut   June 16, 1961
Festival Theatre, Production Department

[Two books. Mimeograph, 8½ x 11; red leather ring binders.]

Cast includes Kim Hunter, Donald Harron, Donald Davis, Hiram Sherman. Designed by Robert O'Hearn and Motley. The first book, called "Rehearsal," has stage business, maps, cues for effects, all roughly penciled; properties list and rough working papers. The second, called "Show Copy," has calls and cues for effects neatly entered.

109. Michael Elliott   Stratford-upon-Avon   July 4, 1961
Shakespeare Centre Library: O.S.71.21/1961A

[Cambridge Pocket Shakespeare, 1957, pasted in a workbook, 8 x 13; red cloth board spring binder; title on spine label.]

Cast includes Vanessa Redgrave, Ian Bannen, Max Adrian, Colin Blakely. Designed by Richard Negri. Cuts on full text, much stage business, cues for effects. Production sheets include wrestling routine, actor lists, 14 maps. Much of the writing has been erased and written over, perhaps when it was moved to the Aldwych in London in 1962.

110. Other books of *As You Like It:*

Brown University: Asa Cushman and Julia Bennett, 1852.

Connecticut State Library: William Gillette, 1877.

Folger: AYL, 1, Modjeska; AYL, 21, 28, 31, anonymous; AYL, 26, Leon John Vincent; AYL, 27, National in Philadelphia, W. E.

Burton and S. C. Ferrers; AYL, 29, John Moore(?); AYL, 30, Miss De Gray; AYL, 35, J. B. Roberts; AYL, 37, A. S. Wright; AYL, 39, Owen Fawcett; AYL, 41, Annette Ince; AYL, 42, Walter Hubbell; AYL, Folio 1, Adelaide Neilson; PR.2803.A421. cop. 2, Mary Anderson.

Harvard Theatre Collection: uncatalogued, W. Riddle and Frank Andrews.

Historical and Philosophical Society of Ohio: 812.3/R283/9, Alvin Read.

Missouri Historical Society: George B. Berrell (apparently a well-marked book, reported by W. G. B. Carson, *Quarterly Journal of Speech,* XLIII, 2, but now missing).

Museum of the City of New York: 32.485.14.C, J. H. Ring, 1838-76.

Princeton University, Seymour Collection: AYL, 9, J. B. Booth, Jr.; AYL, 10, Melbourne MacDowell; AYL, 11, Lydia Eliza Morgan; AYL, 18, A. S. Murray; AYL, 19, Chauncey Davis and Albert Bradley; AYL, 20, J. H. W. Toohey; AYL, 21, George Browne; AYL, 23, Thomas L. Connor.

University of Minnesota: Z820.12/Z11, volume 12, W. S. Forrest.

The Comedy of Errors

1. Joseph Ashbury   Dublin, Smock Alley   1670's
   Folger: Com. Err., Smock Alley
   [Pages 85-100 from a Third Folio, 1663, 7⅞ x 12⅛; red marbled boards and half brown leather; title gilt up spine.]
   Preparation copy. Cuts and alterations, but no stage directions or actors' names.

2. Anonymous   London, Hatton Garden Nursery   c.1672
   University of Edinburgh
   [Pages 85-100 from a First Folio, 1623, 8 x 12⅜; blue marbled boards and half green leather; title gilt up spine.]
   Promptbook thoroughly marked and used. Cuts and alterations. Songs and dances indicated. Entrance cues are long lines with vertical slashes. Names of 11 actors appear in calls. (Published in facsimile in G. Blakemore Evans, *Shakespearean Prompt-Books*.)

3. Anonymous   Douai   1694
   Bibliothèque de Douai: MS.7.87
   [Manuscript, folios 66-93 of a volume, 6¾ x 8⅝; parchment.]
   Manuscript version used for amateur staging at Douai. Few cuts, alterations, little stage business. (See G. Blakemore Evans, *Philological Quarterly*, XLI, 158-172.)

4. John Philip Kemble   London, Covent Garden   April 17, 1811
   Shakespeare Centre Library: 50.04(1811)
   [Kemble edition, 1811, 5 x 8¼; interleaves; brown leather; title gilt on red spine label, "TR/CG/PB/C6" stamped on spine.]
   Promptbook marked in Kemble's hand. Calls, some stage business, maps, cues for effects, timings. Names of minor performers are penciled. From the library of William Creswick, 1888.

5. [Kemble]
   British Museum: 11765.C14
   [Kemble edition, 1811, 5⅜ x 8⅛; red and brown marbled boards and brown leather spine; title gilt up spine.]
   Rehearsal copy marked by Kemble for Jones, who played Antipholus of Syracuse. The markings are confined to Jones's role. New manuscript ending is added.

6. [Kemble]
   Garrick Club

[Kemble edition, 1811, 5⅛ x 8⅜; interleaves; blue cloth boards and brown leather spine; title gilt up spine.]

Promptbook marked in Kemble's hand. Some stage business and maps in addition to contents of preceding books.

7. William B. Wood   Philadelphia

New York Public Library: *NCP.P164540

[Bell edition, 1793, 4⅝ x 7⅜; black cloth boards; title gilt up spine.]

Promptbook marked "From Covent Garden." Cut to 3 acts. Few stage directions.

8. [Wood]

New York Public Library: *NCP.342939

[Reynolds operatic version, 1819, 5 x 8; interleaves; black cloth boards; title gilt up spine.]

Promptbook of the Reynolds operatic version, first done at Covent Garden, December 11, 1819. Cuts, few stage directions.

9. Anonymous   London, Drury Lane   June 1, 1824

University of Nebraska: 822.33/P3r

[Reynolds operatic version, 1819, 5 x 8⅛; interleaves watermarked 1822; brown cloth boards; title gilt down spine and wrongly identified with Covent Garden.]

Promptbook of the Reynolds operatic version lightly but systematically marked for Drury Lane. Complete cast entered. Cuts and additions, some scenic indications, grooves, calls, little stage business, cues for effects.

10. John Gilbert   Boston, Tremont Street   1836-46

Boston Public Library: K.49.10

[Cumberland edition, c.1829, 3¾ x 5¾; interleaves; bound with 8 other plays in marbled boards and maroon leather spine.]

Promptbook cut to 3 acts, checked for Dromio of Syracuse. Cuts, many additions, much stage business, maps, timings. A cast given for 1836.

11. Anonymous   Boston, Tremont Street

Folger: Com. Err., 12

[Cumberland edition, c.1829, 3⅝ x 5½; interleaves; brown paper; title inked up spine.]

Called "Tremont Theatre/Prompt Book." Cut to 3 acts. Calls, some stage business, cues for effects.

12. Noah Ludlow St. Louis 1840's
University of Pennsylvania, Furness Collection: C59.ShlCo
[Cumberland edition, c.1829, 3¼ x 5¾; green interleaves, 3⅞ x 6⅜; blue cloth boards; title gilt up spine.]
Promptbook of 3-act version. Scenic indications, grooves, stage business occasionally detailed, maps, cues for effects, timings. Names of Noah Miller, Anderson, and Smith are also on the book.

13. John Proctor America 1843
New York Public Library: *NCP.255324B
[Cumberland edition, c.1829, 3¼ x 5¼; bound with *The Merchant of Venice* (no. 22) in gray marbled boards and half black leather; title inked on spine.]
Promptbook. Cuts, calls, little stage business, cues for effects. Some Dromio gags from the 1819 operatic version are interpolated.

14. Anonymous America
New York Public Library: *NCVp.v.14.900677
[Cumberland edition, c.1829, 3½ x 5¾; interleaves slightly larger; bound with *Henry IV* and other plays in black cloth boards; title gilt on spine.]
Promptbook cut to 3 acts, with additions of some non-Shakespearean matter. Calls, and some detailed stage business.

15. Henry and Thomas Placide
New York, Niblo's Garden September 23, 1845
Folger: Com. Err., 7
[Pages 5-76 from volume IV of a Chalmers-Steevens *Works*, 5 x 8; blue interleaves; brown cardboard; title, etc., inked on cover.]
Promptbook made up by John Moore after 1848, when he came to America. "Cut into 3 Acts As played by the Two Placides New York." Playbills and reviews of the production at Burton's, December 15, 1853. Cuts, alterations, calls, scenic indications, grooves, considerable stage business.

16. Charles Kean 1850's
Folger: Kean Costume Book, Prints and Engravings, 50

[Scrapbook, 10¾ x 14½; green cloth boards and half green leather gilt.]

Contains tracings for 22 costumes for *Comedy of Errors*, style of c.1598, which Kean prepared but did not use.

17. Samuel Phelps   London, Sadler's Wells   November 8, 1855
Folger: Com. Err., 8

[Pages 5-76 from volume IV of a Chalmers-Steevens *Works*, 5⅜ x 8¾; few small interleaves; cream heavy paper pasted over blue publisher's wrappers (C. and S. Baldwin); title inked on cover.]

Promptbook of Phelps's production with restored text. Cuts, alterations, scenic indications, calls, some stage business, cues for effects. Dated on cover 1856-7-8-9. A list of supers on page of Persons Represented. Contains a review of J. S. Clarke production of 1865.

18. Mercer Hampson Simpson
                    Birmingham, Theatre Royal   April 9, 1862
Enthoven Collection: C. G. Box, 1808

[Cumberland edition, c.1829, 3½ x 5⅞; interleaves; tan cardboard.]

Promptbook of 3-act version. Cuts and interpolations. Calls, grooves, some stage business, many maps, cues for effects. Part of a bill for the above date.

19. George Ellis   London, Princess's   February 27, 1864
Folger: Com. Err., 10

[Pages 5-76 from volume IV of a Chalmers-Steevens *Works*, 1811, 5⅜ x 8¾; interleaves, 7¼ x 9; white cardboard and white cloth backing, unsewn.]

Fine promptbook of an arrangement of the play in 12 scenes, played without entr'actes, produced by Ellis under the management of George Vining. The book is in Ellis' hand. Cast given. Cuts on full text, scenic indications, grooves, much stage business especially for supers, maps.

20. John Sleeper Clarke New York, Winter Garden October 3, 1864
Folger: Com. Err., 3

[Spencer's Boston Theatre, 1856, 4½ x 7⅛; interleaves; black cloth boards and black leather spine; title gilt on spine.]

Owen Fawcett, who played Dromio of Ephesus opposite Clarke,

wrote up this book in 1882 as a present for George Becks. A 3-act version, with scenic indications, much stage business especially for supers, maps, cues for effects.

21. R. H. Horne   c.1876

Folger: Com. Err., 5, 6

[Two books. French edition, $4\frac{1}{4}$ x $7\frac{1}{4}$; slips and manuscript sheets, $8\frac{3}{4}$ x $11\frac{1}{4}$, inserted.]

Horne's alteration, "Reconstructed for the Modern Stage/In Four Acts." Manuscript Preface, and long new scene for Aegeon. Enclosed letter refers to Marie Wilton's interest in producing it.

22. W. H. Crane and Stuart Robson
                                 New York, Park   November 25, 1878

Folger: Com. Err., 4

[Music-Publishing Company issue of Cumberland edition, $3\frac{5}{8}$ x $5\frac{3}{4}$; interleaves, $7\frac{7}{8}$ x 9.]

Promptbook prepared for Robson and Crane by Owen Fawcett, October 21, 1878. Contains casts for 1853, 1859, 1865, 1869. Properties list, stage business, maps, cues for effects. At the front a groundplan and plot of scenes with grooves.

23. Edward Compton   Liverpool, Alexandra   1881

Birmingham, Shakespeare Memorial Library: B54/456353

[E. Saker edition, Liverpool, 1881, $4\frac{1}{2}$ x $6\frac{7}{8}$; interleaves; purple cloth boards; bound with several other Shakespeare plays in green cloth boards.]

"This promptbook was prepared by Edward Compton, in whose handwriting are the textual restorations and stage business." Two casts given, one including Calvert, Wyndham, Miss Bateman. Timings.

24. Frederick Paulding   1890's

Rutgers University: PR.1243.SHA

[French issue of Lacy edition, 1866, $4\frac{1}{8}$ x 7.]

Carelessly marked but rather full promptbook, based on version produced at Drury Lane, 1866. Cuts, scenic indications, some stage business, maps, cues for effects.

25. A. E. F. Horniman London, Duke of York's December 23, 1915

British Drama League

[Temple edition pasted in a workbook, 6¾ x 8⅞; maroon cloth boards and half purple cloth; title page pasted on cover.]

A reduced version (cuts made on full text), played in 42 minutes. Calls, some stage business, maps, cues for effects. Plots for properties, scenes (with groundplans), flys, crowds, dress (with names of some of the actors).

[ACTOR LISTS FOR FOLLOWING BOOKS ARE GIVEN IN THIS ORDER: Antipholus of Ephesus, Antipholus of Syracuse, Dromio of Ephesus, Dromio of Syracuse.]

26. Theodore Komisarjevsky   Stratford-upon-Avon   April 12, 1938
Shakespeare Centre Library: 71.21/1939

[Eversley edition pasted in a workbook, 7 x 9; purple cloth boards; title printed on cover label.]

Cast includes G. Sheldon Bishop, James Dale, Andrew Leigh, Dennis Roberts. Cuts, calls, much stage business especially for minor characters, cues for effects. At the back a duel routine, a dance, opening pantomime, light plot for opening. Production revived April 18, 1939.

27. Walter Hudd   London, Old Vic   April 23, 1957
Old Vic, Publicity Department

[Temple edition pasted in a workbook, 8 x 10½; with *Titus Andronicus* in black ring binder.]

Cast includes Keith Michell, John Humphrey, Dudley Jones, James Culliford. Designed by Paul Mayo. Short version produced with *Titus Andronicus*. Cuts, stage business, maps, cues for effects. Production papers, including groundplans.

28. Other books of *The Comedy of Errors:*

Boston Public Library: K.49.10, no. 2, Joseph Cowell.

Folger: Com. Err., 1, Sedley Brown; Com. Err., 2, Th. Eichhoff; Com. Err., 9, Russell (operatic version, 1819).

Princeton University, Seymour Collection: CE, 5, William Seymour; CE, 10, A. S. H. Murray.

Rutgers University: PR.1243.SHA, J. B. Wright and the Misses Newton.

Coriolanus

1. J. Aickin   London, Drury Lane   February 7, 1789
   Folger: Cor, 19

   [Kemble edition, 1789, 5 x 8⅜; brown boards and gray spine; title on spine label.]

   Rehearsal copy. Cuts and a few bits of stage business for Cominius probably in the hand of the actor.

2. John Philip Kemble   London, Covent Garden   Nov. 3, 1806
   Folger: Cor, 8

   [Kemble edition, 1806, 5⅛ x 8¼; interleaves; brown leather; title and "CG/PB/C/1" stamped on spine.]

   Promptbook marked in Kemble's hand. Calls, properties, some stage business, cues for effects, timings. At the front a 3-page description of the triumphal procession. Letter of gift from William Creswick to Henry Irving, May 18, 1881.

3. [Kemble]
   Garrick Club

   [Kemble edition, 1806, 5 x 8⅛; interleaves watermarked 1807; blue cloth boards and brown leather spine; title gilt up spine.]

   Later promptbook marked in Kemble's hand. Cuts, calls, a property list for stage left, some stage business, cues for effects.

4. [Kemble]
   Folger: T.a.23

   [Manuscript, 7 x 8⅞; brown leather gilt; title gilt up spine.]

   Kemble's 29-page partbook for Coriolanus, in his hand; 668 lines.

5. Joseph Ebsworth   London, Drury Lane   May 8, 1819
   Folger: Cor, 18

   [Kemble edition, C. Lowndes, c.1800, 4¾ x 7⅞; interleaves; gray and green marbled boards and half brown leather; title and "10" gilt on spine.]

   Promptbook generally taken from Kemble's, marked, signed, and dated in the round, neat hand of Joseph Ebsworth, the Drury Lane prompter. Calls, property lists, some stage business, triumphal procession, etc. A few pencilings of light cues and timings appear to be by John Willmott, a later Drury Lane prompter.

6. William Dowton   London, Drury Lane
   Folger: Cor, 5

[Kemble edition, 1814, 4⅛ x 7; gray paper and brown marbled paper, red leather spine.]

Rehearsal copy, checked for Menenius. Cuts, little stage business.

7. William Charles Macready
                London, Covent Garden   November 29, 1819
Folger: Cor, 9

[Kemble edition, 1814, 4⅜ x 7; interleaves watermarked 1816, 1817, 5¼ x 8¼; green marbled boards and half brown leather; title gilt on red leather spine label.]

Transcription of the Covent Garden promptbook (see nos. 2, 3) made by a copyist. A page of costume notes at the front and numerous pencilings throughout are in Macready's hand.

8. William Augustus Conway   New York, Park   January 14, 1824
New York Public Library: *NCP.18155

[Kemble edition, 5 x 7⅞; black cloth boards; title gilt up spine.]

Promptbook given by Conway to T. S. Hamblin, whose first American performance was December 9, 1825. Both actors had played the part in England previously. Supposed to be "By the Kemble Book," but not a transcription; much used, and worked over by several hands. Calls, grooves, properties, some stage business, a few maps, cues for effects.

9. Anonymous   1840's(?)
University of Pennsylvania, Furness Collection: C59.ShlCorK

[Kemble edition (no title page), 5⅛ x 8¼; brown marbled boards and brown cloth spine; title gilt up spine.]

Irregularly marked promptbook. The speeches of some of the principals are numbered—e.g., Marcius to 132, Volumnia to 45. Many brief notes of stage business and histrionic manner. The name W. Padcock stamped at the end is probably of no theatrical significance.

10. George W. Lewis   Philadelphia, Walnut Street   July 29, 1845
Folger: Cor, 1

[Oxberry edition, Boston, 1822, 3½ x 6; interleaves; black cloth boards and black leather spine; title gilt on spine.]

Promptbook originally dated from the Bowery, 1841 (Hamblin?), but mainly marked in 1845 by George Lewis, then a prompter in Philadelphia. Much stage business especially for curtain tableaux, a 3-page procession list, maps and sketches, cues for effects, timing.

11. Noah Ludlow   St. Louis   1845

University of Pennsylvania, Furness Collection: C59.ShlCor

[T. H. Palmer edition, Philadelphia, 1823, $3\frac{5}{8}$ x $5\frac{3}{4}$; interleaves; red cloth boards; title gilt on spine.]

"As performed at the Philadelphia Theatre." A crude but systematically marked promptbook. Cuts and restorations, calls, stage business especially for crowds, maps, procession list, costume list, cues for effects, timing.

12. John Fest   America

Harvard Theatre Collection: uncatalogued

[Cumberland edition, c.1829, $3\frac{5}{8}$ x $5\frac{1}{2}$; interleaves; black cloth boards and black cloth spine; title gilt on spine.]

Promptbook checked for Coriolanus. Costume list, calls, some stage business, maps, cues for sound.

13. Samuel Phelps   London, Sadler's Wells   September 27, 1848

Folger: Cor, 12

[Pages 131-258 from volume IX of a *Works,* $4\frac{3}{4}$ x $8\frac{1}{8}$; smaller interleaves watermarked 1847; white paper, dirty and torn; title inked on cover and dated 1847, 1850, 1857.]

Promptbook of Phelps's version which, except for a bit in Act IV, is all from Shakespeare but much cut and somewhat rearranged. Marked in the hands of Phelps and Williams, the prompter. Calls, grooves, some stage business especially for procession and military movements, maps, cues for sound, list of supers.

14. [Phelps]

Folger: Cor, 13

[Pages 102-242 from volume VII of a *Works,* $5\frac{1}{4}$ x $8\frac{3}{8}$; interleaves; blue and red marbled boards and half maroon leather; title gilt on spine.]

Excellent transcription of Phelps's book. Belonged to Harry Plowman.

15. [Phelps]

Folger: Cor, 15

[Pages 1-113 of a Shakespeare edition, $4\frac{1}{2}$ x $6\frac{1}{2}$; interleaves; black rubberized paper and black cloth spine; title on cover label.]

Transcription of Phelps's book, perhaps made from Plowman's copy. Belonged to Henry Irving.

16. Henry Betty   England   1850's
    Folger: Cor, 4
    [Cumberland edition, c.1829, 3½ x 5¾; interleaves; gray boards
    and green cloth spine.]
    Promptbook with stresses marked for Caius Marcius. Grooves,
    stage business, many notes on interpretation of the role.

17. John Moore   New York   1850's
    Folger: Cor, 11
    [Oxberry edition, Boston, 1822, 3⅞ x 6¼; interleaves; brown
    paper.]
    Very full promptbook compiled by Moore, with references to vary-
    ing arrangements of Hamblin and Forrest. Contains partbook
    for "Volusius." Scenic indications, excellent properties list, much
    stage business especially for crowds, full account of triumphal
    procession and funeral pyre scene.

18. [Moore]
    Folger: T.b.2
    [Notebook, 6⅛ x 10¼; blue boards and black cloth spine.]
    Cues for the band for 48 plays, including *Coriolanus*.

19. Thomas Barry   Boston, Boston Theatre   1854
    Harvard Theatre Collection: uncatalogued
    [Two books. Oxberry edition, 1820. One is 4¾ x 8⅛; gray inter-
    leaves, 5¼ x 8¼; gray boards and black leather spine; title and
    "1" inked on cover. The other is 4¼ x 6¾; gray boards and half
    brown leather; title and "41" inked on cover.]
    Two promptbooks written by Charles Melville, an English
    prompter, whose stage library Thomas Barry brought to Boston
    in 1854. The larger interleaved copy is arranged for 6 acts: calls,
    grooves, some stage business, cues for effects.

20. Mercer Hampson Simpson   Birmingham, Theatre Royal   1860's
    Birmingham, Shakespeare Memorial Library: S.315/1820
    [Oxberry edition, 1820, 4¼ x 7¼; interleaves, 5 x 8; gray card-
    board under blue cloth boards; title gilt on spine.]
    Well-developed promptbook. Some restorations. Cast list, com-
    plete scene plot with grooves, costume list, stage business espe-
    cially for crowds, maps.

21. Charles Dillon   Birmingham, Theatre Royal   1860's
    Birmingham, Shakespeare Memorial Library: S.315/1831
    [Acting edition, 1831, pasted in a workbook, 6½ x 8; yellow paper under blue cloth boards; title gilt on spine.]
    Promptbook made for Dillon by F. C. Hastings of the Theatre Royal, Sheffield. Some restorations. Scenic indications with grooves, stage business for crowds, cues for effects.

22. Edwin Forrest   New York, Niblo's Garden   November 2, 1863
    Folger: Cor, 20
    [Spencer's Boston Theatre, 4½ x 7⅝; interleaves, 7¾ x 9¾; whitish paper, very dirty and torn; title and signature inked on cover.]
    Very full and much used book made by John B. Wright, who was stage manager for Forrest during his latter years. Scenic indications, grooves, much stage business, maps and sketches, notes on interpretation, records of supers, timings. The funeral pyre scene at the end is described, and the dirge given in full. Sketches including George Scharf's 3 drawings of the Macready production of 1838; a Forrest program of December 2, 1864; notes from performances in Boston, Philadelphia, Baltimore. Wright continued to use the book after Forrest's retirement, as at the California Theatre in 1873.

23. [Forrest]   New York, Niblo's Garden   September 5, 1864
    Folger: Cor, 2
    [Spencer's Boston Theatre, 4⅜ x 7; interleaves; black and white cloth boards and black leather spine.]
    A full but little used book made by George Becks, who played in Forrest's company during the 1864 season at Niblo's. Some scenic indications, grooves, calls, stage business, maps, cues for effects. The procession, with map and hymn; text of dirge for the funeral scene; cast list for 1864; program for Forrest's last night at Niblo's on October 21, 1864; engraving of Vandenhoff as Coriolanus.

24. Henry Irving   London, Lyceum   April 15, 1901
    Folger: Cor, 7
    [Irving edition, Chiswick Press, 1901, 5⅜ x 8⅜; green limp leather with red ribbon marker; title gilt down spine.]
    Irving's studybook, much used before being bound (original wrappers soiled). The arrangement is in 3 acts. Cuts, restorations, and many random notes.

25. Ellen Terry   London, Lyceum   April 15, 1901
    Smallhythe
    [Wright edition, 1893, 4½ x 6½; orange boards; title printed on
    cover.]
    Miss Terry's studybook. The date 1907 is inked on the cover, but
    it was used for the 1901 production. Cuts, many notes on the act-
    ing of Volumnia, several comments on Irving's Coriolanus.

26. [Terry]
    Smallhythe
    [Irving edition, 1901, 5⅜ x 8½; tan cloth boards and half green
    leather; title gilt up spine.]
    Miss Terry's second studybook. Most of the notes on Volumnia
    from the preceding book are roughly transcribed; many addi-
    tional jottings.

27. Lewis Waller
    Folger: Cor, 17
    [Windsor Shakespeare, Edinburgh, 1901, 5¼ x 8⅛; red cloth
    boards gilt.]
    Preparation copy, rigorously cut but not developed further.

28. William Poel   London, Chelsea Palace   May 11, 1931
    Enthoven Collection
    [Three typescripts, 8 x 10; orange paper (Poel's), purple paper
    (Poel's), blue paper (Molly Tyson's).]
    Promptbooks. Cuts, calls, little stage business, cues for ad libs and
    effects. Some scenes played "above on the platform stage."

[ACTOR LISTS FOR FOLLOWING BOOKS ARE GIVEN IN THIS ORDER: Coriolanus, Menenius, Tullus Aufidius, Volumnia.]

29. W. Bridges-Adams   Stratford-upon-Avon   April 24, 1933
    Shakespeare Centre Library: 71.21/1933C(6054)
    [Temple edition pasted in a workbook, 6⅝ x 8; tan marbled
    boards and black cloth spine; title on cover and spine labels.]
    Cast includes Anew McMaster, Stanley Lathbury, Laidman
    Browne, Alice O'Day. Cuts, calls, stage business, maps, cues for
    effects. At the front a list of 18 scenes; at the back a sketch of a
    scene. The book had been used for Bridges-Adams' production
    on April 23, 1926; was erased and written over.

30. [Bridges-Adams]

Shakespeare Centre Library: 71.21/1933C(7931)

[Shakespeare edition pasted in a workbook, $7\frac{1}{8}$ x 9; purple cloth boards and half black leather; title on cover and spine labels.]

Unused transcription of the 1933 book. Program pasted in.

31. Federal Theatre   New York   c.1938

New York Public Library: 9-*NCP.978745A

[Typescript, 8 x 11; blue and gray Federal Theatre wrapper under green cloth boards; title gilt on spine.]

A "streamlined" version for the Federal Theatre, arranged by M. Manisoff for use in schools. Complete production book, with plots for costumes, lights, music, and curtains. Several photographs from performances.

32. B. Iden Payne   Stratford-upon-Avon   May 9, 1939

Shakespeare Centre Library: 71.21/1939Cor

[Eversley edition pasted in a workbook, $7\frac{1}{8}$ x 9; purple cloth boards and half black leather; title on cover and spine labels.]

Cast includes Alec Clunes, Andrew Leigh, James Dale, Dorothy Green. Designed by J. Gower Parks. Cuts on full text, calls, some stage business, maps, cues for effects.

33. Glen Byam Shaw   Stratford-upon-Avon   March 13, 1952

Shakespeare Centre Library: O.S.71.21/1952C

[Penguin edition pasted in a workbook, 8 x 13; black cloth spring binder; title on spine label.]

Cast includes Anthony Quayle, Michael Hordern, Laurence Harvey, Mary Ellis. Designed by Motley. Cuts on full text, much stage business, many maps, cues for effects.

34. John Houseman   New York, Phoenix   January 19, 1954

University of California, Los Angeles: Houseman Box 9

[Mimeograph, $8\frac{1}{2}$ x 11; blue leather; title gilt on spine.]

Cast includes Robert Ryan, Alan Napier, John Emery, Mildred Natwick. Designed by Donald Oenslager. Costumes by Alvin Colt. Final or souvenir promptbook, copiously illustrated with photographs from the production; several reviews; many production papers.

35. Michael Benthall   London, Old Vic   February 23, 1954

Old Vic, Publicity Department

[New Temple edition pasted in a workbook, 8 x 10½; black ring binder.]

Cast includes Richard Burton, William Squire, Paul Daneman, Fay Compton. Designed by Audrey Cruddas. Stage business, maps, cues for effects. Many production papers.

36. Peter Hall   Stratford-upon-Avon   July 7, 1959
Shakespeare Centre Library: O.S.71.21/1959C

[Cambridge Pocket Shakespeare pasted in a workbook, 8⅜ x 13; blue cloth ring binder; title on spine label.]

Cast includes Laurence Olivier, Harry Andrews, Anthony Nicholls, Edith Evans. Designed by Boris Aronson and Riette Sturge Moore. Cuts on full text, stage business especially for crowds, cues for effects. Production papers including 36 maps, a battle sequence, the Coriolanus-Aufidius fight, etc.

37. Michael Langham   Stratford, Ontario   June 19, 1961
Festival Theatre, Library

[Two books. Penguin edition pasted in workbooks, 7¾ x 13⅛; blue cloth boards bordered in red; title pasted on cover.]

Cast includes Paul Scofield, Douglas Campbell, John Colicos, Eleanor Stuart. Designed by Tanya Moiseiwitsch. The first book has much stage business, many maps, cues for effects, timings, property plot. The second has calls, cues for effects, many timing sheets.

38. Other books of *Coriolanus:*

Boston Public Library: K.47.13, John G. Gilbert and George W. Fenno.

Folger: Cor, 3, George Berrell; Cor, 6, Walter Hubbell; Cor, 10, Marcus Moriarty; Cor, 14, anonymous; Cor, 16, Mrs. Wallack.

Harvard Theatre Collection: (Widener, 13484.21.5), Henry Placide (with Forrest, January 11, 1838).

Library Company of Philadelphia: Oe2+.11607.D, William Warren.

Princeton University, Seymour Collection: Cor, 3, A. S. H. Murray, 1875.

Cymbeline

1. Thomas Hull   London, Covent Garden   December 28, 1767
   Folger: Cymb, 3

   [Garrick edition, 1767, $3\frac{7}{8}$ x $6\frac{1}{2}$; bound with *Hamlet* and laid in leather cover.]

   Hull's studybook, dated 1767. Checked for Posthumus and Belarius (at Covent Garden Hull regularly played Pisanio). Cuts and alterations, entrances and exits.

2. James Bates   London, Covent Garden   ante 1784
   Harvard Theatre Collection: 13484.22.50

   [An eighteenth-century edition, no title page, 4 x 7; brown marbled boards and brown cloth spine; in box of gray cloth boards and maroon spine; title gilt up spine.]

   Much used and much traveled promptbook. James Bates, whose name is at the head of Act I, was a Covent Garden actor (not identified with a cast of this play) who died in 1784. Also at the head of Act I are the names of Warren and Reinagle of Philadelphia and the date 1807. Other names are J. Jones and Mary Jones Roberts. Cuts, scenic indications, calls, some basic stage business, cues for effects.

3. Lumley St. George Skeffington   Hackney School   c.1785
   Folger: Cymb, 10

   [Garrick edition, 1784, $4\frac{1}{4}$ x $6\frac{5}{8}$; interleaves; green-red marbled boards and brown leather spine.]

   Promptbook of a schoolboy production in which Skeffington played the Queen and spoke the Epilogue. Cuts, restorations, some stage business, cast list, Epilogue (by George Keate). Skeffington's bookplate.

4. William Warren   York   1788
   Library Company of Philadelphia: Oe2+.11608.D

   [Bell edition of a Johnson-Steevens text, 1786, $3\frac{1}{2}$ x $5\frac{1}{2}$; marbled boards and brown leather spine.]

   Promptbook checked for Belarius. Cuts on full text. Cast given for York, 1788 (partly cropped). Bookplate of W. Warren, New Theatre, Philadelphia.

5. J. Megget
   University of Illinois: x792.9/Shl5cy/no.1

   [Kemble edition, 1801, $5\frac{3}{8}$ x $8\frac{7}{8}$; blue cloth boards; title gilt up spine.]

Rehearsal copy. Random penciled notes of stage business for Posthumus. At bottoms of pages copious vocabulary notes. At back, Posthumus' soliloquy in II, 5.

6. George Frederick Cooke

London, Covent Garden   January 18, 1806

Harvard Theatre Collection: 13484.22.45

[Kemble edition, 1801, $4\frac{7}{8}$ x $8\frac{1}{4}$; red cloth boards; in box of gray cloth boards and brown leather spine; title gilt up spine.]

Rehearsal copy marked by Kemble with additions by Cooke. Some stage business. The 1806 cast written in.

7. [Cooke]

Folger: Cymb, 12

[Edition printed for J. Barker, 1795, $4\frac{1}{4}$ x $7\frac{1}{8}$; interleaves; blue and white marbled boards and half brown leather; title on spine label.]

Rehearsal copy, marked in Cooke's hand for Iachimo, and dated inside back cover "Wed. Night, Jan. 22, 1806." Alterations and some detailed stage business for Iachimo.

8. John Philip Kemble   London, Covent Garden   June 3, 1812

Shakespeare Centre Library: 50.06(1810)

[Kemble edition, 1810, 5 x $8\frac{1}{4}$; interleaves; brown leather; title gilt on red spine label, spine stamped "TR/CG/PB/C/13."]

Promptbook originally marked in Kemble's hand, with some stage business, maps, cues for effects, timings, probably from 1812. Kemble's cast of 1816 penciled on page of Persons Represented. Further markings, including a new "Druidical" scene, penciled for May 16, 1827. Many pencilings added when Helen Faucit took a benefit as Imogen on May 18, 1837, including timings and, at the back, a schedule of scenes. Finally belonged to William Creswick, who used it on October 17, 1864, and added, in ink, a cast list, costume list for Iachimo, and many notes on the playing of Iachimo.

9. [Kemble]

Garrick Club

[Kemble edition, 1810, $5\frac{1}{8}$ x $8\frac{1}{4}$; interleaves; blue cloth boards and brown leather spine; title gilt up spine.]

Promptbook marked in Kemble's hand. Calls, some stage business, maps, cues for effects.

10. William Charles Macready   London, Drury Lane   Jan. 21, 1843
    Folger: Cymb, 17

    [Pages 1-139 of a Steevens edition, 6¼ x 9¾; interleaves water-
    marked 1844, 1845, 7¾ x 9½; white cardboard and white cloth
    spine; title inked on cover.]

    George Ellis' penciled transcription of Macready's 1843 prompt-
    book. Cuts and alterations on full text, scenic prescriptions in
    some detail with maps and sketches, grooves, list of property
    manuscripts, calls, stage business, cues for effects, timing. Large
    sketch of banquet scene folded in.

11. [Macready]
    Folger: Cymb, 7

    [Pages 5-128 from volume XI of a *Works,* 5 x 8¼; interleaves,
    7 x 8¾; purple cloth boards and half brown leather; title and
    "C.K." gilt on spine label, "Mr. Charles Kean/Prompt Copy" gilt
    on green leather cover label.]

    Perfected transcription of the Macready book made for Charles
    Kean by George Ellis in January, 1847. Many pencilings appar-
    ently made by Kean. (See no. 15.)

12. [Macready]
    Folger: Cymb, 8

    [Watercolors, 6¾ x 8¾; interleaves; purple cloth boards and half
    brown leather; "Scenery/Cymbeline/C.K." gilt on spine label.]

    Eleven fine watercolor designs of "Scenery, For the Play of Cymbe-
    line, As Acted, at the Theatre Royal, Drury Lane.—Seasons
    1843-4," prepared for Charles Kean by George Ellis. Some are
    done in several depths, the wings, etc., being painted on separate
    pieces laid upon the back-flats. Carpenter's notes.

13. [Macready]
    Folger: Cymb, 9

    [Watercolors watermarked 1845, 1846, 6¾ x 8¾; purple cloth
    boards and half brown leather; "Costumes/Cymbeline/C.K."
    gift on spine label.]

    Thirty-five designs of "Costumes for the Play of Cymbeline, From
    various Authorities, and, as acted, at the Theatre Royal, Drury
    Lane, Seasons 1843-4," prepared for Charles Kean by George
    Ellis. The first 21 are copied from those worn at Drury Lane, the
    last 14 are from "authorities," which are listed.

14. Helen Faucit   c.1845

    Folger: Cymb, 2

    [Knight's Cabinet Edition, 1843, $3\frac{3}{8}$ x $5\frac{1}{2}$; green oilcloth publisher's wrappers.]

    Miss Faucit's promptbook probably used for touring in the 1840's and 1850's. The text reverts to Kemble's naming of certain characters, and "Go to Cumberland" (i.e., Cumberland edition, 1829) is sometimes noted. Cuts, calls, cues for effects. Two sonnets penciled on back fly.

15. Charles Kean   London, Princess's   c.1850

    Harvard Theatre Collection: TS.2438.300

    [Pages 1-138 from volume VIII of a *Works*, $5\frac{1}{4}$ x $8\frac{5}{8}$; interleaves, $7\frac{1}{4}$ x 9; green cloth boards; title inked up spine.]

    Fully developed promptbook of English origin, probably another transcription of the Macready book and used by Kean for a production which did not materialize (see no. 11). Cuts on full text, calls, stage business, maps, cues for effects, timings. The inked cuts and the assignment of a gentleman to Pisanio appear to be in the hand of George Ellis (other markings are perhaps by T. W. Edmonds, the Princess's prompter). The names of Belton and several minor actors are entered. At page 100 are pasted in a lyric poem called "Lily's Footsteps" and 2 interleaves from a promptbook of a version of *The Bride of Lammermoor,* signed by "John Rose—Prompter—1852—Museum—Providence—Rhode Island."

16. John Moore   America   1850's

    Folger: Cymb, 6

    [Bell edition, 1773, $3\frac{7}{8}$ x $6\frac{5}{8}$; lavender interleaves; tan paper, badly torn; title inked on cover.]

    Very old inked cuts, grooves, stage business, etc., on the text pages, supposed to be "Cuts and Transpositions mostly as arranged by David Garrick." Additional notes by Moore on the interleaves.

17. [Moore]

    Folger: Cymb, 5

    [Oxberry edition, Boston, 1823, $3\frac{5}{8}$ x $6\frac{3}{8}$; blue interleaves, $4\frac{1}{4}$ x 6; brown publisher's wrappers under tan cardboard; title inked on cover.]

    A sort of preparation copy, probably not used. Lacks systematic prompter's signs, but contains cuts, many scenic indications, grooves, much stage business, notes on music and other effects.

18. Samuel Phelps   London, Sadler's Wells   September 26, 1857
British Theatre Museum: G 49 1963
[Cumberland edition, 3¾ x 6, and part of another edition; inter-leaves, 4 x 6⅜; tattered brown paper; title and "Prompt Book/ 1857/Theatre Royal Sadlers Wells" inked on cover.]
Promptbook heavily marked in several hands including that of Williams, the prompter. Cuts, some grooves, calls, considerable stage business, maps and sketches, cues for effects, timing (3:00). At the front a full description of the battle scene in Act V. Belonged to Harry Plowman.

19. James Taylor   1867
Harvard Theatre Collection: uncatalogued
[Cumberland edition, 3⅜ x 5⅜; interleaves; green cloth boards.]
Promptbook signed and dated by Taylor, neatly marked in red ink, with calls, cues for effects. Earlier signatures of Geo. W. Gile, M. R. Lewis. From the Edwin Forrest Lodge. Probably a Forrest book of much earlier date.

20. Adelaide Neilson   New York, Daly's Fifth Avenue   May 14, 1877
Harvard Theatre Collection: 13484.22.81
[Davidson issue of Cumberland edition pasted in a workbook, 5 x 8; red cloth boards; in box of tan cloth boards and brown leather spine; title gilt up spine.]
Not a working promptbook, but a partial memorial of the Neil-son production made by John Moore. Cuts, extensive restorations. Costume list "generally like King Lear." Some scenic indications, groundplan of bedroom scene, some vivid stage business, maps, cues for some effects.

21. Miss Alleyn   Stratford-upon-Avon   1884
Shakespeare Centre Library: 50.06(187–)
[French edition, 4¼ x 7¼; publisher's wrappers.]
Text much cut and rearranged according to "Alterations from Miss Allyn's [sic] copy."

22. Helena Modjeska   New York, Fourteenth Street   Feb. 4, 1888
Folger: Cymb, 11
[Cumberland edition, 3⅝ x 5⅝, with added sheets from French's issue of Lacy, 1864; blue interleaves, 5 x 7⅝; black cloth boards and black leather spine; title and "J. Stark" gilt on cover.]

In 1853, G. W. Lewis, prompter at the Broadway, marked this book for James Stark "as played by Mr. McCready at the Walnut Street Theatre, Phila." (It does not resemble known Macready books.) By 1883 it belonged to George Becks, who added pages from the 1864 acting edition and expanded the annotations in red ink. About 1888 Becks marked it further, in blue ink and pencil, with numerous references to Modjeska. Scenic indications, grooves, calls, much stage business, maps.

23. William Seymour   c.1890
    Princeton University, Seymour Manuscripts: Box S—F-z
    [French edition pasted in a workbook, 7 x 11½; red and blue marbled boards and black cloth spine; title pasted on cover.]
    Rough but thorough promptbook. Sketches, stage business, maps, cues for effects.

24. Henry Irving   London, Lyceum   September 22, 1896
    Folger: Cymb, 4
    [Cassell's National Library edition, 1892, 3⅝ x 5⅝; publisher's blue cloth boards.]
    Preparation copy, with extensive cuts.

25. Ellen Terry   London, Lyceum   September 22, 1896
    Smallhythe
    [Longmans, Green, 1890, 4⅛ x 6½; publisher's red boards.]
    Rehearsal copy with many vivid notes in Miss Terry's hand on the playing of Imogen.

26. [Terry]
    Smallhythe
    [Proof copy of Irving edition, 1896, 5½ x 8½.]
    Rehearsal copy with many vivid notes in Miss Terry's hand on her own playing and record of numerous directives by "B.S." (Bram Stoker).

27. [Terry]
    Smallhythe
    [Irving edition, 1896, 5¼ x 8¼.]
    Rehearsal copy marked in Miss Terry's hand. Revisions and restorations of text. A great many very vivid notes on her own playing; occasional references to "Ted," "Ben," and others.

28. Viola Allen   Washington, D.C., New National   October 1, 1906
New York Public Library: *NCP.330695B

[Typescript, 8 x 10⅜; red cloth boards and half red leather; title inked up spine, gilt on cover.]

Promptbook made on a clean carbon of Miss Allen's version. Stage directions underlined in red, with manuscript notes. Scenery described in great detail, elaborate groundplans, much stage business especially of incidental and decorative kind. Cast list and plots of music, scenes, properties are at the front. The producer was Frank Vernon.

29. [Allen]
Folger: Cymb, Folio 1

[Typescript, 8 x 13; blue paper.]

A 96-page Preface and Commentary to Miss Allen's acting version, prepared by William Winter in 1905. Annotation of text, description of characters, interpretation of the play, stage history, list of authorities.

30. [Allen]
Folger: AYL, 22

[Manuscript, 8½ x 11.]

A 4-page description of Miss Allen's *Cymbeline*, dated December 15, 1906. Bound with description of Julia Marlowe's *As You Like It* (see AYL, 85).

31. Charles B. Hanford   America   c.1910
Folger: Cymb, 15, 16

[Two books. Pages of a Shakespeare text pasted in a workbook, 7⅝ x 10; black and white mottled boards and black cloth spine.]

Number 15 is a fully developed promptbook, apparently derived from Viola Allen's (see no. 28), with scenic indications, stage business, etc. A sheaf of publicity notes on Marie Drofnah (Hanford) and the "galaxy of brilliant players" of the company. A program of the Viola Allen production. Number 16 is similar in form, but not developed. These books probably were not used.

[ACTOR LISTS FOR FOLLOWING BOOKS ARE GIVEN IN THIS ORDER: Imogen, Posthumus, Iachimo, Cloten.]

32. W. Bridges-Adams   Stratford-upon-Avon   August 5, 1922
Shakespeare Centre Library: O.S.71.21/1922C

[Favourite Classics edition pasted in a workbook, 7⅞ x 12⅝; black cloth boards and red leather spine; title on cover and spine.]

Cast includes Ethel Carrington, William Stack, Baliol Holloway, Stanley Lathbury. Cuts on full text, calls, stage business, maps, cues for effects. At the back are curtain calls and 3 groundplans.

33. E. H. Sothern and Julia Marlowe
                    New York, Jolson   October 2, 1923
Museum of the City of New York: 43.430.632

[Pages of a Shakespeare text pasted in a workbook, 5½ x 8½; brown limp leather; title pasted on cover.]

Labeled "Julia Marlowe Last Copy." Pencil-marked for stresses, etc. The cuts, scenic arrangements, stage business are tentative, as if it were a preparation copy. Penciled cast with queries. Two 1923 programs (one for *Twelfth Night*) enclosed. Cast includes Julia Marlowe, E. H. Sothern, Frederick Lewis, France Bendtsen.

34. [Sothern and Marlowe]
Museum of the City of New York: 43.430.633

[Pages of a Shakespeare text pasted in a workbook, 6¾ x 8½; brown and red boards and brown cloth spine; title pasted on cover.]

Preparation copy. At the front a properties list and tentative cast for 1923. Penciled scenic indications, stage business, maps.

35. [Sothern and Marlowe]
Museum of the City of New York: 43.430.634

[Pages of a Shakespeare text pasted in a workbook, 6¾ x 8½; green boards.]

Stage directions of the preceding book have been organized, numbered, and entered in pencil on left-hand pages.

36. [Sothern and Marlowe]
New York Public Library: *NCP.280791B

[Temple edition pasted in a workbook, 5½ x 8½; black cloth boards; title inked on spine.]

Preparation copy. Cuts and alterations, stress marks for all characters, notes on vocabulary, scenery, stage business, music.

37. [Sothern and Marlowe]
Museum of the City of New York: 43.430.631A, B, C

[Three typescripts, 8½ x 11; brown paper.]

Final promptbooks made from the preceding books. Plots of lights, scenes. Many additional pencilings: cuts, stage directions, cues.

38. [Sothern and Marlowe]
New York Public Library: *NCP.276566B
[Typescript, 7¾ x 11; red cloth boards; title gilt on spine.]
A carbon copy of the final promptbook, signed by V. H. Collins of Los Angeles. Penciled alterations. Properties list, maps, additional stage business, notes on scenery and effects.

39. B. Iden Payne   Stratford-upon-Avon   April 12, 1937
Shakespeare Centre Library: 71.21/1937C(5329, 8157)
[Two books. Eversley edition pasted in a workbook, 7⅛ x 9; purple cloth boards and half black leather; title on cover and spine labels.]
Cast includes Joyce Bland, Godfrey Kenton, Donald Wolfit, Baliol Holloway. Designed by J. Gower Parks. Cuts on full text, calls, some stage business, maps. The second book is a partial copy of the first.

40. Nugent Monck   Stratford-upon-Avon   April 23, 1946
Shakespeare Centre Library: O.S.71.21/1946C
[Eversley edition pasted in a workbook, 7¾ x 10; tan marbled boards and green cloth spine; title on cover and spine labels.]
Cast includes Valerie Taylor, Myles Eason, David King-Wood, Paul Scofield. Designed by O. P. Smythe and J. Gower Parks. Cuts, some stage business, few maps, cues for effects.

41. Michael Benthall   Stratford-upon-Avon   May 21, 1949
Shakespeare Centre Library: O.S.71.21/1949C
[New Temple edition pasted in a workbook, 8 x 12¾; red cloth boards and red cloth spine; title on cover and spine labels.]
Cast includes Kathleen Michael, Clement McCallin, John Slater, William Squire. Designed by Leslie Hurry. Cuts, calls, much stage business, maps, cues for effects. At the back a fight routine.

42. [Benthall]   London, Old Vic   September 11, 1956
Old Vic, Publicity Department
[New Temple edition pasted in a workbook, 8 x 10½; black ring binder; title on cover and spine.]
Cast includes Barbara Jefford, Leon Gluckman, Derek Godfrey,

John Humphrey. Designed by Audrey Cruddas. Cuts, stage business, maps, cues for effects. Many production papers.

43. Peter Hall   Stratford-upon-Avon   July 2, 1957

Shakespeare Centre Library: O.S.71.21/1957C

[New Temple edition pasted in a workbook, 8 x 13; red cloth spring binder; title on spine label.]

Cast includes Peggy Ashcroft, Richard Johnson, Geoffrey Keen, Clive Revill. Designed by de Nobili and Douboujinsky. Cuts, calls, much stage business, maps, cues for effects. At the back a cast, maps, light plots.

44. Other books of *Cymbeline:*

Folger: Cymb, 1, Arnold Daly(?); Cymb, 13, anonymous; Cymb, 14, Mrs. Cairn (Dublin edition, 1762).

Harvard Theatre Collection: 13484.22.95, John Swinburne.

Shakespeare Centre Library: 50.06(1784), anonymous.

Hamlet

1. Joseph Ashbury   Dublin, Smock Alley   1670's
   University of Edinburgh
   [Pages 729-760 from a Third Folio, 1663, 8 x 12⅛; red marbled boards and half maroon leather; title gilt up spine.]
   Promptbook. Page 729 is the last page of *Macbeth,* with cuts and calls. *Hamlet* begins on page 730. Cuts, calls, scenic indications, cues for effects. Entrance cues are long lines with vertical slashes. The actor Trefusis is named as Messenger. Page 747 partly missing. (See G. Blakemore Evans, *Shakespearean Prompt-Books.*)

2. Anonymous   1700's
   Folger: Hamlet, 55
   [Martyn and Herringman edition, 1676, 6⅞ x 8½; red, yellow, and gray marbled paper; in red leather slip-box.]
   Rehearsal copy of an eighteenth-century actor. Cuts and alterations, but no details of stage arrangements or business.

3. John Ward   England   c.1740
   Folger: Hamlet, 54
   [Heringham and Bentley edition, 1683, 6½ x 8½; red, yellow, and blue marbled boards and half green leather; title gilt up spine.]
   Ward's earlier promptbook. Cuts, a scenic indication, calls, properties, cues for effects (including traps). Entrance cues are long lines with vertical slashes. (See J. C. McManaway, *Papers of the Bibliographical Society of America,* XLIII, 288-320.)

4. [Ward]
   Johns Hopkins University: PO2807.A2.1676
   [Martyn and Herringman edition, 1676, 6 x 8; red, yellow, and blue marbled boards and half leather gilt; title gilt up spine.]
   Ward's fully developed promptbook. Page corners rounded to prevent curling. Cuts, a scenic indication, calls, properties, cues for effects, entrance cues all more systematically entered than in the preceding book. (See McManaway, *op. cit.*)

5. David Garrick   London, Drury Lane   February 10, 1773
   Folger: Hamlet, 16
   [J. & P. Knapton edition, 1747, 3⅞ x 6½; bound with *The Humorous Lieutenant* in red, green, and tan marbled boards and brown leather spine.]

Preparation copy of Garrick's version, which was to "rescue that noble play from all the rubbish of the fifth act." Cuts, alterations, and additions. (See Percy Fitzgerald, *The Theatre*, n.s. XLI, 252-256; G. W. Stone, *PMLA*, XLIX, 890-921; Kalman Burnim, *David Garrick, Director*, pp. 152-173.)

6. [Garrick]
Folger: Hamlet, 1
[Richard Wellington edition, 1703, 6¼ x 8⅞; red leather gilt; title gilt on spine.]
Uncompleted promptbook probably deriving from the Garrick book after 1773. Cuts and alterations are made only through IV, 5. Some stage business.

7. George Frederick Cooke   Chester   1785
Literary and Philosophical Society, Newcastle-on-Tyne: 822.33/63
[C. Bathurst edition, 1782, 3⅞ x 6⅝; interleaves; red cloth boards; title gilt on spine.]
Promptbook checked for Hamlet and thoroughly marked in Cooke's hand. Cuts, calls, copious stage business and notes on customary stage practices, cues for effects. Cast for Chester, 1785. Endorsed by Cooke, Christmas Eve, 1789, Sheffield. (See M. St. C. Byrne, *Theatre Notebook*, XV, 21-31.)

8. Richard Daly   Dublin, Crow Street   c.1788
Folger: Hamlet, 56
[Peter Wilson edition, Dublin, 1750, 3⅝ x 6⅜; interleaves; red, yellow, and blue marbled boards and half blue leather; title gilt on spine.]
Though identified as Daly's prompter's book by an early owner who signs himself "H" (Hitchcock?), it does not have many prompter's markings. Many notes by "H," critical of the play and of performers, including Joseph Holman. Another owner, apparently an actor or producer, has entered a great many notes of stage business, interpretation, staging arrangements. Rough penciled scrawls suggest further use as an actor's rehearsal copy.

9. Thomas Hull   London, Covent Garden   June 2, 1790
Folger: Cymb, 3
[Acting edition, 1763, 3⅞ x 6⅝; bound with *Cymbeline* in brown leather; "Goldsmith's England" on red spine label.]

Rehearsal copy checked for King and Hamlet (Hull played the King). Cuts and a few alterations.

10. Anonymous   c.1800(?)
    The Players

    [Manuscript, 7¼ x 9⅜; blue marbled boards and half green leather; title gilt on spine.]

    Unsigned 98-page manuscript adaptation, "alter'd from Shakespear," which reduces the latter portion of the play more drastically than Garrick did: the catastrophe follows immediately after the closet scene. Given to Edwin Booth, November 23, 1890, by William Bispham, who thought it was Garrick's version.

11. John Philip Kemble   London, Covent Garden   1807-37
    Shakespeare Centre Library: 50.07(1804)

    [Kemble edition, 1804, 5 x 8¼; interleaves watermarked 1807; brown leather; title gilt on red spine label, spine stamped "TR/ CG/PB/H/1."]

    Promptbook originally marked by Kemble: lengths of lesser roles, list of extras, some stage business, maps, cues for effects, procession list for funeral, timing. Much used later, especially between 1831 and 1837, for actors including C. Kemble, Macready, Cooper, Young, Hamblin, C. Kean: many pencilings in various hands show cuts, restorations, stage business, cues for effects, timings.

12. Charles Mayne Young   Brighton   September 10, 1809
    Folger: Hamlet, 62

    [J. Barker edition, 4⅞ x 8¼; interleaves; gray and rose marbled boards, brown leather corners, red leather spine; title and "Plays/ 12" stamped on spine.]

    Although Young's name and the date are written on the title page, the book is probably the official promptbook of a theatre. References to Young, Kemble, Cooper, etc., given in third person. Properties list, list of supers, costume notes at the front. Cuts and restorations, stage business, maps, timings.

13. John Pritt Harley   Gravesend   November 20, 1812
    Folger: S.a.101

    [Manuscript, 6¼ x 7⅝; fragments of leather spine; in brown cloth board box; title gilt on cover.]

    Manuscript partbook (5 leaves) for First Gravedigger. Dated as above; at Hull, November 29, 1813; at Brighton, December 3, 1814. Clipping from Hull playbill, with Charles Kemble as Hamlet.

14. William Charles Macready   London, Covent Garden   June 8, 1821
Folger: Hamlet, 24

[Oxberry edition, 1820, 4 x 6¾; interleaves; green boards and half brown leather, much worn; title stamped on spine.]

Promptbook marked by Macready probably in 1821, and used by him for many years. Lists of properties and dress at the front. Restorations, some stage business, maps, cues for effects. Belonged to the Reverend C. Tisdall in 1876; given to Henry Irving in 1881. (See nos. 28-30, 40, 56.)

15. [Macready]
British Museum: 011768.ff3

[Johnson's edition of *The Plays of William Shakespeare*, 10 volumes, Dublin, 1766, 3¾ x 6½; brown leather.]

The text of *Hamlet*, in volume X, is cut for performance and has a few theatrical marginalia in Macready's hand.

16. Edmund and Charles Kean   Edinburgh   c.1828
Folger: W.a.71

[Kemble edition, 1806, 3¾ x 6⅛; interleaves; bound with other plays in brown leather gilt; "Siddons" gilt on spine.]

George Joseph Bell's commentaries on various stage performances, including notes on both the Keans in *Hamlet*.

17. Edwin Forrest   New York   1830's
Edwin Forrest Home (On loan to the University of Pennsylvania Library, Rare Book Room.)

[Cumberland edition, 3¾ x 5¾; interleaves; green leather.]

Promptbook probably marked by Forrest (in ink), with penciled additions. Restorations, calls, some detailed stage business, cues for effects. Regular key-marks are triple dollar signs. (See nos. 63-68.)

18. [Forrest]
Edwin Forrest Home (On loan to the University of Pennsylvania Library, Rare Book Room.)

[Oxberry edition, 3½ x 5⅝; interleaves; brown marbled boards and half brown leather; title and Forrest's name gilt on spine.]

Promptbook lightly but systematically marked by Forrest. Restorations, calls, some stage business, cues for effects.

19. John H. Oxley   New York, Park   August 16, 1836
University of Pennsylvania: AC85.M9415.820p.47b
[Oxberry edition, Boston, 1822, 3¾ x 6; interleaves; tan cardboard; title inked on cover.]

Promptbook. No stage business, but systematic calls, cues for effects. Inscribed by N. F. Kenny, a Pittsburgh prompter, September 14, 1836, and also by George M. Fenno. Later belonged to James Murdoch.

20. Charles Kean   London, Haymarket   June 1, 1840
Folger: Hamlet, 18
[Kemble edition, 1800, 5 x 7¾; interleaves; marbled boards and half brown leather, much worn and broken.]

Handsome promptbook made for Kean by James Parsloe, the Drury Lane prompter, in August, 1840. (Kean had played Hamlet at Drury Lane on January 8, 1838.) Corrections by A. W. Nimmo, the Edinburgh prompter, in 1842. Eight beautiful ink-wash drawings of the scenes, with groove numbers. Call-lists, stage business, maps, cues for effects, timings. (See nos. 16, 58-61.)

21. [Kean]
Folger: W.a.10
[Notebook, 4¾ x 7¾, sheets watermarked 1837; brown marbled boards and half brown leather gilt; "Theatrical Costumes" inked on spine label.]

Kean's touring wardrobe list for Hamlet is the seventh of 16 such lists in this book.

22. [Kean]
Folger: T.b.15
[Notebook, 7¾ x 12⅝; brown marbled boards and black leather spine.]

Lists of scenery and properties, texts of written papers, call-lists, music cues for several plays, including *Hamlet*, as used by Kean when touring.

23. Fred Coleman Nantz   Bath, Theatre Royal   1839
Folger: Hamlet, 39
[Oxberry edition, 1818, 5⅛ x 8½; interleaves; sewn together with the 1825 reprint of the 1603 *Hamlet*.]

Studybook. Many annotations from Shakespearean critics. Some comments on theatrical practice. Cast for Bath, when Nantz played Laertes to Charles Kean's Hamlet.

24. J. B. Addis   New York, Bowery and Chatham   1839-46
Dartmouth College: Sp.824Sh.Q3o.F

[Oxberry edition, 1820, 4⅛ x 6¾; interleaves; gray marbled boards and half brown leather; title inked on cover label.]

Addis was the prompter at the Bowery, and this is his own book. Cuts and restorations, calls, much stage business, maps and sketches, cues for effects. Casts led by T. S. Hamblin, A. A. Addams, J. B. Booth. A great many notes on the business of Hamblin, who played at the Bowery October 2, 1839. Further notes on Booth, Addams, Charles Kean, J. Wallack, Bass, Mrs. Bland.

25. James H. Hackett   New York, Park   October 21, 1840
Enthoven Collection

[Oxberry edition, Boston, 1822, 3¾ x 6; interleaves; limp brown leather sewn with red tape.]

Studybook, dated 1827. Checked for Hamlet, marked for stresses. Textual notes based on First Folio, etc. Copious annotations of stage business and interpretation.

26. [Hackett]
Enthoven Collection

[Oxberry edition, London, 1827, 4½ x 7½; interleaves; limp brown leather; title inked on cover.]

Another studybook, transcribed and augmented from the preceding book. This copy Hackett loaned to J. Q. Adams in 1838-39. Comments on other actors' Hamlets, many notes from Shakespeare critics, copious and detailed plans for stage business.

27. [Hackett]
Enthoven Collection

[French's Standard Drama, 4⅜ x 7¼; interleaves; brown cloth boards and half brown leather; title gilt on spine.]

Partial promptbook made up long after 1840, when Hackett first played Hamlet. Lightly and randomly marked for stage arrangements and business.

28. William Charles Macready   London, Drury Lane   April 29, 1842
Victoria and Albert, Forster Library, 7918:   F.48.C.16

[Kemble edition, 4¼ x 7¼; interleaves; bound with four other Macready promptbooks in green cloth boards and half tan leather; titles gilt on spine.]

Macready's promptbook at Drury Lane in 1842-43 and probably after: much soiled, last leaves missing, marked by several hands, including Macready's and those of the Drury Lane prompters, Willmott and Ellis. Restorations, some scenic indications, grooves, calls, some stage business, maps, cues for effects. (See nos. 14-15, 40, 56.)

29. [Macready]

The Players: PB.75

[Pages 1-146 (last pages missing) of a Shakespeare text, 5¼ x 8¾; interleaves, 6¼ x 9.]

Fine transcription of Macready's 1842-43 book made for the Theatre Royal, Manchester, by George Ellis, the Drury Lane prompter. Cuts on full text. Many scenic indications, groove numbers, sketches, calls, stage business, maps, cues for effects, timings (but no timing for last act, the end of which is missing). Numerous pencilings indicate Manchester use.

30. [Macready]

University of Illinois: x792.9/Sh15h/no.1

[Pages 1-152 of a Shakespeare text, 5⅛ x 8¼, with half title and Preface from a Steevens edition; interleaves, 7½ x 9; green marbled boards and half maroon leather; title gilt on spine, name of Hermann Vezin gilt on black leather cover label.]

Fine transcription of the Macready book made by George Ellis for Hermann Vezin, who used it much and marked it further. Timings total 3:35.

31. Henry Betty   London, Covent Garden   December 28, 1844

Folger: Hamlet, 2

[Hinds English Stage, 1839, 4⅛ x 7⅛; interleaves; green marbled boards and half black leather; title gilt up spine, "W.H.W. Betty" gilt on black cover label.]

Promptbook of the son of William Henry West Betty, whose name is on the cover. Neatly marked in brown ink, with prompter's cues in red; additional notes in blue ink and pencil. Cuts and restorations, scenic indications, calls, stage business mainly as printed, maps, cues for effects.

32. [Betty]

Folger: Hamlet, 3

[Knight's Cabinet Edition, 1843, 3¼ x 5½; interleaves; gray boards and gray cloth spine; title penciled on cover.]

Promptbook with markings similar to those of preceding book. Cuts on full text, grooves. At the back a dummy playbill with Betty as Hamlet.

33. James E. Murdoch   New York, Park   October 21, 1845

University of Pennsylvania: AC85.M9415.820p.47

[Oxberry edition, Boston, 1822, 3½ x 5⅝; some interleaves; brown cloth boards and half brown leather; title inked on cover label.]

Rehearsal copy, with cuts and restorations, and various reminder notes of effects. At the front are recorded performances in 1845 and 1880.

34. [Murdoch]

University of Pennsylvania: AC85.M9415.820p.47a

[French's Standard Drama, 4½ x 7½; publisher's wrappers under gray cardboard; title inked on cover.]

Promptbook for a cutting of (or group of scenes from) the play, ending with the closet scene. Cues for effects.

35. J. B. Roberts   New York, Chatham   February 26, 1847

Folger: Hamlet, 44

[Cumberland edition, 3¾ x 6; interleaves, 4 x 6⅜.]

Studybook with stresses marked for Hamlet. Cuts and restorations, notes on scenery and furniture, much stage business. Said to be "marked from Mr. C. Kemble's prompt Book" (Kemble played in America in 1832); further notes on stage business of Kean, Booth, Cooper, Wallack, Forrest. (See nos. 71, 99.)

36. [Roberts]

Folger: Hamlet, 43

[Cumberland edition, 3¾ x 6; interleaves, 4 x 6⅜.]

Studybook with stresses marked for Hamlet and Ghost. Costume list. Copious stage business for Hamlet, including some from Hackett. J. S. Woodhouse named as Laertes. References to Newcastle (Delaware), Gosport, Richmond, Norfolk, etc.

37. [Roberts]

Folger: Hamlet, 42

[Cumberland edition, 3¾ x 6; interleaves; publisher's wrappers under brown cardboard.]

Studybook with stresses marked for Hamlet. Copious stage business, including notations of the business of Macready, Vandenhoff, Anderson, Charles Kean, Hackett, Kemble, Booth, Forrest. Detailed fencing routine copied from Kean. Scraps of bills of Roberts' performances in 1843, with Miss Fisher and Mrs. Thoman as Ophelia. Formerly belonged to Jacob Thoman.

38. [Roberts]
Folger: Hamlet, 45
[Cumberland edition, 3¾ x 6; interleaves; brown cardboard.]
Studybook dated 1847 with stresses marked for Hamlet. Copious stage business, maps, fencing routine. A few references to business of other actors (Anderson, Kean). Formerly belonged to Jacob Thoman.

39. Charlotte Cushman   Manchester, Theatre Royal   1847
Folger: Hamlet, 10
[Pages 85-176 from a volume of Knight's Pictorial Edition, 1843, 6⅜ x 9½; interleaves; purple cloth boards.]
Dated London, February 8, 1848. Notes by Miss Cushman for an unnamed addressee, explaining her own conception and acting of Hamlet. Refers to her Manchester performance. (See no. 48.)

40. William Charles Macready
        New York, Niblo's Astor Place   October 12, 1848
New York Public Library: *NCP.342989
[Modern Standard Drama, 4¼ x 7½; gray interleaves; publisher's wrappers under black and green marbled boards and black cloth spine; in brown manila folder.]
Promptbook made by Henry B. Phillips, apparently transcribing from Macready's book. Cast lists for Macready at the Astor Place, and for Conway and Wallack. Cuts and restorations, scenic indications, grooves, calls, stage business, maps, cues for effects, timing. (See nos. 14-15, 28-30, 56.)

41. Asa Cushman   Providence   1850's
Brown University: Eng.P.17
[Modern Standard Drama, 4½ x 7½; tan paper.]
Promptbook checked for Bernardo. Cuts, cues for effects. Clip-

pings of playbills for G. V. Brooke in 1852, and for Mrs. E. S. Conner supported by members of the Cushman family.

42. James Seymour   America   1850's
Princeton University, Seymour Collection
[Modern Standard Drama, 1846, $4\frac{1}{2}$ x $7\frac{1}{2}$; lined paper.]
Promptbook checked for Benvolio, Queen, Gravedigger. Cuts, cues for effects.

43. Henry Farren   America   1850's
Harvard Theatre Collection: uncatalogued
[Oxberry edition, 1827, $4\frac{1}{8}$ x 7; blue interleaves, $4\frac{7}{8}$ x $7\frac{1}{2}$; brown cloth boards.]
Promptbook crudely marked with calls and cues for effects.

44. John Moore   New York   1850's-70's
Folger: Hamlet, 29
[Pages 127-285 from volume IX of a Steevens *Works*, 5 x $8\frac{3}{8}$; small interleaves; brown cardboard, much soiled; title inked on cover.]
Very full promptbook and memorial record. At the front a list of property manuscripts, fencing routine, list of supers. Cuts on full text, calls, copious stage business, maps, cues for effects. Notations of business of Macready, J. Wallack, Eddy, E. Booth. Playbills of Young at Covent Garden, 1819; Macready at Park, 1844; Moore and G. Jordan at Montreal, 1854; Davenport at Park, 1870; Booth at Daly's, 1875. Engravings from Booth's acting edition pasted in.

45. [Moore]
Folger: Hamlet, 72
[French issue of Lacy edition, $4\frac{1}{8}$ x $7\frac{1}{4}$; interleaves, $4\frac{7}{8}$ x $7\frac{3}{4}$; tan paper; title inked on cover.]
Thorough promptbook, apparently by John Moore. Grooves, calls, properties, considerable stage business, maps, cues for effects.

46. [Moore]
Folger: T.b.2
[Notebook, $6\frac{1}{8}$ x $10\frac{1}{4}$; blue boards and black cloth spine.]
Cues for the band for 48 plays, including *Hamlet*.

47. Daniel Wilmarth Waller   New York, Broadway   June 30, 1851
New York Public Library: *NCP.3429

[Hinds English Stage, 1839, 4¾ x 7⅝; interleaves; green cloth boards; title gilt up spine.]

Dated as above and also from Sadler's Wells, 1854. Some scenic indications, a sketch, irregular calls, detailed stage business in early scenes, maps, cues for effects.

48. Charlotte Cushman
New York, Brougham's Lyceum   November 24, 1851
Library of Congress, Manuscripts Division: Cushman Box
[Pages from Verplanck *Works,* 1847, 6¾ x 10⅜; blue cloth boards; title gilt on cover.]

Promptbook "marked for Miss C. Cushman by Henry B. Phillips, Prompter, N.Y." Cuts on full text, calls, some stage business, cues for effects, timings. (See no. 39.)

49. James Stark   New York, Astor Place   September 28, 1852
New York Public Library: *NCP.342977
[Modern Standard Drama, 4½ x 7½; interleaves, 6 x 7½; black cloth boards; title on spine.]

Excellent and much used promptbook, made by Robert Jones, the prompter at the Howard Athenaeum, in 1852. Scenic indications, grooves, calls, stage business, maps, sketches, cues for effects. At the front an unfilled chart for "casts at different localities": Richmond, 1848 (Stark as Hamlet), New Orleans, 1858, San Francisco, 1850, Sydney, 1853.

50. William E. Burton   New York   1852
Folger: Hamlet, 8
French's Standard Drama, 4½ x 7½; laid-in interleaves, 8 x 10; brown paper.]

Excellent promptbook, unused, made by George Becks. "Marked from the Prompt Book of W. E. Burton, with additions." Very similar to the preceding Stark book.

51. George Vandenhoff   London, Haymarket   October 25, 1853
Folger: Hamlet, 53
[Kemble edition, 1814, 3¾ x 6½; interleaves; green marbled boards and half green leather; title and "Vandenhoff's Prompt Copy" gilt on spine.]

Rather haphazard half-studybook, half-promptbook. At the front a description of the fencing match, and Haymarket cast with Vandenhoff as Hamlet. Restorations, some scenic indications, calls, stage business for various roles, maps. At the back a suggested arrangement for a happy ending. Belonged to Thomas Jefferson McKee in 1895.

52. Thomas E. Morris   America   1854

Folger: Hamlet, 38

[Modern Standard Drama, 4½ x 7½; red cloth boards; title written on cover label.]

Studybook checked for Ghost, King, Polonius. Some stage business. Clippings from playbills, 1850-62, with Forrest, Davenport, Couldock, Murdoch, Jamieson.

53. Samuel Phelps   London, Sadler's Wells   September 25, 1854

Shakespeare Centre Library: O.S.P.50.07(1829)

[Davidson issue of Cumberland edition, 3½ x 5¾; blue interleaves; tan marbled boards and half tan cloth; title on cover label.]

Promptbook neatly written in brown ink with red underlinings, thought to be a Phelps book of 1854. Scenic indications, calls, stage business, maps, cues for effects, timing. F. Haywel (Hawley), to whom it belonged, has indicated various restorations.

54. Alexander Burger   1856

Folger: Mac, 15

[French's Standard Drama, 4¼ x 7¼; bound with *Macbeth* and other plays in brown marbled boards and black leather spine; Burger's name gilt on cover and spine.]

Crude promptbook, thoroughly marked but probably unused. At the front a list of properties. Cuts, calls, cues for effects.

55. J. W. Wallack   New York, Wallack's   October 20, 1856

New York Public Library: *NCP.342983

[Oxberry edition, 1820, 4 x 7¼; interleaves; yellow paper under black cloth boards; title gilt on spine.]

Promptbook marked for Wallack, as played by him in 1856, by Henry B. Phillips, the prompter. Cuts, scenic indications, grooves, some stage business, cues for effects.

56. Walter Benn   America   1858

University of North Carolina: Tannenbaum Shakespeare Collection

[Pages 223-352 from volume VII of Knight's Cabinet Edition, $3\frac{3}{8}$ x $5\frac{1}{2}$; interleaves, $4\frac{7}{8}$ x $7\frac{5}{8}$; bound.]

Excellent transcription of a promptbook probably of English origin, at many points verbatim with Macready's; given to the American actor Benn "from his friend A. F. Kiefer"; dated July 30, 1858. Cuts on full text, grooves, calls, stage business, maps and sketches, cues for effects, timings. Benn added in pencil a few bits of business, one or two crude sketches, and a great many naive notes on pronunciations. (See nos. 14-15, 28-30, 40.)

57. Anonymous   Boston, Boston Museum   1859

Princeton University, Seymour Collection

[French's Standard Drama, $4\frac{1}{2}$ x $6\frac{1}{2}$; interleaves; coarse cloth; title, date, and "Boston Museum" inked on cover.]

Crude but thorough promptbook marked by several hands. Cuts, grooves, calls, stage business, cues for effects.

58. Charles Kean   London, Princess's   January 10, 1859

Folger: Hamlet, 21, 20, 19

[Three books. Kean edition, 1859, $5\frac{1}{4}$ x $8\frac{1}{4}$; interleaves, $6\frac{3}{4}$ x 9; tan cloth boards and half brown leather; title gilt up spine.]

Three final or souvenir promptbooks made by T. W. Edmonds, the prompter. Contain fine watercolors of the 11 scenes. Stage directions are mainly as printed. Maps, cues for effects, timings. Of these 3 copies, no. 21 became Kean's touring book and is much soiled; no. 20 is clean and perfect; no. 19 is broken and its watercolors removed. (See nos. 16, 20-22.)

59. [Kean]

Enthoven Collection: Box DT.43

[Watercolors mounted on large display boards.]

Fine watercolors of the 11 scenes, with names of the artists.

60. [Kean]

Folger: Prints and Engravings, 51

[Watercolors, 8 x $5\frac{1}{2}$, mounted in an album, $10\frac{1}{4}$ x $14\frac{1}{8}$; gray cloth boards and half green leather gilt; "Charles Kean/Original Water Color Drawings" gilt on spine.]

Fine watercolor scene designs for 4 plays, including 11 for Hamlet.

61. [Kean]

Folger: T.a.68

[Dummy book of watercolor pages, 4 x 6⅝; purple velvet and glittery paper decorations.]

A letter of gift from F. Belton of the Theatre Royal, Exeter, to Wilson Barrett, states that this is the property prayerbook used by Edmund Kean in *Richard III* and Charles Kean in *Hamlet*. It was doubtless made for Charles Kean in the 1850's: one of the illuminated pages is initialed "F.L." (Lloyds?)

62. Mercer Hampson Simpson   Birmingham, Theatre Royal   1860's

Birmingham, Shakespeare Memorial Library: A15/455853

[Cumberland edition, 3⅝ x 5⅝; gray boards and brown cloth spine; title inked on cover label; bound with other Shakespeare plays in green cloth boards.]

Promptbook much soiled from use. Calls, maps, cues for effects.

63. Edwin Forrest   America   1860's

Folger: Hamlet, 58

[Edition "as played by . . . Forrest," published by W. A. Moore, 4⅝ x 7⅛; interleaves; blue and tan marbled boards and half brown leather; title inked on spine.]

Rather crude promptbook, perhaps Forrest's. Properties list, maps, cues for effects. (See nos. 17-18.)

64. [Forrest]

Folger: Hamlet, 69

[French's Standard Drama, 4½ x 7½; interleaves; gray cardboard; title elaborately inked on cover.]

Well-developed promptbook, apparently Forrest's. Calls, stage business resembling that in J. B. Wright's memorial book (see no. 66), maps, cues for effects. (Compare OTH, 47.)

65. [Forrest]

Edwin Forrest Home (On loan to the University of Pennsylvania Library, Rare Book Room.)

[French's Forrest edition, 1860, 4⅜ x 7¼; interleaves; brown marbled boards and half brown leather gilt; title gilt on spine.]

Excellent promptbook, done in brown ink with red underlinings by a professional prompter or copyist. Calls, much stage business, maps, cues for effects. In lieu of scenic descriptions there are half a dozen neat ink drawings of the scenes. (See KL, 68.)

66. [Forrest]

Folger: Hamlet, 61

[French's Standard Drama, 4½ x 7½; interleaves, 5 x 8; white paper; title pasted on cover.]

Excellent memorial book made by John B. Wright, who was Forrest's stage manager in the later years. An 1860 Baltimore playbill. A great many detailed notes of Forrest's stage business, maps and sketches, cues for effects.

67. [Forrest]

New York Public Library: *NCP.342926

[French's Forrest edition, 1860, 4½ x 7½; interleaves; black cloth boards; title gilt on spine.]

George Becks's "Memory of some of Forrest's business and manner in Hamlet." (Becks played in Forrest's company for four seasons.) Extremely detailed and vivid record of Forrest's performance.

68. [Forrest]

Folger: Hamlet, 50

[French's Standard Drama, 4⅜ x 7⅜; interleaves; black cloth boards and black leather spine.]

Transcription of George Becks's memorial book, owned by James Taylor.

69. Henry Holmes   England   1860's

Enthoven Collection: 1842 Box

[French issue of Lacy edition, 4¼ x 7¼; publisher's wrappers, front cover missing.]

The Hamlet role and some other parts marked for stresses, pauses, etc. Through 2 acts many notes on stage business, maps, notes on lighting.

70. Anonymous   1860's(?)

Harvard Theatre Collection: (Widener, 13484.41.2)

[French's Standard Drama, 4⅜ x 7½; yellow publisher's wrapper under green marbled boards and green cloth spine; title inked up cover.]

Amusing comments on a performance, made by a disgruntled spectator.

71. J. B. Roberts   1861

Folger: Hamlet, 40

[French's Standard Drama, 4⅜ x 7½; interleaves, 4⅞ x 8; brown boards; title, etc., on cover.]

Promptbook dated 1861, much used, marked "Please return after performance." Some stage business, maps, cues for effects. (See nos. 35-38, 99.)

72. Charles Fechter   London, Lyceum   May 21, 1864
Folger: Hamlet, 25

[Lacy edition, 4 x 7¼; interleaves, 5⅛ x 8; brown cloth boards and half black leather gilt; title gilt on cover.]

Fine souvenir promptbook made by W. McIntyre, who played Rosencrantz. Cuts and restorations, several good sketches of scenes, grooves, copious and detailed stage business, maps, cues for effects. Henry Irving bookplate.

73. [Fechter]
Enthoven Collection

[Watercolors, 6½ x 8¼.]

Fine watercolor designs for 5 scenes of Fechter's production, by William Telbin.

74. [Fechter]
Harvard Theatre Collection: (Widener, 13484.42.5)

[Lacy edition, 4⅛ x 7¼; interleaves; gray and red marbled boards and brown cloth spine; title inked up cover.]

Studybook of the actor of Laertes in Fechter's production. Little stage business.

75. Edwin Booth New York, Winter Garden November 26, 1864
The Players

[Tauchnitz edition, 1862, 3½ x 5½; purple cloth boards; in red leather box; title gilt on spine.]

Partial preparation copy inscribed "Found by me at Winter Garden during my 'Hundred Nights' and marked for reference." First act shows cuts, grooves, stage business, maps, cues for effects. (See nos. 86-87, 101-104, 107-113.)

76. [Booth]
The Players

[Booth-Hinton edition, 5⅝ x 9⅛; brown marbled boards and half maroon leather; title gilt on spine.]

Studybook marked "Private." Many notes on interpretation and acting. References to Forrest, Sullivan, Fechter.

77. Lawrence Barrett   Brooklyn, Park   December, 1864
     Harvard Theatre Collection: TS.2272.78

[French's Standard Drama, $4\frac{3}{8}$ x $7\frac{3}{8}$; interleaves, 5 x $7\frac{5}{8}$; red marbled boards and half black leather; title gilt on black leather cover label; in box of gray boards and brown leather spine; title gilt up spine.]

Very full and much used promptbook, written in purple ink by "W. S." At the front a list of doubles. Cuts and restorations, scenic indications, grooves, calls, copious stage business, maps, cues for effects. (See nos. 81-83.) (If "W. S." is William Seymour, this copy was probably made c.1870).

78. George C. Boniface   New York, New Bowery   February 27, 1865
     Folger: Hamlet, 5

[French's Standard Drama, $4\frac{1}{2}$ x $7\frac{5}{8}$; interleaves, 5 x 8; salmon boards and brown velvet spine; title on cover label.]

Elegantly developed promptbook. Calls, properties, some stage business, maps, cues for effects. Contains 1894 flier for his "Shakespearean Readings," which lists the greater actors he has served under.

79. George A. Ober   America   1865-67
     Princeton, Seymour Collection

[French's Standard Drama, $4\frac{1}{8}$ x $6\frac{1}{2}$; tan cardboard.]

Much worn studybook checked for Claudius and Horatio. Notes on lengths of various roles, records of performance. Two sheets of notes on disposition of scenes for the play and list of new scenes to be painted.

80. F. A. Marshall   London, Royal Alfred   February 23, 1869
     Shakespeare Centre Library: 50.07(1855)

[Lacy edition, 4 x $7\frac{1}{4}$; interleaves, $8\frac{1}{2}$ x $7\frac{1}{4}$; blue leather; title gilt on front, inked on spine label.]

Studybook of an actor or reader with detailed notes of business and interpretation for the opening scenes.

81. Lawrence Barrett   1870
     Princeton University, Seymour Collection

[Booth-Hinton edition, $5\frac{3}{4}$ x 9; publisher's wrappers.]

Stage manager's workbook signed and dated by William Seymour. Barrett's name substituted for Booth's on the cover. (See no. 77.)

82. [Barrett]

University of Illinois: x792.9/Shl5h/no.4

[French's Standard Drama, 4½ x 7¼; interleaves; purple cloth boards; title and "Chas. B. Wells [sic]" gilt on cover.]

Transcription of Barrett's promptbook made by Charles B. Welles in 1875. Lists of Hamlet's costumes, doubles, written papers. Cuts, scenic indications, grooves, calls, copious stage business, maps and sketches, cues for effects, timing. At the back a music score for the Dead March.

83. [Barrett]

Harvard Theatre Collection: uncatalogued

[Ten music score books, 9½ x 6¼; brown cloth boards and green cloth spine.]

Complete scores for the band for 9 plays including *Hamlet,* endorsed by musicians in many cities.

84. James E. Kirkwood   Rochester, New York   1870's

University of Illinois: x792.9/Shl5h/no.2

[French's Standard Drama, 4¼ x 6⅜; interleaves; purple marbled boards and brown cloth spine, broken.]

Early promptbook of Kirkwood, the Rochester prompter: cues for effects done in brown and red ink. Much stage business added in pencil, especially for the last acts, perhaps in the hand of William Farnum.

85. [Kirkwood]

University of Illinois: x792.9/Shl5h/no.3

[French's Standard Drama, 4⅜ x 6⅞; interleaves; green marbled boards and blue cloth spine; title inked down spine label.]

Later Kirkwood promptbook: cuts, cues for effects neatly printed in brown and red ink. Rochester playbills pasted in for Edwin Adams in 1875 and Sophia Miles in 1877.

86. Edwin Booth   New York, Booth's   January 5, 1870

Folger: T.b.16

[Double-column journal, 9 x 10½; brown cloth boards and tan leather spine; title gilt on maroon spine label.]

Manuscript description (108 pages) of Booth's Hamlet, written by Charles W. Clarke in the summer of 1870. (See Murray Bundy, *Shakespeare Quarterly,* II, 99-102.)

87. [Booth]
The Players
[Booth-Hinton edition, 5¾ x 9⅛, between leaves of a workbook, 7½ x 9⅛; red marbled boards and red leather spine; in red leather box; titles gilt on spine. Workbook also contains *Richelieu*.]
Well-marked promptbook used on tours. Scenic indications, calls, stage business, cues for effects. Timings for performances in various cities, 1870-77. Playbill for hundredth night, March 22, 1865. (See nos. 75-76, 101-104, 107-113.)

88. Walter Hubbell   Philadelphia   1872
Folger: Hamlet, 14
[French's Standard Drama, 4¼ x 7½; gray cardboard.]
Rehearsal copy, much thumbed but very little marked. (See no. 113.)

89. William Creswick   London, Princess's   November 4, 1873
Shakespeare Centre Library: 50.07(1826)
[Pages 253-410 from volume VIII of Chalmers' *Works,* 1826, 5½ x 8½; interleaves; green cloth boards and half green leather; title gilt on red spine label, Creswick's name gilt on red cover label.]
Promptbook handsomely marked in large clear hand, with penciled additions. Cuts on full text, scenic notes and several sketches, calls, stage business, maps, cues for effects. Programs for Princess's and for Drury Lane, December 15, 1874.

90. Henry Irving   London, Lyceum   October 31, 1874
Harvard Theatre Collection: TS.2272.75
[Pages of a Shakespeare edition pasted in a workbook, 7⅜ x 8⅞; red marbled boards and black cloth spine; in box of green cloth boards and green leather spine; title gilt on spine.]
Excellent souvenir promptbook made by J. H. Allen after the 200-night Lyceum run. Explicit details of stage management. Many maps and sketches, cues for effects.

91. [Irving]
Harvard Theatre Collection: uncatalogued

[Clarendon Press (Clark and Wright), 1873, 4½ x 6⅝; publisher's wrappers.]

Irving's studybook, marked in red, blue, and lead pencil. Cuts on full text, countless notes on the interpretation and playing of his own role, and notes on effects.

92. [Irving]
Folger: Hamlet, 15
[Clarendon Press edition, 1873, 4½ x 6⅝; orange publisher's wrappers, much worn.]
Given by Irving to Charles Lamb Kenney, "with marks, as performed by him at the Lyceum." Cuts and transpositions only.

93. [Irving]   London, Lyceum   December 30, 1878
Shakespeare Centre Library: 72.907/Irving
[Sheets of Irving edition, 1878, tipped to stubs between pages of a workbook, 6⅜ x 7⅞; blue cloth boards and blue leather spine; title gilt on cover.]
Carefully marked promptbook, probably by J. H. Allen, the Lyceum prompter. Scenic indications, grooves, calls, maps, cues for effects, timings. A nice watercolor of Ghost standing on rock backed by the sea.

94. [Irving]
Folger: Hamlet, 17
[Irving edition, 1879, 5¼ x 8¼; yellow leather gilt.]
Studybook with a few penciled jottings.

95. Ellen Terry   London, Lyceum   December 30, 1878
Smallhythe
[Irving edition, 1879, 5¼ x 8; interleaves; maroon leather, much worn.]
Rehearsal book, dated as of Miss Terry's first appearance at the Lyceum. Many notes by Miss Terry on Ophelia's mad scene. Notes on Hamlet's business in play scene in another hand. At the front she has noted "Some of Edward W. G. . . . Henry Irving . . . Edward Gordon Craig."

96. [Terry]
Smallhythe
[Oxford edition, 1876, 4½ x 6½; publisher's orange paper with printed title; "H. I." inked on cover.]
A copy in which Miss Terry has entered many derogatory notes

about somebody's performance of Hamlet, comparing him unfavorably to Irving.

97. [Terry]
Folger: Hamlet, 49
[Irving edition, 1883, 5⅜ x 8¼; gray paper.]
A few notes of stage business in the fourth act.

98. Julian Reed   1880's
Harvard Theatre Collection: uncatalogued
[French's Standard Drama, 4½ x 7½; pink paper.]
"Presented to Julian Reed by Ed. Chas. Voltz." Cuts, some stage business, maps, some cues.

99. J. B. Roberts   1880's
Folger: Hamlet, 41
[Pages 247-394 from volume VII of a *Works*, 6¼ x 9¾; black cloth boards and brown leather spine.]
Cutting of the play for public readings. At the front a list of 12 Shakespeare plays, apparently his reading repertory. At the back an article on Hamlet by Wilson Barrett, a note on Irving's business with the peacock fan, a review of Tree's *Hamlet* in 1892. (See nos. 35-38, 71.)

100. Frederick Warde   America   1880's
W. A. Clarke Library, Los Angeles
[Kean edition, 4 x 6⅝; interleaves; brown leather; title and Warde's name gilt on cover, title gilt on spine.]
Promptbook used by Warde for many years after it was given to him by L. Sola in Dallas in 1882. At the front, plots of scenes and grooves, properties, supers. Calls, some stage business, good groundplans, cues for effects.

101. Edwin Booth   New York   c.1880
Harvard Theatre Collection: uncatalogued
[Booth-Winter edition, 1878, 4⅝ x 7⅛.]
A richly marked copy, checked for Ghost and Rosencrantz, but probably marked by the leader of the orchestra: all music cues are carefully noted. Copious notations of stage business as seen from the front. In all Hamlet passages there are marginal keymarks—a, b, d, e, etc. (but never c)—which correspond to the keymarks in E. T. Mason's books. (See nos. 75-76, 86-87, 107-113.)

102. [Booth]
     Folger: Hamlet, 6
     [Booth-Winter edition, 4¾ x 6¾.]
     Rehearsal copy, with many nearly illegible scribblings probably by Booth. A gift from Booth to Charles Dunphie, October, 1880.

103. [Booth]
     The Players
     [Booth-Winter edition, 1879, 4⅝ x 6½; black limp leather gilt; title gilt on cover.]
     Transcription of Booth's promptbook made by J. R. Pitman as a souvenir for Russ Whytal, autographed by Booth. Excellently marked with scenic indications, groundplans, calls, stage business, maps, cues for effects.

104. [Booth]
     University of Pennsylvania, Furness Collection: C59.ShlHP
     [Booth-Winter edition, 1879, 4¾ x 6¾; gray publisher's wrappers.]
     Carefully marked promptbook by J. R. Pitman, with pencilings showing signs of use. Calls, stage business, several good maps, cues for effects. Probably derived from Booth and related to preceding book.

105. Louis James   1882-83
     University of Pennsylvania, Furness Collection: C59.ShlR3J
     [French's Standard Drama pasted in a workbook of brown paper, 5½ x 8¼; gray marbled boards and blue cloth spine. Workbook also contains James's 1881 book of *Richard III*.]
     Promptbook arranged in 6 acts, very carefully marked. Cuts, some grooves, much stage business, good maps, cues for effects.

106. Helena Modjeska   New York, Broadway   November 4, 1889
     Boston Athenaeum: $VE.S58.1911
     [Pages of Ophelia scenes pasted in a workbook, 6¾ x 8⅛; black leather. Workbook also contains Booth's banquet scene in *Macbeth* (see MAC, 103).]
     Edward Tuckerman Mason's descriptive notes on Modjeska's Ophelia when she played with Edwin Booth.

107. Edwin Booth   America   1890
     Harvard Theatre Collection: TS.2272.73

[Booth-Winter edition, 1890, printed on right-hand pages only, 4¾ x 6¾; publisher's wrappers; in gray cloth board box with maroon leather spine; title gilt up spine.]

Fully though roughly marked book of Booth's final season. Cuts, scenic indications, grooves, calls, much stage business, maps, cues for effects. Last pages missing. (See nos. 75-76, 86-87, 101-104.)

108. [Booth]

Harvard Theatre Collection: TS.665.9.5

[Pages 1-152 of a Shakespeare text, 5¼ x 8¾; interleaves, 7 x 10¼; black cloth boards; title gilt on spine.]

Scrapbook in promptbook form made up by James Taylor, the actor, during the 1890 tour and presented to Booth. Includes title pages and introductions from several editions of the play, two articles on its stage history, several portraits of actors. Many descriptive and interpretive notes by Taylor, and additional notes by Booth and Barrett.

109. [Booth]

The Players

[Booth-Winter edition, 1878, 4¾ x 6¾; interleaves; brown marbled boards and half brown leather; title and Booth's name gilt on spine.]

Private studybook in which Booth wrote about 230 "Rough *mems* for future use. To be put into proper shape at leisure." Notes on stage business, motivation, pronunciations, meanings of words, etc. Many key numerals entered in the text have no corresponding notes, as if the work was in progress.

110. [Booth]

Boston Athenaeum: $VE.S5H.1909

[Booth-Winter edition, 1909, 4½ x 6¾; interleaves; blue cloth boards; title gilt on spine.]

"Some of Edwin Booth's business in Hamlet, observed and noted by Edward Tuckerman Mason, from 1862 to 1891." There are 234 notes, with many maps, recording Booth's varying practices for 30 years.

111. [Booth]

The Players

[Booth-Winter edition, 1888, 4¾ x 6½; interleaves; black cloth; title inked on spine label.]

Another copy of E. T. Mason's notes. This is probably the original, from which the preceding book was transcribed.

112. [Booth]

New York Public Library: *NCP

[Pages of Booth-Winter edition, 4½ x 7⅛, tipped into workbook, 6¾ x 8¼; black boards and tan cloth spine; title typed up spine.]

A promptbook made up by Hallam Bosworth, partly taken from Booth books, partly from George Becks's memorials of Forrest, with references to Sothern. At the front are groundplans for the 6 acts. Plots for properties and lights. Copious stage business, cues for effects. The text is marked for stresses.

113. [Booth]

Folger: Hamlet, 60

[Booth-Winter edition, 1896, 4½ x 7; interleaves; blue cloth boards.]

William Winter's souvenir copy of the edition with numerous photographs and autographs, and a manuscript page of Winter's description of Booth as Hamlet.

114. Frank Lodge   c.1890

Folger: Hamlet, 23

[Booth-Winter edition, 1878, pasted in a workbook, 4½ x 7⅜; brown leather; title on cover label.]

Rehearsal copy. Costume list, random stage business for various minor roles.

115. La Nera

Harvard Theatre Collection: uncatalogued

[Booth-Winter edition, 4¾ x 7⅛; publisher's wrappers.]

Rehearsal copy. Copious stage business for Gertrude's closet scene and Ophelia's mad scene.

116. Walter Hubbell   c.1890

Folger: Hamlet, 73

[Typescripts, 8 x 5¼; blue paper.]

Eighteen partbooks for Hubbell's touring company. An advertising leaflet for him, containing reference to the imminent retirement of Booth. (See no. 88.)

117. Robert Mantell   Troy   March 19, 1890

Folger: Hamlet, 26

[French's Standard Drama, 4½ x 7; interleaves; brown limp leather; title, etc., gilt on cover.]

Promptbook, much used. Cuts and restorations. At the front a list of scenes with grooves, and a dummy cast list. Stage business, maps, cues for effects entered in several colors.

118. Herbert Beerbohm Tree   London, Haymarket   January 21, 1892

Folger: Hamlet, 51

[Memorial Theatre edition, 1882, 4¾ x 7⅛.]

Rehearsal copy checked and cut for Hamlet.

119. [Tree]

Folger: Hamlet, 52

[Wilson Barrett edition, 1886, 5½ x 8⅜.]

Preparation copy. A few notes on scenery and stage business.

120. [Tree]

Enthoven Collection: Tree, 12

[Memorial Theatre edition, 1882, 4¾ x 7¼; interleaves, 6¾ x 9; binding and last pages missing.]

Much used rehearsal promptbook. Cuts and transpositions, stage business roughly penciled, maps, cues for effects. At the front a list of timings and names of minor actors for opening scene.

121. [Tree]

Enthoven Collection: Tree, 12

[Memorial Theatre edition, 1882, 4¾ x 7¼; interleaves, 5¼ x 8½; green boards and green cloth spine, very much worn; title and "1893" inked on cover.]

Promptbook, marked in black and red ink. Cuts, good groundplans, stage business, maps, cues for effects.

122. [Tree]

Enthoven Collection: Tree, 12

[Typescripts, 8⅞ x 7¾; gray paper.]

Partbooks for King, Marcellus, Bernardo, Francisco, Second Player, Player Queen, Priest, Rosencrantz.

123. [Tree]

Enthoven Collection: Tree, 12

[Black leather notebook, 4⅝ x 7.]

Inventory of scenery, properties, wardrobe for American tour.

124. [Tree]   London, His Majesty's   1905

Enthoven Collection: Tree, 12

[Papers.]

Cast lists for 1905, 1906, 1908, 1910. Scenery lists, dressing room lists, property lists, proofs for 1906 program, etc.

125. [Tree]

Enthoven Collection: Tree, 12

[Heinemann's Favourite Classics, 1904, 3¾ x 6; green cloth boards; title gilt up spine.]

Nine rehearsal copies with cuts and some penciled notes: Queen, Polonius, Ghost, Laertes, Ophelia, Horatio, etc.

126. Johnston Forbes-Robertson   London, Lyceum   Sept. 11, 1897

Henry E. Huntington Library: 344883

[Forbes-Robertson edition, 1897, 7¼ x 9½; tan boards and red cloth spine; title in red on cover; in brown leather box, 7⅝ x 10; title and "Prompt Copy" gilt on spine.]

Promptbook marked in ink and pencil along the margins. Some cuts, some stage business, routine for overture and opening, cues for effects. Signed at the back by Charles Chappel of South Kensington.

127. William Poel   London, Carpenter's Hall   February 21, 1900

Enthoven Collection

[Leaves of Cassell's National Library edition, 3⅝ x 5⅝, tipped to stubs between leaves of a workbook, 6⅜ x 8; black imitation leather.]

Incomplete preparation copy. Many passages, cut and rearranged, are in manuscript.

128. [Poel]

Enthoven Collection

[Cassell's National Library edition, 3⅝ x 5⅝; gray publisher's wrappers.]

Preparation copy. Cuts on full text. Various working notes.

129. F. Owen Chambers   c.1900

Shakespeare Centre Library: 72.907CHA

[Cassell's National Library edition pasted in two workbooks, $6\frac{1}{4}$ x $7\frac{7}{8}$, fastened together; black boards; title inked on spine and cover labels.]

Promptbook thought to have been prepared about 1900; does not appear used. Cuts, elaborate scenic indications, grooves, 5 careful groundplans, stage business, cues for effects.

130. E. H. Sothern   New York, Garden   September 17, 1900
The Players: PB.95

[Rolfe(?) edition, $4\frac{5}{8}$ x $6\frac{1}{4}$, sewn between leaves of a workbook, $7\frac{1}{2}$ x $9\frac{5}{8}$; red leather; title, etc., gilt on cover.]

Extremely full preparation book, by Fred Williams, Lyceum Theatre Company, 1899. Cuts on full text, scenic indications, elaborate groundplans, calls, detailed stage business, scores for songs, cues for effects. At the back, 164 pages of manuscript notes on some 20 great Hamlets of the past. Penciled annotations by Sothern.

131. [Sothern]
The Players: TS.104
[Typescript, $8\frac{1}{2}$ x 11; brown paper.]
Early version of Sothern's text. Some stage business.

132. E. H. Sothern and Julia Marlowe
                Chicago, Illinois Theatre   October 4, 1904
The Players: PB.111
[Seven booklets. Typescript, 8 x $10\frac{1}{2}$.]
Early working copy of the 1904 version. Penciled corrections of text. First booklet contains plots of rigging, properties, lights, scenes with groundplans, music, cast. Sixth booklet contains lists of supers and their business. Seventh booklet contains groundplans and stage business.

133. [Sothern and Marlowe]
The Players: TS.106, 112
[Two books. Typescript, 8 x $10\frac{1}{2}$; each book consists of 6 parts bound separately in blue paper.]
Two copies of completed book. Many notes on the text, very full stage business. All the technical data from the preceding book, plus special instructions to house carpenters.

134. [Sothern and Marlowe]
     Museum of the City of New York: 43.430.641
     [Typescript (original), 8½ x 11; black cloth board folder.]
     Final promptbook, much used on the road. Extra pencilings of
     calls, added stage business, maps, cues for effects, timings in sev-
     eral cities.

135. [Sothern and Marlowe]
     Museum of the City of New York: 43.430.640
     [Typescript (carbon of preceding book); acts bound separately.]
     Electrician's copy (W. Stiefell). Large groundplans and sketches
     showing focus of lighting instruments.

136. [Sothern and Marlowe]
     Folger: T.a.81, 82
     [Notebook, 6⅝ x 8⅛; red marbled boards and black cloth spine.]
     "Sothern & Marlowe Elect Dept." Light plots for 5 Shakespeare
     productions, including 11 plots (sketches) for *Hamlet;* instru-
     ments, colors, maps, cues. With it a typed light plot mounted on
     cardboard for use at the controls.

137. [Sothern and Marlowe]
     Folger: Hamlet, 34, 35
     [Two books. Typescript, 8½ x 11; brown paper.]
     Complete book of the production, with stage business and plots
     of lights, properties, music, etc., for each scene. Number 34 is an
     original, and 35 a carbon.

138. [Sothern and Marlowe]
     Folger: Hamlet, Folios 1, 2, 3
     [Two books. Typescript, 8½ x 12; gray cardboard.]
     In these three "folios" are 2 complete copies of a final version
     which differs somewhat from that of Folger nos. 34 and 35. Pre-
     pared by Frederick Kaufman, general stage manager.

139. [Sothern and Marlowe]
     New York Public Library: *NCP.276561B
     [Typescript, 8⅛ x 11; red cloth boards; title gilt on spine.]
     Carbon copy of one of the final versions, used by V. H. Collins.
     Penciled cues for musical flourishes.

140. [Sothern and Marlowe]
New York Public Library: *NCOF.51x304
[Typescript, 8½ x 11; brown cloth boards; title gilt up spine.]
Carbon copy of same text as preceding (Collins) copy, but in a
different typing.

141. [Sothern and Marlowe]
Museum of the City of New York: 43.430.683
[Typescript, 7⅞ x 6½; blue paper.]
Miss Marlowe's partbook for Ophelia, lightly annotated.

142. [Sothern and Marlowe]
Museum of the City of New York: 43.430.684
[Typescript, 7⅞ x 6½; blue paper.]
Sothern's partbook for Hamlet. Costume lists.

143. [Sothern and Marlowe]
Folger: Hamlet, 32
[Shakespeare text pasted in a workbook, 7⅜ x 9½; black cloth
board ring binder.]
Promptbook record of the production made by Lark Taylor,
November, 1906. Cuts on full text. Very detailed stage business.
Playbill for 1906.

144. [Sothern and Marlowe]
Folger: Hamlet, 36
[Sothern edition, 1903, 5½ x 8¾; brown cloth boards and half
brown leather gilt; title and "King Claudius Prompt Book" gilt
on spine.]
Lark Taylor's second record of the production. Casts for 1900,
1907, 1911. Copious stage business, maps. Many anecdotes from
the history of the production, including Taylor's experience in
various roles, the Cincinnati fire, etc.

145. [Sothern and Marlowe]
Joint University Libraries, Nashville: S822.33/S7/H7
[Sothern edition, 1901, 5 x 8½; interleaves; red cloth boards;
title and "Lark Taylor" gilt on cover.]
Lark Taylor's third promptbook record of the production. Casts
for 1907 in London, 1907 in Pittsburgh, 1911, 1912, 1913-14,
groundplans, copious stage business, maps, cues for effects. Exten-

sive notes on the early career of Cissy Loftus (with photographs), on alterations in the company, on the Cincinnati fire, on his own experiences in various roles, etc.

146. [Sothern and Marlowe]
Library of Congress, Batchelder Collection: 382
[Sothern edition, 1903, 5⅝ x 9; publisher's pictorial boards.]
John Davis Batchelder's copy, annotated with comments on Sothern's production and others. Many photographs, playbills, reviews.

147. [Sothern and Marlowe]
Folger: Hamlet, 27
[Pages 9-125 of an acting edition pasted in a workbook, 6½ x 8¼; green and black mottled boards and half black leather.]
A promptbook of doubtful provenience. Cuts, some stage business, cues for effects, a fencing routine. Contains a letter from Miss Marlowe to "Alice" mentioning imminent sailing to America.

148. H. B. Irving   London, Adelphi   April 4, 1905
Harvard Theatre Collection: uncatalogued
[Aldine edition, 1895, 4 x 5⅛; limp red leather; title gilt up spine.]
Rehearsal copy checked for Hamlet and marked for stresses and pauses. Cuts on full text. Little stage business. Casts for Edinburgh and Sunderland, 1895, and for the Adelphi.

[ACTOR LISTS FOR FOLLOWING BOOKS ARE GIVEN IN THIS ORDER: Hamlet, King, Polonius, Gertrude, Ophelia.]

149. Frederick Melville   London, Lyceum   March 13, 1909
Enthoven Collection
[Typescript, 8 x 10; 5 acts bound separately in gray paper.]
Cast includes Matheson Lang, Eric Mayne, George Fitzgerald, Mary Allestree, Hutin Britton. Cuts, elaborate scenic indications, calls, some stage business, maps, cues for effects.

150. Henry Jewett   Boston   1915-29
Folger: Hamlet, Folio 4[1]
[Typescript, 8½ x 11; white canvas over gray cardboard.]
Jewett's stage arrangement, apparently used as a promptbook. Cast, much stage business, maps, cues for effects. Photograph of Jewett.

151. [Jewett]
     Folger: Hamlet, Folio 4²
     [Typescript, 8½ x 11; gray cardboard and green cloth spine.]
     Jewett's partbook for Hamlet. Many pencilings of stage business.

152. F. R. Benson   Stratford-upon-Avon   April, 1916
     Shakespeare Centre Library: 72.907BEN
     [Temple edition pasted in a workbook, 7 x 9; red marbled boards
     and green cloth spine; title printed on cover label.]
     The book of the Benson "North Company" directed by Lady
     Benson; said to have been used in 1921 and perhaps earlier
     (Benson's last *Hamlet* at Stratford was in the spring of 1916).
     Scenic indications, calls, stage business, cues for effects. Plots for
     properties and supers.

153. Lena Ashwell   London   1919-29
     Birmingham, Shakespeare Memorial Library: 421199
     [Temple edition pasted in a workbook, 7 x 9; black oilcloth;
     title gilt up spine.]
     Promptbook of the Lena Ashwell Players. Cues for effects.

154. John Barrymore   New York, Sam Harris   November 16, 1922
     Folger: Hamlet, 30
     [Roycroft edition, 1902, 8 x 10⅛; gray boards and green leather
     spine; title gilt on spine.]
     Promptbook record of the Barrymore production made by Lark
     Taylor, the actor, in 1922-23. Cast includes John Barrymore,
     Tyrone Power, John S. O'Brien, Blanche Yurka, Rosalind Fuller.
     Directed by Arthur Hopkins. Designed by Robert Edmond Jones.
     Cuts on full text, watercolor of the set, groundplan with dimen-
     sions, copious stage business, maps, music scores, program, auto-
     graphs of the actors. "I've marked on this book for several
     months—and have the satisfaction of knowing that not another
     copy of the original cuts and markings—as per rehearsals and
     first performance—exists. . . ."

155. [Barrymore]
     Joint University Libraries, Nashville
     [Temple edition, 1919, 4 x 5⅛; red leather; title gilt on spine.]
     Promptbook record of the Barrymore production in its second
     season, made by Lark Taylor in 1923-24 on his own rehearsal

copy, much of it done in pencil and later inked over. Cuts on full text, groundplans, much stage business, cues for effects. Notes on changes of cast, anecdotes including a visit of the Moscow Art Theatre Company, dates of road performances, many notes on the history of the production.

156. [Barrymore]

Folger: Hamlet, 31

[Roycroft edition, 1902, 8 x 10⅛; gray boards and brown leather spine; title gilt on spine.]

Promptbook record of the Barrymore production in its second season, made by Lark Taylor in 1924, showing alterations made during the run. Crayon drawing of the set, copious stage business, etc., as in preceding book. Anecdotes and observations on the history of the production, including Barrymore's last curtain speech and his farewell party for the company.

157. [Barrymore]

Joint University Libraries, Nashville: S822.33/S7/H8

[Roycroft edition, 1902, copy no. 100 signed by Elbert Hubbard, 8 x 10¼; tan boards and leather spine; title gilt on spine.]

Promptbook record of the Barrymore production made by John Lark Taylor, with his bookplate. Very full copy containing all the matter of the preceding Taylor books. Autographs of the whole company as of November, 1922, and of new members in November, 1923; transcription by Taylor of the autographs and quotations made in January, 1924. At the front an engraving of a pencil portrait of Barrymore, and sketches of Marcellus, Second Player, Taylor as First Player, the Gravediggers. Map of lighting instruments. At the back complete fight routine, curtain plot, property plot, newspaper clipping about Kronborg Castle.

158. [Barrymore]

The Players

[Temple edition, 4 x 5⅛; red cloth boards; title gilt up spine.]

Barrymore's studybook for the 1922-24 production, inscribed to Margaret Carrington. Numerous pencilings: cuts, stresses, some stage business, sketches.

159. Robert Atkins   Egypt   1927

Shakespeare Centre Library: 72.907ATK

[Favourite Classics edition pasted in a workbook, 6¾ x 8⅞; blue marbled boards and red cloth spine.]

Used by Atkins for Egyptian tour, 1927. Cuts on full text, calls, stage business, maps, cues for effects.

160. Esme Percy   London, Court   February 12, 1930
Mander and Mitchenson

[Calvert edition, 1912, 4¾ x 7½; green boards; title printed on cover.]

Cast includes Esme Percy, John Laurie, Charles Macdona, Miriam Lewes, Gabrielle Casartelli. Producer, Peter Godfrey. Cuts, some stage business, maps, cues for effects. Some of the markings said to be by William Poel.

161. Norman Bel Geddes New York, Broadhurst November 5, 1931
University of Texas, Hoblitzelle Theatre Arts Library: DR15, g.1-7

[Seven workbooks, 8½ x 11; gray cloth boards.]

Production books and scrapbook. Cast includes Raymond Massey, David Horne, John Daly Murphy, Mary Servoss, Celia Johnson. Volume 1 contains printed text pasted in; cuts, copious annotations of stage business and interpretation. Volume 2 contains typewritten text called "third revision"; copious stage business, cues for effects. Volumes 3-5 contain complete text as acted, with photographs of stage model and blueprints of groundplans. Volume 6 contains casting charts and lists of actors, list of 128 drawings, light plots, costume lists, music scores and lists, rehearsal schedules, timings, a speech to the cast. Volume 7 contains photographs of rehearsal scenes and all principal performers, programs for Lakewood, Pennsylvania, and New York, reviews, correspondence, a defense of the script. (Not available for use pending publication.)

162. Whitford Kane   1932
New York Public Library: *NCP

[Text pasted in a workbook, 7¼ x 9½; black cloth boards; title gilt on spine.]

An acting version marked for recorded musical accompaniment: Shostakovich, Holst, Mozart, etc.

163. W. Bridges-Adams   Stratford-upon-Avon   July 20, 1933
Shakespeare Centre Library: 71.21/1933H(6055, 7934)

[Two books. Temple edition pasted in workbooks, 7 x 9; first book in blue cloth boards and half red leather; second book in purple cloth boards and half black leather.]

Cast includes Anew McMaster, Stanley Howlett, Stanley Lathbury, Esme Church, Rachel Kempson. Cuts, calls, stage business, maps, cues for effects. The first book was used previously at Stratford in 1929, and for American tours in 1928-30. The second is a neat copy of the first, unused.

164. B. Iden Payne   Stratford-upon-Avon   July 6, 1936
Shakespeare Centre Library: 71.21/1930H

[Temple edition pasted in a workbook, $6\frac{7}{8}$ x 9; purple cloth boards and half black leather; title printed on cover label.]

Not the Bridges-Adams book of 1930, as listed, but Payne's book of 1936. Cast includes Donald Wolfit, Norman Wooland, Eric Maxon, Barbara Couper, Valerie Tudor. Designed by Randle Ayrton. Cuts, calls, stage business, maps, cues for effects.

165. Guthrie McClintic   New York, Empire   October 8, 1936
New York Public Library: *NCP.0643196

[Text pasted in a workbook, 8 x $10\frac{1}{2}$; black cloth boards; title gilt up spine.]

Cast includes John Gielgud, Malcolm Keen, Arthur Byron, Judith Anderson, Lillian Gish. Designed by Jo Mielziner. Acting version with few markings.

166. Leslie Howard   Boston, Boston Opera House   Oct. 19, 1936
University of California, Los Angeles: Houseman Box 13
[Carbon typescript, $8\frac{1}{2}$ x 11.]

Cast includes Leslie Howard, Wilfrid Walter, Aubrey Mather, Mary Servoss, Pamela Stanley. Designed by Stewart Chaney. Promptbook of 3-act version by Schuyler Watts. Copious stage business and cues for effects typed into the text. Much marked for stage use.

167. Margaret Webster   New York, St. James   October 12, 1938
New York Public Library: *ZC.9
[35 mm. negative film.]

Film copy of the promptbook, the original in the possession of Maurice Evans. Cast includes Maurice Evans, Henry Edwards, George Graham, Mady Christians, Katherine Locke. Heavily annotated.

168. Robert Atkins   Stratford-upon-Avon   April 24, 1944
Shakespeare Centre Library: 71.21/1944H
[Temple edition pasted in a workbook, 7⅛ x 9; purple cloth boards and half black leather; title inked on cover label.]
Cast includes John Byron, Raymond Pollett, Michael Martin-Harvey, Viola Lyel, Anna Burden. Designed by Guy Sheppard and Barbara Curtis. Cuts on full text, calls, stage business, maps. The book was originally used by B. Iden Payne in 1936 and 1937, has been erased and reused.

169. Robert Breen   June, 1944
New York Public Library: *NCP
[Typescript, 8 x 10¾; black cardboard and tan cloth spine.]
Version as produced for army audiences.

170. Michael Benthall   Stratford-upon-Avon   April 24, 1948
Shakespeare Centre Library: O.S.71.21/1948H
[Temple edition pasted in a workbook, 8 x 12⅞; green boards and red cloth spine; title printed on cover label.]
Cast includes Robert Helpmann and Paul Scofield alternating, Anthony Quayle, John Kidd, Diana Wynyard, Claire Bloom. Designed by James Bailey. Cuts, calls, much stage business, maps, cues for effects.

171. Robert Breen   Elsinore, Kronborg Castle   June 17, 1949
New York Public Library: *NCP
[Mimeograph, 8½ x 10¾; black cardboard and tan cloth spine.]
Copy of the Elsinore production book belonging to George Quick, stage manager. Copious stage business, cues for effects, maps of lights.

172. Michael Langham   Stratford-upon-Avon   April 10, 1956
Shakespeare Centre Library: O.S.71.21/1956H
[New Temple edition pasted in a workbook, 8 x 12⅞; red cloth board spring binder.]
Cast includes Alan Badel, Harry Andrews, George Howe, Diana Churchill, Dilys Hamlett. Designed by Michael Northen and Desmond Heeley. Cuts, copious stage business typed on facing pages, maps, cues for effects. Production papers include curtain call, duel routine, "reaction" lines, and 27 maps on mimeographed groundplans.

173. [Langham]   Stratford, Ontario   July 1, 1957
Festival Theatre, Library
[Two books. New Temple edition pasted in workbooks, 8 x 12¾; black cloth boards and red cloth spine; title pasted on cover.]
Cast includes Christopher Plummer, Douglas Campbell, William Hutt, Joy Lafleur, Frances Hyland. Designed by Desmond Heeley. The first book has copious stage business, cues for effects. The second has calls, cues for effects.

174. Glen Byam Shaw   Stratford-upon-Avon   June 3, 1958
Shakespeare Centre Library: O.S.71.21/1958H
[Temple edition pasted in a workbook, 7¾ x 12⅞; blue cloth board spring binder.]
Cast includes Michael Redgrave, Mark Dignam, Cyril Luckham, Googie Withers, Dorothy Tutin. Designed by Motley. Cuts, copious stage business, maps, cues for effects. Production papers include plots of scenes and properties, many maps on mimeographed groundplans. The book was used for Russian tour in winter of 1958-59.

175. John Houseman   Stratford, Connecticut   June 19, 1958
Festival Theatre, Production Department
[Two books. Mimeograph, 8½ x 11; first book in black cloth board spring binder, second in black cloth board ring binder.]
Cast includes Fritz Weaver, Morris Carnovsky, Hiram Sherman, Geraldine Fitzgerald, Inga Swenson. Designed by David Hays and Alvin Colt. The first book, called "Original Blocking," has copious stage business, company lists. The second has cues for effects.

176. [Houseman]
University of California, Los Angeles: Houseman Box 10
[Text pasted in a workbook, 8½ x 11; black limp ring binder.]
First production book or preparation copy. Cuts, rough working notes.

177. [Houseman]
University of California, Los Angeles: Houseman Box 10
[Mimeograph, 8½ x 11; blue cloth board ring binder.]
Rough production book. Stage business and other notes. Many production papers.

178. Peter Wood   Stratford-upon-Avon   April 11, 1961
Shakespeare Centre Library: O.S.71.21/1961H

[Cambridge Pocket Shakespeare pasted in a workbook, 8½ x 13; blue cloth board ring binder.]

Cast includes Ian Bannen, Noel Willman, Redmond Phillips, Elizabeth Sellars, Geraldine McEwan. Designed by Leslie Hurry. Cuts on full text, stage business, maps, cues for effects. Production papers include cast lists and 8 maps on mimeographed ground-plans.

179. Other books of *Hamlet:*

Connecticut State Library: William Gillette.

Edwin Forrest Home (on loan to the University of Pennsylvania Library, Rare Book Room): 3 books of Edwin Forrest.

Folger: Ham, 4, Wm. H. P——, Mrs. Bingham; Ham, 7, J. B. Booth, 1839; Ham, 9, Miss F. G. Conkling; Ham, 11, James P. Deuel; Ham, 12, C. W. Folsom; Ham, 13, Joseph Kainz, excellent Regiebuch based on Schlegel translation; Ham, 22, James Lewis; Ham, 28, Emilie Melville; Ham, 37, Muler and Everett; Ham, 46, John Sefton; Ham, 47, John Seymour; Ham, 48, J. H. Smith; Ham, 57, anonymous, excellent German Regiebuch; Ham, 59, George W. Wilson, 1875; Ham, 63, 64, 65, 66, 67, 68 (German with English notations), 70, 71, all anonymous; PR.1243.K3. cop. 2, John Thomas Ambrose; Y.d.38, proofs of Preface to Irving edition, 1878.

Harvard Theatre Collection: "marked as at Drury Lane," c.1800.

Historical and Philosophical Society of Ohio: 812.3/R283/72, Alvin Read.

Library Company of Philadelphia: OEngShak.22418.D.3, Manchester, 1906; Oe2+.11603.D, William Warren.

Library of Congress, Batchelder Collection: 380, C. Leslie Allen; 381, Francis Wilson's partbook for First Gravedigger, Bel Geddes production.

Museum of the City of New York: 32.485.143, J. H. Ring, 1839-77.

New York Public Library: *NCP, typescript of a German version.

Shakespeare Centre Library: 50.07(1909), Eily Malyon.

Rutgers University: PR.1243.SHA, Frederick Paulding and Lillie Eldridge.

Toronto Public Library: 822.33/S.13, Albert Taverner.

University of Minnesota: Z820.12/Z11, volume 12, W. S. Forrest.

Henry IV, Part 1

1. Sir Edward Dering   Surrenden   1620's
   Folger: V.b.34
   [Manuscript, $7\frac{5}{8}$ x $11\frac{5}{8}$; green leather gilt; title gilt up spine.]
   A 110-page manuscript version of a play made from *Henry IV*, parts 1 and 2, used in a performance at Surrenden in Kent. Two actor lists (for *The Spanish Curate*) on the reverse of a sheet of additions. (See S. B. Hemingway, *New Variorum Edition,* pp. 495-501; G. Blakemore Evans, *JEGP*, LIV, 498-503.)

2. Joseph Ashbury   Dublin, Smock Alley   1680's
   Folger: 1 Hen IV, Smock Alley
   [Half a leaf from a Third Folio.]
   Fragment of a promptbook: portion of 2 scenes of the second act. Cuts, one scenic indication, name of the actor Longmore. (See G. Blakemore Evans, *Henry IV, Part 1, A Variorum Supplement,* p. 104.)

3. James Quin   London, Lincoln's Inn Fields   October 28, 1721
   Folger: T.a.121
   [Manuscript, $5\frac{3}{4}$ x $8\frac{5}{8}$, tipped into a made-up book; gray and green marbled boards and half green leather; "Falstaff" gilt on red spine label.]
   Quin's 45-leaf partbook for Falstaff, mainly in the hand of a copyist, with a few notes by Quin. Belonged successively to Garrick, Thomas King, William Dowton (1798). Several eighteenth-century prints and other illustrative matter.

4. Anonymous   Kidderminster   May, 1762
   Folger: T.a.72
   [Manuscript, $6\frac{3}{8}$ x $8\frac{1}{8}$; red, yellow, and blue marbled boards and half red leather gilt; "Play-House MS. of Henry IV" gilt up spine.]
   A 32-page manuscript partbook for Falstaff dated as above. No clue to ownership.

5. Edward Henry King   1790's(?)
   Folger: 1 Hen IV, 17
   [Eighteenth-century edition printed by Augustus Long, Dublin, $3\frac{7}{8}$ x $6\frac{5}{8}$; brown paper.]
   Promptbook probably of late eighteenth century. Cuts and alterations, little stage business, cues for effects, timings. The actor's

name is at the head of Act I. Also endorsed by Thomas Price, Boston (1850's), and W. L. Wainwright.

6. John Philip Kemble   London, Covent Garden   May 12, 1808
   Garrick Club

   [Kemble edition, 1803, 5 x 8¼; interleaves watermarked 1807; blue cloth boards and brown leather spine; title gilt up spine.]

   Promptbook marked by Kemble. List of supers, calls, some stage business, maps, cues for effects, timings.

7. Anonymous   England   c.1810
   New York Public Library: *NCP.709398

   [Bell edition, 1774, 4¼ x 6½; interleaves watermarked 1809; black cloth boards; title gilt up spine.]

   Lightly marked promptbook. Calls, little stage business, cues for effects.

8. George Bartley   London, Drury Lane   April 12, 1815
   University of Nebraska: 822.33/T1h

   [Bell edition, 1773, c.4½ x 5¼; interleaves watermarked 1811, 4¾ x 7⅞; blue cloth boards; title gilt down spine.]

   Promptbook much marked during 3 decades. The original calls, cues for effects, etc., are neatly inked. Many further cues, maps, sketches, notes on the text have been added in ink and pencil down to 1839. One penciled reading is cited from "Prompt Book of TRDL/1773/Hopkins/Prompter." A reference to Bartley probably was made in the 1815 season. A note on "Mr. H." refers to Hackett in November, 1839. A cartoon of Falstaff at page 57 is signed by T. Dibdin. Numerous timings are probably in the hand of John Willmott. Bookplate of Augustus Harris.

9. William B. Wood   Philadelphia   February 21, 1816
   New York Public Library: *NCP.164351

   [Kemble edition, 1815, 4 x 6¾; green cloth boards; title gilt on spine.]

   Lightly marked promptbook. Calls, some stage business, cues for effects.

10. James St. Aubyn   1820's(?)
    Folger: 1 Hen IV, 9

    [Kemble edition, 1815, 4⅜ x 7¼; interleaves; gray cardboard.]

    Lightly marked promptbook. Penciled cast, perhaps for an

amateur production. Some stage business for Hotspur. Belonged to Clement Scott.

11. Thomas Scrivener(?)   America   1821
    New York Public Library: *NCVp.v.14.900677
    [Dramatic Repository, New York, 1811, 3½ x 5¾; interleaves; bound with *Comedy of Errors* and other plays in black cloth boards; title gilt on spine.]
    Promptbook given by Scrivener to Miche· Monier in 1821; by her to F. Johnson. A manuscript cast includes J. H. Hackett, Thomas Barry, Miss Duff, Mrs. Barnes (1830's?). Cuts, scenic indications, grooves, some stage business, cues for effects.

12. James H. Hackett   New York, Park   May 13, 1828
    Enthoven Collection
    [Oxberry edition, 1822, 4¼ x 7½; interleaves; green cloth boards and green leather spine; title, etc., gilt up spine.]
    Promptbook dated 1828, with notes of performances at the Haymarket in London on May 13, 1833, and in New York and Boston in 1833-34. Arranged in both 5-act and 3-act versions. Much stage business, including an interpolated gag in the third act, cues for effects. Some of the interleaves misbound, final pages missing. (See nos. 16-19, 37.)

13. [Hackett]
    Enthoven Collection
    [Oxberry edition, Boston, 1823, 3½ x 6¼; blue interleaves; tan marbled boards and red leather spine; title gilt on spine label.]
    Promptbook arranged in 5 acts, much used. At the front a doubling list for "short company." Calls, little stage business, cues for effects.

14. Stanley Charles Ferrers   New York, Bowery   1837
    New York Public Library: *NCP.255019B
    [Oxberry edition, Boston, 1823, 3½ x 5½; interleaves; gray marbled boards and half black leather; title inked on spine.]
    Excellent promptbook made by the Bowery stage manager transcribing from his own Edinburgh book of 1836, when William Murray and Charles Kean played Falstaff and Hotspur. At the front an account of the order of scenes in which "Mr. Hackett has mutilated the play" for use as an afterpiece. Cuts, restorations, scenic indications, grooves, calls, copious stage business, maps

and sketches, cues for effects, timings. Reference to business of
C. Kemble, Hackett, Dowton, etc. Belonged to John Proctor in
1846.

15. Mercer Hampson Simpson
                        Birmingham, Theatre Royal   1838, 1851
    Birmingham, Shakespeare Memorial Library: A15/455855, 6
    [Two books. Davidson issue of Cumberland, $3\frac{1}{2}$ x $5\frac{7}{8}$; gray
    marbled boards and brown leather spine; bound with other Shake-
    speare plays in green cloth boards.]
    Two promptbooks, lightly marked and much used, one dated
    1838, the other 1851. Lengths of roles noted, calls, cues for effects.

16. James H. Hackett   1840
    Folger: 1 Hen IV, 5
    [Pages 161-226 of volume IV of Knight's Pictorial Edition, 1838,
    $6\frac{3}{4}$ x 10; interleaves; brown mottled boards and brown cloth
    spine; printed title pasted on cover.]
    Book dated "New York, 1840." No prompter's marks or other
    signs of stage usage. A brief Preface by Hackett and numerous
    notes of stage business suggest use for public readings. The
    Hotspur role marked for stresses. (See nos. 12-13, 37.)

17. [Hackett]
    Enthoven Collection
    [Dramatic Repository, New York, 1811, $3\frac{1}{2}$ x $5\frac{3}{4}$; double inter-
    leaves; green cloth boards and brown leather spine, $4\frac{1}{2}$ x $6\frac{1}{4}$;
    title, etc., gilt up spine.]
    Promptbook arranged in 3 acts. Two manuscript title pages.
    Marked by J. W. McCrum, prompter at Vicksburg. Much de-
    tailed stage business, cues for effects.

18. [Hackett]
    The Players: PB.93
    [French's Standard Drama, $4\frac{1}{8}$ x $7\frac{1}{8}$; interleaves; brown paper
    under red cloth boards; title gilt on spine.]
    Transcription of Hackett's Falstaff business made from the pre-
    ceding (McCrum) book by William F. Owen in 1895.

19. [Hackett]   1841
    Enthoven Collection

[Cumberland edition, $3\frac{1}{2}$ x $5\frac{7}{8}$; interleaves; green cloth boards and brown leather spine; title, etc., gilt up spine.]

Promptbook arranged in both 5 and 3 acts. Cast given for the St. Charles in New Orleans, December 6, 1841. More fully developed than preceding books and directions in somewhat different language. Scenic indications, grooves, calls, much stage business, maps and sketches, cues for effects.

20. Henry Betty   London, Covent Garden   February 3, 1845
    Folger: 1 Hen IV, 1, 2

    [Two books. Cumberland edition, $3\frac{5}{8}$ x $5\frac{3}{4}$; interleaves; gray boards and green cloth spine; title penciled on cover.]

    The first is a promptbook marked in colored inks with cuts and alterations, furniture, grooves, stage business, maps; Hotspur marked for stresses. The second has cuts and alterations only.

21. Samuel Phelps   London, Sadler's Wells   July 25, 1846
    Folger: 1 Hen IV, 20

    [Pages 1125-1204 from Rowe edition, 1709, $5\frac{1}{2}$ x $8\frac{5}{8}$; interleaves; no binding.]

    Rough but thorough promptbook, marked in several hands. Cuts, scenic indications, grooves, calls, some stage business, cues for effects.

22. John Moore   c.1850-70's
    Folger: 1 Hen IV, 16

    [French's Standard Drama, $4\frac{3}{8}$ x $7\frac{3}{8}$; interleaves, $5\frac{1}{8}$ x 8; publisher's wrappers under gray paper.]

    Thorough promptbook, often resembling Hackett's and others. List of supers and of doublings. Properties list for each act. Calls, copious stage business, maps, cues for effects. News clipping of 1874 of John Jack as Falstaff.

23. [Moore]
    Folger: T.b.2

    [Notebook, $6\frac{1}{8}$ x $10\frac{1}{4}$; blue boards and black cloth spine.]

    Cues for the band for 48 plays, including *Henry IV*.

24. J. B. Wright   Boston   1850's
    New York Public Library: *NCP.342614

    [Inchbald edition, $3\frac{1}{2}$ x $5\frac{3}{4}$; interleaves; bound with other plays in red cloth boards; title gilt on spine.]

Lightly marked promptbook, checked for Hotspur. Cuts, some stage business, fight routine for Hotspur and Hal. First leaves missing.

25. James Stark   San Francisco, Jenny Lind   January, 1852
New York Public Library: *NCP.343042
[No title page (Oxberry, Boston?), 3¾ x 5¾; interleaves; black cloth boards; title gilt on spine.]
Promptbook. Scenic indications, grooves, some stage business, cues for effects.

26. Charles Kean   London, Princess's   November 22, 1852
Folger: 1 Hen IV, 11
[Oxberry edition, 1822, 5 x 8; interleaves, 7⅛ x 9¼; green cloth boards and half green leather gilt; title gilt on red leather spine label, "Prompt Copy, Mr. Charles Kean" gilt on maroon leather cover label.]
Excellent transcription of the "Drury Lane" promptbook made for Kean by George Ellis in July, 1849. Cuts and restorations, list of property manuscripts, grooves, calls, little stage business, maps and sketches, cues for effects, timings.

27. [Kean]
Folger: 1 Hen IV, 8
[Inchbald edition, 3¾ x 6¼; interleaves; red marbled boards and half brown leather; title gilt on red spine label, Kean's name on maroon leather cover label.]
Promptbook made for Kean by T. W. Edmonds, the prompter. Contents very similar to those of the preceding book, but different timings.

28. [Kean]
Folger: 1 Hen IV, 13
[Pages 381-489 from volume IV of a *Works*, 4¾ x 8⅛; interleaves, 6¾ x 8⅝; tan cloth boards and half brown leather; title gilt up spine, Kean's name gilt on black leather cover label.]
Final or souvenir promptbook made by T. W. Edmonds in 1859. Cuts and alterations on full text. Contents essentially the same as in the preceding book.

29. [Kean]
Folger: Kean Costume Book, Prints and Engravings, 50

[Scrapbook, 10¾ x 14½; green cloth boards and half green leather gilt.]

Contains a group of costume drawings and tracings for *Henry IV* by Charles Hamilton Smith and his daughter Emma Smith.

30. Thomas Barry   Boston, Boston Theatre   1854
Harvard Theatre Collection: uncatalogued
[Oxberry edition, 1822, 5 x 8; gray interleaves; gray boards and brown leather spine; title and "4" inked on cover.]
Systematic promptbook signed by "Charles Melville, Prompter, T.R.D.L.," brought to America by Barry in 1854. Grooves, calls, some stage business, cues for effects, timings.

31. [Barry]
Harvard Theatre Collection: uncatalogued
[Oxberry edition, 1822, 4¼ x 6⅞; tan boards and half red leather; title and "39" inked on cover.]
A less complete promptbook than the preceding, probably made by Melville. Calls, cues for effects.

32. Anonymous   England   c.1855
New York Public Library: *NCP.285344
[Lacy edition with Princess's cast of 1852, 3¾ x 6⅜; blue interleaves watermarked "Glasgow"; green cloth boards; title gilt up spine.]
Full and interesting promptbook, apparently (judging from the rather hasty writing) a copy of some other book, made in England or Scotland after 1852. Often verbatim with Hackett's or Ferrers' or others. Scenic indications, grooves, calls, copious stage business, maps and sketches, cues for effects.

33. John Woodward   Cambridge, St. John's College   c.1855
Folger: 1 Hen IV, 10
[Pages 405-518 from volume IV of a *Works*, 5⅛ x 8½; interleaves; gray and yellow marbled boards and half brown leather; title gilt on spine label.]
Promptbook of an amateur production. Woodward, who played Hotspur, says this book was marked from Charles Kean's, which was itself marked from the Drury Lane book. Text much restored. Footnotes on historical characters. At the back, plots of properties, characters, scenery, grooves. Five sheets of costume sketches, 2

sheets of watercolors, and 2 pages of description of armorial bearings. Printed cast enclosed.

34. F. Chippendale   1857

Harvard Theatre Collection: (Widener, 13485.7.64)

[Modern Standard Drama, 4½ x 7½; publisher's wrappers under gray and red marbled boards and brown cloth spine; title inked up cover.]

Studybook checked for Falstaff, with some stage business for Hotspur. Given to Chippendale by Mary Shaw, December, 1857.

35. William Creswick   London, Drury Lane   March 28, 1864

Shakespeare Centre Library: 50.08(1826)

[Acting edition and portion of another text, 3½ x 5⅞; interleaves, 4¼ x 6¾; green marbled cardboard under brown marbled boards and half tan leather.]

Much used promptbook. Cuts, calls, some scenic indications, occasional stage business, maps, cues for effects, timings. Sketch of council chamber, several sketches of coats of arms with colors noted. Cast for 1864, when Creswick played Hotspur to Phelps's Falstaff. Endorsed by Walter Carle, prompter at the Academy of Music, 1867-78.

36. [Creswick]

Shakespeare Centre Library: 50.08(1864)

[Lacy edition, 4¼ x 7¼; purple cloth boards and half black leather; title gilt up spine.]

Promptbook probably belonging to Creswick. Checked for Falstaff, little stage business.

37. James H. Hackett   1868

Enthoven Collection

[Davidson edition, 3⅜ x 5¾; interleaves; tan marbled boards and half brown leather; printed title pasted on cover.]

Promptbook arranged in 5 acts, dated 1868, much used. At the front a doubling list for "short company." Calls, stage business for supporting roles, maps, cues for effects. (See nos. 12-13, 16-19.)

38. Barton Hill   1879

Folger: 1 Hen IV, 7

[French's Standard Drama; interleaves, 6 x 7½; brown cloth boards and black leather spine; title gilt up spine.]

Fine transcription of somebody's promptbook, made by Robert J. Preston, prompter of the California Theatre, San Francisco, November 9, 1879. Does not appear used. Scenic indications, grooves, calls, copious stage business which resembles that of Hackett and others, maps, cues for effects.

39. George Becks   1880's
New York Public Library: *NCP.343036
[Lacy edition, 4 x 6¾; interleaves; black cloth boards; title gilt up spine.]
Originally a working promptbook, with scenic indications, grooves, calls, maps, cues for effects. Becks has added all the traditional stage business he could find: a very rich accretion.

40. James Taylor   1880's
Harvard Theatre Collection: uncatalogued
[Modern Standard Drama, 4½ x 7⅛; interleaves; black cloth boards and black leather spine; title gilt on spine.]
Like the preceding Becks book, a very rich collection of traditional directions. Scenic indications, grooves, copious stage business, maps, cues for effects.

41. Louis Calvert   Manchester, Queen's   1890's
Enthoven Collection: Tree, 14
[Cassell's National Library edition pasted in a workbook, 6 x 12¾; green cloth boards and red leather spine.]
Among Beerbohm Tree's books, marked "old promptbook." Printed cast gives Calvert as Falstaff, William Mollison as Hotspur, Mrs. Charles Calvert as Quickly. Groundplans signed by W. T. Elworthy. Fully marked and much used. Cuts, stage business, sketches, cues for effects.

42. Julia Marlowe   New York, Palmer's   March 19, 1896
Birmingham, Shakespeare Memorial Library: 370/421200
[Rolfe edition pasted in a workbook, 7⅞ x 10⅛; black cloth boards and half black leather; title and "The Lena Ashwell Players" gilt up spine.]
Promptbook of the production which originated in Milwaukee, Wisconsin, with Miss Marlowe as Prince Hal, Robert Taber as Hotspur, W. F. Owen as Falstaff. Extremely full and interesting book, all stage business given in detail. Plots of cast, makeup, lights, doubles, groundplans for each scene. "Please return to Robert Taber, The Players, 16 Gramercy Park, New York City."

43. Herbert Beerbohm Tree   London, Haymarket   May 8, 1896
Enthoven Collection: Tree, 237

[Cassell's National Library edition pasted in a workbook, $6\frac{7}{8}$ x $8\frac{3}{4}$; red marbled boards and half black leather; title inked on cover label.]

Much used preparation copy. Cuts, copious stage business, maps, cues for effects, all roughly penciled and frequently provisional. At the front are typed sheets of "Suggested Scenery," etc.

44. [Tree]
Enthoven Collection: Tree, 14

[Cassell's National Library edition pasted in a workbook, 7 x $8\frac{7}{8}$; green cloth boards and tan leather spine.]

Much used promptbook, dated March 2, 1896. Penciled cuts, copious stage business, maps, cues for effects. Sketch of one set.

45. [Tree]
Enthoven Collection: Tree, 237

[Cassell's National Library edition, $3\frac{5}{8}$ x $5\frac{5}{8}$; blue cloth boards; title stamped on cover, gilt up spine.]

Partbook for Hotspur, dated 1896.

46. [Tree]   London, His Majesty's   April 24, 1906
Enthoven Collection: Tree, 237

[Eighteen books. Eight of Cassell's Favourite Classics edition, $3\frac{3}{4}$ x 6; green cloth boards. Nine of Cassell's National Library edition, 1905, 4 x $6\frac{1}{8}$; red cloth boards. One Pocket Falstaff edition, $3\frac{5}{8}$ x $5\frac{1}{4}$; red cloth boards.]

Actors' rehearsal copies, variously marked for cuts, stage business, etc. One Falstaff copy is heavily marked and has a sketch of the tavern scene.

47. [Tree]
Enthoven Collection: Tree, 237

[Papers.]

Fine drawing of the tavern scene, $17\frac{1}{2}$ x $11\frac{1}{2}$. Drawings of properties on small cardboards. Cut-outs of tents. Plots of scenes, flys, properties, lights, extras, etc. Other production notes.

48. [Tree]
Enthoven Collection: Tree, 14

[Papers.]
Plots of scenes, properties, flys. Cast for April 24, 25, 1906.

49. The Players   New York, Knickerbocker   May 31, 1926
The Players: PB.37
[New Hudson edition, 1926, pasted in a workbook, 8½ x 14; black imitation leather ring binder.]
Promptbook of The Players' Fifth Annual Classic Revival. Cuts and alterations, scenes introduced from *Henry IV*, part 2. Stage business, maps, cues for effects.

[ACTOR LISTS FOR FOLLOWING BOOKS ARE GIVEN IN THIS ORDER: Falstaff, Hotspur, Hal, the King.]

50. W. Bridges-Adams   Stratford-upon-Avon   April 23, 1932
Shakespeare Centre Library: 71.21/1932H1, Hen1
[Two books. Temple edition pasted in workbooks, 7 x 9; first book in green cloth boards and half red leather, second book in black cloth boards and half black leather; title on cover and spine.]
Cast includes Roy Byford, Wilfrid Walter, Gyles Isham, Randle Ayrton. Opening matinee of the new Memorial Theatre. Cuts, calls, some stage business, maps and sketches, cues for effects. Much erasure and rewriting. Used earlier at Stratford and for the American tour in 1931-32. The second book is a clean, unused copy of the first.

51. B. Iden Payne   Carnegie Institute   1934
Folger: 1 Henry IV, Folio 1
[Arden edition pasted in a workbook, 8⅜ x 11.]
Promptbook of a production done with students. Copious stage business, cues for effects, etc. Words and score for Lady Mortimer's Welsh dialogue and song. Accompanied by a dissertation on the play and production by Franklin Heller.

52. [Payne]   Stratford-upon-Avon   April 25, 1935
Shakespeare Centre Library: 71.21/1935H
[New Temple edition pasted in a workbook, 7 x 9; purple cloth boards and half black leather; title on cover and spine.]
Cast includes Roy Byford, Neil Porter, Ernest Hare, Gerald Kay Souper. Designed by Aubrey Hammond. Cuts, calls, much stage business, maps, notes on some effects.

53. John Kidd and Anthony Quayle
                    Stratford-upon-Avon   April 3, 1951
Shakespeare Centre Library: O.S.71.21/1951Hy4

[New Temple edition pasted in a workbook, 7¾ x 12¾; red cloth boards and red cloth spine; title on cover and spine.]

Cast includes Anthony Quayle, Michael Redgrave, Richard Burton, Harry Andrews. Designed by Tanya Moiseiwitsch. Cuts, calls, much stage business, maps, cues for effects. Two sheets of Welsh dialogue.

54. Anthony Quayle and Raymond Westwell   Australia   1953
Shakespeare Centre Library: O.S.71.21/1953H

[New Temple edition pasted in a workbook, 8 x 13; black cloth board spring binder.]

Revival of the 1951 Stratford production for Australian tour. Cast includes Anthony Quayle, Keith Michell, Terence Langdon, Jack Gwillim. Cuts more extensive than in 1951, much stage business, maps, cues for effects.

55. Michael Langham and George McCowan
                    Stratford, Ontario   June 23, 1958
Festival Theatre, Library

[Two books. Penguin edition pasted in workbooks, 7¾ x 13⅛; blue cloth boards bordered in red; title pasted on cover.]

Cast includes Douglas Campbell, Jason Robards, Jr., Douglas Rain, Max Helpmann. Designed by Tanya Moiseiwitsch and Marie Day. The first book has stage business, many maps on mimeographed groundplans, cues for effects, some production papers. The second has calls, some cues for effects.

56. Dennis Vance   London, Old Vic   February 14, 1961
Old Vic, Publicity Department

[New Temple edition pasted in a workbook, 8 x 10; red ring binder; title on cover and spine.]

Cast includes Douglas Campbell, Tony Britton, John Stride, Robert Harris. Designed by Timothy O'Brien. Cuts, calls, stage business, cues for effects. Many production papers.

57. Other books of *Henry IV*, part 1:

Folger: 1 Hen IV, 3, W. R. Blake; 1 Hen IV, 4, Margaret Freal; 1 Hen IV, 6, Walter Hubbell and John Jack; 1 Hen IV, 14, 15, N. M. Ludlow; 1 Hen IV, 18, 19, Marcus Moriarty; 1 Hen IV,

21, J. B. Roberts; 1 Hen IV, 22, John Sefton; 1 Hen IV, 23, Leon John Vincent; 1 Hen IV, 24, J. W. Wallack; 1 Hen IV, 25, anonymous.

Harvard Theatre Collection: uncatalogued, S. W. Glenn; 13485.6.15, one of J. C. Edwards, one of John Kirkland.

Historical and Philosophical Society of Ohio: 812.3/R283/91, Alvin Read.

Museum of the City of New York: 32.485.192b, W. H. Sedley Smith and J. H. Ring, 1863.

Princeton University, Seymour Collection: HIV¹, 12, George Berrell.

University of Minnesota: Z820.12/Z11, volume 12, W. S. Forrest.

University of Pennsylvania: AC85.M9415.820p.48, James Murdoch, 2 books.

Henry IV, Part 2

1. Anonymous   England   1600's

   Henry E. Huntington Library: 69317

   [Wise and Aspley edition, 1600, 4¾ x 6¾; red leather gilt; title gilt on spine.]

   Promptbook with seventeenth- and eighteenth-century markings. Exits and entrances noted, and one entrance for Falstaff "Singinge." A map or groundplan of unknown provenience is on sig. B2ʳ. Bookplates of Frederick Locker and E. D. Church. Note by J. O. Halliwell, 1866.

2. David Garrick   London, Drury Lane   March 13, 1758

   Folger: 2 Hen IV, 2

   [Tonson edition, 1733, 4 x 7; red and blue marbled boards and brown leather spine.]

   Promptbook. Cuts, properties, calls, little stage business, few cues for effects. At the front a cast list folded in.

3. Thomas King   1794

   Folger: Y.d.41

   [Manuscript, 6¼ x 7¾; heavy tan paper.]

   A 37-page partbook for Falstaff, dated 1794. (Hogan lists no performance of the play that year, nor any for King in any year.) A few restorations and notes of stage business. Belonged to William Dowton.

4. John Philip Kemble   London, Covent Garden   January 17, 1804

   Garrick Club

   [Kemble edition, 1804, 5⅛ x 8¼; interleaves watermarked 1807; blue cloth boards and brown leather spine; title gilt up spine.]

   Promptbook marked by Kemble about 1807, probably a transcription of his 1804 book. At the front a list of supers. Calls, properties, some stage business, maps, cues for effects.

5. Charles Kemble   London, Covent Garden   June 25, 1821

   Shakespeare Centre Library: 50.09(1821)

   [Kemble edition, 1821, "with the Representation of the Coronation as arranged by Mr. Farley," 5½ x 8¼; interleaves; brown leather; title gilt on red leather spine label.]

   Promptbook marked (perhaps) by R. J. Collier, apparently unused. List of supers, grooves, calls, some stage business, maps, cues for effects. Belonged to William Creswick.

6. James H. Hackett   Philadelphia, National   March 15, 1841
Enthoven Collection

[Pages 229-306 from volume IV of Knight's Pictorial Edition, 1839, 6⅝ x 9⅞; interleaves; cloth; title in red on cover.]

Promptbook dated by S. C. Ferrers, the stage manager, who marked it from Hackett's first performance. Playbill for March 15 pasted in; also a manuscript version of an announcement calling it "Falstaff's Latter Days," first performance in 30 years. Extensive cuts on full text, grooves, calls, some stage business, maps, cues for effects. Final scenes in manuscript.

7. [Hackett]
Enthoven Collection

[Manuscript, 4⅝ x 7¼; brown leather; title in red on cover.]

Hackett's partbook for Falstaff, bound with partbook for O'Callaghan in *His Last Legs*. Dated 1841. Note on New Orleans critics, 1843. Loaned to Edwin Booth, April, 1869.

8. William Charles Macready   London, Drury Lane   May 29, 1843
Victoria and Albert, Forster Library, 7919:   F.48.C.17

[Pages from an acting edition, 3½ x 5¾; interleaves; bound with other Macready promptbooks in green cloth boards and half tan leather; titles gilt on spine.]

Promptbook of Macready's display piece called "Act of King Henry 4th," being that portion of the fourth act leading to the death of the King. Scenery carefully described. Cuts, calls, stage business, maps, cues, timing.

9. [Macready]
Folger: 2 Hen IV, 3

[Cumberland edition; interleaves in fourth act, 4⅜ x 7; paper wrapper.]

John Moore's transcription of the Macready "Act."

10. Mercer Hampson Simpson   Birmingham
Birmingham, Shakespeare Memorial Library: A15/455858

[Cumberland edition, 3⅝ x 5⅞; gray paper; title inked on cover label; bound with other Shakespeare plays in green cloth boards.]

Simpson's partial transcription of the Macready "Act."

11. Barry Sullivan   c.1852
Shakespeare Centre Library: 50.09(1797)

[One page of manuscript plus pages 411-412, 441-451 from volume III of the Robinson *Works,* 1797, 6¾ x 9¾; interleaves; tan marbled boards and half brown leather; Sullivan's name gilt on cover label, title gilt on spine.]

Arrangement of the Macready "Act" made by a professional copyist, probably George Hastings; belongs to a set which Sullivan gathered about 1852 when he was at the Haymarket. Pencilings probably by Sullivan. Cuts, scenic indications, stage business, maps. The wording of the directions differs from Macready's.

12. Samuel Phelps London, Sadler's Wells March 17, 1853

Harvard Theatre Collection: TS.2780.17

[Inchbald edition, 3⅞ x 6⅛; cardboard; title, etc., inked on cover; in box of tan cloth boards and blue leather spine; title gilt up spine.]

Promptbook rather lightly marked, probably by Williams, the prompter, with some notations by Phelps. Cuts, grooves, calls, some stage business, cues for effects.

[ACTOR LISTS FOR FOLLOWING BOOKS ARE GIVEN IN THIS ORDER: Falstaff, Pistol, Shallow, Hal, the King.]

13. W. Bridges-Adams Stratford-upon-Avon April 23, 1932

Shakespeare Centre Library: 71.21/1932HII

[Tudor edition pasted in a workbook, 7¼ x 9¼; green cloth boards; title on cover; in brown paper wrapper.]

Cast includes Roy Byford, Wilfrid Walter, Eric Maxon, Gyles Isham, Randle Ayrton. Costumes by Eric Maxon. Opening night of the new Memorial Theatre. Cuts, calls, scenic indications, stage business, maps, cues for effects.

14. Michael Redgrave Stratford-upon-Avon May 8, 1951

Shakespeare Centre Library: O.S.71.21/1951/Hy4.II(4375)

[New Temple edition pasted in a workbook, 7¾ x 12¾; red boards and red cloth spine; title on cover and spine.]

Cast includes Anthony Quayle, Richard Wordsworth, Alan Badel, Richard Burton, Harry Andrews. Designed by Tanya Moiseiwitsch. Cuts, stage business, maps, cues for effects.

15. [Redgrave]

Shakespeare Centre Library: O.S.71.21/1951/Hy4.II(4377)

[New Temple edition pasted in a workbook, 7¾ x 12¾; red boards and red cloth spine; title on cover and spine.]

Redgrave's preparation book for the 1951 production. First half of the play thoroughly marked; 22 pages of typed notes on stage business especially for incidental characters. Partial draft of speech for the birthday luncheon.

16. Douglas Seale   London, Old Vic   April 28, 1955
    Old Vic, Publicity Department
    [New Temple edition pasted in a workbook, 8 x 10½; black ring binder.]
    Cast includes Paul Rogers, John Neville, Paul Daneman, Robert Hardy, Eric Porter. Designed by Audrey Cruddas. Cuts, calls, stage business, maps, cues for effects.

17. Other books of *Henry IV*, part 2:
    Folger: 2 Hen IV, 1, E. Dyas, 1843; 2 Hen IV, 4, anonymous. *University of Pennsylvania:* AC85.M9415.820p.49, James Murdoch.

Henry V

1. John Philip Kemble   London, Covent Garden   March 4, 1811
   Shakespeare Centre Library: 50.01(1806)
   [Kemble edition, 1806, 5 x 8¼; interleaves watermarked 1807; brown leather; title gilt on spine label, spine stamped "T.R./C.G./P.B./K/2."]
   Promptbook marked by Kemble. Names of minor actors and lengths of parts. Some scenic indications and properties lists, calls, some stage business, maps, cues for effects, timings.

2. [Kemble]
   Garrick Club
   [Kemble edition, 1806, 5⅛ x 8⅛; interleaves watermarked 1807; blue cloth boards and brown leather spine; title gilt up spine.]
   Promptbook marked by Kemble. Some scenic indications, grooves, some stage business, maps, cues for effects.

3. [Kemble]
   University of Nebraska: 822.33/T4k
   [Kemble edition, 1801, 4⅜ x 7⅜; interleaves watermarked 1805; brown cloth boards; title gilt down spine and perhaps wrongly identified with Drury Lane.]
   Promptbook lightly marked in pencil. Some stage business, cues for effects. Sketch of city walls in Act III.

4. [Kemble]
   Folger: T.a.38
   [Manuscript, 7 x 8⅞; brown leather gilt; title gilt up spine.]
   Kemble's 39-page partbook for Henry, in his own hand, 814 lines.

5. William Charles Macready
                   London, Covent Garden   October 4, 1819
   Folger: Henry V, 7
   [Kemble edition, 1815, 4¼ x 7¼; interleaves watermarked 1816, 5¼ x 8¼; green marbled boards and half brown leather; title gilt on red spine label.]
   Promptbook much used for over a decade. The heavy cuts were made in December, 1834, when Macready prepared a 3-act version for use at Bath and Bristol. At the front are lists of Henry's dresses and properties. Calls, some stage business, maps, cues for effects, timings.

6. [Macready]   London, Covent Garden   June 10, 1839

Folger: Henry V, 8

[Pages 325-454 from volume VII of a *Works*, 5¼ x 9⅛; interleaves watermarked 1838; brown paper, much worn; title and "P.B." inked on cover.]

Promptbook marked by Macready and John Willmott, the prompter, for the production with restored choruses. Cuts and transpositions on full text. Some scenic indications, grooves, calls, stage business, maps, cues for effects, timings.

7. [Macready]

Enthoven Collection

[Oil painting, 10¾ x 13⅞.]

Design for a battle scene, oil on paper, by Clarkson Stanfield, said to be for Macready's *Henry V*.

8. Barry Sullivan   c.1852

Shakespeare Centre Library: 50.01(1797)

[Pages 473-577 from volume III of the Robinson *Works*, 1797, 6¾ x 9⅝; interleaves; brown marbled boards and half brown leather; title gilt on spine label, Sullivan's name gilt on cover label.]

Neatly marked promptbook, probably prepared by George Hastings; belongs to a set which Sullivan gathered about 1852 when he was at the Haymarket. Inked cuts are said to follow Kemble's version; further cuts in pencil. Some scenic indications, calls, stage business, maps, cues for effects.

9. Samuel Phelps   London, Sadler's Wells   October 25, 1852

Folger: Henry V, 9

[Pages 137-256 from volume V of a Steevens *Works*, 5¼ x 8¾; lavender interleaves watermarked 1852; brown cloth boards; title inked on cover.]

Promptbook used for several seasons. Cuts on full text, with restorations marked for 1853. Scenic indications especially for panoramas of the choruses, grooves, calls, stage business, maps, cues for effects, timings. Belonged to Harry Plowman.

10. Charles Kean   London, Princess's   March 28, 1859

Folger: Henry V, 6

[Kean edition, 1859, 5½ x 8¼; interleaves, 7 x 8⅞; tan cloth boards and half brown leather; title gilt up spine, "Mr. Charles Kean, Prompt Copy" gilt on black cover label.]

Final or souvenir promptbook made by T. W. Edmonds in 1859. Calls, stage business, maps, cues for effects, timings. Procession list contains 142 names. Twenty-one fine watercolor scene designs.

11. [Kean]

Harvard Theatre Collection: TS.2272.90

[Proof sheets of Kean edition, 5½ x 8¼; blue interleaves water-marked 1856, 6¼ x 8; green cloth boards; title inked up spine; in box of tan cloth boards and red leather spine.]

Heavily marked workbook of George Ellis, the stage manager. Not a systematic promptbook, but has many maps and copious notes on stage business, arrangements, and effects.

12. [Kean]

Folger: Henry V, 5

[Proof sheets of Kean edition, 5½ x 8¼; cream wrapper under gray wrapper.]

Kean's rehearsal copy checked for Henry and used on tour in the 1860's. A note by George Becks in 1896 identifies it as originally Kean's, later James Cathcart's, later Mrs. Lander's.

13. [Kean]

Enthoven Collection: Box DT.48a

[Watercolors.]

T. Grieve's preliminary watercolor studies for several scenes.

14. [Kean]

Enthoven Collection: Box DT.45

[Watercolors.]

Fine watercolors of 24 scenes, and 15 watercolor plates of proper-ties and coats of arms, mounted on large display cards.

15. [Kean]

Folger: Prints and Engravings, 52

[Watercolors, 8 x 5½, mounted in an album, 10¼ x 14⅛; gray cloth boards and half green leather gilt; "Charles Kean/Original Water Color Drawings" gilt on spine.]

Fine watercolors of 21 scenes.

16. [Kean]

Folger: Kean Costume Book, Prints and Engravings, 50

[Scrapbook, 10¾ x 14½; green cloth boards and half green leather gilt.]

About 50 tracings by Emma Hamilton Smith of designs for costumes, banners, shields, etc.

17. [Kean]

Folger: Kean Costume Book, Prints and Engravings, 182

[Scrapbook, 15 x 22; brown cloth boards and half brown leather.]

Contains 61 watercolor plates of costume designs.

18. [Kean]

Enthoven Collection: 94G27, plates 1810-14

[Scrapbook, 15¼ x 21⅜.]

Watercolors of 30 costumes.

19. Charles Calvert   Manchester, Prince's   September 16, 1872

Shakespeare Centre Library

[Calvert edition, 1872, 6⅝ x 9¼, pasted in 2 albums, 21½ x 28; brown leather; title gilt on covers, "The Text/Scenery" gilt on spine of volume I, "Heraldry, Costumes, Music" gilt on spine of volume II.]

Splendid souvenir albums of Calvert's Manchester production. In the first volume are the text, playbill, program, a large watercolor of the procession, 18 watercolor scene designs by 7 different artists. In the second volume are 20 pages of designs for shields, banners, etc.; 13 pages (62 figures) of costumes; 57 pages of music score.

20. [Calvert]   New York, Booth's   February 8, 1875

New York Public Library: *NCP+.346542

[Calvert edition, 1875, 5¼ x 8½, pasted on sheets, 7⅛ x 8⅞; another copy with wider margins pasted on sheets, 8 x 12½; 165 pages of music score, 11½ x 9⅜; all bound in blue cloth boards; title gilt on spine.]

Two promptbooks and the music score of Calvert's New York production. The first and smaller book, much used, has at the front a list of extras, and throughout calls, stage business, cues for effects. The second book, less used, is more fully developed: at the front is a property list 2 feet 7 inches long, at the back 2 copies of scene plot with grooves; throughout copious stage business, many maps and sketches, cues for effects. The score is probably the conductor's copy.

21. [Calvert]

New York Public Library: *NCP.172895

[Calvert edition, 1875, 5⅜ x 8⅞; black and white marbled boards and black cloth spine; title inked up spine.]

Well-developed promptbook of the New York production. Some scenic indications, grooves, calls, some stage business, maps, cues for effects. The last 8 pages are missing.

22. [Calvert]

Folger: Henry V, 3

[Calvert edition, 1875, 4⅜ x 7⅝; interleaves, 6⅛ x 7¾; white paper, much torn.]

Well-developed promptbook of the New York production. Calls, properties, stage business, maps and sketches, cues for effects.

23. [Calvert]

New York Public Library: *NCP.172893, 6, 7, 8

[Four books. Proof sheets of Calvert edition, 1875, mostly 5½ x 9; black and white marbled boards and black cloth spine; title inked up spine.]

Four copies apparently used as partbooks. Random pencilings of stage business.

24. [Calvert]

Folger: Henry V, 1

[Charles E. Newton edition, 1875, 4½ x 7⅛; interleaves; black cloth boards and black leather spine; title gilt up spine.]

Newton's edition purports to give the text "as produced at Booth's Theatre," but it differs considerably from Calvert's edition. George Becks, who made up this copy, cut and altered it to match Calvert's, copied the maps and sketches from the official promptbook, and transcribed the stage business with augmentations.

25. [Calvert]

Folger: Henry V, 2

[Lacy edition, 4⅛ x 7; interleaves; brown cloth boards and black leather spine; title gilt up spine.]

George Becks has here attempted to transcribe the Calvert

promptbook onto a Lacy text, with much paging back and forth and "See Calvert Ed." Stage business, cues, etc., are copied fairly completely.

26. [Calvert]

Harvard Theatre Collection: uncatalogued

[Charles E. Newton edition, 4½ x 7½; interleaves; black cloth boards and black leather spine; title gilt up spine.]

Very full transcription of Calvert's New York production made by James Taylor. The calls, copious stage business, maps, sketches, cues for effects are verbatim with various "official" promptbooks. Several prints and engravings pasted in.

27. [Calvert]

Folger: Henry V, 4

[Calvert edition, 1875, 5¼ x 8½; purple cloth boards; title, "Prompt Copy," and "Mr. L. J. Vincent" gilt on cover.]

The book is inscribed "To L. J. Vincent Esq., Compliments of Jarrett & Palmer." Into it someone (probably Leon John Vincent) has penciled the essential data of the promptbook—calls, property list, stage business, cues for effects, etc. Many of the notations are original and descriptive, as if made by an observer seeing the production from the front.

28. John Martin-Harvey   London, His Majesty's   May 29, 1916

London Museum

[Pages of a Shakespeare text pasted in a workbook, 7 x 8⅞; plum-colored boards; title gilt on green cover label.]

Well-developed promptbook, with cast, scenic indications, ground-plans with dimensions, stage business, cues for effects. Accompanied by separate book of Notes by Alfred Rodway, containing also sketches, prints, tracings, watercolors of costumes, arms, etc. Some letters between Harvey and his designers. (This book is the property of Mr. Martin Holmes.)

[ACTOR LISTS FOR FOLLOWING BOOKS ARE GIVEN IN THIS ORDER: Henry, Pistol, Katherine.]

29. Robert Atkins   Stratford-upon-Avon   April 20, 1934

Shakespeare Centre Library: 71.21/1934H

[Temple edition pasted in a workbook, 6¾ x 9; red marbled boards and red cloth spine; title on spine label.]

Cast includes John Wyse, Baliol Holloway, Gwynne Whitby. Designed by Aubrey Hammond. Cuts on full text. Calls, some stage business, cues for effects.

30. [Atkins]

Shakespeare Centre Library: 71.21/1927

[Temple edition pasted in a workbook, 7 x 9; purple cloth boards and half black leather; title on cover and spine labels.]

This is labeled "1927," but appears to be simply a clean copy of the 1934 Atkins book, slightly revised, without cues for effects.

31. B. Iden Payne   Stratford-upon-Avon   April 1, 1937

Shakespeare Centre Library: 71.21/1937HE

[Temple edition pasted in a workbook, 7 x 9; purple cloth boards and half black leather; title on spine and cover labels.]

Cast includes Clement McCallin, Baliol Holloway, Valerie Tudor. Designed by Herbert Norris and Aubrey Hammond. Cuts, calls, stage business, maps, cues for effects.

32. Milton Rosmer   Stratford-upon-Avon   April 25, 1943

Shakespeare Centre Library: 71.21/1943H

[Temple edition pasted in a workbook, $6\frac{7}{8}$ x $8\frac{7}{8}$; blue cloth boards and half black leather; title on spine and cover labels.]

Cast includes Baliol Holloway, Abraham Sofaer, Anna Konstam. Designed by Herbert Norris and Charles Reading. Cuts, calls, stage business, maps, cues for effects. Roughly executed book, which probably had been used for an earlier production.

33. Laurence Olivier   1944

Folger: Henry V, Folio 1

[Mimeograph, 8 x 13; blue cloth boards and blue leather spine; title gilt on black spine label.]

Shooting script for the Olivier film, endorsed by Olivier in 1946.

34. Dorothy Green   Stratford-upon-Avon   May 11, 1946

Shakespeare Centre Library: O.S.71.21/1946H

[Temple edition pasted in a workbook, $7\frac{1}{2}$ x 10; tan marbled boards and green cloth spine; title on spine and cover labels.]

Cast includes Paul Scofield, Vernon Fortescue, Ruth Lodge. Designed by Herbert Norris and Reginald Leefe. Cuts, calls, stage business, maps, cues for effects. Score for the Agincourt Hymn, plots for lights and properties.

35. Anthony Quayle   Stratford-upon-Avon   July 31, 1951
Shakespeare Centre Library: O.S.71.21/1951HyV
[New Temple edition pasted in a workbook, 7¾ x 12⅝; red cloth boards and red cloth spine; title on spine and cover labels.]
Cast includes Richard Burton, Richard Wordsworth, Hazel Penwarden. Designed by Tanya Moiseiwitsch. Cuts, calls, stage business, maps, cues for effects. A special Epilogue.

36. Michael Benthall   London, Old Vic   December 13, 1955
Old Vic, Publicity Department
[New Temple edition pasted in a workbook, 8 x 10½; black ring binder; title on spine and cover labels.]
Cast includes Richard Burton, Richard Wordsworth, Zena Walker. Designed by Audrey Cruddas. Some stage business, a few maps, cues for effects.

37. Michael Langham   Stratford, Ontario   June 18, 1956
Festival Theatre, Library
[Two books. New Temple edition pasted in workbooks, 8 x 12⅝; black cloth boards and red cloth spine; title pasted on cover.]
Cast includes Christopher Plummer, Douglas Campbell, Ginette Letondal. Designed by Tanya Moiseiwitsch. The first book has copious stage business, maps, cues for effects, timings, understudies, cue sheets for music and lights. The second book has calls and little stage business.

38. Michael Benthall   Old Vic, American Tour   1958
Old Vic, Publicity Department
[New Temple edition pasted in a workbook, 8 x 10½; black ring binder.]
Cast includes Laurence Harvey, Richard Wordsworth, Judi Dench. Designed by Audrey Cruddas. Cuts, calls, stage business, cues for effects. Production papers.

39. John Neville   London, Old Vic   May 31, 1960
Old Vic, Publicity Department
[New Temple edition pasted in a workbook, 8 x 10; green ring binder.]
Cast includes Donald Houston, Joss Ackland, Judi Dench. Designed by John and Margaret Bury. Cuts, stage business, maps, cues for effects. Production papers, including several groundplans.

40. Other books of *Henry V:*

> *Folger:* S.a.140, eighteenth-century manuscript of part of the play, intended for theatrical use but not used.
>
> *Harvard Theatre Collection:* 13485.21.20, E. Dyas; 13485.21.50, F. Chippendale.
>
> *Princeton University, Seymour Collection:* Hen V, 15, anonymous.
>
> *Shakespeare Centre Library:* 50.10(1872), Manchester, 1872.

Henry VI

1. Edmund Kean   London, Drury Lane   December 22, 1817

   Folger: Henry VI, 1

   [Pages of *Richard, Duke of York*, London, 1812, 4¾ x 7½; inter-leaves; rose and black marbled boards and half brown leather.]

   The 5-act adaptation of the three parts of *Henry VI* by Soane or Merivale. The title page is overwritten in ink "King Henry VI . . . as altered . . . By Edmund Kean." The notation "Corrected from the Prompt-Book by G. C. Carr, Prompter, Theatre Royal Drury Lane" has been lined out. Many cuts and some restorations. Numerous stage directions have been scratched.

2. G. Osmond Tearle   Stratford-upon-Avon   April 23, 1889

   Shakespeare Centre Library: 71.21(1889)H

   [Memorial Theatre edition, 1888, pasted in a workbook, 7 x 8⅞; black oilcloth; title inked on spine.]

   Promptbook of Tearle's production of part 1 of *Henry VI*, with Erskine Lewis as the King and Ellen Cranston as Margaret. At the front the program copy, with cast, credits, etc. Some stage business, maps. The book is signed by Philip Gordon, the stage manager, who arranged the tableaux, battles, and processions.

3. F. R. Benson   Stratford-upon-Avon   1899

   Shakespeare Centre Library: 72.912BEN

   [Pages of a text pasted in a workbook, 4⅞ x 8; maroon cloth boards and red leather spine; title on spine label.]

   Benson's production of part 2 of Henry VI. This "working stage book," by F. R. Ayrton, is marked only in the first few pages.

4. Douglas Seale   London, Old Vic   October 16, 1957

   Old Vic, Publicity Department

   [New Temple edition pasted in a workbook, 8 x 10½; black ring binder.]

   Production of part 2 of *Henry VI*. Cast includes Paul Daneman, Barbara Jefford. Designed by Leslie Hurry. Cuts, stage business, many maps, cues for effects. Production papers, including maps on mimeographed groundplans.

5. Other books of *Henry VI*:

   Shakespeare Centre Library: 50.11(1883), 50.12(1883), 50.13 (1883), F. Hawley, some cuts and few directions.

Henry VIII

1. Joseph Ashbury   Dublin, Smock Alley   1670's
   Folger: Henry VIII, Smock Alley
   [Pages 541-568 from a Third Folio, 8⅛ x 12¼; blue-green marbled boards and half green leather gilt; title gilt up spine.]
   Promptbook. Cuts and small additions to bridge the cuts. Call-lists, a few properties. (See G. Blakemore Evans, *Shakespearean Prompt-Books*.)

2. James Quin   London, Covent Garden   April 16, 1751
   Folger: T.a.118
   [Manuscript, 6½ x 8¼; brown paper.]
   Quin's 24-page partbook for Henry.

3. David Beatt and James Love   Edinburgh   1761
   University of Pennsylvania, Furness Collection: C59.Sh1H8
   [Manuscript, 7⅜ x 9⅝; red, green, and yellow marbled boards and half brown leather; title inked on cover label.]
   Fully developed promptbook, apparently not used. The manuscript title page, signed by the managers Beatt and Love, states "Entrances and Exits properly mark'd, To the Use of the Edinburgh Theatre." Cuts, alterations, scenic indications, calls, some stage business. At the back a map of the trial scene, a plot of scenes (no grooves), a 5-page list of the coronation procession, a 1-page list of the procession to fetch the champion.

4. Anonymous   London, Haymarket   1780
   Folger: Henry VIII, 22
   [Bell edition, 1773, 4½ x 7¾; interleaves; unbound.]
   Promptbook done in at least 2 hands. Cast list for 1780 includes 23 names (Hogan gives smaller casts for preceding and following years but not for 1780). Cuts and restorations, calls, properties, scenic indications, little stage business, cues for effects.

5. William Warren   Philadelphia, Chestnut Street   Feb. 2, 1803
   Folger: Henry VIII, 20
   [Bell edition, 1773, 3⅞ x 6½; interleaves watermarked 1800(?); red marbled boards and half brown leather.]
   Promptbook owned by Warren and Wood, the Philadelphia managers. Warren entered a York cast of 1792, with Tate Wilkinson as Wolsey, himself as Cranmer. Calls, some stage business,

maps, procession lists, cues for effects. Later pencilings of calls, supers, grooves, and references to Covent Garden.

6. [Warren]
Library Company of Philadelphia: Oe2+.11600.D
[Edition of 1786, 4¼ x 7; tan cloth boards; title gilt up spine.]
Promptbook owned by Warren and Wood. Checked for the King. Cuts and a few pencilings of stage business.

7. Snelling Powell   Boston   c.1805
Folger: Henry VIII, 17
[Kemble edition, 1804, 5 x 8; gray marbled boards and brown suede spine; title inked on cover label.]
Preparation copy. Cuts and a few pencilings of stage business.

8. John Philip Kemble   London, Covent Garden   April 23, 1806
The Players
[Kemble edition, 1804, 5⅛ x 8¼; interleaves; brown leather; title and "Edwin Booth" inked on cover label.]
Edwin Booth wrote on the title page "Cooke's prompt-book," and it is checked for the King (Cooke played the King at Covent Garden beginning May 5, 1810). The copious original markings are in the hand of Kemble. Calls, stage business, maps, procession lists, cues for effects, timings which total 3:10. Some inked notations in the hand of Booth's prompter of the 1870's; some penciled additions by Booth himself. (See nos. 10-11.)

9. Sarah Siddons
Folger: W.a.70
[Inchbald edition, 1808, 3¾ x 6⅛; interleaves; bound with *Macbeth* and *Winter's Tale* in brown leather gilt; "Siddons" gilt on spine.]
George Joseph Bell's notes on Mrs. Siddons as Queen Katharine.

10. George Frederick Cooke   New York, Park   October 2, 1811
Harvard Theatre Collection: TS.2272.100
[Inchbald edition, 4 x 5¾; interleaves; red cloth boards; title gilt up spine.]
Promptbook of the Park Theatre when Cooke and T. A. Cooper played together. Entire cast given, with a list of supers. Cuts, calls, some stage business, maps, cues for effects. Last pages missing.

11. [Cooke]

Birmingham, Shakespeare Memorial Library: S649.28/526709

[C. Bathurst edition, 1786, 4 x 7; interleaves; brown leather; title gilt on spine.]

Promptbook inscribed "With all the stage Directions marked by the celebrated George F. Cooke, given to me by Mr. E. Simpson Manager of the Park Theatre New York. Edward Knight. 1827." A note by Cooke speaks of the time span of the play and the author's error in dating the death of Katharine. Checked for the King and for Wolsey. Cuts and alterations, stage business. At the back a list of scenes.

12. Edmund Kean   London, Drury Lane   May 20, 1822

Shakespeare Centre Library: 50.14(1804)

[Kemble edition, 1804, 5¼ x 8¼; interleaves watermarked 1815, 1817, 1819; brown marbled boards and half brown leather; title gilt up spine.]

Much used promptbook, marked in ink and pencil in several hands. Cast given with Kean as Wolsey and another with Macready as Wolsey at the Princess's in 1847. Costume list for Wolsey. Calls, stage business, maps, cues for effects entered in a neat flowing hand. Procession lists, etc., added in a neat round hand. Several nice sketches, watercolored rose and gray. Timings total 3:15. (See no. 21.)

13. William Charles Macready

                    London, Covent Garden   January 15, 1823

Victoria and Albert, Forster Library, 7920:   F.48.C.18

[Kemble edition, 1804, 5⅛ x 8¼; bound with other Macready promptbooks in green cloth boards and half tan leather; titles gilt on spine.]

Studybook for Wolsey, given to Macready by John Philip Kemble. The stage business is in Kemble's hand. At the front, penciled notes on the character of Wolsey. Stress marks and marginalia in Macready's hand. Marked only to the end of Act III. (See nos. 21-23.)

14. Anonymous   London, Covent Garden   c.1825

University of Nebraska: 822.33/T3k

[Kemble edition, 1804, 5 x 8⅛; interleaves watermarked 1824; yellow cloth boards; title printed in black down spine.]

Promptbook very neatly marked for grooves, calls, some stage business, maps, cues for effects. Crude penciled notes of a prompter, including timing, initialed "J W Ptr" (John Willmott?).

15. Charles Kemble   London, Covent Garden   October 24, 1831
    Garrick Club
    [Kemble edition, 1804, 5½ x 8¼; interleaves watermarked 1825; blue cloth boards and brown leather spine; title gilt up spine.]
    Much used promptbook written in a clear flowing hand, in or after 1825, and probably used for the above date. When the book was cropped for binding the marginalia were preserved by folding back. Some stage business, maps, cues for effects. Marked only to the end of Act III.

16. Fanny Kemble
    Shakespeare Centre Library: 50.14(1815)
    [Kemble edition, 1815, 4¼ x 6⅞; bound with three other plays in green cloth boards.]
    "This is volume one of a collection of prompt-copies used by Fanny Kemble and presented by Charles Kemble to Helen Faucit in 1838." Checked for the Queen. A few notations. (Fanny Kemble played the Queen to her father's King on October 24, 1831.)

17. Mercer Hampson Simpson Birmingham, Theatre Royal c.1840
    Birmingham, Shakespeare Memorial Library: C53/455747
    [Kemble edition, 1815, 4¼ x 7¼; blue cardboard; bound with other Shakespeare plays in green cloth boards.]
    Promptbook sparsely marked in several hands, perhaps partly from a Kemble book. Calls, some stage business, cues for effects.

18. [Simpson]
    Birmingham, Shakespeare Memorial Library: B53/455809
    [Cumberland edition, 3¾ x 6; gray cardboard; bound with other Shakespeare plays in green cloth boards.]
    Much used promptbook. Scenic indications, grooves, some stage business, cues for effects.

19. James E. Murdoch   America
    University of Pennsylvania: AC85.M9415.820p.50
    [Kemble edition, 1815, 4¼ x 7¼; interleaves; brown paper, much worn; title inked on cover.]
    Promptbook belonging to Murdoch, but apparently marked by an

earlier owner. Calls, cues for effects. Before the christening scene is a 4-page addition of a "carpenter's scene" (compare to Barry's book, no. 34).

20. Samuel Phelps London, Sadler's Wells April 10, 1845
   Folger: Henry VIII, 16
   [Cumberland edition, $3\frac{1}{2}$ x $5\frac{7}{8}$; interleaves, 4 x $6\frac{1}{4}$; tan wrappers with title and dates inked, under gray wrappers, much worn.]
   Promptbook dated for 9 seasons between 1845 and 1862, marked by both Phelps and Williams, the prompter. Scenic indications, grooves, calls, some stage business, maps, sketches, procession lists, cues for effects. The fifth act not marked.

21. William Charles Macready
   London, Princess's October 13, 1847
   Victoria and Albert, Forster Library, 7919: F.48.C.17
   [Cumberland edition, $3\frac{1}{2}$ x 6; bound with other Macready promptbooks in green cloth boards and half tan leather; titles gilt on spine.]
   A Macready promptbook, though probably of later usage than the above date. The 1847 and 1848 performances at the Princess's seem to have been prompted from the Edmund Kean book of 1822 (see no. 12). John Ryder is listed for the King: this suggests use in America in the fall of 1848. Calls, cues for effects. Marked through the fifth act.

22. [Macready]
   Folger: Henry VIII, 19
   [Pages 1-126 from a *Works*, $5\frac{3}{8}$ x $8\frac{3}{8}$; blue interleaves; reddish marbled boards and half brown leather; title gilt on spine, "Mr. Rogers" gilt on red cover label.]
   "Marked by G. Hastings, T. R. Haymarket from Mr. Macready's P.Book—May 1852." Cuts, some stage business, maps.

23. [Macready]
   Toronto Public Library: Taverner Collection
   [Small notecard in a manila envelope.]
   Manuscript notes on Macready's acting of Wolsey, by J. W. Taverner, the elocutionist.

24. Charles Kean May, 1848
   Folger: Henry VIII, 7
   [Pages 1-126 from a *Works*, 5 x $8\frac{7}{8}$; interleaves, 7 x 9; blue cloth

boards and half brown leather; title gilt on black spine label, "Prompt Copy, Mr. C. Kean" gilt on cover label.]

Beautiful transcription (and augmentation) of the traditional Covent Garden promptbook made for Charles Kean by George Ellis in May, 1848. Not used. Cuts on full text, grooves, calls, properties, some stage business, maps and sketches, procession lists, cues for effects, timing (2:40). Notes on music added in pencil. Cast is given including Kemble, Cooke, and Mrs. Siddons. (See nos. 8-11, 36-46.)

25. John Moore   New York   1848-c.1870
Folger: Henry VIII, 13

[Title page of Modern Standard Drama, 1848, but text of Oxberry edition, 1823, 4⅜ x 7⅜; interleaves; yellow wrapper; title, etc., inked on cover.]

A full and much used promptbook, dated London, 1848, but principally used in New York and with Charlotte Cushman. At the front, a 4-page account of the dance routine in I, 4. Some detailed scenic indications, grooves, calls, much stage business, maps, procession lists, cues for effects. At the back a list of doubles. The fifth act is marked in brown ink as of 1848, but is not worked over, and apparently was not used. An 1857 playbill of Cushman's Katharine and one of her Wolsey. News clippings of Cushman and Genevieve Ward.

26. [Moore]
Folger: T.b.2
[Notebook, 6⅛ x 10¼; blue boards and black cloth spine.]
Cues for the band for 48 plays, including *Henry VIII*.

27. George W. Lewis   1849
New York Public Library: *NCP.342995
[Cumberland edition, 3½ x 5¾; gray interleaves; black cloth boards; title gilt up spine.]
Carefully developed promptbook ending with the death of the Queen. Some scenic indications, grooves, calls, considerable stage business, good maps and sketches, procession lists, cues for effects, timing (2:08). Fifth act marked but not used. Later belonged to James Stark and to George Becks. (See no. 33.)

28. John Proctor   Philadelphia
New York Public Library: *NCP.267586B

[Cumberland edition, 3¼ x 5½; interleaves; gray marbled boards and half black leather; title inked on spine.]

Uncompleted promptbook marked through the first act. Grooves, calls, some stage business, maps and sketches, cues for effects. Resembles the preceding (Lewis) book.

29. Charlotte Cushman   New York, Broadway   September 15, 1849
  Folger: Henry VIII, 4
  [Modern Standard Drama, 1848, 4⅜ x 7; blue interleaves; brown cloth boards and half red leather gilt; title, etc., gilt on black cover label.]
  Promptbook carefully prepared in blue ink, with additions in brown ink and pencil. A scene restored from the original is called Act III, and the whole is divided into 5 acts, though Shakespeare's fifth act is omitted. Grooves, calls, properties, some stage business, detailed procession list and dance routine, several good maps, cues for effects. At the front a good watercolor design for the trial scene. Page 48 badly stained.

30. [Cushman]
  Folger: Henry VIII, 3
  [French's Standard Drama, 4¼ x 7; interleaves; gray mottled boards and half black leather gilt; title gilt up spine and "C. Cushman" gilt on black cover label.]
  Promptbook similar to the preceding book but not verbatim: some directions omitted, some given in greater detail. So-called "Act III" given in manuscript. Notes on shortening the play. Purple ink sketch of Buckingham going to execution, and sketch of the vision.

31. [Cushman]
  Library of Congress, Manuscripts Division: Cushman Box
  [Manuscript, 6½ x 8; bound with partbook for Evadne in *The Bridal*.]
  Miss Cushman's partbook for Queen Katharine, apparently for the full-length version.

32. E. Dyas   Manchester, Theatre Royal
  Harvard Theatre Collection: (Widener, 13485.33.5)
  [Two books. Cumberland edition, 3¼ x 5⅜ (second copy slightly larger); brown paper under brown cloth boards; title gilt up spine.]

The second copy, signed F. E. Simon and checked for the King and Queen, is a crude promptbook. List of written letters, calls, cues for effects.

33. George W. Lewis   New York, Broadway   1853
New York Public Library: *NCP.342929
[Modern Standard Drama, 4½ x 7¼; gray interleaves; black cloth boards; title gilt up spine.]
Promptbook "Marked as played by Mr. Macready, Charlotte Cushman, &c.—at the Broadway Theatre N. York, 1853, George W. Lewis Prompter." Fifth act not marked. Playing time is 2:08. Generally very similar to Lewis' 1849 book (see no. 27). Some notes added by George Becks.

34. Thomas Barry   Boston, Boston Theatre   1854
Harvard Theatre Collection: uncatalogued
[Oxberry edition, 1823, 4½ x 7; bound with *The Tempest* in brown boards and half red leather; title and "42-43" inked on cover label.]
"Marked from C. Garden Pt.Book" by Charles Melville, an English prompter, and brought to Boston by Barry in 1854. Grooves, calls, some stage business, maps, cues for effects. Before the christening scene there is an invented "carpenter's scene" (compare to Murdoch's book, no. 19).

35. William E. Burton
Harvard Theatre Collection: uncatalogued
[Longworth edition, 1811, 3½ x 5¼; marbled paper and green leather spine; title inked up spine label and on cover.]
Rather sparsely marked promptbook in which Burton's name is written several times; also "Boston Theatre" and names of Wm. B. Spooner, James Taylor. Calls, little stage business, cues for effects.

36. Charles Kean   London, Princess's   May 16, 1855
Folger: Henry VIII, 12
[Pages 433-521 from Knight's National Edition, 1852, 5¾ x 8⅞; lavender interleaves, 7⅛ x 8⅞; white cardboard and canvas spine; title inked on cover.]
Preparation copy and stage manager's workbook in the hand of George Ellis. Cuts on full text do not correspond to the traditional Kemble cutting, which Ellis had given Kean earlier (see no. 24).

Many rough maps and many jottings of stage business. Manuscript version of V, 1, probably in Kean's hand.

37. [Kean]

Folger: Henry VIII, 8

[Kean edition, 1855, 5¼ x 8⅜; interleaves, 6¾ x 8⅞; brown cloth boards and half brown leather, covers broken away; title gilt up spine, "Henry Irving" inked on cover where Kean's name was originally gilt on a cover label.]

Promptbook made by T. W. Edmonds, the prompter during the first (1855) season of Kean's production of the play: includes the fifth act. Calls, some stage business, cues for effects, timings (3:20). Originally contained 13 watercolor scene designs, but only 5 of them remain (see no. 40).

38. [Kean]

Folger: Henry VIII, 10

[Same format as preceding book, but with Kean's name gilt on cover label.]

Transcription of the preceding book made by Edmonds during or after the second season: does not include the fifth act. Contains 11 watercolor scene designs for the first 4 acts.

39. [Kean]

Folger: Henry VIII, 9

[Kean editions of Henry VIII and other plays; brown leather; "Princess's Theatre" gilt on spine.]

A gift volume. Notation in Kean's hand on omission of the fifth act.

40. [Kean]

Enthoven Collection: 94G27, plates 1770-91

[Scrapbook, 15¼ x 21⅜; blue cloth boards and half blue cloth.]

Two sets of watercolors of the scenes, one set painted on white paper and one set on brown. The brown paper set is complete (13 scenes) except for the fifth-act panorama of London. The white paper set consists of the 8 plates torn out of Folger, Henry VIII, 8 (see no. 37), and also the panorama, a strip over 4½ feet long showing continuous views of London from the Bridewell to Greenwich.

41. [Kean]

Enthoven Collection: Box DT.45

[Watercolors.]

Watercolors of 16 scenes from the play and 9 plates of properties, mounted on large display boards.

42. [Kean]

Enthoven Collection: Box DT.48a

[Watercolor.]

Preliminary sketch of a scene outside Westminster Abbey, by T. Grieve.

43. [Kean]

Folger: Kean Costume Book, Prints and Engravings, 182

[Scrapbook, 14⅜ x 21¼; brown cloth boards and half brown leather.]

Six colored scenes of the play as published in 1855 by Joseph, Myers & Co.

44. [Kean]

Folger: Kean Costume Book, Prints and Engravings, 49

[Scrapbook, 10¾ x 14½; green cloth boards and half green leather gilt.]

Contains about 70 watercolor plates and tracings for costume designs, made by Charles Hamilton Smith and his daughter Emma Smith.

45. [Kean]

Enthoven Collection: 94G26, plates 1739-44

[Scrapbook, 15¼ x 21⅜; blue cloth boards and half blue cloth.]

Six watercolor costume plates showing 16 figures.

46. [Kean]

Enthoven Collection

[Two brochures, 14½ x 8¾.]

Printed costume plates from Joseph, Myers & Co. Part 1, colored, consists of plates 1 to 6 with about 6 figures each (no. 3 is missing). Part 2, plain, consists of plates 7 to 12 (no. 10 is missing).

47. James Edwards   1856

Folger: Henry VIII, 6

[Kean first edition, 4½ x 7⅞; interleaves; brown and blue marbled boards and half black leather; title gilt up spine.]

Not a finished promptbook, but an observation and preparation copy. Alterations of Kean's text generally tend toward restoration of the Kemble version. Some scenic indications, calls, cues for effects. Several maps, which do not square with Kean's arrangements. Dated within January 25, 1856.

48. W. J. Le Moyne   Philadelphia   1860's
Folger: Henry VIII, 11
[Davidson issue of Cumberland edition, $3\frac{5}{8}$ x $5\frac{5}{8}$; interleaves; heavy brown paper.]
Neatly though sparsely marked promptbook. Some stage business.

49. Charles Dornton   Liverpool, Theatre Royal   February 2, 1866
Birmingham, Shakespeare Memorial Library: B53/455729
[Davidson edition, $3\frac{1}{4}$ x $5\frac{3}{4}$; interleaves; gray paper; bound with other Shakespeare plays in green cloth boards.]
Lightly marked promptbook. Partial cast for above date.

50. Jean Davenport Lander   America   1868
New York Public Library: *NCP.342928
[French's Standard Drama, $4\frac{1}{2}$ x $7\frac{1}{4}$; interleaves; blue cloth boards; title gilt on cover.]
Promptbook marked by George Becks "with 3rd Act for Catherine as played by Mrs. F. W. Lander." At the front, music cues and scene plot with grooves. Cuts, calls, stage business, maps, sketches, cues for effects. Maps of Kemble's "situations" and Lander's for trial scene. Two versions indicated, one to include the fall of Wolsey. Contains embossed colored portraits of Creswick as Cromwell and Phelps as Wolsey.

51. [Lander]
New York Public Library: *NCP.342930
[Lacy edition, $4\frac{1}{4}$ x $7\frac{1}{4}$; interleaves; brown cloth boards and half black leather, front cover and leaves missing.]
Mrs. Lander's working promptbook, dated 1868, probably in the hand of George Becks. Scenic indications, grooves, calls, much stage business, maps, sketches, procession list, Kemble's "situations," cues for effects. Music plot at front is partly missing. Frequently verbatim with the preceding book.

52. [Lander]
Harvard Theatre Collection: uncatalogued
[French's Standard Drama, $4\frac{1}{2}$ x $7\frac{3}{8}$; interleaves; black cloth boards and black leather spine; title gilt up spine.]

James Taylor's promptbook of a production ending with the death of the Queen, probably Mrs. Lander's. Fifth act very lightly marked as if not used. Scenic indications, grooves, calls, much stage business, maps, sketches, procession list, cues for effects. This is the fuller of Taylor's two books.

53. [Lander]

Harvard Theatre Collection: uncatalogued

[Lacy edition, 4½ x 7¼; interleaves; black cloth boards and black leather spine; title gilt on spine.]

James Taylor's promptbook of a version ending with the death of the Queen, probably Mrs. Lander's. Cuts, some scenic indications, grooves, some stage business, Kemble's "situations," procession list, maps and sketches, cues for effects.

54. Genevieve Ward   New York, Booth's   September 23, 1878

New York Public Library: *NCP.342931

[Kean edition(?), 4¼ x 7; interleaves, 7⅛ x 9¼; maroon cloth boards; title gilt on spine.]

Elaborate promptbook of the Jarrett and Palmer production with Genevieve Ward; arranged for touring, marked by E. Edmonds. Fifth act included. Cuts marked "for the country." Cues entered on circles or squares of bright watercolor. Calls, stage business, processions, notes on dances, excellent maps and sketches of major scenes, cues for effects. At the back are production booklets of Frank Little, the stage manager: maps of scenes with supers, gas plot, inventory of costumes and properties.

55. Louis Besn   America   1882

Harvard Theatre Collection: uncatalogued

[French's Standard Drama, 4⅜ x 7⅜; publisher's wrappers.]

Partbook of a minor actor with Fanny Janauschek, checked for Brandon, Surveyor, Clerk, etc. Cuts and scenic indications.

56. Anonymous   America   1890's

New York Public Library: *NCP

[Pages of French's Standard Drama pasted in a workbook, 6¾ x 8⅜; black and white paper cover.]

Carefully developed promptbook of a touring production. Ends with death of the Queen. Some stage business, maps, cues for effects. Acts end with tableaux. At the back are plots of properties, lights, music.

57. Henry Irving   London, Lyceum   January 5, 1892
   Folger: Henry VIII, 1
   [Kean edition, 5 x 8; interleaves; black cloth boards and black leather spine; title gilt up spine.]
   A professional observer's notes on Irving's production. Several maps. Several hostile notes on the acting and scenic arrangements. "Terry comic laugh." Belonged to George Becks.

58. George Becks   c.1895
   Folger: S.b.20
   [Pages 211-303 from a *Works*, 4 x 7; interleaves, 8 x 10; in red cloth board box; title and "Becks' Henry VIII" gilt on brown spine label.]
   Becks planned but did not publish *The Actor's Shakespeare*. His gathering of traditional materials for *Henry VIII* was completed even to a manuscript title page and Dedication. Includes prefaces from French's Standard Drama, and from editions of Charles Kean and Henry Irving. Describes 70 scenic units and their use for the 15 scenes of the play. Discusses versions "for Wolsey," "for Queen Katherine." Plots of properties, gas lights, limes, costumes. Cuts on full text, following Calvert's and Kean's versions. Copious stage business follows the Genevieve Ward production at Booth's (see no. 54) and incorporates details from Kemble, Siddons, the Keans, Cushman, Lander, Calvert, Modjeska, Irving, and Terry.

59. Ellen Terry   Stratford-upon-Avon   April 23, 1902
   Smallhythe
   [Irving edition, 1892, 5¼ x 8⅛; interleaves; maroon leather, much worn and broken; title gilt up spine.]
   Copy inscribed to Miss Terry from Irving in 1892. "Notes entered from a copy used at Stratford on Avon for study." Many detailed and vivid notes on how to play the Queen.

60. [Terry]
   Smallhythe
   [Henry Altemas edition, Philadelphia, 4 x 5½; red limp leather cover from Temple edition; title gilt up spine.]
   Rehearsal copy dated 1902, checked and cut for Katharine. A few notes on the acting.

61. Herbert Beerbohm Tree
      London, His Majesty's   September 1, 1910
      Enthoven Collection: Tree, 223

      [Pages of a text pasted in a workbook, 7 x 9; black limp cloth boards and black leather spine.]

      Preparation book. Cuts (44 of 127 pages) and roughly penciled directions, much of it in Tree's hand. Remarks on historical truth and archaeological accuracy.

62. [Tree]

      Enthoven Collection: Tree, 223

      [Pages of a text pasted in a workbook, 7 x 9; green marbled boards and half black leather; "Early Rehearsals, Unfinished Script, *not* correct" inked on cover.]

      Rehearsal promptbook signed by Claude Rains. List of entrances. Much stage business, list of scenes, timings.

63. [Tree]

      Enthoven Collection: Tree, 223

      [Cassell's National Library edition pasted in a workbook, 7 x 9; red marbled boards and red cloth spine; "Finished copy but not correct" inked on cover.]

      Very full rehearsal promptbook signed by William Abingdon. Cuts, copious stage business, groundplans, cues for effects, timings.

64. [Tree]

      Enthoven Collection: Tree, 223

      [Cassell's National Library edition pasted in a workbook, 6⅞ x 9; dark blue cardboard, spine patched with brown paper, much worn.]

      Promptbook signed by Cecil King. At the front a list of scenes. Cuts, much stage business, maps, cues for effects, many rough sketches of characters. Originally marked to the end, later cut back to the death of the Queen.

65. [Tree]

      Enthoven Collection: Tree, 250

      [Cassell's National Library edition pasted in a workbook, 7 x 9; red marbled boards and green cloth spine, much worn.]

      Fully developed promptbook ending with death of the Queen. Cuts, much stage business (some typed on slips and pasted in), maps, cues for effects. Overture time 8 minutes. Prologue spoken by a Jester.

66. [Tree]

Enthoven Collection: Tree, 250

[Papers.]

Plots of scenes, principals, supers, lights. Ten neat groundplans.

67. [Tree]

Enthoven Collection: Tree, 239

[Papers.]

Production papers relating to special matinee on July 5, 1915.

[Actor Lists for Following Books Are Given in This Order: King Henry, Wolsey, Queen Katharine.]

68. B. Iden Payne   Stratford-upon-Avon   April 24, 1938

Shakespeare Centre Library: 71.21/1938H

[Eversley edition pasted in a workbook, 7⅛ x 9; purple cloth boards and half black leather; title on spine and cover labels.]

Cast includes Gyles Isham, James Dale, Phyllis Neilson-Terry. Designed by Herbert Norris. Cuts, calls, stage business, a few maps, cues for effects.

69. Robert Atkins   Stratford-upon-Avon   May 17, 1945

Shakespeare Centre Library: 71.21/1945H

[Eversley edition pasted in a workbook, 7⅛ x 9; purple cloth boards and half black leather; title on spine and cover label.]

Cast includes Antony Eustrel, George Skillan, Viola Lyel. Designed by Herbert Norris and Guy Sheppard. Cuts, calls, stage business, maps, cues for effects. The book had been a second copy for Payne's 1938 production, was erased and reused.

70. Tyrone Guthrie   Stratford-upon-Avon   July 23, 1949

Shakespeare Centre Library: O.S.71.21/1949H

[Temple edition pasted in workbook, 8 x 12¾; red cloth boards; title on spine label.]

Cast includes Anthony Quayle, Harry Andrews, Diana Wynyard. Designed by Tanya Moiseiwitsch. Cuts, calls, much stage business, cues for effects. At the front a carefully drawn groundplan.

71. [Guthrie]   April 20, 1950

Shakespeare Centre Library: O.S.71.21/1950H

[New Temple edition pasted in a workbook, 8 x 12¾; red cloth boards; title on spine label.]

Cast includes Anthony Quayle, Andrew Cruickshank, Gwen Ffrangcon-Davies. Revision of the 1949 book for revival. Production papers including supers and plot of changing properties.

72. [Guthrie]   London, Old Vic   May 6, 1953

Old Vic, Publicity Department

[New Temple edition pasted in a workbook, 8 x 10½; black ring binder; title on spine and cover labels.]

Cast includes Paul Rogers, Alexander Knox, Gwen Ffrangcon-Davies. Designed by Tanya Moiseiwitsch. Calls, stage business, maps, cues for effects. Production papers: calls, properties, timings, etc.

73. Michael Benthall   London, Old Vic   May 13, 1958

Old Vic, Publicity Department

[New Temple edition pasted in a workbook, 8 x 10½; black ring binder; title on spine and cover labels.]

Cast includes Harry Andrews, John Gielgud, Edith Evans. Designed by Loudon Sainthill. Cuts, calls, stage business, many maps, cues for effects. Many production papers, including groundplans.

74. George McCowan   Stratford, Ontario   June 20, 1961

Festival Theatre, Library

[Two books. Penguin edition pasted in workbooks, 7¾ x 13⅛; one in buff boards, one in blue cloth boards bordered in red; title pasted on cover.]

Cast includes Douglas Campbell, Douglas Rain, Kate Reid. Designed by Tanya Moiseiwitsch. The first book has much stage business, maps (some on mimeographed groundplans), cues for effects, timings. The second has calls, cues for effects, many timing sheets.

75. Other books of *Henry VIII:*

Connecticut State Library: William Gillette.

Folger: Henry VIII, 2, Edw. Butler, Birmingham cast for 1868; Henry VIII, 5, John de Bonay; Henry VIII, 14, Marcus Moriarty; Henry VIII, 15, Mude; Henry VIII, 18, J. B. Roberts; Henry VIII, 21, 23, anonymous; x.d.231, key to the painting of the trial scene called "The Kemble Family."

Harvard Theatre Collection: *61.2357, Russell Bassett.

Historical and Philosophical Society of Ohio: 812.3/R283/92, Alvin Read.

Library Company of Philadelphia: OEngShak.Log2074.0.3, anonymous early American(?) with cast badly cropped.

Museum of the City of New York: 45.265.A, Henry Placide.

Princeton University, Seymour Collection: HVIII, 1A, E. L. Davenport; HVIII, 5, L. R. Shervell.

Shakespeare Centre Library: O.S.P.50.14(1803), F. Haywel; O.S.P.50.14(1824), William Cooper, Manchester, 1846.

Julius Caesar

1. Joseph Ashbury   Dublin, Smock Alley   1670's
   Folger: Timon, Smock Alley
   [Pages 667-688 of a Third Folio, 8 x 12¼; maroon cloth boards and half brown leather gilt; title gilt up spine.]
   The Smock Alley promptbook of *Julius Caesar* was destroyed by fire at the Shakespeare Memorial Library, Birmingham, in 1879, but its cast list of 13 names appears on the last page (688) of *Timon of Athens*, which preceded *Caesar* in the Folio.

2. Anonymous   1670's(?)
   Folger: V.a.85
   [Manuscript, pages 74-140 in a commonplace book, 4⅛ x 6½; brown leather.]
   Manuscript version thought to be transcribed from a lost seventeenth-century prompt copy. Alterations and some stage business. Last leaves missing. (See G. Blakemore Evans, *JEGP*, XLI, 401-417.)

3. Anonymous   Douai   1694
   Bibliothèque de Douai: MS.7.87
   [Manuscript, folios 131-170 of a volume, 6¾ x 8⅝; parchment.]
   Manuscript version closely resembling the preceding one, used for amateur staging at Douai. Alterations and some stage business. (See G. Blakemore Evans, *Philological Quarterly,* XLI, 158-172.)

4. George Garrick(?)   London, Drury Lane   January 24, 1780(?)
   Folger: Julius Caesar, 8
   [Herringman and Bentley edition, 1684, 7 x 9¼; brown leather gilt; title gilt up spine.]
   Promptbook said to be marked in the hand of George Garrick, who kept the Drury Lane Diary, 1760-69. (Hogan does not list the play at Drury Lane between 1747 and 1780.) Cuts and additions including a final appearance of the Ghost at Philippi. Scenic indications, property manuscript list, calls, some stage business, cues for effects.

5. John Philip Kemble   London, Covent Garden   February 29, 1812
   Garrick Club
   [Kemble edition, 1812, 5⅛ x 8⅛; interleaves; blue cloth boards and brown leather spine; title gilt up spine.]
   Promptbook marked in Kemble's hand. Calls, some stage business,

maps, procession list (106 figures), cues for effects. Detailed map of senate scene.

6. [Kemble]
Folger: Julius Caesar, 13
[Kemble edition, 1811, 5 x 8¼; interleaves; brown leather; title and "TR/CG/MB/J/4" stamped on spine.]
A note of gift from Charles Kemble in 1840 identifies it as his brother's promptbook, "marked in his own hand for representation." Cuts, some stage business, maps, cues for some effects. Not so complete a book as the preceding one.

7. Henry Siddons   Edinburgh, Theatre Royal   c.1812
Folger: Julius Caesar, 24
[Kemble edition, 1812, 5⅛ x 8⅛; interleaves watermarked 1812; brown boards and half brown leather.]
Promptbook of Henry Siddons, "Marked & corrected from Mr. J. Kemble's Own Copy" by J. L. Anderson, the Edinburgh prompter. Some scenic indications, calls, stage business (full account of the murder), procession list, maps, cues for effects. Contains more matter than either of the preceding books. Additional pencilings show extended use. Belonged to Henry Irving.

ad 7. See Addenda, p. 507.

8. Richard Jones   Edinburgh, Theatre Royal   1817
Shakespeare Centre Library: 50.15(1814)
[Kemble edition, 1814, 4¼ x 7¼; interleaves; brown and yellow marbled boards and half brown leather; title gilt on red leather spine label.]
Promptbook of Richard Jones, 1816, "Mark'd & corrected according to Mr. J. Kemble's copy." Cast for Edinburgh, 1817, with Jones as Antony. Lengths of roles noted. A full book, very similar to the preceding (Siddons-Anderson) book. Later belonged to William Creswick, who entered an 1845 Liverpool cast with Macready and an 1846 Sadler's Wells cast with Phelps. At the back are sketches of three scenes from the Booth's Theatre production in which Creswick played in March, 1872. Additional stage business, cues, timings, etc., by Creswick.

9. William B. Wood Philadelphia, Chestnut Street Feb. 14, 1817
New York Public Library: *NCP

[Kemble edition, 1814, 4¼ x 7¼; black cloth boards; title gilt up spine.]

Crudely marked promptbook. Cuts, calls, some stage business, cues for effects. Checked for Casca.

10. Henry Betty   1840's
    Folger: Julius Caesar, 1
    [Cumberland edition, 3½ x 5¾; interleaves; gray boards and green cloth spine; title penciled on cover.]
    Promptbook lacking regular prompter's markings and perhaps not used. Brutus marked for stresses. Grooves, some stage business. At the back are lists of properties, scenes with grooves, calls, cues for some effects, a model playbill, lengths of parts, sketches of Roman footwear.

11. George Bennett   London   1840's
    New York Public Library: *NCP.342984
    [Oxberry edition, 1822, 4⅛ x 6⅞; interleaves; black cloth boards; title gilt up spine.]
    On November 28, 1850, W. Waller transcribed this promptbook from George Bennett's; in 1855 it belonged to W. H. Wilder; in 1858 to James Stark; in 1883 to George Becks. List of supers, calls, maps and sketches, cues for effects.

12. John G. Gilbert
    Harvard Theatre Collection: (Widener, 13485.47.12)
    [Acting edition, Edinburgh, 3¾ x 6; gray boards and brown cloth spine; title gilt up cover.]
    Promptbook crudely but heavily marked, checked for Cassius. Cuts, cues for effects.

13. William Charles Macready   London, Drury Lane   May 1, 1843
    Folger: Julius Caesar, 16
    [Oxberry edition, 1822, 4½ x 7¼; interleaves watermarked 1837, 7⅞ x 9¾; white cardboard and canvas spine.]
    Transcription of Macready's promptbook made by George Ellis, the prompter: cuts and key-marks in ink, notations on interleaves in pencil. Contains, as if intended for publication, a Preface, a Dramatis Personae, histories of characters, notes on Roman customs. Scenic indications, list of property manuscripts, calls, stage business, maps and sketches, cues for effects, timings. Huge groundplan (21 x 13) of senate scene, detailed chart of scenes and

grooves. Callbook (3⅞ x 9) "scratched out temp^y, for rehearsal, and is incorrect, in many particulars."

14. [Macready]

Folger: Julius Caesar, 12

[Oxberry edition, 1822, 4¾ x 8¼; interleaves, 7¼ x 9⅛; green cloth boards and half green leather gilt; title gilt on red leather spine label, "Prompt Copy, Mr. Charles Kean" gilt on maroon leather cover label.]

Beautiful transcription of the Macready promptbook made by George Ellis in December, 1849, for Charles Kean's Windsor Castle production of February 1, 1850.

15. [Macready]

University of Illinois: x792.9/Shl5j/no.1

[Pages 259-351 from volume IX of a *Works*, 4⅞ x 8⅛; interleaves, 7½ x 9; blue marbled boards and half maroon leather; title gilt on spine, "Hermann Vezin" on black leather cover label.]

Beautiful transcription of the Macready book made by George Ellis for Hermann Vezin. Cuts on full text.

16. Samuel Phelps   London, Sadler's Wells   May 5, 1846

Folger: Julius Caesar, 21

[Kemble edition, 1814, 4 x 6⅞; interleaves; brown cloth boards embossed and half brown leather; title gilt on black spine label, "S.P./T.R.D.L." stamped on spine.]

Promptbook originally marked in a fine round hand, with rough additions for 1846 and 1849 by Williams, the prompter. Cuts and restorations, some scenic indications, grooves, calls, stage business, maps, processions, list of supers, cues for effects, timing (3:05). Belonged to Harry Plowman.

17. [Phelps]

New York Public Library: *NCP.343411

[Steevens edition, 5⅞ x 8¾; interleaves watermarked 1840; blue cloth boards; title gilt on spine.]

Promptbook originally marked by a skilled copyist, with additions in the hand of Williams, the prompter. Cuts on full text. At the front, a list of 44 supers. Scenic indications, grooves, calls, stage business, processions, maps, cues for effects. Given to George Becks in 1891 by William J. Le Moyne.

18. John Moore   New York   c.1850-70's
    Folger: Julius Caesar, 14
    [Cumberland edition, $3\frac{1}{2}$ x 6; interleaves; purple wrapper; title inked on cover.]
    Promptbook dated 1845 and "Marked from a book of Mr. John Kemble's in the possession of W. H. Murray, Esq." (see nos. 5-8). Much used in New York theatres, and with many additions by Moore. At the front, lines from *Childe Harold*. Property lists for each act. Much stage business, and notes on effects. Elaborate final tableau of Brutus' funeral pyre, which was not used in *Julius Caesar* until the Barrett-Davenport production of 1875 (see nos. 38-43).

19. [Moore]
    Folger: T.b.2
    [Notebook, $6\frac{1}{8}$ x $10\frac{1}{4}$; blue boards and black cloth spine.]
    Cues for the band for 48 plays, including *Julius Caesar*.

20. N. B. Clarke   New York, National   July 1, 1853
    Harvard Theatre Collection: (Widener, 13485.48.5)
    [Two books bound together. French's Standard Drama, $4\frac{3}{8}$ x $7\frac{1}{2}$; second copy interleaved; brown cloth boards; title inked up spine.]
    The first copy is marked "Prompt Book. National. N.Y." Cues for effects. The second has a procession list, some stage business, a rough map, some cues for effects.

21. [Clarke]
    Harvard Theatre Collection: (Widener, 13485.47.25)
    [Cumberland edition, New York, 1830, $3\frac{5}{8}$ x $5\frac{3}{4}$; stiff brown paper under red cloth boards; title gilt up spine.]
    Promptbook lightly marked. Cues for effects.

22. Thomas Barry   Boston, Boston Theatre   1854
    Harvard Theatre Collection: uncatalogued
    [Kemble edition, 1812, $5\frac{1}{8}$ x $8\frac{1}{4}$; few interleaves; blue marbled boards and brown leather spine; title and "190" inked on cover label.]
    Much used promptbook with early nineteenth-century markings probably derived from Kemble, and with additions apparently by Charles Melville, the English prompter, who then made his own (the following) copies from it. Barry brought all these books to

Boston in 1854. Some scenic indications, calls, stage business, maps, cues for effects, timings.

23. [Barry]

Harvard Theatre Collection: uncatalogued

[Oxberry edition, 1822, 4⅛ x 6⅞; gray interleaves; bound with unmarked *Henry V* in gray boards and half red leather; titles and "44-45" inked on cover label.]

Promptbook marked by Charles Melville, partly verbatim from preceding book. Grooves, stage business, maps, cues for effects.

24. [Barry]

Harvard Theatre Collection: uncatalogued

[Oxberry edition, 1822, 4⅛ x 7⅛; interleaves; blue marbled boards and black cloth spine; title and "251" inked on cover label.]

Promptbook marked by Charles Melville. Calls, stage business mostly verbatim with preceding books, maps, cues for effects.

25. J. B. Wright   Boston

New York Public Library: *NCP.342981

[Oxberry edition, 1822, 4¾ x 8¼; gray interleaves; black cloth boards; title gilt on spine.]

Promptbook which belonged to Wright, but was probably marked by Charles Melville (see 3 preceding books). Grooves, calls, stage business, maps, cues for effects.

26. Sydney Wilkins   America   1860's

Folger: Julius Caesar, 26

[Cumberland edition, 3⅝ x 5⅝; stiff brown paper.]

Crudely marked promptbook. Cuts, cues for effects. At the front the characters are marked for "lengths."

27. W. H. Stephens   1860's

Harvard Theatre Collection: (Widener, 13485.47.30)

[Cumberland edition, 3¾ x 6; gray publisher's wrappers under green cloth boards; title gilt up spine.]

Promptbook and rehearsal copy, checked for Decius Brutus. Some stage business and rough cues for effects.

28. J. B. Roberts   America   1866

Folger: Julius Caesar, 22

[French's Standard Drama, 4⅜ x 7⅜; interleaves; brown cardboard.]

A touring promptbook, dated 1866: "Please return this Book after Performance." List of doubles, grooves, calls, stage business, procession lists, maps, cues for effects, timings (2:45).

29. [Roberts]

Folger: Julius Caesar, 23

[Large paper edition, 6½ x 10; black cloth boards and brown leather spine.]

Copy prepared for public readings, cut and marked for stresses.

30. Harry B. Hudson   Chicago   1867

Harvard Theatre Collection: *61.2356

[French's Standard Drama, 4⅜ x 7¼; paper; title and Hudson's name pasted on cover; in box of gray cloth boards and green leather spine; title gilt up spine.]

Rehearsal copy checked for Trebonius and Lucius. Cuts, costume notes, some penciled stage business.

31. James E. Kirkwood   Rochester, New York   1870's

University of Illinois: x792.9/Sh15j/no.2

[Lacy edition, 4 x 6⅞; interleaves; purple marbled boards and brown cloth spine, broken; title inked up spine label.]

Promptbook neatly marked in brown and red ink through first act only: some stage business, maps, cues for effects. Further stage business and maps roughly penciled. Belonged in 1880 to Charles B. Welles.

32. Edwin Booth   New York, Booth's   December 25, 1871

New York Public Library: *NCP+.346672

[French's Standard Drama, 4 x 7⅜; interleaves, 7¾ x 12½; brown and red marbled boards and half brown cloth; title inked up spine.]

Much used promptbook, probably Booth's. The text as partly restored does not square with his later (1878) acting edition; but the binding resembles that of the Booth books at The Players, and a scenic notation at II, 3—"W.T.Sc. in 2"—recalls that *Winter's Tale* was produced at Booth's in the preceding spring (1871). Some stage business, cues for effects, itemization of supers used on 4 different days. A news clipping concerning the play at the Haymarket, 1898.

(NOTE: It is not here possible to distinguish with certainty between many of the following Booth and Barrett books and the productions they reflect.)

33. Lawrence Barrett   c.1872
New York Public Library: *NCP.285341
[Music-Publishing Company issue of Cumberland edition, $3\frac{1}{2}$ x
$5\frac{3}{4}$; interleaves, $6\frac{1}{8}$ x 8; brown cloth boards; title gilt on spine.]
Well-developed promptbook, probably used for touring. At the
back a gas and calcium plot "as Done by Mr. Lawrence Barrett,
Fred P. Barton Stage Mgr." At the front a plot of supers listing
14 women and about 85 men. Calls, much stage business, processions, cues for effects.

34. [Barrett]
W. A. Clark Library, Los Angeles
[Printed sheet, $10\frac{1}{4}$ x $19\frac{3}{8}$.]
Scene plot for touring, giving description of scenes and wings and
the groove numbers. Fred P. Barton, stage manager.

35. [Barrett]   San Francisco, California Theatre
University of Pennsylvania, Furness Collection: C59.Sh1J
[French's Standard Drama, $4\frac{1}{4}$ x $7\frac{1}{4}$; interleaves, 6 x $7\frac{3}{4}$; red
leather gilt; title and "California Theatre" gilt on cover.]
Very fine, full promptbook which may have been transcribed
from Barrett's when he visited the California in 1872 or when
he and Booth were there in 1889. Scenic indications, grooves, calls,
much stage business, good maps and sketches, cues for effects.

36. [Barrett]   Boston, Boston Museum
University of Pennsylvania, Furness Collection: C59.Sh1JP
[French's Standard Drama pasted in a workbook, $7\frac{5}{8}$ x $9\frac{3}{4}$; paper
wrapper with publisher's wrapper pasted on it and endorsed
"Prompt Book, Property of J. R. Pitman"; in red cloth board
folder; title gilt on cover.]
Very fine, full promptbook made by J. R. Pitman for the Boston
Museum, containing a cast list for March, 1878 (Barrett as Cassius, Charles Barron as Brutus, Frank Colter as Antony). Generally verbatim with the preceding (California) book, and probably transcribed from the same original. (See no. 47.)

37. [Barrett]
Harvard Theatre Collection: uncatalogued
[Ten music score books, $9\frac{1}{2}$ x $6\frac{1}{4}$; brown cloth boards and green
cloth spine.]

Complete scores for the band for 9 plays including *Julius Caesar,* endorsed by musicians in many cities.

38. Lawrence Barrett and E. L. Davenport
                      New York, Booth's   December 27, 1875
    New York Public Library: *NCOFp.v.190.384095B

    [French edition of the Booth's Theatre version, 5 x 8; interleaves; bound with 6 other promptbooks in black cloth boards; title gilt on spine.]

    Apparently a transcription by Leon John Vincent of the official promptbook of the Barrett-Davenport-Bangs production, very thorough though written hastily and probably unused. At the front a list of doubles, a list of supers, a note on variant stagings of the ghost scene. Copious stage business, detailed cues for effects including scene change by sink and fly. At the end a good sketch of the funeral pyre scene, which was introduced in the Barrett-Davenport-Bangs production.

39. [Barrett and Davenport]
    New York Public Library: *NCP.285343

    [Modern Standard Drama, 4¼ x 6⅞; interleaves; black cloth boards; title gilt up spine.]

    George Becks's very full memorial book of the Barrett-Davenport-Bangs production, "marked from observations & notes taken during the performance," with additions "kindly furnished by my friend Mr. E. T. Mason," and "with supplementary stage directions, 1883." Engravings of Barrett, Davenport, Bangs; engravings of 4 scenes; details of costume and armor. Scenic indications, grooves, calls, much detailed stage business, maps, cues for effects. Map of the funeral pyre scene.

40. [Barrett and Davenport]
    New York Public Library: *NCP.342996

    [French's Standard Drama, 4½ x 7; interleaves; black and white marbled boards and green cloth spine; title inked up spine.]

    Another book of George Becks, less fully marked than the preceding. Some scenic indications, grooves, calls, some stage business, cues for effects. At the front a descriptive list of banners of Caesar, Brutus, Cassius, Marc Antony.

41. [Barrett and Davenport]
    Harvard Theatre Collection: uncatalogued

[French's Standard Drama, 4½ x 7; interleaves; black cloth boards and black leather spine; title gilt up spine.]

James Taylor's very full memorial book of the Barrett-Davenport-Bangs production. Many engravings of Roman costume, scenes from the play. Gérôme's painting of the death of Caesar, etc., pasted in. Very detailed accounts of stage business, cues for effects.

42. [Barrett and Davenport]

New York Public Library: *NCP.52x296

[Booth Prompt Book edition, 1912, 4⅜ x 7¼; interleaves, 6⅛ x 8¼; brown cloth boards; title gilt up spine.]

Hallam Bosworth's promptbook taken mainly from the George Becks book (see no. 39).

43. [Barrett and Davenport]

Boston Athenaeum: $VE.S5I.19

[French's Standard Drama, 4½ x 7½; interleaves; green cloth boards; title gilt on spine.]

Edward Tuckerman Mason's record of the business of Davenport as Brutus and Barrett as Cassius. More than 100 very vivid and detailed notes.

44. Frederick Warde   America   1880's

W. A. Clark Library, Los Angeles

[French's Standard Drama, 4⅜ x 7⅛; interleaves, 4⅞ x 7⅛; brown limp leather; title gilt on spine.]

Promptbook "mark'd from Rehearsals of Fred'k Warde by J. L. Laphore," and used by Warde for many years. Grooves, stage business, maps, crowd responses, cues for effects. Typed plots of scenery, supers, properties. Text of song for Lucius. Playbills of the 1875 Barrett tour in which Warde played Antony; an 1885 performance with Warde as Brutus; a Denver bill of 1910-11. Several prints of scenes from the play.

45. Frederick Paulding   1882

Rutgers University: PR.1243.SHA

[Two books. French's Standard Drama, 4½ x 7½; publisher's wrappers.]

Rehearsal copies, one merely checked for Cassius, the other with many brief notations of the actor's business and manner.

46. Edwin Booth and Lawrence Barrett
         New York, Academy of Music   December 26, 1887
    The Players
    [French's Standard Drama pasted in a workbook, 5¾ x 8¾; red marbled boards and half green leather gilt; title gilt on spine.]
    Souvenir promptbook of the Booth-Barrett production, "Bound and prepared for my dear Friend Edwin Booth as a memento of our Season of 1887/8 with the enduring love and respect of/Lawrence Barrett."

47. [Booth]
    The Players
    [French's Standard Drama pasted in a workbook, 5½ x 8⅝; limp black leather gilt; title gilt on cover.]
    Excellent transcription of Booth's promptbook made by J. R. Pitman as a souvenir for Russ Whytal, autographed by Booth. Similar to Pitman's own Boston Museum book (see no. 36) and to various Barrett books.

48. [Booth and Barrett]
    Folger: Julius Caesar, 9
    [French's Standard Drama interleaved into a stapled workbook, 4⅜ x 8.]
    A roughly made promptbook owned by Charles B. Hanford, who played Antony with Booth and Barrett. Some stage business, maps, sketches, cues for effects.

49. [Booth and Barrett]
    Folger: Julius Caesar, 7
    [Oxberry edition, 1822, 5 x 8⅛; paper wrapper, much worn.]
    Rehearsal copy of Owen Fawcett, who played First Citizen with Booth and Barrett, variously dated from New York, Detroit, London, in 1886 and 1887. Few markings. Several prints of scenes pasted in.

50. [Booth]
    Folger: Julius Caesar, 4
    [French's Standard Drama tipped into a workbook, 4½ x 7⅜; brown leather; title on cover label.]
    Rehearsal copy checked for Soothsayer. Notes on Brutus' costume, on Brutus' character.

51. [Booth and Barrett]

Folger: Julius Caesar, 3

[Booth-Winter edition, 1898, 4⅝ x 7¼; publisher's wrappers.]

William Winter's copy of the edition. Contains photograph of Booth as Brutus, engraving of Barrett as Cassius, a note from Booth in 1877 discussing publication of his promptbooks, a note from Barrett in 1882 concerning Ludwig Barnay.

52. Anonymous

The Players: PB.85

[French's Standard Drama, 4½ x 7⅜; interleaves, 5 x 7⅞; laid in black cloth boards.]

Neatly marked promptbook. Cuts and additions, calls, some stage business, cues for effects.

53. Osmond Tearle   Stratford-upon-Avon   1889

Shakespeare Centre Library: 71.21(1889)J

[French issue of Lacy edition, 4¼ x 7¼; interleaves; publisher's wrappers pasted on boards and black cloth spine.]

Promptbook marked by C. Rainbow and owned by Charles Flower. Cuts, some scenic indications, some stage business, sketches, cues for effects.

54. George Rignold   Sydney, Her Majesty's   August 24, 1889

Folger: Julius Caesar, 11

[Rignold edition, Sydney, 5⅜ x 8½; brown cardboard and green cloth spine.]

Henry Jewett's rehearsal copy, checked for Cassius. Photograph on the cover said to be of Jewett. Rignold's Preface explains staging arrangements.

55. Anonymous   c.1895

Folger: Julius Caesar, Folio 1

[Booth-Barrett edition, 1895, pasted on left-hand pages of a workbook, 7⅞ x 12½; gray cloth boards and half red leather gilt.]

Stage manager's cuebook, probably unused. Cues for effects fairly complete.

56. Herbert Beerbohm Tree   London, Her Majesty's   Jan. 22, 1898

Enthoven Collection: Tree, 1

[Temple edition, 1896, pasted in a workbook, 7 x 9; red marbled boards and green cloth spine.]

Rehearsal promptbook done in pencil and red ink, signed by Arthur Coe. Partial cast, stage business, maps.

57. [Tree]

Enthoven Collection: Tree, 1

[Same format as preceding book.]

Rehearsal promptbook roughly penciled, signed by Alfred Wigley. Much stage business, maps, cues for effects.

58. [Tree]

Enthoven Collection: Tree, 33

[Same format as preceding book, but black cloth spine.]

Very full and much used promptbook done mainly in red ink, signed by Arthur Coe. Cast list, cuts, calls, very full stage business, cues for effects. List of supers inserted.

59. [Tree]

Enthoven Collection: Tree, 33

[Temple edition pasted in a workbook, $7\frac{1}{2}$ x $9\frac{1}{4}$; white vellum boards; title on cover label.]

Promptbook even more fully developed than the preceding one. Full stage business, cues for effects. Printed sketches of all scenes. The forum scene is overcrowded with directions.

60. [Tree]

Enthoven Collection: Tree, 33

[Same format as preceding book, but slightly smaller.]

Final development of the stage manager's book, signed by Arthur E. Coe, July 15, 1898. Printed cast and list of scenes. Printed sketches of all scenes. All stage business necessary to the stage manager. Cues for effects in colored inks. Good groundplans. Text of forum scene especially printed with space to accommodate notes of crowd responses, etc.

61. [Tree]

British Theatre Museum: G 58 1963

[Mixture of a Shakespeare edition and portions of (probably) Tree edition pasted in a workbook, $7\frac{1}{2}$ x $9\frac{1}{4}$; white vellum boards; title and decorations on cover label.]

Unused or souvenir copy of Tree's version made up by G. H. Croxon, the prompter. Few markings. Many illustrations pasted throughout. Cast list from a program at the front and a souvenir booklet at the back.

62. [Tree]   London, His Majesty's   April 29, 1905
Enthoven Collection: Tree, 33
[Eight books. Two Cassell's National Library, 1904, 4 x 6; red cloth boards. Four Heinemann edition, 1904, 3¾ x 6; green cloth boards. Two Tree edition, 1898, 4⅛ x 5⅜; tan boards.]
Rehearsal copies for Cassius and several minor characters. Some stage business.

63. [Tree]
Enthoven Collection: Tree, 36
[Pamphlet, 5¾ x 11.]
Many copies of a 17-page forum scene especially printed with cues and crowd responses.

64. [Tree]
Enthoven Collection: Tree, 1A
[Pamphlet, 6 x 9¾.]
Many copies of a 24-page printed booklet of Granville-Barker's forum scene, used for "Coronation Gala Performance," June 16, 1911. The crowd of nearly 100 was divided into 11 groups, each assigned words, business, and motivation.

65. [Tree]
Enthoven Collection: Tree, 33
[Pamphlet, 5¾ x 8¾.]
Copies of a 9-page forum scene printed for touring company.

66. [Tree]
Enthoven Collection: Tree, 39, 41
[Papers.]
Printed plots for calls, crowds, costume changes, properties, limes, electrics, supers. Mimeographed plots of costumes.

67. Winthrop Ames   Boston, Castle Square   February 26, 1906
New York Public Library: *NCP+.41371B
[Typescript, 8 x 12¾; green cloth boards; title gilt on spine.]
Final promptbook. Stage directions underlined in red. Cast, synopsis of scenery, extremely detailed stage business, excellent groundplans. Penciled rehearsal notes. Crowds were divided into teams

of Reds, Yellows, Greens, Blues. The production was revived on
October 26, 1906.

68. [Ames]

New York Public Library: *NCP+.41406B

[Temple edition pasted in a workbook, 15 x 13; blue cloth boards;
title gilt on spine.]

Huge workbook with hundreds of preparation notes for Ames's
production.

69. [Ames]

New York Public Library: *NCP+.83541B

[Blueprints; blue cloth boards, 12½ x 17¾; title gilt on spine.]
Seven blueprint groundplans, mounted on linen and folded.

70. [Ames]

New York Public Library: *NCP+.41370B

[Carbon typescript, 8 x 13; blue cloth boards; title gilt on spine.]
Cues and detailed directions for crowds. Plots of properties, music,
costumes, lights.

71. [Ames]

New York Public Library: *NCP+.41369B

[Carbon typescripts, 8 x 6½; blue cloth boards; title gilt on spine.]
Partbooks for 23 roles, much used, each bearing name of actor on
brown paper cover. Plots for properties, lights, scenery, costumes,
music.

72. Robert Mantell   New York, Academy of Music   Nov. 26, 1906
Folger: Julius Caesar, 17

[Pages of a Shakespeare text, 4¾ x 7¼; interleaves, 6 x 8½; blue
cloth boards and half blue leather gilt; title and owner's name
gilt on cover.]

Excellent and much used promptbook "as played by Edwin
Booth," prepared by William H. Young, 1906 (see nos. 32, 46-51).
The cuts made on a full text do not exactly square with Booth's
acting edition. Scenic indications, grooves, calls, detailed stage
business, maps, sketches, cues for effects.

73. Oscar Asche   Australia and South Africa   1909, 1912
Shakespeare Centre Library: 72.915ASC

[Temple edition pasted in a workbook, 8¾ x 11; green marbled boards, much worn; title gilt on cover and spine labels; in white paper wrapper.]

Heavily marked and much used promptbook signed by J. Fritz Russell. Some scenic indications, much stage business especially for crowds, maps, cues for effects. At the back a cast list and plot of properties.

74. [Asche]

Shakespeare Centre Library: 72.915ASC

[Temple edition pasted in a workbook, 6⅝ x 9; green cloth boards; title inked on spine label.]

Stage manager's book for Asche's touring production. Cuts on full text. Stage business for crowds, cues for effects.

75. Henry Jewett   Boston, Boston Opera House   January 25, 1915

Folger: Julius Caesar, 31

[Typescript, 8½ x 11; gray cardboard and green cloth spine.]

Much used promptbook of the Henry Jewett Players. Cast lists, properties, some stage business, cues for effects, timing sheets for a 3-week run, light plot. Advertisement for several plays. Program for October 21, 1929.

76. Lena Ashwell   London   1919-29

Birmingham, Shakespeare Memorial Library: 370/421201

[Temple edition pasted in a workbook, 7 x 9; tan marbled boards and brown cloth spine; title gilt up spine.]

Promptbook of the Lena Ashwell Players. Some stage business, cues for effects. Plots of properties and scenes. Advertisement for performances at Winchmore Hill, October 1, 1923.

77. F. R. Benson   England   1921

Shakespeare Centre Library: 72.915BEN

[Favourite Classics edition pasted in a workbook, 7⅞ x 10; blue cloth boards; title inked on spine and cover labels.]

Promptbook of Benson's North Company in 1921 and earlier. Cuts, some stage business including crowd responses, maps, cues for effects. At the back a plot of business for 20 supers.

[ACTOR LISTS FOR FOLLOWING BOOKS ARE GIVEN IN THIS ORDER: Brutus, Cassius, Antony, Caesar.]

78. The Players   New York, New Amsterdam   June 6, 1927

The Players: PB.38

[Pages of a Shakespeare text pasted in a workbook, 8 x 12½; limp black imitation leather.]

Promptbook of The Players' Sixth Annual Classic Revival. Cast includes Tyrone Power, Basil Rathbone, James Rennie, William Courtleigh. Prologue by Percy Mackaye. Blueprint groundplans for all scenes. Call sheets, stage business, cues for effects, timings.

79. W. Bridges-Adams   Stratford-upon-Avon   April 26, 1932
Shakespeare Centre Library: 71.21/1932J
[Temple edition pasted in a workbook, 7 x 9; blue cloth boards and half black leather; title on cover and spine labels.]
Probably Bridges-Adams' book for his 1932 production, of which the cast includes Gyles Isham, Eric Maxon, Wilfrid Walter, Randle Ayrton. Designed by Aubrey Hammond. Much stage business, maps, some cues for effects.

80. [Bridges-Adams]   Stratford-upon-Avon   April 19, 1934
Shakespeare Centre Library: 71.21/1934J
[Temple edition pasted in a workbook, 7 x 9; green cloth boards and half red leather; title on cover and spine labels.]
Cast includes John Wyse, Baliol Holloway, Neil Porter, Eric Maxon. Designed by Aubrey Hammond. Much stage business, maps, sketches, cues for effects. Earlier markings, as for 1928 and 1932, erased.

81. John Wyse   Stratford-upon-Avon   April 14, 1936
Shakespeare Centre Library: 71.21/1936J
[New Temple edition pasted in a workbook, 6⅞ x 9; purple cloth boards and half black leather; title on cover and spine labels.]
Cast includes James Dale, Donald Wolfit, Peter Glenville, Donald Eccles. Designed by James Cox and Barbara Curtis. Director's workbook, not used in performance. Stage business, maps, notes on music.

82. Orson Welles   New York, Mercury   November 11, 1937
New York Public Library: 8-*NCP+.319879B
[Carbon typescript, 8 x 11; gray cloth boards; title gilt up spine.]
Cast includes Orson Welles, Martin Gabel, George Coulouris, Joseph Holland. Designed by Samuel Leve. Much used promptbook used in stage management. Properties list, cues for effects.

83. [Welles]

Folger: Julius Caesar, 29

[Typescript, 8½ x 11; black binder; title and "Mercury Theatre" inked on cover label.]

Unused copy of the Mercury Theatre version, endorsed by Orson Welles.

84. Andrew Leigh   Stratford-upon-Avon   April 16, 1941

Shakespeare Centre Library: 71.21/1941J

[New Temple edition pasted in a workbook, 7 x 9; purple cloth boards and half black leather; title on cover and spine labels.]

Cast includes George Hayes, Baliol Holloway, Godfrey Kenton, G. Kay Souper. Designed by Barbara Curtis. Lightly marked with stage business, maps, cues for effects. The book had been used in 1936. Was erased and reused.

85. National Broadcasting Company   April 3, 1949

Folger: Julius Caesar, Folio 2

[Two books. Mimeograph, 8½ x 11; in black file box.]

Shooting script of the NBC-TV production of the Amherst College Masquers playing in the Folger Shakespeare Library Theatre.

86. Anthony Quayle and Michael Langham
                    Stratford-upon-Avon   May 2, 1950

Shakespeare Centre Library: O.S.71.21/1950J

[New Temple edition pasted in a workbook, 8 x 12¾; red cloth boards; title on cover and spine labels.]

Cast includes Harry Andrews, John Gielgud, Anthony Quayle, Andrew Cruickshank. Designed by Warwick Armstrong. A partial promptbook only: stage business given for part of Act I. Calls and cues for effects *passim*.

87. Loew's Incorporated   July, 1952

Folger: Julius Caesar, 30

[Mimeograph, 8½ x 11; yellow paper.]

Shooting script of the film directed by Joseph L. Mankiewicz.

88. Michael Langham   Stratford, Ontario   June 27, 1955

Festival Theatre, Library

[Two books. New Stratford Shakespeare pasted in workbooks, 8 x 12¾; black cloth boards and red cloth spine; title pasted on cover.]

Cast includes Lorne Greene, Lloyd Bochner, Donald Davis, Robert Christie. Designed by Tanya Moiseiwitsch. The first book has copious stage business, maps, cast list. The second has cues for effects.

89. Michael Benthall   London, Old Vic   September 7, 1955
Old Vic, Publicity Department
[New Temple edition pasted in a workbook, 8 x 10½; black ring binder; title on cover and spine labels.]
Cast includes Paul Rogers, Richard Wordsworth, John Neville, Gerald Cross. Designed by Audrey Cruddas. Cuts, calls, stage business, maps, cues for effects. Many production papers.

90. Glen Byam Shaw   Stratford-upon-Avon   May 28, 1957
Shakespeare Centre Library: O.S.71.21/1957J
[New Temple edition pasted in a workbook, 8 x 13; red cloth board spring binder; title on spine label.]
Cast includes Alec Clunes, Geoffrey Keen, Richard Johnson, Cyril Luckham. Designed by Motley. Very full stage business, maps, cues for effects. Production papers: working divisions, effects cues, plot of screens, 5 maps on large mimeographed groundplans.

91. Douglas Seale   London, Old Vic   October 8, 1958
Old Vic, Publicity Department
[Temple edition pasted in a workbook, 8 x 10½; green ring binder; title on cover and spine labels.]
Cast includes John Phillips, Michael Hordern, Peter Moynihan, Jack May. Designed by Berkeley Sutcliffe. Typewritten stage business, careful maps, cues for effects. Production papers: flys, properties, effects cues, understudies, etc.

92. Other books of *Julius Caesar:*
Boston Public Library: K.47.13 no. 2, Thomas Barry and John Gilbert.
Connecticut State Library: William Gillette, 2 books.
Folger: Jul Caes, 2, J. B. Booth, Jr.; Jul Caes, 5, W. E. Burton, Philadelphia, 1840; Jul Caes, 6, Sidney A. Carey, Bowery; Jul Caes, 10, Charles Hill, 1838; Jul Caes, 15, H. V. Lovell; Jul Caes, 18, William A. Minards; Jul Caes, 19, 20, Marcus Moriarty; Jul Caes, 25, James Taylor; Jul Caes, 27, George W. Wilson; Jul Caes, 28, anonymous; PR.2796.G3.J1.A1, D. Neuffer, a German book based on the Schlegel translation.

Harvard Theatre Collection: K.47.13, John Gilbert, Boston, 1841, New York, 1849, Philadelphia, 1852.

Historical and Philosophical Society of Ohio: 812.3/R283/90, Alvin Read.

Library of Congress, Batchelder Collection: 375, J. W. Wallack; 376, Edwin Adams, Baltimore, 1855.

Princeton University, Seymour Collection: JC.15, A. S. H. Murray, Boston, 1871.

University of Minnesota: Z820.12/Z11, volume 12, W. S. Forrest.

University of Pennsylvania: AC85.M9415.820p.51, James Murdoch, 2 books.

King John

1. Anonymous   1700's
   Folger: John, 24
   [Pages 165-252 from volume III of Theobald's *Works*, 4⅞ x 7½.]
   Eighteenth-century promptbook. Cuts, entrances and exits, cues
   for effects.

2. David Garrick   London, Drury Lane   February 20, 1745
   Folger: A.a.22
   [Manuscript, 6⅜ x 8; soft tan paper wrapper; in red slip-case;
   title gilt on black spine label.]
   Garrick's partbook for King John, made by a copyist, with cuts
   and notes in Garrick's hand. Lines added in the first act and at
   the death of John.

3. William Powell(?)   London, Drury Lane   1766(?)
   Folger: John, 17
   [Pages 3-70 of an eighteenth-century edition, no title page, 5⅛ x
   7¾; blue, green, and yellow marbled boards and half brown
   leather; title gilt on red cover and spine labels and on cover label
   also the letters "R.K.B."]
   An inserted slip identifies this promptbook with one of the
   Powells. (William Powell played John at Drury Lane March 20,
   1766; John Powell played Pandulph at Drury Lane November
   20, 1800.) Extensive cuts. Scenic indications, list of property manuscripts, calls, stage business, some cues for effects.

4. William B. Wood   1807
   New York Public Library: *NCP.164554
   [C. Bathurst edition, 1784, 4 x 6½; black cloth boards; title gilt
   up spine.]
   Lightly marked promptbook. Cuts, some stage business. Cast for
   1807 including Wood, the Warrens, Fennell, etc.

5. [Wood]
   Folger: John, 21
   [Inchbald edition, 3⅝ x 6; some interleaves; gray marbled boards
   and half red, half brown leather.]
   Crude promptbook. Cuts, restorations, little stage business.

6. John Philip Kemble   London, Covent Garden   May 1, 1810
   Folger: John, 10
   [Kemble edition, 1804, 5 x 8¼; interleaves watermarked 1807;

brown leather; title gilt on red spine label, spine stamped "TR/ CG/PB/I."]

Much used promptbook marked in Kemble's hand. Calls, stage business, maps, cues for effects, timings (3:10). Names of several minor actors are given in the calls.

7. [Kemble]

Garrick Club

[Kemble edition, 1800, 5⅛ x 8¼; interleaves watermarked 1809; blue cloth boards and brown leather spine; title gilt up spine.]

Promptbook lightly marked in Act I mainly in Kemble's hand, in later acts by other hands.

8. [Kemble]

Folger: T.a.25

[Manuscript, 7 x 8⅞; brown leather gilt; title gilt up spine.]

Kemble's 23-page partbook for John, in his own hand, 441 lines. Dated December 10, 1783, but probably written much later.

9. R. J. Collier   London, Drury Lane

Folger: John, 9

[Kemble edition, 1804, 4⅞ x 8⅛; interleaves; handsome brown leather gilt; title and "MSS.NOTES.—KEMBLE" gilt on black spine label.]

A note at the front of this promptbook asserts that it is "Mr. J. Kembles own Stage Copy—Authentic notes in his autograph." Most of the markings, however, are by R. J. C[ollier], whose initials are at the back. Probably therefore it belonged to Drury Lane rather than Covent Garden Theatre. Calls, stage business, maps, cues for effects. (See no. 11.)

10. Edmund Kean   London, Drury Lane   June 1, 1818

Folger: John, 23

[Kemble edition, Lowndes, 4⅞ x 7¾; interleaves; blue, yellow, and red marbled boards and half blue leather, front cover broken; title gilt up spine, spine stamped "D.L./PB/29."]

A copyist or prompter with a round, curling hand has transcribed the Covent Garden book (see no. 6) for Drury Lane. Kemble's "R.H." and "L.H." are generally, but not always, translated into "OP." and "PS." The Covent Garden act timings are carried over, but a penciled note totals them not at 3:10 but 2:35 or 2:26. The Edmund Kean cast of 1818 is written in.

11. R. J. Collier   Bath, Theatre Royal   1823

Shakespeare Centre Library: 50.16(1800)KEM

[Kemble edition, 1800, 4¾ x 7⅞; interleaves watermarked 1817; tan and green marbled boards and brown leather spine, much worn; title gilt on spine.]

Adaptation of the Kemble book signed by R. J. Collier, who was prompter at Bath in 1823. Occasional scenic indications, one groove, calls, stage business, cues for effects, timings (3:00). Additional markings in pencil. (See no. 9.)

12. Fanny Kemble   1830's

Shakespeare Centre Library: 50.16(1814)

[Kemble edition, 1814, 4¼ x 6⅞; bound with other plays in green cloth boards.]

Miss Kemble's rehearsal copy, given to Helen Faucit by Charles Kemble in 1838. Checked for Constance. Marked for stresses, probably by Miss Faucit.

13. Noah Ludlow and Sol Smith   Mobile and St. Louis   1830's

Harvard Theatre Collection: TS.2355.50

[Cumberland edition, 3½ x 5¾; gray paper with title inked under white pamphlet boards.]

Promptbook of simplified version reduced to 3 acts. Cuts, little stage business, some cues for effects.

14. J. B. Wright   Boston   1830's

Folger: John, 22

[Cumberland edition, 3¾ x 5⅞; blue interleaves, 4 x 6¼; gray cardboard with publisher's cover pasted on.]

Promptbook owned by Wright, but the markings suggest it is of English origin deriving from Kemble. Some grooves, some stage business, maps, sketches, cues for effects. Playbills of Macready in 1831, Kean in 1852.

15. Thomas Barry   New York, Park   October 1, 1832

The Players

[Cumberland edition, 3¾ x 6; interleaves; coarse tan cloth; title inked on cover.]

Promptbook used when Barry played John, with Charles and Fanny Kemble as Faulconbridge and Constance. Cast penciled in. Calls, some stage business, cues for effects. Notes by Barry on the playing of John. Two reviews of Miss Kemble's Constance.

16. Robert Hamilton   Liverpool, Theatre Royal   1835
University of Illinois: x792.9/Sh15k/no.4
[Cumberland edition, 3⅝ x 5⅝; brown marbled boards and brown leather spine; title on cover label.]
Promptbook marked for two acts only: calls, some stage business, maps, some cues for effects. Later acts checked as a rehearsal copy for John and Faulconbridge. Belonged in 1858 to John Kirley(?) of the Boston Museum.

17. William Charles Macready   London, Drury Lane   Oct. 24, 1842
University of Illinois: x792.9/Sh15k/no.1
[Pages 293-395 from volume IV of a *Works*, 1825, 4⅝ x 7⅛; interleaves; tan marbled boards and half brown leather; title gilt on spine.]
Macready's preparation copy marked in his hand, signed in the front cover and dated September 8, 1842. Cuts on full text. At the front, 5 pages of calls. Much stage business, maps, cues for effects. (See nos. 24, 26, 27, 29, 37, 42, 45.)

18. [Macready]
Folger: John, 12
[Pages 213-302 from volume V of a Steevens *Works*, 5⅛ x 8¼; interleaves watermarked 1840; white cardboard, very worn; title and date inked on cover.]
The working promptbook of Macready's Drury Lane production. Contains all the matter of the preceding book, transcribed by a professional copyist. Prompter's additions in ink and pencil in the hand of John Willmott include a list of 53 supers, bits of stage business, maps, cues for effects, timings.

19. [Macready]
Newberry Library: Case YS.737.8
[Pages 195-287 from volume IV of Knight's Cabinet Edition, 3⅜ x 5½; interleaves watermarked 1843, 4⅞ x 7⅝; blue cloth boards and half brown leather gilt, broken; title gilt on red spine label, "Prompt Book" gilt on black spine label; in brown cloth board box; title gilt on spine.]
Excellent transcription of Macready's promptbook of the 1842 production. The manuscript title page calls it "The Private Property of the T.R.D.L." Stage business is in brown ink underlined with red; calls and cues for effects are in blue ink. Endorsed

"H. Scharf/Novr. 1844." A later owner has penciled at the end "time notes of Mantell in Garrick Theatre, Chicago, 6 April, 1915," and a few scattered notes of Mantell's business.

20. [Macready]
Folger: John, 8
[Watercolors, 7⅛ x 8⅞; interleaves; red and brown marbled boards and half black leather gilt.]
William Telbin's 14 watercolor scene designs for Macready's 1842 production, which George Ellis sent to Charles Kean in America in March, 1846. Carpenter's notes by Ellis on facing pages. (See Charles H. Shattuck, *William Charles Macready's "King John."*)

21. [Macready]
University of Illinois
[Watercolors, 4 x 6½.]
Twelve plates (15 figures) of costume designs by Charles Hamilton Smith. (See Charles H. Shattuck, *William Charles Macready's "King John."*)

22. Helen Faucit   London, Drury Lane   October 24, 1842
University of Pennsylvania, Furness Collection: C59.Sh1KJ
[Manuscript, 6⅜ x 8⅛; brown paper with title inked, under rose and white marbled boards and half red leather gilt; title and "Queen Constance (Lady Martin)" gilt up spine.]
Partbook for Constance. Marked for stresses throughout, and many faint notes by Miss Faucit on the acting. Letter of gift from Sir Theodore Martin to H. H. Furness.

23. Elizabeth Mary Anne Shaw New York, Bowery October 16, 1843
Harvard Theatre Collection: TS.2355.53
[Longman edition, 1804, 3¾ x 6⅛; interleaves including several double-size ones (folded) with maps and sketches; green leather gilt; title and "E.M.A.Shaw" gilt on red cover label.]
Full and much used promptbook. Scenic indications, grooves, calls, some stage business, maps, cues for effects. Names of some actors are penciled in.

24. John Moore   c.1845
Folger: John, 14
[Pages 193-290 from volume IV of a *Works*, 5⅛ x 8; interleaves; tan cardboard, very soiled; title and signature inked on cover.]

Somewhat simplified transcription of the Macready promptbook or one of its derivatives. Not much used. (See nos. 17-19.)

25. [Moore]

   Folger: T.b.2

   [Notebook, 6½ x 10¼; blue boards and black cloth spine.]

   Cues for the band for 48 plays, including *King John*.

26. Samuel Phelps   London, Sadler's Wells   September 30, 1844

   Folger: John, 16

   [Pages 297-395 from volume IV of a Steevens *Works*, 4¾ x 7⅜; interleaves watermarked 1840, 5⅜ x 7⅝; marbled boards worn to gray and half brown leather; title and "SP/TRDL" gilt on red spine labels.]

   Excellent transcription of the Macready Drury Lane book (see no. 18) made by George Ellis in May, 1843. Phelps has added a list of supers, some stage business. At the front, several pages of costume notes on sheets watermarked 1847. Used by Phelps for many years.

27. Charles Kean   New York, Park   November 16, 1846

   Folger: John, 7

   [Pages 193-290 from volume IV of a Steevens *Works*, 5½ x 8⅞; interleaves, 7⅛ x 8⅞; red and brown marbled boards and half black leather gilt; title gilt on spine, "Mr. Charles Kean" gilt on black leather cover label.]

   Excellent transcription of the Macready Drury Lane book (see no. 18) made by George Ellis in March, 1846. Used by Kean for the Park Theatre production and for London productions at the Princess's on February 9, 1852, and October 18, 1858 (see nos. 37-41). Kean and his prompters have entered cuts and restorations, revisions of scenery and stage business, and timings. (See facsimile reproduction in Charles H. Shattuck, *William Charles Macready's "King John."*)

28. James B. Roberts   1847

   Folger: John, 18

   [Modern Standard Drama, 1846, 4⅝ x 7⅝; interleaves; gray cardboard; title, signature, and date inked on cover.]

   Promptbook based on the newly published "Kean" version. Cuts, little stage business beyond that printed. Checked for John and marked for stresses.

29. William Creswick   London, Surrey   April 2, 1851
Shakespeare Centre Library: 50.16(1765)
[Pages 401-504 from volume III of Tonson's *Works*, 1765, 4¾ x 7⅞; interleaves watermarked 1847, 6⅝ x 8¾; tan marbled boards and half brown leather; title gilt on black leather spine label.]
Excellent transcription of the Macready Drury Lane book (see no. 18) made for Creswick by George Ellis.

30. Thomas Barry   Boston, Boston Theatre   March 12, 1855
Harvard Theatre Collection: uncatalogued
[Oxberry edition, 1819, 5 x 7¾; gray interleaves, 5¼ x 8¼; gray boards and brown leather spine; title and "2" inked on cover label.]
Promptbook made by Charles Melville, the English prompter, and brought to America by Barry in 1854. Scenic indications, maps, cues for effects. Used by Barry in 1855, with certain alterations of Melville's arrangements which suggest influence by the Macready-Kean productions. Cast is given, with James Bennett as John.

31. [Barry]
Harvard Theatre Collection: uncatalogued
[Acting edition, no title page, 4¼ x 7⅜; brown cloth boards; title gilt on cover, "11" inked on cover label.]
Another Melville promptbook in Barry's collection. Cuts and restorations, calls, some stage business, cues for effects. Probably not used by Barry.

32. James Bennett   Pittsburgh   1855
Folger: John, 3
[French's Standard Drama, 4¼ x 7⅜; interleaves.]
Promptbook marked by T. A. Dow, the prompter, "as played by Mr. Jas. Bennett." Marked in ink through 2 acts, then pencil. Cuts, scenic indications, grooves, calls, maps, cues for effects.

33. W. H. Stephens   New York, Bowery   December 29, 1856
Harvard Theatre Collection: (Widener, 13485.40.6)
[Modern Standard Drama, 4½ x 7¾; small interleaves; brown paper under green marbled boards and blue cloth spine; title inked up cover.]
Promptbook dated 1858, but apparently taken from that of the

Brougham-Davenport revival of 1856. Cuts, calls, stage business, cues for effects.

34. J. B. Booth, Jr.   San Francisco   July 23, 1857
Folger: John, 1
[Modern Standard Drama, 1846, 4¼ x 7⅜; gray cardboard.]
Crude promptbook. Cuts, scenic indications. Clippings of play-bills for the Wallacks, the Booths with McCullough, Mrs. Julia Dean Hayne.

35. [Booth]
Folger: John, 2
[Modern Standard Drama, 1846, 4⅝ x 7½; interleaves; coarse net cloth.]
Crude promptbook. Scenic indications, some stage business, maps, cues for effects. An announcement for Agnes Booth and Joseph Wheelock.

36. Anonymous   America
Folger: John, 27, 28
[Two books. French's Standard Drama, 4¼ x 7⅜; interleaves, 9¼ x 11⅞; black cloth boards.]
Two promptbooks in the same format. The first shows only cuts. The second is systematically developed and used: specific though primitive scenic indications, large maps. At the beginning of each scene is a chart of scene, borders, wings, lights, props.

37. Charles Kean   London, Princess's   October 18, 1858
Folger: John, 6
[Kean edition, 1858, 5 x 8; interleaves, 6⅞ x 9; tan cloth boards and half brown leather; title gilt up spine, "Mr. Charles Kean/ Prompt Copy" gilt on black leather cover label.]
Final or souvenir promptbook made for Kean by T. W. Edmonds, the prompter. The text is somewhat cut from the 1846 version as provided by Ellis (see no. 27). Stage directions are slightly reduced but generally verbatim from Ellis. Fourteen watercolor scene designs for the 1858 production. (The scenes are repro-duced in Charles H. Shattuck, *William Charles Macready's "King John."*) (See nos. 43-44.)

38. [Kean]
Folger: Kean Costume Book, 49

[Scrapbook, 10¾ x 14½; green cloth boards and half green leather gilt.]

Lying loose at the front of this scrapbook is a variant watercolor scene design for Act I.

39. [Kean]

Enthoven Collection: Box DT.46

[Watercolors.]

Fourteen watercolor scene designs and 6 plates of banners and arms, mounted on large display boards. These are substantially the same as those in the Edmonds promptbook (see no. 37).

40. [Kean]

Enthoven Collection: 94G26, plates 1732-34

[Scrapbook, 15¼ x 21⅜; blue cloth boards and half blue cloth.]

Three provisional watercolor scenes for the play (the death of Arthur and 2 versions of the death of John) which differ from other representations.

41. [Kean]

Folger: Kean Costume Book, Prints and Engravings, 182

[Scrapbook, 14⅜ x 21¼; brown cloth boards and half brown leather.]

Contains 67 watercolor plates of costume designs.

42. Hermann Vezin   London, Surrey   July 13, 1859

University of Illinois: x792.9/Sh15k/no.2

[Kean edition, 5¼ x 8; interleaves, 7½ x 9⅛; red, yellow, and blue marbled boards and half brown leather, broken; title and "Hermann Vezin" gilt on red leather cover label.]

Excellent transcription of the Macready Drury Lane book (see no. 18) made for Vezin by George Ellis. Bits of Macready's text not printed by Kean are restored in longhand.

43. Charles Kean   New York, Broadway   May 3, 1865

New York Public Library: *NCP.342968

[Modern Standard Drama, 4¼ x 7; interleaves; bound with an unmarked eighteenth-century edition in blue cloth boards; title gilt on spine.]

Promptbook made during Kean's last American tour. Calls, little stage business beyond that printed (which is full and authentic), cues for effects. Cast of the Kean company. (See nos. 27, 37-41.)

44. [Kean]

New York Public Library: *NCP.343030

[French's Standard Drama, 4¼ x 6¾; interleaves; gray cloth boards; title gilt on spine.]

Promptbook. Cuts, calls, little stage business beyond that printed, cues for effects.

45. Barry Sullivan   London, Drury Lane   September 22, 1866

Shakespeare Centre Library: 50.16(1797)

[Pages 81-168 from volume III of the Robinson *Works*, 1797, 6¾ x 9⅝; interleaves; tan marbled boards and half brown leather; title gilt on black leather spine label, Sullivan's name as of Haymarket gilt on cover label.]

Partial transcription from the Phelps book (see no. 26) by "G. Hastings, 2 Grafton Street East, Fitzroy Square," made for Sullivan when he was at the Haymarket about 1852. Stage business is given, but most of the calls, maps, cues for effects are omitted.

46. Lawrence Barrett San Francisco, California Theatre April, 1875

Harvard Theatre Collection: TS.2355.52

[French's Standard Drama, 4½ x 7½; interleaves, 4½ x 9½; black leather; title and "R. J. Preston to L. P. Barrett" gilt on cover; date and place inked within on original gray paper cover; in box of gray cloth boards and half black leather; title gilt up spine.]

Sparsely and irregularly marked promptbook, with a few restorations, little stage business beyond that printed, cues for effects.

47. George B. Berrell   Cincinnati Dramatic Festival   May, 1883

University of Pennsylvania, Furness Collection: C59.Sh1KJ[a]

[French's Standard Drama, 4⅜ x 7¼; red cloth boards; title gilt up spine.]

Promptbook of George Berrell, of St. Louis, who was commissioned to prepare *King John* for the Cincinnati Dramatic Festival. Scenic indications, grooves, some stage business, cues for effects. Enclosed is an old advertisement for the Hamblin-Shaw production at the Bowery, May 17, 1849.

48. H. B. Irving   Oxford, New College   1890's

Harvard Theatre Collection: uncatalogued

[Clarendon Press edition, 4½ x 6½, printed on right-hand pages only; limp red leather; title gilt on spine.]

Irving's studybook when he played John as an undergraduate. Cast entered in pencil. Cuts on full text. Stage business penciled on facing pages.

49. Herbert Beerbohm Tree

London, Her Majesty's   September 20, 1899

Enthoven Collection: Tree, 141

[Temple edition, 1894, 4 x 5¼; red cloth boards; title gilt up spine.]

Tree's rehearsal copy for John. Cuts, stage business for various roles penciled in.

50. [Tree]

Enthoven Collection: Tree, 141

[Temple edition pasted in a workbook, 7 x 9; red marbled boards and red leather spine; title on cover label.]

Rehearsal promptbook signed by A. Wigley. Cuts, cast, much stage business, maps, cues for effects, done in pencil and red ink.

51. [Tree]

Enthoven Collection: Tree, 142

[Temple edition pasted in a workbook, 7 x 9; red marbled boards and red leather spine, much worn; cover label effaced.]

Very full and much used promptbook signed by A. Wigley and A. Coe. Cast at the front, including Ellen Terry as Constance. Cuts, copious stage business, cues for effects, done in pencil and colored inks. Packaged in 1902 and labeled "old book."

52. [Tree]

Enthoven Collection: Tree, 142

[Temple edition pasted in a workbook, 7 x 9; red marbled boards and red leather spine.]

Fully developed stage manager's book, signed by Cecil King, done in red ink. Cast at the front. Cuts blocked out in red watercolor. Copious but selective stage business, maps, cues for effects. "Tableau of Battle" is noted. Packaged in 1902 and labeled "old book."

53. [Tree]

Enthoven Collection: Tree, 141

[Temple edition pasted in a workbook, 7 x 9; red marbled boards and red leather spine.]

Fully developed stage manager's book, done in red ink. Cuts blocked out in red. Stage business copious but selective as in the preceding book, maps, cues for effects. Magna Charta tableau is noted. Typed notes of September, 1899, for corrections and improvements of performance.

54. [Tree]

Enthoven Collection: Tree, 141

[Temple edition pasted in a workbook, 6¾ x 9½; white vellum boards; title on cover label.]

Perfected stage manager's book. Cast and scene lists from printed program pasted at the front. Printed sketches of all scenes and photographs of battle tableau, Magna Charta tableau. Cuts are scissored out. Excellent groundplans in black and red ink. Stage business, cues for effects.

55. [Tree]

Enthoven Collection: Tree, 40

[Papers.]

Mimeographed plots of supers, properties, lights. Printed fly plots, 12 x 22½.

56. Robert B. Mantell
                        Chicago, Grand Opera House   November 18, 1907

Folger: John, 13

[French's Standard Drama, 4½ x 7; interleaves; limp brown leather; title, etc., gilt on cover.]

Rehearsal copy. Some cues for effects. (See no. 19.)

[ACTOR LISTS FOR FOLLOWING BOOKS ARE GIVEN IN THIS ORDER: King John, Faulconbridge, Constance.]

57. W. Bridges-Adams   Stratford-upon-Avon   July 13, 1925

Shakespeare Centre Library: 71.21/1925K

[Favourite Classics edition pasted in a workbook, 6¾ x 8⅞; blue marbled boards and blue cloth spine; title on cover and spine labels.]

Cast includes Randle Ayrton, James Dale, Florence Saunders. Costumes by Tom Heslewood. Cuts on full text, stage business, maps, cues for effects, special notes for stagehands.

58. B. Iden Payne   Stratford-upon-Avon   May 8, 1940

Shakespeare Centre Library: 71.21/1940K

[Eversley edition pasted in a workbook, 7 x 9; blue cloth boards and half black leather; title on cover and spine labels.]

Cast includes George Skillan, Baliol Holloway, Joan Sanderson. Costumes by Barbara Curtis. Cuts on full text, stage business, maps, cues for effects. Small red callbook.

59. Michael Benthall   Stratford-upon-Avon   April 15, 1948
Shakespeare Centre Library: O.S.71.21/1948K

[Temple edition pasted in a workbook, 8 x 12⅞; green cloth boards and red cloth spine; title on cover and spine labels.]

Cast includes Robert Helpmann, Anthony Quayle, Ena Burrill. Designed by Audrey Cruddas. Very full stage business keyed to text by numbers, cues for effects. Production papers include Latin lines for priests.

60. George Devine   London, Old Vic   October 27, 1953
Old Vic, Publicity Department

[New Temple edition pasted in a workbook, 8 x 10½; black ring binder.]

Cast includes Michael Hordern, Richard Burton, Fay Compton. Designed by Motley. Cuts, calls, stage business, maps, cues for effects. Many production papers including battle routines.

61. John Houseman and Jack Landau
                 Stratford, Connecticut   June 26, 1956
Festival Theatre, Production Department

[Two books. Mimeograph, 8½ x 11; interleaves; one in black cloth board ring binder, one unbound.]

Cast includes John Emery, Fritz Weaver, Mildred Dunnock. Designed by Rouben Ter-Arutunian. The first book has copious stage business, maps on mimeographed groundplans, cues for effects, property list, company lists. The second, signed by Ben Janney, has stage business and cues for effects roughly penciled; production papers much used and written upon.

62. Douglas Seale   Stratford-upon-Avon   April 16, 1957
Shakespeare Centre Library: O.S.71.21/1957K

[Temple edition pasted in a workbook, 8 x 11⅞; red cloth board spring binder; title on spine label.]

Cast includes Robert Harris, Alec Clunes, Joan Miller. Designed by Audrey Cruddas. Very full stage business, cues for effects. At the back a fight routine.

63. [Seale]   Stratford, Ontario   June 27, 1960
    Festival Theatre, Library
    [Penguin edition pasted in a workbook, 7¾ x 13⅛; blue cloth
    boards bordered in red; title pasted on cover.]
    Cast includes Douglas Rain, Christopher Plummer, Ann Casson.
    Designed by Tanya Moiseiwitsch. Calls and cues for effects.

64. Peter Potter   London, Old Vic   September 19, 1961
    Old Vic, Publicity Department
    [Temple edition pasted in a workbook, 8 x 10; gray ring binder;
    title on cover and spine labels.]
    Cast includes Maurice Denham, Paul Daneman, Maxine Audley.
    Designed by Audrey Cruddas. Cuts, stage business, maps, cues for
    effects. Production papers.

65. Other books of *King John:*
    Folger: John, 4, William Ellis and John Spelman; John, 5,
    Walter Hubbell, E. M. Post; John, 11, A. B. Lindsley, 1825-30;
    John, 15, J. Neville, TRDL; John, 19, Crom^ll Price, Crow Street,
    Dublin; John, 20, T. J. Serle, G. S. Bennett; John, 25, anonymous;
    John, 26, J. B. Roberts.

    Historical and Philosophical Society of Ohio: 812.3/R283/93,
    Alvin Read.

    Library Company of Philadelphia: OEngShak.Log2074.0.2, anon-
    ymous, Tonson edition, 1734.

    Princeton University, Seymour Collection: KJ, 3, E. L. Daven-
    port; KJ, 4, Fanny Davenport; KJ, 7, A. S. H. Murray; KJ, 8,
    Jeanne Macpherson; KJ, 9, 10, books of Chatillon and Constance.

    University of Illinois: x792.9/Sh15k/no.3, John Bignall, W. R.
    Blake, J. W. Wallack.

    University of Pennsylvania: AC85.M9415.820p.52, James Mur-
    doch, 1839, with Charles Kean as John.

King Lear

1. Joseph Ashbury   Dublin, Smock Alley   1670's
   Folger: Lear, Smock Alley
   [Pages 761-787 from a Third Folio (page 788 is first page of
   Othello), 8 x 12⅛; red marbled boards and half maroon leather;
   title gilt up spine.]
   Promptbook. Cuts and alterations. Some scenic indications, calls.
   One cue for "Drum Colours." (See G. Blakemore Evans, *Shake-
   spearean Prompt-Books*.)

2. Anonymous   1700's
   Folger: Lear, 30
   [Tonson edition, 1734, 4 x 6⅝; white paper wrapper and purple
   paper spine.]
   Preparation copy of a Shakespeare text (retaining the Fool), incompletely marked. Cuts *passim*. A few notes of stage business
   and arrangements.

3. David Garrick   London, Drury Lane   October 28, 1756
   Harvard Theatre Collection: TS.2355.60
   [Bell edition, 1773, 4⅝ x 7½; brown marbled boards and brown
   leather spine; in box of tan cloth boards and blue leather spine;
   title gilt up spine.]
   Uncompleted promptbook lightly marked through 3 acts, thought
   to be a late record of some of Garrick's preferences. Slight cuts,
   little stage business, some cues for effects especially for the storm
   scenes. Garrick's bookplate. (See G. W. Stone, *Studies in Philology*,
   XLV, 89-103; Kalman Burnim, *David Garrick, Director*, pp. 141-
   151.)

4. George Colman   London, Covent Garden   c.1768
   Shakespeare Centre Library: 50.17(1768)
   [Colman edition, London, 1768, 4⅞ x 8¼; gray and red marbled
   boards and half brown leather; title gilt up spine.]
   Neatly marked promptbook probably of Covent Garden. Scenic
   indications, calls, little stage business, cues for effects. Belonged
   to John Adolphus.

5. William Macready   London, Covent Garden   1789
   Boston Public Library: G.4012.45
   [Colman edition, London, 1768, 5½ x 8½; green marbled boards
   and yellow cloth spine; title gilt up red leather spine label.]

Crude rehearsal copy belonging to the elder Macready. Cuts and some restorations; part of Tate's ending is added. Macready played Cornwall and Edmund in various Covent Garden performances after 1789; this book is of questionable relevance, however, as the Colman version was no longer in use at Covent Garden.

6. Anonymous　　　　　　　Bath, Theatre Royal　　　　　　1790's(?)
Folger: Lear, 29
[Colman edition (no title page), 4⅝ x 7⅞; interleaves; red and blue marbled boards and brown leather spine; title and identification on cover label.]
Promptbook based on the Colman version, but with passages from the Bell(?) edition inserted on the interleaves mainly to restore the Tate love story. Calls, little stage business.

7. John Philip Kemble　　London, Drury Lane　　November 20, 1795
Garrick Club
[Kemble edition, Lowndes, 4½ x 7¼; interleaves watermarked 1794; blue cloth boards and brown leather spine; title gilt up spine.]
Study and preparation copy, marked in Kemble's hand, much used. Though lacking many prompter's cues, it is more fully marked for stage business than Kemble books of most plays. (See nos. 11, 13.)

8. [Kemble]
Folger: T.a.17
[Manuscript, 7 x 8⅞; brown leather gilt; title gilt up spine.]
Kemble's 32-page partbook for Lear, in his own hand. Dated January 21, 1788, but probably written much later.

9. William B. Wood　　Philadelphia, Chestnut Street　　c.1804
Harvard Theatre Collection: uncatalogued
[Garrick (Bathurst) edition, 1786, 4¼ x 6⅜; interleaves; green marbled boards and half brown leather.]
Crudely marked promptbook. Cuts. The Tate dialogue of Edgar and Cordelia restored after the throne scene. Calls, some cues for effects.

10. George Frederick Cooke
                    London, Covent Garden   May 21, 1807
    University of Michigan: PR.2819.A22.K32
    [Kemble edition, Lowndes, 5¼ x 8⅜; brown cloth boards; title
    gilt up spine.]
    Promptbook marked by Cooke. The dating, the inked cast on the
    page of Dramatis Personae, and the many numbered items of
    stage business at the bottoms of the pages are in Cooke's hand.
    On the title page are the words "The signature of J. P. Kemble,"
    but Kemble's hand does not appear. Later belonged to John
    Duff, who probably added most of the calls, maps, cues for
    effects, and about 1826 a cast with Edwin Forrest. Still later the
    book belonged to the Boston Museum. (See no. 14.)

11. John Philip Kemble   London, Covent Garden   February 27, 1809
    Harvard Theatre Collection: TS.2355.78
    [Kemble edition, 1808, 5 x 8¼; interleaves; red leather gilt; title
    and identification gilt on spine; in box of tan cloth boards and
    green leather spine; title gilt up spine.]
    Handsomely marked promptbook in Kemble's hand, probably
    made as a souvenir for his library rather than for use in the
    theatre. List of 32 extra characters, calls, much stage business,
    maps, cues for effects. (See nos. 7-8, 13.)

12. Thomas Jones   England
    Folger: Lear, 13
    [Kemble edition, 1808, 5⅛ x 8⅜; red marbled boards and half
    red leather gilt; title gilt up spine.]
    Rough promptbook. Some penciled stage business.

13. James Harvey   England
    Boston Public Library: G.4012.48
    [Inchbald edition, 1808, 3½ x 6⅛; gray cardboard under brown
    marbled boards and blue leather spine; title gilt on spine.]
    Promptbook "Marked from Mr. Kemble's Book," checked for
    Edmund and Lear. Conscientious transcription of most of
    Kemble's notations, badly crowded into the margins of the
    printed text. (See nos. 7-8, 11.)

14. George Frederick Cooke   New York, Park   February 20, 1811
    Harvard Theatre Collection: TS.2355.65
    [Inchbald edition, 4 x 6¼; interleaves; green cloth boards; title

gilt up spine; in box of tan cloth boards and brown leather spine; title gilt up spine.]

Promptbook of the Park Theatre marked in several hands and used for Cooke's performances in February and March, 1811. Complete cast for Cooke is entered. Cuts and restorations, calls, some stage business occasionally corrected to Cooke's practice, maps, cues for effects. (See no. 10.)

15. Brown   America   1820's

Folger: Lear, 33

[Longworth edition, New York, 1811, 3¾ x 5⅞; "No. 3" on cover.]

Crude promptbook. Calls, cues for effects. Perhaps belonged to a Shakespearean actor named Frederick Brown who was playing tragic roles in New York and Boston in the early 1820's.

16. Edmund Kean   London, Drury Lane   April 24, 1820

London Museum: Sp.822.33

[Kemble edition, 1808, 5⅛ x 8⅛; tan paper; title inked on cover; in box of green cloth boards; title gilt up spine.]

Promptbook originally checked for Cordelia and marked through the Tate happy ending. For Kean's restoration of the tragic ending, pages from another edition were pasted in. The original markings, generally derived from Kemble's (see no. 11), are in a tiny round hand at the bottoms of the pages, and some are illegible from wear. Numerous entries, including a list of extras pasted at the front, appear to be in the later hand of John Willmott. Grooves, calls, stage business, cues for effects.

17. [Kean]

Harvard Theatre Collection: TS.2355.76

[Oxberry edition, 1820, 4 x 6⅞; tan and red marbled boards and tan cloth spine; title inked up cover; in box of gray cloth boards and black leather spine; title, etc., gilt up spine.]

Transcription of the Drury Lane (Kean) promptbook of G. C. Carr, made in April, 1827, by the Glasgow prompter S. C. Ferrers. Not a very detailed book, but the inked cuts and restorations, a few bits of stage business, a map, and the cues for effects probably are Kean's. Later cuts are penciled.

18. Charles Kemble   London, Covent Garden   1820's

University of Nebraska: 822.33/T2k

[Kemble edition, 1808, 5⅛ x 8⅛; interleaves watermarked 1817; brown cloth boards; title gilt down spine.]

Transcription with some alterations of the J. P. Kemble promptbook (see no. 11) done in a neat sloping hand and initialed "GWC." At the front a list of extras. Some parts marked for lengths. Calls, grooves, 43 numbered items of stage business, maps, cues for effects. Prompter's pencilings include timings, references to Young and Kean, and a specific timing for Edmund Kean's performance at Covent Garden on March 10, 1828.

ad18. See Addenda, p. 507.

19. S. W. Kellogg   1830's(?)
    Harvard Theatre Collection: TS.2355.62
    [Acting edition, no title page, last leaves missing, 3⅝ x 5¾; interleaves; yellow paper with title and "41" inked on cover, under maroon cloth boards; title gilt up spine.]

    Crude but adequate promptbook. Calls, some stage business, cues for effects. Supers are referred to as "Soups." It has been called a "Kean" book, but it is not. Later belonged to W. Shires.

20. Anonymous   Boston, Tremont Street   1830's(?)
    Folger: Lear, 27
    [Longworth edition, 1811, 3¾ x 5⅞; interleaves; limp brown leather; title inked on cover.]

    Neatly made promptbook. Tate's scene of the ruffians sometimes pinned shut, but the happy ending retained. Calls, maps, cues for effects. Reference to Forrest in the storm scene.

21. Anonymous   1830's(?)
    New York Public Library: *NCP.164545
    [Kemble edition, 1815, 4¼ x 7⅜; black cloth boards; title gilt up spine.]

    Promptbook sparsely marked "from Oxberry's edition." Tate's ruffians are cut out, but the happy ending is retained. Checked for Edgar. Calls, some stage business, cues for effects. Belonged to George Becks.

22. J. M. Maddox   London, Princess's(?)   1830's
    London Museum: F1.SHA
    [Cumberland edition, 3¾ x 6; slips laid in; publisher's wrappers; in box of green cloth boards; title gilt up spine.]

    Lightly marked promptbook. Grooves, calls, little stage business, maps, cues for effects. The text does not include the Fool, hence is an "old" one, perhaps antedating Maddox's management of the Princess's.

23. H. C. Charnock   New York, Park   March 12, 1831
University of Pennsylvania, Furness Collection: C59.Sh1LrC
[Edition with Tate alterations, William Smith, Dublin, 1758, 3¾ x 6⅝; bound with *Life's Vagaries* and *The Iron Chest* in black cloth boards; title gilt on red spine label.]
Promptbook used for performances of Mr. Barton, whose American debut was in March, 1831. (Charnock, once an actor himself, had turned prompter.) Cuts, scenic indications, some grooves, calls, some stage business, maps, cues for effects.

24. William Elton   London, Haymarket   1833
Folger: Lear, 28
[Kemble edition, Miller, 4⅜ x 7½; interleaves; unsewn, in white paper wrapper; title inked on cover.]
Promptbook. Cast list with Elton and Miss Pelham. Calls, some stage business, cues for effects.

25. William Charles Macready
         London, Drury Lane   May 23, 1834
Victoria and Albert, Forster Library, 7919:   F.48.C.17
[Pages 3-154 of a Shakespeare edition, 4 x 6½; bound with other Macready promptbooks in green cloth boards and half tan leather; titles gilt on spine.]
A studybook or preparation copy, heavily cut, the Fool deleted. Several roles numbered for lengths. Many curious marginalia, some in Latin and Greek. (See nos. 27-29, 34, 38, 49.)

26. John G. Gilbert   Boston, Tremont Street   1835
Boston Public Library: K.47.13
[Oxberry edition, Boston, 1822, 3¾ x 5¾; publisher's wrappers; bound with other Shakespeare plays in marbled boards and maroon leather spine.]
Promptbook or rehearsal copy. Checked for Kent, Edmund, Gloster. Cuts, calls. Tragic ending restored "as acted by Mr. Forrest."

27. William Charles Macready
         London, Covent Garden   January 25, 1838
Victoria and Albert, Forster Library, 7920:   F.48.C.18

[Jennens edition, 1770, 4⅞ x 8⅛; interleaves; bound with other Macready promptbooks in green cloth boards and half tan leather; titles gilt on spine labels.]

Heavily marked and much used promptbook of Macready's production with the Fool restored, done in the hand of a copyist, with additions by Macready and Willmott, the prompter. Cast list as originally set up, but corrected. Cuts on full text, and major transpositions and alterations in longhand. Some scenic indications, grooves, calls, stage business, procession lists, maps and sketches, cues for effects, timings. Words and music of the Fool's songs bound in. (See nos. 25, 34, 38, 49.)

28. [Macready]

Folger: Lear, 5

[Jennens edition, 1770, 5 x 8; interleaves; red and yellow marbled boards and half green leather; title gilt on spine.]

Handsome transcription of Macready's promptbook very much resembling the one endorsed by E. L. Davenport in 1851 (see no. 49). This one is inscribed "to Mr. Sinclair with Annie Ness's Kindest regards" and "From him to his dear Ned"—i.e., from John Sinclair to his son-in-law Edwin Forrest (probably given in the fall of 1838). Cuts on full text. Calls, some stage business, maps, cues for effects.

29. [Macready]

Folger: Lear, 16

[Bell edition, 1773, augmented by scraps of other texts and by longhand, 3⅞ x 6⅝; interleaves, 4½ x 7⅛; cream paper; title and "Theatre Royal Covent Garden 1839" inked on cover.]

Transcription of Macready's promptbook made by John Moore in 1839 (see Moore's other copy, no. 41). Cuts and alterations, some scenic indications, grooves, calls, stage business, maps, cues for effects.

30. Mercer Hampson Simpson Birmingham, Theatre Royal 1840's

Birmingham, Shakespeare Memorial Library: B53/455730

[Cumberland edition, 3¾ x 6⅛; gray cardboard with title inked on cover; bound with other Shakespeare plays in green cloth boards.]

Promptbook made from the Tate version, roughly modernized by manuscript restoration of the Fool scenes, some of Gloster's blinding, etc. In Act V, "This, or the Scene in Tate may be played according to the judgement of the manager." Some stage business, maps, cues for effects.

31. James H. Hackett   New York, Park   September 30, 1840
Enthoven Collection
[Oxberry edition, Boston, 1822, 3¾ x 6⅛; interleaves; gray cardboard; title inked on cover.]
Promptbook marked for Hackett by "Alex MacKenzie Prompter Theatre Mobile Jany 23, 1843." Cuts and restorations. Ruffians' scene marked for performance but pinned shut, the blinding of Gloster reduced, the ending revised to make it tragic. Scenic indications, grooves, calls, some stage business, maps, cues for effects. Note of acknowledgment to Mrs. Hackett from J. W. Taverner, the elocutionist, in 1872. (See no. 38.)

32. [Hackett]
Enthoven Collection
[Manuscript, 6½ x 8; brown paper.]
Hackett's 32-page partbook for Lear, dated 1840. A few notes of stage business and some hostile comments on Forrest's playing of Lear.

33. W. H. Sedley Smith   Boston   1843
Harvard Theatre Collection: uncatalogued
[Oxberry edition, 1820, 4 x 6¾; cardboard; title, etc., inked on cover.]
Lightly marked promptbook. Calls, cues for effects. Combat routine at the back. "Bought of A. B. Sutherland, Boston, Jany. 20th, 1843."

34. William Charles Macready   c.1844
Victoria and Albert, Forster Library, 7918: F.48.C.16
[Pages 1-103 of a Shakespeare edition, 3¾ x 6½; interleaves; bound with other Macready promptbooks in green cloth boards and half tan leather; titles gilt on spine labels.]
Transcription of Macready's promptbook of 1838 (see nos. 27-29), made by a copyist, with additions by prompters but not by John Willmott. Much used. Probably Macready's touring book after 1843.

35. B. Mulford   Bristol, Theatre Royal   April 15, 1845
The Players: PB.89

[Oxberry edition, 4 x 6½; interleaves; blue marbled boards and half brown leather.]

Promptbook of B. Mulford, a Bristol prompter, marked by 2 or 3 hands. The Tate alterations largely cut: ruffians suppressed, Aranthe retained, tragic ending given in longhand. Calls, stage business, maps, cues for effects. (Compare to Forrest books, nos. 44-47, 68-72.)

36. Samuel Phelps   London, Sadler's Wells   November 5, 1845

Folger: Lear, 19

[Pages 5-111 from an eighteenth-century *Works,* 4 x 6¾; interleaves; green marbled boards and half black leather, much worn; title, Phelps's name, and "T.R.S.W." gilt on spine.]

Phelps's first, full, and much used promptbook of his restored version. Cuts on full text, the blinding scene marked with pinholes as if sometimes omitted. Grooves, calls, stage business, maps, sketches, cues for effects, timings (3:15). (See nos. 53, 74.)

37. [Phelps]

Harvard Theatre Collection: TS.2780.22

[Pages 391-471 from volume I of Knight's Pictorial Edition, 6⅛ x 10; tan paper.]

Rough preparation copy. Cuts on full text. Calls, little stage business. A Phelps cast penciled in.

38. William Charles Macready

               New York, Astor Place   September 13, 1848

Enthoven Collection (Hackett Books)

[Shakespeare edition, 2½ x 4⅞; blue interleaves, 4 x 6¼; gray marbled boards and half black leather; "Plays" gilt on spine.]

James Hackett wrote at the front in 1848, "I gave H. B. Phillips my Prompter during Macready's Engagement at the Astor Place Five dollars to make a perfect copy of Macready's Prompt Book of King Lear." Cuts on full text, major alterations in longhand. Scenic indications, grooves, calls, stage business, cues for effects. Phillips appears to have added some bits of stage business from observation. (See nos. 25, 27-29, 34, 49.)

39. C. W. Couldock   New York, Broadway   September 20, 1849

New York Public Library: *NCP.285349

[Modern Standard Drama, 4½ x 7½; interleaves, 5⅛ x 8; black cloth boards and half black leather; title gilt on cover.]

Sparsely marked but much used promptbook, checked for Edgar, signed in St. Paul, Minnesota. Calls, some stage business, maps, cues for effects.

40. James W. Wallack, Jr.   New York, Bowery   October 29, 1849
University of Illinois: x792.9/Sh15ki/no.1
[Shakespeare edition with double border lines around text and with frontispiece of Cordelia, 6½ x 10⅛; interleaves; brown marbled boards and half brown leather, spine patched with brown canvas; title and "Mr. J. W. Wallack" gilt on black leather cover label.]
Fine promptbook of a restored version. Cuts on full text. Scenic indications, calls, stage business, maps, cues for effects. Playbill of the Wallacks at the Boston Museum, 1859. Wallack's widow gave this book to William H. Young. Later belonged to Robert Mantell (see no. 101).

41. John Moore   c.1850-70's
Folger: Lear, 17
[Shakespeare edition with double border lines around text, 6½ x 10¼; interleaves; brown paper, much worn.]
John Moore's second transcription (see no. 29) of Macready's 1838 promptbook, filled out with business of J. W. Wallack, Forrest, and others. Moore has copied the 3 drawings of Macready's scenes from George Scharf's *Recollections of the Scenic Effects*, 1839, and pasted in an engraving of Forrest in the mad scene of Act IV, and part of the Bowery bill of March 28, 1850, when Moore played Gloster to Wallack's Lear. Cuts on full text, calls, stage business, maps, cues for effects.

42. [Moore]
Folger: T.b.2
[Notebook, 6⅛ x 10¼; blue boards and black cloth spine.]
Cues for the band for 48 plays, including *King Lear*. Three musical arrangements as for Eddy, Macready, and Forrest in 1867.

43. Henry Betty   c.1850
Folger: Lear, 1
[Pages 247-364 from volume VIII of Knight's Cabinet Edition, 1843, 3¼ x 5⅜; interleaves; yellow marbled boards and half brown leather; title gilt on spine.]
Much used promptbook. Cuts on full text. Calls, grooves, stage business, maps, sketches, cues for effects.

44. Edwin Forrest   New York   1850's

Folger: Lear, 6

[Oxberry edition, Boston, 1822, $3\frac{3}{4}$ x 6; blue interleaves, 5 x $7\frac{1}{2}$; blue marbled boards and maroon leather spine; title gilt on spine.]

Promptbook "Marked as played by Mr. Forrest by Geo. W. Lewis Prompter Broadway 1851" and "Marked as played by Mr. Booth & Mr. Forrest & E. Kean." Forrest's tragic ending is given in longhand at the front. Scenic indications, grooves, calls, stage business, maps, sketches, cues for effects. (See nos. 28, 68-72.)

45. [Forrest]

Folger: Lear, 8

[Oxberry edition, 1820, $4\frac{3}{8}$ x $7\frac{3}{8}$; interleaves; brown paper.]

An "old" promptbook revised to match Forrest's version: the early Edgar-Cordelia dialogue is penciled out as "in Forrest," and the happy ending, though marked for performance, has been pinned shut as if the tragic ending were to be substituted. A very full book, with calls, much stage business (some of it specifically Forrest's), maps, cues for effects. Forrest bill for the Broadway Theatre pasted on cover.

46. [Forrest]

New York Public Library: *NCP.342935

[Double-column edition of Shakespeare, $7\frac{3}{8}$ x $10\frac{3}{4}$; double interleaves; black cloth boards; title gilt on spine.]

Preparation copy of a restored version, unused, made by J. B. Wright of the Broadway Theatre in 1854. George Becks, to whom the book belonged, says that Wright made it at a time when Forrest considered staging the Fool. Cuts on full text. Scenic indications, much stage business, sketches, cues for effects. Several prints of actors in roles from various Shakespeare plays. Two clippings from the 1890's concerning Irving's and Warde's Lears.

47. [Forrest]

New York Public Library: *NCP.342941

[Cumberland edition, $3\frac{1}{2}$ x $6\frac{1}{8}$; interleaves, $4\frac{5}{8}$ x $7\frac{1}{2}$; red cloth boards; title gilt on spine.]

Book used by John Wright to prompt Forrest. The Tate alterations are much cut or supplanted in longhand, or marked "lines here by Forrest." Grooves, calls, stage business, maps and sketches, cues for effects.

48. N. B. Clarke   1850's

Harvard Theatre Collection: TS.2355.76.2

[Oxberry edition, 1822, $3\frac{1}{2}$ x $5\frac{5}{8}$; gray boards and blue cloth spine.]

Promptbook or rehearsal copy checked for Gloster, Edgar, Regan. Names of other owners or users are C. L. Stone, F. E. Davis, Stephens, and John Williams. Cuts and some stage business. Notation beside old Drury Lane (Kean) cast: "5 damned good Actors." Part of a Forrest playbill pasted at the back.

49. William Charles Macready
                  London, Haymarket   February 3, 1851

Folger: Lear, 4

[Pages 339-470 from volume VIII of a *Works*, $4\frac{7}{8}$ x $7\frac{7}{8}$; blue interleaves watermarked 1850; red marbled boards and half black leather; title gilt on spine.]

Handsome transcription of Macready's promptbook, signed "Edw$^\text{d}$. L. Davenport/Theatre Royal/Haymarket/1851." A photograph of Davenport is pasted beside his signature. Partial cast of Macready's last performance of *King Lear*. The text is close to, but not identical with, Macready's version of a dozen years earlier, and the book much resembles that which went to Edwin Forrest (see no. 28). Cuts on full text. Calls, some stage business, maps, cues for effects. In 1887 Davenport's widow gave it to an actor named Smith. (See nos. 25, 27-29, 34, 38.)

50. James Stark   New York, Astor Place   September 27, 1852

New York Public Library: *NCP+.407868

[Manuscript, 8 x $13\frac{3}{4}$; black cloth boards; title gilt on spine.]

Promptbook of Stark's arrangement of *King Lear* "without any Interpolations whatever." Cast for the Jenny Lind Theatre in San Francisco, November, 1850. Many pencilings indicate prolonged use. Scenic indications, grooves, some stage business, cues for effects. At the back are music scores for the Fool.

51. [Stark]

New York Public Library: *NCP.346656

[Manuscripts, $7\frac{3}{4}$ x $6\frac{1}{4}$; black and white marbled boards and blue cloth spine; title inked on spine.]

Collection of 26 partbooks for *King Lear*, done in various hands on various kinds of paper (watermarks of the 1850's), perhaps from several productions. Actors' names include Stark, McCullough, Mayo. George Becks's partbook for Oswald is at the front.

52. Joe Taylor

New York Public Library: *NCP.342957

[Modern Standard Library, 4½ x 7¼; interleaves, 5¾ x 7⅜; white paper under black cloth boards; title gilt on spine.]

Joe (J. B.) Taylor appears to have been a prompter. His markings drop off in the fifth act, and George Becks has completed the book. Cuts and restorations, basic stage business, maps, cues for effects.

53. Samuel Phelps   London, Sadler's Wells   1855

Shakespeare Centre Library: 50.17(1854)

[Pages 247-364 from volume III of Knight's Cabinet Edition, but issued separately as a 6d. booklet, 3⅜ x 5½; green publisher's wrappers under tan cardboard with inked title under gray cardboard with title on cover and spine labels.]

F. Haywel's promptbook of "Nov. 1855/Sadler's Wells." Shows Phelps's version when he had somewhat modified his restorations. Some scenic indications, grooves, calls, considerable stage business, maps, cues for effects, timing (3:15). (See nos. 36-37, 74.)

54. Charles Kean   London, Princess's   April 17, 1858

Harvard Theatre Collection: TS.2355.73

[Proof sheets of Kean edition, 5½ x 8¼; gray interleaves, 7⅛ x 9; gray cardboard with title and "G. E. 1858" inked on cover; in box of tan cloth boards and brown leather spine; title gilt up spine.]

The penciled workbook of George Ellis, the stage manager. Countless notes on backstage activity. Cuts, grooves, calls, stage business, maps, cues for effects, timings. Contains an 8-page callbook; a 12-page callbook with notes on costumes and properties; a set of 9 sheets of random rehearsal notes; a booklet of special cues and warnings. (See no. 90.)

55. [Kean]

Folger: Lear, 11

[Kean edition, 1858, 5⅛ x 8¼; interleaves, 6⅞ x 9; tan cloth boards and half brown leather; title gilt up spine, "Mr. Charles Kean/Prompt Copy" gilt on blue leather cover label.]

Final or souvenir promptbook made in 1859 by T. W. Edmonds, the prompter. Calls, stage business, maps, cues for effects, timings (2:45). Fine watercolor designs of the 13 scenes. Additional pencilings indicate later use.

56. [Kean]

Folger: Lear, 12

[Same format as preceding book.]

Clean second copy of Edmonds' final promptbook, but its 13 watercolor scene designs have been removed.

57. [Kean]

University of Illinois: x792.9/Sh15ki/no.2

[Kean edition, 5⅛ x 7¾; interleaves, 7½ x 9⅛; blue marbled boards and half maroon leather, much worn and broken; title and "Hermann Vezin" gilt on black leather cover label.]

Excellent transcription of the Kean promptbook made by George Ellis for Hermann Vezin. Grooves, calls, stage business, maps, sketches, cues for effects.

58. [Kean]

Enthoven Collection: DT.46

[Watercolors.]

Fine watercolor designs of 13 scenes and 10 plates of properties, mounted on large display boards.

59. [Kean]

Folger: Prints and Engravings, 51

[Watercolors, 8 x 5½, mounted in an album, 10¼ x 14⅛; gray cloth boards and half green leather gilt; "Charles Kean/Original Water Color Drawings" gilt on spine.]

Fine watercolor designs of 13 scenes.

60. [Kean]

Enthoven Collection: 94G26, plates 1705-25

[Scrapbook, 15¼ x 21⅜; blue cloth boards and half blue cloth.]

Provisional watercolor designs of 8 scenes; 13 watercolor costume plates, each containing about 6 figures.

61. [Kean]

Folger: Kean Costume Book, 49, 50

[Scrapbooks, 10¾ x 14½; green cloth boards and half green leather gilt.]

Book 49 contains a watercolor costume plate for Lear and several pages of designs and tracings by Emma Hamilton Smith probably for this production. Book 50 contains a fine sketch for the throne scene.

62. [Kean]

Folger: Kean Costume Book, Prints and Engravings, 182

[Scrapbook, 14⅜ x 21¼; brown cloth boards and half brown leather.]

Contains 62 watercolor plates of costume designs.

63. James B. Roberts   New York, Burton's   September, 1858

Folger: Lear, 23

[Kean edition, 5¼ x 8; interleaves; brown cardboard; title and "1858" inked on cover.]

Roberts' studybook. Detailed description of Charles Kean's stage business and readings. Grooves, maps. Long note on Lear's curse of Goneril. Two notes on Macready's business in first scene.

64. [Roberts]

Folger: Lear, 22

[Kean edition, 5¼ x 8; interleaves; brown and yellow marbled boards and half black leather; title gilt on spine.]

Promptbook developed by Roberts on a copy of the play given him by Kean. Cuts, calls, stage business, cues for effects. "Please return this book when play is over."

65. [Roberts]

Folger: Lear, 21

[Kean edition, 5¼ x 8; blue interleaves, 6 x 8¼; brown and yellow marbled boards and half black leather; title gilt on spine.]

Fully developed and much used promptbook, dated 1858. Cuts, grooves, stage business, maps, sketches, cues for effects. Roberts imitated Kean's staging arrangements and probably his business. Engraving of Kean's throne scene, playbills of Roberts' *Lear* at Burton's in 1858, at Walnut Street in 1858, at Metropolitan in 1863.

66. [Roberts]

Folger: Lear, 24

[Modern Standard Drama, 4⅜ x 7½; brown interleaves; gray cardboard; title inked on cover.]

Studybook, with the role of Lear marked for stresses. Some stage business, partly derived from Forrest. Maps.

67. [Roberts]

Folger: S.a.50-64

[Manuscripts, 8 x 6¼; brown paper.]

Fifteen partbooks for *King Lear,* some written by Roberts, some by O. S. Fawcett. Costume notes and names of various actors.

68. Edwin Forrest   New York   1860's

Edwin Forrest Home (On loan to the University of Pennsylvania Library, Rare Book Room.)

[Forrest edition, no. 3, 1860, 4½ x 7⅛; interleaves; red marbled boards and half black leather; title gilt up spine.]

Beautifully made promptbook done by the same hand as the *Hamlet* book at the Forrest Home, in black and red inks (see HAM, 65). Call-lists are set off on drawings of appropriate scenic objects—walls, gates, flag, serpent, spear, etc. Grooves, calls, much stage business, cues for effects. (See nos. 28, 44-47.)

69. [Forrest]

Folger: Lear, 9

[Forrest edition, no. 1, 1860, 4⅝ x 7⅞; interleaves; publisher's wrapper under ragged paper.]

Fully developed promptbook made by J. B. Wright. Grooves, calls, stage business, sketches, cues for effects. A Forrest bill for Philadelphia, March 24, 1863.

70. [Forrest]

Folger: Lear, 7

[Forrest edition, no. 3, 1860, 4½ x 7½; interleaves; green and black boards and green cloth spine; title and "Prompt/J. H. Browne" inked on cover label.]

Promptbook marked from Forrest's book by J. H. Browne, a Boston prompter, in December, 1868. Calls, stage business, maps, sketches, cues for effects. William Winter's bookplate.

71. [Forrest]

New York Public Library: *NCP.343043

[Forrest edition, 4½ x 7¼; interleaves; blue cloth boards; title gilt up spine.]

Promptbook of Forrest's Lear made by George Becks early in his own career and later augmented with many vivid details. Calls, stage business, maps, cues for effects. Remarks copied from Henry Chorley, the critic, comparing Forrest and Macready. Photograph of Becks as Oswald.

72. [Forrest]

Harvard Theatre Collection: uncatalogued

[Davidson issue of Cumberland edition, $3\frac{1}{2}$ x $5\frac{5}{8}$; interleaves; black cloth boards and black leather spine; title gilt on spine.]

Memorial reconstruction of Forrest's Lear by James Taylor. Calls, much stage business, cues for effects. Passages copied from Alger and Rees (Forrest's biographers) describing Forrest's points.

73. Frank Mayo   1860's

Museum of the City of New York: 48.194.135

[French's Standard Drama, $4\frac{3}{8}$ x $6\frac{7}{8}$; blue interleaves; brown cloth boards and half black leather; title and "Frank Mayo" gilt on cover.]

Fairly thorough promptbook. Cast for Memphis with Mayo, Mrs. Moore, Mrs. Waldron. Cuts, calls, stage business, maps, sketches, cues for effects. Some curious suggestions for stage business.

74. Samuel Phelps   London, Sadler's Wells, Drury Lane   1860-66

Folger: Lear, 20

[Pages 5-133 from volume VIII of a *Works,* $5\frac{1}{4}$ x $8\frac{1}{2}$; interleaves; gray marbled boards and half black leather; title gilt on brown leather spine label, "S. Phelps, Esq." gilt on black leather cover label.]

Handsome promptbook made in 1861 by G. H. Gates, the copyist. Cuts on full text (modified restoration: blinding scene sewn shut). Casts given for the Wells, 1860, 1861; "super plot" for Drury Lane, 1864, 1865, 1866. Contents mainly transcribed from Phelps's earlier books (see nos. 36-37, 53).

75. H. C. Davis   Nashville   1866

New York Public Library: *NCP.343418

[Pages 3-133 from volume VII of a *Works,* $5\frac{1}{2}$ x $8\frac{5}{8}$; interleaves; dark marbled boards and half black leather; title on spine label.]

Uncompleted promptbook. Cuts on full text, stage business, maps, cues for effects all carefully entered in first 2 acts and part of the third.

76. James E. Kirkwood   Rochester, New York   1870's

University of Illinois: x792.9/Sh15ki/no.4

[Lacy edition, 4 x 7; interleaves; red marbled boards and brown cloth spine, broken.]

Promptbook which first belonged to Kirkwood, who underlined

the stage business. Belonged in 1880 to Charles B. Welles. The penciled stage business and cues for effects are probably in the hand of William Farnum.

77. James Taylor   1870's(?)
Harvard Theatre Collection: (Widener, 13485.78)
[French's Standard Drama, 4½ x 7¼; yellow publisher's wrappers; bound with several other French copies in green cloth boards; title gilt up spine.]
Roughly marked studybook. Cuts and restorations, Lear's pauses marked, stage business for Gloster, Kent, and Lear, some cues for effects.

78. Hermann Vezin   1870's(?)
Folger: Lear, 37
[Reprint of the Steevens edition, 6 x 8⅞; gray interleaves; brown leather gilt; title and "M.L." gilt on spine; in carrying case of blue and white striped canvas containing also the canvas covers for 20 partbooks.]
Handsome promptbook prepared by G. Johnson Frampton, altered and corrected by its owner (Hermann Vezin or "M. L."). A sketch showing throne up center is scratched and throne at left is substituted; some of Goneril's violence during the curse is canceled; the blinding scene is pinned shut, etc. Cuts on full text, grooves, calls, much stage business, maps, sketches, cues for effects. The 20 partbooks are missing.

79. William Creswick   Newcastle-on-Tyne   November 9, 1873
Shakespeare Centre Library: 50.17(1851)
[Pages 293-374 of Pattie(?) acting edition, 3½ x 5¾; interleaves; red marbled boards and half red leather; title gilt up spine, Creswick's name (misspelled) gilt on cover label.]
Promptbook signed and dated from Newcastle: "I play'd Lear *the first time* I *ever* play'd it, in 1843, at the T. R. in this city." Creswick cast for the Surrey Theatre. Cuts and restorations, scenic indications, grooves, calls, stage business, maps, cues for effects. About a dozen sketches of scenes, the throne scene resembling that in Scharf's *Recollections of the Scenic Effects*. (See nos. 92, 94.)

80. Edwin Booth   New York, Fifth Avenue   November 16, 1875
The Players
[French issue of Lacy edition, 4 x 7¼; brown marbled boards and half maroon leather; title gilt on spine.]

Preparation copy. Cuts and alterations.

(NOTE: The books of Booth's *Lear,* made at various times over 15 years, are here listed together.)

81. [Booth]

The Players

[Pages 5-71 from a double-column pictorial edition, 6⅝ x 10¾; brown and red marbled boards and half brown leather; title gilt on spine, inked on cover label; in red leather slip-box; title gilt on spine.]

Preparation copy. Cuts on full text, scenic indications (some of them provisional), stage business, maps, sketches, cues for some effects.

82. [Booth]

The Players

[Manuscript, 7⅝ x 10⅛; brown marbled boards and half maroon leather; title gilt on spine.]

Early manuscript promptbook, much used. Calls, some stage business, cues for effects. Act V is misbound at the front. Portion of a partbook for Lear (8 x 6¼) is fastened in.

83. [Booth]

The Players

[Typescript, 8 x 10; orange marbled boards and brown leather spine; title from playbill as cover label; in red leather slip-box; title gilt on spine.]

Improved copy of the preceding book. At the front, plots of scenes and grooves, properties, cast. Calls, stage business, cues for effects. Timings for New York and Chicago, 1877. Partbook for Regan autographed by several actresses and signed "Willie Seymour Scrib."

84. [Booth]

The Players

[Booth edition, 1878, 4¾ x 6⅝; brown marbled boards and half maroon leather; title gilt on spine.]

Corrected for reprinting by William Winter. Several notations by Booth.

85. [Booth]

The Players

[Booth edition, 4⅝ x 6½; limp black leather gilt; title gilt on cover.]

Fine transcription of Booth's perfected promptbook made by J. R. Pitman as a souvenir for Russ Whytal, autographed by Booth. Scenic indications, calls, stage business, maps, cues for effects.

86. [Booth]

University of Pennsylvania, Furness Collection: C59.Sh1LrP

[Booth edition, 4⅝ x 6½; red cloth boards; title gilt on spine.]

Transcription of Booth's promptbook signed "Property of J. R. Pitman." Calls, some stage business, maps, cues for effects.

87. [Booth]

Library of Congress, Batchelder Collection: 393

[Booth edition, 4¾ x 6⅝; in box of brown leather; title gilt on red leather spine label.]

Letter of gift from William Seymour to J. D. Batchelder in 1930 attests this was Booth's promptbook during a 16-week engagement at the Boston Museum in the middle 1880's. Partly in ink, partly in pencil. Calls, some stage business, maps, cues for effects. Magazine article on the career of William Seymour enclosed.

88. Lawrence Barrett   New York, Booth's   December 4, 1876

University of Pennsylvania, Furness Collection: C59.Sh1LrB

[Clarendon edition, 4⅝ x 6½; interleaves, 5 x 8; green leather gilt; title and identification gilt on spine.]

Excellent promptbook of a spectacular production. Cuts on full text. Scenic indications, grooves, much stage business, fine maps and sketches, cues for elaborate effects.

89. [Barrett]

Harvard Theatre Collection: TS.2355.77

[Two title pages: French's Standard Drama and Forrest edition, no. 3, 1860, 4⅝ x 6½; interleaves, 6 x 7¾; maroon cloth boards and half red leather; title gilt on cover and spine; in box of gray cloth boards and red leather spine; title gilt up spine.]

The hand-drawn title page declares this to be Barrett's promptbook as taken from John McCullough's, by R. J. Preston, 1876. Most of the text is in longhand. Almost no stage business or prompter's cues or signs of use. Does not seem to derive from the McCullough book.

90. John McCullough   New York, Booth's   April 23, 1877
Harvard Theatre Collection: TS.2355.75

[Proof sheets of Kean edition, $5\frac{1}{4}$ x $7\frac{3}{4}$; double interleaves, one set blue and watermarked 1858, the other set white, $6\frac{1}{2}$ x $7\frac{7}{8}$; black leather; title and "John McCullough" gilt on cover; in box of tan cloth boards and brown leather spine; title, etc., gilt up spine.]

Very full promptbook much used by McCullough, said to have been made by Harry Edwards (see following book). It was originally marked by T. W. Edmonds, who was Kean's prompter at the Princess's. Kean's cast was inked in, and on the blue interleaves Edmonds penciled alterations, calls, stage business, maps, cues for effects. All these pencilings were erased by Edwards and redone in ink. On the white interleaves are Edwards' additional markings. (On the first blue interleaf is discernible, though erased, the original map of Kean's throne scene.) (See nos. 54-62.)

91. [McCullough]
New York Public Library: *NCP.342994

[Shakespeare edition, $4\frac{1}{4}$ x $7\frac{1}{8}$; interleaves; black cloth boards; title gilt on spine.]

Transcription of McCullough's promptbook by George Becks. Becks says that McCullough's book was made by Harry Edwards and "it is but a variation of Charles Kean's." Cuts on full text. Becks transcribed much of Kean's printed matter (Preface, scenic indications, vocabulary notes, etc.) as well as the Edwards-McCullough markings.

92. William Creswick   Sydney, Victoria   December, 1877
Shakespeare Centre Library: 50.17(1857)

[Lacy edition, 4 x $7\frac{1}{4}$; purple cloth boards and half black leather; title gilt up spine.]

Much used promptbook and rehearsal copy checked for Kent, Fool, and Edgar. List of Kent's properties. Scenic indications, grooves, stage business in abbreviated form, cues for effects. Several special warnings for stage managers. (See nos. 79, 94.)

93. W. E. Sheridan Melbourne, Theatre Royal September 25, 1882
Folger: Lear, 25

[French issue of Lacy edition, 4 x $7\frac{1}{8}$; interleaves, $6\frac{1}{4}$ x $8\frac{1}{4}$; gray marbled boards and blue cloth spine; title and identification printed on cover label.]

Well-made, much used promptbook, first marked by a professional copyist in brown ink, augmented by several hands in inks and pencils. Cuts and restorations, calls, some stage business, cues for effects.

94. William Creswick   Stratford-upon-Avon   1883

Shakespeare Centre Library: 50.17(187–)

[French issue of Lacy edition, 4 x 7¼; interleaves, 4⅝ x 7¼; purple cloth boards; title gilt on spine.]

According to notes within signed "JSW," this promptbook was used at Stratford (probably by Creswick in 1883). Calls, some stage business, cues for effects. (See nos. 79, 92.)

95. Henry Irving   London, Lyceum   November 10, 1892

Folger: Lear, 10

[Pages 319-487 from volume IX of a *Works*, 3⅞ x 6⅜; brown leather gilt; title gilt on cover and spine.]

Preparation copy. Penciled cuts.

96. [Irving]

Folger: Lear, 31

[Kean edition, 1858, 5⅛ x 8; publisher's wrappers.]

A few notes on Irving's performance by an anonymous spectator.

97. Ellen Terry   London, Lyceum   November 10, 1892

Smallhythe

[Proof copy of Irving edition, 1892, 5¼ x 8½; interleaves; maroon leather; title gilt up spine.]

Book inscribed to Miss Terry by Irving, June 21, 1892. Names of actors entered in green ink. In Act IV Miss Terry transcribes part of a letter from Irving on the effect he intended in the mad scene. Note on a visit to an insane asylum.

98. Frederick Warde   Salt Lake City   February, 1896

University of California, Los Angeles: Special collections 669, Box 1

[Edition pasted in thick workbook, 6⅜ x 8¼; brown leather; title and Warde's name gilt on cover.]

Promptbook and souvenir collection accumulated by Warde during two decades. Stage business, cues for effects. Two playbills, 7 reviews down to 1916, 33 photographs of Warde as Lear, his son as the Fool, and other actors and scenes from his productions.

99. E. H. Sothern   c.1898

Museum of the City of New York: 43.430.648

[Partly printed text and partly manuscript in a workbook, $5\frac{1}{2}$ x $8\frac{5}{8}$; limp brown leather; title on cover label.]

Preparation copy made by William Harris, who discusses the state of the text in an appendix. Signed by Sothern, as of Daly's Theatre, at the front. Interesting descriptions of scenes, including Camelot, Stonehenge. Apparently not used.

100. Julia Marlowe

Museum of the City of New York: 43.430.649

[Shakespeare edition pasted in a workbook, $5\frac{1}{4}$ x $8\frac{1}{2}$; limp brown leather; title printed on cover label.]

Incomplete preparation copy made by Julia Marlowe. Cuts and some stage business for first act.

101. Robert B. Mantell   New York, Garden   November 27, 1905

Folger: Lear, 15

[Booth edition, 1904, $4\frac{5}{8}$ x $6\frac{7}{8}$; interleaves; limp red leather, worn and broken.]

Much used promptbook. Cuts and restorations, stage business, maps, cues for effects.

102. Anonymous   October 10, 1913

Folger: Folios 2, 3

[Two books. Pages 381-486 from an edition of Shakespeare, $4\frac{3}{4}$ x $7\frac{1}{4}$; interleaves, $7\frac{7}{8}$ x $11\frac{3}{4}$; limp black cloth boards.]

Two copies of the director's book for an amateur production. Stage business given in great detail. Lear's daughters have been translated into sons named Cordelius, Godfred, Botolf.

103. Anonymous

Folger: Lear, Folio 1

[Booth edition, 1911; interleaves, $8\frac{3}{8}$ x $11\frac{7}{8}$; limp black cloth boards; title gilt on cover.]

Stage manager's book for an amateur production (see preceding book), marked with sign of the cross and "A.M.D.G." Cuts, restorations, "professional" scenic indications, maps, cues for effects.

[ACTOR LISTS FOR FOLLOWING BOOKS ARE GIVEN IN THIS ORDER: Lear, Fool, Goneril, Regan, Cordelia.]

104. W. Bridges-Adams   Stratford-upon-Avon   May 3, 1932

Shakespeare Centre Library: 71.21/1932

[Temple edition pasted in a workbook, $6\frac{7}{8}$ x 9; red cloth boards; title inked on cover; in brown paper wrapper.].

Cast includes Randle Ayrton, Geoffrey Wilkinson, Dorothy Massingham, Dorothy Francis, Hilda Coxhead. Scenic indications, considerable stage business, maps, cues for effects. The book had been used in 1924, 1931, and for the American tour of 1931-32.

105. Theodore Komisarjevsky   Stratford-upon-Avon   April 20, 1936

Shakespeare Centre Library: 71.21/1936K

[New Temple edition pasted in a workbook, 7 x 9; purple cloth boards and half black leather; title on cover and spine labels.]

Cast includes Randle Ayrton, Geoffrey Wilkinson, Barbara Couper, Buena Bent, Rosalind Iden. Unused copy of the 1936 book. Cuts on full text, a groundplan, stage business, cues for effects.

106. [Komisarjevsky]   Stratford-upon-Avon   March 30, 1937

Shakespeare Centre Library: 71.21/1937K

[Same format as preceding book.]

Cast includes Randle Ayrton, Andrew Leigh, Joyce Bland, Clare Harris, Rosalind Iden. Similar in contents to the preceding book.

107. John Gielgud   London, Old Vic   April 15, 1940

Folger: T.b.17

[Typescript, $7\frac{3}{4}$ x 10; red cloth boards; title printed on spine label.]

Unpublished study by Hallam Fordham called *Player in Action, John Gielgud as "King Lear,"* with notes by Gielgud and photographs by Edwin Smith. Cast includes John Gielgud, Stephen Haggard, Cathleen Nesbitt, Fay Compton, Jessica Tandy. Directed by Lewis Casson, assisted by Harley Granville-Barker.

108. Peter Creswell   Stratford-upon-Avon   May 2, 1943

Shakespeare Centre Library: 71.21/1943K

[Eversley edition pasted in two workbooks. Acts I-IV in book, $5\frac{7}{8}$ x $9\frac{1}{8}$; blue cloth boards and red leather spine. Act V in book, 6 x 8; red cloth boards.]

Cast includes Abraham Sofaer, Geoffrey Wincott, Patricia Jessel, Alison Pickard, Anna Konstam. Designed by Barbara Curtis and Charles Reading. Cuts on full text, some stage business, maps, cues for effects.

109. John Gielgud and Anthony Quayle
    Stratford-upon-Avon   July 18, 1950
    Shakespeare Centre Library: O.S.71.21/1950K
    [New Temple edition pasted in a workbook, 8 x 12½; red cloth
    boards; title on cover and spine labels.]
    Cast includes John Gielgud, Alan Badel, Maxine Audley, Gwen
    Ffrangcon-Davies, Peggy Ashcroft. Designed by Leslie Hurry. Cuts
    on full text. Copious stage business, maps, cues for effects.

110. John Houseman   New York, National   December 25, 1950
    New York Public Library: *NCP
    [Mimeograph, 8 x 11; black boards; title typed up spine.]
    Cast includes Louis Calhern, Norman Lloyd, Jo Van Fleet, Edith
    Atwater, Nina Foch. Designed by Ralph Alswang and Dorothy
    Jeakins. Kurt Richard's copy, checked for Oswald and Fool. Cuts,
    restorations, notations for these 2 roles. At the back many re-
    hearsal notes.

111. [Houseman]
    University of California, Los Angeles: Houseman Box 13
    [Mimeograph, 8½ x 11; black cloth board spring binder.]
    Rough production book with some working notes.

112. [Houseman]
    University of California, Los Angeles: Houseman Box 9
    [Mimeograph, 8½ x 11; blue leather; title gilt on spine; in slip-
    case of brown marbled boards.]
    Final or souvenir promptbook copiously illustrated with photo-
    graphs.

113. George Devine   Stratford-upon-Avon   July 14, 1953
    Shakespeare Centre Library: O.S.71.21/1953K
    [New Temple edition pasted in a workbook, 8 x 13; green cloth
    board spring binder; title on spine label.]
    Cast includes Michael Redgrave, Marius Goring, Joan Sanderson,
    Rachel Kempson, Yvonne Mitchell. Designed by Robert Colqu-
    houn. Cuts on full text. Copious stage business, many maps on
    mimeographed groundplans, sketches, cues for effects.

114. [Devine]   London, Palace   July 26, 1955
    Shakespeare Centre Library: O.S.71.21/1955K
    [New Temple edition pasted in a workbook, 8 x 12½; green cloth
    boards and red cloth spine; title on spine label.]

Cast includes John Gielgud, David O'Brien, Helen Cherry, Moira Lister, Peggy Ashcroft. Designed by Isamu Noguchi. Cuts on full text. Copious stage business, cues for effects. Production papers, including groundplans. This book used for London and the Continental tour.

115. Douglas Seale   London, Old Vic   February 19, 1958
Old Vic, Publicity Department
[New Temple edition pasted in a workbook, 8 x 10½; black ring binder.]
Cast includes Paul Rogers, Paul Daneman, Coral Browne, Barbara Jefford, Rosemary Webster. Designed by Leslie Hurry. Cuts, calls, stage business, maps, cues for effects. Many production papers.

116. Glen Byam Shaw   Stratford-upon-Avon   August 18, 1959
Shakespeare Centre Library: O.S.71.21/1959K
[New Temple edition pasted in a workbook, 8 x 13; blue cloth board ring binder; title on spine label.]
Cast includes Charles Laughton, Ian Holm, Stephanie Bidmead, Angela Baddeley, Zoe Caldwell. Designed by Motley. Cuts, copious stage business, maps on mimeographed groundplans, cues for effects.

117. Other books of *King Lear:*
Boston Public Library: K.47.13, no. 3, anonymous.
Brown University: Eng.P.17a, Asa Cushman.
Folger: Lear, 2, Agnes Booth; Lear, 18, Marcus Moriarty; Lear, 32, anonymous.
Harvard Theatre Collection: (Widener 13485.78), F. Chippendale.
Historical and Philosophical Society of Ohio: 812.3/R283/94, Alvin Read.
Museum of the City of New York: 32.485.175A, J. H. Ring.
The Players: MSS.97, manuscript promptbook in German.
Princeton University, Seymour Collection: KL.2, 3, 4, William Seymour, 1872.
University of Illinois: x792.9/Sh15ki/no.5, E. L. Davenport and W. H. Sedley Smith.
University of Minnesota: Z820.12/Z11, volume 12, W. S. Forrest.

Love's Labor's Lost

1. David Garrick   c.1773
   Folger: LLL, 1
   [Tonson edition, 1735, $4\frac{1}{8}$ x 7; interleaves, $6\frac{1}{4}$ x $7\frac{5}{8}$; blue-gray paper; title inked on cover.]
   Preparation copy of an operatic version arranged for Garrick about 1773 by Captain Edward Thompson, not produced. Contains 21 songs adapted from Shakespeare's lines. (See G. W. Stone, *Review of English Studies,* XV, 323-328.)

2. Elizabeth Vestris   London, Covent Garden   September 30, 1839
   Folger: LLL, 2
   [Pages 109-217 from volume III of a *Works,* $5\frac{1}{4}$ x 9; interleaves watermarked 1838; brown paper, much worn; title inked on cover.]
   Thoroughly developed promptbook mainly marked in pencil. Cuts on full text. Cast list marked for lengths, and a list of supers. Calls, considerable stage business, maps, cues for effects, timings. Description of the processions of Spring, Winter, and the Nine Worthies.

3. Samuel Phelps   London, Sadler's Wells   September 30, 1857
   Folger: LLL, 8
   [Pages 105-198 from volume III of a *Works,* 4 x $6\frac{5}{8}$; lavender interleaves watermarked 1857; white paper, much worn; title inked on cover.]
   Phelps's promptbook partly in Phelps's hand, partly by Williams, the prompter. Cuts on full text. Cast list and list of 16 supers. Calls, stage business, maps, cues for effects, timing (2:55). A formal march of all the characters at the end.

4. [Phelps]
   Shakespeare Centre Library: 50.18(1851)
   [Pages 149-244 from Knight's Cabinet Edition, 1851, $3\frac{1}{2}$ x 5; interleaves, $4\frac{5}{8}$ x $7\frac{1}{4}$; stiff paper under brown marbled boards and half brown leather; title gilt on red leather spine label.]
   Inscribed "Phelps/Marked Books." Cuts on full text. List of 16 supers. Calls, stage business, maps, cues for effects, timing (2:55). Pageant in fifth act. Belonged to William Creswick.

5. [Phelps]
   Shakespeare Centre Library: 39(183?-186?)
   [Duncombe issue of Cumberland edition, $3\frac{5}{8}$ x $5\frac{7}{8}$; interleaves,

$4\frac{1}{2}$ x $6\frac{7}{8}$; blue marbled boards and blue cloth spine; publisher's wrapper pasted on cover.]

Promptbook which belonged to Charles Flower and was probably used in the Stratford production of 1885 by Charles Bernard and Miss Alleyn; appears to be a transcription from the preceding Phelps book. Pencilings suggest further cutting.

6. Augustin Daly   New York, Fifth Avenue   February 21, 1874
   Folger: LLL, 3
   [Daly edition, 1874, $5\frac{5}{8}$ x $8\frac{3}{4}$; interleaves, 6 x 10; brown paper; title inked on cover.]
   Promptbook of John Moore, the stage manager, made on Daly's acting edition. List of property manuscripts, calls, considerable stage business, maps, cues for sounds. Nine sheets of production papers: groundplans, descriptions of scenery, property lists. Copies of playbill, advertisement, 3 reviews.

7. [Daly]
   Folger: LLL, 4, 5, 6, 7
   [Four books. Cumberland (3 copies) and Spencer (1 copy) editions; publisher's wrappers except no. 4, which is pasted in a workbook, $5\frac{1}{2}$ x $8\frac{3}{4}$.]
   Rehearsal copies for the 1874 production checked for various characters. Cuts and very little stage business.

8. [Daly]   New York, Daly's   March 28, 1891
   New York Public Library: 8*T-*NCP+.686465
   [Daly edition, 1891, $5\frac{3}{4}$ x $9\frac{1}{8}$, mounted in window pages, $9\frac{3}{4}$ x $13\frac{7}{8}$; red marbled boards and half brown leather gilt, front cover missing; title gilt on spine.]
   Souvenir album containing Daly's edition, a silk program of the opening night, a Boston playbill, several old engravings, several magazine engravings, and 25 photographs of scenes and characters in Daly's production. Belonged to Ada Rehan.

9. [Daly]
   Folger: Prints and Engravings
   [Daly edition mounted in an album, $9\frac{7}{8}$ x $13\frac{7}{8}$; red marbled boards and half brown leather gilt; title gilt on spine.]
   Souvenir album containing Daly's edition, numerous old prints and old playbills, Daly's bill for 1874, Daly's silk bill for 1891,

26 photographs of the actors, and 42 watercolor costume designs for Daly's production.

[ACTOR LISTS FOR FOLLOWING BOOKS ARE GIVEN IN THIS ORDER: Don Adriano, Biron, Rosaline, Princess.]

10. W. Bridges-Adams Stratford-upon-Avon April 23, 1934
Shakespeare Centre Library: 71.21/1934L
[Two books. Temple edition pasted in workbooks, 7 x 9; the first in blue cloth boards and red leather spine, the second in purple cloth boards and half black leather; title on spine labels.]
Cast includes Baliol Holloway, Neil Porter, Dorothy Black, Rachel Kempson. Designed by Aubrey Hammond. Considerable stage business, maps, cues for effects. The first book had been used for the 1925 production, was erased and reused; the second is a clean copy of the first.

11. Peter Brook Stratford-upon-Avon April 26, 1946
Shakespeare Centre Library: O.S.71.21/1946L
[Temple edition pasted in a workbook, 7⅝ x 10; tan marbled boards and green cloth spine; title on cover and spine labels.]
Cast includes Paul Scofield, David King-Wood, Ruth Lodge, Valerie Taylor. Designed by Reginald Leefe. Copious stage business, maps, cues for effects.

12. [Brook] April 14, 1947
Shakespeare Centre Library: O.S.71.21/1947L
[New Temple edition pasted in a workbook, 7⅞ x 12⅞; tan boards; title on cover and spine labels.]
Cast of the 1947 revival includes Paul Scofield, Lawrence Payne, Helen Burns, Veronica Turleigh. The stage business less fully but more carefully entered than in the preceding book. Cue sheet for the scene of the Nine Worthies.

13. Frith Banbury London, Old Vic October 20, 1954
Old Vic, Publicity Department
[New Temple edition pasted in a workbook, 8 x 10½; black ring binder; title on cover and spine labels.]
Cast includes Paul Rogers, John Neville, Virginia McKenna, Gwen Cherrell. Designed by Cecil Beaton. Calls, stage business, maps, cues for effects. Many production papers: cast, properties, groundplans, timings.

14. Peter Hall   Stratford-upon-Avon   July 3, 1956
    Shakespeare Centre Library: O.S.71.21/1956L

    [New Temple edition pasted in a workbook, 8 x 13; black cloth board spring binder; title on spine label.]

    Cast includes Harry Andrews, Alan Badel, Jeannette Sterke, Greta Watson. Designed by James Bailey. Copious stage business, many maps on mimeographed groundplans, cues for effects.

15. Michael Langham   Stratford, Ontario   June 21, 1961
    Festival Theatre, Library

    [Penguin edition pasted in a workbook, 7¾ x 13⅛; blue cloth boards bordered in red; title pasted on cover.]

    Cast includes Paul Scofield, John Colicos, Zoe Caldwell, Michael Learned. Designed by Tanya Moiseiwitsch. Copious stage business, maps, cues for effects.

16. Other books of *Love's Labor's Lost:*
    Brown University: Eng.P.17, Celia Logan.

Macbeth

1. Anonymous   England   c.1640

Biblioteca Universitaria, Padova

[Pages 131-151 in an unbroken First Folio, 1623, $8\frac{1}{2}$ x $12\frac{7}{8}$; brown leather, newly bound.]

Promptbook marked in the early seventeenth century. Names of several minor actors. Cuts, some properties, calls, cues for effects. (See G. Blakemore Evans, *Shakespearean Prompt-Books.*)

2. Joseph Ashbury   Dublin, Smock Alley   1670's

Folger: Mac, Smock Alley

[Pages 711-728 (last sheet missing) from a Third Folio, 1663, 8 x $12\frac{1}{8}$; red marbled boards and half brown leather gilt; title gilt up spine.]

Promptbook. Cuts, a few scenic indications, calls, cues for effects. On the first page are copied some lines from *Julius Caesar*, the preceding play in the Folio. For the last page see HAM, 1. (See G. Blakemore Evans, *Shakespearean Prompt-Books.*)

3. Anonymous   Douai   1694

Bibliothèque de Douai: MS.7.87

[Manuscript, folios 171-209 of a volume, $6\frac{3}{4}$ x $8\frac{1}{8}$; parchment.]

Manuscript version used for amateur staging at Douai. Cuts and alterations, stage business. (See G. Blakemore Evans, *Philological Quarterly*, XLI, 158-172.)

4. Edward Salmon   Edinburgh   1753

New York Public Library: NCOFp.v.156.300583B

[Cheyne edition, Edinburgh, 1753, $4\frac{3}{4}$ x 8; bound with four other promptbooks in black cloth boards; title gilt on spine.]

Lightly marked promptbook signed "Edward Salmon prompter" on the title page. Some cuts and restorations, little stage business. Belonged to William B. Wood, the Philadelphia manager.

5. [Salmon]

Shakespeare Centre Library: 50.19(1753)

[Cheyne edition, Edinburgh, 1753, $4\frac{3}{4}$ x $7\frac{3}{4}$; brown marbled paper and brown leather, much torn; title once inked on cover.]

Promptbook signed on the title page by Edward Salmon, the prompter, and identified (in pencil) as in the adaptation of J. Lee.

At the back, among various scribblings, are the names of West Digges and John Bland. On the half title, "Samuel Hindley's/ Book/1785" and "F. Faraday." Initials of a cast are entered along the Dramatis Personae. Cuts, calls, stage business for Banquo, cues for effects.

6. West Digges   Edinburgh, Concert Hall   December 26, 1757
Harvard Theatre Collection: uncatalogued
[Cheyne edition, Edinburgh, 1753, 4⅞ x 8; interleaves; brown leather gilt; title, etc., gilt on cover; in box of gray cloth boards and red leather spine; title gilt up spine.]
Promptbook signed on the title page by Edward Salmon, the prompter. Cuts, calls, some stage business, cues for effects. Belonged to West Digges (see also the preceding book). A note by T. L. Dick, 1803, tells how the book passed from Digges to a relative of the Dick family in lieu of room rent.

7. David Beatt and James Love   Edinburgh   1761
University of Pennsylvania, Furness Collection: C59.Sh1MCB
[Manuscript, 7½ x 9½; blue marbled boards and half brown leather; title gilt on spine, inked on cover.]
Handsomely written manuscript version as "Adapted to yᵉ Edinburgh Theatre." Stage directions are set into the dialogue in a bold hand. Much used, and additional directions entered in margins in a lighter hand. Complete cast. Scenic indications, grooves, stage business, cues for effects.

8. David Garrick   London, Drury Lane   c.1773
Folger: Mac, 13
[Bell edition, 1773, 3⅞ x 6½; red and blue marbled boards, very faded, and brown leather spine.]
Promptbook marked in two hands: in brown ink (said to be in the hand of William Hopkins) and in red crayon. Cuts, scenic indications, some grooves, calls, little stage business, cues for effects. A note of gift from C. Roeder to Henry Irving in 1894 asserts that the book served Garrick. Garrick did not play Macbeth as late as 1773, but the book doubtless reflects his earlier practice. (See G. W. Stone, *Studies in Philology*, XXXVIII, 625; Kalman Burnim, *David Garrick, Director*, pp. 103-126.)

9. Anonymous   Wynnstay   1784
Folger: Mac, 43

[Bell edition, 1773, 4 x 6½; interleaves; brown boards and half black leather; title gilt on spine.]

Well-developed promptbook probably of the private theatre at Wynnstay, marked in three hands: in red ink, in lead pencil repeating the red ink markings, in brown ink. Cast given in pencil. Scenic indications including names of the painters Wilkinson, Sandby, and Richards, who all had worked at Wynnstay. Cuts, some stage business, cues for effects. (See G. W. Stone, *Studies in Philology*, XXXVIII, 626-627.)

10. John Philip Kemble   London, Drury Lane   March 31, 1785
    Folger: T.a.11

    [Manuscript, 7 x 8⅞; brown leather gilt, cover detached; title gilt up spine.]

    Kemble's 36-page partbook for Macbeth, in his own hand, 796 lines. Dated from Drury Lane as above, but probably written much later. (See no. 15.)

11. John Palmer   London, Drury Lane   April 21, 1794
    Garrick Club

    [Kemble edition, 1794, 4⅞ x 8⅛; bound, together with an incomplete copy of "Macbeth Reconsidered," 1786, inscribed "From the Author to Mr. Kemble," in blue cloth boards and brown leather spine; title gilt up spine.]

    Rehearsal copy checked for Macduff, probably marked by Palmer, who played Macduff. Some stage business. Some special business and readings of Kemble and Mrs. Siddons are noted and commented on.

12. George Frederick Cooke
                        London, Covent Garden   April 22, 1807
    New York Public Library: *NCP.285342

    [Inchbald edition, 3⅞ x 6⅛; interleaves; brown cloth boards; title gilt on spine.]

    Study or rehearsal copy largely in Cooke's hand, giving detailed stage business for the scenes in which Macbeth appears. Partial cast with Cooke is given for 1806, but this is probably an error for 1807: the book was made up sometime later, perhaps for Cooke's first American performance on December 10, 1810. Belonged to J. B. Wright and George Becks.

13. Sarah Siddons
    Folger: W.a.70

[Inchbald edition, 1808, 3¾ x 6⅛; interleaves; bound with *Henry VIII* and *Winter's Tale* in brown leather gilt; "Siddons" gilt on spine.]

George Joseph Bell's copious notations of Mrs. Siddons' performance of Lady Macbeth, and a few hostile comments on Kemble's Macbeth.

14. James Grice(?)

The Players: PB.66

[Longman edition, 1794, 4⅜ x 7⅛.]

Promptbook inscribed "James Grice's Property," marked in the manner of the early nineteenth century. Some scenic indications, calls, some stage business, cues for effects.

15. Anonymous   London, Covent Garden   1820-37

Shakespeare Centre Library: 50.19(1803)

[Kemble edition, 1803, 5¼ x 8⅜; interleaves watermarked 1814, 1816; brown leather; title gilt on red leather spine label, spine stamped "TR/CG/PB/I." The spine is a replacement of the original.]

Though probably a transcription from J. P. Kemble's promptbook, it is not in his hand: perhaps marked by R. J. Collier. The signature "J. Toovey[?] Pro 1820" appears on the title page. A note by William Creswick, to whom it once belonged, identifies it as "Covent Garden Prompt Book/Used 1828." Fourteen of the lesser roles are marked for lengths. List of supers. Some scenic indications, grooves, calls, some stage business, maps, properties, cues for effects, timings (3:20). A great many dated pencilings show use from about 1824 to 1837. These include cuts and restorations, names of minor actors, calls, cues for effects, many timings. References to business of Kean, Mason, C. Hill, Meadows, Vandenhoff, C. K., etc., and especially Macready.

16. William Charles Macready

                    London, Covent Garden   June 9, 1820

Victoria and Albert, Forster Library, 7920: F.48.C.18

[Kemble edition, 1814, 4 x 7⅜; interleaves watermarked 1817, 5 x 8¼; bound with other Macready promptbooks in green cloth boards and half tan leather; titles gilt on spine labels.]

Early Macready promptbook, much used, mainly in his own hand but with prompter's additions. At the front, lists of costumes and properties and the signature "W. C. M'Cready." Grooves, calls, stage business, maps, sketches, cues for effects. (See nos. 25, 27, 43-44.)

17. H. C. Charnock   Boston   1826
University of Pennsylvania, Furness Collection: C59.Sh1MCC
[Longman edition, 1794, 4½ x 7¼; interleaves; green marbled boards and half brown leather.]
Well-marked promptbook dated 1810; a list of actors for the apparitions of Kings has been identified by A. C. Sprague with a Boston performance of 1826. Cuts and restorations, some scenic indications, grooves, calls, stage business, maps, cues for effects. A reference to Macready, whom Charnock would have seen and perhaps prompted in 1826.

18. Sol Smith   Montgomery   1830's
Folger: Mac, 39
[Oxberry edition, Boston, 1823, 3½ x 5½.]
A crude but much used promptbook. Cuts, calls, cues for effects.

19. N. M. Ludlow   Nashville   1830's
Folger: Mac, 23
[Longworth edition, New York, 1816, 3⅜ x 5⅝; interleaves; gray cardboard; title inked on cover.]
Lightly marked promptbook. Calls, stage business, cues for effects. Also used as actor's studybook, with many notations of interesting business. At the back routines for "Caldwell's fight with me" and "Pelby's fight."

20. Charles Kean   Dublin   1835
Folger: Mac, 18
[Kemble edition, 1814, 4⅛ x 7; interleaves; gray boards and half green leather, much worn; title and "Mr. C. Kean" gilt on spine.]
Promptbook made for Kean in 1835 by the prompter R. J. Collier, "TRD" (Dublin). Cuts and restorations, grooves, calls, some stage business, maps, cues for effects. Some later pencilings by George Ellis, who was Kean's stage manager in the 1850's. (See nos. 27, 48-54.)

21. [Kean]
Folger: Mac, 19
[Kemble edition, 1803, 5 x 7¾; interleaves; yellow and blue

marbled boards and half brown leather; title and "M^rC^hsKean" gilt on blue leather spine labels.]

Transcription of the preceding book made for Kean by J. Parsloe, the Drury Lane prompter, probably during Kean's engagement at Drury Lane early in 1838.

22. [Kean]

Folger: W.a.10

[Notebook of sheets watermarked 1837, $4\frac{3}{4}$ x $7\frac{3}{4}$; brown marbled boards and half brown leather gilt; "Theatrical Costumes" inked on spine label.]

Kean's touring wardrobe list for Macbeth is the tenth of 16 such lists in this book.

23. [Kean]

Folger: T.b.15

[Notebook, $7\frac{3}{4}$ x $12\frac{5}{8}$; brown marbled boards and black leather spine.]

Touring book of scene plots, property plots, text of written papers, call-lists, music cues, for many plays including *Macbeth*.

24. Stanley Charles Ferrers

Edinburgh, Theatre Royal   November, 1836

Princeton University, Seymour Collection: MAC, 9

[Cumberland edition, $3\frac{1}{2}$ x $5\frac{1}{2}$; blue cardboard and white paper spine.]

Neat though sparse promptbook marked by Ferrers, the Edinburgh stage manager and prompter, and brought by him to America. Calls, cues for effects. Variously belonged to James Gallagher, James Seymour, Barton Hill, William Seymour.

25. William Charles Macready

London, Covent Garden   November 6, 1838

Victoria and Albert, Forster Library, 7918:   F.48.C.16

[No title page, but apparently the edition of 1814 as "Revived at the Theatre Royal, Drury Lane," $4\frac{1}{4}$ x $7\frac{1}{4}$; interleaves; bound with other Macready promptbooks in green cloth boards and half tan leather; titles gilt on spine labels.]

Very much used promptbook (fouled and torn) made by a professional copyist, with additional notes by Macready and his prompters, John Willmott and George Ellis. The notes in Ellis' hand are of 1841-43 at Drury Lane. Provisional cuttings "at the pleasure of the Theatre" prove its use on tour. At the front, a list of supers. Grooves, calls, stage business, maps, sketches, cues for effects, some timings. (See nos. 16, 27, 43-44.)

26. C. Butcher   Calcutta, New Sans Souci   November 10, 1841

Folger: Mac, 44

[Englishman Press, Calcutta, $4\frac{3}{8}$ x $7\frac{1}{4}$.]

Rehearsal copy checked and marked for Malcolm. Cast list. Cues for effects.

27. William Charles Macready
                 London, Drury Lane   March 28, 1842

Folger: Mac, 20

[Hinds English stage, 1839, $4\frac{7}{8}$ x $8\frac{1}{8}$; interleaves, $7\frac{1}{4}$ x 9; white cardboard, covers loose; title inked on cover.]

Excellent transcription of Macready's Drury Lane promptbook made by George Ellis in 1846 and sent by him to Charles Kean in America. Some scenic indications with interesting carpenter's notes, calls, properties, stage business, fine maps and sketches, cues for effects. (See nos. 16, 25, 43-44.)

28. Helen Faucit   Dublin   June 6, 1842

Shakespeare Centre Library: 50.14(1815)

[Edition of 1814 as "Revived at the Theatre Royal, Drury Lane," $4\frac{1}{4}$ x $6\frac{7}{8}$; bound with 3 other plays in blue-green cloth boards.]

Fanny Kemble's rehearsal copy given by her father to Helen Faucit in 1838. Many pencilings by Miss Faucit: stresses, pauses, admonitions about the acting. Miss Faucit first played Lady Macbeth on the above date.

29. Samuel Phelps   London, Sadler's Wells   May 27, 1844

Folger: Mac, 41

[Pages 83-188 from volume IV of a *Works*, $5\frac{1}{4}$ x $7\frac{1}{2}$; gray interleaves watermarked 1845; marbled boards and half black leather, cover broken loose; title and "Mrs. Warner" gilt on spine.]

Very full, handsomely written, much used promptbook prepared for Mrs. Warner during the second season of Phelps's first production of *Macbeth*, with additional notations by Williams and other prompters. Scenic indications, grooves, calls, much stage business, maps, sketches, cues for effects, timings (3:00). One note on Modjeska, one on Edwin Booth. (See nos. 35-36, 56, 63.)

30. James H. Ring   Boston, Boston Museum   1845
Museum of the City of New York: 32.485.235
[Acting edition, $3\frac{3}{8}$ x $5\frac{5}{8}$; interleaves.]
Crude but workable promptbook from the Boston Museum
dated 1845 and 1858, checked for Third Witch and Physician.
Cues for effects. *Macbeth* was not produced at the Boston
Museum until October 14, 1850, when the Wallacks did it.

31. Henry Betty   London, Covent Garden   January 3, 1845
Folger: Mac, 3
[Cumberland edition, $3\frac{1}{2}$ x $5\frac{3}{4}$; interleaves watermarked 1841;
gray boards and green cloth spine.]
Neatly marked promptbook showing signs of use. Cuts and restorations. Scenic indications, grooves, calls, stage business, maps,
cues for effects. Dummy playbill entered at the back.

32. James Murdoch   New York, Society Library   April 18, 1845
Harvard Theatre Collection: Murdoch Collection
[Three manuscript volumes, $10\frac{3}{8}$ x $12\frac{3}{8}$; brown cloth boards;
title inked on cover labels.]
A version of the play made up in 3 books, used by Murdoch for
public readings. Written in a huge hand, about 20 lines per page.
A prefatory essay and interspersed commentary.

33. [Murdoch]   New York, Park   October, 1845
Harvard Theatre Collection: Murdoch Collection
[Oxberry edition, New York, 1829, $3\frac{1}{2}$ x $5\frac{1}{2}$; limp brown marbled
boards and brown leather spine.]
"The first book used by James E. Murdoch in studying Macbeth."

34. [Murdoch]
University of Pennsylvania: AC85.M9415.820p.53
[Modern Standard Drama, $4\frac{3}{8}$ x 7; stiff brown marbled paper
and brown leather spine.]
Studybook. A few notes on the role of Macbeth.

35. Samuel Phelps   London, Sadler's Wells   September 27, 1847
Folger: Mac, 31
[Knight's Cabinet Edition, $3\frac{3}{8}$ x $5\frac{1}{2}$, pasted in a workbook
(both sides of sheets), $6\frac{1}{2}$ x $8\frac{7}{8}$; several layers of brown paper,
much soiled and torn; title inked on cover.]
Very full, much used promptbook of Phelps's second production

of *Macbeth,* with restored text, mainly in Phelps's hand with additions by Williams, the prompter. Restored scenes later penciled out. Full cast. Cuts on full text. Scenic indications (some of them detailed), grooves, calls, stage business, maps, cues for effects, timings (3:00). (See nos. 29, 56, 63.)

36. [Phelps]

Folger: Mac, 33

[Jennens edition, 1773, 5 x 7¾; gray and blue interleaves water-marked 1846, 1847; blue marbled boards and half brown leather; title gilt on spine.]

Handsome transcription of Phelps's 1847 promptbook, apparently unused.

37. Charlotte Cushman   New York, Broadway   September 10, 1849

Library of Congress, Manuscripts Division: Cushman Box

[Modern Standard Drama, 4½ x 7⅝; blue interleaves, 6⅛ x 7¾; gray cloth boards and half green leather gilt; title gilt on cover and green spine label.]

Excellent promptbook much used in touring, made for Miss Cushman by R. J. Jones, then a New York prompter. Other prompters who signed it are John Rose of Providence in 1852 and William Mearchael of Baltimore in 1858. At the front a list of property manuscripts and a set of timings (3:00). Calls, some stage business, maps, detailed cues for effects.

38. John Moore   1850's

Folger: Mac, 28

[Pages 83-188 from volume IV of a *Works,* 5⅛ x 8; interleaves; brown paper; title inked on cover.]

Excellent and much used promptbook of the 1850's and after. Probably taken initially from the Phelps-Warner book at Sadler's Wells (see no. 29). Cuts and additions of traditional non-Shake-spearean elements tend to restore it to the Kemble version. Scenic indications, grooves, calls, stage business, cues for effects. Nota-tions of special business of Hamblin, Wallack, Forrest, Macready, Fisher, Eddy, Faucit, Montague, Cushman. List of supers at the Park. Editorial matter from Lacy's 1853 edition. News clippings about Garrick, Siddons, and Cushman, and Abraham Lincoln's letter to Hackett about Falstaff.

39. [Moore]

Folger: Mac, 27

[Eighteenth-century acting edition, 3⅞ x 6⅜; interleaves.]
Rehearsal copy checked for Rosse. Cues and lines in Moore's hand at the back.

40. [Moore]
Folger: T.b.2
[Notebook, 6⅛ x 10¼; blue boards and black cloth spine.]
Cues for the band for 48 plays, including *Macbeth*.

41. Asa Cushman   Providence   1850's
Brown University: Eng.P.17
[French's Standard Drama, 4½ x 7¼; interleaves, 6 x 8; lined paper.]
Ambitious but not quite literate promptbook finished only through 4 acts. Scenic indications ("Set Cheve Aux de Friez Walls"), grooves, calls, much stage business, good maps, cues for effects.

42. C. M. Davis   Boston, Howard Athenaeum   September, 1850
Folger: Mac, 10
[Modern Standard Drama, 4½ x 7⅛; blue interleaves, 6⅝ x 7⅛; brown leather gilt; title gilt down black leather spine label, Davis' name gilt on cover label.]
Good and much used promptbook. At the front a cast for September, 1850, with Charlotte Cushman. Restorations, calls, some stage business, maps, sketches, cues for effects. A special cue for Sullivan, another for E. Booth.

43. William Charles Macready
            London, Haymarket   October 28, 1850
Princeton University, Seymour Collection: Mac, 12
[Oxberry edition, 1821, 4¼ x 7; interleaves; marbled boards and half brown leather, broken and unsewn; title gilt on black spine label.]
Fine transcription of Macready's latest promptbook apparently made by George Hastings, the copyist, much used and augmented by E. L. Davenport, whose signature is on the title page. Davenport entered the cast for "1st night Mr. Macready's farewell engagement," when he himself played Macduff. Cuts and restorations, grooves, calls, stage business, maps, cues for effects. (See Alan S. Downer, *Quarterly Journal of Speech*, XXXIII, 172-181.) (See nos. 16, 25, 27.)

44. [Macready]

Shakespeare Centre Library: 50.19(1797)

[Pages 1-80 from volume III of the Robinson *Works*, 1797, 6¾ x 9⅝; interleaves; brown marbled boards and half brown leather; "Barry Sullivan/Theatre Royal Haymarket" gilt on red leather cover label, title gilt on black leather spine label.]

Fine transcription of Macready's latest promptbook made by George Hastings for Barry Sullivan, part of a collection gathered by Sullivan when he was at the Haymarket in 1852. The contents very similar to the preceding book. Penciled alterations by Sullivan.

45. John G. Gilbert

Philadelphia, Chestnut Street   December 1, 1851

New York Public Library: *NCP.342998

[Oxberry edition, Boston, 1823, 3¾ x 6; green cloth boards; title gilt up spine.]

Gilbert's promptbook originally checked for Macduff and dated 1827, but giving cast for 1851, when Gilbert played Macbeth with Charlotte Cushman. Calls, cues for effects. Two references to Edwin Forrest.

46. Robert Jones   Boston, Howard Athenaeum   1852

New York Public Library: *NCP.343040

[Modern Standard Drama, 4¼ x 7½; blue-gray interleaves, 5⅞ x 7⅝; black cloth boards; title gilt up spine.]

Excellent promptbook frequently verbatim with Charlotte Cushman's book (see no. 37), which Jones also prepared, and sometimes with George Lewis' and J. B. Wright's books (see nos. 47, 57). Exact scenic indications, grooves, calls, some stage business, good maps and sketches, cues for effects, timings.

47. George W. Lewis   New York, Broadway   1852

New York Public Library: *NCP.342940

[Modern Standard Drama, 4¾ x 7⅜; interleaves; black cloth boards; title gilt up spine.]

Very full and interesting promptbook, "Marked as played by Messrs. Forrest—Macready—Booth &c," and including references to Hamblin and J. W. Wallack. Scenic indications, calls, stage business, maps and sketches, cues for effects. Some elaborate effects including tableau of the murder of Duncan.

48. Charles Kean   London, Princess's   February 14, 1853

Folger: Mac, 17

[Lacy edition, 4¼ x 7½; interleaves, 7 x 8⅞; green cloth boards and half purple leather; title gilt up spine, Kean's name gilt on green leather cover label.]

The Lacy edition was made from Kean's promptbook and antedated Kean's own edition in 1853. Kean's prompter, T. W. Edmonds, used the Lacy issue to make up this promptbook on August 18, 1853. Scenic indications, grooves, list of property manuscripts, calls, much stage business, good maps, cues for effects, timings (3:00). A few penciled additions by George Ellis, the stage manager. (See nos. 20-23, 27.)

49. [Kean]

Folger: Mac, 16

[Kean edition, 1853, 5¼ x 7⅞; interleaves, 6⅞ x 8¾; tan cloth boards and half brown leather; title gilt up spine, Kean's name gilt on blue leather cover label.]

Final or souvenir promptbook made by T. W. Edmonds in 1859. Emended transcription of the 1853 book. Contains fine watercolors of the 18 scenes. At the back is the sales catalogue description of the 65-volume collection of Kean promptbooks to which this one belonged.

50. [Kean]

Folger: Mac, 21

[Same format as preceding book.]

Another copy of the Edmonds final promptbook, later used for touring. Some new cuts. Contains the 18 watercolor scene designs. Much worn, cover detached. A Memphis prompter, C. D. Lovett, signed it in 1865.

51. [Kean]

Folger: Prints and Engravings, 51

[Watercolors, 8 x 5½, mounted in an album, 10¼ x 14⅛; gray cloth boards and half green leather gilt; "Charles Kean/Original Water Color Drawings" gilt on spine.]

Contains fine watercolors of the 18 scenes.

52. [Kean]

Enthoven Collection: Box DT.47

[Watercolors mounted on large display boards.]

Twenty-three fine watercolor scene designs (compare with those in the Edmonds 1859 books) and 6 plates of properties.

53. [Kean]

Enthoven Collection: 94G26, plates 1726-31

[Scrapbook, 15¼ x 21⅜; blue cloth boards and half blue cloth.]

Six provisional watercolor scene designs.

54. [Kean]

Folger: Kean Costume Book, 181

[Scrapbook, 14⅛ x 16⅝; green cloth boards and half green leather gilt.]

Contains 19 handsome plates of costume designs (47 figures) for *Macbeth*, by "P. Bishop 1853."

55. Anonymous   England   c.1853

University of California, Los Angeles: Special Collection 714, Box 6

[Lacy edition, 4¼ x 7¼; interleaves.]

Promptbook neatly marked in ink with some penciled revisions. Some cuts, grooves, calls, some stage business, cues for effects.

56. Samuel Phelps   London, Sadler's Wells   August 27, 1853

Shakespeare Centre Library: O.S.P.50.19(1827)

[Davidson issue of Cumberland edition, 3½ x 5¾; blue interleaves; reddish marbled stiff paper; title inked on cover.]

Promptbook signed "F. Haywel/Sept. 1854" and "with Shakespearian Restorations by F. Haywell." Said to be taken from Phelps's book of that time, when Phelps had reintroduced some of the traditional non-Shakespearean elements. Rather sparsely marked. Grooves, calls, cues for effects. (See nos. 29, 35-36, 63.)

57. J. B. Wright   New York, Broadway   1854

New York Public Library: *NCP.285353

[Lacy edition (Kean cast of 1853), 4⅛ x 7⅛; interleaves, 4¾ x 7¼; black cloth boards; title gilt on spine.]

Transcription of a London promptbook, very like Macready's book as prepared by George Ellis for Charles Kean, also resembling the Phelps-Warner book (see nos. 27, 29). Belonged to Wright, but except for some pencilings not in his hand. Scenic indications, grooves, calls, stage business, maps and sketches, cues for effects.

58. [Wright]   Boston

New York Public Library: *NCP.342965

[Dolby's British Theatre, 1824, $3\frac{1}{2}$ x $5\frac{1}{2}$; interleaves, 5 x $5\frac{1}{2}$; black cloth boards; title gilt on spine.]

Promptbook resembling the preceding one but much less fully developed. Some scenic indications, calls, some stage business, maps, some cues for effects. One reference to Wallack.

59. J. B. Roberts   1855

Folger: Mac, 36

[Pages 1-70 of a Shakespeare edition, $4\frac{1}{4}$ x $6\frac{7}{8}$; blue interleaves; stiff brown paper; title, etc., inked on cover.]

Actor's studybook. The Macbeth role marked for stresses and heavily annotated for stage business and histrionic manner. Some stage business for other roles, maps. Note on Macready and the daggers. At the back a fight routine.

60. [Roberts]

Folger: Mac, 38

[Pages 171-262 from a *Works*, $6\frac{3}{8}$ x $9\frac{3}{4}$; black cloth boards and brown leather spine.]

Copy used for public readings, marked for stresses. Program for Irving and Terry in Philadelphia.

61. Alexander Burger (or Berger)   New York   1856

Folger: Mac, 15

[French's Standard Drama, $4\frac{1}{4}$ x $7\frac{1}{4}$; bound with other plays in brown marbled boards and black leather spine; Burger's name gilt on spine and cover.]

Crude promptbook, thoroughly marked but probably not used. At the front a list of properties and a drawing of the banquet scene. Cuts, calls, cues for effects.

62. William H. Stephens   1860's

Folger: Mac, 42

[Modern Standard Drama, $4\frac{1}{2}$ x $7\frac{1}{2}$; blue cardboard; title inked on cover.]

Crudely penciled promptbook, checked for Second Witch. Cues for effects. Also signed by William H. Whalley.

63. Samuel Phelps   London, Sadler's Wells   November 10, 1860
Folger: Mac, 32

[Pages 1-107 from volume VI of a *Works*, 5⅜ x 8¾; interleaves watermarked 1860; brown marbled boards and half brown leather; title gilt on spine, identifications gilt on brown leather cover label.]

Handsomely written promptbook of Phelps's later productions (after 1853) when he had reintroduced some of the traditional non-Shakespearean elements. Much used, and augmented with prompters' notations. Cuts on full text. List of supers (45) as of 1860, stage business, maps, cues for effects, timings. (See nos. 29, 35-36, 56.)

64. Edwin Booth   New York, Winter Garden   February 4, 1861
The Players

[Pages 77-177 from volume IV of a *Works*, 5⅜ x 8⅜; interleaves; green leather fold-over cover; title and Booth's name gilt on cover.]

This book is not marked, but it belongs to a set of promptbooks in similar format which Booth prepared in the 1860's. (See nos. 102-105.)

65. [Booth]
Museum of the City of New York: 35.339.28

[French's Standard Drama, 4½ x 7¼; heavy brown paper, front cover missing.]

Promptbook belonging to W. Henry Flohr, the stage manager. Cuts and restorations, scenic indications, grooves, some stage business, cues for effects. References to Booth.

66. J. C. Cowper   England   1864
Folger: Mac, 9

[Lacy edition, 1853, 4¼ x 7⅛; blue interleaves; gray cloth boards and maroon leather spine.]

Actor's studybook. The Macbeth role marked for stresses and annotated for stage business. Lists of costumes, properties, doubles (at Jersey). Five fight routines as used by Joseph Proctor, Meads, T. C. King, G. V. Brooke, Cowper. Three essays on Macbeth. Programs for 1864 and for Leeds in 1868. Review of Cowper's Macbeth from the *Liverpool Porcupine*; news note of his being cut up in *Richard III*. Vivid notes on Macready's points; notes on B. S., Charles Kean; much about Mme. Ristori's text, costume, and interpretation.

67. Frank Mayo

San Francisco, Maguire's Opera House   April 23, 1864
Museum of the City of New York: 48.194.138
[French's Standard Drama, 4⅜ x 6⅞; blue interleaves; brown cloth boards and half black leather; title and Mayo's name gilt on cover.]

Thorough promptbook in Mayo's hand with rough penciled corrections. Cuts and restorations, calls, some stage business, cues for effects. At the back a fight routine. Cast for Mayo's first performance of Macbeth at the "Triennial Centennial."

68. William Creswick   London, Drury Lane   November, 1864
Shakespeare Centre Library: 50.19(1864)
[Lacy edition, 5½ x 8½; publisher's wrappers, loosely laid into cover of purple cloth boards and half black leather; title gilt on spine.]

Studybook copiously annotated for Creswick's own business and histrionic manner. Some restorations. List of Macbeth's costumes, sketch of opening scene, notes on music, a fight routine. The cast as printed is emended to show that in November, 1864, Creswick shared the roles of Macbeth with Phelps and of Macduff with H. Marston.

69. Edwin Forrest   c.1868
Harvard Theatre Collection: 13486.12.6
[Forrest edition, no. 4, 1860, 4½ x 7⅜; interleaves; limp purple cloth boards; title gilt on cover; in box of tan cloth boards and brown leather spine; title gilt up spine.]

Fully developed promptbook by George H. Clarke, who was stage manager to Forrest in 1868-69. Calls, much stage business, maps, sketches, cues for effects. Symbolic interpretation of the apparitions.

70. [Forrest]
New York Public Library: *NCP.342970
[Forrest edition, 4⅜ x 7; interleaves; black cloth boards; title gilt up spine.]

George Becks's memorial reconstruction of Forrest's stage business and manner through 4 acts (the fifth act marked only lightly).

Grooves, calls, stage business, maps, cues for effects. Very vivid accounts of Forrest and Mme. Ponisi in major scenes.

71. Fanny Davenport   America   1870's
Harvard Theatre Collection: TS.2405.50
[French's Standard Drama pasted in a workbook, 7¾ x 10¼; red marbled boards and half black leather.]
Roughly developed promptbook marked in ink, purple pencil, lead pencil. Some scenic indications, some stage business, crude maps and sketches, some cues for effects.

72. Charles Waverly   1870's
The Players: PB.67
[French's Standard Drama, 4⅜ x 7¼; interleaves; heavy blue paper and red cloth spine.]
Rehearsal copy checked for Banquo, Rosse, Physician. Expanded into a promptbook by the addition of interleaves bearing key words to mark insertion: calls, some stage business, cues for effects. Later augmentations in ink and pencil. One reference to Wallack.

73. James E. Kirkwood   Rochester, New York   1870's
University of Illinois: x792.9/Sh15m/no.1
[French's Standard Drama, 4¼ x 7½; interleaves; green marbled boards and faded red cloth spine, broken.]
Promptbook neatly marked in brown and red ink. Cues for effects, properties plot. Toronto playbill for 1877 pasted in.

74. [Kirkwood]
University of Illinois: x792.9/Sh15m/no.2
[Lacy edition, 1865, 3¾ x 6⅝; interleaves; brown marbled boards and brown cloth spine; title inked down spine label.]
Promptbook neatly marked in brown and red ink: cues for effects. Belonged in 1880 to Charles B. Welles. Later belonged to William Farnum, who probably added the considerable penciled stage business.

75. J. R. Pitman   Boston, Boston Museum   1870
University of Pennsylvania, Furness Collection: C59.Sh1MCP
[French's Standard Drama, 4½ x 7½; interleaves, 6½ x 7¾; soft tan paper; title and identification inked on cover; in red cloth board folder; title gilt on cover.]

Carefully marked and much used promptbook. Scenic indications, grooves, calls, much stage business, maps, sketches, cues for effects.

76. Annie Clarke   Boston, Boston Museum

   Library of Congress: PR.2823.A2.F73

   [French's Standard Drama, 4½ x 7½; interleaves, 5⅛ x 8¼; brown paper, publisher's wrapper pasted on cover.]

   Transcription of the preceding book made for Miss Clarke by J. R. Pitman.

77. Anonymous

   New York Public Library: *NCP.342991

   [French's Standard Drama, 4 x 7; interleaves; green cloth boards; title gilt up spine.]

   Interesting promptbook apparently taken from one of Pitman's books. Scenic indications, grooves, much stage business, maps, some cues for effects.

78. John McCullough

          San Francisco, California Theatre   c.1873

   Harvard Theatre Collection: 13486.12.5

   [Forrest edition, no. 4, 1860, 4¼ x 7¼; interleaves; blue cloth boards; in box of gray cloth boards and black leather spine; title gilt up spine.]

   Full promptbook largely derived from Edwin Forrest's, marked in several inks and pencil, one of the hands being that of Barton Hill, acting manager at the California. Cuts, scenic indications, grooves, calls, stage business, maps, cues for effects.

79. Marcus J. Moriarty   1875

   Folger: Mac, 30

   [French's Standard Drama, 4 x 7; brown cloth boards, detached; title and Moriarty's name gilt on cover.]

   Rehearsal copy checked for Lennox and Rosse; contains Cushman bill of 1875 in which Moriarty played those roles. At the front his analysis of Macbeth's character and some historical notes; throughout notes on acting the role.

80. Mrs. James Hackett   Brooklyn   March 20, 1875

   Folger: MW, 20

   [See MWW, 18.]

Folded into James Hackett's *Merry Wives* are relics of Mrs. Hackett's first season on the stage: an Albany bill of *Medea;* an Albany review of her Lady Macbeth; her property manuscript for the first scene of Lady Macbeth.

81. Henry Irving   London, Lyceum   September 25, 1875
University of Pennsylvania, Furness Collection: C59.Sh1Mc1
[Clarendon Press edition, 1874, 4½ x 6⅝; publisher's orange covers; in slip-box of red cloth boards and red leather spine; title gilt on spine.]
Irving's studybook. Cuts on full text. Some passages marked for stresses, key words at the head of certain scenes, many notes on stage business and manner. Music cues are systematically entered, perhaps by Robert Stoepel, composer and director of the Lyceum band. Stoepel gave the book to Henry Miller, who gave it to Charles Rann Kennedy, who gave it to Dr. Furness. (See nos. 90-96.)

82. Henry Holmes   England   1880's
Enthoven Collection
[French issue of Lacy edition, 4⅛ x 7¼; publisher's wrappers under blue cardboard.]
Lightly marked promptbook. At the front a plot of the 18 scenes. Cues for effects throughout.

83. Frank Lodge   1880's
Folger: Mac, 37
[Booth-Winter edition pasted in a workbook, 4⅝ x 7½; brown leather; title pasted on cover.]
Rehearsal copy. Costume list and notes throughout about changing costume.

84. Charles Leslie Allen   1880's
Folger: Mac, 1
[Modern Standard Drama, 4 x 6¼; publisher's wrappers under brown paper.]
Rehearsal copy checked for Macbeth. Many notations of business and manner especially for Lady Macbeth. Belonged to Viola Allen.

85. Lawrence Barrett   1880's
Harvard Theatre Collection: uncatalogued
[Ten music score books, 9½ x 6¼; brown cloth boards and green cloth spine.]

Complete scores for the band for 9 plays including *Macbeth,* endorsed by musicians in many cities.

86. Tommaso Salvini   Philadelphia   April, 1880

Folger: Mac, 35

[Parallel text edition, London, 1876, 5¼ x 8¼; green publisher's wrappers.]

J. H. Ring's rehearsal copy, checked for First Murderer and Doctor. (See no. 89.)

87. J. H. Barnes and Adelaide Ristori

                    London, Drury Lane   July 3, 1882

Harvard Theatre Collection: TS.2405.50.4

[French edition, Drury Lane production of 1865, 4¼ x 7¼; gray interleaves, 6⅝ x 8¼; brown cardboard; title inked on cover; in box of tan cloth boards and brown leather spine; title gilt up spine.]

"Prompt Book of Macbeth as played at Drury Lane Theatre by me 1882. JB." Barnes was Macduff to William Rignold's Macbeth and Madame Ristori's Lady Macbeth. At the front a plot of scenes with grooves, and throughout specific scenic indications, very little stage business, maps, cues for effects.

88. George C. Miln   Brooklyn, Academy of Music   Feb. 15, 1884

Folger: Mac, 25

[Booth-Winter edition, 1878, 4½ x 6⅝; interleaves; limp brown leather; title and Miln's name gilt on cover.]

Actor's studybook. Some stage business, notes on dagger soliloquy, fight routine. Photograph of a company of men in front of a "Theatre Royal" showing posted bills of Miln's last week in *Richelieu, Macbeth,* and *Hamlet.*

89. Tommaso Salvini   London, Covent Garden   March, 1884

Folger: Mac, 26

[Clarendon Press edition, 1877, 4½ x 6⅝; brown publisher's wrappers.]

William A. Minard's "Notes made during Salvini's performance": many maps, copious notations of moves and positions of the characters. (See no. 86.)

90. Henry Irving   London, Lyceum   December 29, 1888

Folger: Mac, 48

[Pages 1-95 of a Shakespeare edition, 5 x 8¼, tipped onto pages of a workbook, 7 x 9; gray cardboard and green cloth spine.]

Extensive compilation of "Notes and Suggestions for Macbeth" assembled for Irving by Percy Fitzgerald. Copious notes on acting and production of the play gathered from study of Garrick, Siddons, Edmund Kean, Macready, Charles Kean, etc. A few pencilings by Irving. (See no. 81.)

91. [Irving]

Smallhythe

[Cassell(?) edition, 4¼ x 6⅜; thin paper interleaves; black leather.]

Very full preparation and studybook in Irving's hand. Long notes of analysis of Macbeth's character. Dozens of pencilings of stage business. Much provisional detail of scenic and stage effects, maps, sketches.

92. [Irving]

Harvard Theatre Collection: uncatalogued

[Proof copy of Irving edition, 1888, 5⅛ x 8⅛; limp red leather gilt; title gilt up spine.]

Preparation book for the whole production done in red, blue, and black pencil in Irving's hand. Synopsis of scenery, notes on lighting. Notes on stresses, pronunciation, the acting. Many notes on effects.

93. [Irving]

Harvard Theatre Collection: uncatalogued

[Irving edition, 1889, 5⅜ x 8¼.]

Lightly marked studybook. Some cuts and some stage business. Engraving of his Macbeth from *Illustrated London News,* December 15, 1875.

94. [Irving]

Folger: Mac, 14

[Irving edition, 1889, 5⅜ x 8¼; gray publisher's wrappers.]

Spectator's copy. Large number of descriptive and critical notes on Irving's performance and production, mostly hostile; some written on letterhead paper of the London *Daily News.*

95. [Irving]

Folger: Mac, Folio 1

[Huge type edition, 1890, 13 x 16; brown cloth boards.]

Special printing of the play "as arranged for the public readings of Henry Irving and Ellen Terry." Some blue-penciled cuts.

96. [Irving]

Harvard Theatre Collection: TS.10075.10F

[Huge type edition, 1890, 13¼ x 16¾; green leather gilt; title and Irving's name gilt on cover.]

Another copy of the book printed for public readings, heavily scored in blue and red crayon. Program for a reading in St. James Hall.

97. Ellen Terry   London, Lyceum   December 29, 1888

Smallhythe

[Proof copy of Irving edition, 1888, 5⅛ x 8⅛; red leather; title gilt up spine.]

Miss Terry's studybook, with dozens of notes on her own and Irving's acting, the play, the text, and the production.

98. [Terry]

Smallhythe

[Proof copy of Irving edition, 1888, 5½ x 8¼; bound with J. Comyns Carr's essay on "Macbeth and Lady Macbeth," 1889, in maroon leather, much worn; title gilt on cover.]

Study and souvenir book, heavily annotated. Analyses of characters, many details of specific business, vivid impressions of dramatic moments. Contains program of December 29, 1888, an anecdote about Kean, a lock of Irving's hair, many of Partridge's illustrations of the production, photograph of Sargent's original sketch for his portrait of her, many photographs of her as Lady Macbeth.

99. [Terry]

Smallhythe

[Irving edition, 1890, 5¼ x 8⅜; gray publisher's wrappers.]

Rehearsal copy. Several notes by Miss Terry criticizing use of music, commenting on tempo of scenes, mentioning the public readings.

100. [Terry]

British Theatre Museum

[Pamphlet, 5⅜ x 8½; blue leather; title gilt on spine.]

An essay-review of Knight's Cabinet Edition, from *Westminster Review*, August 12, 1843. This first belonged to Helen Faucit, later to Ellen Terry, later to T. H. "She told me this criticism on 'Macbeth' had influenced Irving's & her reading of the characters more than anything else. T.H." Copiously marked and annotated by Miss Terry.

101. [Terry]
Smallhythe
[Temple edition, 1914, 3⅞ x 5½; red leather; title gilt on spine.]
Personal copy. Photograph of Edith Craig dated 1919, and note by Miss Terry: "Wouldn't E. C. be a good lady Macbeth."

102. Edwin Booth   New York, Broadway   November 18, 1889
The Players
[Booth-Winter edition, 1878, 4⅝ x 6½, printed on right-hand pages only; limp black leather gilt; title gilt on cover.]
Handsome transcription of Booth's promptbook made by J. R. Pitman as a souvenir for Russ Whytal, autographed by Booth. Scenic indications, grooves, calls, stage business (some very detailed), excellent maps, cues for effects. (See nos. 64-65.)

103. [Booth]
Boston Athenaeum: $VE.S58.1911
[Pages of banquet scene pasted in a workbook, 6¾ x 8⅛; with two scenes of Modjeska's Ophelia; black leather.]
Detailed notes of Booth's business during the banquet scene by Edward Tuckerman Mason. Good map.

104. [Booth]
Folger: Mac, 5
[Booth-Winter edition, 1878, 4½ x 6½.]
Crudely developed promptbook. Some stage business, rough maps, cues for effects.

105. [Booth]
Folger: Mac, 4
[Booth-Winter edition, 1897, 4½ x 6½; maroon cloth boards; title gilt up spine.]
William Winter's copy of the edition. Engraving of Booth as Macbeth, note on the setting, picture of Cushman as Lady Mac-

beth, note on her reputed remark that Macbeth was the "ancestor of all the Bowery ruffians."

106. George Becks   1890's
Folger: S.b.19
[Alden's Ideal edition, 4¼ x 7¼; interleaves, 7⅞ x 9⅞; also much manuscript matter; in 4 red cloth board folders contained in red cloth board slip-box, 8¾ x 10⅞; title gilt on brown leather spine label.]

Becks's compilation of *Macbeth* material for his projected but unpublished *The Actor's Shakespeare*, apparently complete. In folder 1, plots of scenes, properties, and costumes, notes on music, and the promptbook: traditional non-Shakespearean elements restored to the text, coventional nineteenth-century scenery and effects; stage business derived from Kemble, Siddons, Macready, Phelps, Forrest, Warner, C. Kean, Murdoch, Cushman, Glyn, Hamblin, Wallack, Lander, Ponisi, E. Booth, Modjeska, Irving, Terry, and others. In folder 2, music scores. In folder 3, hundreds of pages of transcribed and printed matter concerning the interpretation of the play and its characters; its stage history. In folder 4, engravings of actors and a bundle of notes on the text.

107. William Harris   c.1900
Harvard Theatre Collection: uncatalogued
[Partly manuscript and partly printed pages pasted in a workbook; black cloth boards and half red leather, 8¼ x 10½; title printed on cover label.]

Incomplete and unused preparation copy put together by an old stager (Harris died in 1916 at the age of 93). The first 3 acts (dialogue, directions, maps) are almost entirely in longhand; the last 2 acts use more printed pages. Some vivid effects.

108. Hallam Bosworth   c.1900
New York Public Library: *NCP.52x296
[American Academy of Dramatic Arts edition, 1901, 5¾ x 8⅛; interleaves, 6½ x 8¼; black boards; title gilt up spine.]

Promptbook made up by transcribing traditional stage arrangements and business from many sources: from George Becks's memorial book of Edwin Forrest, from George Lewis' book, from records of Siddons, Cushman, Edwin Booth, Salvini, Ellen Terry, etc.

109. Minnie Maddern Fiske   c.1903
     Folger: S.b.137
     [Shakespeare text pasted on stiff sheets, 8⅞ x 11⅞; not bound
     but tied between brown marbled boards.]
     Preparation book which William Winter undertook for Mrs. Fiske
     but did not complete. Statement of his principles in a long
     Preface. Scenery described for the first 3 acts. Printed articles on
     Phelps's restorations, Locke's music, Mrs. Siddons' farewell per-
     formance.

110. Anonymous   c.1905
     Folger: Mac, 8
     [American Academy of Dramatic Arts edition, 1901, decayed
     sheets mounted on gauze; in box of blue boards, 6⅜ x 8⅜.]
     Penciled preparation copy badly disintegrated but carefully re-
     stored. Cuts, grooves, some cues for effects.

111. Robert B. Mantell   New York, Garden   November 13, 1905
     Folger: Mac, 24
     [American Academy of Dramatic Arts edition, 5¾ x 8¾; inter-
     leaves; limp red leather.]
     Much used promptbook done in several colors of ink and pencil.
     Cuts and restorations. At the front a plot of scenes. Some stage
     business added to that already printed, cues for effects, fight
     routine. Sketches of Macbeth's headdress.

112. Tyrone Power   Philadelphia   October 17, 1907
     Folger: Mac, 34
     [Elizabethan Shakespeare edition, 1903, 6¾ x 9½; publisher's
     red cloth boards; title gilt on spine.]
     Preparation copy dated as above; in 1916 given to William
     Winter. Copiously annotated in margins, on endpapers, and on
     scraps of hotel stationery. Long notes on interpretation of the
     play, some scenic notes with sketches and a watercolor, stage
     business, maps, notes on effects, a fight routine. Contains a 1915
     letter from Power to Winter on the "beastly & ridiculous" *Mid-
     summer Night's Dream* of Granville-Barker.

113. E. H. Sothern and Julia Marlowe
                           New Haven   November 10, 1910
     Museum of the City of New York: 43.430.654

[Temple edition pasted in a workbook, 6 x 9½; black leather ring binder.]

Preparation copy for the 1910 production. Marked for stresses. Notes on the text and on the play. Much stage business.

114. [Sothern and Marlowe]

Museum of the City of New York: 43.430.655

[Rolfe edition, 1903, 4⅝ x 6⅜; limp green leather gilt; title gilt on spine.]

Preparation copy copiously annotated, much of it verbatim from the preceding book.

115. [Sothern and Marlowe]

Folger: Mac, Folio 8

[Shakespeare text pasted on pages of a workbook, 8 x 10½; black boards.]

Preparation copy of Frederick Kaufman, general stage manager: "The rough copy which I compiled and from which the newer copy was made." Cast list, plots of scenery and properties, much stage business, maps, cues for effects.

116. [Sothern and Marlowe]

Folger: Mac, Folios 3, 4, 5, 6, 7

[Five books. Typescript, 8½ x 11; brown paper.]

Five clean copies (unused carbons) apparently containing all the matter in the preceding book.

117. [Sothern and Marlowe]

The Players: TS.118A

[Typescript, 8 x 10½; the 6 acts separately bound in blue covers.]

In this typing there is relatively little stage business.

118. [Sothern and Marlowe]

The Players: TS.118B, C

[Two books. Typescript, 8 x 10½; B in manila wrapper, C in limp leather.]

Later version than the preceding book. Very full stage business and cues for effects. Copy C lacks ending. Copy B much used as a promptbook: penciled maps give names of many of the minor actors.

119. [Sothern and Marlowe]
    New York Public Library: *NCP.276569B
    [Carbon typescript, 8 x 10½; the 6 acts separately bound in green paper; all in brown manila folder.]
    Much used promptbook. Text is marked for stresses. Stage directions underlined in red. Much stage business and many notes on scenic arrangements added in pencil and red ink.

120. [Sothern and Marlowe]
    Folger: Mac, Folio 2
    [Pages 424-480 of a *Works* pasted in a workbook, 7½ x 9½; black boards.]
    Promptbook record of the production made by the actor Lark Taylor, who played various small roles. Cuts on full text. Record of variation of cuts. Detailed notes of scenery and stage business, with maps and sketches. Cast list. Anecdotes from the history of the production.

121. [Sothern and Marlowe]
    W. A. Clark Library, Los Angeles
    [Acting edition, 4¾ x 7⅛; interleaves; brown cloth boards; title gilt on spine.]
    Promptbook record made by Lark Taylor "with all the cuts . . . used by them in their first production of the play." Cast as of 1911. Copious stage business, groundplans, notes on lighting and special effects, anecdotes.

122. Herbert Beerbohm Tree
                    London, Her Majesty's   September 5, 1911
    Enthoven Collection: Tree, 160
    [Shakespeare text pasted in a workbook, 6⅞ x 8¾; red marbled boards and half black leather, much worn and loose.]
    Rehearsal promptbook, roughly penciled, much used, signed by Cecil King. Cuts, much stage business, maps, cues for effects.

123. [Tree]
    Enthoven Collection: Tree, 250
    [Cassell's National Library edition pasted in a workbook, 7 x 9; red marbled boards and blue cloth spine, much worn.]
    Promptbook roughly penciled, much used. Groundplans, stage business essential to stage management, maps, cues for effects carefully entered and boxed.

124. [Tree]

Enthoven Collection: Tree, 160

[Seven books. Eversley, 1911; Macmillan, 1908; Favourite Classics, 1904.]

Rehearsal copies with cuts and random stage business for various characters.

125. [Tree]

Enthoven Collection: Tree, 160

[Papers.]

Actor lists, plots of properties, scenes and lights, 6 groundplans, rehearsal notes, etc.

126. F. R. Benson   1917-18

Shakespeare Centre Library: 72.919BEN

[French acting edition pasted in a workbook, 7 x 9; bound with *Don Caesar de Bazan* in red marbled boards and black cloth spine; title inked on cover and spine labels.]

Promptbook "Probably used 1917-18 on 14 week tour of army camps with twice nightly Shakespeare." Cuts and restorations. Scenic indications, calls, maps, cues for effects. Stage business usually entered only as "Business."

127. [Benson]

Shakespeare Centre Library

[Cassell's National Library edition (mainly) pasted in a workbook, 8 x 10; blue cloth and half black leather, worn and broken.]

Promptbook marked by several hands, owned by Dennis Roberts, the stage manager, used from early in the century down to at least 1923. Program for March 16 pasted in. Scenic indications, calls, much stage business, cues for effects, list of properties, timings for several towns. This book is on loan to the library from Mr. and Mrs. Dennis Roberts of Shottery.

128. Lena Ashwell   London   1919-29

Birmingham, Shakespeare Memorial Library: 370/421202

[Temple edition pasted in a workbook, 6½ x 8; tan marbled boards and black cloth spine; title gilt up spine.]

Promptbook of the Lena Ashwell Players. Careful groundplans, some stage business, maps.

129. James K. Hackett   London, Aldwych   November 2, 1920

Folger: Mac, 11, 12

[Two books. Brandes edition, 1912, 3⅝ x 5⅝; publisher's green cloth boards. Rolfe edition, 1905, 4⅝ x 6¼; green limp leather gilt.]
The first is a rough preparation copy for the production with Mrs. Patrick Campbell. Severe cuts, some stage business, cues for effects. The other is a rehearsal copy.

130. [Hackett]
Princeton University, Seymour Collection: MAC, 13B
[Rolfe edition pasted in a workbook, 8 x 13.]
Preparation copy labeled on the cover "James K. Hackett's original prompt copy" and dated 1914. A typed note at the back declares that "whatever ideas of value may be contained in these notes . . . are my own, absolutely," and this is attested by 2 witnesses. Some scenic indications and many notes on mood and motivation. Later belonged to and probably used by George Tyler (see nos. 133-136).

131. Henry Jewett   Boston, Boston Repertory   March 7, 1927
Folger: Mac, Folio 9
[Typescript, 8½ x 11; gray cardboard and green cloth spine.]
Much used promptbook. Explanatory footnotes, stage business, maps, cues for effects. News clipping celebrating the 14-year history of the Jewett Company and their fourth anniversary in the new theatre, photograph of Frances Jewett, *Macbeth* program for 1927 with photograph of Henry Jewett, program for Providence.

[ACTOR LISTS FOR FOLLOWING BOOKS ARE GIVEN IN THIS ORDER: Macbeth, Lady Macbeth, Macduff, Banquo.]

132. Barry Jackson   London, Royal Court   February 6, 1928
British Drama League
[Shakespeare edition pasted in a workbook, 7 x 9; green cloth boards and red cloth spine.]
Promptbook of Matthew Forsyth, the stage manager for Jackson's modern-dress *Macbeth*, which originated at the Birmingham Repertory Theatre. Cast includes Eric Maturin, Mary Merrall, Scott Sunderland, Marshall Sheppard. Cuts on full text. Copious stage business, maps. Production papers at the back include calls, plot of scenes and costumes, etc. Program for the Royal Court.

133. George C. Tyler   New York, Knickerbocker   November 19, 1928
New York Public Library: *NCP.920354A

[Shakespeare text pasted in a workbook, 6¼ x 9¼; old brown leather with remains of metal clasp; title inked on spine.]

Cast includes Lyn Harding, Florence Reed (replacing Margaret Anglin), Basil Gill, William Farnum. Designed by Gordon Craig. Fully developed promptbook: cuts, copious stage business, maps, cues for effects. (See no. 130.)

134. [Tyler]
Princeton University, Seymour Collection: MAC, 13

[Temple edition (with some French's Standard Drama) pasted in a workbook, 6¾ x 8⅞; blue-green boards and black cloth spine.]

Promptbook and preparation copy. "Used for making Tyler's prod. 1928-29. See also Hackett's." Considerable cuts, scenic indications, much stage business, cues for effects. Signed by E. M. Beckley, 25 Wimpole St.

135. [Tyler]
Princeton University, Seymour Collection: MAC

[Booth-Winter edition pasted in a workbook, 7¾ x 10¼; yellow cover; title and Tyler's name on cover.]

Promptbook. Scenic indications, stage business, cues for effects.

136. [Tyler]
Princeton University, Seymour Collection: MAC, 13C

[Shakespeare edition pasted in a workbook, 7 x 12; cloth boards; "RECORD" embossed on cover.]

Promptbook. Much stage business, cues for effects. At the front a list of scenes, and printed casts for Drury Lane and Covent Garden in 1823, Paris in 1847.

137. Theodore Komisarjevsky   Stratford-upon-Avon   April 18, 1933
Shakespeare Centre Library: 71.21/1933MA(6056,7935)

[Two books. Temple edition pasted in workbooks, 7 x 9; purple cloth boards and half black leather; title on spine label.]

Cast includes George Hayes, Fabia Drake, Anew McMaster, R. Eric Lee. The first book has cuts on full text, stage business, maps, cues for effects, but has mostly been erased; contains production papers. The second is a clean unused copy lacking only some of the cues for effects.

138. Philip Merivale   New York, Ethel Barrymore   October 7, 1935
New York Public Library: *NCP.328671B
[Carbon typescript, 8½ x 11; black cloth boards; title gilt up spine.]
Cast includes Philip Merivale, Gladys Cooper, Kenneth Mac-Kenna, Charles Francis. Staged by Henry Herbert. Designed by P. Dodd Ackerman and Charles Falls. Copy used in stage arrangement, copiously marked for effects. Some stage business is in the typed text.

139. [Merivale]
New York Public Library: *NCP+.899318A
[Carbon typescript, 8¼ x 10¾; blue cloth boards; title gilt up spine.]
Alexandra Carlisle's copy of the preceding book. A few pencilings.

140. Orson Welles   New York, Lafayette   April 14, 1936
New York Public Library: *NCP+.978746A
[Mimeograph, 8 x 11; brown cloth boards; title gilt up spine.]
Complete working script of the WPA Negro version, "Conceived * Arranged * Staged by Orson Welles." Cast includes Jack Carter, Edna Thomas, Maurice Ellis, Canada Lee. Designed by Nat Karson. Blueprint groundplans, 9 photographs of scenes.

141. B. Iden Payne   Stratford-upon-Avon   April 11, 1938
Shakespeare Centre Library: 71.21/1938MA
[Penguin edition pasted in a workbook, 7 x 9; purple cloth boards and half black leather; title on cover and spine labels.]
Cast includes James Dale, Phyllis Neilson-Terry, Gyles Isham, Guy Belmore. Designed by Osborne Robinson. A clean unused copy. Cuts on full text. Stage business, maps, cues for effects.

142. [Payne]   April 14, 1942
Shakespeare Centre Library: 71.21/1942MA
[Same format as preceding book.]
Cast includes George Skillan, Margaretta Scott, Duncan Yarrow, George Hayes. Designed by Osborne Robinson. The book, originally used for the 1938 production, contains the same stage business, more cues for effects.

143. Robert Atkins   Stratford-upon-Avon   April 12, 1944
Shakespeare Centre Library: 71.21/1944MA

[Temple edition pasted in a workbook, 7 x 9; blue cloth boards and half red leather; title on cover and spine labels.]

Cast includes George Hayes, Patricia Jessel, Antony Eustrel, Raymond Pollett. Designed by Guy Sheppard. The book had been used by Bridges-Adams in 1929-30, was erased and written over. Stage business, maps, cues for effects. Small blue callbook.

144. Anthony Quayle   Stratford-upon-Avon   April 16, 1949
Shakespeare Centre Library: O.S.71.21/1949MA
[Temple edition pasted in a workbook, 8 x 13; green cloth boards; title on cover and spine labels.]

Cast includes Godfrey Tearle, Diana Wynyard, Leon Quartermaine, Harry Andrews. Designed by Edward Carrick. Cuts on full text. Copious stage business, maps, cues for effects.

145. [Quayle]   Australia   November 20, 1949
Shakespeare Centre Library: O.S.71.21/1949MA
[Mimeograph, 8 x 13, in envelope.]

A 36-page radio version as performed by the Memorial Theatre Company in Australia.

146. John Gielgud   Stratford-upon-Avon   June 10, 1952
Shakespeare Centre Library: O.S.71.21/1952M
[New Temple edition pasted in a workbook, 8 x 13; black cloth board spring binder; title on spine label.]

Cast includes Ralph Richardson, Margaret Leighton, Jack Gwillim, Raymond Westwell. Designed by Michael Northen and Kenneth Rowell. Cuts on full text. Copious stage business, cues for effects.

147. Glen Byam Shaw   Stratford-upon-Avon   June 7, 1955
Shakespeare Centre Library: O.S.71.21/1955M
[New Temple edition pasted in a workbook, 8 x 13; black cloth board spring binder; title gilt on cover, inked on spine label.]

Cast includes Laurence Olivier, Vivien Leigh, Keith Michell, Ralph Michael. Designed by Roger Furse. Very full stage business, maps on mimeographed groundplans, cues for effects. Production papers include fight routines.

148. Douglas Seale   London, Old Vic   December 17, 1958
Old Vic, Publicity Department
[New Temple edition pasted in a workbook, 8 x 10; blue ring binder.]

Cast includes Michael Hordern, Beatrix Lehmann, John Phillips, Jack May. Designed by Desmond Heeley. Cuts, calls, stage business, maps, cues for effects. Production papers.

149. Jack Landau   Stratford, Connecticut   June 18, 1961
Festival Theatre, Production Department
[Mimeograph, 8½ x 11; interleaves; blue cloth board ring binder.]
Cast includes Pat Hingle, Jessica Tandy, Richard Waring, Donald Harron. Designed by Robert O'Hearn and Motley. Copious stage business, maps. Production papers include company lists, property list, large blueprint of stage.

150. Other books of *Macbeth:*
Brown University: Eng.P.17, Asa Cushman, 1852.
Connecticut State Library: William Gillette.
Folger: Mac, 2, Gorman T. Bell; Mac, 6, E. W. Boyle; Mac, 7, Sedley Brown, 1877; Mac, 22, James Lewis; Mac, 40, Felix A. Vincent, 1853-55; Mac, 45, 46, 47, anonymous.
Historical and Philosophical Society of Ohio: 812.3/R283/112, Alvin Read.
Princeton University, Seymour Collection: MAC, 1, William Seymour and Angela Sefton; MAC, 10, T. H. Evans, Boston Museum; MAC, 11, P. E. Sullivan; MAC, 25, anonymous.
Rutgers University: PR.1243.SHA, Barry Sullivan, April 7, 1860.

Measure for Measure

1. Anonymous   England   c.1640
Biblioteca Universitaria, Padova
[Pages 61-84 in an unbroken First Folio, 1623, 8½ x 12⅞; brown leather, newly bound.]
Promptbook marked in the early seventeenth century. Cuts, calls, some cues for effects. (See G. Blakemore Evans, *Shakespearean Prompt-Books*.)

2. Thomas Betterton   London, Lincoln's Inn Fields   1704
Folger: Measure, 2
[Gildon version, 1700, 6⅜ x 8; gray cardboard under blue paper.]
Promptbook of Charles Gildon's operatic version subtitled *Beauty the Best Advocate*, in the hand of John Downes, the prompter. Calls with names of actors and cues for music, badly cropped.

3. Anonymous   Covent Garden   c.1780
New York Public Library: *NCP.285347
[Bell edition, 1773, 4¼ x 6¾; black cloth boards; title gilt up spine.]
Promptbook lightly marked in a flowing hand. Some restorations, list of property manuscripts, scenic indications (including "Dall's Hall," "Dall's Town," "Perseus' Town"), calls.

4. John Philip Kemble   London, Drury Lane   December 30, 1794
Folger: T.a.35
[Manuscript, 7 x 8⅞; brown leather gilt; title gilt up spine.]
Kemble's 38-page partbook for Vincentio, in his own hand, 826 lines. Dated from Drury Lane as above but probably written long afterwards.

5. [Kemble]   London, Covent Garden   October 30, 1811
Garrick Club
[Kemble edition, 1803, 5 x 8¼; interleaves watermarked 1807; blue cloth boards and brown leather spine; title gilt up spine.]
Promptbook marked by Kemble. List of supers, properties list, grooves, calls, some stage business, maps, timing (2:56).

6. [Kemble]   November 21, 1815
The Players
[Kemble edition, Lowndes, n.d., 4¾ x 7⅞; red and green marbled boards and brown leather spine.]

Transcription of Kemble's promptbook in two or more hands. On the title page marked "Theatre Royal/Drury Lane"; on the page of Dramatis Personae marked "Theatre Royal, Covent Garden/ By Command of their Majes/Monday Evening, November 21st/ 1815." Two Kemble casts. Cuts, property list, calls, some stage business, some cues for effects. Earlier markings are in a neat round hand, later ones in a rough hand. Given to Edwin Booth by E. S. Conner.

7. Anonymous   London, Drury Lane   c.1824
University of Nebraska: 822.33/Ulk
[Kemble edition, 1803, 4¾ x 7⅞; interleaves; black cloth boards; title gilt down spine, attributed to Covent Garden.]
Promptbook neatly but lightly marked in same hand as CE, 9. Calls, little stage business, some maps, procession list for Act V, some timings. No sign of use.

8. Samuel Phelps London, Sadler's Wells November 4, 1846
Folger: Measure, 3
[Cumberland edition, 3¾ x 5⅞, with pages from some other edition; interleaves, 4¼ x 7⅜; paper, much worn; title and identification inked on cover.]
Much used promptbook in the rough hand of Williams, the prompter. Cuts and many restorations. Grooves, calls, stage business, maps, cues for effects, timing.

9. [Phelps]
Shakespeare Centre Library: 50.20(18—)
[Pages 257-394 from volume II of a *Works,* 4 x 6¼; interleaves; blue-green marbled boards and half red leather; title gilt on spine.]
Very neatly marked, unused promptbook owned by William Creswick, thought to be a transcription from the Sadler's Wells book. Cuts on full text. Scenic indications, grooves, calls, stage business, maps, sketches, cues for effects, timing (2:35).

10. Henry Betty
Folger: Measure, 1
[Pages 287-380 from volume III of Knight's Cabinet Edition, 1843, 3⅜ x 5½; green publisher's wrappers.]
Uncompleted, unused promptbook. Cuts and transpositions marked on full text. Calls.

11. Thomas Barry   Boston, Boston Theatre   1854
Harvard Theatre Collection: uncatalogued
[Oxberry edition, 1822, $4\frac{1}{8}$ x $6\frac{7}{8}$; bound with *Twelfth Night* in brown boards and half brown leather; title and "37-38" inked on cover labels.]
Promptbook signed by Charles Melville, the English prompter, and "Marked from Covent Garden Book." Brought to Boston by Barry in 1854. Grooves, calls, some stage business, maps, cues for effects.

12. George Becks   New York   1880's
New York Public Library: *NCP.342992
[French issue of Cumberland edition, 4 x $7\frac{1}{4}$, pasted on sheets bearing advertisement for Madison Square Theatre, $9\frac{1}{4}$ x $7\frac{7}{8}$; black cloth boards; title gilt on spine.]
Lightly marked preparation copy for a version in 3 acts. Heavy cuts. Some scenic indications, grooves, some stage business, few cues for effects. Enclosed sheets of advertising for a farce with George Fawcett Rowe at Palmer's Madison Square Theatre.

13. [Becks]
New York Public Library: *NCP.342943
[Cumberland edition, $3\frac{1}{4}$ x $5\frac{1}{2}$; interleaves; brown cloth boards; title gilt on spine.]
Full and interesting preparation copy, not used. Provisional cuts and directions. Scenic indications, grooves, calls, much stage business, cues for effects.

14. James Taylor(?)
New York Public Library: *NCP.276100B
[Lacy issue of Cumberland edition, $3\frac{3}{4}$ x 6; interleaves; black cloth boards and black leather spine; title gilt on spine.]
Apparently a transcription, not quite complete, from the preceding book.

15. Oscar Asche   London, Adelphi   March 20, 1906
Shakespeare Centre Library: 79.920ASC
[Temple edition pasted in a workbook, $6\frac{3}{4}$ x 9; blue cloth boards and red leather spine; title gilt on cover and spine labels.]
Fair copy of Asche's promptbook. Heavily cut. Some scenic indications, little stage business.

16. Ellen Terry   London, Adelphi   April 28, 1906
    Smallhythe
    [Temple edition, 1906, $3\frac{7}{8}$ x $5\frac{1}{2}$: Oscar Asche's acting version and also a full text; limp maroon leather; "Adelphi Theatre" gilt on cover.]
    Miss Terry's rehearsal copy for the part of Francisca the nun, which she played on the occasion of her Jubilee.

17. William Poel   Manchester, Gaiety   April 11, 1908
    Enthoven Collection
    [Shakespeare edition pasted in a workbook, 7 x 9; red marbled boards and red cloth spine.]
    Promptbook of Poel's "Elizabethan" production for Miss Horniman at Manchester and on April 21 at Stratford-upon-Avon. Cuts on full text. Calls, some stage business, maps, cues for effects.

18. [Poel]
    British Drama League
    [Heinemann edition, 1904, pasted in a workbook, 7 x 9; black cloth boards and red cloth spine; title page pasted on cover.]
    Miss A. E. F. Horniman's copy of the Poel promptbook, carefully marked, not much used. Cuts on full text. Some stage business, maps, cues for effects.

19. E. H. Sothern and Julia Marlowe
    Museum of the City of New York: 43.430.658
    [Temple edition pasted in a workbook, 5 x 8; black rubberized cloth; printed title as cover label.]
    Preparation copy signed "Julia Marlowe Sothern," not used in production. Several notes on the playing of Isabella.

20. Henry Jewett   Boston, Boston Repertory   November 16, 1929
    Folger: Measure, Folio 1
    [Typescript, $8\frac{1}{2}$ x 11; gray cardboard and green cloth spine.]
    Promptbook of Jewett's own adaptation. Descriptions of costumes. Much stage business. Timing sheet for 2 weeks of performances.

21. [Jewett]
    Joint University Libraries, Nashville
    [Temple edition, 1911, 4 x $5\frac{1}{8}$; red leather, loose; title gilt on spine.]

Rehearsal copy of Lark Taylor, checked for the Duke. Cuts on full text, little stage business.

[ACTOR LISTS FOR FOLLOWING BOOKS ARE GIVEN IN THIS ORDER: Duke, Angelo, Isabella.]

22. W. Bridges-Adams   Stratford-upon-Avon   April 16, 1931
Shakespeare Centre Library: 71.21/1931MEA
[Temple edition pasted in a workbook, 6¾ x 8⅞; blue marbled boards and red cloth spine; title on cover label; in brown paper wrapper.]
Cast includes Randle Ayrton, Gyles Isham, Hilda Coxhead. Costumes by Eric Maxon. Calls, stage business, maps, some cues for effects.

23. Frank McMullan   Stratford-upon-Avon   August 24, 1946
Shakespeare Centre Library: O.S.71.21/1946M
[New Temple edition pasted in a workbook, 7⅞ x 12¾; blue cloth boards and red cloth spine; title on cover and spine labels.]
Cast includes David King-Wood, Robert Harris, Ruth Lodge. Designed by Otis Riggs. Cuts on full text, calls, copious stage business, maps, cues for effects.

24. Ronald Giffen   Stratford-upon-Avon   April 13, 1947
Shakespeare Centre Library: O.S.71.21/1947MEA
[Eversley edition pasted in a workbook, 7⅛ x 9; blue cloth boards and half black leather; title on cover and spine labels.]
Cast includes Michael Golden, Robert Harris, Beatrix Lehmann. Designed by Otis Riggs. The book had been used for the 1940 production by B. Iden Payne, was erased and reused by Giffen for revival of the McMullan production of 1946. Calls, stage business and maps only partially developed, cues for effects.

25. Peter Brook   Stratford-upon-Avon   March 9, 1950
Shakespeare Centre Library: O.S.71.21/1950ME(7437)
[New Temple edition pasted in a workbook, 8 x 13; red cloth boards; title on cover and spine labels.]
Cast includes Harry Andrews, John Gielgud, Barbara Jefford. Designed by Brook, Michael Northen, Keegan Smith. Cuts on full text. Calls, copious stage business, maps, cues for effects.

26. [Brook]   April 23, 1950
Shakespeare Centre Library: O.S.71.21/1950ME

[Mimeograph, 8 x 13; in manila envelope.]

The 55-page script of the radio version of Brook's production, broadcast on Shakespeare's birthday.

27. Cecil Clarke   Stratford, Ontario   June 28, 1954

Festival Theatre, Library

[Two books. Temple edition pasted in workbooks, $7\frac{3}{4}$ x $12\frac{1}{2}$; one in red cloth boards and red cloth spine; one in black cloth boards and red cloth spine; title pasted on cover.]

Cast includes Lloyd Bochner, Donald Davis, Frances Hyland. Designed by Tanya Moiseiwitsch. Calls, much stage business, many maps, cues for effects. The second has cues for effects.

28. Michael Benthall   Old Vic, Australian Tour   1955

Old Vic, Publicity Department

[New Temple edition pasted in a workbook, $8\frac{1}{4}$ x 13; blue ring binder.]

Cast includes Leon Ryan, Robert Helpmann, Katharine Hepburn. Designed by Leslie Hurry. Cuts on full text, much stage business, maps, cues for effects. Arrangements for street scene enclosed.

29. [Benthall]

Old Vic, Publicity Department

[Same format as preceding book.]

Perfected copy of the preceding book, with all stage directions typewritten, used for the Australian tour.

30. John Houseman and Jack Landau

           Stratford, Connecticut   June 27, 1956

Festival Theatre, Production Department

[Mimeograph, $8\frac{1}{2}$ x 11; black spring binder.]

Cast includes Arnold Moss, Kent Smith, Nina Foch. Designed by Rouben Ter-Arutunian. This copy, which also served at the Phoenix in New York in 1957, is signed by Robert Leaf. Stage business, maps, cues for effects, cast list.

31. [Houseman and Landau]

New York Public Library: *NCP

[Mimeograph, $7\frac{3}{4}$ x $10\frac{7}{8}$; red cloth boards; title gilt up spine.]

Unused copy of the preceding book.

MEASURE FOR MEASURE 275

32. [Houseman and Landau]
    University of California, Los Angeles: Houseman Box 13
    [Two books. Mimeograph, 8½ x 11; black cloth board spring binders.]
    One rough production book with a few working notes. One unmarked copy.

33. Anthony Quayle   Stratford-upon-Avon   August 14, 1956
    Shakespeare Centre Library: O.S.71.21/1956M
    [New Temple edition pasted in a workbook, 8 x 13; red cloth board spring binder; title on spine label.]
    Cast includes Anthony Nicholls, Emlyn Williams, Margaret Johnston. Designed by Tanya Moiseiwitsch. Copious stage business, many maps on mimeographed groundplans, cues for effects. Many production papers.

34. Margaret Webster   London, Old Vic   November 19, 1957
    Old Vic, Publicity Department
    [New Temple edition pasted in a workbook, 8 x 10½; black ring binder.]
    Cast includes Anthony Nicholls, John Neville, Barbara Jefford. Designed by Barry Kay. Cuts, stage business, many maps, cues for effects. Many production papers including groundplans.

35. Other books of *Measure for Measure:*
    Brown University: Eng.P.17, Celia Logan.
    Folger: Measure, 4, 5, anonymous.
    Library Company of Philadelphia: Oe2+.11602.D, William Warren.
    Shakespeare Centre Library: 39(1833-186?), Charles Flower, with cuts from Miss Alleyn's book.

The Merchant of Venice

1. Anonymous   1600's
University of Michigan
[Pages 163-184 from a Second Folio.]
Preparation copy. Rough cuts through 2 acts.

ad1. See Addenda, p. 507.

2. William Ward   Doncaster   October 25, 1772
Folger: Y.d.42
[Manuscript, 5 x 6½; gray cardboard; title inked on cover.]
Ward's 10-leaf partbook for Shylock, called 10 lengths, well thumbed. Once belonged to William Dowton.

3. Anonymous   London, Covent Garden   c.1780
Folger: Merch, 16
[Bell edition, 1773, 4½ x 7½; red marbled boards and half black leather gilt; title gilt on spine.]
Promptbook handsomely marked in a perfect round hand. Cuts and restorations, list of property manuscripts, scenic indications (including "Athens," "Ryalto," "French Town," "Roman Hall," "Waltham Cross"), grooves, calls, little stage business, cues for effects. (Compare AW, 1; AYL, 4; R&J, 4; TEM, 2.)

4. John Philip Kemble   London, Drury Lane   January 22, 1784
Folger: T.a.30
[Manuscript, 7 x 8⅞; brown leather gilt; title gilt up spine.]
Kemble's 24-page partbook for Shylock, in his own hand, 431 lines. Dated from Drury Lane as above but probably written long afterwards.

5. [Kemble]   c.1797
Harvard Theatre Collection: 13486.38.5
[Kemble edition, 1797, 5½ x 8⅝; red cloth boards.]
Promptbook lightly marked in Kemble's hand. Cuts, some stage business, maps, few cues for effects.

6. [Kemble]   London, Covent Garden   c.1810
Garrick Club
[Kemble edition, 1810, 5⅛ x 8⅜; interleaves; blue cloth boards and brown leather spine; title gilt up spine.]
Promptbook lightly marked in Kemble's hand. Some properties,

some stage business, maps. Some of Portia's lines marked for stresses.

7. [Kemble]   1810-37
   Shakespeare Centre Library: 50.21(1810)
   [Kemble edition, 1810, 5 x 8¼; interleaves; brown leather; title gilt on red leather spine label, spine stamped "TR/CG/PB/M/ 15."]
   Promptbook originally marked by Kemble: calls, some stage business, map of trial scene, some cues for effects, timings (3:10). Later markings, in ink and pencil, show use from 1825 to 1837. Lesser roles marked for lengths. Grooves, stage business, cues for effects, notes on omission of songs, many timing notes. Actors named include Kean, Webster, Wood, C. Kemble, Fawcett, Heath, Wilson, the Misses Paton, Romer, Kemble, Faucit.

8. William B. Wood   Philadelphia, Chestnut Street   April 10, 1811
   Folger: Merch, 49
   [Longworth edition, 1811, 3¾ x 6; gray stiff paper; title and Wood's name inked on cover.]
   Lightly marked rehearsal copy. Penciled cuts, marks for stresses. Inked cast for 1811 with Cooke as Shylock.

9. Edmund Kean   London, Drury Lane   January 26, 1814
   Folger: W.a.71
   [Inchbald edition, 1808, 3¾ x 6⅛; interleaves; bound with *Hamlet* and *King Lear* in brown leather gilt; "Siddons" gilt on spine.]
   George Joseph Bell's notes describing points in Kean's Shylock. Also his description of Mrs. Siddons in her public readings of the play.

10. Laurence Macdonald   1820's
    Folger: T.a.76
    [Manuscript, 5⅞ x 7½; bound with several non-Shakespearean parts.]
    A 6-page partbook for Gratiano, apparently of the early nineteenth century. Macdonald ("scripsit") was perhaps a copyist rather than an actor.

11. Mark Allen   1830's
    Harvard Theatre Collection: 13486.39.20
    [Cumberland edition, 3⅜ x 5¾; gray interleaves, 4 x 6; tan marbled boards and yellow cloth spine; title inked on cover.]

Lightly marked but much used promptbook of the early nineteenth century. Calls, cues for effects, some timings. Last act pinholed for omission.

12. Charles Kean   London, Drury Lane   April 5, 1838
    Folger: Merch, 22

    [Kemble edition, 1810, 5 x 7¾; interleaves; marbled boards, very worn, and half brown leather; title and Kean's name gilt on spine.]

    Promptbook made for Kean in 1838 by James Parsloe, the Drury Lane prompter, and used for many years. Penciled cast. Non-Shakespearean songs deleted; arrangements provided to end with the trial scene. Scenic indications, grooves, calls, stage business, maps, cues for effects, timings. On the interleaves, 7 fine drawings of the sets, washed with color. Signatures of prompters: John George Steele of New Orleans, C. D. Lovett of Memphis, W. E. Anderton of Charleston. A reference to Mrs. Kean. (See nos. 17, 30, 34-41.)

13. [Kean]
    Folger: W.a.10

    [Notebook of sheets watermarked 1837, 4¾ x 7¾; brown marbled boards and half brown leather gilt; "Theatrical Costumes" inked on spine label.]

    Kean's touring wardrobe list for Shylock is the fourteenth of 16 such lists in this book.

14. J. H. Ring   Boston, Tremont Street   1839
    Folger: Merch, 33

    [Oxberry edition, Boston, 1823, 3½ x 5⅝; brown marbled paper and black leather spine.]

    Rehearsal copy checked for several characters but especially for Old Gobbo. Cuts, little stage business, some cues for effects.

15. William P. Davidge   London   1840's
    Harvard Theatre Collection: (Widener: 13486.39.11)

    [Dolby edition, 1824, 3⅜ x 5½; brown cloth boards; title gilt up spine.]

    Studybook checked for Bassanio and Shylock. Some notes on the acting. At the front a 31-line lyric poem.

16. William Charles Macready
                              London, Drury Lane   December 27, 1841
    Folger: Merch, 24

[Pages 3-100 from volume III of a *Works*, 5 x 7⅝; interleaves watermarked 1845, 7¼ x 8¾; white cardboard, broken; title inked on cover.]

Transcription of the promptbook of Macready's Drury Lane production made by George Ellis. Cuts in ink, notations on interleaves in pencil. Property lists, grooves, calls, stage business, maps, sketches, cues for effects, timings (2:35).

17. [Macready]

Folger: Merch, 17

[Pages 5-100 from volume XII of a *Works*, 5 x 8½; interleaves watermarked 1844, 7 x 8⅞; green cloth boards and half brown leather, broken; title gilt on maroon spine label, "Mr Charles Kean/Prompt Copy" gilt on black leather cover label.]

Excellent transcription of Macready's Drury Lane promptbook made by George Ellis for Charles Kean in November, 1846. Cuts on full text. Unused. (See nos. 12-13, 30, 34-41.)

18. [Macready]

University of Illinois: x792.9/Sh15mer/no.1

[Pages 469-563 from volume II of a *Works*, 5½ x 8¾; interleaves watermarked 1847, 7⅝ x 9½; brown marbled boards and half green leather, broken; title and Hermann Vezin's name gilt on maroon leather cover label.]

Excellent transcription of Macready's Drury Lane promptbook made by George Ellis for Hermann Vezin in the 1850's. Cuts on full text. Much used by Vezin, many penciled additions.

19. [Macready]

Folger: Merch, 18

[Watercolors, 7 x 8⅞; interleaves watermarked 1846; green cloth boards and half brown leather; title and "Scenery" gilt on maroon spine label.]

Fine watercolor designs for 9 scenes, probably Charles Marshall's originals for the Drury Lane production, with identifying notes by George Ellis on facing pages. Sent to Kean with the promptbook in 1846. (See no. 17.)

20. [Macready]

Folger: Merch, 19

[Watercolors on sheets watermarked 1846, 7¼ x 9⅜; green cloth boards and half brown leather; title and "Costume" gilt on maroon spine label.]

Thirty-four sheets of fine watercolor costume designs sent to Charles Kean by George Ellis in 1846, probably drawn and painted by Ellis. Two pages of explanatory notes including historical authorities. A cast list penciled by Kean. (See no. 17.)

21. [Macready]
University of Illinois
[Watercolors, $4\frac{1}{2}$ x $8\frac{5}{8}$.]
Five plates of watercolor costume designs (6 figures) made for Macready by Colonel Charles Hamilton Smith. The costumes of Morocco and Arragon, here included, were not used.

22. John Proctor   Philadelphia   1843
New York Public Library: *NCP.255324B
[Oxberry edition, Boston, 1823, $3\frac{1}{4}$ x $5\frac{1}{4}$; bound with *Comedy of Errors* (see no. 13) in gray marbled boards and half black leather.]
Nicely marked promptbook, with numerous comments on staging and arrangement of text. Grooves, calls, little stage business, cues for effects. A penciled cast.

23. Henry Betty   c.1845
Folger: Merch, 4
[Pages 179-267 from volume II of Knight's Cabinet Edition, $3\frac{3}{8}$ x $5\frac{1}{8}$; interleaves; gray boards and green cloth spine; title penciled on cover.]
Thoroughly marked but not much used promptbook. Cuts on full text. Scenic indications, grooves, stage business and comments on the acting, cues for effects.

24. John Moore   1845-75
Folger: Merch, 28
[Cumberland edition, $3\frac{3}{4}$ x 6; interleaves; purple paper, much worn.]
Promptbook begun in England and used for many years in America: references to Helen Faucit, Edward Eddy, Edwin Booth. List of distribution of supers, cuts, calls, considerable stage business, maps, cues for effects, timings. (See no. 53.)

25. John B. Wright   Boston   c.1850
New York Public Library: *NCP.343037

[National Acting Drama Office, London, 1848, 4¼ x 7¼; blue interleaves; red cloth boards; title gilt up spine.]

Promptbook. Cuts, little stage business, maps. Costume notes for Shylock. Printed Kean cast of 1848.

26. [Wright]
New York Public Library: *NCP.342615

[Roach edition, London, 1804, 3½ x 5¾; interleaves; bound with *Henry IV* and *All in the Wrong* in red cloth boards; "Henry IV" gilt on spine.]

An older promptbook which belonged to Wright. References to Cooper (c.1815) and Mr. B. Costume notes for Shylock. Cuts, some stage business, a map.

27. [Wright]
Folger: Merch, 50

[Cumberland edition, 3½ x 5⅝; interleaves; green marbled boards and brown leather spine.]

Rehearsal copy. Some cuts, some music cues. Playbills for Kean at Drury Lane, December 29, 1823; F. Robson at the Olympic, July 18, 1853; McCullough in Dayton, March 13, 1866.

28. Anonymous   Boston, Boston Museum   1850's
Princeton University, Seymour Collection: MV, 5

[Modern Standard Drama, 4½ x 7½; coarse cloth; title and "Boston Museum" inked on cover.]

Promptbook of a version cut to 4 acts, checked for Jessica and Bassanio. References to Mrs. Wallack, Miss Shaw. Cuts, calls, some stage business, cues for effects.

29. James Stark   California   1850's
New York Public Library: *NCP.342973

[Modern Standard Drama, 4¼ x 7¼; interleaves; black cloth boards; title gilt up spine.]

Lightly marked promptbook checked for Antonio. Maps, cues for effects. Amusing note by Sarah Stark. Reference to Irving's conduct of trial scene perhaps added by George Becks, to whom the book later belonged.

30. Charles Kean   London, Princess's   November 2, 1850
New York Public Library: *NCP.342960

[Mixture of a Shakespeare edition with some leaves of French's

Standard Drama, 4⅛ x 7⅛; interleaves; black cloth boards; title gilt on spine.]

George Becks's transcription, "Kindness Mr. Schonberg," of Kean's promptbook of 1850-51, by T. W. Edmonds. Cuts and transpositions on nearly full text; non-Shakespearean songs introduced. Grooves, calls, some stage business, maps, sketches, cues for effects, timings. (See nos. 12-13, 17, 34-41.)

31. James Anderson   America   c.1852

Folger: Merch, 2

[Pages 345-382 from a double-column *Works*, 7¾ x 11⅛.]

Promptbook of Anderson, the American stage manager, also signed "George W. Muir, Cin. Ohio." At the end of Act I Morocco and Arragon are introduced in a manuscript scene on sheets watermarked 1852. Cuts, calls, some stage business, cues for effects, timings with waits.

32. May Vandenhoff   c.1855

Harvard Theatre Collection: 13486.39.31

[Modern Standard Drama, 4⅛ x 7⅛; interleaves; marbled boards, leather corners, brown cloth spine.]

Promptbook owned by Mrs. Vandenhoff and also signed before 1855 in her maiden name, Miss M. E. J. N. Makeah. Calls, little stage business, cues for effects.

33. Edwin Booth   New York, Burton's New   May 7, 1857

Folger: Merch, 9

[Modern Standard Drama, 4¼ x 7⅛; interleaves; black cloth boards; Booth's name gilt on cover.]

Early Booth promptbook, neatly written by a copyist, with additions in Booth's hand. Marked for whole play, but fifth act has sometimes been pinned shut. Calls, stage business, maps, sketches, cues for effects. (See nos. 46, 48, 70-71, 79-80.)

34. Charles Kean   London, Princess's   June 12, 1858

Folger: Merch, 23

[Proof sheets of Kean edition, 1858, 7 x 9⅛; interleaves, 7½ x 9; white cardboard; title inked on cover.]

Rehearsal workbook of George Ellis, the stage manager, signed "G. E. June, 1858." Copious penciled notes of stage business, rough maps, sketches. Large sheet of notes on costumes of minor characters. (See nos. 12-13, 17, 30.)

35. [Kean]

Folger: Merch, 20

[Kean edition, 1858, 5 x 8; interleaves, 6⅞ x 8⅞; tan cloth boards and half brown leather, broken; "Mr. Charles Kean/Prompt Copy" gilt on brown leather cover label.]

Final or souvenir promptbook made by T. W. Edmonds, the prompter. Calls, stage business, maps, cues for effects. Originally contained 11 watercolor scene designs, but only the one of Shylock's house on the canal remains. Much used by Kean on tour in the 1860's; soiled and broken.

36. [Kean]

Folger: Prints and Engravings, 52

[Watercolors, 8 x 5½, mounted in an album, 10¼ x 14⅛; gray cloth boards and half green leather gilt; "Charles Kean/Original Water Colors" gilt on spine.]

Fine watercolor scene designs for 3 plays, including 10 for *The Merchant of Venice*.

37. [Kean]

Enthoven Collection: Box DT.47

[Watercolors.]

Thirteen fine watercolor scene designs and 7 plates of properties mounted on large display boards.

38. [Kean]

Enthoven Collection: 94G26, plates 1683-1704

[Scrapbook, 15¼ x 21⅜; blue cloth boards and blue cloth spine; "Kean Theatrical Scenery" gilt up spine.]

Eight watercolor scene designs; 12 plates of watercolor costume designs, 6 figures each; 1 plate of the gondola; 1 plate each of Shylock's and Portia's costume.

39. [Kean]

Enthoven Collection: 94G27, plates 1803-06

[Same format as preceding book.]

Four pages of watercolor costume designs, 24 figures.

40. [Kean]

Folger: Kean Costume Book, Prints and Engravings, 182

[Scrapbook, 14⅜ x 21¼; brown cloth boards and half brown leather.]

Contains 65 plates of watercolor costume designs and 4 plates of banners and properties for *The Merchant of Venice*.

41. [Kean]

Folger: Kean Costume Book, Prints and Engravings, 50

[Scrapbook, 10¾ x 14½; green cloth boards and half green leather gilt.]

Contains 44 sheets of tracings by Emma Hamilton Smith for costumes and properties for *The Merchant of Venice*.

42. Barry Sullivan   New York, Broadway   c.November 25, 1858

Shakespeare Centre Library: 50.21(1797)

[Pages 93-180 from volume II of the Robinson *Works*, 1797, 6¾ x 9⅝; interleaves; brown marbled boards and half brown leather; title gilt on spine label, Sullivan's name and "T.R. Haymarket" gilt on black leather cover label.]

Transcription probably by George Hastings, perhaps from Macready's Drury Lane promptbook; part of a set gathered by Sullivan when at the Haymarket in 1852. Cuts on full text. Some grooves, calls, some stage business, maps including a good one of the trial scene, cues for effects.

43. [Sullivan]

Shakespeare Centre Library: 50.21(1840)

[Lacy edition, 4½ x 7, with passages from another edition pasted in; interleaves; tan marbled boards and half black leather; title gilt up spine.]

Promptbook signed by Sullivan as of London, New York, Melbourne. Arranged to play the whole or to end with the trial scene. Scenic indications, some stage business, cues for effects. At the back a plot of scenes and grooves.

44. J. W. Wallack   New York, Wallack's   December 9, 1858

New York Public Library: *NCP.342979

[Kean edition, 1858, 5 x 8; interleaves, 6¼ x 8; black cloth boards; title gilt on spine.]

Lightly marked but much used promptbook inscribed "To Jas. Wᵐ Wallack from his Brother H. J. Wallack." Cast for Wallack's Theatre, 1858, with J. W. and Lester Wallack. Grooves, calls, some stage business, maps, sketches, cues for effects.

45. J. B. Roberts   c.1860-1900

Folger: Merch, 35

[Lacy edition, 4¼ x 7⅜; interleaves, 6½ x 8⅛; black and white boards and red leather spine.]

Good promptbook of a 6-act version, with copious reference to other actors. Many notes on Irving's Shylock, some on Mansfield's, and some of the business of Cooke, Kean, the elder Booth. Scenic indications, grooves, stage business, many fine maps, cues for effects. Two Irving playbills: Lyceum, 1897, and Chestnut Street Opera House. (See no. 74.)

46. Edwin Booth   London, Haymarket   September 30, 1861
The Players

[Pages 7-92 from volume III of a *Works*, 5¼ x 8⅜; interleaves; green leather fold-over cover; title and Booth's name gilt on cover.]

Transcription by a professional copyist of an older book, probably English, in which the fifth act was to be played; additional pencilings. Cuts on full text. Some stage business, maps, cues for effects. Nice drawings of Shylock with moneybags, exterior of Shylock's house, trial scene. Partial cast for the Haymarket. (See nos. 33, 48, 70-71, 79-80.)

47. James H. Hackett   1862
Enthoven Collection

[Manuscript, 6¾ x 8⅛; orange and brown marbled paper.]

Hackett's partbook for Shylock, dated 1862. Several bits of stage business.

48. Edwin Booth   New York, Winter Garden   January 28, 1867
Harvard Theatre Collection: (Widener, 13486.40.11)

[Booth-Hinton edition, 1867, 5¾ x 9; pictorial publisher's wrapper under gray and red marbled boards and brown cloth spine; title inked on cover.]

The Winter Garden promptbook, with calls and some stage business crudely penciled and cues for effects inked. At the back, 3 rough maps. (See nos. 33, 46, 70-71, 79-80.)

49. James E. Kirkwood   Rochester, New York   1870's
University of Illinois: x792.9/Sh15mer/no.3

[Lacy edition, 4⅛ x 7¼; interleaves; green marbled boards and brown cloth spine.]

Promptbook of a 4-act version neatly marked in brown and red ink. Cuts, stage business, maps, cues for effects. Belonged in 1880 to Charles B. Welles. Penciled additions of stage business are perhaps in the hand of William Farnum.

50. J. B. Booth, Jr.   c.1870
The Players
[Modern Standard Drama, 4½ x 7½; publisher's wrappers, torn.]
Crudely marked promptbook checked for Bassanio. Cuts, few scenic indications, calls, cues for effects.

51. E. L. Davenport   c.1870
Folger: Merch, 27
[French's Standard Drama, 4⅜ x 7½; interleaves; tan paper; title written on cover.]
Promptbook of a version "Condensed in 3 Acts Ending with Trial Scene by ELD." He proposes to find "some good tag" to end the play. Cuts, scenic indications, grooves, cues for effects. Belonged to John Moore.

52. [Davenport]
New York Public Library: *NCP.164543
[French's Standard Drama, 4¼ x 7¼; green and black marbled boards and black cloth spine; in manila folder.]
E. T. Taylor's copy, "cut as Mr. Davenport Plays it 3 Acts." Cuts, cues for effects.

53. John Moore   c.1875
Folger: Merch, 25
[Booth-Hinton edition, 1867, pasted in a workbook, 6 x 9¼; tan paper, much worn.]
Promptbook of a version which ends with the trial scene. Scenic indications, grooves, calls, considerable stage business, cues for effects. Much printed matter pasted in: a Gravesend playbill of 1839 with Moore as Salarino; an advertisement for Wallack; an 1868 essay on Shylock; reviews of C. Kean and E. Booth. Probably used for Augustin Daly's production at the New Fifth Avenue Theatre on January 11, 1875. (See nos. 24, 84-85.)

54. William Creswick   Melbourne   December 10, 1877
Shakespeare Centre Library: 50.21(1840)
[Lacy edition, 4⅜ x 7⅜; publisher's wrappers under blue cloth boards and half black leather; title gilt up spine.]

Studybook checked for Shylock. Costume list, a few rough notes on stage business and interpretation.

55. Henry Irving   London, Lyceum   November 1, 1879
Folger: Merch, 15
[Pages 475-563 from volume II of Collier's *Works*, 1842, 5¼ x 7½; interleaves; purple cloth boards and half red leather; title gilt up spine, Irving's name gilt on cover.]
Early Irving promptbook, finely prepared by a professional copyist, with jottings and sketches by Irving. Cuts on full text. Grooves, calls, some stage business, maps, cues for effects.

56. [Irving]
Museum of the City of New York: 43.156.15
[Mixture of French's Standard Drama and other texts pasted in a workbook, 7¾ x 10; blue cloth boards and half red leather gilt.]
Extremely full and careful copy (probably an augmented transcription) of Irving's promptbook. In 1909 Fuller Mellish told Eleanor Robson that it is "exactly as produced by Irving at the Lyceum Theatre." Used by Winthrop Ames to prepare his production in 1928. Detailed scenic indications, excellent groundplans, vivid accounts of stage business, sketches, cues for effects.

57. [Irving]
Harvard Theatre Collection: uncatalogued
[Irving edition, 1881, 5 x 8; red leather gilt; title gilt up spine.]
Studybook for Shylock. Call-list for first scene. Some markings for stresses, words of the text jotted in margins, a few notes on the acting.

58. [Irving]
Folger: Merch, 14
[Irving edition, 1879, 5⅜ x 8½; publisher's wrappers.]
Spectator's notes on the performances of Irving and Ellen Terry.

59. [Irving]
Folger: Merch, 13
[French edition (Irving version), 5½ x 8¾; some interleaves; green paper with publisher's wrapper pasted on cover.]
Spectator's notes on the performances of Irving and Ellen Terry made by Charles Bamburgh in 1888. Some property lists, some stage business, effects.

60. Ellen Terry   London, Lyceum   November 1, 1879
    Smallhythe
    [French edition, $4\frac{1}{4}$ x $7\frac{1}{8}$; publisher's wrappers.]
    Rehearsal copy signed "E.T." Cuts and comments on the tradi-
    tional acting version. Random notes on the playing of Antonio
    and Shylock.

61. [Terry]
    Smallhythe
    [Pages 395-498 from volume II of a *Works,* Chiswick Press, $4\frac{1}{8}$ x
    $6\frac{5}{8}$; black oilcloth.]
    Studybook, much used. Cuts on full text. List of properties for
    Portia. Notations of time of day of the scenes.

62. [Terry]
    Smallhythe
    [Pages 355-431 from a *Works,* $4\frac{1}{2}$ x $6\frac{1}{4}$; white vellum boards;
    title gilt on spine.]
    Souvenir book signed by Miss Terry on the flyleaf. Several photo-
    graphs of Irving and Terry in their own persons; a Christmas
    card with a watercolor of Terry as Portia; many photographs of
    Venetian scenes, details from paintings, etc.; pictures of Irving
    and Terry in character. Cuts and revisions on full text. A few
    notes on the playing of Antonio.

63. [Terry]
    Smallhythe
    [Clarendon Press edition, 1879, $4\frac{1}{2}$ x $6\frac{1}{2}$; publisher's orange
    paper cover and green cloth spine.]
    Rehearsal copy. Cuts on full text. A few notes on the playing of
    Portia.

64. [Terry]
    Smallhythe
    [Irving edition, 1880, $5\frac{1}{8}$ x $8\frac{1}{8}$; interleaves; maroon leather,
    much worn.]
    Rehearsal copy, signed from the Lyceum as of 1879. Many printed
    illustrations of the production by E. Abbey, 1882. Cuts. Many
    notes on the playing of Portia.

65. [Terry]
    Smallhythe

[Irving edition, 1880, 5⅛ x 8⅛; white boards; title gilt on cover celebrating the hundredth performance on February 14, 1880.]
Rehearsal copy signed by Miss Terry. Cuts. Numerous rehearsal notes mainly descriptive of the playing of Antonio. Program of the hundredth performance.

66. [Terry]
Smallhythe
[Irving edition, 1879, 5¼ x 8¼; white boards; title on cover.]
"Illustrated by Miss E. Webling, the drawings being made at the Lyceum Theatre." Along the margins over 30 delicate drawings of characters from the Irving-Terry production, dated 1880. Belonged to L. D. Nicholson.

67. [Terry]
Smallhythe
[Temple edition, 1895, 3⅞ x 5; limp maroon leather; title gilt up spine.]
Miss Terry's critical notes on an unidentified production.

68. [Terry]
Folger: Merch, 45
[Clarendon Press edition, 1897, 4⅜ x 6⅝; red cardboard cover.]
Studybook signed by Miss Terry in 1904. The Introduction underscored. A few cuts and jottings of stage business.

69. William H. Gillette   Boston, Globe   c.1880
Connecticut State Library
[French's Standard Drama, 4⅜ x 7½; publisher's wrapper.]
Studybook. Considerable stage business for Shylock for the trial scene only.

70. Edwin Booth   c.1880
The Players
[Booth-Winter edition, 1878, 4⅝ x 6½; limp black leather gilt; title gilt on cover.]
Fine transcription of Booth's promptbook made by J. R. Pitman as a souvenir for Russ Whytal, autographed by Booth. Scenic indications with excellent groundplans, calls, stage business, maps, cues for effects. A non-Shakespearean song introduced. Ends with trial scene. (See nos. 33, 46, 48, 79-80.)

71. [Booth]

University of Pennsylvania, Furness Collection: C59.Sh1MeP

[Booth-Winter edition, 1881, 4⅝ x 6½; interleaves, 5 x 8; bound with *Katherine and Petruchio* in gray cardboard publisher's cover.]

Transcription from Booth's book made by J. R. Pitman, who used it at the Castle Square Theatre, Boston, in 1901-03. Ends with trial scene. Calls, stage business, maps, sketches, cues for effects. Two Castle Square playbills. (See no. 87.)

72. James L. Carhart   c.1880

Harvard Theatre Collection: 13486.39.30

[Modern Standard Drama, 4½ x 7⅜; tan paper under green marbled boards and green cloth spine; title inked on cover.]

Promptbook originally marked in ink by John W. Buck— (Buckland?, 1850's); later pencilings by Carhart. Cuts, grooves, calls, some stage business, cues for effects. Checked for Duke, Salarino, Old Gobbo.

73. Fred G. Ross   c.1880

Museum of the City of New York: 48.194.113

[Booth-Winter edition, 1878, 4¾ x 6¾; front wrapper missing.]

Lightly marked promptbook and studybook, checked for Bassanio. Calls, some stage business, cues for effects.

74. J. B. Roberts   1880

Folger: Merch, 34

[Pages 167-252 from a *Works,* 6¼ x 9¾; black cloth boards and maroon leather spine.]

Copy used for public readings. Heavy cuts. Shylock speeches marked for stresses. Essay on Shylock pasted in the front. (See no. 45.)

75. Frederick Warde   America   1880's

University of California, Los Angeles: Special Collections 669, Box 1

[Shakespeare edition, 5 x 7½; interleaves, 6 x 7½; brown limp leather; title gilt on spine.]

Promptbook used by Warde for many years after it was given him by O. W. Blake in 1882. Some stage business, maps and sketches, cues for effects. Over 2 dozen pictures and photographs, including many from Calvert's production at the Prince's Theatre in Manchester in 1870, when Warde played Bassanio.

76. John Musgrove　　　　London, Drury Lane　　　　1881
Harvard Theatre Collection:　(Widener, 13486.39.22)
[Davidson issue of Cumberland edition, $3\frac{1}{2}$ x $5\frac{1}{2}$; lavender interleaves watermarked "LONDON"; brown cloth boards; title gilt up spine.]
Promptbook. Cuts, maps, cues for effects. List of actors' names at the back. A reference to John McCullough, who visited Drury Lane in May of 1881, though not with this play.

77. Frederick Paulding　　　　　　　　　　1882
Rutgers University:　PR.1243.SHA
[Two books. French's Standard Drama, $4\frac{1}{2}$ x $7\frac{1}{2}$; one has publisher's wrappers.]
One rehearsal copy checked for Bassanio. One lightly marked promptbook: some stage business, maps, cues for effects.

78. Louis James　　　New York, Windsor　　　December 10, 1886
New York Public Library:　*NCP
[French's Standard Drama pasted in a workbook, $6\frac{1}{2}$ x $8\frac{1}{4}$; in manila folder.]
Promptbook of a version in 6 acts, used for many years. Calls, copious stage business, maps, cues for effects. A non-Shakespearean song introduced. James played Bassanio in Daly's production of January, 1875; he first played Shylock in New York as above.

79. Edwin Booth　　　　　　　　　　1887
University of Pennsylvania, Furness Collection:　C59.Sh1MeB
[Booth-Winter edition, 1878, $4\frac{3}{4}$ x $6\frac{3}{4}$; publisher's wrappers; in red cloth folder and red leather gilt slip-box; title gilt on spine.]
More than 100 notes on Shylock, endorsed "To Rabbi Furness, the Scribe—from his disciple E. T[ubal] Booth—1887." Most but not all of these are printed in the Furness Variorum edition. (See nos. 33, 46, 48, 70-71.)

80. Edwin Booth and Lawrence Barrett　　　　1887-88
Harvard Theatre Collection:　TS.2424.110
[French's Standard Drama tipped into a workbook, $7\frac{1}{2}$ x $9\frac{1}{2}$; tan cloth boards and half red leather; title, Barrett's name, and

prompter's name inked on cover; in box of tan cloth boards and blue leather spine; title gilt up spine.]

Crude but much used promptbook, "marked by Oliver Doud 1887." Last act cut and restored as if to be played. Scenic indications, excellent groundplan of opening scene. Some stage business penciled. Cues for effects.

81. [Barrett]

Harvard Theatre Collection: uncatalogued

[Ten music score books, 9½ x 6¼; brown cloth boards and green cloth spine.]

Complete scores for the band for 9 plays including *The Merchant of Venice,* endorsed by musicians in many cities.

82. Charles B. Hanford   1890's

Folger: Merch, 12

[French's Standard Drama pasted in a workbook, 7½ x 9½; limp green leather; title on cover label.]

Fully developed promptbook of a version ending with the trial scene, probably unused. Scenic indications, grooves, much stage business especially for act-end tableaux, cues for effects. Postcard of Columbian Exposition, 1893.

83. George Becks   1890's

New York Public Library: *NCP.343044

[Lacy edition, 4 x 7½; interleaves; black cloth boards; title gilt up spine.]

Promptbook marked through the whole play, but Dr. Valpy's alteration is suggested for reducing it to 4 acts. Calls, much stage business, maps, cues for effects. Illustrations from the Booth-Hinton edition and an engraving of Irving and Terry in the trial scene.

84. Augustin Daly   New York, Daly's   November 19, 1898

Folger: Prints and Engravings

[Daly edition, 1898, mounted in pages of albums (2 volumes), 12 x 16⅞; green and gold marbled boards and half brown leather gilt; title gilt on spines.]

Souvenir album in 2 volumes. The first volume contains many prints of old actors, many prints and photographs of Venetian scenes, a long series of watercolors of past actors of Shylock and Portia, reviews of Daly's production, 24 photographs of actors, and 18 photographs of scenes from Daly's production. The second volume contains many prints of old actors, many eighteenth- and nineteenth-century playbills, and 53 watercolor costume designs for Daly's production. (See no. 53.)

85. [Daly]
New York Public Library: 8*T-*NCP+
[Daly edition, 1898, mounted in a scrapbook, 12¼ x 16¾; brown and green marbled boards and half brown leather, broken; title gilt on spine.]
Souvenir album given to Ada Rehan by Augustus Toedteberg in 1901. Dozens of photographs of characters and scenes of the Daly production, playbills, etc.

86. William Poel   London, St. George's Hall   November 29, 1898
Enthoven Collection
[Shakespeare edition pasted in a workbook, 4½ x 7; black imitation leather boards.]
Preparation copy only partially marked. Calls and properties given for two acts.

87. J. R. Pitman   Boston, Castle Square   April 1, 1901
University of Pennsylvania, Furness Collection: C59.Sh1MeP^2
[French's Standard Drama, 4½ x 7½; interleaves, 5½ x 7¾; tan paper; title and "Property of J. C. Pitman, Prompter" inked on cover; in red cloth board folder; title gilt on cover.]
Promptbook considerably more fully developed than the Pitman one listed above as a transcription of Booth's (see no. 71). Ends with the trial scene. Casts from Castle Square playbills, 1901 and 1903, pasted in. Detailed scenic indications, grooves, much stage business, fine maps, sketches, cues for effects.

88. F. R. Benson   c.1905
Shakespeare Centre Library: 72.921BEN
[Chiswick edition, 1904(?), pasted in a workbook, 7 x 9; red marbled boards and green cloth spine; title on cover and spine labels.]
Thoroughly marked promptbook. Scenic indications, calls, much stage business, maps, cues for effects. Names of actors appear in the directions. At the back lists of supers and hand properties. Separate list of larger properties folded in a pocket.

89. E. H. Sothern and Julia Marlowe
New York, Knickerbocker   October 30, 1905
Museum of the City of New York: 43.430.659
[Shakespeare edition pasted in a workbook, 5⅞ x 9; black leather.]
Preparation copy, roughly written. Marked for stresses. Scenic indications and list of extras at the front. Much stage business.

90. [Sothern and Marlowe]
Museum of the City of New York: 43.430.660
[Shakespeare edition pasted in a workbook, 5½ x 8½; brown leather.]
Preparation copy in which stage directions of the preceding book have been organized, numbered, and entered on the left-hand pages.

91. [Sothern and Marlowe]
Folger: Merch, 43
[Shakespeare edition pasted in a workbook, 8 x 10½; black cloth board and half red leather ring binder.]
Perfected promptbook made by Francis Powell, the stage manager, and Frederick Kaufman, assistant. At the front a 5-page plot of properties. Excellent groundplan at head of each scene. Copious stage business fully described in numbered notations on left-hand pages. Cues for effects (with scenic gondolas).

92. [Sothern and Marlowe]
Folger: Merch, 38, 40, 41
[Three books. Typescripts, 8⅜ x 10⅞; brown paper wrappers.]
Copies of a version which includes scenic gondolas, compiled and used by Frederick Kaufman, general stage director. Of these, 38 is an original and 40 a carbon; 41, in a different typing, is soiled and was perhaps a working promptbook.

93. [Sothern and Marlowe]
Folger: Merch, 36, 37, 39
[Three books. Typescripts, 8⅜ x 10⅞; brown paper wrappers, except no. 36, which is in gray cardboard.]
Copies of a version without scenic gondolas, compiled and used by Frederick Kaufman, general stage director. Full-page sketch or map of each set. Of these, 36 was probably a working promptbook.

94. [Sothern and Marlowe]
    The Players: TS.114
    [Typescript, 8½ x 11; brown paper wrapper.]
    Copy of the version with scenic gondolas, and with notation on
    reducing it when gondolas were not used.

95. [Sothern and Marlowe]
    New York Public Library: *NCP.276568B
    [Typescript, 8¼ x 11; red cloth boards; title gilt up spine.]
    Copy of the version with scenic gondolas, and with notation on
    reducing it when gondolas were not used. Soiled from use. Be-
    longed to V. H. Collins.

96. [Sothern and Marlowe]
    Princeton University, Seymour Collection
    [Carbon typescript, 8½ x 11; brown paper.]
    Stage manager's copy of the version with scenic gondolas, much
    used. Belonged to Mr. Tilden. Calls, maps, cues for effects, tim-
    ings.

97. [Sothern and Marlowe]
    New York Public Library: *NCP+.51x304
    [Typescript, 8 x 10¾; blue cloth boards; title gilt up spine.]
    Clean copy of one of the versions, in different typing from the
    preceding book.

98. [Sothern and Marlowe]
    Folger: T.a.81, 82
    [Notebooks, 6⅝ x 8⅛; brown and red marbled boards and black
    cloth spine.]
    "Sothern & Marlowe Elect Dept." Light plots for 5 Shakespearean
    productions, including 8 plots (sketches) for *The Merchant of
    Venice*: instruments, colors, maps, cues. With it a typed plot
    mounted on cardboard for use at the controls.

99. [Sothern and Marlowe]
    University of Illinois: x792.9/Sh15mer/no.2
    [Acting edition, 4¾ x 7⅛; interleaves; brown cloth boards; title
    gilt on spine.]
    Promptbook record of the production made in 1906 by Lark Tay-
    lor, the actor. Gives cast of Daly's production in 1898 when

Taylor played Leonardo. Cast of Sothern and Marlowe production in 1906 with Taylor in several roles. Cuts, copious stage business, maps, notes on effects.

100. [Sothern and Marlowe]
Folger: Merch, 42
[Shakespeare edition pasted in a workbook, 6¾ x 8¼; red paper and black cloth spine; title on cover label.]
Another promptbook record made by Lark Taylor. Cuts on full text. Full account of stage business and effects, and many notes on the history of the production.

101. Winthrop Ames   Boston, Castle Square   January 15, 1906
Harvard Theatre Collection: uncatalogued
[American Academy of Dramatic Arts edition (Irving version), 5¾ x 8⅞.]
Preparation copy. Production notes penciled throughout. The production was revived on April 1, 1907. (See nos. 117-118.)

102. [Ames]
New York Public Library: *NCP+.40736B
[Carbon typescript, 8 x 12⅞; green cloth boards; title gilt on spine.]
Promptbook called "Castle Square Theatre Version," though heavily revised in ink and pencil as if for later use (see no. 117). At the front a penciled cast and synopsis of scenes. Excellent groundplans for all scenes. Copious stage business. Critical and interpretive notes from standard authorities. Notes on earlier productions of Irving, Booth, Tree, Novelli, Forbes-Robertson, etc.

103. Robert B. Mantell   Buffalo   October 20, 1906
Folger: Merch, 8
[Mixture of a Shakespeare edition and a bowdlerized text, 4¾ x 6⅝; interleaves, 5¾ x 8¼; black cloth boards and half black leather; title and Mantell's name gilt on cover.]
Handsome promptbook prepared by William H. Young in 1906, "as played by Edwin Booth." Marked both to end with the trial scene and to include the fifth act. Much used by Mantell. Scenic indications with excellent groundplans, grooves, stage business, maps, fine sketches, cues for effects.

104. Herbert Beerbohm Tree

London, His Majesty's   April 4, 1908

Folger: Merch, 44

[Pages of a Shakespeare edition, 4 x 6, pasted in a workbook, 10⅛ x 8½; black cloth boards and half black leather.]

Tree's preparation copy. Copious penciled notes on the acting and production.

105. [Tree]

Enthoven Collection: Tree, 205

[Cassell's National Library edition pasted in a workbook, 7 x 9; red marbled boards and red cloth spine.]

Rehearsal promptbook initialed by Cecil King. Cuts and stage business crudely penciled.

106. [Tree]

Enthoven Collection: Tree, 205

[Same format as preceding book but black cloth spine.]

Rehearsal promptbook initialed "S.B." Stage business and cues for effects crudely penciled.

107. [Tree]

Enthoven Collection: Tree, 251

[Cassell's National Library edition pasted in a workbook, 6½ x 8¾; red marbled boards and red cloth spine, very worn and broken; title typed on cover label.]

Final, very full promptbook as "produced April 4, 1908—May 30th 1908/59 performances," signed by Courtice Pounds and Claude Rains. Much used. At the front an itemization of the 90 roles. Each scene has plots of properties, lights, crowd business, music, excellent groundplans. Stage business in great detail. Last page missing. Program pasted in.

108. [Tree]

Enthoven Collection: Tree, 205

[Cassell's National Library edition, 1906, 4 x 6; red publisher's boards.]

Rehearsal copy of Mr. Bellew. Cuts, notes on music, etc.

109. [Tree]

Enthoven Collection: Tree, 257

[Papers.]

Partbook for Portia. Designs and swatches of materials for all footwear. Good watercolor designs for 5 scenes.

110. [Tree]

Enthoven Collection: Tree, 204A

[Papers.]

Plots of properties, limes, electrics, cast, dressing rooms; 5 ground-plans with list of scenic pieces for each.

111. Oscar Asche   Australia and South Africa   1909-13

Shakespeare Centre Library: 72.921ASC(5407)

[Temple edition pasted in a workbook, 7 x 9; black oilcloth boards; title on cover and spine labels.]

Promptbook of the Asche-Brayton tours of Australia in 1909-10 and Australia–South Africa in 1912-13. Calls, much stage business, maps, cues for effects. Good sketches of 3 scenes. Names of actors are jotted throughout. Production papers at the back.

112. [Asche]

Shakespeare Centre Library: 72.921ASC(5408)

[Cassell's National Library edition pasted in a workbook, 8 x 10⅛; red marbled boards and black cloth spine; title on cover label.]

Another promptbook, much used, of the Asche-Brayton tours. Calls, much stage business, cues for effects, timings. Many casual sketches of heads, scenery, furniture, etc. At the back production papers: lights, properties, trumpet scores.

113. Hallam Bosworth

New York Public Library: *NCP

[American Academy of Dramatic Arts edition (Irving version), 5½ x 9; interleaves, 7½ x 9¾; blue cloth boards; title gilt up spine.]

Promptbook compiled by transcribing stage business, maps, sketches from older books. Plots of properties, lights, etc., from various old promptbooks.

114. Henry Jewett   Boston, Boston Opera House   February 8, 1915

Folger: Merch, 21

[Typescript, 8½ x 11; gray cardboard and green cloth spine.]

Promptbook of the Henry Jewett Players used in 1915, 1921, 1929. The production resembles that of Sothern and Marlowe. Scenic indications, copious stage business, maps, cues for effects, time sheet.

[ACTOR LISTS FOR FOLLOWING BOOKS ARE GIVEN IN THIS ORDER: Shylock, Portia, Antonio.]

115. David Belasco   New York, Lyceum   December 21, 1922
    New York Public Library: *NCP.388978B
    [Belasco edition, 1922, 6¼ x 9¾; blue cloth boards; title gilt on spine.]
    Cast includes David Warfield, Mary Servoss, Ian MacLaren. This is not a marked copy, but an unusually interesting acting edition, privately printed, containing an Introduction justifying Belasco's principles of production and all major stage business and effects.

116. Percival Vivian
    Folger: Merch, 47
    [Ben Greet edition, 1912, 4¾ x 7¼; green cloth boards; title gilt on cover and spine.]
    Rehearsal copy for Old Gobbo in the Belasco production. Much scribbled stage business. Inscribed to Belasco.

117. Winthrop Ames   New York, Broadhurst   January 16, 1928
    New York Public Library: *NCP+.40735B
    [Shakespeare edition pasted in a workbook, 8 x 10½; black cloth boards; title gilt on spine.]
    Cast includes George Arliss, Peggy Wood, Leonard Willey. Synopsis of scenes, groundplans, copious stage business, maps. At the back plots of music, properties, lights, rehearsals, and a road sheet. (See nos. 101-102.)

118. [Ames]
    New York Public Library: 8-*NCP.37087B
    [Tudor edition, 1927, 3⅞ x 5⅜; red cloth boards; title gilt on spine.]
    Souvenir volume given to Ames by the 1928 company. Nineteen photographs of the actors and 6 of the sets.

119. Maude Adams   Cleveland   November 3, 1931
    New York Public Library: *NCP+.279441B
    [Typescript, 8¼ x 11⅞; red cloth boards; title gilt up spine.]
    Clean first copy of a 3-act "prose" version as played by Maude Adams and Otis Skinner for Erlanger Productions, Inc.

120. Theodore Komisarjevsky   Stratford-upon-Avon   July 25, 1932
    Shakespeare Centre Library: 71.21/1933ME

[Two books. Temple edition pasted in a workbook, 7 x 9; blue cloth boards and half red leather; title on cover and spine labels.] Cast includes Randle Ayrton (1932) and George Hayes (1933), Fabia Drake, Wilfrid Walter (1932) and Laidman Browne (1933). Designed by Mrs. Lesley Blanch. The first book had been used for the 1929 production; was erased and reused for the 1932 production, which was revived in 1933. Cuts, sketch of the scenery, considerable stage business, maps, cues for effects. The second book is an unused copy, less thoroughly marked.

121. B. Iden Payne   Stratford-upon-Avon   April 4, 1942
Shakespeare Centre Library: 71.21/1942
[Temple edition pasted in a workbook, 7 x 9; purple cloth boards and half black leather; title on cover and spine labels.]
Cast includes Baliol Holloway, Margaretta Scott, George Skillan. Designed by Peggy Neale. The book had been used for productions in 1936, 1940, 1941. Rather sparsely marked: cuts, some stage business, maps, irregular cues for effects.

122. Robert Atkins   Stratford-upon-Avon   April 8, 1944
Shakespeare Centre Library: 71.21/1944
[Penguin edition pasted in a workbook, 6¾ x 9; green cloth boards and blue cloth spine; title on cover and spine labels.]
Cast includes George Hayes, Helen Cherry, Antony Eustrel. Designed by Guy Sheppard. The book had been used before; was erased and rewritten. Cuts, stage business, maps, cues for effects.

123. Michael Benthall   Stratford-upon-Avon   July 11, 1947
Shakespeare Centre Library: O.S.71.21/1947
[New Temple edition pasted in a workbook, 8 x 12¾; blue cloth boards; title on cover and spine labels.]
Cast includes John Ruddock, Beatrix Lehmann, Walter Hudd. Designed by Sophie Fedorovitch. Cast and understudy list, much stage business, maps, cues for effects. Revived in 1948.

124. Denis Carey   Stratford-upon-Avon   March 17, 1953
Shakespeare Centre Library: O.S.71.21/1953
[New Temple edition pasted in a workbook, 8 x 13, red cloth board spring binder; title on spine label.]
Cast includes Michael Redgrave, Peggy Ashcroft, Harry Andrews. Designed by Hutchinson Scott. Cuts on full text, copious stage

business, maps (many of them on mimeographed groundplans), cues for effects. Production papers.

125. Michael Benthall
             Sydney (Old Vic, Australian Tour)   May 14, 1955
     Old Vic, Publicity Department
     [Temple edition pasted in a workbook, 8¼ x 13; bound with *Taming of the Shrew* in blue ring binder.]
     Cast includes Robert Helpmann, Katharine Hepburn, David Dodimead. Designed by Loudon Sainthill. Cuts, much stage business, cues for effects.

126. Tyrone Guthrie   Stratford, Ontario   June 29, 1955
     Festival Theatre, Library
     [Two books. New Stratford Shakespeare pasted in a workbook, 8 x 12¾; black cloth boards and red cloth spine; title pasted on cover.]
     Cast includes Frederick Valk, Frances Hyland, Robert Goodier. Designed by Tanya Moiseiwitsch. The first book has much stage business, maps, cues for effects, cast list. The second, a rougher copy, has stage business, maps, cues for effects.

127. Margaret Webster   Stratford-upon-Avon   April 17, 1956
     Shakespeare Centre Library: O.S.71.21/1956
     [New Temple edition pasted in a workbook, 8 x 13; red and black cloth board spring binder; title on spine label.]
     Cast includes Emlyn Williams, Margaret Johnston, Anthony Nicholls. Designed by Alan Tagg. Cuts on full text, copious stage business, maps (many on mimeographed groundplans), cues for effects. Production papers.

128. Jack Landau   Stratford, Connecticut   July 10, 1957
     University of California, Los Angeles: Houseman Box 14
     [Mimeograph, 8 x 11; blue stiff paper binder.]
     Cast includes Morris Carnovsky, Katharine Hepburn, Richard Waring. Designed by Rouben Ter-Arutunian. Unmarked copy of the acting version owned by John Houseman.

129. [Landau]
     University of California, Los Angeles: Houseman Box 9
     [Mimeograph, 8½ x 11; red cloth board ring binder.]
     Final or souvenir promptbook owned by John Houseman. Stage business typed along margins. Many production papers.

130. Michael Langham   Stratford-upon-Avon   April 12, 1960
     Shakespeare Centre Library: O.S.71.21/1960
     [Cambridge Pocket Shakespeare pasted in a workbook, 8 x 13;
     black cloth board spring binder; title on spine label.]
     Cast includes Peter O'Toole, Dorothy Tutin, Patrick Allen. De-
     signed by Desmond Heeley. Cuts on full text, copious stage busi-
     ness, many maps on mimeographed groundplans, cues for effects.
     Production papers.

131. Peter Potter   London, Old Vic   May 30, 1961
     Old Vic, Publicity Department
     [New Temple edition pasted in a workbook, 8 x 10; red ring
     binder; title on cover and spine labels.]
     Cast includes Robert Harris, Barbara Leigh-Hunt, George Baker.
     Designed by Felix Kelly and Rosemary Vercoe. Cuts, calls, stage
     business, maps, cues for effects. Production papers, including
     groundplans.

132. Other books of *The Merchant of Venice:*
     British Drama League: Edith Craig.
     Brown University: Eng.P.17a, Asa Cushman.
     Essex Institute, Salem: 822.08/S24/61, Harry George.
     Folger: Merch, 1, 3, 6, 26, 31, 32, anonymous; Merch, 5, Alfred
     Bucklaw; Merch, 7, William Winter; Merch, 10, George Becks;
     Merch, 11, R. H. Fitzgerald; Merch, 29, Marcus Moriarty, 1874;
     Merch, 30, Julia M. Powell; Merch, 46, H. B. Tree; Merch, 48,
     J. W. Wallack; Merch, 51, V. Wyngate; Merch, Folio 1, Adelaide
     Neilson.
     Harvard Theatre Collection: 13486.40.30, anonymous; TS.2424.-
     109, Maude Adams.
     Historical and Philosophical Society of Ohio: 812.3/R283/123,
     Alvin Read.
     Museum of the City of New York: 32.485.253A, Joseph Kirby
     and Boston Museum; 32.485.253c, anonymous.
     Princeton University, Seymour Collection: MV, 1, 4, William
     Seymour; MV, 6, Mueller and Everett.

The Merry Wives of Windsor

1. Anonymous   1630's

   Boston Public Library: G.17b.21

   [R. Meighen, London, 1630, $5\frac{1}{8}$ x 7; red leather gilt; title gilt up spine.]

   Calls to "Entter" through the first 4 acts are given in a seventeenth-century hand. These are probably only a reader's markings, not of theatrical significance.

2. Joseph Ashbury   Dublin, Smock Alley   1670's

   Folger: MW, Smock Alley

   [Pages 39-60 from a Third Folio, 1663, $7\frac{3}{4}$ x $12\frac{1}{8}$; red marbled boards and half maroon leather gilt; title gilt up spine; pages 53-56 missing.]

   Promptbook marked comparatively generously. Cuts, scenic indications, calls, cues for entrances (horizontal line with vertical slashes), cues for music. (See G. Blakemore Evans, *Shakespearean Prompt-Books*.)

3. [Ashbury]

   Folger: V.b.240

   [Manuscript, $7\frac{1}{2}$ x $11\frac{3}{4}$; red marbled boards and half green leather gilt; title gilt up spine.]

   An 8-leaf manuscript of a portion of *The Merry Wives* done in a seventeenth-century hand, being a replacement of the pages missing from the preceding book. No theatrical markings.

4. Anonymous   1700's

   Folger: Second Folio, 41

   [Pages 39-60 in a complete Second Folio, 1632, $8\frac{1}{2}$ x $12\frac{3}{4}$; brown leather, broken.]

   Promptbook probably of the latter part of the eighteenth century. (In this Folio only *The Merry Wives* has been marked for performance.) Cut, calls, some cues for act endings. Belonged to Chr. E. Merrett.

5. George Colman   London, Haymarket   August 24, 1781

   Folger: MW, 3

   [Pages 5-70 from volume III of a *Works*, $4\frac{1}{2}$ x 8; interleaves, 5 x $7\frac{1}{2}$; once bound in brown leather, but now only spine remaining; title gilt on spine.]

Promptbook endorsed by Colman and dated from the Haymarket; also marked "Promptbook/Hitchcock." Most of the markings in a clear round hand; additions and timings in Hitchcock's more careless, sloping hand. Cuts, scenic indications, calls, some stage business, cues for effects, timings.

6. S. Powell   London, Covent Garden(?)   February 13, 1797(?)
Folger: MW, 27
[Kemble edition, 1797, 5 x 8¼; blue marbled boards and brown leather spine; title and Powell's name printed on cover label.]
Promptbook endorsed "S.Powell." Sparks Powell died in 1798. Snelling Powell of Boston and New York lived into the nineteenth century. Another Powell is listed as Page in both Arnold's and West's promptbooks of c.1813 (see nos. 10, 11). Cuts, some scenic indications, calls, stage business, cues for effects.

7. George Frederick Cooke   London, Covent Garden   April 28, 1802
Folger: MW, 32
[Manuscript, 6⅜ x 8.]
Cooke's 14-leaf partbook for Falstaff, in his own hand. Property list. Endorsed on the front from "Boulton Street, (4) Piccadilly/ Tuesday./Half past Eleven, at Night,/April the 27th,/1802./ Coo[ke]."

8. John Philip Kemble   London, Covent Garden   May 10, 1808
Folger: MW, 36
[Kemble edition, 1804, 5⅛ x 8¼; interleaves watermarked 1805 or 1807; brown leather; title and "C.G./P.B./M/3" stamped on spine.]
Promptbook originally marked by Kemble: calls, some stage business, cues for effects, timings (2:40). Lengths are marked for several short roles. Additional markings by a prompter in 1831. Sometime later the prompter George Ellis inserted some groove numbers and a note objecting to an interpolated gag.

9. [Kemble]
Boston Public Library: G.4013.18
[Kemble edition, 1797, 5 x 8; red and blue marbled boards and maroon leather spine; title gilt up spine.]
Rehearsal copy for Mrs. Page, with a few directions marked by Kemble. A signature or the name of the assigned actress has been cut from the top of the title page.

10. S. J. Arnold   London, Drury Lane   c.1813
    Folger: MW, 1
    [Kemble edition, 1797, 5⅛ x 8⅜; green marbled boards and brown leather spine, broken; title gilt down spine.]
    Rough promptbook or preparation copy with penciled marginalia, owned by Arnold, the Drury Lane manager in 1812, but perhaps dating from earlier. Penciled cast list. Calls, little stage business, cues for effects.

11. W. H. West   London, Drury Lane   c.1813
    Folger: MW, 2
    [Kemble edition, 1797, 5¼ x 8¼; gray-green marbled boards and brown leather spine, broken; title gilt down spine.]
    Probably a transcription from the Drury Lane promptbook, and "Mark'd by W. West." Cuts and additions, calls, some stage business, cues for effects. In a cast list marked "OTRDL," Robin is by "Master West" and Shallow and Slender are "Both W. West." In a cast list marked "NTRDL, 1813" the name of West does not appear. The terms "OP" and "PS" are noted as meaning "RH" and "LH."

12. William B. Wood   Philadelphia, Chestnut Street   Feb. 20, 1818
    Folger: MW, 29
    [Kemble edition, 1815, 4 x 6¾; gray marbled boards and brown leather spine.]
    Lightly marked book: cuts, little stage business. Belonged to George Becks.

13. Anonymous   London, Drury Lane   February 20, 1824
    University of Nebraska: 822.33/U2k
    [Kemble edition, 1804, 4¾ x 7⅞; interleaves watermarked 1819; red cloth boards; title gilt down spine and identified perhaps wrongly with Covent Garden.]
    Promptbook heavily marked in several hands at several times; probably originally used for the dramatic version and finally as preparation copy for the Reynolds operatic version. Cast given with Madame Vestris. Cuts, alterations, additions, and notes for insertion of songs. Projected but canceled final scene of revelry at Page's villa. Calls, some stage business, cues for effects.

14. Mrs. Edward Wright   1830's
    Harvard Theatre Collection: (Widener, 13486.47.6)

[Longworth edition, New York, 1817, $3\frac{5}{8}$ x $6\frac{3}{8}$; interleaves; green cloth boards; title gilt up spine.]

Promptbook revised to match the Reynolds operatic version of 1824. Cuts and restorations, notes for insertion of songs, some stage business.

15. Anonymous   1830's

Harvard Theatre Collection: (Widener, 13486.47.5)

[Longworth edition, New York, 1817, $3\frac{1}{2}$ x $6\frac{1}{8}$; some interleaves; tan paper under green cloth boards; title gilt up spine.]

Promptbook "Corrected and Cut according to Prompt Book T.R.D.L." and "From Wilmott's correction T.R.D.L.," roughly revised to match the Reynolds operatic version. Cuts and restorations, notes for insertion of songs, some grooves, some stage business, cues for effects.

16. James H. Hackett   1832-70

Enthoven Collection

[Dolby edition, $3\frac{1}{2}$ x $5\frac{1}{2}$; interleaves; tan cardboard; title inked on cover.]

Promptbook of a 3-act version, marked for Hackett by S. C. Ferrers at the Park Theatre, in September, 1841. Appears to have been marked originally for 5 acts, later much cut. Cast for 1838 is entered. Calls, stage business, sketch, cues for effects.

[NOTE: Hackett played Falstaff in *The Merry Wives*, sometimes in 5 acts and sometimes in 3, from 1832 to about 1869. His many promptbooks are here listed together.]

17. [Hackett]

Enthoven Collection

[Cumberland edition, $3\frac{1}{2}$ x $5\frac{3}{4}$; interleaves, $3\frac{1}{2}$ x $6\frac{5}{8}$; red cloth and leather spine.]

Promptbook of a 5-act version marked for Hackett by Augustus C. Lewis at the Park Theatre in 1843. Casts for the Park in 1843 and Boston in 1848. Grooves, calls, stage business slightly fuller than in preceding book, cues for effects.

18. [Hackett]

Folger: MW, 20

[Pages 637-685 from an illustrated *Works*, $6\frac{1}{2}$ x 10; interleaves; brown cloth boards and half black leather; title gilt on spine, printed on cover label.]

Promptbook of a 5-act version marked for Hackett by H. B. Phillips at the Astor Place Opera House in 1848. Also dated 1861, 1862. Cuts on full text, grooves, calls, stage business, maps and sketches, cues for effects.

19. [Hackett]

Enthoven Collection

[Pages 3-52 from a double-column illustrated edition, 6¾ x 10½; interleaves; tan marbled boards and half black leather; title printed on cover label.]

Promptbook of a 5-act version marked for Hackett by Henry B. Phillips at Niblo's in 1849. Also signed by John W. Clifford of Buffalo, 1856. Cuts on full text. Markings transcribed from the preceding book.

20. [Hackett]

Enthoven Collection

[Spencer's Boston Theatre, 1855, 4¼ x 7¼; interleaves; brown cloth boards and half black leather; title gilt on spine.]

Promptbook of a 5-act version marked for Hackett by F. G. Crocker at Laura Keene's Theatre on May 31, 1858 ("and very badly marked too"). Signed by prompters John G. Steele of New Orleans, J. Whitaker of Detroit, and T. V. Jones of Cleveland in 1866 and 1867. Casts entered for Laura Keene's in 1858, the St. Charles in 1866, Memphis in 1868. Some scenic indications, maps and sketches. Stage business not written out because already printed in Spencer's acting edition.

21. [Hackett]

Enthoven Collection

[Davidson issue of Cumberland edition, 3¾ x 5⅝; interleaves; tan marbled boards and half black leather; title printed on cover label.]

Promptbook dated 1868. A scrap of playbill shows E. L. and Fanny Davenport as Mr. and Mrs. Ford. In early scenes the stage business is generously marked though in a shaky hand; later scenes sparsely marked.

22. [Hackett]

Folger: MW, 19

[Davidson issue of Cumberland edition, 3¾ x 5¾.]

Promptbook "To be returned to J H Hackett 1868."

23. [Hackett]

    Folger: MW, 18

    [Dunigan issue of Cumberland edition, 3½ x 5¾; tan paper wrapper.]

    Promptbook of a 3-act version. Cuts, calls, and notes on doubling "as reduced to three acts for a small company."

24. [Hackett]

    Folger: MW, Folio 2

    [Pages 81-120 from Halliwell's *Works*, 7⅝ x 11⅛; brown paper wrappers.]

    Promptbook of a 3-act version. Cuts on full text.

25. [Hackett]

    Library of Congress, Batchelder Collection: 410

    [Longworth edition, New York, 1817, 3⅞ x 6; blue interleaves; stiff brown paper; title inked on cover.]

    Promptbook "Marked from Hackett" and owned by S. T. Naylor. Cuts, scenic indications, grooves, calls, much stage business, maps, cues for effects. This transcription is fuller and more orderly than most of the Hackett books, but its contents are perhaps not entirely authentic Hackett.

26. [Hackett] and Charles Bass

    New York Public Library: *NCP. 342959

    [Spencer's Boston Theatre, 1855, 4¼ x 6⅞; interleaves; brown cloth boards; title gilt on spine.]

    Promptbook compilation of mid-century directions made by George Becks, taken from the promptbooks of James Hackett and Charles Bass (Bass played *The Merry Wives* in New York on June 24, 1850). At the front a list of property manuscripts and a detailed description of Falstaff's makeup. Scenic indications, grooves, calls, copious stage business, cues for effects, timing (2:40).

27. Stanley Charles Ferrers   New York, National   1837; May 30, 1839

    Folger: MW, 14

    [Two books. Cumberland edition, 3¼ x 5½; interleaves. Oxberry edition, Boston, 1822, 3¼ x 5½. Bound together in gray marbled boards and half green leather.]

    The Cumberland copy is a well-developed promptbook of the operatic version, made by Ferrers, the prompter, in 1837: cuts, scenic indications, grooves, calls, some stage business, maps, cues for effects. The Oxberry non-operatic copy is crudely and lightly marked as of May, 1839, probably for John Dwyer's final performance of Falstaff at the National on May 30.

28. Mercer Hampson Simpson   Birmingham, Theatre Royal   1840's
Birmingham, Shakespeare Memorial Library: B53/455732
[Cumberland edition, 3¾ x 6; bound with other plays in green cloth boards; "Shakespeare's Separate Plays" gilt on spine.]
Carefully marked promptbook, much used, checked for Ford. Calls, some stage business, maps, cues for effects, timings.

29. Anonymous
Birmingham, Shakespeare Memorial Library: B54/456354
[Shakespeare edition, 3¼ x 5½; interleaves, 4¼ x 7; blue paper; title inked on cover; bound with other plays in green cloth boards; "Shakespeare's Separate Plays" gilt on spine.]
Promptbook thoroughly marked in a small neat hand. Groundplans, grooves, calls, much stage business, maps, cues for effects.

30. Elizabeth Vestris   London, Covent Garden   September 11, 1840
Folger: MW, 25
[Shakespeare edition, 6½ x 10½; blue interleaves; heavy tan paper; title and "London 1840" in blue ink on cover.]
Extremely full and interesting promptbook compiled by John Moore. The original markings, in blue ink, are a transcription of Madame Vestris' book of 1840. Cuts on full text. Addition of songs and other non-Shakespearean matter to match the Reynolds operatic version as Vestris used it. Scenic indications, grooves, much stage business, cues for effects. After 1848, in America, Moore added, in brown ink and in pencil, further details from Hackett and from William Burton's 1853 production. Finally, in 1872 and perhaps again in 1886, Moore used the book in helping prepare Augustin Daly's productions: further cuts and alterations including the addition of a Falstaff Epilogue; scenic indications, property lists, much stage business, cues for effects. Extra matter fastened in includes: 10 printed casts from French's Standard Drama, clippings of a Covent Garden playbill of 1840, 3 Burton playbills, a Hackett playbill of 1869, 2 Daly playbills, 4 reviews from 1850 to 1869, an obituary of Hackett, comic engravings, a Daly property list, a list of rehearsal absences. (See nos. 41, 44-45, 48-50.)

31. George Bartley   London, Covent Garden   September 11, 1840
The Players: PB.79

[French issue of Lacy edition, 4⅜ x 7; interleaves; limp green leather gilt; title and "Property of W. F. Owen" gilt on cover.]

W. F. Owen's transcription of a promptbook of Edward Hastings, prompter at Brighton, which is a partial record of Madame Vestris' 1840 production and in some scenes a detailed record of George Bartley's stage business for Falstaff.

32. [Bartley]

New York Public Library: *NCP.342938

[Spencer's Boston Theatre, 1855, 4¼ x 7⅜; interleaves; brown cloth boards; title gilt on spine.]

Transcription of the preceding book made by W. F. Owen as a gift for George Becks. Explanatory notes by Owen, and a few additions of what "E. H. told me," especially about stage business of Falstaff.

33. W. H. Sedley Smith   1848

Harvard Theatre Collection: uncatalogued

[Oxberry edition, Boston, 1822, 3⅝ x 6; interleaves; publisher's wrappers under tan cardboard; title inked on cover.]

Lightly marked studybook, checked for Falstaff and Shallow, with bits of stage business. Also dated 1853.

34. Henry Farren   St. Louis   1850's

Harvard Theatre Collection: TS.2424.125

[Oxberry edition, 1820, 4⅛ x 7½; interleaves, 4⅞ x 7¾; marbled boards and black leather spine; title inked on cover.]

Lightly marked promptbook: cuts, some stage business, cues for effects. Originally belonged to E. W. Danforth of Boston.

35. Charles Kean   London, Princess's   November 22, 1851

Folger: MW, 21

[Pages 175-279 from volume I of a *Works*, 4¾ x 7⅜; blue interleaves, 6⅜ x 8; white cardboard; title and "Mr. Geo. Ellis" inked on cover.]

Promptbook or stage manager's workbook of George Ellis. Cuts on full text. Stage business, maps entered in ink in a small round hand. Many further notes, sketches, and warnings penciled by Ellis.

36. [Kean]

Folger: MW, 22

[Pages 205-309 from volume I of a *Works*, 5¼ x 8½; interleaves, 6¾ x 8½; tan cloth boards and half brown leather; title gilt up spine and "Mr. Charles Kean/Prompt Copy" gilt on blue leather cover label.]

Final or souvenir promptbook made by T. W. Edmonds, the prompter, in 1859. Cuts on full text. Grooves, calls, stage business, maps and sketches, cues for effects, timings (2:20).

37. [Kean]
Enthoven Collection: 94G27, plates 1807-09
[Scrapbook, 15¼ x 21⅜; blue cloth boards and blue cloth spine; "Kean Theatrical Scenery" gilt up spine.]
Three pages of watercolor costume designs (16 figures).

38. [Kean]
Folger: MW, 15
[Lacy edition, 4 x 7⅜; gray cardboard.]
Book marked for scenery, signed by Randle Fitzgerald, "Supt. St. Scene." Notations of stock sets to be used, partly in the hand of George Ellis. The sets include "Thompson's Chamber," "Bowley Hall," "Man of Quality," "Led Astray."

39. John G. Gilbert   Philadelphia, Chestnut Street   January 12, 1853
Boston Public Library: K.47.13
[Oxberry edition, Boston, 1822, 3¾ x 5¾; bound with 5 other plays in marbled boards and maroon leather spine; "Shakespeare" gilt on spine.]
Promptbook checked for Ford and Mrs. Quickly. Cuts, grooves, calls, cues for effects. Dated 1838. Philadelphia cast for January 12, 1853.

40. [Gilbert]
Harvard Theatre Collection: uncatalogued
[Two books. Cumberland edition, 3¾ x 5⅞; bound with William Davidge's copy (also Cumberland) in green cloth boards; title gilt up spine.]
Gilbert's copy, checked for Falstaff, is dated London, January, 1848, and gives Philadelphia cast for 1853. Davidge's copy is dated Norwich, May, 1840, when Davidge played Shallow, and contains an Augustin Daly bill for 1872, when he played Sir Hugh Evans.

41. William Burton   New York, Burton's   March 14, 1853
[See John Moore's book of Mme. Vestris' production (no. 30).]

42. John B. Wright   Boston, Boston Theatre   c.1854

New York Public Library: *NCP.342962

[Cumberland edition, 3¾ x 5⅞; gray interleaves; blue cloth boards; title gilt on spine.]

Very full promptbook made by John Wright, the stage manager, probably to be associated with John Gilbert, who was the Falstaff of the Boston Theatre Stock Company in 1854-58. Scenic indications, grooves, calls, copious stage business, maps. This book appears to be the source of Spencer's Boston Theatre edition of 1855.

43. [Wright]   Boston, Boston Theatre   c.1854

Harvard Theatre Collection: uncatalogued

[French's Standard Drama, 4⅜ x 7½; interleaves, 5 x 8; publisher's wrappers.]

Lightly marked promptbook: cuts, some stage business, maps.

44. Augustin Daly   New York, Fifth Avenue   November 19, 1872

Folger: MW, 8

[French edition, 4½ x 7⅜; interleaves, 5 x 8¾; tan paper; title inked on cover.]

Preparation copy for Daly's production made by John Moore, the stage manager. Cuts and transpositions, scenic indications for the first act, some detailed stage business. (See no. 30 for fuller record of the Daly production, and see nos. 48-50.)

45. [Daly]

Folger: MW, 11, 12

[Manuscripts, c.7½ x c.6¼.]

Partbooks for Shallow, Host, Caius, in the hand of John Moore. One large folded sheet of maps and scenery for 4 acts.

46. George B. Berrell   St. Louis   1875

Princeton University, Seymour Collection: MWW, 5

[French edition, 1855, 4⅜ x 7⅝; interleaves.]

Promptbook in preparation. Many careful notes on interleaves which are inserted, but not bound, in an acting edition. Cuts, scenic indications, stage business, maps, cues for effects.

47. Frederick Paulding   1880's

Rutgers University: PR.1243.SHA

[French edition, 4½ x 7½.]

Carelessly marked promptbook. Cuts, some stage business, maps, some cues for effects.

48. Augustin Daly   New York, Daly's   January 14, 1886
Harvard Theatre Collection: uncatalogued
[Shakespeare edition pasted in a workbook, 7½ x 9¼; in box of tan cloth boards and green leather spine; title gilt up spine.]
Partial preparation copy marked by William Winter through only 2 acts. Cuts, schedule of scenes, lists of properties, some stage business. (See nos. 30, 44-45.)

49. [Daly]
Folger: MW, 5, 6, 7, 9, 35
[Daly edition, 1886, 5¾ x 9⅛.]
Rehearsal copies for Mrs. Ford, Nym, Bardolph, Evans, Fenton. Some contain notes of stage business.

50. [Daly]
Folger: Prints and Engravings
[Daly edition, 1886, with facsimile of the 1602 Quarto, mounted in an album, 11⅞ x 15⅞; red and green marbled boards and half brown leather gilt; title gilt on spine.]
Souvenir album with many old prints of actors and scenes from the play, many old playbills, the Lucy coat of arms colored, the Cruikshank cartoons of Falstaff, playbills of Daly's productions, 30 photographs of Daly's actors in the play.

51. Herbert Beerbohm Tree   London, Haymarket   January 2, 1889
Enthoven Collection: Tree, 17
[Tree edition, 4 x 6¼; brown paper.]
Preparation copy. Cuts and revisions, stage business lightly developed in the margins. (See nos. 57-62.)

52. [Tree]
Enthoven Collection: Tree, 17
[Typescript, 8 x 10; brown papers; title typed on cover labels.]
Rehearsal promptbook of Tree's 5-act version, the acts bound separately. Some stage business and cues for effects added in pencil.

53. [Tree]
Folger: MW, 13

[Tree edition, 1889, 4⅛ x 6⅜; interleaves; publisher's wrapper.]
Originally the rehearsal copy for Ford. Name of James Ferndey
(Fernandez?) and date of January 19 on the cover. Two penciled
sketches of Ford's costume. Cuts and restoration of traditional gag
lines. Copious record of stage business, hastily penciled.

54. [Tree]
Folger: MW, 30
[Tree edition, 1889, 4¼ x 6⅜; publisher's wrappers.]
Spectator's comments on the Tree production.

55. William Seymour   Saratoga   August 2, 1895
Princeton University, Seymour Collection: MWW, 4
[Spencer's Boston Theatre, 1855, 4½ x 7½.]
Incompletely marked promptbook. Calls, some stage business, a
map at the foot of nearly every page, some cues for effects.

56. [Seymour]
Princeton University, Seymour Collection: MWW, 8, 9
[Two books. French's Standard Drama, 4½ x 7⅜.]
One is the stage manager's book with music cues. The other is
Mrs. John Drew's rehearsal copy for Dame Quickly. Both are
dated as of the Saratoga production.

57. Herbert Beerbohm Tree   London, His Majesty's   June 10, 1902
Enthoven Collection
[Tree edition, 1889, 4 x 6⅜; publisher's wrappers.]
One of Tree's studybooks, checked for Falstaff. Cuts, a few bits of
stage business probably for 1902. (See nos. 51-54.)

58. [Tree]
Enthoven Collection: Tree, 250
[Tree edition pasted in a workbook, 7 x 9; tan marbled boards
and green cloth spine, much worn.]
Completed and much used promptbook of Tree's 3-act version.
Cast of 1902. Cuts, copious stage business in red ink with pen-
ciled additions; maps, sketches, cues for effects.

59. [Tree]
Enthoven Collection: Tree, 143
[Tree edition pasted in a workbook, 6⅞ x 9; red marbled boards
and black cloth spine, much worn; title on cover label.]

Fullest promptbook of Tree's 3-act version. Printed cast of 1889 pasted in; 1902 cast written in. Cuts, good groundplan for each scene, much stage business typewritten and in longhand, cues for effects, timings.

60. [Tree]
Enthoven Collection: Tree, 143
[Mixture of a Shakespeare edition and Tree edition pasted in a workbook, 7 x 9; red marbled boards and black spine; title on cover label.]
Cleaned-up copy of the 3-act version, but not as complete as the preceding book.

61. [Tree]
Enthoven Collection: Tree, 250, 48, 143
[Papers.]
Plots of scenes, properties, lights. Printed work-sheets for use on tour: scenes, properties, flys, limes, electrics, etc. Program for the Festival of 1908. Cast lists, a hundred or more printed copies of the fairies' songs. Typescript partbooks for Falstaff and Mrs. Ford.

62. [Tree]
Enthoven Collection: Tree, 144
[Notebook, 45/8 x 7; black leather.]
Contains inventory of scenery, properties, wardrobe for an American tour.

63. Ellen Terry   London, His Majesty's   May 30, 1908
Smallhythe
[Temple edition, 1908, 37/8 x 5; limp maroon leather; title gilt up spine.]
Gift copy from an admirer used as a rehearsal copy. Cuts, several bits of stage business.

64. [Terry]
Smallhythe
[Temple edition, 1919, 37/8 x 5; limp maroon leather; title gilt up spine.]
One scene marked for a public reading. At the front a list of selections for the program of readings.

65. Winthrop Ames   New York, New Theatre   November 7, 1910
Harvard Theatre Collection: uncatalogued

[French's Standard Drama, 4½ x 7½; interleaves; publisher's wrappers.]

Preparation copy, signed also by W. C. Masson. Cuts and restorations, properties plot, calls, some stage business.

66. [Ames]

New York Public Library: *NCP+.42608B

[Typescript, 8½ x 13; green cloth boards; title gilt on spine.]

Clean first copy of "New Theatre Version," arranged in 12 scenes. Complete stage business, maps. At the back are plots of properties, lights, scenery, etc.; references to *Henry IV* for illumination of characters. Timing (1:46).

67. Henry Jewett   Boston, Boston Opera House   January 18, 1915

Folger: MW, Folio 1

[Typescript, 8½ x 11; gray cardboard and green cloth spine.]

Much used promptbook of a 4-act version. Stage business typed into the text, with penciled additions, maps, cues for effects. Printed programs of the 1915 production, an unpublished Preface, penciled cast of a later company.

68. James K. Hackett   New York, Criterion   March 20, 1916

Library of Congress, Manuscripts Division: Fiske Box 31

[Shakespeare edition tipped into a workbook, 9 x 14½; heavy black cloth boards and black imitation leather spine.]

Hackett's promptbook, owned by Minnie Maddern Fiske but marked "Nothing to do with the Fiske production." Cuts on full text; a Falstaff Epilogue. Copious penciled stage business, maps, cues for effects, timings. At the back a complete light plot, a dressing room list, addresses of the actors.

69. Lena Ashwell   London   1919-29

Birmingham, Shakespeare Memorial Library: 370/421203

[Favourite Classics edition pasted in a workbook, 6¼ x 8; black oilcloth; title gilt up spine.]

Promptbook of the Lena Ashwell Players. Scenic indications, properties, some stage business, maps, cues for effects.

70. Minnie Maddern Fiske   Philadelphia   October 31, 1927

Library of Congress, Manuscripts Division: Fiske Box 31

[Shakespeare edition pasted in 5 booklets, 8½ x 11; brown paper covers.]

Preparation copy. Cuts, alterations, little stage business, synopsis of scenes.

71. [Fiske]

Library of Congress, Manuscripts Division: Fiske Box 31
[Carbon typescript, 8½ x 11; green paper cover.]
Rehearsal copy, not much marked, of the version as "arranged and edited for stage representation by Harrison Grey Fiske, September 1927."

72. [Fiske]

Library of Congress, Manuscripts Division: Fiske Box 31
[Typescript, 8½ x 11; green paper cover.]
Perfected and clean copy of the final promptbook, marked in ink in a neat hand. Cuts and alterations, interpolated final song, scenic indications, copious stage business, light plot.

73. [Fiske]

Library of Congress, Manuscripts Division: Fiske Box 31
[Typescript, 8½ x 11; black cloth board binder.]
Promptbook used in production. Cuts and alterations. List of understudies. Much stage business but less complete than in the preceding book. Cues for effects.

74. [Fiske]

Library of Congress, Manuscripts Division: Fiske Box 32, 33
[Papers.]
Many folders of production and business papers. Ink drawings of properties. Sketches of Otis Skinner and Harrison Grey Fiske. Plots of properties, lights, dressing rooms. Testimonials from distinguished Shakespeareans. Publicity releases. Weekly financial statements, October 29, 1927, to May 19, 1928. Box office reports, contracts, salary lists, inventories of wardrobe and properties, routing plans, etc.

75. George E. Lask   1927

University of California, Los Angeles: Special Collections 714, Box 6
[Vade Mecum edition, 1900, 3⅞ x 5¾; publisher's gray boards; title in red down spine.]
Rehearsal copy. Rough cuts, some stage business, some notes on scenery.

[ACTOR LISTS FOR FOLLOWING BOOKS ARE GIVEN IN THIS ORDER: Falstaff, Ford, Mrs. Ford, Mrs. Page.]

76. W. Bridges-Adams   Stratford-upon-Avon   July 5, 1928
Shakespeare Centre Library: O.S.71.21/1928M
[Temple edition pasted in a workbook, 8 x 10; green cloth board spring binder; title on cover and spine labels.]
Cast includes Roy Byford, Wilfrid Walter, Mary Holder, Dorothy Massingham. Cuts on full text, stage business, some cues for effects. The book had been used by Bridges-Adams for production at Stratford and at the Lyric, Hammersmith, in 1923.

77. [Bridges-Adams]   June 30, 1931
Shakespeare Centre Library: 71.21/1931ME, 1934MER
[Two books. Temple edition pasted in a workbook, 7 x 9; blue cloth boards; title on cover label.]
Cast includes Roy Byford, Randle Ayrton, Dorothy Francis, Dorothy Massingham. Costumes by Eric Maxon. Clean copy, incompletely marked. The second book (which is in blue cloth boards and half red leather) is erroneously marked 1934; apparently it is another copy of the 1931 book, with much business, cues for effects.

78. Theodore Komisarjevsky   Stratford-upon-Avon   April 18, 1935
Shakespeare Centre Library: 71.21/1935MERR, M
[Two copies. Temple edition pasted in a workbook, 7⅛ x 9; purple cloth boards and half black leather; title on cover and spine labels.]
Cast includes Roy Byford, Roy Emerton, Gwynne Whitby, Catherine Lacey. Cuts, calls, map at the front, some stage business. The second copy is very similar to the first.

79. H. K. Ayliff   Stratford-upon-Avon   April 5, 1937
Shakespeare Centre Library: 71.21/1937ME
[Eversley edition pasted in a workbook, 7 x 9; purple cloth boards and half black leather; title on cover and spine labels.]
Cast includes Baliol Holloway, Donald Wolfit, Joyce Bland, Valerie Tudor. Costumes by Barbara Harris. Most of the writing has been erased; can be made out with close inspection.

80. F. Owen Chambers   Leamington Spa, Loft   May, 1938
Shakespeare Centre Library: 72.922CHA, 1 and 2

[Collins edition pasted in two workbooks, 6¼ x 8; gray boards and red (1), green (2) cloth spines; title on cover and spine labels.] Promptbook. Cuts, copious stage business. At the front a ground-plan.

81. Robert Atkins   Stratford-upon-Avon   April 3, 1945
Shakespeare Centre Library: 71.21/1945ME
[Eversley edition pasted in a workbook, 7⅛ x 9; blue cloth boards and half black leather; title on cover and spine labels.]
Cast includes Robert Atkins, Antony Eustrel, Claire Luce, Viola Lyel. Designed by Martin Battersby. Stage business, maps, some cues for effects. The book had been used by B. Iden Payne in 1940; was erased and reused.

82. Romney Brent   March 14, 1948
New York Public Library: *NCP+
[Three books. Typescript, 7¾ x 11; black boards.]
Three books of a production which toured the United States from March 14 to June 3, 1948. One of them, marked no. 7, has a special Prologue and some introductory scenes from *Henry IV*. Another is without these additions. The third, marked no. 13 and signed by Lionel Ince, was much used on the tour.

83. Glen Byam Shaw   Stratford-upon-Avon   July 12, 1955
Shakespeare Centre Library: O.S.71.21/1955ME
[New Temple edition pasted in a workbook, 8 x 13; blue cloth board spring binder; title on spine label.]
Cast includes Anthony Quayle, Keith Michell, Joyce Redman, Angela Baddeley. Designed by Motley. Very full stage business, maps, mimeographed groundplans, cues for effects. Cast lists. Television script of Act II.

84. Douglas Seale   London, Old Vic   September 27, 1955
Old Vic, Publicity Department
[New Temple edition pasted in a workbook, 8 x 10½; black ring binder.]
Cast includes Paul Rogers, Richard Wordsworth, Margaret Rawlings, Wendy Hiller. Designed by Paul Shelving. Cuts, calls, stage business, maps, cues for effects. Many production papers including a callbook.

85. Michael Langham   Stratford, Ontario   June 19, 1956
Festival Theatre, Library

[Two books. New Temple edition pasted in workbooks, 8 x 12¾; black cloth boards and red cloth spine; title pasted on cover.]

Cast includes Douglas Campbell, William Hutt, Helen Burns, Pauline Jameson. Designed by Tanya Moiseiwitsch. The first book has copious stage business. The second book has cues for effects, cast list, some production papers, and the stage manager's notes on the effectiveness of various actors and performances.

86. John Houseman and Jack Landau
                       Stratford, Connecticut   July 8, 1959
Festival Theatre, Production Department
[Two books. Mimeograph, 8½ x 11; one in blue cloth board ring binder, one in black ring binder.]
Cast includes Larry Gates, Hiram Sherman, Nancy Wickwire, Nancy Marchand. Designed by Will Steven Armstrong and Motley. The first book has copious stage business, maps. The second, signed "Goodman," has random stage business.

87. [Houseman]
University of California, Los Angeles: Houseman Box 12
[Mimeograph, 8½ x 11; rose interleaves; red cloth boards; title gilt on cover.]
Final or souvenir promptbook prepared for Houseman by the Connecticut stage managers. Stage business typed on interleaves. Full set of production papers at the back.

88. John Hale   London, Old Vic   December 22, 1959
Old Vic, Publicity Department
[Temple edition pasted in a workbook, 8 x 10½; black ring binder with green spine and corners.]
Cast includes Joss Ackland, Alec McCowen, Maggie Smith, Moyra Fraser. Designed by Carl Toms. Cuts, much stage business, cues for effects. Production papers.

89. Other books of *The Merry Wives of Windsor:*
Boston Public Library: G.176.21, G.4013.18, anonymous.
British Drama League: Edith Craig.
Brown University: Eng.P.17, Asa Cushman.
Connecticut State Library: William Gillette, 2 books.
Folger: MW, 4, Thomas Shirley and Geo. W. Clarke, Baltimore, 1858; MW, 16, D. J. Palmer, P. E. Elliott, W. C. Forbes; MW, 17,

Miss Gwynne; MW, 23, N. M. Ludlow; MW, 24, Marcus Moriarty, 1874; MW, 26, F. W. Percy and George Brown, 1848; MW, 28, S. J. Willis; MW, 31, 33, anonymous; MW, 34, marked libretto of Nicolai opera.

Historical and Philosophical Society of Ohio: 812.3/R283/124, Alvin Read.

Missouri Historical Society: John W. Norton.

New York Public Library: *NCP, Peter Richings.

Princeton University, Seymour Collection: MWW, 1, anonymous; MWW, 12, A. D. Bradley; MWW, 19, A. S. H. Murray, 1874.

A Midsummer Night's Dream

1. Joseph Ashbury   Dublin, Smock Alley   1670's
   University of Edinburgh
   [Pages 145-162 from a Third Folio, 1663, 8⅛ x 12¼; blue boards and half blue leather; title gilt up spine.]
   Perhaps a preparation copy: lacks calls and entrance signals. Cuts and alterations, scenic indications, some bits of stage business, one cue for music. (See G. Blakemore Evans, *Shakespearean Prompt-Books*.)

2. Anonymous   London, Hatton Garden   c.1672
   University of Edinburgh
   [Pages 145-162 from a First Folio, 1623, 8 x 12½; red marbled boards and half blue leather; title gilt up spine.]
   Preparation copy. Cuts for 3 acts. (See G. Blakemore Evans, *Shakespearean Prompt-Books*.)

3. David Garrick and George Colman
                  London, Drury Lane   November 23, 1763
   Folger: MND, 6
   [Tonson edition, 1734, 4¼ x 7⅛; red marbled boards and brown leather spine.]
   Garrick's preparation copy, which Colman altered and produced during Garrick's trip to the Continent. Developed as a promptbook: scenic indications, calls, stage business, cues for effects. Numbers in margins mark insertions of 23 songs. (See G. W. Stone, *PMLA*, LIV, 467-482.)

4. [Garrick and Colman]
   Folger: A.b.49
   [Manuscripts; red cloth board box, 8½ x 10¾; title gilt on black spine label.]
   Manuscripts related to the 1763 production: (1) provisional cast list and notice of rehearsal absences initialed by Garrick; (2) partial cast list; (3) prompter's callbook, being a large sheet, 8¼ x 13, folded into 6 columns, 3¼ x 8¼, with 32 calls; (4) and (5) parts for Moth and Peaseblossom; (6) list of songs, in Garrick's hand; (7) song for a fairy, in the hand of Edward Capell; (8) Colman's commentary on Garrick's proposed text.

5. [Garrick and Colman]
   Henry E. Huntington Library: Larpent, 229

[Manuscript, 6⅝ x 8¼; gray paper under blue cardboard; title inked on cover.]

Additions to the play as submitted by Colman for licensing.

6. [Colman]   London, Haymarket   July 18, 1777
    Folger: *A Fairy Tale* (promptbook)
    [Tonson edition of *A Fairy Tale,* 1763, 5¼ x 8¼; interleaves; red and yellow marbled boards and half brown leather, broken; title gilt on black spine label.]
    Promptbook of the 2-act afterpiece which Colman substituted for the *Dream* at Drury Lane in 1763, and produced at the Haymarket in 1777. (This is the Haymarket promptbook.) Cuts, scenic indications, properties list, calls, assignment of songs, cues for effects.

7. John Philip Kemble   London, Covent Garden   January 17, 1816
    Folger: MND, 19
    [Tonson edition of Garrick-Colman version, 1763, 5 x 7⅞; black cloth boards and brown leather spine; title gilt up spine.]
    Preparation copy of Frederic Reynolds' operatic version, based upon the Garrick-Colman version. Provisional cast. Copious notes for revising the text and on staging arrangements.

8. [Kemble]
    Folger: MND, 18
    [Kemble edition, 1816, 5⅜ x 8¼; interleaves; brown leather; title gilt on spine, spine stamped "TR/CG/PB/M/24."]
    Promptbook of the operatic version marked by Kemble. Cuts, scenic indications, calls, some stage business, cues for effects.

9. Edmund Kean(?)   London, Drury Lane   c.1824
    Folger: MND, 8
    [Kemble edition, 1816, 5¼ x 8⅜; interleaves watermarked 1824; reddish boards and half brown leather; title stamped up spine.]
    Promptbook which sometime belonged to Charles Kean and according to a notation of questionable authority had belonged to his father. The original markings of cuts, calls, stage business, cues for effects are in the hand (steady, light hand with divided letters) of a prompter who marked numerous books in the early 1820's. Additional markings in ink and pencil and the manuscript last page appear to be in the hand of Charles Kean. (See nos. 15-17.)

10. William E. Burton   New York, Burton's   February 3, 1854
Folger: MND, 21

[Shakespeare edition, 6⅝ x 10⅜; blue interleaves; heavy brown paper; title and John Moore's signature on cover.]

Promptbook record of Burton's production done in brown ink by John Moore, the stage manager, who played Egeus. Occasional notes on Madame Vestris' Covent Garden production of November 16, 1840; cast for Covent Garden. At the front full plots of scenes, grooves, properties, costumes. Cuts on full text, calls, much detailed stage business, maps, cues for effects. Pasted in are Burton's 24-page pamphlet on his production, 2 Burton playbills and some advertisements, 9 reviews of the productions by Burton and Thomas Barry (which were simultaneous). There are also many penciled notes referring to Augustin Daly's production, either that of August 19, 1873, at the Grand Opera House, or that of January 31, 1888, at Daly's. Moore would have used this book to help prepare the Daly productions. (See nos. 14, 23-25.)

[NOTE: All Burton, Barry, Wright, Moore, and Becks books of the *Dream* need comparative analysis.]

11. [Burton]
Folger: MND, 15

[French's American Drama, no. 1, 4⅝ x 7¼; publisher's wrappers under tan paper.]

Contains John Moore's manuscript partbook for Egeus, 8 x 6¼, by "Jas. E. Bell copyist."

12. Thomas Barry   New York, Broadway   February 6, 1854
New York Public Library: *NCP.343412

[Pages 5-73 from volume II of a *Works*, 6⅝ x 10; double interleaves, 7½ x 10; tan paper under red cloth boards; title gilt on spine.]

Very full promptbook of the Barry production by John B. Wright, the stage manager. Cuts on full text, very detailed scenic indications, grooves, much stage business, processions, maps, sketches, cues for effects.

13. [Barry] and William E. Burton
Folger: MND, 20

[French's American Drama, CVI, 4⅜ x 7; interleaves; black and white cloth boards and black leather spine; title gilt up spine.]

Composite promptbook made by George Becks based on an acting edition apparently derived from the Barry production. In brown ink Becks has entered much data from John Wright's (Barry) book, which belonged to him; in black ink he has entered details from the following (John Moore?) book, which also belonged to him. At the front plots of scenes, grooves, properties, processions. Calls, much stage business, maps, sketches, cues for effects.

14. [Barry and Burton]
New York Public Library: *NCP.164552
[French's American Drama, CVI, 4½ x 7½; interleaves, 5 x 8; green and black boards and black cloth spine; title inked on spine.]
Unidentified promptbook compilation of stage business and scenic indications and effects which seems to derive from both the Barry and Burton productions. Very full and interesting; at many points provisional and advisory in tone. It is perhaps John Moore's preparation book for the Daly production of 1873. (See nos. 10, 23-25.)

15. Charles Kean   London, Princess's   October 15, 1856
Folger: MND, 9
[Proof pages of Kean edition, 1856, 5¼ x 8¼; gray interleaves, 7⅛ x 9; gray cardboard; title and "G.E./R.P.T.-Oct^r-1856" inked on cover.]
Workbook of George Ellis, the stage manager. Cuts on provisional acting version. Copious penciled notations of stage business and the working of machinery. Dance routine at end of third act. Timing (2:40). On large enclosed sheets, lists of properties and supers. Three small sheets of rehearsal notes. (See no. 9.)

16. [Kean]
Folger: Kean Costume Book, Prints and Engravings, 181
[Scrapbook, 14⅛ x 16⅝; green cloth boards and half green leather gilt.]
Contains a group of small plates of watercolor costume designs (nearly 50 figures) for the Dream.

17. [Kean]
Enthoven Collection: Box DT.43
[Watercolors mounted on large display boards.]
Fine watercolor designs of 10 scenes, and 5 plates of properties.

18. Laura Keene   New York, Laura Keene's   April 18, 1859
New York Public Library: NCOFp.v.194.385194B

[French's American Drama, CVI, 4½ x 7¼; gray interleaves, 5½ x 7¼; bound with 4 other books in brown paper under black cloth boards; title gilt on spine.]

Roughly marked promptbook or stage manager's workbook. Cuts and restorations, calls, maps, cues for effects. Many warnings for the working of machines.

19. Samuel Phelps   London, Sadler's Wells   October 19, 1861
Folger: MND, 13

[Pages 307-387 from volume II of a *Works*, 5⅛ x 8⅞; blue interleaves watermarked 1858, 5½ x 9¼; green marbled boards and black leather spine; title gilt up spine.]

A beautifully written promptbook apparently made for Phelps's 1861 revival (he had produced the *Dream* in 1853, 1855, 1856). Cuts on full text, scenic indications, grooves, calls, copious stage business, maps, sketches, cues for effects, timings. Occasional notice to "Go back to old book." Belonged to Harry Plowman.

20. [Phelps]   Manchester, Prince's   c.1870
Folger: MND, 14

[Mixture of Calvert edition, Manchester, 1865, 4¾ x 7¼, and a Shakespeare edition mounted between the leaves of a workbook, 7½ x 9; black cloth boards and half black leather; title and "Prince's Theatre, Manchester" inked on cover label.]

Rough promptbook probably made for one of Phelps's engagements with Charles Calvert at Manchester. Some scenic indications, calls, stage business, maps, cues for effects. One note to "Go to Mr. Phelps Book." Belonged to Harry Plowman.

21. William Seymour   1880's
Princeton University, Seymour Collection: MND, 2

[French's American Drama, CVI, 4⅛ x 7¼; interleaves, 5¼ x 8; paper wrappers.]

Promptbook. Cuts, some stage business, maps, many cues for music and lights.

22. [Seymour]
Princeton University, Seymour Collection: MND, 3

[Laura Keene edition, 1859, 4¼ x 7¼; interleaves of hotel stationery dated 188–, 4¼ x 8¼; paper wrappers.]

Crudely penciled promptbook mainly concerned with music and lights.

23. Augustin Daly   New York, Daly's   January 31, 1888
    Folger: MND, 5
    [Daly edition, 1888, 7 x 11; gray paper under gray cardboard.]
    Promptbook based on Daly's edition in which most of the stage directions are printed. Some cuts, calls, additional stage business, maps, cues for effects. Several photographs of the production pasted in. Cue sheet for "Calcium Light in front of house." (See nos. 10, 14.)

24. [Daly]
    Folger: MND, 4
    [Manuscript, 7¾ x 6½.]
    Partbooks, in the hand of John Moore, the stage manager, for Cobweb, First Fairy, Moth, Mustard Seed.

25. [Daly]
    New York Public Library: 8-*NCP.686464
    [Daly edition, 1888, 6½ x 10¾, expanded into an album; leather gilt; title gilt on cover and spine.]
    Ada Rehan's souvenir album, given her by Daly in 1888. About 30 old engravings and contemporary cartoons, and about 75 photographs of scenes and characters in the production, some printed on satin.

26. George Becks
    New York Public Library: *NCP.342976
    [Lacy edition, 4⅛ x 7; interleaves; green cloth boards; title gilt up spine.]
    Not a complete promptbook, lacking calls and regular cues; perhaps notes made by Becks as a spectator at some production. (The date on the book—1861—is probably not the date of the notes.) Some scenic indications, some grooves, interesting but random stage business, maps, sketches, some cues for effects.

27. F. R. Benson   London, Globe   December 19, 1889
    Shakespeare Centre Library: 72.923BEN
    [Memorial Theatre edition pasted in a workbook, 4½ x 7⅜; black cloth boards; title on cover and spine label.]
    "Working Stage Book for Music, Gas, Limes, Supers and Chil-

dren's Entrances," signed and dated (1897) by F. R. Ayrton. (The date given above is that of Benson's important first London production.) Names of actors, crowd movements and responses, cues for effects, timings (3:10).

28. Herbert Beerbohm Tree

London, Her Majesty's   January 10, 1900

Enthoven Collection: Tree, 144

[Temple edition pasted in a workbook, 8 x 12½; tan marbled boards and black cloth spine, much worn.]

Rehearsal promptbook. Cuts, much stage business roughly entered in pencil and red ink.

29. [Tree]

Enthoven Collection: Tree, 144

[Temple edition pasted in a workbook, 7 x 9; blue marbled boards and red leather spine, much worn.]

Rehearsal promptbook done in red ink with penciled additions. Cuts blocked out in red wash. Copious stage business, maps, cues for effects. Good groundplan for last scene.

30. [Tree]

Enthoven Collection: Tree, 144

[Temple edition pasted in a workbook, 7 x 9¾; white vellum boards, very soiled; title on cover label.]

Final promptbook, carefully written in red ink with penciled additions. Cuts, good groundplans, essential stage business, cues for effects. Printed cast and scene lists pasted in.

31. [Tree]

Folger: MND, 7

[Clarendon Press edition, 1888, 4¼ x 6½; interleaves; red cloth boards; title and "F. Grove" gilt on green spine label.]

Souvenir promptbook of Tree's production made by Fred Grove. Cuts, scenic indications, very detailed stage business, some maps.

32. [Tree]

Enthoven Collection: Tree, 144

[Two books. Eversley edition, 1908, 4½ x 6¾; Favourite Classics edition, 1904, 3⅝ x 6.]

Rehearsal copies, with cuts and some stage business.

33. [Tree]
Enthoven Collection: Tree, 144
[Papers.]
Property list, cast list, distribution charts, etc.

34. [Tree]
Enthoven Collection: Tree, 144
[Notebook, 4⅝ x 7; black leather.]
Inventory of scenery, properties, wardrobe for an American tour.

35. Harley Granville-Barker   London, Savoy   February 6, 1914
University of Michigan, Shakespeare Collection
[Favourite Classics edition, 1912, tipped between sheets of a workbook, 9⅞ x 11¾; red cloth boards; title gilt up spine.]
Very full prompt or production book. Copious stage business, excellent maps and groundplans, cues for effects. At the front, program, plots of lights, arcs, properties, and 8 large photographs of the sets. At the back, a 32-page book of Cecil Sharp's songs and incidental music for the production. (This book or any part of it cannot be copied without the written permission of Mr. C. B. Purdom, 39 Woodland Rise, Welwyn Garden City, Hertfordshire, England.)

36. Henry Jewett   Boston, Boston Opera House   March 1, 1915
Folger: MND, 12
[Typescript, 8½ x 11; gray cardboard and green cloth spine.]
Much used promptbook. Cast, scenic indications, much stage business, cues for effects. Many songs added. Photograph of Green Room of the theatre. Program, which lists about 180 productions by Jewett's company from 1915 to 1926.

37. F. Owen Chambers   c.1920
Shakespeare Centre Library: 72.923CHA
[Favourite Classics edition pasted in a workbook, 7 x 9; black cloth boards and black leather spine; title on cover and spine labels.]
Promptbook probably for an amateur performance. Groundplans, much stage business, cues for effects. Photograph of a woods scene as model for set. Production papers: cast, costumes, wigs, scenes, properties, dances, lights.

[ACTOR LISTS FOR FOLLOWING BOOKS ARE GIVEN IN THIS ORDER: Bottom, Puck, Hermia, Helena.]

38. W. Bridges-Adams   Stratford-upon-Avon   April 28, 1932
Shakespeare Centre Library: 71.21/1932
[Temple edition pasted in a workbook, 7 x 9; blue cloth boards and half black leather; title on cover and spine labels.]
Cast includes Roy Byford, Geoffrey Wilkinson, Hilda Coxhead, Fabia Drake. Designed by Norman Wilkinson. Stage business, maps, cues for effects.

39. [Bridges-Adams]   1934
Shakespeare Centre Library: 71.21/1934MI
[Temple edition pasted in a workbook, $6\frac{7}{8}$ x $8\frac{7}{8}$; blue cloth boards and half red leather; title on cover label.]
Cast includes Roy Byford, John Denis, Gwynne Whitby, Dorothy Black. Designed by Norman Wilkinson. Stage business, maps, some cues for effects. The book had been used in 1928, 1930, 1932, and for an American tour in 1928-29.

40. Robert Atkins   London, Regent's Park   July 21, 1936
Shakespeare Centre Library: 72.923ATK
[Shakespeare edition pasted in a workbook, $6\frac{7}{8}$ x $8\frac{7}{8}$; tan boards and green cloth spine, much worn; title on spine label.]
Cast includes Baliol Holloway, Leslie French, Margaretta Scott, Rosalyn Boulter. Stage business, maps, cues for effects, 5 pages of timings. Plots of properties, lights, cast, etc. The book was used also in following seasons in the Open Air Theatre and at Eastbourne.

41. [Atkins]   Stratford-upon-Avon   May 9, 1944
Shakespeare Centre Library: 71.21/1944MI
[Penguin edition pasted in a workbook, 7 x 9; purple cloth boards and half black leather; title on cover and spine labels.]
Cast includes Cliff Weir, Mary Honer, Anna Burden, Viola Lyel. Designed by Guy Sheppard. Stage business, maps, some cues for effects. The book had been used in 1938; was erased and reused.

42. Michael Benthall   Stratford-upon-Avon   April 23, 1949
Shakespeare Centre Library: O.S.71.21/1949MI
[Shakespeare edition pasted in a workbook, $7\frac{3}{4}$ x $12\frac{3}{4}$; red cloth boards; title on cover and spine labels.]

Cast includes John Slater, Philip Guard, Penelope Munday, Diana Wynyard. Directed by Anthony Quayle. Designed by James Bailey. Copious stage business, maps, cues for effects.

43. George Devine   Stratford-upon-Avon   March 23, 1954
Shakespeare Centre Library: O.S.71.21/1954M
[New Temple edition pasted in a workbook, 8 x 13; red cloth board spring binder; title on spine label.]
Cast includes Anthony Quayle, David O'Brien, Zena Walker, Barbara Jefford. Designed by Motley. Copious stage business, cues for effects. At the back 19 maps on mimeographed groundplans.

44. Jack Landau   Stratford, Connecticut   June 20, 1958
Festival Theatre, Production Department
[Two books. Mimeograph, 8½ x 11; one in cream cloth board ring binder, one in black board ring binder.]
Cast includes Hiram Sherman, Richard Easton, Barbara Barrie, Inga Swenson. Designed by David Hays and Thea Neu. The first book has copious stage business typed on facing pages, cues for effects typed on text pages; production papers include 19 pages of ad libs and business for walk-ons, hanging section, plots for flys, traps and machines, properties, wigs and beards. The second book has cues for effects and timings.

45. [Landau]
University of California, Los Angeles: Houseman Box 11
[Mimeograph, 8½ x 11; white cloth board ring binder.]
Final or souvenir promptbook which belonged to John Houseman. Stage business typed along margins. Production papers at the back.

46. Peter Hall   Stratford-upon-Avon   June 2, 1959
Shakespeare Centre Library: O.S.71.21/1959M
[New Temple edition pasted in a workbook, 8 x 13; in 2 green cloth board spring binders.]
Cast includes Charles Laughton, Ian Holm, Priscilla Morgan, Vanessa Redgrave. Designed by Lila de Nobili. Copious stage business typed on interleaved sheets, many maps on mimeographed groundplans, cues for effects.

47. Douglas Campbell   Stratford, Ontario   June 28, 1960
Festival Theatre, Library

[Two books. Penguin edition pasted in workbooks, 7¾ x 13⅛; blue cloth boards bordered in red; title pasted on cover.]

Cast includes Tony van Bridge, Jake Dengel, Helen Burns, Kate Reid. Designed by Brian Jackson. The first book has copious stage business, cues for effects. The second has calls.

48. Michael Langham   London, Old Vic   December 20, 1960
Old Vic, Publicity Department
[New Temple edition pasted in a workbook, 8 x 10; green ring binder.]

Cast includes Douglas Campbell, Tom Courtenay, Judi Dench, Barbara Leigh-Hunt. Designed by Carl Toms. Cuts, much stage business, maps, cues for effects. Many production papers: cast, singers, flys, properties, etc.

49. Other books of *A Midsummer Night's Dream:*
Folger: MND, 1, 2, George Becks; MND, 3, William Winter and Augustin Daly; MND, 10, 11, Emilie Melville; MND, 16, James Taylor; MND, 17, anonymous.

Historical and Philosophical Society of Ohio: 812.3/R283/125, Alvin Read.

Princeton University, Seymour Collection: MND, 13, A. S. H. Murray, 1875.

Much Ado About Nothing

1. Anonymous   1600's
   Victoria and Albert: Dyce 8980
   [Wise and Aspley Quarto, 1600.]
   Preparation copy probably of the seventeenth century. Dramatis Personae, cuts, and speeches checked for retention. (See G. Blakemore Evans, *Shakespearean Prompt-Books*.)

2. John Philip Kemble   London, Drury Lane   April 30, 1788
   Folger: T.a.34
   [Manuscript, 7 x 8⅞; brown leather gilt; title gilt up spine.]
   Kemble's 23-page partbook for Benedick, in his own hand, 577 lines. Dated from Drury Lane as above, but probably written much later. (See nos. 5-7.)

3. William Warren and William Wood
                    Philadelphia, Chestnut Street   March 16, 1804
   Harvard Theatre Collection: (Widener, 13486.69)
   [Bell edition, 1773, 4¼ x 6⅞; interleaves; brown cloth boards; title gilt on spine.]
   Promptbook of eighteenth-century English origin, more generously marked than most Warren and Wood books. Cuts, scenic indications, grooves, calls, some stage business, maps, cues for effects. Penciled additions, including the names of some actors, are Philadelphian. (See no. 9.)

4. Anonymous   London, Drury Lane   c.1805
   Harvard Theatre Collection: uncatalogued
   [Kemble edition, 1797, 5 x 8⅛; gray paper.]
   Promptbook "Marked as at Drury Lane." Hasty copy with minimal stage business. (See OTH, 5.)

5. Maria Foote   London, Covent Garden   c.1815
   Folger: Mu Ad, 3
   [Kemble edition, 1810, 5 x 8¼; orange leather and half red leather; title gilt on blue leather cover label.]
   Partbook for Beatrice, marked by John Philip Kemble. Cuts, calls, stage business and maps for Beatrice. Additional dialogue for Beatrice-Benedick at end of the church scene. A note by an owner in 1870 identifies "these plays" as the acting copies of Miss Foote.

6. Charles Kemble   London, Covent Garden   c.1820
   Garrick Club

[Kemble edition, 1810, 5 x 8½; interleaves; blue cloth boards and brown leather spine; title gilt up spine.]

Transcription of John Philip Kemble's promptbook in a clear flowing hand, probably made for Charles Kemble in the early 1820's. Considerable stage business, maps. Additional dialogue for Beatrice and Benedick at end of the church scene. (See no. 20.)

7. [Kemble]

Harvard Theatre Collection: uncatalogued

[Kemble edition, 1810, 4⅞ x 8; interleaves; red marbled boards and half red leather; title gilt on spine.]

Transcription of the preceding book made by Walter Lacy at the Garrick Club in 1859. Cuts, stage business, maps. Some additions to stage business by Lacy. Several notes about Lacy, personal and professional, entered by himself. (See no. 32.)

8. J. W. Wallack   1823-59

Folger: Mu Ad, 24

[Oxberry edition, 1823, 4 x 6½; interleaves; green cloth boards; title gilt up spine, Wallack's name gilt on cover.]

Promptbook carefully marked in ink with penciled additions, checked for Don Pedro. Cuts and restorations, grooves, calls, stage business, cues for effects. Wallack's farewell to the stage was as Benedick at Wallack's Theatre in New York on May 14, 1859.

9. William B. Wood   Baltimore   February 11, 1829

Folger: Mu Ad, 27

[Inchbald edition, 4⅛ x 6⅝; interleaves; limp brown leather; title and Wood's name inked on cover.]

Promptbook with cast for above date. Cuts and restorations, calls, some stage business, cues for effects. Kemble's additional dialogue for Beatrice-Benedick at end of the church scene. (See no. 3.)

10. Charles Kean   1830's

Folger: Mu Ad, 12

[Kemble edition, 1810, 4⅞ x 8⅛; interleaves; gray cloth boards and half black leather; title and Kean's name gilt on spine.]

Early Kean promptbook used for many years. Marked originally in a light neat hand transcribing the essentials of the Kemble book: grooves, calls, stage business, maps, cues for effects, additional dialogue for Beatrice and Benedick at end of the church scene. Additional markings in darker ink, rougher style (probably Kean's hand): cuts and restorations, further stage business, etc. One note signed by J. B. Addis, the American prompter, and many other prompters' jottings. A note about stone benches in the hand of George Ellis (1858). Timings range from 2:25 to 2:35. (See nos. 18, 26-31.)

11. [Kean]
    Folger: W.a.10
    [Notebook of sheets watermarked 1837, 4¾ x 7¾; brown marbled boards and half brown leather gilt; "Theatrical Costume" inked on cover label.]
    Kean's touring wardrobe list for Benedick is the fifth of 16 such lists in this book.

12. Frederick Vining   London, Haymarket   June 23, 1832
    Harvard Theatre Collection: (Widener, 13486.69.4)
    [Kemble edition, 1815, 4¼ x 7⅛; interleaves; gray boards and green cloth spine; title inked on cover.]
    Rehearsal copy dated from the Haymarket, May, 1833. Few scenic indications and properties, considerable stage business for Benedick personal to Vining, few cues for effects. Additional dialogue for Beatrice and Benedick at end of the church scene.

13. James E. Murdoch   New York, Park   June 4, 1838
    University of Pennsylvania: AC85.M9415.820p.54a
    [French's Standard Drama, 4½ x 7½; interleaves, 4⅞ x 7¾; purple and yellow marbled boards and brown leather spine; title on cover label.]
    Thorough promptbook. Scenic indications, grooves, calls, some stage business, maps, dance routine, cues for effects. Additional dialogue for Beatrice and Benedick at end of the church scene and in the final scene.

14. [Murdoch]
    University of Pennsylvania: AC85.M9415.820p.54
    [Kean edition, 1859, 4¼ x 6⅝; gray pamphlet boards.]
    Rehearsal copy of Murdoch's later 3-act version checked for Don John. Cuts, a few scenic notes.

15. William Charles Macready
                     London, Drury Lane   February 24, 1843
    British Theatre Museum: G 49 1963

[Pages 275-366 from volume II of a *Works,* 5⅛ x 8; interleaves, 6¼ x 8; tattered brown paper.]

Promptbook marked in several hands including the round ink hand of a copyist and pencilings by John Willmott and George Ellis. Cuts on full text, some grooves, some stage business, several rough sketches and maps, cues for effects, timings (2:35). Belonged to George Wightwick, later to Henry Irving.

16. [Macready]

Harvard Theatre Collection: uncatalogued

[Pages 217-312 from volume XII of a *Works,* 5½ x 8¼; interleaves; gray cardboard; title and "GE—TRDL—1845" inked on cover; in box of tan cloth boards and black leather spine; title gilt up spine.]

Transcription of Macready's promptbook done in pencil by George Ellis in 1845. Cuts on full text. Additional dialogue for Beatrice and Benedick at end of the church scene. Scenic indications, calls, stage business, fine maps, cues for effects, timings (2:35). Contains Ellis' 1843 callbook: 12 pages, 3 x 8, gray paper in tan cover.

17. [Macready]

Victoria and Albert, Forster Library, 7918:   F.48.C.16

[Pages 8-208 (last pages missing) of a Shakespeare edition, 4½ x 7½; bound with other Macready promptbooks in green cloth boards and half tan leather; titles gilt on spine.]

Macready's study copy, probably older than the preceding book. Marked for stresses. Numerous marginal notes of stage business, in English, Latin, Greek.

18. [Macready]

Folger: Mu Ad, 13

[Pages 205-301 from volume II of a Steevens *Works,* 5¼ x 8½; interleaves, 7⅛ x 9⅛; reddish brown marbled boards and half green leather gilt; title gilt on red leather spine label, "Prompt Copy/Mr. Charles Kean" gilt on black leather cover label.]

Excellent transcription of Macready's book made by George Ellis for Charles Kean in 1850. Cuts on full text. Scenic indications, grooves, calls, stage business, maps, sketches, cues for effects, timings (2:25). Pencilings indicate use by Kean. Contains 2 copies of a poem to "My dearest Jane" on paper watermarked 1862, in Kean's hand. (See nos. 10-11, 26-31.)

19. [Macready]

University of Illinois: x792.9/Sh15mu/no.1

[Pages 205-301 from volume II of a Steevens *Works*, 5⅜ x 8¾; gray interleaves, 7¼ x 8¾; blue marbled boards and half green leather, broken; title gilt up spine, "Hermann Vezin" gilt on red cover label.]

Excellent transcription of Macready's book "as acted at the TRDL" made by George Ellis for Hermann Vezin. Cuts on full text. Scenic indications, grooves, calls, stage business, maps and sketches, cues for effects, timings (2:35).

20. [Macready] and Charles Kemble

New York Public Library: *NCP.342944

[Cumberland edition, 3¼ x 5½; interleaves, 3¾ x 6; black cloth boards; title gilt up spine.]

Promptbook compilation made by George Becks: "N.B. From Promptbook under Mr. Macready's Direction, T.R.D.L. 1842. Where the bus. of C. Kemble differed from Mr. M—a note is made of same." Restorations of text, scenic indications, grooves, calls, stage business, maps and sketches, cues for effects, timings (2.35). (See nos. 6, 38.)

21. John Moore   New York, Burton's   1846-70

Folger: Mu Ad, 17

[Cumberland edition, 3½ x 6; interleaves, 4⅞ x 8; tan paper; title inked on cover.]

Promptbook first marked by Moore in England in 1846, and used in America (mainly at Burton's) for many years. Checked for Verges, which Moore often played. At the front a dance routine. Grooves, calls, stage business, maps, cues for effects, timings. References to particular business of Helena Faucit, Mrs. Nisbett, Mrs. Kean, Mrs. Barrow. Playbills of Charles Kemble, 1818; James Murdoch, 1857; Belton, Barrow, and Burton, 1857; Barry Sullivan, 1858; Lester Wallack, 1869; Scott-Siddons, 1870. Reviews of the Wallack production (4), Scott-Siddons (2), Adelaide Neilson (1).

22. [Moore]

Folger: Mu Ad, 18

[Modern Standard Drama, 4½ x 7½; interleaves, 5 x 8; publisher's wrappers under blue paper.]

Unfinished promptbook. At the front good plots of scenes with grooves, gas, properties, supers.

23. E. F. Taylor   1850's

New York Public Library: *NCP.164541

[French's Standard Drama, 4¼ x 7⅜; green cloth boards; title gilt up spine.]

Lightly marked promptbook of a 4-act version. Calls, some stage business, cues for effects.

24. Barry Sullivan   1850's

Shakespeare Centre Library: 50.24(1797)

[Pages 419-505 from volume I of the Robinson *Works,* 1797, 6¾ x 9⅝; interleaves; brown marbled boards and half brown leather; title gilt on black spine label, Sullivan's name and "T.R. Haymarket" gilt on black cover label.]

Neat but sparsely marked promptbook, probably a transcription by George Hastings from some earlier book. Cuts on full text, some stage business, maps, cues for effects. Part of a set of books gathered by Sullivan while at the Haymarket in 1852.

25. T. Agnew Dow   Philadelphia, Arch Street   December 7, 1854

Folger: Mu Ad, 2

[Modern Standard Drama, 1848, 4 x 6⅝; interleaves; white paper spine.]

Carefully prepared promptbook checked for Don John. Cuts, scenic indications, grooves, calls, stage business resembling Kemble's, map, sketches, cues for effects.

26. Charles Kean   London, Princess's   November 19, 1858

Folger: Mu Ad, 10

[Kean edition, 1858, 5⅛ x 8; interleaves, 6⅞ x 8⅝; tan cloth boards and half brown leather; title gilt up spine, "Prompt Copy/ Mr. Charles Kean" gilt on blue leather cover label.]

Final or souvenir promptbook made by T. W. Edmonds in 1859. Contents generally similar to the book George Ellis made for Kean in 1850 (see no. 18); notes on mechanics of lighting. Fine watercolor designs of 8 scenes. (See nos. 10-11.)

27. [Kean]

Folger: Mu Ad, 11

[Same format as preceding book.]

Another copy of Edmond's final promptbook (with scene designs) used on tour by Kean after 1859.

28. [Kean]

Folger: Prints and Engravings, 51

[Watercolors, 8 x 5½, mounted in an album, 10¼ x 14⅛; gray cloth boards and half green leather gilt; "Charles Kean/Original Water Color Drawings" gilt on spine.]

Fine watercolor scene designs for 4 plays, including 8 for *Much Ado*.

29. [Kean]

Enthoven Collection: Box DT.46

[Watercolors mounted on large display boards.]

Fine watercolor designs for 8 scenes.

30. [Kean]

Folger: Kean Costume Book, Prints and Engravings, 182

[Scrapbook, 14⅜ x 21¼; brown cloth boards and half brown leather.]

Contains 25 watercolor plates of costume designs for *Much Ado*.

31. [Kean]

Enthoven Collection: 94G27, plate 1815

[Scrapbook, 15¼ x 21⅜; blue cloth boards and half blue cloth; "Kean Theatrical Scenery" gilt up spine.]

A plate of watercolor costume designs (6 figures).

32. Walter Lacy   London, Haymarket   September 21, 1859

Folger: Mu Ad, 9

[Oxberry edition, 1823, 4⅜ x 7¼; interleaves; reddish brown marbled boards and half green leather; title gilt on spine.]

Promptbook originally marked by Lacy as a transcription of the Kemble book at the Garrick Club (see his other copy, no. 7), then bound and dated June 15, 1859; then augmented with "The Bus: from Haymarket Prompt Book" when he played Benedick at the Haymarket in September of 1859. Cuts, calls, stage business, maps, cues for effects. Many notes on the differences in text and business between the Kemble book, the Haymarket book, and T. H. Lacy's edition. References to Macready and Charles Kean. Contains Benjamin Webster's addition to the Kemble addition to the

Beatrice-Benedick dialogue in the church scene. Belonged to Henry Irving.

33. J. B. Roberts   c.1860

Folger: Mu Ad, 20

[Pages 423-507 from volume I of a *Works,* 6⅜ x 9⅝; black cloth boards and maroon leather spine; "12" on spine label.]

Rehearsal and reading copy, checked for Benedick. Cuts.

34. Kate Terry   c.1860

Smallhythe

[Kean edition, 1858, 5⅛ x 7⅞; interleaves; green cloth boards; "Miss Kate Terry" gilt on cover.]

Promptbook carefully marked by "B.T." (Ben Terry). At the front 3 pages of notes on sixteenth-century costume for women. Page references listed for Hero and Beatrice. Scenic indications, stage business, maps, cues for effects.

35. James Taylor   Boston, Boston Theatre   c.1860

Harvard Theatre Collection: uncatalogued

[Davidson issue of Cumberland edition, 3⅝ x 5⅜; interleaves; brown cloth boards and black leather spine; title gilt up spine.]

Promptbook "copied from Boston Theatre Prompt Book," checked for Leonato. Cuts, calls, stage business, maps and sketches, cues for effects.

36. E. L. and Fanny Davenport   1870's

Princeton University, Seymour Collection: M Ado, 7

[French's Standard Drama, 4½ x 7½; interleaves; publisher's wrappers.]

Carefully written but mechanical promptbook "as played by" the Davenports. Scenic indications, some stage business, dance routine, maps, cues for effects.

37. William Seymour   Boston, Boston Museum   1870's

Princeton University, Seymour Collection: M Ado, 9

[Modern Standard Drama, 4½ x 7½; coarse cloth; title and "Boston Museum" inked on cover.]

Crude promptbook which belonged to Seymour but is of earlier vintage, checked for Claudio. Cues for effects. Partial cast with Eliza Logan. Timing for Mr. and Mrs. Davenport (2:10).

38. George Becks 1870's

New York Public Library: *NCP.285345

[French issue of Booth-Hinton edition, 5¼ x 8¼; interleaves; black cloth boards; title gilt up spine.]

Promptbook of a version in 6 acts marked throughout at one time and emended with additions later; belonged to George Becks perhaps as a user, perhaps only as a collector. Calls, considerable stage business, maps and sketches, cues for effects. The arrangements frequently recall Macready's and there are explicit references to Charles Kemble's. (See no. 20.)

39. [Becks]

New York Public Library: *NCP.342986

[Music-Publishing Company edition, 3½ x 5½; interleaves; black cloth boards; title gilt on spine.]

Promptbook very similar in contents to the preceding book but somewhat less full, and probably written much later. At end of the first act an elaborate notation of pantomime and music from Modjeska's production.

40. Edwin Booth 1871-90

Museum of the City of New York: 35.339.20

[Booth-Winter edition, 1878, 4⅝ x 6⅞; publisher's wrappers.]

Lightly marked promptbook of W. Henry Flohr, the stage manager. A few maps and cues for effects.

41. [Booth]

Folger: Mu Ad, 25

[Booth-Winter edition, 1890, 4½ x 6¼; red cloth boards; title gilt up spine.]

William Winter's souvenir copy. Contains a letter from Booth, November 17, 1889, discussing problems of admission to The Players, his health, rehearsals, newspaper attacks; a printed itinerary of the 1889-90 tour with Modjeska; a letter from J. H. Magonigle, January 9, 1893, about Booth's illness.

42. Junius Brutus Booth, Jr. c.1875

Folger: Mu Ad, 1

[French's Standard Drama, 4½ x 7⅝; interleaves; yellow publisher's wrappers.]

Promptbook crudely penciled. Abbreviated stage business, a few maps, cues for effects. Part of a playbill for January 11, 1875, with Agnes Booth and Joseph Wheelock.

43. George B. Berrell
          Indianapolis, Academy of Music   January 31, 1876
University of Pennsylvania, Furness Collection: C59.Sh1Mu
[Modern Standard Drama, 1845, 5½ x 9; interleaves, 6¾ x 9½; purple cloth boards and half black cloth; title gilt up spine.]
Thinly marked promptbook. Some scenic indications and grooves, some stage business, some cues for effects. Cast for above date with Agnes Booth and J. W. Norton.

44. William Creswick   Melbourne, Bijou   November 26, 1877
Shakespeare Centre Library: 50.24(1873)
[French issue of Lacy edition, 4 x 7¼; few interleaves; publisher's wrappers under purple cloth boards and half black leather; title gilt up spine.]
Partial promptbook. Cuts, some stage business for Benedick, maps, a sketch, cues for music, timings. Some pencilings by "G. Tharp."

45. Henry Irving   London, Lyceum   October 11, 1882
Folger: Mu Ad, 8
[Irving edition, 1882, 5 x 8; red leather gilt; title gilt up spine.]
Rehearsal copy. Cuts, insertion of the traditional extra dialogue for Beatrice and Benedick at end of the church scene, notes on scenery, many jottings about Benedick, partial cast.

46. [Irving]
Folger: Com Err, 11
[Pages 80-182 from volume II of Aldine edition; green cloth publisher's boards of the whole volume; titles gilt on spine.]
Rehearsal and preparation copy. Cuts on full text. Notes on extras, scenery. Sketches of garden scene. Dozens of notes on the playing of Benedick.

47. [Irving]
New York Public Library: *NCP.342969
[Modern Standard Drama, 4½ x 7¼; gray interleaves, 5 x 7½; blue cloth boards; title gilt up spine.]
Hastily written but very thorough promptbook record of Irving's production as played at the Star Theatre in New York, March 31, 1883; belonged to George Becks, probably his transcription of

Irving's promptbook. Scenic indications, grooves, much stage business, maps and sketches, cues for effects.

48. Ellen Terry   London, Lyceum   October 11, 1882
    Smallhythe
    [Longmans, Green edition, 4⅛ x 6½; purple cloth boards; title stamped on cover.]
    Rehearsal copy dated from the Lyceum, 1880, checked for Beatrice. Several notes on the acting, a few on music and other effects.

49. Henry Holmes   1884
    Enthoven Collection
    [French issue of Lacy edition, 4⅛ x 7⅜; brown paper.]
    Lightly marked promptbook. Cuts, maps, cues for effects.

50. Edward Gordon Craig   London, Lyceum   January 5, 1891
    University of California, Los Angeles: Craig Collection
    [Irving edition, 1887, 5⅜ x 8⅜.]
    Studybook for the Messenger in the first scene. Lines marked for stresses, notes of stage business and motivation.

51. Augustin Daly   New York, Daly's   December 21, 1896
    New York Public Library: *NCP.686459
    [Daly edition, 1897, 6¼ x 10; interleaves; blue publisher's wrappers under red cloth boards; title gilt up spine.]
    Well-developed promptbook owned by Ada Rehan. Fine sketches of the principal scenes, with descriptive notes. Calls, some stage business in addition to that which is printed, cues for effects.

52. [Daly]
    New York Public Library: *NCP.52x296
    [French's Standard Drama, 4½ x 7½, tipped into a workbook, 7¾ x 9⅞; gray boards and black cloth spine; title gilt up spine.]
    Transcription of Daly's promptbook by Hallam Bosworth. Cuts and restorations, stage business, cues for effects, etc.

53. [Daly]
    Library of Congress, Batchelder Collection: 412
    [Daly edition, 1897, 6½ x 10; publisher's wrappers.]
    Partial promptbook marked only through the first act. Calls, stage business, cues for effects.

54. [Daly]

Folger: Prints and Engravings

[Daly edition, 1897, mounted in pages of an album, 12⅜ x 16¾; green and gold marbled boards and half brown leather gilt; title gilt on spine.]

Souvenir album with many old prints of actors and scenes from the play, many nineteenth-century playbills, bills and review of Daly's production, several photographs of Ada Rehan.

55. [Daly]

New York Public Library: 8*T*NCP+

[Daly edition, 1897, mounted in pages, 12¼ x 16¾; bound with *The Tempest* in brown cloth boards; "The Tempest" gilt on spine.]

Ada Rehan's souvenir book. A few old prints, an engraving of Irving and Terry, a playbill, several photographs of Miss Rehan.

56. Charles B. Hanford   c.1900

Folger: Mu Ad, 5

[Mixture of a Shakespeare edition and French's Standard Drama pasted in a workbook, 7⅛ x 9¼; red cloth boards; title on cover label.]

Full and much used promptbook of Hanford's touring company. Scenic indications, copious stage business, cues for effects. At the back a dummy playbill with Hanford and Marie Drofnah.

57. William Poel   London, Court   March 19, 1904

Enthoven Collection

[Shakespeare edition pasted in a workbook, 4½ x 7; black imitation leather.]

Rehearsal promptbook. Cuts on full text, calls, some stage business, cues for music. Names of actors.

58. E. H. Sothern and Julia Marlowe   Chicago   September 27, 1904

Folger: Mu Ad, Folio 2

[Typescript, 8½ x 11; limp brown leather.]

Rough promptbook of Frederick Kaufman, the stage manager, much used, revised, patched, written upon. Pages bound out of order. Some scores for songs.

59. [Sothern and Marlowe]

Folger: Mu Ad, Folio 1

[Typescript, 8½ x 11; brown paper wrappers.]
Clean copy of version as perfected by Frederick Kaufman, the stage manager. At the front plots of properties, furniture, calciums, lights, cast. Copious stage business, cues for effects.

60. [Sothern and Marlowe]
New York Public Library: *NCP.276554B
[Carbon typescript, 8¼ x 10⅞; black cloth boards; title gilt on spine.]
Another copy of the preceding book.

61. [Sothern and Marlowe]
The Players: PB.103
[Typescript, 8 x 10½; blue paper wrappers.]
Much used, much marked promptbook of a different version from that of preceding books. Plots of calciums, lights. Three casts. Copious stage business, maps.

62. [Sothern and Marlowe]
W. A. Clark Library, Los Angeles
[Acting edition, 4¾ x 7⅛; interleaves; brown cloth boards; title gilt on spine.]
Souvenir promptbook made by Lark Taylor, the actor. Cast of 1906 and notes on Taylor's various roles. Copious stage business, groundplans, cues for effects underlined as printed.

63. [Sothern and Marlowe]
Folger: Mu Ad, 22
[Irving edition, 5½ x 8⅞; interleaves; blue cloth boards; title and "Prompt Book" gilt on cover.]
Souvenir promptbook made in the summer of 1911 by Lark Taylor, who played Borachio in 1906, later Dogberry, later Leonato. Cuts, very detailed stage business, maps, sketches, a drawing of himself as Dogberry, costume notes.

64. George E. Lask
University of California, Los Angeles: Special Collections 714, Box 6
[French issue of Irving edition, 5¾ x 9⅛; publisher's gray wrappers under brown paper.]
Partial promptbook or spectator's notes, marked in the first 2 acts. Some stage business, rough maps, cues for music and dance.

65. Herbert Beerbohm Tree   London, His Majesty's   Jan. 24, 1905
    Enthoven Collection: Tree, 179

    [Temple edition pasted in a workbook, 7 x 9; red marbled boards and green cloth spine, broken.]

    Rehearsal promptbook roughly penciled. Cuts, much stage business, cues for effects.

66. [Tree]

    Enthoven Collection: Tree, 179

    [Temple edition pasted in a workbook, 7 x 9; black oilcloth, much worn.]

    Rehearsal promptbook or preparation book roughly penciled. Cuts, some stage business, maps, some cues for effects.

67. [Tree]

    Enthoven Collection: Tree, 179

    [Cassell's National Library edition pasted in a workbook, 7 x 9; red marbled boards and green cloth spine, damaged.]

    Uncompleted promptbook. Some good groundplans.

68. [Tree]

    Enthoven Collection: Tree, 179

    [Temple edition pasted in a workbook, 7 x 9; red marbled boards and purple cloth spine, broken.]

    Final promptbook, probably the one used for performances, done in ink with penciled additions. Cuts, groundplans, much stage business, maps, cues for effects.

69. [Tree]

    Enthoven Collection: Tree, 179

    [Cassell's National Library edition pasted in a workbook, 7 x 9; red marbled boards and red cloth spine; title on cover label.]

    Final promptbook, clean and perhaps unused. Cuts are scissored out. Seven excellent groundplans, copious stage business, maps, cues for effects, neatly inked.

70. [Tree]

    Enthoven Collection: Tree, 179

    [Eighteen books. Cassell's National Library edition (12), 4 x 6; Temple edition, 1904 (6), 4 x 5¼.]

    Rehearsal copies, 7 of them assigned, with cuts and bits of stage business.

71. [Tree]

Enthoven Collection: Tree, 185

[Oil paintings on wooden panels, 4⅞ x 8½; papers.]

Five costume designs done in oil on wood; 21 sheets of sketches for women's costumes; 52 sheets of sketches for men's costumes, some in watercolor.

72. [Tree]

Enthoven Collection: Tree, 178, 179

[Papers.]

Plots of properties, limes, electrics, sound, cast, dressing rooms, etc.

73. Fred Grove   London

Folger: Mu Ad, 4

[Cassell edition, 1904, 3⅞ x 5¾; interleaves; green cloth boards; title gilt on green spine label.]

Rehearsal copy checked for Antonio, Dogberry. Cuts, random stage business.

74. Winthrop Ames   Boston, Castle Square   October 30, 1905

New York Public Library: *NCP+.55875B

[Typescript, 7¾ x 12¾; green cloth boards; title gilt on spine.]

Very thorough promptbook. Synopsis of scenes, much detailed stage business, excellent groundplans, light plots. Copious annotation of the text. Many notes on the Irving and Booth productions. The production was revived on April 22, 1907.

75. [Ames]

New York Public Library: *NCP+.55874B

[Typescripts, 7¾ x 6½; green cloth boards; title gilt on spine.]

Eighteen partbooks. Plots of costumes, properties, lights, music. At the front a typescript of the program.

76. [Ames]

New York Public Library: *NCP+

[Music scores; tan boards, 10¾ x 13¼; title on cover label.]

Five copies of the Bridal Chorus from *The Rose Maiden;* 4 copies of "Pardon Goddess" for the tomb scene.

77. A. E. F. Horniman   Manchester, Gaiety   December 27, 1909

British Drama League

[Shakespeare edition pasted in a workbook, 7 x 9; red marbled boards and red cloth spine.]

Promptbook fully developed for two acts; thereafter only stage manager's penciled cues. Calls, much stage business, maps, cues for effects. Music scores.

78. [Horniman]

British Drama League

[Temple edition, 1894, 4½ x 7; blue cloth boards; title gilt up spine.]

Workbook to accompany the preceding book. Cuts, scenic notes, some stage business, many maps, cues for effects. Names of actors.

79. Charles Frohman   New York, Empire   September 1, 1913

New York Public Library: *NCP.53x300

[Carbon typescript, 7¼ x 10¼; gray boards and black cloth spine; title gilt up spine.]

Unused copy of an acting version prepared by John Drew. Some stage business. Cast includes Laura Hope Crews, John Drew, Hubert Druce.

80. Albert Lang   1921

Princeton University, Seymour Collection

[Irving edition, 1882, with some leaves of French's Standard Drama, pasted in a workbook, 7⅛ x 9¼; black cloth boards and half red leather; title page pasted on cover.]

Excellent promptbook of an itinerant producer from Fort Lee, N.J. Dated by an enclosed costume rental list from Waas & Son, Philadelphia. Synopsis of scenes, 2 scaled groundplans, very full stage business, maps, cues for effects, light chart, music chart.

81. Henry Jewett   Boston, Boston Repertory   January 11, 1926

Folger: Mu Ad, Folio 3

[Typescript, 8½ x 11; gray cardboard and green cloth spine.]

Much used promptbook. Copious stage business of a traditional sort, partly typewritten, partly longhand. Additional dialogue for Beatrice and Benedick at end of the church scene. Maps, cues for effects, cast. Contains programs and a 12-page brochure, "Story of the Play."

82. Robert Edmond Jones   New York, Theatre Guild   1928

New York Public Library: *NCP.57x10

[Carbon typescript, 7¾ x 11; black cloth boards; title gilt up spine.]

Rehearsal promptbook of a version conceived and directed by Robert Edmond Jones, with Alfred Lunt and Lynn Fontanne. Rehearsed but never performed. Penciled notes throughout.

83. Minnie Maddern Fiske Boston, Hollis Street November 19, 1928
   Library of Congress, Manuscripts Division: Fiske Box 34
   Shakespeare edition pasted in four folders, 8½ x 11; brown paper.]
   Preparation copy made in August, 1928, by Harrison Grey Fiske. Cuts.

84. [Fiske]
   Library of Congress, Manuscripts Division: Fiske Box 35
   [Three books. Typescript, 8½ x 11; each of the 4 acts bound in green paper wrappers.]
   One book is a clean copy of the final version. One has notes on music. One is a rehearsal promptbook, crudely marked, with much stage business, cues for effects.

85. [Fiske]
   Library of Congress, Manuscripts Division: Fiske Box 35
   [Papers.]
   Notes on music, words for final song, properties plot, 15 ground-plans (9 x 12), salary lists, expenses of production, booking sheets, cast lists, inventories of scenery and properties, timing sheets, contracts, box office reports, financial statements, etc.

[ACTOR LISTS FOR FOLLOWING BOOKS ARE GIVEN IN THIS ORDER: Beatrice, Benedick, Dogberry.]

86. W. Bridges-Adams   Stratford-upon-Avon   July 3, 1929
   Shakespeare Centre Library: 71.21/1929MU
   [Favourite Classics edition pasted in a workbook, 6½ x 9; green cloth boards and tan canvas spine; title on cover and spine labels.]
   Cast includes Dorothy Massingham, Wilfrid Walter, Roy Byford. Designed by Conrad Leigh and Eric Maxon. Stage business, maps, cues for effects. The book had been used in 1922, 1923, 1925, 1927.

87. [Bridges-Adams]   April 17, 1933
   Shakespeare Centre Library: 71.21/1933MU
   [Temple edition pasted in a workbook, 7 x 9; purple cloth boards and half black leather; title on cover and spine labels.]

Cast includes Fabia Drake, George Hayes, Stanley Lathbury. Costumes by Mrs. Lesley Blanch. Clean, unused copy: much stage business, maps, cues for effects.

88. [Bridges-Adams]   April 18, 1934
Shakespeare Centre Library: 71.21/1934MU
[Temple edition pasted in a workbook, 8 x 10; blue oilcloth boards gilt; title on cover and spine labels.]
Cast includes Dorothy Black, Baliol Holloway, Roy Byford. Much stage business, maps, some cues for effects. A music score. The book had been used for the 1929-30 tour, and in 1930 and 1933.

89. B. Iden Payne   Stratford-upon-Avon   April 23, 1936
Shakespeare Centre Library: 71.21/1936MU
[Temple edition pasted in a workbook, 7⅛ x 9; purple cloth boards and half black leather; title on cover and spine labels.]
Cast includes Barbara Couper, James Dale, Roy Byford. Designed by Aubrey Hammond. Much stage business, maps, cues for effects.

90. Columbia Broadcasting System   July 19, 1937
Folger: Mu Ad, 4
[Mimeograph, 8½ x 11¼; green paper.]
Radio adaptation by Brewster Morgan, as broadcast with Rosalind Russell and Leslie Howard.

91. Robert Atkins   Stratford-upon-Avon   March 31, 1945
Shakespeare Centre Library: 71.21/1945MU
[New Temple edition pasted in a workbook, 6⅞ x 8⅞; purple cloth boards and half black leather; title on cover and spine labels.]
Cast includes Claire Luce, Antony Eustrel, George Skillan. Designed by J. Gower Parks. Considerable stage business, maps, cues for effects. The book had been used for the Payne production of 1939, was erased and reused.

92. John Gielgud and Anthony Quayle
                         Stratford-upon-Avon   April 20, 1949
Shakespeare Centre Library: O.S.71.21/1949MU
[Temple edition pasted in a workbook, 7¾ x 12⅝; maroon cloth boards and red cloth spine; title on spine label.]

Cast includes Diana Wynyard, Anthony Quayle, George Rose. Designed by Mariano Andreu. Very much stage business, maps, cues for effects. Cast lists and understudies.

93. John Gielgud   Stratford-upon-Avon   June 6, 1950
Shakespeare Centre Library: O.S.71.21/1950MU
[New Temple edition pasted in a workbook, 8 x 12¾; red cloth boards; title on spine label.]
Cast includes Diana Wynyard, Anthony Quayle, George Rose. Designed by Mariano Andreu. Very much stage business, maps, cues for effects. Many production papers.

94. [Gielgud]   London, Palace   July 21, 1955
Shakespeare Centre Library: O.S.71.21/1955M
[New Temple edition pasted in a workbook, 7⅞ x 12¾; green cloth boards and red cloth spine; title on cover and spine label.]
Revival of 1949 and 1950 productions. Cast includes Peggy Ashcroft, John Gielgud, George Devine. Designed by Mariano Andreu. Very much stage business typed and pasted in, maps, cues for effects.

95. Denis Carey   London, Old Vic   October 23, 1956
Old Vic, Publicity Department
[New Temple edition pasted in a workbook, 8 x 10½; black board ring binder.]
Cast includes Barbara Jefford, Keith Michell, Dudley Jones. Designed by Peter Rice. Cuts, calls, stage business, maps, cues for effects. Many production papers.

96. John Houseman and Jack Landau
        Stratford, Connecticut   August 7, 1957
Festival Theatre, Production Department
[Mimeograph, 8½ x 11; heavy blue paper.]
Cast includes Katharine Hepburn, Alfred Drake, Larry Gates. Designed by Rouben Ter-Arutunian. Much roughly penciled stage business, maps. Signed by B. Gersten.

97. [Houseman]
University of California, Los Angeles: Houseman Box 14
[Mimeograph, 8½ x 11; black cloth board spring binder.]
Rough production book. Some stage business and other working notes.

98. [Houseman]
University of California, Los Angeles: Houseman Box 11
[Mimeograph, 8½ x 11; green cloth board ring binder.]
Final or souvenir promptbook. Stage business typed along margins. Production papers at the back.

99. Michael Langham   Stratford, Ontario   June 24, 1958
Festival Theatre, Library
[Two books. New Clarendon edition pasted in workbooks, 7¾ x 13⅛; dark blue cloth boards bordered in red.]
Cast includes Eileen Herlie, Christopher Plummer, Tony Van Bridge. Designed by Desmond Heeley. The first book has much stage business, many maps on mimeographed groundplans, cues for effects. The second has calls.

100. Douglas Seale   Stratford-upon-Avon   August 26, 1958
Shakespeare Centre Library: O.S.71.21/1958M
[New Temple edition pasted in a workbook, 8 x 13; red cloth board spring binder; title on spine label.]
Cast includes Googie Withers, Michael Redgrave, Patrick Wymark. Designed by Tanya Moiseiwitsch and Motley. Much stage business, cues for effects.

101. Michael Langham   Stratford-upon-Avon   April 4, 1961
Shakespeare Centre Library: O.S.71.21/1961M
[Cambridge Pocket Shakespeare pasted in a workbook, 8 x 13; red cloth board spring binder; title on cover label.]
Cast includes Geraldine McEwan, Christopher Plummer, Newton Blick. Designed by Desmond Heeley. Unused copy: copious stage business, cues for effects.

102. Other books of *Much Ado About Nothing:*
Boston Public Library: K.37.22, Mrs. John Gilbert.
Brown University: Eng.P.17a, Asa Cushman and Anna Cora, Mowatt, 1850.
Essex Institute, Salem: 822.S52.78, John B. Adams, 1867.
Folger: Mu Ad, 6, George Holland and Harry Crisp; Mu Ad, 7, Walter Hubbell; Mu Ad, 14, James Lewis; Mu Ad, 15, Frank Lodge; Mu Ad, 16, C. Meggett; Mu Ad, 19, Marcus Moriarty, 1876; Mu Ad, 21, Charles Seabert; Mu Ad, 23, Felix A. Vincent;

Mu Ad, 26, William Winter; Mu Ad, 28, William Hildebrand; Mu Ad, 29, anonymous; Mu Ad, 30, W. M. Cambridge.

Harvard Theatre Collection: Emma Reignolds.

Historical and Philosophical Society of Ohio: 812.3/R283/134, Alvin Read.

Missouri Historical Society: John W. Norton.

The Players: PB.74, Irving edition, anonymous.

Princeton University, Seymour Collection: M Ado, 12, book for Beatrice; M Ado, 22, Albert Bradley, 1851.

Shakespeare Centre Library: O.S.P.50.24(1831), F. Haywel.

Smallhythe: 3 books of Ellen Terry, including an Irving edition checked for Beatrice.

University of Minnesota: Z820.12/Z11, volume 12, W. S. Forrest.

University of Pennsylvania: AC85.M9415.820p.54b, c, James Murdoch, 2 books.

Othello

1. Anonymous   England   1600's
   Henry E. Huntington Library: 69337
   [Sheets of 1622 Quarto, 5⅜ x 6⅞, mounted in window pages, 6⅝ x 8½; red leather gilt; title gilt on cover and up spine.]
   Promptbook with several bits of stage business in an apparently seventeenth-century hand (e.g., page 81, "gives up ye gost"). Belonged to George Steevens, who entered certain notes on the text. Later belonged to J. P. Kemble, who numbered the scenes, mounted it in the window pages, and marked it "collated & perfect, J.P.K.—1804."

2. Joseph Ashbury   Dublin, Smock Alley   1670's
   Folger: Oth, Smock Alley
   [Pages 789-816 from a Third Folio, 1663, 8 x 12¼; maroon cloth boards and half maroon leather gilt; title gilt up spine.]
   Promptbook marked in some detail. The first page of this book is the last page of *King Lear*. Pages 795-800 are missing. Cuts, scenic indications, calls, cues for effects. Entrance cues are horizontal lines with vertical slashes. Names of several actors. (See G. Blakemore Evans, *Shakespearean Prompt-Books*.)

3. John Palmer   London, King's and Haymarket   August 8, 1766
   Folger: Oth, 27
   [C. Hitch acting edition, 1761, 4 x 6⅝; white paper and purple spine.]
   Neatly marked promptbook. Cuts, scenic indications, grooves, some stage business, cues for effects, list of property manuscripts. Palmer played Montano.

4. Richard Power   Kilkenny   October 29, 1803
   Folger: Oth, 38
   [Garland edition, 1765, 3⅞ x 6½; interleaves watermarked 1801; green marbled boards and half red leather gilt; title gilt on spine.]
   Promptbook of the private theatre of Kilkenny, where *Othello* was often produced from 1803 to 1819. Cast list with amateur gentlemen and professional ladies. Cuts and restorations, some stage business, many notes on histrionic manner.

5. Anonymous   London, Drury Lane   c.1805
   Harvard Theatre Collection: uncatalogued
   [Kemble edition, 1804, 5 x 8; gray paper.]

Unidentified promptbook, apparently a companion to a *Much Ado* book at Harvard which was "marked as at Drury Lane." Minimal stage business. (See MA, 4.)

6. George Frederick Cooke   New York, Park   May 8, 1811
   Harvard Theatre Collection: TS.2493.50
   [West issue of Kemble edition, Boston, 1807, 3¾ x 5⅝; interleaves; brown cloth boards; in box of tan cloth boards and red leather spine; title gilt up spine.]
   Promptbook of the Park Theatre when Cooke played Iago to Cooper's Othello. A note or two on Cooke's special business. Cast given. Cuts, calls, some stage business, cues for effects. Note on use of supers.

7. John Howard Payne
   Folger: Oth, 28
   [Pages 192-286 from volume VIII of a *Works*, 3¾ x 6⅝; interleaves; gray marbled boards and half red leather; title and Payne's name gilt on spine.]
   Rehearsal copy. Cuts, little stage business.

8. Sarah Siddons   c.1815
   Birmingham, Shakespeare Memorial Library: S639.41/666730
   [Garland edition, 1765, 4⅞ x 8; brown leather gilt; title gilt up spine.]
   Copy marked for a reading at Mrs. Weddel's. Introductory remarks, cuts, transitions. Explanatory notes by Mrs. C. Fitzhugh, to whom Siddons gave it. Belonged to Fanny Kemble, R. J. Lane, John Pritt Harley. Description from Maggs Bros. Catalogue 871, 1960, pasted at the back.

9. John Philip Kemble   London, Covent Garden   October 10, 1816
   Folger: Oth, 19
   [Kemble edition, 1804, 5⅛ x 8¼; interleaves watermarked 1816; brown leather; "Othello/MB/10" gilt on vestiges of spine.]
   Promptbook marked by Kemble. Cuts, calls, stage business, maps, cues for effects, timings (3:35). Given to Thomas Powrie by the actor Frank Cooke, who entered at the back an authentication of the book by George Bartley.

10. James Burchall
    Folger: Oth, 37

[Kemble edition, 1804, 5⅛ x 8⅜; interleaves watermarked 1816; gray marbled boards and half brown leather gilt; title gilt on spine.]

Probably a transcription from some Kemble book: each interleaf is given act, scene, and page number, as if for insertion after marking. Cuts and alterations, some stage business, some cues for lights.

11. Edmund Kean   London, Drury Lane   c.1818
    Folger: Oth, 18

[Rodwell issue of Kemble edition, 1818, 4⅛ x 7⅛; interleaves; marbled boards worn to common brown and half brown leather, broken.]

"Corrected from the Prompt-Book" for Kean by G. C. Carr, the Drury Lane prompter. Cuts, calls, some stage business, maps, cues for effects, timing (3:27). Note on redivisioning of last act. Pencilings of a later prompter. Given to Henry Irving in 1876 by the Baroness Burdett-Coutts. (See no. 16.)

12. Anonymous   London, Drury Lane   c.1820-43
    Folger: Oth, 20

[Kemble edition, 1804, 4⅝ x 7¾; interleaves; gray marbled boards and half brown leather; title gilt on spine.]

The official "T.R.D.L./P.B." as inscribed at head of Act I, but *not* used by Kemble and Siddons, as stated in an inscription by E. T. Smith, since they did not play at Drury Lane after 1802. Cuts and corrections, grooves, calls, stage business, maps and sketches, cues for effects. Many entries by John Willmott and a few by George Ellis, prompters in the 1830's and early 1840's: note on the "Great Row/Kean v. Cox" on January 28, 1825; anecdote of Kean's last performance; list of supers for October, 1836; timings showing the hour of Half Price in May, 1838; Macready cast for June 8, 1843; variant entrances and arrangements for Macready, Forrest, Charles Kean. A cartoon, some prompter's jokes. (See no. 24.)

13. Thomas Abthorpe Cooper
                Boston,Tremont Street   March 19, 1824
    Folger: Oth, 5

[Kemble edition, 1814, 4¼ x 7⅜; gray marbled boards and half brown leather; title inked on cover label.]

Promptbook used for many years belonging to a prompter or a theatre rather than to the actor. Cooper cast for 1824. Arrangements for Macready on March 7, 1827. A prompter named Nelson Wentworth marked it "as played by Mr. Forrest" on May 5, 1842. Cuts, scenic arrangements, calls, cues for effects, timings.

14. James Henry Hackett   New York, Park   April 10, 1828
Folger: Oth, 8
[Cumberland edition, 3¾ x 5⅞.]
Rehearsal copy dated 1827, checked for Roderigo, Iago, Othello. Cuts, some stage business. "For Readings & Comments See 8ᵛ⁹ Copy."

15. Charles Kean   New York, Park   September 7, 1830
Folger: Oth, 11
[Kemble edition, 1804, 5⅛ x 8⅜; interleaves; green marbled boards and half green leather, much worn; title and "Mr. C. Kean" gilt up spine.]
Kean's early promptbook and studybook. Notes on meanings of words. Calls, stage business, maps, irregular cues for effects. (See nos. 21-23, 25-27.)

16. Edmund Kean   1831
Folger: Oth, 17
[Oxberry edition, 1822, 4⅛ x 7; interleaves; green marbled boards and half brown leather, broken.]
Promptbook mainly transcribed from Kean's earlier book (see no. 11). Inscribed "Edmundi Kean/Theatrum, Mundi,—/1831." Request to prompters to mark only in pencil. Note on scene "always omitted in the country."

17. W. H. Smith   Boston, Tremont Street   1832
Folger: Oth, 10
[Cumberland edition, 3⅝ x 5⅞; interleaves.]
Studybook for Iago and partial promptbook. Smith's name is scratched and the book given by J. Jones to John Burroughs Wright on November 23, 1840. Marginal notes on the playing of Iago. Irregular cues for effects.

18. William Charles Macready
          London, Drury Lane   November 26, 1832
Victoria and Albert, Forster Library, 7919:   F.48.C.17
[Cumberland edition, 3½ x 6; bound with other Macready promptbooks in green cloth boards and half tan leather; titles gilt on spine.]

Macready's studybook for Iago, not dated but probably of the early 1830's. Marked for stresses. Penciled marginal notes of stage business and histrionic manner, some in Latin. (See nos. 24-28, 29, 44.)

19. Stanley Charles Ferrers   Edinburgh, Theatre Royal   1836

New York Public Library: *NCP.343041

[Cumberland edition, 3¼ x 5½; interleaves; black cloth boards; title gilt on spine.]

Fully developed promptbook which Ferrers, the prompter, brought from Edinburgh to New York. Belonged to James Stark and later (1883) to George Becks, who augmented its markings. Grooves, calls, stage business, many maps, cues for effects, timings (3:20). Notes on arrangements or business of J. Wallack, Booth, Hamblin, Scott, Kean, Brooke, Forrest, Mrs. Farren, Mme. Ponisi.

20. J. W. Wallack   New York, National   October 24, 1837

Folger: Oth, 7

[Acting edition, 3½ x 5½; a few interleaves; green cloth boards; title gilt up spine, "J. W. Wallack" gilt on cover.]

Promptbook marked for Wallack by S. C. Ferrers, the prompter. Call-lists at the front. Some stage business, maps, cues for effects. Checked for Othello and Emilia. Last pages missing. Later belonged to or signed by George Washington Barton, D. D. McKinney, George F. Rowe.

21. Charles Kean   London, Drury Lane   May 16, 1838

Folger: Oth, 12

[Kemble edition, 1804, 5 x 7¾; interleaves; marbled boards and half brown leather, much worn; title and "Mr Chs Kean" gilt on black spine labels.]

Promptbook much used and marked by many hands: neat markings by the original copyist (probably Parsloe), Kean's additions, prompters' pencilings. Cast for Drury Lane, September 21, 1838. Cuts, grooves, calls, stage business, maps and sketches, cues for effects, timings (3:10). Excellent ink-wash drawings of the 8 scenes. (See nos. 15, 25-27.)

22. [Kean]

Folger: T.b.15

[Notebook, 7¾ x 12⅝; brown marbled boards and black leather spine.]

Touring book of scene plots, property plots, calls, etc., for *Othello* and 3 other plays.

23. [Kean]
Folger: W.a.10
[Notebook of sheets watermarked 1837, 4¾ x 7¾, brown marbled boards and half brown leather gilt; "Theatrical Costumes" inked on spine label.]
Kean's touring wardrobe list for Othello is the eleventh of 16 such lists in this book.

24. William Charles Macready   London, Drury Lane   May 23, 1842
Folger: Oth, 16
[Hinds English Stage, 1838, 6⅜ x 10; interleaves, 7¼ x 9; white cardboard.]
Corrected transcription of Macready's promptbook of Drury Lane, 1842, done in pencil by George Ellis. The original of this (the book Macready used) was probably the old "T.R.D.L./P.B." (see no. 12). The Hinds edition was apparently derived from Macready's Covent Garden promptbook of 1838. Cuts, list of property manuscripts, scenic indications, grooves, stage business, timings (3:20). Enclosed papers: list of supers, notes on costumes for supers, plan for a program of readings. (See nos. 18, 29, 44.)

25. [Macready]
Folger: Oth, 13
[Hinds English Stage, 6¼ x 10; blue interleaves watermarked 1846, 7⅝ x 10; green cloth boards embossed in floral pattern and half brown leather; title gilt up spine, "Mr. Charles Kean/Prompt Copy" gilt on maroon leather cover label.]
Excellent transcription of the preceding book made by Ellis for Charles Kean in 1846. Unused. (See nos. 15, 21-23.)

26. [Macready]
Folger: Oth, 14
[Watercolors, 7½ x 10⅛; interleaves; same binding as preceding book, broken; "Othello/Scenery" gilt up spine.]
Excellent watercolor designs of the 7 scenes of Macready's production, with identifications and grooves on facing pages. Given to Charles Kean by George Ellis with the promptbook. A note that the council chamber scene is identical with the trial scene in *The Merchant of Venice*.

27. [Macready
    Folger: Oth, 15
    [Watercolors, 8⅜ x 10⅜; same binding as preceding book, broken;
    "Othello/Costumes" gilt up spine.]
    Fine watercolor designs for 13 costumes probably drawn and
    painted by George Ellis, who sent them to Charles Kean with the
    promptbook. An inventory, and explanatory notes showing the
    identity of many costumes with those of *The Merchant of Venice*.

28. [Macready]   1843-51
    Victoria and Albert, Forster Library, 7918: F.48.C.16
    [Kemble edition, 1814, 4 x 7¼; gray interleaves; bound with
    other Macready promptbooks in green cloth boards and half tan
    leather; titles gilt on spine.]
    Promptbook mostly in Macready's hand, with notes and signatures
    of prompters: W. E. Anderton of Charleston and Savannah;
    George James Wilton, 1850. Used in touring, probably from
    1843 on. Cuts and restorations, careful scenic indications, grooves,
    stage business, pauses, maps, sketches, cues for effects.

29. Samuel Phelps   London, Sadler's Wells   June 3, 1844
    Folger: Oth, 24
    [Hinds English Stage, 1838, 4½ x 8; interleaves; green cloth
    boards and half brown leather; title gilt down green spine label.]
    Excellent transcription of Macready's promptbook (see no. 24)
    made by George Ellis for Samuel Phelps, used by Phelps for many
    years. Cuts, lists of supers for Sadler's Wells and for Drury Lane
    in 1860 and 1861, additional stage business entered by Phelps and
    his prompters. Given to Henry Irving by Frank Paul, comedian.

30. James E. Murdoch   New York, Park   c.October 23, 1845
    University of Pennsylvania: AC85.M9415.820p.55a
    [Turner's Dramatic Library, Philadelphia, 3¾ x 6; interleaves;
    green marbled boards and red leather spine.]
    Promptbook marked for Murdoch in 1845 by George W. Lewis,
    the prompter at the Walnut Street Theatre in Philadelphia. Some
    scenic indications, grooves, calls, stage business, maps, sketches,
    cues for effects, timing (3:15).

31. [Murdoch]
    University of Pennsylvania: AC85.M9415.820p.55
    [Oxberry edition, Boston, 1822, 3½ x 5½; bound with other plays

in brown marbled boards and half black leather; title inked on spine label.]

Studybook checked for Othello, signed and dated by Murdoch at Louisville, March 13, 1849. Cuts and restorations, a few notes on the acting.

32. John Moore   Edinburgh and New York   1846-70

Folger: Oth, 26

[Pages 291-424 from volume IX of a *Works,* 5⅛ x 8⅝; interleaves; black paper; title inked on cover label.]

Very full promptbook, marked at Edinburgh from some English original in blue and red inks, brought to America about 1848, and further marked over the years in brown ink and in pencil. Cuts on full text. Lists of property manuscripts, properties, supers. Scenic indications, grooves, calls, copious stage business, maps, cues for effects, timings. Arrangements are noted for Edmund Kean, Forrest, Macready, J. W. Wallack, J. R. Scott, Hamblin, Gilbert, Anderson, Graham, Fisher, Eddy, Edwin Booth, Miss Wemyss, Miss Montague, Mrs. Hamblin, Mrs. Warner. Part of a playbill with Charles Fisher as Othello; playbills for Burton's, September 24, 1858, with H. Loraine and J. B. Roberts.

33. James Stark   New York, Park   September 15, 1846

New York Public Library: *NCP.343039

[Hinds English Stage, 1838, 4¾ x 7¾; blue interleaves, 6 x 7¾; brown marbled boards and half black leather; title gilt up spine.]

Carefully marked promptbook with additional notes by George Becks (1883). Cuts and restorations, scenic indications, grooves, calls, stage business, maps and sketches, cues for effects. Stark was Cassio in Forrest's company on the above date; he played Othello at the Jenny Lind in San Francisco on November 5, 1850.

34. E. F. Taylor   1850's

New York Public Library: *NCP.285354

[Davidson issue of Cumberland edition, 3½ x 6; interleaves; green and black boards and black cloth spine; title inked up spine.]

Lightly marked promptbook, done in pencil. Cues for effects.

35. James B. Roberts   1850

Folger: Oth, 30

[Modern Standard Drama, 4½ x 7⅜; brown interleaves; brown paper; title, etc., inked on cover.]

Studybook dated 1850. Copious notations of stage business and histrionic manner for Iago and Othello. Lines marked for stresses. Maps, some cues for effects. Many notations of the stage business of other actors: Anderson, Kean, Macready, Booth, etc. A Philadelphia review of Macready's Othello.

36. [Roberts]

Folger: Oth, 31

[Pages 395-518 from a *Works,* 6¼ x 9¾; black cloth boards and maroon leather spine.]

Book cut and marked for public reading, dated 1851.

37. George W. Lewis   New York, Broadway   1851
New York Public Library: *NCP.342999

[Modern Standard Drama, 4½ x 7½; gray interleaves; blue cloth boards; title gilt up spine.]

Well-developed promptbook often resembling that of S. C. Ferrers (see no. 19), marked by George W. Lewis, the prompter, "as played by Mr. Forrest" and "as played at Broadway Theatre— Walnut St. Theatre—by Mr. Forrest, Booth, & c." At the front a good drawing of the bedroom scene. Scenic indications, grooves, calls, stage business, maps, cues for effects, timings (3:20). Notes on arrangements of J. Wallack, Hamblin, Conway, Brooke, Mme. Ponisi. Later markings by George Becks.

38. Thomas Barry   Boston, Boston Theatre   1854
Harvard Theatre Collection: uncatalogued

[Oxberry edition, 1819, 4⅞ x 8; gray interleaves; blue marbled boards and black cloth spine; title and "10" inked on cover label.]

Promptbook marked in England by Charles Melville and brought to Boston by Barry in 1854, with penciled additions suggesting later use. Cuts, grooves, calls, stage business, maps, cues for effects.

39. [Barry]

Harvard Theatre Collection: uncatalogued

[Cumberland edition, 3⅝ x 6⅛; gray interleaves, 4⅞ x 7⅞; gray boards and red leather spine; title and "253" inked on cover label.]

Another Melville promptbook. At the front a plot of scenes with grooves and wings. Calls, stage business, maps, cues for effects. Penciled additions suggest later use.

40. Anonymous   Boston, Boston Museum   October, 1854
Princeton University, Seymour Collection: Othello, 8
[Modern Standard Drama, 4½ x 7½; rough cloth; "Boston Museum" inked on cover.]
Crude but workable promptbook. At the front a list of supers. Calls, cues for effects. Reference to Couldock.

41. Alexander Burger   1856
Folger: Mac, 15
[French's Standard Drama, 4¼ x 7¼; bound with *Macbeth* and other plays in brown marbled boards and black leather spine; Burger's name gilt on cover and spine.]
Crude promptbook thoroughly marked but probably unused. At the front a list of properties. Cuts, calls, cues for effects.

42. James Taylor   March 25, 1857
Harvard Theatre Collection: uncatalogued
[French's Standard Drama, 4½ x 7½; blue interleaves; tan cardboard.]
Lightly marked rehearsal copy. Cuts, some stage business, maps. Playbills with Taylor as Othello and Iago.

43. [Taylor]
Harvard Theatre Collection: uncatalogued
[Notebook, 4⅝ x 7⅛; limp green cloth boards.]
Manuscript studybook for Othello. A 6-page list of entrances, crosses, cues, exits; a 15-page transcription from a *Life* of Kean; an 8-page transcription of Mrs. Mowatt's essay "The Stage." Many Othello passages marked with numerals keying the phrases to accompanying lists of appropriate emotions, manners, tones.

44. Hermann Vezin   London, Surrey   July 9, 1859
University of Illinois: x792.9/Sh15o/no.1
[Hinds English Stage, 5 x 8½; interleaves, 7¼ x 9⅛; blue marbled boards and half maroon leather, worn; title gilt on spine, title and "Hermann Vezin" gilt on black cover label.]
Excellent transcription of Macready's promptbook (see no. 24), made by George Ellis for Hermann Vezin. Much used, with additional markings, cuts, maps, etc., by Vezin and his prompters.

45. J. C. Cowper England 1860's
Folger: Oth, 6

[Fechter edition, 1861, 4⅝ x 6⅞; interleaves; limp green cloth boards.]

Lightly marked promptbook based on the Fechter version.

46. Mercer Hampson Simpson
Birmingham, Theatre Royal 1860's
Birmingham, Shakespeare Memorial Library: C52/455740

[Lacy edition, 4¼ x 7½; gray cardboard; title inked on cover; bound with other plays in green cloth boards; "Shakespeare's Separate Plays" gilt on spine.]

Promptbook lightly marked in ink with penciled additions. Calls, little stage business, cues for effects.

47. Edwin Forrest 1860's
Folger: Oth, 41

[French's Standard Drama, 4½ x 7⅜; stiff gray paper; title elaborately inked on cover.]

Lightly marked promptbook. Cuts, calls, some stage business, maps, cues for effects. (Compare the cover with that of HAM, 64.) (See nos. 52, 56.)

48. George Becks September, 1861
New York Public Library: *NCP.342977

[Forrest edition, 4¼ x 7; interleaves; blue cloth boards; title gilt up spine.]

Rehearsal copy and partial promptbook for "Eng^t of Sepr 1861," probably with Forrest. Becks variously played Messenger, Duke, Montano, Roderigo, Cassio. Random notes of stage business, maps, some cues for effects. Numerous penciled references to McCullough.

49. William Creswick London, Drury Lane October 8, 1864
Shakespeare Centre Library: 50.25(1851)

[Pages 241-352 from volume I of Knight's *Works*, 5½ x 8½; gray marbled boards and half black leather; title gilt up spine.]

Studybook for Iago. At the front a list of actors, a list of Iago's dresses. Cuts on full text. A great many notations of Iago's stage business and manner, cues for effects. Shakespeare Penny Memorial stamp, 1864. Advertisement for Drury Lane performance.

50. [Creswick]

Shakespeare Centre Library: 50.25(1838)

[Hinds English Stage, 1838, 5⅝ x 9¼; interleaves; brown marbled boards and half brown leather; title gilt on red leather spine label.]

Well-developed promptbook. Scenic indications, 4 good sketches of scenes, stage business, maps, cues for effects, timings. Shakespeare Penny Memorial stamp. Playbill and prospectus of Drury Lane performance on October 8, 1864. Signed in 1878 by W. Curle, the prompter at the Academy and Opera, Melbourne.

51. W. H. Lewellyn   Louisville   November 5, 1867

Folger: Oth, 21

[Modern Standard Drama, 4½ x 7½; interleaves.]

Stage manager's promptbook which claims to show the "Business of Edwin Booth" but in fact records only cues for effects.

52. Edwin Forrest   New York, Niblo's Garden   October 21, 1868

Harvard Theatre Collection: 13486.75.6

[Forrest edition, 4½ x 7¼; interleaves; purple cloth; title gilt on cover; in box of tan cloth boards and green leather spine; title gilt up spine.]

Promptbook signed and dated (November) by George H. Clarke, who played Iago and appears to have been Forrest's stage manager. Some restorations, calls, some stage business, good maps, cues for effects. At the front a costume note. (See nos. 47, 56.)

53. Edwin Booth   New York, Booth's   April 12, 1869

New York Public Library: *NCP.342993

[Booth-Hinton edition, 5¼ x 7½; interleaves, 6 x 7½; blue cloth boards; title gilt up spine.]

Promptbook of Booth's first production of *Othello* at his own theatre. At the front a list of minor actors and supers. Cuts, some scenic indications, grooves, calls, some stage business, maps and sketches, cues for effects. Notes on doubling. Proposal dated May 19 to shorten the third act in some future revival. (See nos. 55, 59, 65, 67-70, 74, 76-78, 90.)

54. Edwin Adams   Detroit   June 1, 1870

Harvard Theatre Collection: uncatalogued

[Booth-Hinton edition, 5 x 7¼; interleaves; green leather gilt; title and Adams' name gilt on cover.]

Well-developed promptbook for instruction of stage managers, used by Adams on tour. No stage business, but cuts, careful scenic indications, grooves, cues for effects.

55. Edwin Booth   New York, Booth's   March 20, 1871
The Players

[Pages 415-541 from volume VIII of a *Works*, 5⅜ x 8⅜; interleaves; green leather fold-over cover; title and Booth's name gilt on cover.]

Excellent promptbook marked by William Seymour and dated April 1, 1871. Cast for March 20 for a run in which Booth and Barrett alternated Othello and Iago. Cuts on full text. At the front detailed plots of scenes with grooves, properties. Very good groundplans, calls, stage business, cues for effects, timings (3:10). (See nos. 53, 59, 65, 67-70, 74, 76-78, 90.)

56. Edwin Forrest   c.1872
New York Public Library: *NCP.342933

[Forrest edition, 1860, 4½ x 7½; interleaves, 4⅜ x 8; black cloth boards; title gilt up spine.]

Promptbook record of Forrest's production by John B. Wright, who was Forrest's last stage manager. Lacks the cues of a working promptbook. Scenic indications, much stage business, maps, sketches. (See nos. 47, 52.)

57. John McCullough
          San Francisco, California Theatre   c.1873
Harvard Theatre Collection: 13486.75.11

[Forrest edition, 1860, 4¼ x 7⅛; interleaves; green cloth boards; title gilt on cover and up spine; in box of tan cloth boards and red leather spine; title gilt up spine.]

Promptbook much used on tour, roughly marked by several hands, one of them said to be that of Barton Hill of the California Theatre. Calls, much stage business, maps, cues for effects. At the back a list of supers and a timing note for Providence.

58. [McCullough]
New York Public Library: NCOFp.v.140.304766B

[French's Standard Drama, 4¼ x 7; bound with 11 other books in black cloth boards; title gilt on spine.]

Studybook for Othello elaborately marked with notes and symbols denoting emotion and vocal effects. Many maps.

59. Edwin Booth   New York, Booth's   November, 1873
The Players

[Booth-Hinton edition, 1868, 5⅞ x 8⅜; tan paper under brown marbled boards and half maroon leather; title gilt on spine.]

Fully marked promptbook mainly in pencil. Cuts, scenic indications, calls, stage business, maps, cues for effects. Minor actors mentioned in calls. Reference in a scenic note to "Winters Tale platform circle" : the only production of *Winter's Tale* in these years was at Booth's in April, 1871; the next *Othello* at Booth's was as dated above. Enclosed is a playbill for December 29, 1866, when Booth played Iago in English to Bogumil Dawison's German Othello. (See nos. 53, 55, 65, 67-70, 74, 76-78, 90.)

60. Tommaso Salvini   Hartford   May 15, 1874
Connecticut State Library

[Salvini bilingual edition, 1873.]

Notes on Salvini's stage business and histrionic manner made by William Gillette. (See nos. 64, 80-81.)

61. Marcus J. Moriarty   c.1875
Folger: Oth, 40

[French's Standard Drama, 4¼ x 7⅜; torn and unsewn.]

Rehearsal copy checked for Iago. Several sheets of manuscript notes on the playing of Iago and Othello. Clippings of playbills for Edwin Booth, December, 1874, and McVicker's Theatre, April 14, 1876.

62. Leon John Vincent   Cleveland   c.1875
Folger: Oth, 34

[French's Standard Drama, 4¼ x 7; interleaves; brown paper; title inked on cover.]

Crude but thorough promptbook. Cuts, calls, little stage business, maps, cues for effects.

63. William H. Gillette   Boston, Globe   c.1875
Connecticut State Library

[French's Standard Drama, 4½ x 7½.]

Rehearsal copy checked for Duke, Montano. Provisional or descriptive notes of the stage business of Othello.

64. Tommaso Salvini   London, Drury Lane   April 1, 1875
Folger: Oth, 32

[Salvini parallel text edition, London, 1876, 5¼ x 8⅜; purple publisher's wrappers.]

Spectator's notes on Salvini's performance. (See nos. 60, 80-81.)

65. Edwin Booth   New York, Lyceum   January 18, 1877
The Players
[Pages of Booth-Hinton edition, 5¼ x 7½, tipped to stubs between leaves of a workbook, 6⅞ x 8¼; red marbled boards and half red leather; in slip-box of red leather; title gilt on spine.]
Well-developed (though ill-spelled) promptbook much used on tour in the 1870's. Cuts and corrections, calls, stage business, maps, cues for effects. Names of minor actors mentioned in calls. Printed cast for Booth's Theatre in 1869. Timings for several cities, including New York for 1877. (See nos. 53, 55, 59, 67-70, 74, 76-78, 90.)

66. Stella Boniface   New York   April, 1878
Folger: Oth, 2
[French's Standard Drama, 4⅝ x 7½; publisher's yellow wrappers, torn.]
Rehearsal copy checked for Desdemona. Some stage business.

67. Edwin Booth   1880's
The Players
[Booth-Winter edition, 1878, 4⅝ x 6½; limp brown leather gilt; title gilt on spine.]
Excellent transcription of Booth's promptbook made by J. R. Pitman as a souvenir for Russ Whytal, autographed by Booth. Very good groundplans, calls, stage business, maps, cues for effects. (See nos. 53, 55, 59, 65, 74, 76-78, 90.)

68. [Booth]
The Players
[Booth-Winter edition, 4½ x 6⅝; brown marbled boards and half maroon leather.]
Roughly penciled but used promptbook. Maps, cues for effects.

69. [Booth]   Chicago, McVickers
New York Public Library: *NCP.5954B
[Booth-Winter edition, 1878, 4¾ x 6½; black cloth boards; title gilt on spine.]

Lightly marked promptbook. Some stage business, a few maps, cues for effects, timing (3:00).

70. [Booth]

Folger: Oth, 3

[Booth-Winter edition, 4¼ x 7¼; tipped into brown leather notebook.]

Preparation copy. Some cuts; 3 elaborate costume lists for Iago.

71. Lawrence Barrett   1880's

Harvard Theatre Collection: uncatalogued

[Ten music score books, 9½ x 6¼; brown cloth boards and green cloth spine.]

Complete scores for the band for 9 plays including *Othello,* endorsed by musicians in many cities.

72. Frederick Paulding   1880's

Rutgers University: PR.1243.SHA

[Booth-Hinton edition, 1869, 5 x 7½; publisher's wrappers.]

Liberally but randomly marked book, as if the actor were observing and recording a performance. Stage business with especial attention to Iago, maps, cues for effects.

73. Henry Irving   London, Lyceum   May 2, 1881

Harvard Theatre Collection: uncatalogued

[Clarendon Press edition, 4⅛ x 6¼; interleaves; limp brown leather gilt; title gilt on cover.]

Studybook for Iago and Othello, marked in red, blue, and lead pencil. Cuts on full text. Hundreds of jottings on the acting of the two roles.

74. Edwin Booth   Paris   1883

The Players

[*Othello, Le More de Venise,* Paris, 1882, 4⅞ x 7½; brown marbled boards and half maroon leather.]

"Arranged for my performance at the Odeon—Paris, which did not occur." (See nos. 53, 55, 59, 65, 67-70, 76-78, 90.)

75. Thomas W. Keene   Philadelphia, Arch Street   February 15, 1883

Harvard Theatre Collection: (Widener, 13486.78.5)

[Keene edition (French), 5⅝ x 9; pictorial paper wrapper under maroon cloth boards; title gilt up spine.]

Probably a spectator's copy with copious notes in the last 3 acts on Keene's stage business.

76. Edwin Booth   April, 1885
University of Pennsylvania, Furness Collection: C59.Sh1OB
[Booth-Winter edition, 1878, 4¾ x 6¾; gray publisher's wrappers under red leather gilt and silk-lined; "Prompt Book of Othello" gilt on spine.]
"Some notes for ye Novice, H.H.F." More than 280 notes by Booth on the roles of Iago and Othello and on production of the play, done in April, 1885. Most but not all are printed in the Furness Variorum edition. (See nos. 53, 55, 59, 65, 67-70, 74, 90.)

77. [Booth]   New York, Academy of Music   April 26, 1886
The Players
[Mixture of bilingual Booth-Salvini edition, 5¼ x 8⅜, and French's Standard Drama.]
Heavily marked promptbook of a 6-act version used for the occasions when Booth played Iago to Salvini's Italian Othello. Cuts, stage business, cues for effects.

78. [Booth]
The Players
[Two books. Booth-Salvini edition in English, 5¾ x 8¼; brown marbled boards and half maroon leather.]
One of these lists performances in New York, Philadelphia, and Boston. Both have a few pencilings.

79. Robert B. Mantell   Reading   February 18, 1888
Folger: Oth, 25
[French's Standard Drama, 4¼ x 6¾; interleaves; limp maroon leather; title and Mantell's name gilt on cover.]
Touring promptbook. At the front a dummy cast list and plot of scenes with grooves. Cuts and restorations, some stage business, maps, cues for effects.

80. Tommaso Salvini   New York, Palmer's   October 16, 1889
New York Public Library: *NCP.342932
[Salvini's Farewell American Tour edition, 1889, 6½ x 9; black cloth boards.]
George Becks's record of Salvini's performance: costume notes,

maps, copious annotation of stage business and histrionic manner. (See nos. 60, 64.)

81. [Salvini]
New York Public Library: 8-*T-*NCVF.70727B
[Manuscript, 7⅞ x 9¾; red cloth boards; title gilt up spine.]
Manuscript of an Italian translation of E. T. Mason's book about Salvini's Othello (published in 1890). At the back about 20 corrections apparently by Salvini: "Tutto il resto e perfettamente esatto." Many good maps by Robert Blum.

82. Robert S. Taber   c.1890
Library of Congress, Batchelder Collection: 415
[Booth-Winter edition, 1878, 4½ x 6⅝; limp green cloth; title gilt on cover.]
Randomly marked studybook, with stage directions lightly penciled in third and fourth acts, literary and critical notes *passim*, Booth's autograph on a card.

83. Frederick Warde   America   1892
University of California, Los Angeles: Special Collections 669, Box 1
[French's Standard Drama, 4¼ x 7⅜; interleaves, 6 x 7½; brown leather; title gilt on spine.]
Promptbook used between 1892 and 1895, when Warde was partnered with Louis James, and probably before and after. Some stage business, cues for effects. Several playbills including one of Edwin Booth in Baltimore in 1876; several reviews of the 1880's and 1890's; many prints and photographs including several of James and Warde.

84. Charles B. Hanford   c.1895
Folger: Oth, 9
[Booth-Winter edition, 4½ x 6½; gray cloth boards and half black leather, back missing; title and Hanford's name gilt on cover.]
Studybook for Othello. Cuts, stage business for Othello, a few cues for effects.

85. Henry Jewett   New York, Broadway   1895-96
Folger: Oth, Folio 1
[Typescript, 8½ x 11; gray cardboard under gray canvas.]

Promptbook of Jewett's arrangement as acted at the Broadway in 1895-96, and produced some 30 years later for the Boston Repertory Theatre. Stage business is typed, with penciled additions. Maps, cues for effects. Two photographs of the library of the Boston Repertory.

86. Ellen Terry   London, Lyceum   c.1898
Smallhythe

[Temple edition, 1897, 3⅞ x 5; limp maroon leather; title gilt up spine.]

Much used rehearsal copy, "No. 1/Ellen Terry/Ilkley/August/ Fulham." Cuts on full text, Bianca scene pinned shut. Initials of a cast. Copious notes on the acting of Desdemona and comments on Iago and Othello and the production.

87. [Terry]
Smallhythe

[Same as preceding book.]

Rehearsal copy checked for Desdemona, dated Fulham, August, 1898. Cuts on full text, Bianca scene pinned shut. Costume notes. A few notes on the acting of Desdemona.

88. [Terry]
Smallhythe

[Irving edition, 1899, 4 x 5⅞; green cloth boards gilt; title gilt up spine.]

Rehearsal copy cut and checked for Desdemona. A few notes on the acting.

89. F. R. Benson   c.1900
Shakespeare Centre Library: 72.925BEN

[Heinemann edition pasted in a workbook, 6¾ x 9; red marbled boards and red cloth spine, much worn; title inked on spine label.]

Preparation copy. Cuts, stage business, some groundplans, cues for effects, all roughly entered.

90. J. R. Pitman   Boston, Castle Square   February 23, 1903
University of Pennsylvania, Furness Collection: C59.Sh1OP

[Booth-Winter edition, 1878, 4¾ x 6¾; gray publisher's wrappers.]

Carefully marked promptbook largely derived from Booth's (see no. 67). Scenes and grooves indicated on excellent groundplans.

Calls, stage business, cues for effects. Playbill of Pitman's production.

91. Lewis Waller   London, Lyric   May 17, 1906
Folger: Oth, 35

[Shakespeare edition pasted in a workbook, 9¾ x 7¾; limp brown leather.]

Promptbook for only the second half (from middle of Act III) of Waller's production. Heavy cuts on full text, calls, much stage business, cues for effects. For Act V, property lists and 2 excellent groundplans. Notes on the text as used at the Lyric and "Variations done at Stratford-on-Avon." Waller played Othello at Stratford with the Benson company in 1907.

92. Oscar Asche London, His Majesty's November 7, 1907
Shakespeare Centre Library: 72.925ASC

[Shakespeare edition pasted in a workbook, 6⅜ x 8; black oilcloth boards, front cover missing; tied in white cardboard wrapper.]

Much used promptbook. Cast, groundplans, stage business, cues for effects.

93. [Asche]
Shakespeare Centre Library: 72.925ASC

[Temple edition pasted in a workbook, 6¼ x 8; gray boards and half black leather, much worn; title gilt up spine.]

Full and well-made promptbook much used at Kennington and on tour. Stage business, maps and groundplans, cues for effects. Names of actors. Many sketches of the principal characters.

94. C. W. Buchanan   January, 1912
Folger: Oth, 4

[Lacy edition, 4¼ x 7⅜; stiff white paper.]

The book first owned (1861) but not written in by Harry Cox, Theatre Royal, Sunderland. In 1912, Buchanan, a Londoner, filled it with strangely naive notes on acting and production.

95. Herbert Beerbohm Tree
     London, His Majesty's April 9, 1912
Enthoven Collection: Tree, 228

[Two books. Favourite Classics edition, 1904, 3½ x 5¾; interleaves; blue cloth boards; title gilt on spine.]

The first is a full and systematic promptbook done in pencil by

Stanley Bell. At the front good groundplans. Cuts, much stage business, cues for effects. The second is an inked transcription completed through only 3 acts.

96. [Tree]

Enthoven Collection: Tree, 228

[Temple edition pasted in a workbook, 6¼ x 7⅞; black oilcloth.]

Preparation copy marked in red ink perhaps by Tree. Stage directions for Act III only.

97. [Tree]

Enthoven Collection: Tree, 228

[Temple edition, 1899, 4 x 5⅛; maroon limp leather.]

Tree's rehearsal and preparation book checked for Othello. Cuts, some stage business, provisional notes on effects.

98. [Tree]

Folger: Oth, 33

[French issue of Lacy edition, 4⅛ x 7¼.]

Rehearsal copy. First scene of Act III penciled for Iago's stage business.

99. [Tree]

Enthoven Collection: Tree, 228

[Six books. Temple edition (5), 1899; Favourite Classics edition (1), 1904.]

Rehearsal copies for various roles. One unassigned book has cuts, stage business, cues for effects.

100. [Tree]

Enthoven Collection: Tree, 228

[Papers.]

Plots of costumes, properties, cast, supers' entrances, etc.; 2 sketches of scenes, several sketches of properties.

101. Hallam Bosworth   c.1915

New York Public Library: *NCP.52x296

[Booth-Winter edition, 1911, 4 x 7¼; interleaves, 6 x 8; black cloth boards; title gilt on spine.]

Penciled transcription of traditional matter from several old promptbooks, especially Booth's. At the front, groundplans, plots of properties and lights. Copious stage business, cues for effects.

102. Robert Atkins   Egypt   October, 1927

Shakespeare Centre Library: 72.925ATK

[Heinemann edition pasted in a workbook, $6\frac{3}{4}$ x 9; green marbled boards and blue cloth spine; title inked on spine label.]

Roughly made promptbook used by Atkins' company during tours to Egypt in 1927 and 1928. Stage business, cues for effects, timings.

[ACTOR LISTS FOR FOLLOWING BOOKS ARE GIVEN IN THIS ORDER: Othello, Iago, Desdemona, Emilia.]

103. W. Bridges-Adams   Stratford-upon-Avon   April 23, 1930

Shakespeare Centre Library: 71.21/1930 O

[Favourite Classics edition pasted in a workbook, $6\frac{5}{8}$ x 9; blue cloth boards and red cloth spine, much worn; title inked on cover label.]

Cast includes Wilfrid Walter, George Hayes, Joyce Bland. Costumes by Eric Maxon. Stage business, cues for effects roughly entered. The book had been used in 1924; was erased and rewritten.

104. Maurice Browne   London, Savoy   May 19, 1930

Folger: Oth, Folio 2

[Shakespeare edition pasted in a workbook, $8\frac{7}{8}$ x $12\frac{3}{4}$; heavy maroon binder; title gilt on spine.]

Cast includes Paul Robeson, Maurice Browne, Peggy Ashcroft, Sybil Thorndike. Directed by Ellen van Volkenburg. Cuts on full text. Good groundplans, calls, stage business, maps, cues for effects, timings (3:05). Photographs of the 7 sets designed by James Pryde. At the back plots of properties, armour, electrics. Fourteen-page description of George Sheringham's costumes.

105. [Browne]

University of Michigan, Shakespeare Collection

[Temple edition pasted in a workbook, $9\frac{5}{8}$ x 12; black cloth boards and red leather spine.]

"Preliminary prompt-copy" of the Browne-Robeson production. Cuts on full text, scenic indications, calls, stage business, maps, cues for effects.

106. Philip Merivale   New York, Ethel Barrymore   September 27, 1935

New York Public Library: *NCP+.329226-7B

[Two books. Carbon typescript, $7\frac{3}{4}$ x 11; black cloth boards; title gilt up spine.]

Cast includes Philip Merivale, Kenneth MacKenna, Gladys Cooper, Alexandra Carlisle. Directed by Henry Herbert. Designed by P. Dodd Ackerman. Produced by Crosby Gaige. First book much used in stage management: cues for effects. The second unused.

107. [Merivale]

Princeton University, Seymour Collection

[Typescript, 8½ x 11; blue paper wrapper; title on orange cover label.]

Unused copy of preceding book identified as the production of Crosby Gaige.

108. Margaret Webster   New York, Shubert   October 19, 1943

New York Public Library: *NCP+.344134B

[Carbon typescript, 8 x 11, and photostats of music score, 10¼ x 13⅜; blue cloth boards; title gilt up spine.]

Cast includes Paul Robeson, Jose Ferrer, Uta Hagen, Margaret Webster. Music by Tom Bennett. Designed by Robert Edmond Jones. Unused copy of the version, arranged as prose, with basic stage business and effects.

109. Robert Atkins   Stratford-upon-Avon   April 4, 1945

Shakespeare Centre Library: 71.21/1945 O

[Eversley edition pasted in a workbook, 7 x 9; blue cloth boards and half black leather; title on cover and spine labels.]

Cast includes George Skillan, Antony Eustrel, Moira Lister, Viola Lyel. Designed by Martin Battersby. Stage business, cues for effects. The book had been used for Atkins' 1939 production.

110. Godfrey Tearle   Stratford-upon-Avon   July 31, 1948

Shakespeare Centre Library: O.S.71.21/1948 O

[Temple edition pasted in a workbook, 8 x 12⅞; green boards and red cloth spine; title on cover and spine labels.]

Cast includes Godfrey Tearle, Anthony Quayle, Diana Wynyard, Ena Burrill. Designed by Joseph Carl and Audrey Cruddas. Much stage business, cues for effects. Used again for the 1949 revival.

111. Anthony Quayle   Australia   1953

Shakespeare Centre Library: O.S.71.21/1953

[New Temple edition pasted in a workbook, 8 x 13; black cloth board spring binder.]

Cast includes Anthony Quayle, Leo McKern, Barbara Jefford. Designed by Tanya Moiseiwitsch. Very much stage business, maps, cues for effects. At the back a fight routine.

112. [Quayle]   Stratford-upon-Avon   March 16, 1954
Shakespeare Centre Library: O.S.71.21/1954
[New Temple edition pasted in a workbook, 8 x 13; blue cloth board spring binder; title on spine label.]
Cast includes Anthony Quayle, Raymond Westwell, Barbara Jefford, Joan MacArthur. Designed by Tanya Moiseiwitsch. Very much stage business, maps on mimeographed groundplans, cues for effects. This was a revival of the 1953 Australian production.

113. Glen Byam Shaw   Stratford-upon-Avon   May 29, 1956
Shakespeare Centre Library: O.S.71.21/1956 O
[New Temple edition pasted in a workbook, 8 x 13; blue cloth board spring binder; title gilt on red cloth cover label, inked on spine label.]
Cast includes Harry Andrews, Emlyn Williams, Margaret Johnston, Diana Churchill. Designed by Motley. Very full stage business, maps on mimeographed groundplans, cues for effects. Many production papers.

114. John Houseman   Stratford, Connecticut   June 23, 1957
University of California, Los Angeles: Houseman Box 13
[Mimeograph, 8½ x 11; black cloth board spring binder.]
Cast includes Earle Hyman, Alfred Drake, Jacqueline Brooks, Sada Thompson. Designed by Rouben Ter-Arutunian. Rough production book. Some stage business and other working notes.

115. [Houseman]
University of California, Los Angeles: Houseman Box 9
[Mimeograph, 8½ x 11; brown cloth board ring binder.]
Final or souvenir promptbook. Stage business typed along margins.

116. Tony Richardson   Stratford-upon-Avon   April 7, 1959
Shakespeare Centre Library: O.S.71.21/1959 Oth
[New Temple edition pasted in a workbook, 8 x 13; blue cloth board spring binder.]
Cast includes Paul Robeson, Sam Wanamaker, Mary Ure, Angela

Baddeley. Designed by Loudon Sainthill. Much stage business, maps, cues for effects.

117. Jean Gascon and George McCowan
                    Stratford, Ontario   June 30, 1959
Festival Theatre, Library
[Two books. Penguin edition pasted in workbooks, $8\frac{1}{4}$ x $13\frac{5}{8}$; green cloth boards; title pasted on cover of first book.]
Cast includes Douglas Campbell, Douglas Rain, Frances Hyland, Kate Reid. Designed by Robert Prévost. The first book has roughly entered stage business, maps, cues for effects. The second has calls, cues for effects.

118. Franco Zeffirelli   Stratford-upon-Avon   October 10, 1961
Shakespeare Centre Library: O.S.71.21/1961 O
[Cambridge Pocket Shakespeare pasted in a workbook, 8 x 13; red cloth board spring binder; title on spine label.]
Cast includes John Gielgud, Ian Bannen, Dorothy Tutin, Peggy Ashcroft. Costumes by Peter Hall. Very full stage business, cues for effects.

119. Other books of *Othello*:
Brown University: Eng.P.17, Asa Cushman, 1852, Providence casts with G. V. Brooke and J. B. Booth.
Connecticut State Library: William Gillette.
Essex Institute, Salem: 822.08/S24/no. 23, John B. Adams, Boston Museum, 1851.
Folger: Oth, 1, 22, 42, anonymous; Oth, 23, F. G. Lowe (England), cast with Wallack and John Child; Oth, 29, L. D. Ross, 1850, and George W. Furber; Oth, 36, Jefferson Winter; Oth, 39, M. C. Snowdon or Seaman; Oth, 43, Jean Aicard translation, addressed to Paul Mounet, cut and heavily marked promptbook.
Harvard Theatre Collection: 13486.72.25, anonymous, eighteenth century; uncatalogued, G. Reignolds.
Missouri Historical Society: John W. Norton.
Museum of the City of New York: 32.485.294A, C, one of J. H. Ring and one anonymous.
New York Public Library: *NCP+.963717A, manuscript Italian version of Ermete Novelli, 1907.
Princeton University, Seymour Collection: OTH, 7, William

Cutter of the Broadway, James Seymour, William Seymour, play-bill of J. W. Lonergan.

Shakespeare Centre Library: 50.14(1815), Fanny Kemble and Helen Faucit; 50.25(1856), F. A. Marshall.

W. A. Clark Library, Los Angeles: Temple edition, anonymous.

Pericles

1. Samuel Phelps   London, Sadler's Wells   October 14, 1854

   Folger: Per, 1

   [Shakespeare edition pasted in 5 booklets, 4½ x 7¼; heavy brown paper.]

   Phelps's original promptbook probably in his own hand, with prompter's pencilings added. Text much cut, rearranged, and augmented. Scenic indications, grooves, calls, stage business, maps and sketches, cues for effects. Diorama show in the last act.

2. [Phelps]

   Folger: Per, 2

   [Shakespeare edition pasted in a workbook, 4¾ x 8; blue boards and canvas spine; title inked on cover.]

   Transcription and expansion of the preceding book, used. Scenery and stage business given more fully, cues for effects more regularly.

3. [Phelps]

   Shakespeare Centre Library: 50.26(1805)

   [Pages 237-334 from volume VIII of Chalmers' *Works,* 1805, 5¼ x 8⅝; a few interleaves; tan marbled boards and half black leather; title gilt up spine.]

   Transcription of Phelps's promptbook made by William Creswick. In the front cover the Shakespeare Penny Memorial stamp of 1864.

[ACTOR LISTS FOR FOLLOWING BOOKS ARE GIVEN IN THIS ORDER: Pericles, Marina, Gower.]

4. Nugent Monck   Stratford-upon-Avon   August 16, 1947

   Shakespeare Centre Library: O.S.71.21/1947

   [New Temple edition pasted in a workbook, 8 x 12¾; black boards and red cloth spine; title on cover and spine labels.]

   Cast includes Paul Scofield, Daphne Slater, Dudley Jones. Designed by Barry Jackson. Much stage business, maps, cues for effects, timings.

5. Tony Richardson   Stratford-upon-Avon   July 8, 1958

   Shakespeare Centre Library: O.S.71.21/1958P

   [New Temple edition pasted in a workbook, 8 x 13; red cloth board spring binder; title on spine label.]

Cast includes Richard Johnson, Geraldine McEwan, Edric Connor. Designed by Loudon Sainthill. Additions to text, very much stage business, maps on mimeographed groundplans, cues for effects.

Richard II

1. Thomas Elrington   Dublin, Smock Alley   c.1720
   Folger: Rich II, 7
   [Theobald alteration, 1720, 4⅝ x 7½.]
   Promptbook with cast inked in, most of whom are known to be
   Smock Alley actors of about 1720. Cuts and alterations, calls, en-
   trance signals (horizontal line with vertical slashes), cues for ef-
   fects.

2. John Roberts   London, Covent Garden   March 6, 1738
   Folger: R II, Second Folio
   [Pages 23-46 from a Second Folio, 1632, 8⅞ x 12⅝ (ends folded),
   tipped between leaves of an album, 9⅝ x 11⅞; brown cloth
   boards and red leather spine; "Shakespeare's Original Edition
   1623" gilt up spine.]
   Preparation copy, "Correct cum Libr Theatr." Cuts and a few
   alterations. Excellent large maps of the combat scene and the
   Parliament scene. Decorated title page of album by T. Purland
   dated September 11, 1847. Playbill of Kean's *Richard II* for October 23, 1815, tinted print of Kean as Richard, Shakespeareana,
   portion of original manuscript cover with Roberts' signature,
   etc. (See J. G. McManaway, *Shakespeare Quarterly*, XV, 2, 161-
   175.)

3. Edmund Kean   London, Drury Lane   March 9, 1815
   Folger: Rich II, 3
   [Wroughton edition, 1815, 5⅛ x 8½; interleaves watermarked
   1818; green marbled boards and half brown leather; title and
   "Mʳ. Kean" gilt up spine.]
   Transcription from the 1815 promptbook by G. C. Carr, the
   Drury Lane prompter, probably for Kean's later use. Cuts, calls,
   little stage business, maps, cues for effects, timing (2:45).

4. [Kean]   Philadelphia   January 22, 1819
   Harvard Theatre Collection: TS.2587.63
   [Wroughton edition, 1815, 5½ x 8½; brown leather; in box of
   tan cloth boards and red leather spine; title gilt up spine.]
   Promptbook, "Marked from Mr. Kean's Book," which belonged
   to William B. Wood. Philadelphia cast with J. W. Wallack as the
   King. Cuts, scenic indications, calls, stage business, cues for ef-
   fects, timing.

5. William Charles Macready

           London, Haymarket   December 2, 1850

Victoria and Albert, Forster Library, 7919:   F.48.C.17

[Acting edition, 1812, $3\frac{1}{2}$ x 6; interleaves, $3\frac{1}{2}$ x 7; bound with other Macready promptbooks in green cloth boards and half tan leather; titles gilt on spine.]

Promptbook marked by Macready in the margins, by a prompter on the interleaves. Cuts, some scenic indications, some stage business, maps, cues for effects.

6. [Macready]

Victoria and Albert, Forster Library, 7915:   F.48.C.15

[Pages 3-112 from volume V of Pickering edition, 1825, $4\frac{7}{8}$ x $7\frac{1}{4}$; interleaves; green cloth boards and half tan leather; title gilt on spine label.]

Preparation copy. Cuts on full text. Some stage business.

7. Charles Kean   London, Princess's   March 12, 1857

Folger: Rich II, 2

[Reprint from Steevens edition, $5\frac{3}{4}$ x 9; gray interleaves, $7\frac{1}{4}$ x $8\frac{7}{8}$; white cardboard and canvas spine.]

Penciled workbook of George Ellis, the stage manager. Cuts on full text. List of supers and their wages. Copious stage business, maps, notes on effects. At the back a detailed description of the murder scene. (NOTE: There is no proper "final" promptbook of Kean's production.)

8. [Kean]

Folger: T.a.75

[Manuscript, $5\frac{1}{4}$ x $6\frac{5}{8}$.]

Cuebook for *Richard II* and *The Tempest* in the hand of George Ellis, the stage manager. Calls, maps and sketches, procession list for the "Historical Episode," cues for effects, special warnings on handling of scenery, sounds, etc.

9. [Kean]

Folger: Rich II, 8

[Kean edition, 1857, $4\frac{3}{4}$ x $7\frac{3}{4}$; interleaves; brown marbled boards and half green leather; title gilt up spine.]

Incomplete promptbook apparently used after 1859: complete Kean cast which is not that of the Princess's production. Few pencilings.

10. [Kean]

Folger: Rich II, 4

[Kean edition, 1857, 5¼ x 8¼; publisher's wrappers.]

Workbook. Cuts, notes on doubling lesser characters. The name "Mills" inked on cover.

11. [Kean]

Enthoven Collection: Box DT.44

[Watercolors mounted on large display boards.]

Fine watercolor designs of 17 scenes; 16 watercolor plates of properties, banners, etc.

12. [Kean]

Folger: Kean Costume Book, 33, Prints and Engravings, 182

[Scrapbook, 14⅜ x 21¼; brown cloth boards and half brown leather; "Charles Kean's Scrap Book" gilt on spine and red leather cover label.]

Contains 176 fine watercolor plates of costumes, properties, scenes.

13. [Kean]

Enthoven Collection: 94G26, plates 1735-38

[Scrapbook, 15¼ x 21⅜; blue cloth boards and half blue cloth; "Kean Theatrical Scenery" gilt up spine.]

Watercolor designs of 4 scenes, with figures.

14. [Kean]

Enthoven Collection: 94G27, plates 1764, 1767, 1792-1854

[Scrapbook like the preceding book.]

Plates 1764 and 1767 are watercolors of figures in the "Historical Episode." Plates 1792-99 are watercolor designs of 8 scenes of the play; these are in the style of those which usually appear in the Edmonds final or souvenir promptbooks at the Folger, but for this play there is no Edmonds book. Plates 1800-1802 are designs of properties. Plates 1816-37 are drawings for costumes. Plates 1838-39 are newspaper engravings of scenes. Plates 1840-54 are oval engravings of all scenes of the play and a color print of the interior of the Princess's.

15. [Kean]

Enthoven Collection: Box DT.48a

[Watercolors.]

Preliminary watercolor designs by T. Grieve for 10 scenes.

16. John Moore   New York, Daly's Fifth Avenue   November 8, 1875
Folger: Rich II, 5
[Pages 295-399 from volume IV of a *Works*, 5⅛ x 8; interleaves; buff paper.]
Thorough and carefully written promptbook for Booth's production mostly done in blue ink. Unlike most of Moore's books this one apparently was not taken from an English or earlier American original. Cuts on full text. Scenic indications, grooves, calls, copious stage business, cues for effects. Numerous penciled references to the arrangements of Kean's production, presumably that at the Broadway Theatre on September 15, 1865. Enclosures: a list of doubling characters, a newspaper account of the first American production in 1819, several reviews of Kean's London production in 1857, a review of Kean's New York production in 1865, announcements of Booth's 1875 production (for which this promptbook was made), a review of Booth's production in 1878.

17. Edwin Booth   New York, Daly's Fifth Avenue   Nov. 8, 1875
The Players
[French issue of Cumberland edition, 3⅝ x 5⅜; brown marbled boards and half maroon leather; title gilt on spine.]
Preparation copy with some cuts and notes, inscribed "Keep this as a Curiosity of the *Palmy days!*" The version was rejected because of its corruption, which "beats Colly Cibber & Tate."

18. [Booth]
The Players
[Dicks Standard Plays, 4¾ x 7⅜; brown marbled boards and half maroon leather; title gilt on spine.]
Preparation copy. A few notes.

19. [Booth]
The Players
[Clarendon Press edition, 1874, 4⅜ x 6⅝; limp brown cloth boards; in slip-box of red leather; title gilt on spine.]
Preparation copy. Cuts, alterations, some grooves.

20. [Booth]
The Players
[Shakespeare edition pasted in a workbook, 6⅞ x 8¼; bound with *Richard III* in orange marbled boards and black leather spine; in slip-box of red leather; title gilt on spine.]
Preparation copy. Cuts, scenic indications with rough sketches.

21. [Booth]
    The Players
    [Manuscript, 7¾ x 10⅛; tan boards and brown cloth spine; title penciled on cover; in slip-box of red leather; title gilt on spine.] Manuscript promptbook, much used. At the front a cast, list of doubles, notes on music. Scenic indications, grooves, calls, stage business, maps, cues for effects. Program for the first performance.

22. [Booth]   New York, Lyceum   December 4, 1876
    The Players
    [Typescript, 7¾ x 9¾; gray marbled boards and half green leather; title on cover label; in slip-box of red leather; title gilt on spine.]
    Typescript promptbook, much used. At the front plots of scenes with grooves, properties, characters; 3 large penciled sketches of scenes. Scenic indications, calls, cues for effects. Timing for the Lyceum in 1876-77 (2:57).

23. [Booth]
    The Players: MSS.23
    [Twenty-six booklets. Manuscript, 8 x 6¼; some in tan paper.]
    Partbooks. One set of 17 books, another of 9, all much used. Most of them bear names of actors.

24. [Booth]
    The Players
    [Booth-Winter edition, 1878, 4¾ x 7⅛; brown marbled boards and half maroon leather; title gilt on spine.]
    Book "Marked for corrections" by William Winter in preparation for reprinting. Some stage business added.

25. William Poel   London, University of London   Nov. 11, 1899
    Enthoven Collection
    [Shakespeare edition pasted in a workbook, 4 x 6¼; black imitation leather; title on cover label.]
    Partial promptbook. Cuts on full text. Notes on music and properties.

26. Herbert Beerbohm Tree
                London, His Majesty's   September 10, 1903
    Enthoven Collection: Tree, 152
    [Temple edition pasted in a workbook, 6⅞ x 8¾; black oilcloth.]

Preparation copy marked by Tree. Cuts (22 of 62 pages), stage business, notes on scenery and effects. At the back numerous historical notes, plans for production, plans for an advertising brochure.

27. [Tree]

Enthoven Collection: Tree, 152

[Temple edition pasted in a workbook, 7 x 9; red marbled boards and blue cloth spine.]

Rehearsal promptbook. Much stage business roughly penciled. Partial cast.

28. [Tree]

Enthoven Collection: Tree, 152

[Temple edition pasted in a workbook, 7 x 9; red marbled boards and purple spine; title on cover label.]

Very full rehearsal promptbook. Much stage business, maps, cues for effects. Typewritten plots of scenes, cast, entrance of champions, procession list, etc.

29. [Tree]

Enthoven Collection: Tree, 250

[Shakespeare text pasted in a workbook, 7 x 9; red marbled boards and red cloth spine, much worn; title on cover label.]

Fully developed promptbook. Copious stage business done in red ink, with additional business typewritten and pasted in. Maps and sketches. List of scenes.

30. [Tree]

Enthoven Collection: Tree, 152

[Shakespeare text pasted in a workbook, $6\frac{7}{8}$ x $8\frac{7}{8}$; red marbled boards and green cloth spine, much worn; title on cover label.]

Final promptbook signed by Edgar Ruthven in 1904. Cast and scenes from printed program pasted in. Fine sketches of 6 scenes washed with colored inks, excellent groundplans, copious stage directions partly typewritten and partly in red ink, typewritten light plots.

31. [Tree]

Enthoven Collection: Tree, 152

[Temple edition, $4\frac{1}{2}$ x 7; blue cloth boards; title stamped on cover and gilt up spine.]

Stage manager's cuebook. Cuts partly inked, partly scissored, partly covered with blank paper. Some groundplans, some stage business, cues for effects.

32. [Tree]
Enthoven Collection: Tree, 152
[Temple edition, 4 x 5⅛; red leather; title gilt up spine.]
Cuebook. Cuts, some stage business, cues for effects.

33. [Tree]
Enthoven Collection: Tree, 152
[Twelve books. Favourite Classics edition (11), 1904, 3¾ x 6; green cloth boards. Temple edition (1), 4 x 5¼; red cloth boards.]
Rehearsal copies, all with cuts, a few with stage business.

34. [Tree]
Enthoven Collection: Tree, 151, 152
[Papers.]
Plots for calls, cast, supers, dressing rooms, properties, limes; groundplans, score and words for a song, etc.

[ACTOR LISTS FOR FOLLOWING BOOKS ARE GIVEN IN THIS ORDER: Richard, Bolingbroke.]

35. W. Bridges-Adams   Stratford-upon-Avon   April 16, 1929
Shakespeare Centre Library: 71.21/1929R
[Favourite Classics edition pasted in a workbook, 6½ x 8⅞; blue cloth boards and red cloth spine; title on cover and spine labels.]
Cast includes George Hayes, Wilfrid Walter. Little stage business, maps, cues for effects. The book had been used for the 1924 production.

36. [Bridges-Adams]   July, 1930
Shakespeare Centre Library: 71.21/1930R
[Temple edition pasted in a workbook, 6¾ x 9; blue cloth boards and half red leather; title on cover and spine label.]
Cast includes George Hayes, Wilfrid Walter. Costumes by Eric Maxon. Some stage business, maps, cues for effects. A sheet of music.

37. Tyrone Guthrie   Stratford-upon-Avon   April 21, 1933
Shakespeare Centre Library: 71.21/1933RI

[Temple edition pasted in a workbook, 7 x 9; purple cloth boards and half black leather; title on cover and spine labels.] Cast includes George Hayes, Anew McMaster. Unused copy. Some stage business, maps, cues for effects.

38. Margaret Webster   New York, St. James   February 5, 1937
New York Public Library: *NCP +.76440B
[Dent edition pasted in a workbook, 8½ x 11; blue cloth boards; title gilt on spine.]
Cast includes Maurice Evans, Ian Keith. Promptbook of Edward P. Dimond, the stage manager, used through the first season. Cuts on full text. Cast, copious stage business, maps, cues for effects, timings, dates of the run (133 performances).

39. [Webster]
New York Public Library: *NCP
[Photostat of Dent edition pasted in a workbook, 8½ x 11; blue cloth boards; title gilt on spine.]
Photographic copy of Dimond's final promptbook as used during the second season and on tour until June, 1940. Much detail of the preceding book has been eliminated. Notes on timing (2:24) and length of the run (458 performances).

40. Robert Atkins   Stratford-upon-Avon   May 22, 1944
Shakespeare Centre Library: 71.21/1944RI
[Temple edition pasted in a workbook, 7⅛ x 9; purple cloth boards and half black leather; title on spine label.]
Cast includes George Hayes and Antony Eustrel. Designed by Herbert Norris. A groundplan, much stage business, maps, cues for effects. Yellow callbook enclosed. The book had been used in Guthrie's 1933 production; was erased and reused.

41. Walter Hudd   Stratford-upon-Avon   June 14, 1947
Shakespeare Centre Library: O.S.71.21/1947RI
[Temple edition pasted in a workbook, 8 x 12¾; maroon cloth boards and maroon leather spine; title on cover and spine label.]
Cast includes Robert Harris and Michael Golden. Designed by Hal Burton. Much stage business, maps, cues for effects. Production papers including groundplan. Aumerle scenes in Act V are marked but sealed shut.

42. Anthony Quayle   Stratford-upon-Avon   March 24, 1951
Shakespeare Centre Library: O.S.71.21/1951R
[New Temple edition pasted in a workbook, 8 x 12¾; red cloth boards; title on cover label.]
Cast includes Michael Redgrave, Harry Andrews. Designed by Tanya Moiseiwitsch. Very full stage business, maps, cues for effects. Aumerle scenes in Act V are marked but sealed shut.

43. Michael Benthall   London, Old Vic   January 17, 1955
Old Vic, Publicity Department
[Two books. Temple edition pasted in a workbook, 8 x 10½; black ring binder.]
Cast includes John Neville, Eric Porter. Designed by Leslie Hurry. Stage business, maps, cues for effects. Production papers. Second copy, similar to first, used for revival on July 3, 1956, with Charles Gray replacing Eric Porter.

44. Other books of *Richard II:*
Folger: Rich II, 1, Eichhoff, ed. 1868, cuts; Rich II, 6, James B. Roberts; Rich II, 9, anonymous, ed. 1815, marked for stresses; Rich II, 10, anonymous.

Richard III

1. Thomas Blackburn   Lowestoff   July, 1785
   Harvard Theatre Collection: TS.2587.110.10
   [Bell(?) edition, $3\frac{7}{8}$ x $6\frac{3}{4}$; brown cardboard under green marbled boards; title inked up cover.]
   Preparation copy for a provincial, perhaps amateur, production in which Blackburn played Tressel. Cuts, 2 casts, some stage business, some cues for effects. Many notes on costume with especial attention to colors.

2. Anonymous   1790's
   Folger: R III, 29
   [Barker edition, 1794, $4\frac{1}{8}$ x $6\frac{7}{8}$; brown marbled boards and black leather spine.]
   Promptbook or rehearsal copy, the markings badly cropped. Some stage business, cues for effects.

3. George Frederick Cooke
                    London, Covent Garden   October 31, 1800
   Folger: Rich III, 4
   [Lowndes edition, 1793, $4\frac{1}{8}$ x 7; interleaves; red cloth boards and red leather spine; title gilt up spine.]
   Promptbook marked by Cooke apparently for the instruction of provincial managers, signed and dated 1808. At the front, cast lists for 1800 and 1807 and a 2-page properties list. Cuts and restorations, provisional scenic indications, calls, some stage business, cues for effects. In a note, all such technical symbols as "1.E," "LH," "X" are translated. Belonged after Cooke's death to James Brandon, whose daughter gave it to J. P. Hicks in 1879. At the front, a 4-page penciled account of Cooke's death written by an eyewitness. (See no. 5.)

4. William B. Wood   Philadelphia, Chestnut Street   March 19, 1804
   New York Public Library: *NCP.164553
   [Lowndes edition, 1793, $3\frac{3}{4}$ x $6\frac{1}{2}$; brown cloth boards; title gilt up spine.]
   Lightly marked promptbook. Cuts, calls, some stage business, cues for effects.

5. George Frederick Cooke
                    London, Covent Garden   January 8, 1810
   Harvard Theatre Collection: TS.2587.64

[Roach edition, 1802, 3¼ x 5⅜; interleaves; green leather gilt; title gilt on red leather spine label.]

Promptbook marked in Cooke's hand. Restorations, many bits of stage business keyed to the text with numerals, occasional cues for effects. Notes of performances on October 31, 1800; March 22, 1805; January 8, 1810. Given to C. Smith by W. Clunes in 1842. (See no. 3.)

6. John Philip Kemble   London, Covent Garden   April 1, 1811
Folger: Rich III, 14
[Kemble edition, 1810, 5 x 8¼; some interleaves; red marbled boards and half blue leather gilt; title gilt up spine.]
Promptbook marked by Kemble. Some stage business, procession list for funeral, maps, cues for effects.

7. [Kemble]
Folger: T.a.13
[Manuscript, 7 x 8⅞; brown leather gilt; title gilt up spine.]
Kemble's 43-page partbook for Richard in his own hand.

8. [Kemble]
Folger: W.b.67(94-121)
[Pamphlet mounted in a volume of Shakespeareana.]
Remarks on the character of Richard the Third, as played by Cooke and Kemble, London, 1801. Annotated by Kemble.

9. T. Russell
Folger: Rich III, 35
[Kemble edition, 1811, 5 x 8; brown leather; title gilt up red spine label.]
Partial transcription from Kemble's book. A few restorations, some stage business.

10. Junius Brutus Booth   Ostend   1813
Folger: Rich III, 3
[Acting edition with frontispiece of Edmund Kean dated 1814, 3⅝ x 5½; tan paper.]
Promptbook marked after 1814, but with inked cast for Ostend, 1813. Cuts and restorations, some scenic indications, stage business and a few notes on interpretation, cues for effects.

11. Anonymous c.1820

New York Public Library: *NCP.342947

[Oxberry edition, 1819, 4½ x 6¾; interleaves; green cloth boards; title gilt up spine.]

Lightly marked promptbook apparently of English origin. Some scenic indications, calls, procession list, maps, cues for effects.

12. William Charles Macready

London, Covent Garden after March 12, 1821

Folger: Rich III, 15

[Mixture of Oxberry edition, 1819, 4⅜ x 7⅜, and Stodart edition, 1821; interleaves, 4⅝ x 7¾; greenish marbled boards and half brown leather; title gilt up red spine label.]

Promptbook made up by Macready after the failure of the production with his restored Shakespeare text, combining some of his version (Stodart) with some of the traditional Cibber version (Oxberry). List of persons represented, grooves, calls, stage business, maps, cues for effects. Penciled marginalia, some in Latin and Greek. Belonged to E. Y. Lowne, Henry Irving.

13. R. J. Collier(?) Bath, Theatre Royal(?) c.1823

Shakespeare Centre Library: 50.28(1811)

[Kemble edition, 1811, 4¾ x 7¾; interleaves watermarked 1815; gray marbled boards and brown leather spine, much worn.]

Promptbook similar in style to Collier's promptbook of *King John* (see KJ, 11). Some grooves, property lists, some stage business, maps, cues for effects, timings. Two leaves have been replaced by leaves from a later acting edition. A later owner has added cuts, restorations, scenic indications, and other notes.

14. Edmund Kean New York, Park November 14, 1825

Enthoven Collection

[Oxberry edition, Boston, 1822, 3¾ x 6⅛; interleaves; tan leather; title inked on cover.]

Promptbook of James H. Hackett in which he recorded all the readings and stage business of Edmund Kean, together with critical notes and additional business of his own. Hackett first played Richard at the Park "in imitation of Kean" on December 12, 1826. Gloster's lines marked for stresses. Calls, copious stage business, cues for effects. (See selective facsimile reproduction in Alan S. Downer, *Oxberry's 1822 Edition of King Richard III*.)

15. John Gilbert   1828
    Harvard Theatre Collection: (Widener, 13486.91.20)
    [Oxberry edition, New York, 1828, 3¾ x 6; gray paper with inked
    title and signature under brown cloth boards; title gilt up spine.]
    Promptbook dated 1828 and containing a clipping of a playbill
    for May 21, 1860, when Gilbert played Henry VI to Booth's
    Richard. Calls, cues for effects.

16. Charles Kean   New York, Park   September 1, 1830
    Folger: Rich III, 12
    [Oxberry edition, 1819, 4 x 6⅞; interleaves; green marbled boards
    and half brown leather, broken.]
    Kean's early promptbook, "correctly mark'd agreeably to Mᴿ. C.
    Kean's Business by John W. Wilton Promptor"; in March of
    1837, "Corrected for Mᴿ. Kean by S. C. Ferrers Pᴿ. T. R. Edin-
    burgh." Calls, stage business, procession list for the funeral, list
    of military entrances in Act IV, maps, cues for effects. Ferrers, in
    light blue ink, has corrected the calls, added maps, many cues for
    effects, timings. (See nos. 20-22, 29, 38-41, 47-48.)

17. John B. Wright   Boston, Tremont Street   1834-35
    Folger: Rich III, 32
    [Cumberland edition, 3¾ x 5⅞; interleaves, 3⅞ x 6½; gray
    paper; title inked on cover.]
    Promptbook used for several starring actors: four special key-
    marks denote text preferences and stage business of the elder
    Booth, Forrest, Cooper, Charles Kean; a few notes on Anderson,
    Wallack. Cuts, calls, some stage business, cues for effects.

18. [Wright]
    New York Public Library: *NCP.343033
    [Modern Standard Drama, 4½ x 7⅜; interleaves; black cloth
    boards; title gilt up spine.]
    Roughly written promptbook. Restorations, some scenic indica-
    tions, grooves, some stage business, cues for effects.

19. William Creswick   May 8, 1837
    Shakespeare Centre Library: O.S.P.50.28(1829)
    [Cumberland edition, 3¾ x 6; blue cardboard; title inked on
    cover.]

Early Creswick studybook. At the front a costume list, at the back a fight routine. Many details of stage business for Gloster. (See no. 27.)

20. Charles Kean   London, Drury Lane   February 5, 1838
Folger: Rich III, 11
[Kemble edition, 1811, 5 x 7⅞; interleaves; faded greenish marbled boards, much worn, and half brown leather; title and "Mr Chs Kean" gilt on black spine labels.]
Promptbook made for Kean in 1838 by Parsloe, the Drury Lane prompter, and used for many years. Penciled cast for 1838 nearly obliterated by thumbing. Restorations, scenic indications, grooves, stage business, maps, cues for effects. Fine brown ink-wash drawings of 14 scenes. Several notations in the hand of George Ellis, the stage manager at the Princess's in the 1850's. (See nos. 16, 29, 38-41, 47-48.)

21. [Kean]
Folger: W.a.10
[Notebook made of sheets watermarked 1837, 4¾ x 7¾; brown marbled boards and half brown leather gilt; "Theatrical Costumes" inked on spine label.]
Kean's touring wardrobe list is the twelfth of 16 such lists in this book.

22. [Kean]
Folger: T.b.15
[Notebook, 7¾ x 12⅝; brown marbled boards and black leather spine.]
Touring book of scene plots, property plots, etc., for *Richard III* and 3 other plays.

23. William Mitchell   Scarborough   c.1840
Folger: Rich III, 17
[Oxberry edition, 1818, 4 x 6⅝; interleaves; gray cardboard; title inked on cover.]
Promptbook. The stage directions, said to be Mitchell's, appear often to be derived from Charles Kean's. Tinted designs of 6 scenes, said to be by Bengough, much resemble the corresponding scenes in Kean's book. (See no. 20.)

24. Samuel Phelps   London, Sadler's Wells   February 20, 1845

Folger: T.a.83-92

[Two books. Two manuscripts, each in 5 parts, c.7½ x 9; all 10 parts in tan paper wrappers.]

Preparation copies for Phelps's production of the restored Shakespeare text. Both these manuscripts are partially developed as promptbooks. Scenic indications, grooves, calls, stage business, cues for effects. (See nos. 33, 50.)

25. [Phelps]

Folger: Rich III, 24

[Pages 7-159 from volume IX of a *Works*, 4⅛ x 6⅝; interleaves, 4½ x 7⅜; yellow and green marbled boards and half black leather, broken; title gilt on red spine label.]

Fully developed promptbook done in a neat hand "under the direction of W. C. Williams," who was Phelps's prompter; corrections and additions made by Phelps and Williams. Cast for March, 1845, with later substitutions penciled. Some cuts on full text, but some compressed scenes are given in longhand. Copious scenic indications, grooves, property manuscripts list, calls, stage business, maps and sketches, cues for effects, timings (2:50). Fine brown ink-wash drawings of 11 scenes. Belonged to Harry Plowman.

26. [Phelps]

New York Public Library: *NCP.164551

[Pages 363-398 from a *Works*, 4¾ x 7¼; blue interleaves; black cloth boards; title gilt up spine.]

Fine transcription of Phelps's promptbook done in ink and pencil in a small neat hand. Cuts on full text. Scenic indications, grooves, calls, stage business, good maps and sketches, cues for effects.

27. [Phelps]

Shakespeare Centre Library: 50.28(1806)

[Pages 1-142 from volume IX of a *Works*, 5¼ x 8; gray interleaves; blue marbled boards and half brown leather; title gilt on spine.]

Fine transcription of Phelps's promptbook done in a neat round hand, unused. Cuts on full text. Scenic indications, grooves, stage business, maps, cues for effects. Belonged to William Creswick. (See no. 19.)

28. R. W. M. Klanert

Harvard Theatre Collection: Phelps Collection

[Oxberry edition, 1818, 4½ x 7¼; publisher's wrappers under gray paper; title inked on cover.]

Promptbook kept among Phelps's papers, but probably not related to Phelps's productions. Cuts, scenic indications, grooves, calls, some cues for effects.

29. Charles Kean   New York, Park   January 7, 1846
New York Public Library: *NCP.343045

[Modern Standard Drama, 4½ x 7¼; interleaves, 5 x 7¼; blue cloth boards; title gilt up spine.]

Partial transcription as "Reproduced at Park, Jan 7, 1846," by George Becks. Also marked "Situations of J W Wallack but not his text." Few scenic indications, grooves, some stage business, maps and sketches, cues for effects. (See nos. 16, 20-22, 38-41, 47-48.)

30. J. B. Roberts   New York, Chatham   February 21, 1847
Folger: Rich III, 7

[Cumberland edition, 3¾ x 6⅛; interleaves, 3⅞ x 6½; stiff brown paper.]

Roberts' studybook for Gloster. Cuts, comments on the Cibber version, the Gloster lines marked for stresses, note on elocutionary techniques, description of Gloster's costume, grooves, much stage business. References to the acting of Anderson, Charles Kean, Lambert, Wallack.

31. [Roberts]
Folger: Rich III, 27

[Oxberry edition, 1819, 4¼ x 7⅛; stiff brown paper.]

Studybook. Gloster's lines marked for stresses.

32. [Roberts]
Folger: Rich III, 25

[Modern Standard Drama pasted in a workbook, 7⅜ x 9¾; black cloth boards and red leather spine; title, Roberts' name, and injunction to prompters inked on cover label.]

Promptbook fully developed though not much used. Grooves, calls, stage business, cues for effects.

33. Samuel Phelps   London, Sadler's Wells   March 21, 1849
Folger: Rich III, 22

[Pages 1-133 from volume VII of a *Works,* 4⅛ x 6½; interleaves,

4⅜ x 7⅛; brown marbled boards and half black leather; title gilt on red spine label.]

Promptbook made up to replace Phelps's 1845 book (see no. 25). Contains all the essential matter except the 11 scene designs. At the back, penciled notes on the final battle and the working of profile figures.

34. Robert Jones　　　　Boston, Howard Athenaeum　　　　1852
New York Public Library:　*NCP.200785B
[Modern Standard Drama, 4½ x 7½; blue interleaves, 6 x 7½; brown cloth boards; title gilt up spine.]

Excellent promptbook, perhaps derived from Charles Kean's Park Theatre production of 1846 or Hamblin's revival of it in 1848 (see no. 29). Careful scenic indications, grooves, calls, considerable stage business, procession lists, very good maps and sketches, cues for effects. Warning against beards and moustaches.

35. Asa Cushman　　　　Providence　　　　1852
Brown University:　Eng.P.17
[Modern Standard Drama, 4½ x 7½; tan paper; title and "The Property of A. Cushman/No. 60" inked on cover.]

Lightly marked promptbook. Cuts, cues for effects. Playbills for G. V. Brooke and J. B. Booth, with Cushman as Tyrrel.

36. J. H. Ring　　　　Boston, Boston Museum　　　　1853
Folger:　Rich III, 26
[Modern Standard Drama, 4⅛ x 6½; heavy tan paper; title and signature inked on cover.]

Casual but much used promptbook. Cuts, cues for effects. Used to prompt J. H. Firm, Charles Couldock in 1857, James Wallack in 1858, John Wilkes Booth in 1861, Walter Montgomery in 1871.

37. Anonymous　　　　Boston, Boston Museum
Princeton University, Seymour Collection: R III, 5
[French's Standard Drama, 4½ x 7½; interleaves; coarse cloth; "Boston Museum" inked on cover.]

Crude but much used promptbook. Cuts, maps, cues for effects.

38. Charles Kean　　　　London, Princess's　　　　February 20, 1854
Folger:　Rich III, 10
[Lacy edition (Kean version), 1854, 4 x 7⅜; interleaves, 6⅞ x 8⅝; tan boards and half brown leather, broken; title gilt up

spine, "Mr. Charles Kean/Prompt Copy" gilt on blue leather cover label.]

Final or souvenir promptbook made in 1859 by T. W. Edmonds, the prompter. Grooves, calls, some stage business, maps, cues for effects, timings (3:00). There were once watercolor designs of 13 scenes, but these have been cut out. Opposite the stubs where the scenes once were are maps showing the disposition of characters. (NOTE: The Lacy edition is used because it is the "official" Kean version; for this play Kean did not publish his own edition.) (See nos. 16, 20-22, 29, 47-48.)

39. [Kean]

Folger: Prints and Engravings, 52

[Watercolors, 6 x 4, mounted in an album, $10\frac{1}{4}$ x $14\frac{1}{8}$; gray cloth boards and half green leather gilt; "Charles Kean/Original Water Color Drawings" gilt on spine.]

Fine watercolor designs of 13 scenes.

40. [Kean]

Enthoven Collection: Box DT.44

[Watercolors mounted on large display boards.]

Twenty watercolor scene designs.

41. [Kean]

Folger: Kean Costume Book, Prints and Engravings, 49

[Scrapbook, $10\frac{3}{4}$ x $14\frac{1}{2}$; green cloth boards and half green leather.]

Contains 38 plates of watercolors and tracings for costumes for *Richard III* made for Kean by Charles Hamilton Smith and his daughter Emma.

42. John Moore   New York, Burton's   c.1857

Folger: Rich III, 20

[Lacy edition (Kean version), 1854, $4\frac{1}{4}$ x $7\frac{3}{8}$; lavender interleaves; publisher's wrappers of a New York bookseller under tan paper; title inked on cover.]

Promptbook made by Moore after 1854, transcribing from some original: the interleaves have key words to guide insertion. Penciled additions indicate continued use. Grooves, calls, stage business, cues for effects, timings. Sketch and description of a paneled wall. Restoration of lines in the throne scene for Forrest. Production papers: properties list, funeral procession, map of last scene, fight routine. Other enclosures: introduction to Cumberland edition; printed cast lists with Adams, Booth, Scott, Wallack; introduction to Modern Standard Drama and Kean's cast for the Park in 1846; part of a playbill for Hamblin's 1848 production; playbill with Moore as Henry VI; review of Count Joannes' performance on February 6, 1878; portrait of Richard; a cut-out model of Henry's bier.

43. [Moore]

Folger: Rich III, 18

[Turner's Dramatic Library, Philadelphia, $3\frac{1}{2}$ x $5\frac{7}{8}$; interleaves, $3\frac{3}{4}$ x $6\frac{1}{8}$; heavy brown paper; title inked on cover.]

Promptbook probably made by an American prompter and acquired by Moore after he came to America in 1848 (see American imprint; see timing note for October 20, 1845). Some scenic indications, grooves, calls, some stage business, cues for effects.

44. [Moore]

Folger: Rich III, 19

[Modern Standard Drama, $4\frac{3}{8}$ x $7\frac{5}{8}$; heavy gray-brown paper.]

Rehearsal copy checked for Stanley.

45. [Moore]

Folger: T.b.2

[Notebook, $6\frac{1}{8}$ x $10\frac{1}{4}$; blue boards and black cloth spine.]

Cues for the band for 48 plays, including *Richard III*: one set for Wallack, another for Forrest.

46. George C. Boniface   New York, Bowery   June 24, 1859

Folger: Rich III, 2

[French's Standard Drama; interleaves, 5 x 8; tan boards and brown velvet spine.]

Carefully marked promptbook probably used on tour. Calls, cues for effects. A leaflet of November, 1894, advertising Boniface's Shakespearean readings.

47. Hermann Vezin   London, Surrey   June 27, 1859

Folger: Rich III, 31

[Hinds English Stage, 1839, $4\frac{1}{2}$ x 8; interleaves; red-brown boards and half black leather; title and "Hermann Vezin" gilt on black cover label.]

Promptbook done in a neat round hand, apparently a transcription from Charles Kean's book (see no. 38). Belonged to Hermann Vezin. Calls, procession lists, stage business, maps and sketches, cues for effects.

48. [Vezin]

University of Illinois: x792.9/Sh15ri/no.1

[Hinds English Stage, 1839, 4¾ x 8⅜; interleaves, 7½ x 9¼; blue marbled boards and half maroon leather; title gilt up spine, "Hermann Vezin" gilt on black leather cover label.]

Excellent transcription of Kean's promptbook (see no. 38) made by George Ellis for Hermann Vezin. List of property manuscripts, grooves, calls, some stage business, good maps and sketches, cues for effects.

49. J. C. Cowper   Manchester, Theatre Royal   c.1860

Folger: Rich III, 5

[Lacy edition (Kean version), 4⅛ x 7⅛; blue interleaves watermarked 1855; gray cloth boards and maroon leather spine.]

Studybook for Richard. At the front, a 3-page description of Edmund Kean's Richard, a 4-page analysis of the character, a 4-page discussion of Lady Anne, a list of doubling parts. Notes on Charles Kean's Richard with special attention to his costume. Notes throughout on the stage business and histrionic manner of the part. At the back a fight routine as of 1860, and others as done by Lunt, Creswick, Brooke.

50. Samuel Phelps   London, Sadler's Wells   November 23, 1861

Folger: Rich III, 23

[Lacy edition (Kean version), 4⅛ x 7; interleaves; blue marbled boards and green leather spine; title gilt up spine.]

Phelps's promptbook after he abandoned his restored version and returned to a "Cibber" text. Cast, grooves, calls, some stage business, maps and sketches, cues for effects. (See nos. 24-27, 33.)

51. John Wilkes Booth   New York, Mary Provost's   March 17, 1862

Harvard Theatre Collection: uncatalogued

[French's Standard Drama, 4⅜ x 6⅞; interleaves; brown marbled boards and half brown leather; title and "Wilkes Booth" gilt on leather cover label; in box of gray cloth boards and black leather spine; title gilt up spine.]

Much used promptbook written in ink and pencil. Cuts, some stage business, maps, cues for effects. Signatures include "E. P.

Wilks, Phila., Call Boy Arch St. Theatre" and "Thos. W. Davey, St. Louis, Mo, Southern Confederacy."

52. [Booth]

University of Texas

[French's Standard Drama, 4½ x 7¼; interleaves; green and black marbled boards and half brown leather; title and "Wilkes Booth" on cover.]

Much used promptbook mainly in ink with penciled additions. Cuts, some scenic indications and grooves, some stage business, maps, cues for effects especially numerous and detailed in last act. Near the front a brief newspaper review of Booth's performance at the "Gayety," mentioning supporting cast for his forthcoming Hamlet. Booth's name occurs in one stage direction.

53. Edwin Forrest   New York, Niblo's Garden   October 20, 1864

New York Public Library: *NCP.342980

[Forrest edition, 1860, 4¼ x 6⅞; interleaves; red cloth boards; title gilt up spine.]

Carefully written promptbook by George Becks. Scenic indications, grooves, calls, considerable stage business with references to Forrest, cues for effects. Contains a newspaper engraving of Charles Kean as Richard, playbill for Forrest in 1864 with Becks as Lord Mayor; prefatory matter of the Niblo's Garden edition of April, 1871, when Jarrett and Palmer revived the Shakespearean version of Charles Calvert.

54. Edwin Adams   Chicago, McVicker's   February, 1866

Harvard Theatre Collection: uncatalogued

[French's Standard Drama, 4½ x 7⅜; interleaves; black cloth boards and half black leather; title and Adams' name gilt on cover.]

Well-marked, much used promptbook made for Adams by William H. Daly, the stage manager. Some scenic indications, grooves, calls, stage business, maps, cues for effects.

55. F. Haywel   January, 1867

Shakespeare Centre Library: 50.28(1854)

[Lacy edition, 4¼ x 7⅛; interleaves; tan cardboard and canvas spine; title inked on cover.]

Preparation book. Calls and some cues for effects. Mainly a commentary on the non-Shakespearean elements in the acting edition.

56. William Seymour   New Orleans   October 24, 1868
Princeton University, Seymour Collection: R III, 3
[Turner's Dramatic Library, 3⅝ x 5¾; torn covers.]
Rehearsal copy signed by James Seymour, checked for several
characters. Cast list includes William Seymour as Duke of York.

57. Junius Brutus Booth, Jr.   1870's
The Players
[French's Standard Drama, 4½ x 7½; publisher's wrappers.]
Crude book signed within by William H. Daly, the stage manager.
Cuts, some scenic indications, cues for effects.

58. Frank Roche   St. John, Royal Lyceum   1870's
Harvard Theatre Collection: 13486.93.5
[Modern Standard Drama, 4¼ x 7; interleaves; black cloth
boards; title gilt on cover.]
Promptbook neatly written and much used, inscribed "Royal
Lyceum, St. John, N. B." Calls, maps, cues for effects.

59. J. R. Pitman   c.1870
University of Pennsylvania, Furness Collection: C59.Sh1R3P
[Booth's Series of Acting Plays, no. 4, pasted in a workbook, 7⅝ x
9¼; paper wrappers; in red cloth board folder; title and Pitman's
name gilt on cover.]
Well-developed promptbook made by J. R. Pitman, using Edwin
Booth's early (Cibber) version. At the front plots of properties,
scenes, funeral procession. Scenic indications, grooves, calls, some
stage business, excellent maps and groundplans, cues for effects.

60. Marcus J. Moriarty   Chicago   1874
Folger: Rich III, 21
[French's Standard Drama, 4⅜ x 7; black cloth boards; title and
Moriarty's name gilt on cover.]
Rehearsal copy and studybook, checked for Buckingham and var-
ious lesser roles. Several notes on the stage business of Richard.
Penciled cast for Booth at McVicker's in December, 1874. Clip-
pings of playbills for Barry Sullivan on November 30, 1875; Ed-
mund Collier on June 16, 1888.

61. Lawrence Barrett   New York, Booth's   December 16, 1876
Harvard Theatre Collection: TS.2587.110.5
[French's Standard Drama with leaves from other texts for Act V,

4½ x 7¼; interleaves; plum cloth boards and black leather spine; title and Barrett's name gilt on cover.]

Much used promptbook marked in many inks at different times. Scenic indications, grooves, calls, stage business, maps, cues for effects.

62. Edwin Booth   New York, Lyceum   December 25, 1876
The Players

[A double-column acting edition tipped to stubs between leaves of a workbook, 7⅝ x 9½; red marbled boards and half black leather; title on cover label; in slip-box of red leather; title gilt on spine.]

Promptbook based on a Cibber text with timings for the Lyceum, 1876. Calls, stage business, maps, cues for effects. (See nos. 59, 66-74, 79.)

63. Henry Irving   London, Lyceum   January 29, 1877
Harvard Theatre Collection: uncatalogued

[Longmans edition, 1874, 4½ x 6½; interleaves; gray cloth; title stamped on cover.]

Studybook and preparation copy. Cuts on full text. Gloster's lines marked for stress, pause, stage business, and histrionic manner. Notes on scenery. Maps. At the back, some costume notes. (See no. 82.)

64. [Irving]
Folger: Rich III, 8

[Lacy edition (Kean version) pasted in a workbook, 7¼ x 8¾; brown marbled boards and half maroon leather.]

Promptbook of some earlier actor(?) who marked it very carefully with calls, cues for effects, and timings, and pasted into it some very amusing cartoons (*Bab Ballads*?). Belonged to Irving, who used it as a preparation book, marking the margins in blue and red to distinguish the Cibber and Shakespeare elements, and entering restorations.

65. [Irving]
London Museum: 822.33

[Irving edition, 1877, pasted in a workbook, 7⅜ x 9; red marbled boards and black imitation leather spine; title page pasted on cover.]

Promptbook made by H. J. Loveday, the stage manager, to whom it is inscribed by Irving as of February 6, 1878. Several excellent ink drawings and sketch-maps of the scenes. Some grooves, some stage business, cues for effects, timings.

66. Edwin Booth   1877
    The Players

[Mixture of several editions pasted in a workbook, 6¾ x 8⅛; bound with *Richard II* in brown marbled boards and black leather spine; in slip-box of red leather; title gilt on spine.]

Preparation copy of Booth's Shakespeare version (completed by the fall of 1877). At the front a Dramatis Personae. Provisional text querying inclusion of Clarence. Scenic indications referring comparatively to scenes in *Henry VIII* (at Booth's January 12, 1877). Some cues for effects. (See nos. 59, 62, 79.)

67. [Booth]
    The Players

[Shakespeare edition pasted in a workbook, 6¼ x 7½; black and rose marbled boards and half brown leather; in slip-box of red leather; title gilt on spine.]

Preparation copy of the Shakespeare version. Cuts, some scenic indications, grooves. At the back, a Dramatis Personae and list of doubles.

68. [Booth]
    The Players

[Manuscript, 7¾ x 10⅛; brown marbled boards and half maroon leather.]

Preparation copy or earliest promptbook of the Shakespeare version. Scenic indications, some stage business. Shows signs of stage use, but the text is still being mended.

69. [Booth]   New York, Booth's   January 7, 1878
    The Players

[Typescript, 7½ x 10; gray marbled boards and half black leather; title on cover label; in slip-box of red leather; title gilt on spine.]

Completed and much used promptbook of the Shakespeare version. Calls, stage business, cues for effects. Printed cast of the company at Chicago. Timings for McVicker's on October 2, 1877, and for Buffalo, Baltimore, and New York.

70. [Booth]
    The Players: MSS.24, 78

[Twenty-seven booklets. Manuscript (5), 7 x 9; brown paper. Manuscript (22), 8 x 6¼; heavy tan paper.]

Two packs of partbooks. The larger group are for the Shakespeare version, including Clarence, Margaret, etc. Some have jottings of stage business.

71. [Booth]
The Players
[Booth-Winter edition, 1878, 4¾ x 6⅝; gray publisher's wrappers.]
Rough but used promptbook. Calls, stage business, cues for effects.

72. [Booth]
Museum of the City of New York: 35.339.22
[Booth-Winter edition, 1878, 4¾ x 6⅝; gray publisher's wrappers.]
Promptbook lightly marked by Booth's stage manager, W. Henry Flohr. Calls, cues for effects.

73. [Booth]
The Players
[Booth-Winter edition, 1878, 4½ x 6⅝; brown marbled boards and half maroon leather; title gilt on spine.]
"Marked for corrections" for future editions by William Winter.

74. [Booth]
The Players
[Booth-Winter edition, 1878, 4½ x 6½; limp black leather gilt; title gilt on cover.]
Fine transcription of Booth's perfected promptbook made by J. R. Pitman as a souvenir for Russ Whytal, autographed by Booth. Cuts, scenic indications, excellent groundplans, calls, stage business, maps, processions, cues for effects.

75. Frederick Paulding   1880's
Rutgers University: PR.1243.Sha
[French's Standard Drama, 4½ x 7½; publisher's wrappers.]
Carelessly marked promptbook. Some stage business, maps, cues for effects.

76. Lawrence Barrett   1880's
Harvard Theatre Collection: uncatalogued

[Ten music score books, 9½ x 6¼; brown cloth boards and green cloth spine.]

Complete scores for the band for 9 plays including *Richard III*, endorsed by musicians in many cities.

77. Frank Mayo   New York, Olympic   April 17, 1880
Museum of the City of New York: 48.194.124
[French's Standard Drama, 4⅜ x 6⅞; blue interleaves; brown cloth boards and half black leather; title and Mayo's name gilt on cover.]
Rather crude promptbook originally marked by Mayo, with additional pencilings by prompters. Some scenic indications, calls, some stage business, cues for effects. At the back a fight routine.

78. Thomas W. Keene New York, Niblo's Garden January 28, 1884
Folger: Rich III, Folio 1
[French's Standard Drama pasted in a workbook, 7⅝ x 12¼; gray canvas boards and half red leather.]
Promptbook from the "Keene sale, 1904," carefully marked in colored inks and pencils but not much used. Arranged in 6 acts. Cues for effects only.

79. Edwin Booth   American Tour   1886-87
The Players
[French's Standard Drama, 4⅜ x 7½; leaves tipped to stubs between leaves of a workbook, 6⅝ x 8⅛; red marbled boards and brown cloth spine; title on cover label.]
Well-developed promptbook of the Cibber version used by Booth on tour in 1886-87, prepared by Oliver Doud. Arranged in 7 acts. Cast list. Scenic indications, grooves, calls, stage business, cues for effects. (See nos. 59, 62, 66-74.)

80. Richard Mansfield   London, Globe   March 16, 1889
New York Public Library: *NCP.342934
[Mansfield edition, 6¾ x 9⅜; interleaves; black cloth boards; title gilt on spine.]
Promptbook record rather than a working promptbook, copiously annotated by George Becks. Cuts and alterations, considerable stage business, maps, sketches, notes on effects. Many reviews of Mansfield's production especially from New York and Boston papers.

81. Louis James   New York, Windsor   September 26, 1889
University of Pennsylvania, Furness Collection: C59.ShlR3J
[French's Standard Drama pasted in a workbook, 5½ x 8¼;
bound with *Hamlet* in gray marbled boards and blue cloth spine;
title on cover label, cover endorsed and dated by James.]
Good promptbook dated 1881, carefully and fully marked in red
ink. At the front, a fight routine. Cuts, scenic indications, grooves,
stage business, maps, cues for effects.

82. Henry Irving   London, Lyceum   December 19, 1896
Folger: Rich III, 9
[Irving edition, 1896, 5¼ x 8¼; limp maroon leather; title gilt
up spine.]
Rehearsal copy. Cuts. Many marginal jottings in lead pencil and
orange and blue crayons of significant words, stage business, histrionic manner. (See nos. 63-65.)

83. Robert B. Mantell   South Bend   October 12, 1901
Folger: Rich III, 16
[French's Standard Drama pasted in a workbook, 6⅛ x 9¼; limp
maroon leather; title and Mantell's name gilt on cover.]
Fine promptbook prepared by C. W. Vance, New York, June 30,
1901. For each act are detailed plots of scenery, properties, lights.
Much stage business, maps, tableaux, cues for effects.

84. Seymour Hicks   London   1908
Mander and Mitchenson
[Edition pasted in a workbook, 6⅛ x 7¾; limp blue leather.]
Preparation book for a production at the Aldwych which did not
materialize. Copious stage business, maps, sketches, cues for effects. Watercolors of medieval scenes, photographs of the Tower,
four pencil sketches of Irving's Richard, etc.

85. [Hicks]
Mander and Mitchenson
[Mansfield edition, 6¾ x 10¾; brown cloth boards; title and
Hicks's name gilt on cover.]
Rehearsal promptbook. Cuts and restorations, copious stage busi-
ness, maps, groundplans. Watercolor scene designs of the Tower,
a battlefield. News clippings.

[ACTOR LISTS FOR FOLLOWING BOOKS ARE GIVEN IN THIS ORDER: Richard, Buckingham, Anne, Margaret.]

86. W. Bridges-Adams   Stratford-upon-Avon   July 4, 1928
    Shakespeare Centre Library: 71.21/1928R, RI
    [Two books. Favourite Classics edition pasted in a workbook, 6⅞ x 9; red marbled boards and black cloth spine, much worn; title on cover and spine labels. Temple edition pasted in a workbook, 7¾ x 9½; blue cloth boards and half red leather; title on spine.]
    Cast includes George Hayes, Wilfrid Walter, Cecily Wilson, Georgina Wynter. Costumes by Tom Heslewood. The first book has calls, some stage business, cues for effects. The second book is marked on only 2 or 3 pages.

87. [Bridges-Adams]   American Tour   1928-29
    Shakespeare Centre Library: 71.21/1928-29
    [Temple edition pasted in a workbook, 8 x 10; blue cloth boards and half red leather; title on cover and spine labels.]
    Partial transcription of the preceding book: calls and cues but no stage business.

88. B. Iden Payne   Stratford-upon-Avon   April 7, 1939
    Shakespeare Centre Library: 71.21/1939R
    [Eversley edition pasted in a workbook, 7 x 9; blue cloth boards and half black leather; title on cover and spine labels.]
    Cast includes John Laurie, James Dale, Joyce Bland, Dorothy Green. Designed by Don Finley and Herbert Norris. Calls, considerable stage business, maps, cues for effects. A fine map of the funeral procession in colored inks.

89. Glen Byam Shaw   Stratford-upon-Avon   March 24, 1953
    Shakespeare Centre Library: O.S.71.21/1953R
    [New Temple edition pasted in a workbook, 8 x 13; black cloth board spring binder with black leather spine; title up spine.]
    Cast includes Marius Goring, Harry Andrews, Yvonne Mitchell, Joan Sanderson. Designed by Motley. Very full stage business, maps, cues for effects. A scaled groundplan.

90. Tyrone Guthrie   Stratford, Ontario   July 13, 1953
    Festival Theatre, Library
    [Mimeographed text pasted in a workbook, 7¾ x 12½; maroon cloth boards and maroon spine.]

Cast includes Alec Guinness, Robert Christie, Amelia Hall, Irene Worth. Designed by Tanya Moiseiwitsch. Calls, cues for effects.

91. William Gaskill   Stratford-upon-Avon   May 24, 1961
Shakespeare Centre Library: O.S.71.21/1961R
[Cambridge Pocket Shakespeare pasted in a workbook, 8 x 13; red cloth board spring binder; title on spine label.]
Cast includes Christopher Plummer, Eric Porter, Jill Dixon, Edith Evans. Designed by Jocelyn Herbert. Much stage business, cues for effects. Production papers include cast, groundplan, timings.

92. Other books of *Richard III:*
Brown University: Eng.P.17a, Asa Cushman, with Keene as Richard.
Connecticut State Library: William Gillette, 1876.
Folger: Rich III, 1, George Becks, 1861; Rich III, 6, Henrietta Crosman; Rich III, 13, David C. Johnston; Rich III, 28, John Sefton; Rich III, 30, T. W. Tyrrell; Rich III, 33, 34, 37, 38, anonymous; Rich III, 36, Dan Haskins.
Harvard Theatre Collection: 13486.91.10, William Wood.
Historical and Philosophical Society of Ohio: 812.3/R283/168, Alvin Read.
Princeton University, Seymour Collection: R III, 7, W. J. Le Moyne; R III, 19, James W. Bates, Cincinnati, 1848; R III, 21, Tell Taylor, Chicago, 1892.
University of Minnesota: Z820.12/Z11, volume 12, W. S. Forrest.
University of Pennsylvania: AC85.M9415.820p.56, James Murdoch.
W. A. Clark Library, Los Angeles: French's Standard Drama, anonymous.

Romeo and Juliet

1. Anonymous   1600's
   Yale University, Elizabethan Club
   [Cuthbert Burby Quarto, 1599, 4⅞ x 6⅝; red leather gilt; "G.D."
   gilt on cover.]
   Lightly marked cuebook. Music at ends of acts. Signature of
   George Steevens on title page.

2. Anonymous   Douai   1694
   Bibliothèque de Douai: MS.7.87
   [Manuscript, folios 94-130 of a volume, 6¾ x 8⅝; parchment.]
   Manuscript version used for amateur staging as Douai. Cuts and
   alterations, stage business. (See G. Blakemore Evans, *Philological
   Quarterly*, XLI, 158-172.)

3. Anonymous   England   1700's
   Folger: Rom, 39
   [Tonson edition, 1763, 4 x 6⅝; white paper and purple paper
   spine; title on spine label, inked on cover.]
   Rehearsal copy marked in a neat hand. Cuts and very little stage
   business.

4. Anonymous   London, Covent Garden   c.1780
   New York Public Library: *NCP.709397
   [Bell edition, 1773, 4⅜ x 7⅜; brown cloth boards; title gilt up
   spine.]
   Well-marked promptbook done in ink in a perfect round hand.
   Scenic indications, grooves, calls, entrances, funeral procession,
   cues for effects. (Compare AW, 1; AYL, 4; MV, 3; TEM, 2.)

5. William Warren   York   1789
   Library Company of Philadelphia: Oe2.11604.D
   [Bell edition, 4 x 6⅞; bound with *Rule a Wife and Have a Wife*
   in red and blue marbled boards and brown leather spine.]
   Lightly marked promptbook checked for Juliet. Cuts, little stage
   business. Cast for York, 1789. Warren given as Friar Lawrence at
   Philadelphia, 1822.

6. James William Wallack
   Folger: Rom, 31
   [Harding edition (Steevens text), 1798, 3¾ x 6¼; blue marbled
   boards and brown cloth spine; Wallack's name on cover label.]

Preparation copy, uncompleted. Apparently an early attempt to restore the text. Cuts, little stage business. Inscribed within "Anne D. Wallack, London."

7. William B. Wood   Philadelphia, Chestnut Street   Dec. 19, 1803
   Folger: Rom, 33

   [Lowndes edition, 1793, 4¼ x 6⅝; tan and blue marbled boards and half brown leather.]

   Promptbook arranged in 6 acts, the funeral procession being an act. Cuts, few scenic indications, little stage business, cues for effects. Cast of 15 for Philadelphia in 1804, with Cooper as Romeo.

8. John Philip Kemble   London, Covent Garden   c.1811
   New York Public Library: *NCP.709142

   [Kemble edition, 1811, 4⅞ x 7¾; interleaves; brown cloth boards; title gilt up spine.]

   Promptbook sparsely marked in Kemble's hand. Calls, some stage business, cues for effects, timing (3:10). First interleaf misbound: belongs at page 45.

9. [Kemble]
   Garrick Club

   [Kemble edition, 1811, 5⅛ x 8¼; interleaves; blue cloth boards and brown leather spine; title gilt up spine.]

   Studybook for Capulet or Mercutio. Some of Juliet's lines pencil-marked for stresses.

10. [Kemble]
    University of Nebraska: 822.33/W5g

    [Kemble edition, 1811, 4⅞ x 7⅞; interleaves watermarked 1811; black cloth boards; title gilt down spine.]

    Promptbook very neatly and fully marked through 2 acts: cuts, grooves, calls, stage business, cues for effects. Later acts have only prompter's rough markings, including timings.

11. Maria Foote   London, Covent Garden   c.1815
    Folger: Rom, 35

    [Kemble edition, 1811, 5⅛ x 8⅛; orange leather and half red leather; title gilt on black cover label.]

    Rehearsal copy marked for Juliet by John Philip Kemble, with a few pencilings by the actress. Associated with Miss Foote because of the distinctive binding (see MA, 5). Cuts, some scenic indica-

tions, some stage business for the Juliet scenes, cues for effects.
ad11. See Addenda, p. 507.

12. T. O. Smith   Liverpool   1815
   New York Public Library: *NCP.164549
   [Kemble edition, 1814, 4¼ x 6¾; brown cloth boards; title gilt
   up spine.]
   Much used promptbook worked over in ink and pencil by several
   hands. Many of the original markings are scratched out or pasted
   over with bits of paper. Scenic indications, grooves, calls, cues
   for effects, timings (3:08). Smith, the first owner, was a Liverpool
   prompter. Also dated 1818 and Manchester, 1843. Later owned
   by Edwin Booth, who noted various peculiarities of this "quaint
   old book."

13. Chris John Smith   November, 1827
   Folger: Rom, 28
   [Dolby's British Theatre, 1825, 3⅝ x 5⅝; green paper; title inked
   on cover.]
   Promptbook of a much cut version arranged in 3 acts. Grooves,
   cues for effects, timing (2:14).

14. Helen Faucit   London, Covent Garden   March 10, 1836
   Folger: Rom, 8
   [Cumberland edition, 3⅞ x 6; tattered paper.]
   Rehearsal copy inscribed "Helen Faucit/1st Book," checked for
   Juliet. Penciled cuts and restorations. At the end of Act I it is
   dated January 17, 1845. (See no. 21.)

15. B. K. Brown and Walter Leman   1838-86
   Folger: Rom, 15
   [Longworth edition, New York, 1817, 3½ x 5⅜; buff paper; title
   inked on cover.]
   Rehearsal copy, its history told in enclosed notes. Originally used
   by Brown at the National Theatre in Boston about 1838. Then
   used by Leman for nearly 50 years to play Mercutio and Friar
   Lawrence with many Juliets, the last being Adelaide Neilson.
   Cast for St. Louis, 1850. In October of 1886 Leman restored it to
   its original owner.

16. Charles Kean   London, Haymarket   July 12, 1841
   Folger: Rom, 13
   [Kemble edition, 1811, 4⅞ x 7⅞; interleaves watermarked 1836;

greenish marbled boards and half maroon leather; title gilt on spine.]

Very full promptbook of Kean's Haymarket production with Ellen Tree. Cuts, scenic indications, grooves, calls, some stage business, maps showing disposition of vast numbers of supers, cues for effects, timings (2:45). Fine watercolor designs of 13 scenes. In 1842, A. W. Nimmo of the Edinburgh Theatre Royal entered at the front a 2-page dance routine which he credits to Frederick Webster of the Haymarket, and added other notations.

17. [Kean]

Folger: Rom, 10

[Cumberland edition, $3\frac{7}{8}$ x 6; interleaves; unsewn.]

Fine transcription of the preceding promptbook, lacking only the watercolors. Belonged to W. M. Fleming.

18. [Kean]

Folger: W.a.10

[Notebook made of leaves watermarked 1837, $4\frac{3}{4}$ x $7\frac{3}{4}$; brown marbled boards and half brown leather gilt; "Theatrical Costumes" inked on spine label.]

Kean's touring wardrobe list for Romeo is the ninth of 16 such lists in this book.

19. William Charles Macready   1841
University of Illinois

[Watercolors, $4\frac{1}{2}$ x $8\frac{5}{8}$.]

Thirteen plates of watercolor costume designs (16 figures) made for Macready by Colonel Charles Hamilton Smith. The production, planned in November of 1841, did not materialize.

20. Henry Betty   Bath, Theatre Royal   January 30, 1843
Folger: Rom, 2

[Cumberland edition, $3\frac{5}{8}$ x $5\frac{7}{8}$; interleaves; green boards and green cloth spine; title on cover label.]

Promptbook not marked in great detail but considerably used. Cuts, some grooves, some stage business, cues for effects.

21. Helen Faucit   c.1845
Folger: Rom, 9

[Pages 119-220 from volume VII of Knight's Cabinet Edition, 1843, $3\frac{3}{4}$ x $5\frac{5}{8}$; green publisher's wrappers and cloth spine.]

Rehearsal copy probably used from about 1845 after Miss Faucit abandoned the Garrick version (see no. 14) for the Shakespearean. Cuts on full text, a few warnings.

22. John Moore   1845-77
    Folger: Rom, 19
    [Cumberland edition, 3¾ x 6½; interleaves; stiff red paper.]
    Promptbook of the Garrick version used in England to prompt Helen Faucit and later in America to prompt Mrs. Conway, Mrs. Butler, Miss Wallack, Adelaide Neilson. Cuts, grooves, calls, stage business and some notes on histrionic manner, cues for effects.

23. [Moore]
    Folger: Rom, 18
    [Pages 7-122 from volume IX of a *Works*, 5⅛ x 8⅜; blue interleaves; stiff green paper; title inked on cover.]
    Promptbook of a Shakespeare version used for many years. Cuts on full text. At the front, a 2-page scene plot. Scenic indications, grooves, calls, copious stage business, maps, cues for effects. Contains playbills of Charles Kemble and Miss O'Neill at Covent Garden in 1818; Davenport and Mrs. Mowatt at the Marylebone; Fanny Vining as Romeo in 1849; Anna Hathaway as Romeo at Hartford; the Cushman sisters at Burton's on September 30, 1857; Mrs. Wallack as Romeo at Wallack's; Davenport and Avonia Jones at Wallack's on July 18, 1864; Mrs. Chanfrau as Juliet at the Broadway on September 7, 1867; Sheridan and Miss Proudfoot at the Broadway on September 28, 1867. Reviews of Avonia Jones, Amy Elliott, Mary Anderson, Mme. Modjeska, Margaret Mather, a German production in 1871. Various news clippings.

24. [Moore]
    Folger: Rom, 20
    [French's Standard Drama, 4⅜ x 7½; publisher's wrappers.]
    Rehearsal copy checked for Balthazar.

25. [Moore]
    Folger: T.b.2
    [Notebook, 6⅛ x 10¼; blue boards and black cloth spine.]
    Cues for the band for 48 plays, including *Romeo and Juliet*.

26. Samuel Phelps   London, Sadler's Wells   September 16, 1846
    Folger: Rom, 25

[Pages 9-114 from volume XII of Thomas Tegg's (Reed text) *Works*, 1815, 5⅛ x 8¼; interleaves, 7 x 8⅞; stiff buff paper, much worn; title, date, etc., inked on cover.]

Promptbook of Phelps's Shakespeare version. Cuts on full text. One scenic indication, calls, some stage business, maps, cues for effects.

27. [Phelps]

Folger: **Rom, 24**

[Pages 119-220 from volume VII of Knight's Cabinet Edition, 1843, 3⅝ x 5⅝; interleaves.]

Promptbook marked partly by Phelps and partly by Williams, the prompter. Improved over the preceding book but not as fully developed as most Phelps books. Cuts on full text, calls, some stage business, cues for effects.

28. J. B. Robert   New York, Chatham   March 3, 1847

Folger: **Rom, 27**

[Dolby's British Theatre, 3¼ x 5¼; interleaves; stiff brown paper; title, date, etc., inked on cover.]

Studybook checked for Romeo, the lines marked for stresses. Cuts, some calls, stage business, some cues for effects.

29. [Roberts]

Folger: **Rom, 26**

[Pages 135-246 from a *Works*, 6⅜ x 9¾; black cloth boards and maroon leather spine.]

No. 7 of Roberts' collection of plays cut and marked for public readings.

30. James R. Anderson   New York, Broadway   May, 1848

New York Public Library: *NCP.265143B

[Pages 1-60 from a double-column pictorial edition of Shakespeare, 6½ x 10½; interleaves; blue cloth boards; title gilt on spine.]

Promptbook of a Shakespeare version signed "J.R. Anderson, New York, May 10th, 1848." This is doubtless the English actor Anderson, who had engagements at the Broadway in the spring of 1848 and produced a Shakespeare version of *Romeo and Juliet* there on May 22. A note entered in the book in 1902 identifies it rather with James Anderson, the American stage manager who about the mid-century was at the Bowery, and says that Anderson made the book for Kean, but that it passed to Edward

Eddy and through various hands to the Actors' Fund in 1902. Whichever Anderson made it, he was endeavoring, as the notes "in Miss C.," "out Miss C." show, to follow the restoration which Charlotte Cushman introduced at the Haymarket in 1845. Cuts on full text, some scenic indications, many cues for effects. Partial cast of a later performance with Miss Cushman as Romeo.

31. Charlotte Cushman   c.1852

Harvard Theatre Collection: uncatalogued

[Modern Standard Drama, 4⅝ x 7⅛; gray interleaves; tan cardboard; title on cover label; in box of gray cloth boards and black leather spine; title gilt up spine.]

Very full promptbook signed by Asa Cushman, the prompter at Providence. Cuts, grooves, calls, much stage business, maps, cues for effects. Part of a playbill for March 5, 1852, with Miss Cushman as Romeo.

32. John B. Adams   Boston, Boston Museum   1854

Essex Institute, Salem: 822.S52.34

[Modern Standard Drama, 4½ x 7½; black cloth boards; title on cover label.]

Promptbook "Cut & Marked from Mrs. Farren's Book." Checked for Benvolio, Tybalt. Cuts, cues for effects.

33. John B. Wright   1858

New York Public Library: *NCP.342958

[Lacy edition, 1855, 4 x 7½; interleaves, 7¼ x 9¾; blue cloth boards; title gilt up spine.]

Promptbook not in Wright's hand but dated by him as of 1858. The acting edition, which prints Charlotte Cushman's Haymarket cast of 1855, is a Shakespeare version. Cuts, restorations, some scenic indications, grooves, calls, considerable stage business, maps and sketches, cues for effects.

34. [Wright]

New York Public Library: *NCP.347168

[Modern Standard Drama, 4¼ x 7½; gray interleaves; brown cloth boards; title gilt on spine.]

Not a complete promptbook (lacks most cues for effects) but an interesting record of a production based on the Garrick version. Scenic indications, grooves, calls, considerable stage business, maps, notes on lights.

35. Edwin Booth   c.1860
   Folger: Rom, 14
   [Modern Standard Drama, 4¼ x 7⅛; interleaves; brown cloth boards; title and Booth's name gilt on cover.]
   Clara Louisa Kellogg's copy marked for her by Edwin Booth. Cuts, some scenic indications, some grooves, some stage business, description of a quadrille, maps, cues for effects, note on music. Tom M. Davey of New Orleans signed it on January 20, 1860. (See nos. 37-39.)

36. F. T. Doyle   Manchester, Prince's   October, 1864
   Mander and Mitchenson
   [French issue of Cumberland edition, 3⅝ x 5¾; interleaves, 5⅛ x 8⅜; maroon leather; title gilt on cover.]
   Promptbook made by F. T. Doyle, the stage manager. Cuts, scenic indications, calls, little stage business, map of a minuet.

37. Edwin Booth   New York, Booth's   February 3, 1869
   Harvard Theatre Collection: TS.2588.300
   [Booth-Hinton edition pasted in a workbook, 6¼ x 7⅝; tan paper under gray pamphlet binder and blue cloth spine.]
   Very full promptbook of the production which opened Booth's Theatre, marked by Henry L. Hinton. Calls, copious stage business especially for crowds and supers, cues for effects especially interesting for the scene changes. (See no. 35.)

38. [Booth]
   The Players
   [Booth-Hinton edition, 1868, 5⅛ x 7¾; brown leather; title and date of opening gilt on cover.]
   Booth's souvenir book of the production which opened his theatre. Cast. Cuts.

39. [Booth]
   Folger: Rom, 3
   [Booth-Hinton edition, 1868, 5¾ x 8⅛; stiff tan paper; "Edwin Booth Prompt Book/1868" inked on cover.]
   Preparation copy marked for reprinting. Penciled notations referring to the stage production and to the edition. Cuts, notes about supers, some grooves, some stage business, maps, cues for effects.

40. Junius Brutus Booth, Jr.   1870's
   Folger: Rom, 4

[French's Standard Drama, 4½ x 7⅝; some interleaves; stiff gray paper; title pasted on cover.]

Crude promptbook. Cuts and restorations, little stage business, cues for effects. Signature of H. C. Ford of Ford's Theatre, Washington, on the cover. Clippings of two playbills, one for Booth's Theatre on February 21, 1874, with Agnes Booth and Joseph Wheelock.

41. George Becks   c.1870

New York Public Library: *NCP.342974

[Booth-Hinton edition, 1868, 5 x 7⅜; interleaves; black cloth boards; title gilt on spine.]

Well-developed promptbook. Grooves, calls, considerable stage business, maps and rough sketches, cues for effects.

42. Adelaide Neilson   New York, Daly's Fifth Avenue   May 21, 1877

Folger: Rom, 21

[Lacy edition, 4¼ x 7⅜; interleaves; blue publisher's wrappers under heavy tan paper; title inked on cover.]

Rather crude promptbook of a 6-act arrangement marked in the hand of John Moore. Cuts and restorations, some grooves, some stage business, cues for effects. Collapsible paper model of the Capulet tomb, 5 x 4¾ x 3.

43. [Neilson]

Folger: Rom, 22

[Lacy edition, 4¼ x 7⅜; interleaves; heavy gray paper and purple cloth spine; title stamped on cover label, "Miss Neilson 76" inked on cover.]

Promptbook of a 6-act arrangement, dated 1876, much more carefully developed than the preceding book. At the front, a list of supers for 1878 and a good drawing of a house fronting on a garden. Calls, some stage business, cues for effects.

44. Henry Irving   London, Lyceum   March 8, 1882

Folger: Rom, 12

[Pages 105-245 from volume VIII of a *Works*, 4 x 6⅜; interleaves; brown leather gilt; title gilt on spine and cover.]

Preparation copy. Cuts on full text. (See no. 83.)

45. [Irving]

Princeton University, Seymour Collection: R&J

[Irving edition, 1882, 5½ x 8½; gray publisher's wrappers.]
Spectator's comments on an Irving-Terry performance.

46. [Irving]

Folger: Rom, 23

[Irving edition, 1882, 5½ x 8½; gray publisher's wrappers.]
Analysis of Irving's cuts and alterations by Alan Park Paton,
August, 1897.

47. Ellen Terry　　　　　London, Lyceum　　　　　March 8, 1882

Harvard Theatre Collection:　TS.2588.305

[Irving edition, 1882, 5½ x 8½; interleaves; limp tan leather
gilt; title gilt on cover.]
Rehearsal copy. Dozens of vivid notes by Miss Terry on her stage
business, moods, and histrionic manner in playing Juliet; several
notes on Irving's Romeo. (See no. 88.)

48. Adelaide Moore　　　　　　　　　　　　September, 1884

Enthoven Collection

[French issue of Lacy, 4¼ x 7¼; publisher's wrappers under gray
cardboard; title inked on cover.]
Promptbook of a 6-act arrangement roughly marked by Henry
Holmes for "Miss Adelaide Moore's Tour. Sep. 1st 1884." The
opening fight deleted. Some stage business, maps, cues for effects.

49. Mary Anderson　　　　London, Lyceum　　　　November 1, 1884

New York Public Library:　*NCP.181757B

[Anderson edition, 1884, 5⅝ x 8½; interleaves; green cloth
boards; title gilt up spine.]
Studybook checked for Juliet, but not certainly Miss Anderson's.
The many penciled notes about scenery, stage business, and productional effects may be a spectator's observations.

50. [Anderson]

Folger: Rom, 1

[Anderson edition, 1884, 5⅝ x 8⅞; publisher's wrappers.]
William Winter's copy. Two notes from Miss Anderson, one with
pressed flowers from Stratford. Two bits of manuscript in Winter's
hand, one on the play, one on the costumes. Winter's review from
the *Tribune* of November 12, 1885.

51. Margaret Mather　　New York, Union Square　　October 13, 1885

New York Public Library:　*NCP

[French's Standard Drama, 4½ x 7½; interleaves, 5½ x 8⅝; green cardboard; title and Miss Mather's signature on cover.]

Promptbook of the Garrick version arranged in 7 acts, the opening scene omitted. Cuts, some scenic indications, grooves, some stage business especially for tableaux at the curtains, cues for effects. Partial cast of *Cymbeline*.

52. [Mather?]

New York Public Library: *NCP.465040B

[French's Standard Drama, 4⅛ x 6⅞; interleaves; black cloth boards; title gilt up spine.]

Unidentified promptbook written in faint green ink with music cues in red, perhaps an improved version of the preceding book which in some details it resembles. Arranged in 6 acts, some of the Garrick matter suppressed. Some scenic indications, grooves, some stage business, maps, cues for effects.

53. Robert B. Mantell   Dayton   October 1, 1887

Folger: Rom, 17

[French's Standard Drama, 4¼ x 6¾; interleaves; limp brown leather; title and Mantell's name gilt on cover.]

Promptbook efficiently marked for touring. At the front a dummy cast list and synopses of scenes. Scenic indications and grooves (purple), stage business for crowds, maps, cues for effects (lights in red, scene change in blue). The 21 scenes are reduced to 17.

54. Julia Marlowe   New York, Star   December 12, 1887

Museum of the City of New York: 43.430.664

[Rolfe edition, 5 x 6⅝, tipped between leaves of a workbook, 6 x 8⅝; black cloth boards.]

Probably Miss Marlowe's early promptbook. Cuts on full text. The many stage directions are all entered on the interleaves in a single clear hand. (See nos. 65-78.)

55. Albert Taverner   Toronto   1890's

Toronto Public Library: 822.33/S.13

[American Book Exchange, 1880, 4 x 6⅛; blue paper; bound with 7 other Shakespeare plays in green cloth boards.]

Rehearsal copy checked for Romeo. Cuts, lines marked for stresses, notes on scenery, costumes, stage business.

56. [Taverner]

Toronto Public Library: Taverner Collection

[Music scores, 10½ x 13½; tan paper.]

Orchestral parts (8 instruments) of music for *Romeo and Juliet,* dated 1891-2.

57. Frederick Warde   America   1890's

University of California, Los Angeles: Special Collections 669, Box 1

[Edition pasted in a workbook, 8½ x 7½; brown leather; title gilt on cover.]

Promptbook used over several decades. Some stage business, cues for effects. Playbill for Washington, D.C., in 1893; about 20 prints and photographs of Warde as Romeo, actors of his company, Adelaide Neilson, Mary Anderson, Elinor Aickin, Ella Sturgis, Sothern and Marlowe, and others.

58. Augustin Daly   New York, Daly's   March 3, 1896

Folger: Rom, 7

[Thirteen books. DeWitt edition (Irving version), 4⅝ x 7½; publisher's wrappers.]

Rehearsal copies probably for the production with Mrs. James Brown Potter and Kyrle Bellew. In some of the books cuts and bits of stage business.

59. Blanche Bates   c.1899

Museum of the City of New York: 43.98.189

[Rolfe edition, 4½ x 6¼, tipped between leaves of a workbook, 7¼ x 9¼; limp brown leather; title and Miss Bates's name gilt on cover.]

Excellent promptbook, "arranged and marked by Fred Williams, Stage Director, Lyceum Theatre, New York, 1899," apparently not used by Miss Bates. Cuts on full text. Full scenic indications, calls, copious stage business, maps, cues for effects. Action of the ball scene is given in a long appendix.

60. Julia Arthur   Chicago, Grand Opera House   April 12, 1899

Harvard Theatre Collection: TS.2588.310

[Rolfe edition, 5 x 6⅝; interleaves; paper cover and title on leather cover label under gray pamphlet binder and blue cloth spine.]

Well-marked and much used promptbook. Cuts on full text. Some scenic indications, grooves, stage business, maps, cues for effects, timings, special warnings. Photographs, clippings, and playbills of Chicago, April 12, and Boston, May 15, 1899.

61. Margaret Anglin   c.1900
New York Public Library: *NCP.54x218
[Rolfe edition pasted in a workbook, 7⅜ x 9¼; typewritten interleaves tipped in; red cloth boards; title gilt on spine.]
Promptbook of an arrangement in which the opening fight is not shown but is expressed by noise and music. Cuts on full text. Much stage business with occasional notation, "Business from here on is purely personal business." Cues for effects.

62. John Doud   c.1900
Folger: Rom, 41
[French's Standard Drama pasted in a workbook, 7½ x 9½; bound with other books in gray canvas boards and half red leather.]
Promptbooks, etc., of John Doud inscribed to Curtis Cooksey by Harriette Weems (Mrs. Doud). The volume contains a promptbook for *Romeo and Juliet,* one for *The Bells,* notes for an original play, a description of J. B. Booth's costumes for 7 Shakespearean roles and his fight routine for Macbeth. The *Romeo* book shows cuts, some scenic indications, grooves, some stage business, cues for effects.

63. F. Owen Chambers   c.1900
Shakespeare Centre Library: 72.929CHA
[Cassell's National Library edition pasted in a workbook, 8 x 10⅛; red cloth boards; title on cover and spine labels.]
Perhaps a transcription of Forbes-Robertson's Lyceum production of 1895: contains illustrations from his acting edition. Carefully drawn groundplans with scenic units indicated, copious stage business, cues for effects.

64. Winthrop Ames   Boston, Castle Square   March 20, 1904
New York Public Library: *NCP.52443B
[Nineteen books. Typescript, 8 x 6⅜; blue cloth boards; title gilt on spine.]
Partbooks assigned to actors of two different companies, most of the books marked with notes on vocabulary and interpretation. The production revived April 16, 1906.

65. E. H. Sothern and Julia Marlowe

                  Chicago, Illinois Theatre   September 19, 1904

New York Public Library: *NCP.280656B

[Cut text pasted in a workbook, 7¼ x 9½; black cloth boards; title on cover and up spine.]

Preparation copy. Text partly in print, partly in longhand. Scenic indications, grooves, much stage business. Several drawings of scenes. (See no. 54.)

66. [Sothern and Marlowe]

New York Public Library: NCOF.51x304

[Carbon typescript, 8¾ x 11; brown paper; in manila folder.]

Unmarked copy of the completed Sothern-Marlowe version. Detailed production plans: plots of properties, scenery, music, supers, opening fight, etc.

67. [Sothern and Marlowe]

The Players: TS.113

[Typescript, 8 x 10½; acts bound separately in blue paper.]

Copy of a 6-act version giving the text only, marked "Prompting."

68. [Sothern and Marlowe]

The Players: PB.100

[Four booklets. Typescript, 8 x 10½; acts bound separately in blue paper.]

Much used promptbook of the 6-act version, with copious stage business and detailed production plans: plots of properties, scenery, music, etc. Acts II and VI are missing. Penciled cast, inked maps.

69. [Sothern and Marlowe]

The Players: TS.117A, B

[Two books. Typescript, 8 x 10½; limp brown leather.]

Complete copies of the 6-act version, very similar to the preceding book but in a different typing. Plots of properties, scenes, music, etc., and much stage business.

70. [Sothern and Marlowe]

Folger: Rom, Folio 5

[Typescript, 8 x 11; gray cardboard.]

Promptbook of the 6-act version used by Frederick Kaufman, the general stage manager. At the front, detailed production plans:

a 17-page plot of properties, a synopsis of the 16 scenes, a music plot, etc. Copious stage business, cues for effects.

71. [Sothern and Marlowe]
Folger: Rom, Folios 2, 3, 4
[Three books. Typescript, 8½ x 11; gray cardboard.]
Clean copies of the 6-act version. Folio 2 is a first copy, Folio 3 a carbon, Folio 4 a carbon with stage directions underscored in red.

72. [Sothern and Marlowe]
Museum of the City of New York: 43.430.665
[Typescript, 8½ x 11; black cardboard.]
Much used promptbook. Pencilings of additional stage business, maps, cues for effects, timings for several cities.

73. [Sothern and Marlowe]
Princeton University, Seymour Collection
[Typescript in red and black, 8½ x 11; brown paper.]
Excellent copy said to be a duplicate from the Museum of the City of New York.

74. [Sothern and Marlowe]
Princeton University, Seymour Collection
[Carbon typescript, 8½ x 11; red paper.]
Stage manager's copy, much used. Belonged to V. H. Collins.

75. [Sothern and Marlowe]
Princeton University, Seymour Collection
[Carbon typescript, 8½ x 11.]
Stage manager's copy, much used, in a different typing from the preceding Princeton books. Belonged to W. Stiefel.

76. [Sothern and Marlowe]
Folger: T.a.81
[Notebook, 6⅝ x 8⅛; brown and red marbled boards and black cloth spine.]
"Sothern & Marlowe Co Elect Dept" by M. E. McGarry. Light plots for 5 Shakespeare productions, including 16 plots (sketches) for *Romeo and Juliet*: instruments, colors, maps, cues.

77. [Sothern and Marlowe]
Folger: Rom, 29

[Shakespeare edition pasted in a workbook, 6½ x 8⅛; stiff brown paper; title pasted on cover.]

Thorough promptbook record made by Lark Taylor, the actor, who played Balthazar, Capulet, Benvolio during several seasons beginning in January, 1906. Cuts on full text, properties list, music plot, copious stage business, cues for effects. Clipping of the 1906 program.

78. [Sothern and Marlowe]

Joint University Libraries, Nashville

[Temple edition, 1904, 4 x 5⅛; red leather; title gilt on spine.]

Promptbook record made by Lark Taylor in April, 1923, "as they played R & J in 1906-7-8-10-11-12." Cuts on full text, 10 ground-plans, some stage business, cues for effects. The book had been Taylor's original rehearsal copy, inscribed "John Taylor/Marlowe & Sothern/New Orleans—March 14, 1906."

79. F. R. Benson   c.1905

Shakespeare Centre Library: 72.929BEN(4172)

[Collins edition, 1903, pasted in a workbook, 6⅜ x 8; black oil-cloth boards; title on cover and spine labels.]

Preparation copy. Stage business and cues for effects through the first act.

80. [Benson]

Shakespeare Centre Library: 72.929BEN(4296)

[Pocket Falstaff edition pasted in a workbook, 7¼ x 9; red marbled boards and half black leather, much worn; title on cover and spine labels.]

Much used promptbook. Much stage business roughly entered, groundplans, cues for effects. At the back cast lists and a partial scene plot.

81. Priestley Morrison   c.1905

New York Public Library: 9*NCP+p.v.5.143137 and B

[Two books. French's Standard Drama pasted in a workbook, 7 x 9¼; French's Standard Drama pasted in a workbook, 7 x 11½; bound together with an *As You Like It* (see AYL, 82) in black cloth boards; title gilt on spine.]

The first, called "Farnum production," is the promptbook of a 7-act version, heavily cut, with copious stage business, inserted typed slips giving maps, dance routine, cues for effects. The second, heavily cut, is the promptbook of a 6-act version with synopsis of scenes and grooves, copious stage business.

82. Anonymous c.1905
New York Public Library: *NCP.283818B
[Shakespeare edition pasted in a workbook, 7¼ x 10; red cloth boards; title gilt on spine.]
Unidentified director's book. Cuts on full text. Copious stage business, maps and sketches, notes on effects. Critical notes from William Poel.

83. Lewis Waller London, Imperial April 22, 1905
Folger: Rom, 32
[Irving edition, 5⅞ x 7½; interleaves; blue cloth boards and blue leather spine; title and Henry Irving's name gilt on cover.]
Studybook marked in blue, red, and black crayon and lead pencil in a round strong hand said to be that of Lewis Waller. Random jottings of stage business, some sketches, cues for effects. (See nos. 44-46.)

84. William Poel London, Royalty May 5, 1905
Enthoven Collection
[Cassell's National Library edition, 3⅝ x 5⅝; tipped to stubs between leaves of a workbook, 7¼ x 8⅝; red marbled boards and half black leather.]
Rough promptbook. Cuts on full text, some stage business, cues for effects.

85. Herbert Beerbohm Tree
London, His Majesty's June 30, 1913
Enthoven Collection: Tree, 232
[Six books. Favourite Classics edition, 3¾ x 6; green cloth boards; title gilt up spine.]
Rehearsal copies.

86. [Tree]
Enthoven Collection: Tree, 232
[Papers.]
Cast lists, dressing room assignments.

87. Henry Jewett Boston, Boston Opera House January 11, 1915
Folger: Rom, Folio 1

[Typescript, 8½ x 11; gray cardboard and green cloth spine.]
Promptbook of Jewett's first production at Boston, reused later.
Copious typewritten stage business with penciled augmentations.
Cues for effects. Program for one company, and penciled cast of
a different company.

88. Ellen Terry   London, Lyric   April 12, 1919
    Smallhythe
    [Temple edition, 1919, 3⅞ x 5; limp maroon leather; title gilt
    up spine.]
    Studybook for the Nurse. Cuts and underscorings. (In the copy
    of the Globe Shakespeare beside Miss Terry's bed at Smallhythe
    are her comments on having played the Nurse.) (See no. 47.)

89. Albert Lang   c.1920
    Princeton University, Seymour Collection
    [Maude Adams edition, 1899, pasted in a workbook, 7½ x 10⅛;
    brown marbled boards and black cloth spine; title pasted on
    cover.]
    Very full promptbook of an itinerant producer. Cuts, much stage
    business, very careful maps, cues for effects, photographs from
    the Adams production, properties list, printed cast lists.

[ACTOR LISTS FOR FOLLOWING BOOKS ARE GIVEN IN THIS ORDER:
Romeo, Juliet, Mercutio, Nurse.]

90. Nicholas Hannen   London, Everyman   November 18, 1920
    New York Public Library: *NCP.278922B
    [Shakespeare edition pasted in a workbook, 6⅝ x 8⅞; red cloth
    boards; title gilt on spine.]
    Cast includes Nicholas Hannen, Muriel Pratt, Laurence Hanray,
    Agnes Thomas. Directed by Edith Craig. Promptbook of Audrey
    Cameron, the assistant stage manager. Cuts on full text, some stage
    business, maps and sketches.

91. Jane Cowl   New York, Henry Miller   January 24, 1923
    Harvard Theatre Collection: TS.2588.315
    [Shakespeare edition pasted in a workbook, 7½ x 9⅜; black
    cloth boards and half red leather; title on red leather cover
    label.]
    Cast includes Rollo Peters, Jane Cowl, Dennis King, Jessie Ralph.
    Promptbook made by Edward Broadley, the stage manager for
    J. Sayre Crawley, who assisted in the direction of this production

and played various roles. Copious stage business, maps, cues for effects.

92. Eva LeGallienne   New York, Civic Repertory   April 21, 1930
Yale University, Beinecke Rare Book Library
[Aldus Shakespeare edition, 1909, pasted in a workbook, 5½ x 8½; blue ring binder.]
Cast includes Donald Cameron, Eva LeGallienne, Edward Bromberg, Leona Roberts. Designed by Aline Bernstein. Promptbook of the stage manager. Cuts and rearrangements, little stage business, all cues for effects. Working papers include property list, synopsis of scenes, curtain calls. With it a Boston review of October, 1933, and about 4 dozen photographs.

93. W. Bridges-Adams   Stratford-upon-Avon   June 20, 1933
Shakespeare Centre Library: 71.21/1933RO
[Temple edition pasted in a workbook, 7 x 9; purple cloth boards and half black leather; title on cover and spine labels.]
Cast includes John Wyse, Rachel Kempson, George Hayes, Alice O'Day. Designed by Norman Wilkinson. Stage business, maps. This copy not used in performance.

94. [Bridges-Adams]   April 22, 1934
Shakespeare Centre Library: 71.21/1934R
[Temple edition pasted in a workbook, 6¾ x 9; purple cloth boards and half black leather; title on spine label.]
Cast includes John Wyse, Rachel Kempson, Baliol Holloway, Barbara Gott. Preparation copy, unused. Stage business entered roughly.

95. Katharine Cornell   New York, Martin Beck   December 23, 1935
New York Public Library: *NCP+
[Typescript, 8¼ x 11; gray boards and tan cloth spine; title typed up spine.]
Cast of this second-season revival includes Maurice Evans, Katharine Cornell, Ralph Richardson, Florence Reed. Directed by Guthrie McClintic. This is not a promptbook, but a record of the production made by Fitzroy Davis during the Chicago run in November, 1935. Lines marked for stresses and intonation with a key to the symbols used. Stage business entered roughly but profusely. Sketches of some scenes. Notes on the use Davis made of the play in his novel *Quicksilver*.

96. B. Iden Payne   Stratford-upon-Avon   May 2, 1941
Shakespeare Centre Library: 71.21/1941RO
[Penguin edition pasted in a workbook, 7 x 9; purple cloth boards and half black leather; title on cover and spine labels.]
Cast includes Godfrey Kenton, Margaretta Scott, George Hayes, Freda Jackson. Designed by Peggy Neale and Barbara Harris. Much stage business, maps, cues for effects. The book had been used for Payne's 1938 production.

97. Robert Atkins   Stratford-upon-Avon   June 7, 1945
Shakespeare Centre Library: 71.21/1945R
[New Temple edition pasted in a workbook, 7⅛ x 9; purple cloth boards and half black leather; title on cover and spine labels.]
Cast includes David Peel, Moira Lister, Antony Eustrel, Viola Lyel. Little stage business, cues for effects. The book had been used for Payne's 1936 production; was erased and reused.

98. Basil C. Langton   Hammersmith, King's   March 1, 1946
Mander and Mitchenson
[Shakespeare edition tipped into a workbook, 7 x 9; blue cardboard and red cloth spine; title on cover label.]
Good promptbook of the Touring Repertory Theatre production. Cuts, calls, much stage business, cues for effects.

99. [Langton]
Mander and Mitchenson
[Shakespeare edition pasted in a workbook, 8 x 10; blue-gray marbled boards and blue cloth spine; title on cover label.]
Stage manager's book of the Touring Repertory Theatre production. Much stage business, cues for effects. Contains a large character chart and properties list.

100. Peter Brook   Stratford-upon-Avon   April 6, 1947
Shakespeare Centre Library: O.S.71.21/1947RO
[Temple edition pasted in a workbook, 8 x 13; red cloth boards; title on cover and spine labels.]
Cast includes Laurence Payne, Daphne Slater, Paul Scofield, Beatrix Lehmann. Designed by Rolf Gérard. Calls, stage business, many maps, cues for effects. The production was moved to His Majesty's in London.

101. Glen Byam Shaw   Stratford-upon-Avon   April 27, 1954
Shakespeare Centre Library: O.S.71.21/1954R
[Penguin edition pasted in a workbook, 8 x 11; red cloth board
spring binder; title on spine label.]
Cast includes Laurence Harvey, Zena Walker, Tony Britton, Rosalind Atkinson. Designed by Motley. Much stage business, maps,
cues for effects.

102. [Shaw]   April 8, 1958
Shakespeare Centre Library: O.S.71.21/1958R
[Penguin edition pasted in a workbook, 8 x 13; red cloth board
spring binder; title on spine label.]
Cast includes Richard Johnson, Dorothy Tutin, Edward Wood-
ward, Angela Baddeley. Designed by Motley. Much stage business,
maps, cues for effects. The book also used for the Russian tour in
December, 1958.

103. Jack Landau   Stratford, Connecticut   June 12, 1959
Festival Theatre, Production Department
[Three books. Mimeograph, 8½ x 11; black board ring binders.]
Cast includes Richard Easton, Inga Swenson, William Smithers,
Aline Macmahon. Designed by David Hays and Dorothy Jeakins.
The first book has much stage business, maps (some on mimeographed groundplans), company lists, rehearsal schedule. The second, signed by Bernard Gersten, has copious stage business, some
cues roughly written, and production papers including plots of
properties, wigs, and ad libs, a groundplan, company list, production schedule. The third has cues for effects.

104. [Landau]
University of California, Los Angeles: Houseman Box 11
[Mimeograph, 8½ x 11; yellow interleaves; brown cloth boards;
title gilt on cover.]
Final or souvenir promptbook of the Connecticut production prepared for John Houseman by the stage managers. Stage business
typed on interleaves. Full set of production papers at the back.

105. Michael Langham   Stratford, Ontario   June 29, 1960
Festival Theatre, Library
[Penguin edition pasted in a workbook, 7¾ x 13⅛; blue cloth
boards bordered in ink; title pasted on cover.]
Cast includes Bruno Gerussi, Julie Harris, Christopher Plummer,

Kate Reid. Designed by Tanya Moiseiwitsch. Calls and cues for effects.

106. Peter Hall   Stratford-upon-Avon   August 15, 1961

Shakespeare Centre Library: O.S.71.21/1961R

[Cambridge Pocket Shakespeare pasted in a workbook, 8 x 12⅛; blue cloth board ring binder; title on spine label.]

Cast includes Brian Murray, Dorothy Tutin, Ian Bannen, Edith Evans. Designed by Sean Kenney. Much stage business, cues for effects. Production papers: cast, understudies, 8 maps on mimeographed groundplans, fight routine.

107. Other books of *Romeo and Juliet:*

Brown University: Eng.P.17, Asa Cushman.

Connecticut State Library: William Gillette.

Edwin Forrest Home (on loan to the University of Pennsylvania, Rare Book Room):   Edwin Forrest.

Folger: Rom, 5, William E. Burton; Rom, 6, Coplestone; Rom, 11^1, Mr. Solomon; Rom, 11^2, E. G. Gladstone; Rom, 16, John T. Malone; Rom, 30, Forbes-Robertson; Rom, 34, A. M. Young; Rom, 36, 37, 38, anonymous; Rom, 40, Sullivan.

Harvard Theatre Collection: uncatalogued, Annie M. Clarke.

Historical and Philosophical Society of Ohio: 812.3/R283/175, Alvin Read.

Mander and Mitchenson: Carlotta Addison, 1864.

New York Public Library: *NCP, anonymous; *NCV.p.v.15, A. B. Davis.

Shakespeare Centre Library: 82.5(1657), F. Haywel; O.S.P.50.29 (1825), William Creswick.

The Taming of the Shrew

1. John Philip Kemble   London, Drury Lane   March 13, 1788
University of Pennsylvania, Furness Collection: C59.ShlTaK
[Garrick's *Catherine and Petruchio*, Bathurst, 1786, 4⅛ x 6⅞; interleaves; all sheets tipped into binding of maroon and blue marbled boards and half red leather gilt; title gilt on spine.]
Promptbook marked by Kemble: "The Acting Copy, with the MS. additions, of Mr. John Philip Kemble," given to H. H. Furness by Mrs. F. A. Kemble in 1874. Cuts, some stage business, cues for effects. (See nos. 3-4.)

2. Anonymous   c.1792
Folger: Shrew Ad, 12
[Silvester Doig, *Katharine and Petruchio*, Edinburgh, 1792, 3⅞ x 6⅞; red marbled boards and half green leather gilt; title gilt up spine.]
Promptbook. Cuts, calls, cues for effects.

3. John Philip Kemble   London, Covent Garden   c.1810
Garrick Club
[Kemble's *Katherine and Petruchio*, 1810, 5 x 8¼; interleaves; blue cloth boards and brown leather spine.]
Promptbook marked by Kemble. Some stage business, maps. (See no. 1.)

4. [Kemble]
Garrick Club
[Kemble's *Katherine and Petruchio*, 1810, 5⅛ x 8½; interleaves; blue cloth boards and brown leather spine.]
Promptbook checked for Petruchio. Not in Kemble's hand but contents similar to those of preceding book. Cuts. Additional bits of stage business.

5. John Pritt Harley   Canterbury   June 6, 1812
Folger: S.a.102
[Manuscript, 6⅜ x 7⅞; in box of brown cloth boards; title, etc., gilt on cover.]
Partbooks in Harley's hand for the Tailor and Grumio in *Catharine and Petruchio,* dated as above for "Mr. & Mrs. Meggett's Night."

6. Charles Kemble
Folger: Shrew Ad, 13

[Volume III of *Farces,* 4⅛ x 7; gray boards and half red leather; "Farces" gilt on spine.]

Crude promptbook. Cast with Charles Kemble. Cuts, some stage business.

7. J. W. Wallack   c.1825

Folger: Shrew Ad, 3

[Kemble's *Katherine and Petruchio,* 1810, 5⅛ x 8¼; interleaves watermarked 1825; green cloth boards; title gilt up spine and Wallack's name gilt on cover.]

Promptbook endorsed "J W Wallack from J. P. Kemble" but not marked by Kemble. Cuts, calls, some stage business, cues for effects.

8. John G. Gilbert   1832

Boston Public Library: K.49.10

[Cumberland edition, *Katharine and Petruchio,* 3¾ x 5¾; bound with 8 other plays in marbled boards and maroon leather spine; "Shakespeare" gilt on spine.]

Promptbook. Cuts, calls, some stage business, cues for effects.

9. Benjamin Webster   London, Haymarket   March 16, 1844

Folger: Shrew, 2

[Pages 263-328 from volume I of an illustrated *Works,* 6¾ x 10; gray interleaves; buff paper; title inked on cover.]

According to George Becks's note in the following book, this is "Phelps' promptbook as/marked by G. Hastings/copyist/34 New Hampstead Road/Kentish town/1856." It is not Phelps's book (for which, see no. 16). Internal evidence (use of placards, presence of Sly throughout the play, etc.) indicates Webster's production. Few cuts. Calls, considerable stage business, maps, cues for effects. Contains a transcription of Henry Morley's 1856 review of Phelps's production taken from *The Journal of a London Playgoer.*

10. [Webster]

New York Public Library: *NCP.285352

[Shakespeare edition, 4 x 6¾; interleaves, 4½ x 7⅛; black cloth boards; title gilt on spine.]

Transcription of the preceding promptbook (Hastings' transcription of Webster's) made by George Becks.

11. James E. Murdoch   Philadelphia, Walnut Street   August 31, 1848

University of Pennsylvania: AC85.M9415.820p.57

[Cumberland edition, *Katharine and Petruchio,* 3⅞ x 5⅞; interleaves; brown marbled boards and red leather spine.]
Much used promptbook, marked and dated by G. W. Lewis, the
Philadelphia prompter. Cuts and additions, grooves, calls, considerable stage business, maps, cues for effects.

12. John Moore   1850's
    Folger: Shrew Ad, 5
    [Thomas's Burlesque Drama, *Katharine and Petruchio,* London,
    1838, 4 x 6⅛; interleaves, 4⅞ x 8; stiff brown paper; publisher's
    wrapper pasted on cover.]
    Fully developed promptbook. Cuts and additions, calls, some
    scenic indications, grooves, stage business, cues for effects. One
    gag attributed to Kemble. Playbills for R. Johnstone and Mrs.
    Abbott, 1856; C. Fisher and Mrs. A. Parker; C. Plukkett and Mrs.
    Frank Rea, Troy, 1859; Edwin Booth and Mrs. Davenport.

13. James Stark   1850's
    New York Public Library: *NCP.164537
    [Modern Standard Drama, *Katherine and Petruchio,* 5 x 7⅛; in-
    terleaves; blue cloth boards; title gilt up spine.]
    Well-marked promptbook, aranged to be done in 1 act. Heavy
    cuts, calls, copious stage business, cues for effects.

14. Samuel Phelps   London, Sadler's Wells   1850
    Folger: Shrew Ad, 6
    [Kemble's *Katherine and Petruchio,* 1810, 4⅞ x 8⅛; gray paper
    and red leather spine; "Prompt Book/1850" inked on cover.]
    Promptbook partly marked by earlier owners (Charles Elliston
    and Mr. Goodwin, whose names are scratched), partly by Phelps.
    Cuts, additions, calls, some stage business, a map, cues for effects.
    (See no. 16.)

15. Hermann Vezin   August 18, 1856
    Folger: Shrew, 9
    [Hinds English Stage, *Katharine and Petruchio,* 1839, 4⅝ x 7⅞;
    interleaves; blue-gray marbled boards and half green leather gilt,
    broken; title gilt up spine.]
    Promptbook in the hand of George Hastings, the copyist. Cuts and
    additions, grooves, calls, stage business, maps, cues for effects.

16. Samuel Phelps   London, Sadler's Wells   November 15, 1856
Folger: Shrew, 6
[Pages 331-430 from volume III of Chalmers' *Works*, 5½ x 8¾; a few lavender interleaves; buff paper, torn; title, theatre, etc., inked on cover.]
Promptbook of Phelps's restoration of the Shakespeare play, marked by Phelps and Williams, the prompter. Cuts on full text. Includes the Induction. Some scenic indications, grooves, calls, some stage business, cues for effects. (See no. 14.)

17. J. B. Roberts   1860's
Folger: Shrew Ad, 7
[French's Standard Drama, *Katharine and Petruchio* pasted in a workbook, 7¾ x 9¾, which also contains *The Ragpicker of Paris;* black cloth boards and red leather spine; title inked on cover label.]
Promptbook. Cuts, some scenic indications, grooves, some stage business, cues for effects.

18. Mercer Hampson Simpson   Birmingham, Theatre Royal   1860's
Birmingham, Shakespeare Memorial Library: C52/455742
[Lacy edition, *Katharine and Petruchio*, 4 x 7⅜; gray cardboard; bound with other plays in green cloth boards; "Shakespeare's Separate Plays" gilt on spine.]
Promptbook of Sara Lewis. Addition of traditional gags, calls, some stage business, cues for effects.

19. Owen J. Fawcett   1864
New York Public Library: *NCP.164366
[Music-Publishing Company, *Katharine and Petruchio*, 3½ x 5½; interleaves; black cloth boards; title gilt up spine.]
Promptbook derived from James Stark's (see no. 13), divided into acts but provisionally cut to 1 act. Calls, copious stage business verbatim with Stark's, cues for effects. Fawcett gave it to George Becks in 1865.

20. Barry Sullivan
Folger: Shrew Ad, 1
[Hinds English Stage, *Katharine and Petruchio*, 1839, 4⅝ x 7⅞; bound with *Twelve Precisely!* in purple cloth boards.]
Association value only. A note by David Belasco explains that

Barry Sullivan gave him these plays "when I was a lad"; Belasco sold them; Jean Davenport Lander got them; George Becks bought them in 1903; Belasco bought them from Becks: "And, goodbye, old friend—Where, I wonder, will you go now?"

21. Adelaide Neilson

Folger: Shrew, Folio 1

[Shakespeare Press edition, 12¼ x 16⅝; green cloth boards and half brown leather; title gilt up spine and on red leather cover label.]

Reading copy. Portions heavily cut and emended to conform to the *Katherine and Petruchio* version.

22. J. R. Pitman   1880's

University of Pennsylvania, Furness Collection: C59.Sh1MeP

[Booth-Winter edition, *Katharine and Petruchio,* published with *The Merchant of Venice,* 1881, 4⅝ x 6½; gray publisher's wrappers.]

Promptbook lightly marked, perhaps unused. Scenic indications, grooves, cues for effects.

23. William Seymour   Boston, Boston Museum   1880's

Princeton University, Seymour Collection: K and P, 6

[Modern Standard Drama, *Katharine and Petruchio,* 4½ x 7¾; interleaves, 4⅞ x 8; publisher's wrappers.]

Promptbook fully marked and much used, checked for Petruchio. Cuts, grooves, calls, considerable stage business, maps, cues for effects.

24. [Seymour]

Princeton University, Seymour Collection: K and P, 1

[Modern Standard Drama, *Katharine and Petruchio,* 4½ x 7½; interleaves; stiff canvas.]

Lightly marked promptbook. Cuts, calls, cues for effects.

25. [Seymour]

Princeton University, Seymour Collection: K and P, 3

[French's Standard Drama, *Katharine and Petruchio,* 4½ x 7¾; interleaves not sewn, 5 x 8; in a paper wrapper.]

Uncompleted promptbook. Opening pages heavily marked for scenery and stage business; thereafter only cuts and some sheets of notes on business in the first act.

26. Edwin Booth   New York, Booth's   October 19, 1881

Folger: Shrew Ad, 2

[Booth-Winter edition, *Katharine and Petruchio*, 1878, 4⅝ x 6⅝; gray publisher's wrappers.]

Promptbook roughly marked but much used. Partial cast including Mrs. Pateman. Scenic indications, properties list, calls, stage business, cues for effects, timings.

27. [Booth]

Folger: Shrew Ad, 9

[Booth-Winter edition, *Katharine and Petruchio*, 4⅜ x 6⅜; maroon cloth boards; title gilt up spine.]

William Winter's copy. Winter's manuscript description of Booth's Petruchio. Note from Booth about his failure in management.

28. Augustin Daly   New York, Daly's   January 18, 1887

Folger: Shrew, 3

[Daly first edition, 1887, 6 x 9½; interleaves; publisher's wrappers, unsewn.]

Very full promptbook in the hand of John Moore, the stage manager. Daly's version was "arranged to be played in four acts," but Moore corrects the title page to *five* acts. Contains a second title page for the "Centenary Edition" as printed for April 13, 1887. Calls, properties, copious stage business, maps and sketches, cues for effects. Playbill for November 27, 1891.

29. [Daly]

New York Public Library: 8-*NCP.686481, 3

[Two books. Daly first edition, 1887, 5¾ x 9¼; publisher's wrapper under green cloth boards; title gilt on spine.]

Rehearsal copies. The first was used by Frederick Bond for Tranio and First Player; contains notes on pronunciation and some stage business. The second, checked for Petruchio and Lucentio, was perhaps John Drew's book; brief pencilings of stage business; some alterations of text which were later printed in the Centenary edition.

30. [Daly]

New York Public Library: 8-*NCP.686482

[Daly Centenary edition, 1887, 5¾ x 9¼; publisher's wrapper under green cloth boards: title gilt on spine.]

Rehearsal copy, checked for Petruchio; probably not John Drew's book but that of a later Petruchio. Marked for pauses, laughs, exclamations, stage business, manner, tone.

31. [Daly]

New York Public Library: 8-*NCP.686484

[Fifteen booklets. Typescript, 8¼ x 6½; green cloth boards; title gilt on spine.]

Partbooks, much marked and used, several of them bearing names of actors not in Daly's original company.

32. [Daly]

New York Public Library: *NCP.343000

[Daly Centenary edition, 1887, 6 x 9¼; interleaves; black cloth boards; title gilt on spine.]

Heavily annotated by George Becks, perhaps in preparation for his projected *The Actor's Shakespeare*. Scenic indications, grooves, calls, copious stage business from the tradition including, for instance, all of James Stark's, maps and sketches, cues for effects. Program of Daly's hundredth performance, 4 illustrations of scenes from Daly's production, music score for "Should she Upbraid" as sung by Daly's chorus in the last act.

33. [Daly]

Folger: Prints and Engravings

[Daly edition, 1887, mounted in pages of an album, 11⅞ x 17⅞; red marbled boards and half brown leather; title gilt on spine.]

Souvenir album with Daly's version, many old prints, many nineteenth-century playbills, Daly's silk playbills, 57 photographs of actors, and 10 photographs of scenes in Daly's production.

34. [Daly]

Folger: Shrew, 1

[Daly edition, 1887, 6 x 9½; interleaves; gray cardboard and green cloth spine.]

Promptbook based on Daly's 4-act version, which belonged to George Clarke, an actor in Daly's company (probably later belonged to Henry Jewett). Lists of properties grouped by acts, calls, much stage business, maps and sketches, cues for effects, curtain calls.

35. [Daly]

Joint University Libraries, Nashville: S822.33/Q3/D1

[Daly Centenary edition, 1887, 5¾ x 9½; interleaves; red cloth boards; title gilt on spine, Lark Taylor's name on cover.]

Souvenir promptbook made by Lark Taylor, marked "Property of Jack Taylor" on the title page. Very full record, with descriptions of scenery, copious stage business, groundplans for each scene, cues for effects. Record of Taylor's several roles in the play with Daly, with Rehan, with Sothern and Marlowe. Photograph of Ada Rehan and lengthy note on her costume; photographs of John Drew and the banquet scene. (See no. 55.)

36. Herbert Beerbohm Tree

London, Her Majesty's   November 1, 1897

Enthoven Collection: Tree, 7

[Two books. Typescript of *Katherine and Petruchio,* 8 x 10; the acts bound separately.]

Rehearsal promptbooks. One marked in pencil, signed by A. Wigley: much stage business. One marked in red ink and blue and black pencil: much stage business, cues for effects.

37. [Tree]

Enthoven Collection: Tree, 7

[Typescript, 8 x 10; gray cover.]

Final promptbook marked in pencil and red ink. Groundplans, stage business, maps, cues for effects.

38. [Tree]

Enthoven Collection: Tree, 7

[Seven books. French edition, *Katherine and Petruchio,* 4 x 7⅛; publisher's wrappers under brown paper.]

Rehearsal copies.

39. [Tree]

Enthoven Collection: Tree, 7

[Two booklets. Typescript, 8½ x 7; brown paper.]

Partbooks for Katherine and Petruchio.

40. Charlotte Lambert   1898

Museum of the City of New York: 32.109.13

[French's Standard Drama, *Katharine and Petruchio,* 4½ x 7½; interleaves, 5¼ x 8; paper wrapper; title pasted on cover.]

Very fully developed promptbook prepared by William Seymour, July, 1898. At the front, a list of characters and doubles and an elaborate properties list. Detailed scenic indications, calls, very full stage business, good maps, cues for effects, timing (1:00).

41. Charles B. Hanford   c.1900
    Folger: Shrew, Folio 7
    [Carbon typescript, 8 x 10½; each of the 4 acts in a brown paper wrapper.]
    Promptbook of Hanford's touring company. Cuts (the Induction is omitted), typewritten stage business augmented in longhand, cues for effects.

42. F. R. Benson   c.1900
    Shakespeare Centre Library: 72.930BEN
    [Temple edition pasted in a workbook, 7 x 9; red marbled boards and green cloth spine; title on cover and spine labels.]
    Promptbook. Much stage business roughly entered, maps, cues for effects. At the front a cast list, a time chart. At the back, plots of properties, supers.

43. Oscar Asche   London, Adelphi   November 29, 1904
    Shakespeare Centre Library: 72.930ASC
    [Temple edition pasted in a workbook, 7 x 9; red marbled boards and tan cloth spine, broken; title on cover and spine labels.]
    Much used promptbook. Much stage business, groundplans, cues for effects.

44. E. H. Sothern and Julia Marlowe Cleveland September 18, 1905
    Museum of the City of New York: 43.430.667
    [Shakespeare edition pasted in a workbook, 5½ x 8½; limp brown leather.]
    Preparation copy, pencil-marked for stresses, stage business, effects. The directions are numbered and entered on facing pages.

45. [Sothern and Marlowe]
    New York Public Library: *NCP.276567B
    [Carbon typescript, 8 x 10½; red cloth boards; title gilt on spine.]
    Early version with the text of the Induction given but not marked for use. Groundplans, copious stage business, maps.

46. [Sothern and Marlowe]
    New York Public Library: *NCP.51x304
    [Carbon typescript, 8½ x 11; brown cloth boards; title gilt up spine.]

Later version without the Induction. Copious stage business. Plots of lights, properties, and music given for each act.

47. [Sothern and Marlowe]
Folger: Shrew, Folio 2
[Shakespeare edition pasted in a workbook, 8 x 10½; ring binder of black cloth boards and half red leather.]
Souvenir promptbook made by Francis S. T. Powell, the stage manager, assisted by Frederick Kaufman. Scenic indications, copious stage business, maps, cues for effects. Powell declares that all is "exactly as used in the presentation." It differs from arrangements in the following books.

48. [Sothern and Marlowe]
Folger: Shrew, Folios 3, 6
[Two books. Original and carbon typescript, 8½ x 11; brown paper.]
The production as arranged by Frederick Kaufman, the general stage manager. For each major scene, plots of lights, properties, music, and a carefully drawn red ink groundplan. Folio 6 has the program for Jolson's 59th Street Theatre, October 15, 1923.

49. [Sothern and Marlowe]
Folger: Shrew, Folios 4, 5
[Two books. Original and carbon typescript, 8½ x 11; brown paper.]
Clean retyping of the preceding book.

50. [Sothern and Marlowe]
Museum of the City of New York: 43.430.668
[Carbon typescript, 8½ x 11; blue ring binder.]
Stage manager's copy for lighting. Red ink maps and sketches showing the placing and focus of lamps.

51. [Sothern and Marlowe]
Princeton University, Seymour Collection
[Carbon typescript, 8½ x 11; red paper.]
Stage manager's copy, much used. Belonged to V. H. Collins of 1119 Rosalind Avenue, Los Angeles.

52. [Sothern and Marlowe]
Princeton University, Seymour Collection

[Typescript in black and red, 8½ x 11; blue paper.]
Stage manager's copy, much used. Belonged to W. Stiefel.

53. [Sothern and Marlowe]
Folger: T.a.81, 82
[Notebook, 6⅝ x 8⅛; brown and red marbled boards and black cloth spine.]
"Sothern & Marlowe Co Elect Dept" by M. E. McGarry. Light plots for 5 Shakespeare productions, including 8 plots (sketches) for the *Shrew:* instruments, colors, maps, cues. With it a typed light plot mounted on cardboard for use at the controls.

54. [Sothern and Marlowe]
W. A. Clark Library, Los Angeles
[Shakespeare edition, 4⅝ x 7⅛; interleaves; brown cloth boards; title gilt on spine.]
Composite promptbook made by Lark Taylor, combining elements of the "Daly version as played by Rehan" (with whom Taylor worked in 1899/1900), and the Sothern and Marlowe production (in which Taylor worked for 8 seasons commencing in 1906). Daly cast of 1887, Rehan's cast, a Sothern and Marlowe cast. Notes on the cuttings, groundplans, copious stage business, cues for effects, costume notes.

55. [Sothern and Marlowe]
Folger: Shrew, 7
[Shakespeare edition pasted in a workbook, 6¾ x 8¼; stiff brown paper.]
Promptbook record of the production made by Lark Taylor "as done by Sothern and Marlowe—with most important points from Daly's book" (see no. 35). Taylor played the Page and a servant at Daly's in 1898, and Hortensio, Tranio, Gremio with Sothern and Marlowe. Copious stage business, maps and sketches, critical notes on both productions.

56. [Sothern and Marlowe]
Folger: Shrew, 8
[Shakespeare edition pasted in a workbook, 7⅜ x 9½; stiff brown paper.]
Lark Taylor's transcription of all the matter in the preceding book except notes about himself, made in 1922 for Curtis Cooksey.

57. Margaret Anglin   Melbourne   October 10, 1908
New York Public Library: 8-*NCP.54x218
[Rolfe edition pasted in a workbook, $7\frac{1}{2}$ x $9\frac{1}{2}$; black cloth boards; title inked on spine.]
Promptbook or preparation copy. Copious stage business, maps.

58. John Martin-Harvey   London, Prince of Wales   May 10, 1913
London Museum
[Shakespeare edition pasted in a workbook, $6\frac{7}{8}$ x 9; black imitation leather.]
Preparation copy. Cuts on full text, additions from *Taming of a Shrew* and ad lib lines added for Sly. Much stage business, rough maps, notes on effects. Many notations are by William Poel, who advised on the production.

59. Henry Jewett   Boston, Boston Opera House   February 22, 1915
Folger: Shrew, Folio 9
[Carbon typescript, $8\frac{1}{2}$ x 11; gray cardboard and green cloth spine.]
Promptbook of the Jewett company in their first season. Typewritten stage directions augmented with pencilings. Program.

60. Mrs. C. H. Jones
Folger: Shrew, Folio 8
[Typescript, 8 x $10\frac{1}{2}$.]
The play "adapted . . . into tabloid form." Apparently a scenario for a silent movie.

61. Maude Adams
Museum of the City of New York: 48.367.132A, B, C
[Three books. Typescript, 8 x $10\frac{5}{8}$; each of 3 acts bound in blue paper.]
Much cut version arranged in 3 acts.

[ACTOR LISTS FOR FOLLOWING BOOKS ARE GIVEN IN THIS ORDER: Petruchio, Katharine.]

62. Barry Jackson   London, Royal Court   April 30, 1928
British Drama League
[Shakespeare edition pasted in a workbook, 7 x 9; blue cloth boards and black cloth spine.]
Promptbook of Matthew Forsyth, the stage manager of Jackson's

modern-dress production, which originated at the Birmingham Repertory Theatre and later played at the Royal Court in London. Cast includes Scott Sunderland, Eileen Beldon. Cuts, cast list, many notes on costume and properties, much stage business, maps. Bits of music score. Program for the Royal Court.

63. W. Bridges-Adams   Stratford-upon-Avon   May 23, 1933
Shakespeare Centre Library: 71.21/1933T(6058)
[Temple edition pasted in a workbook, 7 x 9; purple cloth boards and half black leather; title on spine label.]
Cast includes Anew McMaster, Madge Compton. Designed by Reginald Leefe. Much stage business, maps, cues for effects.

64. [Bridges-Adams]
Shakespeare Centre Library: 71.21/1933T(7930)
[Same format as preceding book but blue cloth boards.]
Preparation copy for the preceding book. Slightly different stage business roughly entered, few cues for effects.

65. Alfred Lunt and Lynn Fontanne
                    New York, Theatre Guild   September 30, 1935
New York Public Library: *NCP.57x10
[Two books. Typescript, 7½ x 10¾; black cloth boards; title gilt on spine.]
Cast includes Alfred Lunt, Lynn Fontanne. Directed by Harry Wagstaff Gribble. Designed by Carolyn Hancock. The first book is the stage manager's, marked with additional stage business and cues for effects. The second, signed by Carolyn Simonson, is marked for curtain cues.

66. B. Iden Payne   Stratford-upon-Avon   April 13, 1936
Shakespeare Centre Library: 71.21/1936TA
[New Temple edition pasted in a workbook, 7 x 9; purple cloth boards and half black leather; title on spine label.]
Cast includes Peter Glenville, Barbara Couper. Costumes by Eric Maxon and Barbara Curtis. Text augmented with Sly passages from *Taming of a Shrew*. Much stage business, maps, cues for effects. The book had been used for Payne's 1935 production.

67. F. Owen Chambers   Leamington Spa, Loft   May 14, 1936
Shakespeare Centre Library: 72.930CHA, 1 and 2
Cassell's National Library edition pasted in two workbooks, 7 x 9;

part 1 bound in black oilcloth boards, part 2 in gray boards and black cloth spine; title on cover and spine labels.]

Promptbook of amateur(?) production. Much stage business, maps, cues for effects. Plots of scenes and properties, a program.

68. Columbia Broadcasting System   August 2, 1937

Folger: Shrew, Folio 10

[Mimeograph, 8½ x 11; decorated green paper wrappers; title on cover.]

Radio adaptation by Gilbert Seldes. Cast includes Edward G. Robinson, Frieda Inescort.

69. Theodore Komisarjevsky   Stratford-upon-Avon   April 3, 1939

Shakespeare Centre Library: 71.21/1939TA

[Eversley edition pasted in a workbook, 7 x 9; blue cloth boards and half black leather; title on cover and spine labels.]

Cast includes Alec Clunes, Vivienne Bennett. Some stage business, maps, cues for effects.

70. Robert Atkins   Stratford-upon-Avon   April 11, 1944

Shakespeare Centre Library: 71.21/1944TA

[New Temple edition pasted in a workbook, 7 x 9; gray boards and blue cloth spine; title on cover and spine labels.]

Cast includes Antony Eustrel, Patricia Jessel. Designed by Guy Sheppard. Stage business, maps, cues for effects. Formerly used at Open Air Theatre in 1941.

71. Michael Benthall   Stratford-upon-Avon   May 7, 1948

Shakespeare Centre Library: O.S.71.21/1948T

[New Temple edition pasted in a workbook, 8 x 12¾; green cloth boards and red cloth spine; title on cover and spine labels.]

Cast includes Anthony Quayle, Diana Wynyard. Designed by Rosemary Vercoe. Much stage business, maps, cues for effects. Production papers include lights, cast, music, timings.

72. George Devine   Stratford-upon-Avon   June 9, 1953

Shakespeare Centre Library: O.S.71.21/1953T

[Penguin edition pasted in a workbook, 8 x 13; blue cloth spring binder; title on spine label.]

Cast includes Marius Goring, Yvonne Mitchell. Designed by Vivienne Kernot. Very much stage business, maps on blueprint groundplans, cues for effects.

73. [Devine]   June 1, 1954
Shakespeare Centre Library: O.S.71.21/1954T
[Same format as preceding book.]
Cast includes Keith Michell, Barbara Jefford. Designed by Vivi-
enne Kernot. Very much stage business, 15 maps on mimeographed
groundplans, cues for effects.

74. Tyrone Guthrie   Stratford, Ontario   June 29, 1954
Festival Theatre, Library
[Two books. New Temple edition pasted in workbooks, 8¼ x
13⅝; one in green cloth boards, one in black cloth boards and
red cloth spine; second has title pasted on cover.]
Cast includes William Needles, Barbara Chilcott. Designed by
Tanya Moiseiwitsch. The first book has much stage business, many
maps. The second has cues for effects.

75. Denis Carey   London, Old Vic   November 30, 1954
Old Vic, Publicity Department
[Two books. New Temple edition pasted in a workbook, 8 x 10½;
black ring binder. New Temple edition pasted in a workbook,
8¼ x 13; blue ring binder.]
Cast includes Paul Rogers, Ann Todd. Designed by Kenneth
Rowell. The first book has cuts, stage business, maps, cues for
effects, and production papers: calls, properties, flys, cast. The
second, used for a 1955 revival, has cuts, much stage business carefully entered, maps, cues for effects.

76. Michael Benthall   Old Vic, Australian Tour   May, 1955
Old Vic, Publicity Department
[New Temple edition pasted in a workbook, 8¼ x 13; bound with
The Merchant of Venice in blue ring binder.]
Cast includes Robert Helpmann, Katharine Hepburn. Designed
by Peter Rice. Markings originally penciled but erased and typed.
Calls, stage business, cues for effects. Production papers: music,
properties.

77. Norman Lloyd   Stratford, Connecticut   August 5, 1956
Festival Theatre, Production Department
[Three books. Mimeograph, 8½ x 11; interleaves in first and second; one in stiff black paper, one in stiff brown paper, one in
black board spring binder.]

Cast includes Pernell Roberts, Nina Foch. Designed by Rouben Ter-Arutunian, Jack Landau, Dorothy Jeakins. The first book has copious stage business, maps on mimeographed groundplans, cues for effects, properties plot. The second is a neat transcription of the first. The third, which served at the Phoenix, New York, and belonged to Paul Leaf, has much stage business, cues for effects, plots of properties, costumes, wigs and beards.

78. [Lloyd]
New York Public Library: *NCP
[Mimeograph, 7½ x 10¾; brown cloth boards; title gilt up spine.]
Unused copy of the preceding book.

79. John Barton   Stratford-upon-Avon   June 21, 1960
Shakespeare Centre Library: O.S.71.21/1960TA
[New Temple edition pasted in a workbook, 8 x 13; green cloth board spring binder; title on spine label.]
Cast includes Peter O'Toole, Peggy Ashcroft. Designed by Alix Stone. Very much stage business, cues for effects. Production papers: cast, music cues.

80. Other books of *Katharine and Petruchio* and *The Taming of the Shrew:*
Boston Public Library: K.49.10, anonymous.
Connecticut State Library: William Gillette.
Folger: Shrew Ad, 4, Moffitt; Shrew Ad, 8, Ludlow and Smith, 1842; Shrew Ad, 10, 11, anonymous; Shrew, 4, James Lewis; Shrew, 5, anonymous.
Princeton University, Seymour Collection: K and P, 4, E. L. Davenport.
Shakespeare Centre Library: 50.30(1865), promptbook and 4 rehearsal copies of an amateur production at the home of C. E. Flower.
University of Minnesota: Z820.12/Z11, volume 12, W. S. Forrest.

The Tempest

1. David Garrick   London, Drury Lane   February 11, 1756
   Henry E. Huntington Library: Larpent 123
   [Manuscript, 6⅝ x 8⅜; gray paper under blue cardboard; title inked on cover.]
   Manuscript of Garrick's operatic version as he submitted it to the Lord Chamberlain's Office. Dialogue Prologue, songs. Garrick's note to the Examiner.

2. Anonymous   London, Covent Garden   c.1780
   New York Public Library: *NCP.709081
   [Bell edition, 1774, 4½ x 7¾; brown cloth boards; title gilt up spine.]
   Promptbook marked in a perfect round hand. Cuts and alterations: the storm deleted, in Act II original dialogue inserted to explain the storm, a song added, a song cut. Scenic indications (including "Carvers Rock"), calls, stage business, cues for effects. (Compare AW, 1; AYL, 4; MV, 3; R&J, 4.)

3. Elizabeth Farren   London, Drury Lane   October 13, 1789
   Folger: Temp, 9
   [Kemble edition, 1789, 5 x 8; some interleaves; bound with other plays in brown-green boards and half brown leather.]
   Rehearsal copy of an operatic version with Miss Farren's name on the title page; Michael Kelly entered for Ferdinand. Later (1811) belonged to William Foster of the York Theatre. The name of Mrs. Jarman written beside the Epilogue. Roles marked for lengths. Printed songs pasted on the interleaves.

4. Charles Brood   Dublin   June 23, 1818
   Folger: Temp, 16
   [Kemble edition, 1806, 5¼ x 8⅜; interleaves; gray-green marbled boards and half brown leather, broken.]
   Promptbook marked for Dublin by Brood in 1818; became promptbook no. 4 of the Theatre Royal of Manchester in 1843. Cuts, scenic indications, cues for effects.

5. William Wood   Philadelphia   October 12, 1831
   New York Public Library: *NCP.342945
   [Kemble edition, 1815, 4 x 7; some interleaves; black cloth boards; title gilt up spine.]
   Promptbook. Cast including Maywood, Mrs. Rowbotham. Scenic

indications, calls, some stage business, cues for elaborate scenic effects (especially for the storm, which is moved to the second act), timings. Belonged to William Burton, who perhaps did some of the marking. A note by George Becks that the markings follow those of the Oxberry edition of 1823, "the base of all productions in America until done in NY—Broadway by Barry & John Wright." (Becks is confused: he means Burton's production of 1854 or Barry's production in Boston in 1855—see nos. 15, 16.)

6. Henry Betty   c.1845
Folger: Temp, 6
[Pages 115-192 from volume IV of Knight's Cabinet Edition, 1843, $3\frac{1}{4}$ x $5\frac{1}{8}$; interleaves; gray boards and green cloth spine.]
Promptbook of a restored version probably derived from Macready's production of 1838 or from the edition of J. Pattie, 1839, which was printed from Macready's promptbook. Cuts on full text, scenic indications, grooves, calls, stage business, cues for effects.

7. [Betty]
Mander and Mitchenson
[Knight's National Edition, $5\frac{5}{8}$ x $8\frac{1}{2}$; interleaves; green boards and green cloth spine; Betty's name on cover.]
Carefully marked promptbook, probably taken from Macready's. Cuts on full text, scenic indications, stage business, cues for effects.

8. Samuel Phelps   London, Sadler's Wells   April 7, 1847
Folger: Temp, 13
[Pages 5-107 from volume I of a *Works*, $5\frac{3}{8}$ x $8\frac{3}{4}$; interleaves; canvas boards; title inked on cover.]
Promptbook of Phelps's restored version mainly marked by Phelps, with additions by Williams, the prompter. Cuts on full text, list of supers, detailed scenic indications, grooves, calls, copious stage business, maps and sketches, cues for elaborate effects, timings (2:45).

9. [Phelps]
Harvard Theatre Collection: Phelps Collection
[Eight booklets. Some manuscript, some printed, various sizes.]
Partbooks. One copy of the Pattie edition, 1839, is signed by H. Scharf. Caliban's part is printed and interleaved. Juno's part is 2 sheets of manuscript. Trinculo's part (4 sheets of manuscript) was Lewis Hall's in 1849. Iris' part (1 sheet of manuscript) was

Miss Huddart's in 1849. Stephano's part (5 sheets of manuscript and a music score) was Mr. Ray's in 1849, G. Fisher's in 1862. Antonio's part (3 leaves of manuscript) was Meagreson's and Perfitt's. Alonzo's part (mixture of manuscript and print) was Mr. Marston's in 1860.

10. [Phelps]
Shakespeare Centre Library: 50.31(1709)
[Pages 1-62 from volume I of Tonson edition, 1709, 5¼ x 8½; interleaves; blue marbled boards and half blue leather; title gilt on cover and red spine label.]
Excellent transcription of Phelps's promptbook made for William Creswick. At the front a note on the storm scene probably in the hand of Williams, the prompter. Creswick has copiously augmented it with provisional notes on further stage business and elaborate scenic effects. (See no. 30.)

11. [Phelps]
Shakespeare Centre Library: 50.31(1870)(1661)
[French edition, 4¼ x 7⅛; interleaves; pink publisher's wrapper pasted on boards and black cloth spine.]
Transcription of the preceding promptbook (Phelps's with Creswick's additions) prepared for Charles E. Flower of Stratford. A note on the simplification of contemporary German productions.

12. [Phelps]
Shakespeare Centre Library: 50.31(1870)(3047)
[French edition, 4⅛ x 6½; interleaves; publisher's wrapper over cardboard.]
Crude transcription of one of the preceding Phelps-Creswick promptbooks, "sent by Mr. Bernard"; made for Charles E. Flower.

13. John Moore   New York, Bowery   March 7, 1853
Folger: Temp, 7
[Cumberland edition, 3½ x 6; interleaves; stiff brown paper; title inked on cover.]
Promptbook of the unrestored (Kemble-Dryden) version probably as given at the Bowery in 1853. Grooves, calls, some stage business, maps, cues for effects.

14. James R. Anderson   London, Royal Standard   March 29, 1853
Folger: Temp, 1

[Pattie edition, 1839, $3\frac{5}{8}$ x $5\frac{5}{8}$; interleaves; brown paper; title inked on cover.]

Promptbook based on the Pattie edition, 1839, which was printed from Macready's promptbook. Sketches of 2 scenes, grooves, some stage business, tableaux, cues for effects.

15. William Burton   New York, Burton's   April 11, 1854
Folger: Temp, 12

[Pages 1-77 of a *Works*, $6\frac{5}{8}$ x $10\frac{1}{2}$; interleaves; stiff buff paper; title printed on cover label.]

Very full promptbook by John Moore, "Cut and Marked as played at various Theatres in England and America—some of the Business and suggestions for Scenic effect original." The red ink cuts give Macready's version "as played at Covent Garden Theatre 1839." The penciled cuts give William Burton's version of 1854. Detailed scenic indications, grooves, copious stage business, maps, cues for elaborate effects. A plot of properties divided by acts, a list of entr'acte music with timings, a plot of scenes as done at Burton's, 4 pages of Moore's own ideas for scenic effects, a description of costumes for the masque, a dance of "Shapes" by Mr. Frederick, a dance of "Reapers and Nymphs."

16. Thomas Barry   Boston, Boston Theatre   December 24, 1855
New York Public Library: *NCP.164548

[French's Standard Drama, $4\frac{1}{4}$ x $6\frac{3}{4}$; interleaves; black cloth boards; title gilt up spine.]

Reconstruction of the Thomas Barry–John Wright promptbook of the Boston Theatre production, made by George Becks. The edition here used was in fact printed from Wright's Boston promptbook. Becks has supplemented it with notes on spectacular scenic effects taken from John Wright's promptbook used for a New York revival on September 14, 1863, at the New Bowery (Becks confusedly refers to it as at the Broadway). Numerous details of technical operations.

17. [Barry]

Harvard Theatre Collection: uncatalogued

[Kemble edition, 1806, $5\frac{1}{4}$ x $8\frac{3}{8}$; blue cloth boards and black cloth spine; title and "5" inked on cover label.]

Lightly marked promptbook of the unrestored version, probably by Charles Melville, the English prompter, brought to Boston by

Barry in 1854. Cuts, calls, cues for effects. Not used for the Boston Theatre production.

18. [Barry]

Harvard Theatre Collection: uncatalogued

[Oxberry edition, 1823, 4⅛ x 7; bound with *Henry VIII* in brown boards and half red leather; title and "42-43" inked on cover label.]

Promptbook similar to the preceding one.

19. Charles Kean   London, Princess's   July 1, 1857

Folger: Temp, 10

[Kean edition, 1857, 5⅛ x 8¼; interleaves, 6¾ x 8¾; tan cloth boards and half brown leather; title gilt up spine, "Mr. Charles Kean/Prompt Copy" gilt on blue cover label.]

Final or souvenir promptbook made in 1859 by T. W. Edmonds, the prompter. Calls, stage business, maps, cues for elaborate effects, timings (3:20). Fine watercolor designs of 14 scenes.

20. [Kean]

Folger: Temp, 18

[Pages 138-216 of volume IV of an illustrated *Works*, 5⅜ x 8⅞; brown boards.]

Uncompleted transcription of the Kean promptbook. Many key-marks refer to interleaves, but the interleaves were never inserted. Pencilings in the hand of George Ellis, the stage manager. Cuts on full text. Brief scenic notations, grooves, cues for effects.

21. [Kean]

Folger: Temp, 11

[Shakespeare edition (Steevens text), 5¼ x 7⅜; lavender interleaves, 7 x 9; white cardboard; title and "G.E." inked on cover.]

Rehearsal workbook of George Ellis, the stage manager. Cuts on full text, much stage business, maps and sketches, cues for effects, many carpenters' warnings. Production papers: cast list, call sheet, lists of supers, carpenters, dresses, salary list for supers, copious rehearsal notes.

22. [Kean]

Folger: T.a.75

[Manuscript booklet, 5¼ x 6⅝.]

Cuebook for *Richard II* and *The Tempest* in the hand of George

Ellis, the stage manager. Cues for *The Tempest* go only to the middle of Act II. Excellent notes on spectacular effects. Drawing of the ship.

23. [Kean]

Enthoven Collection: 94G27, plates 1765-66

[Scrapbook, 15¼ x 21⅜; blue cloth boards and half blue cloth; "Kean Theatrical Scenery" gilt up spine.]

Two watercolor costume plates (about a dozen figures).

24. [Kean]

Enthoven Collection: Box DT.44

[Watercolors mounted on large display boards.]

Fine watercolor designs for 13 scenes. See also in Box DT.43 the design for a diorama of Iris and Ceres and the Temple of Eleusis.

25. [Kean]

Folger: Kean Costume Book, Prints and Engravings, 56

[Scrapbook, 10¾ x 14¼; green cloth boards and half green leather gilt.]

Contains 14 sheets of tracings for costumes, the ship, etc., and 3 sheets of notes by the Hamilton Smiths in preparation for Kean's production. At the front a large watercolor cartoon based on III, 3, "Marvellous sweet music," showing a band of monster musicians, dated December 27, 1853.

26. [Kean]

Folger: Kean Costume Book, Prints and Engravings, 182

[Scrapbook, 14⅜ x 21¼; brown cloth boards and half brown leather; "Charles Kean's Scrap Book" gilt on spine and red leather cover label.]

Contains 42 plates of watercolor designs of costumes for *The Tempest*.

27. Anonymous   Baltimore, Holliday Street   1858

Folger: Temp, 2

[Acting edition, 4¼ x 7; interleaves; black cloth boards and black leather spine.]

Transcription of the Baltimore promptbook made by George Becks. Cuts and restorations, calls, some stage business, maps, cues for elaborate effects. At the front a long folded strip called "Baltimore Plot" which gives scenic indications and grooves.

28. Anonymous   Philadelphia

   Folger: Temp, 3

   [Shakespeare edition, 4 x 6; interleaves, $4\frac{7}{8}$ x $7\frac{7}{8}$; black cloth
   boards and black leather spine.]

   Transcription of the Philadelphia promptbook made by George
   Becks. Cuts, scenic indications, calls, copious stage business, maps
   and sketches, cues for elaborate effects. Many details of this production come from the promptbook of Samuel Phelps. (See nos.
   8-12.)

29. E. L. Davenport and Frank Mayo
                New York, Grand Opera House   March 31, 1869

   Folger: Temp, 5

   [Shakespeare edition, $4\frac{1}{8}$ x $6\frac{7}{8}$; interleaves, $4\frac{7}{8}$ x $7\frac{1}{4}$; black
   cloth boards and black leather spine.]

   Transcription of the Davenport-Mayo promptbook made by
   George Becks. Cuts, scenic indications, calls, some stage business,
   maps, cues for elaborate effects, timing (3:18).

30. William Creswick   London, Crystal Palace   December 7, 1875
   Shakespeare Centre Library: O.S.P.50.31(1843)

   [Knight's Cabinet Edition, 1843, $3\frac{1}{2}$ x $5\frac{1}{2}$; green publisher's
   wrappers under tan cardboard; title inked on cover.]

   Preparation copy. Provisional notes about stage business and
   effects. (For Creswick's major book, transcribed from Phelps's, see
   no. 10.)

31. George Becks   1890's

   Folger: Temp, 4

   [Mixture of a Shakespeare edition, 4 x 7, and scraps of various
   acting editions; interleaves, $5\frac{1}{2}$ x $8\frac{3}{4}$; black cloth boards and
   leather spine; title gilt on spine.]

   Said to be the Davenport-Mayo promptbook of 1869 (see no.
   29), but George Becks made it into a composite of all the
   American productions (New York, Boston, Philadelphia, Baltimore, Chicago) which he could find records of, plus Macready's
   Covent Garden production in 1839. Cuts, detailed scenic indications, grooves, calls, much stage business, maps, cues for elaborate
   effects. Plots of scenes, properties, music. Two descriptions of
   the storm scene. A manuscript Preface, the Cumberland Preface,
   the Lacy Preface, several sheets of printed casts, printed costume

notes, an 1871 review by Dutton Cook, a clipping of the Grand Opera House playbill.

32. James Taylor   1890's
Harvard Theatre Collection: uncatalogued
[Davidson edition, $3\frac{1}{2}$ x $5\frac{5}{8}$; interleaves; black cloth boards and black leather spine; title gilt on spine.]
Excellent compilation of notes on productions at Covent Garden, in New York, Boston, Philadelphia, Chicago. Copious details of scenic arrangements, much stage business, many elaborate effects.

33. Augustin Daly   New York, Daly's   April 6, 1897
New York Public Library: 8*T*NCP+
[Daly edition, 1897, mounted in an album, $12\frac{1}{4}$ x $16\frac{3}{4}$; bound with *Much Ado* in brown cloth boards; title gilt on spine.]
Ada Rehan's souvenir album given her by Daly. Contains the Daly version, 5 photographs of Miss Rehan, and 1 old print.

34. [Daly]
Folger: Prints and Engravings
[Daly edition, 1897, mounted in pages of an album, $12\frac{1}{4}$ x $16\frac{7}{8}$; green and gold marbled boards and half brown leather gilt; title gilt on spine.]
Souvenir album with many old prints of scenes from the play and of historical persons associated with the play, many nineteenth-century playbills, magazine photographs of F. R. Benson's 1897 company, 17 watercolor costume designs for Daly's production, reviews from the *Tribune* and *Times,* a few magazine photographs of Daly's actors.

35. [Daly]
Folger: Temp, 8
[Daly edition, 1897, $5\frac{7}{8}$ x $9\frac{1}{8}$; gray publisher's wrapper.]
Rehearsal copy for Iris played by Miss Hoswell; marked for revisions of text.

36. Herbert Beerbohm Tree
            London, His Majesty's   September 14, 1904
Enthoven Collection: Tree, 175
[Memorial Theatre edition pasted in a workbook, 7 x 9; black oilcloth, worn.]

Preparation copy done in pencil. Provisional cuts, some stage business, notes on effects.

37. [Tree]

    Enthoven Collection: Tree, 175

    [Three books. Memorial Theatre edition pasted in workbooks, 7 x 9; red marbled boards and green cloth spine; title on cover labels.]

    Rehearsal promptbooks. The first, roughly penciled and partly in red ink, has cuts, calls, stage business, maps, cues for effects, cast. The second, much worn, roughly penciled with music cues in red ink, has cuts, stage business, maps, cues for effects, a sketch of the cave. The third, much used, is heavily marked for the last act only.

38. [Tree]

    Enthoven Collection: Tree, 175

    [Tree edition, 1904, pasted in a workbook, $7\frac{3}{4}$ x $9\frac{3}{4}$; gray cardboard and black cloth spine, much worn.]

    Final or souvenir promptbook of Fred Grove neatly though illiterately written in black and red ink. Good groundplans, copious stage business, cues for elaborate effects.

39. [Tree]

    Folger: Temp, 15

    [Same format as preceding book.]

    Final promptbook of Fred Grove, probably a transcription of the preceding book. Very full record of the production.

40. [Tree]

    Enthoven Collection: Tree, 175

    [Ten books. Memorial Theatre edition (2), $4\frac{5}{8}$ x $7\frac{1}{4}$; Tree edition (3), 5 x $7\frac{1}{2}$; Temple edition (4), Favourite Classics edition (1), $3\frac{3}{4}$ x 6.]

    Rehearsal copies, most of them with cuts and bits of stage business.

41. [Tree]

    Enthoven Collection: Tree, 175, 177

    [Papers.]

    Partbook for Adrian, lists of actors, dressing room assignments, cast for 1906, plots of lights, limes, properties, etc.

42. E. H. Sothern and Julia Marlowe

   Museum of the City of New York: 43.430.675

   [Prospero scenes and Leontes scenes (*Winter's Tale*) from Temple edition pasted in a workbook, 4 x 6⅛; black oilcloth.]

   Intended as a partbook for Prospero but unmarked and unused.

43. [Sothern and Marlowe]

   Museum of the City of New York: 43.430.669

   [Miranda scenes and Hermione-Perdita scenes (*Winter's Tale*) pasted in a workbook, 4 x 6⅛; black oilcloth.]

   Intended as a partbook for Miranda but unused.

44. Lena Ashwell   London   1919-29

   Birmingham, Shakespeare Memorial Library: 370/421204

   [Temple edition pasted in a workbook, 7 x 9; red marbled boards and black cloth spine; title gilt up spine.]

   Promptbook of the Lena Ashwell Players. Some stage business, cues for effects.

45. Henry Jewett   Boston, Boston Repertory   November 19, 1928

   Folger: Temp, Folio 1

   [Typescript, 8½ x 11; gray cardboard and green cloth spine.]

   Promptbook of Jewett's 4-act arrangement. Copious stage business, maps, cues for effects. Program. Souvenir postcard of the theatre.

[ACTOR LISTS FOR FOLLOWING BOOKS ARE GIVEN IN THIS ORDER: Prospero, Miranda, Caliban, Ariel.]

46. W. Bridges-Adams   Stratford-upon-Avon   July, 1930

   Shakespeare Centre Library: 71.21/1930TE

   [Favourite Classics edition pasted in a workbook, 6¾ x 9; blue cloth boards and red cloth spine, much worn; title on spine label.]

   Cast includes Wilfrid Walter, Joyce Bland, George Hayes, Miriam Adams. Costumes by Eric Maxon. Little stage business, cues for effects, crude sketches at back. The book had been used for the 1926 production.

47. [Bridges-Adams]   April 16, 1934

   Shakespeare Centre Library: 71.21/1934TE

   [Temple edition pasted in a workbook, 6⅞ x 9; purple cloth boards and half black leather; title on spine label.]

   Cast includes Neil Porter, Gwynne Whitby, Baliol Holloway,

Rachel Kempson. Designed by Aubrey Hammond and Rex Whistler. Good groundplans, stage business, cues for effects.

48. Randle Ayrton   Stratford-upon-Avon   April 26, 1935
Shakespeare Centre Library: 71.21/1935TE
[Temple edition pasted in a workbook, 7 x 9; purple cloth boards and half black leather; title on cover and spine labels.]
Cast includes Neil Porter, Gwynne Whitby, Roy Emerton, Margaret Field-Hyde. Designed by Aubrey Hammond and Rex Whistler. Considerable stage business, cues for effects.

49. B. Iden Payne   Stratford-upon-Avon   April 17, 1942
Shakespeare Centre Library: 71.21/1942TE
[Temple edition pasted in a workbook, 7 x 9; purple cloth boards and half black leather; title on spine label.]
Cast includes George Hayes, Barbara White, Baliol Holloway, Sara Jackson. Designed by Peggy Neale and J. Gower Parks. Considerable stage business, cues for effects. The book had been used for productions of 1938 and 1941.

50. Eric Crozier   Stratford-upon-Avon   April 20, 1946
Shakespeare Centre Library: O.S.71.21/1946T
[Temple edition pasted in a workbook, 7⅝ x 10; tan marbled boards and green cloth spine; title on cover and spine labels.]
Cast includes Robert Harris, Joy Parker, Julian Somers, David O'Brien. Designed by Paul Shelving. Much stage business, cues for effects. Four sheets of music.

51. Norman Wright   Stratford-upon-Avon   May 10, 1947
Shakespeare Centre Library: O.S.71.21/1947TE
[New Temple edition pasted in a workbook, 8 x 13; red cloth boards and red leather spine; title on cover and spine labels.]
Cast includes Robert Harris, Daphne Slater, John Blatchley, Joy Parker. Designed by Paul Shelving. Stage business, cues for effects. Cast list and memo sheet.

52. Michael Benthall   Stratford-upon-Avon   June 26, 1951
Shakespeare Centre Library: O.S.71.21/1951T
[New Temple edition pasted in a workbook, 8 x 12⅝; red boards and red cloth spine; title on cover and spine labels.]
Cast includes Michael Redgrave, Hazel Penwarden, Hugh Griffith,

Alan Badel. Directed by Anthony Quayle. Designed by Loudon Sainthill. Very much stage business, cues for effects.

53. [Benthall]   March 25, 1952
Shakespeare Centre Library: O.S.71.21/1952T
[New Temple edition pasted in a workbook, 8 x 13; black cloth board spring binder; title on spine label.]
Cast includes Ralph Richardson, Zena Walker, Michael Hordern, Margaret Leighton. Designed by Loudon Sainthill. Very much stage business, cues for effects.

54. Peter Brook   Stratford-upon-Avon   August 13, 1957
Shakespeare Center Library: O.S.71.21/1957T
[Two books. New Temple edition pasted in a workbook, 8 x 12¾; red cloth board spring binder; title on spine label.]
Cast includes John Gielgud, Doreen Aris, Alec Clunes, Brian Bedford. The first book has much stage business for the early scenes, cues for effects. The second, used when the production was taken to Drury Lane, has much stage business but some scenes in the middle are not marked.

55. Douglas Seale   London, Old Vic   June 9, 1959
Old Vic, Publicity Department
[Mimeograph, 8½ x 11; green ring binder.]
Revival of Dryden and Davenant's *The Tempest, or, The Enchanted Island*. Cast includes John Phillips, Natasha Parry, Joss Ackland, Jeanette Sterke, Juliet Cooke (Dorinda), Christine Finn (Hippolito). Designed by Finlay James. Stage business, maps, cues for effects. Production papers: Prologue, properties, cast, groundplans, sound effects, flys, timings.

56. William Ball   Stratford, Connecticut   June 19, 1960
Festival Theatre, Production Department
[Two books. Mimeograph, 8½ x 11; interleaves; blue cloth board ring binders.]
Cast includes Morris Carnovsky, Joyce Ebert, Earle Hyman, Clayton Corzatte. Designed by Robert Fletcher. The first book has copious stage business typed on the interleaves, cues for effects typed on text pages; production papers include music scores, curtain call, plots of properties, traps and machines, flys, banners and curtains, sound, light, costumes, wigs and beards. The second book has cues for effects, lists of properties, children, understudies.

57. Other books of *The Tempest:*
  Boston Public Library: G.4013.41, J. Dobbs.
  Folger: Temp, 14, 19, anonymous; Temp, 17, William Winter.
  University of Minnesota: Z820.12/Z11, volume 12, W. S. Forrest.

Timon of Athens

1. Joseph Ashbury   Dublin, Smock Alley   1670's
   Folger: Timon, Smock Alley
   [Pages 667-688 from a Third Folio, 1663, 8 x 12¼; maroon cloth boards and half brown leather gilt; title gilt up spine.]
   Unmarked copy, not used for production. On the last page is the cast list for *Julius Caesar,* the book of which is lost (see JC, 1).

2. John Philip Kemble
   Folger: S.b.125
   [Manuscript, 8⅛ x 10⅜; brown leather gilt, broken; title gilt on spine.]
   Manuscript adaptation of four acts only of the play, in Kemble's hand. Of Shakespeare's Dramatis Personae, Kemble kept 3 names, dropped 14, added 32. Not produced.

3. Edmund Kean   London, Drury Lane   October 28, 1816
   University of Nebraska: 822.33/X7h
   [Bell edition, 1773, 4 x 6¾; interleaves watermarked 1812, 5¼ x 8¼; maroon cloth boards; title gilt down spine.]
   Preparation copy copiously marked with cuts, alterations, restorations, and provisional scenic arrangements, some stage business, and notes on effects. Complete Kean cast. Probably not used as a promptbook. The writing, nearly all in one hand, resembles Kean's but probably is not his.

4. [Kean]
   New York Public Library: *NCP.709219
   [Chappell edition, 1816, 4⅞ x 7¾; interleaves; orange and gray marbled boards and half brown leather; title gilt down spine.]
   Interleaved but unmarked book of the version Kean used, "altered and adapted . . . by the Hon. George Lamb."

5. Samuel Phelps   London, Sadler's Wells   September 15, 1851
   Folger: Timon, 2
   [Bell edition, 1785, 5⅛ x 7⅞; interleaves watermarked 1849; brown marbled boards and brown cloth spine.]
   Promptbook marked by Phelps and Williams, the prompter, used by Phelps for several years. Casts for 1851 and 1856. List of supers for 1856. Cuts on full text. Scenic indications, grooves, calls, stage business, maps and sketches, cues for effects.

6. [Phelps]

Shakespeare Centre Library: 50.32(1805)

[Pages 1-99 from volume VII of Chalmers' *Works*, 1805, 5 x 8; interleaves; purple cloth boards; title gilt on maroon spine label.]

Transcription of Phelps's promptbook in a round neat hand. Belonged to William Creswick.

7. [Phelps]

Shakespeare Centre Library: 50.32(1815)

[Pages 129-218 from volume XI of the Tegg *Works*, 1812-15, 4¾ x 7⅞; interleaves; blue marbled boards and half brown leather; title gilt up red leather spine label.]

Another transcription of Phelps's promptbook which belonged to Creswick, occasionally differing from the preceding book in wording and productional details.

8. [Phelps]

Folger: Timon, 6

[Pages 1283-1318 from a double-column *Works* cut and pasted in a workbook, 7½ x 9¾; brown paper; title inked on cover.]

Version of Phelps's promptbook made by John Moore, who sometimes transcribes and sometimes augments the original with observations taken (by Moore?) at Sadler's Wells Theatre. Cuts are verbatim, as are many of the directions.

9. [Phelps]

Folger: Timon, 5

[Pages 1283-1318 from a double-column *Works*, 8½ x 11⅜; blue interleaves; heavy brown paper.]

Approximate transcription of the preceding promptbook, not quite so complete, made by John Moore. (Note that the same text is used but the construction of the book is different.) Inscribed "To John McCullough with best wishes of Edwin Booth 1878."

10. [Phelps]

New York Public Library: *NCP.342924

[Cumberland edition, 3½ x 5⅞; blue interleaves of American manufacture, 5⅝ x 8¼; black cloth boards; title gilt on spine.]

Very full promptbook derived from Phelps's production perhaps by way of John Moore's book. Belonged to John B. Wright and dated September, 1852.

11. [Phelps]

Folger: Timon, 4

[Pages 97-168 from a *Works*, $4\frac{1}{8}$ x $7\frac{1}{8}$; interleaves, $4\frac{7}{8}$ x 8; black cloth boards and black leather spine; title gilt up spine.]

Promptbook derived from Phelps's production, often verbatim with Phelps's promptbook. An explanatory note on one of the cuts; numerous literary or critical notes on the play. Perhaps belonged to George Becks, though not in his hand.

12. "George Frederick Cooke"   c.1854

Folger: Timon, 1

[Bell edition, 1785, 5 x $7\frac{5}{8}$; two lavender leaves at the end watermarked 1854; red marbled boards and half brown leather; title and "G. F. Cooke" gilt on spine.]

Fully developed but unused promptbook which is *not* derived from the Phelps production. Cuts, stage business, cues for effects. The last 11 lines in longhand. At the end a detailed plot of scenes with grooves. Given to Thomas Jefferson McKee by G. W. Frederickson in 1886; described in the sales catalogue (item 1454) of the McKee library, 1902. The Cooke in question may be the actor who first appeared at the Park Theatre in the spring of 1839; or the book may have been fabricated as a joke. (A transcription of this book, which belonged to George Becks, is listed at the New York Public Library but cannot be found.)

13. Frederick Warde   Lancaster, Fulton Opera House   Oct. 3, 1910

Folger: Timon, 3

[Shakespeare edition pasted in a workbook, $7\frac{3}{4}$ x $9\frac{7}{8}$; limp red leather.]

Promptbook of a version "abridged, transposed, and with interpolations of dialogue, incidents & business." Much stage business, maps, cues for effects. Typed program note, list of doubles, plot of scenes, typed transcript of Sadler's Wells playbill of 1851, review of Charleston, S.C., performance in October, 1911.

[ACTOR LISTS FOR FOLLOWING BOOKS ARE GIVEN IN THIS ORDER: Timon, Apemantus.]

14. W. Bridges-Adams   Stratford-upon-Avon   April 23, 1928

Shakespeare Centre Library: 71.21/1928T, TI

[Two books. Favourite Classics edition pasted in a workbook,

$6\frac{7}{8}$ x $8\frac{7}{8}$; blue marbled boards and half red cloth; title on cover and spine labels. Temple edition pasted in a workbook, 7 x 9; blue cloth boards and half black leather; title on spine label.]
Cast includes Wilfrid Walter, George Hayes. Cues for effects. The second book is a copy of the first.

15. Michael Benthall   London, Old Vic   September 5, 1956
Old Vic, Publicity Department
[New Temple edition pasted in a workbook, 8 x $10\frac{1}{2}$; black ring binder.]
Cast includes Ralph Richardson, Dudley Jones. Designed by Leslie Hurry. Cuts, much stage business, maps, cues for effects. Production papers: cast lists, properties plot, time sheets.

16. Other books of *Timon of Athens:*
Library Company of Philadelphia: Oe2+.11605.D, William Warren.
Shakespeare Centre Library: O.S.P.50.32(1803), F. Haywel, rehearsal book.

Titus Andronicus

[ACTOR LISTS FOR FOLLOWING BOOKS ARE GIVEN IN THIS ORDER: Titus, Aaron, Tamora.]

1. Peter Brook   Stratford-upon-Avon   August 16, 1955

   Shakespeare Centre Library: O.S.71.21/1955TI, 1957 Tour

   [Two books. New Temple edition pasted in a workbook, 8 x 13; green cloth board spring binder; title inked on spine.]

   Cast includes Laurence Olivier, Anthony Quayle, Maxine Audley. Copious stage business, maps, cues for effects. Second book, fully developed, used for Continental tour in 1957.

2. Walter Hudd   London, Old Vic   April 23, 1957

   Old Vic, Publicity Department

   [New Temple edition pasted in a workbook, 8 x 10½, with *Comedy of Errors;* black ring binder; title on cover and spine labels.]

   Cast includes Derek Godfrey, Keith Michell, Barbara Jefford. Designed by Paul Mayo. Much cut version. Stage business, cues for effects. Many production papers including properties and groundplans.

Troilus and Cressida

1. John Philip Kemble
   Folger: Troil, 1
   [Shakespeare edition, 5¼ x 8½; brown leather gilt, broken; title and "Revised by Kemble" gilt on spine.]
   Preparation copy marked by Kemble but not produced. Penciled cast. Heavy cuts and alterations. Some scenic indications.

2. R. J.   1810
   Folger: S.a.81
   [Manuscript, 7¼ x 9; red and blue marbled boards and brown leather spine.]
   Manuscript version "altered from Shakespeare and Dryden," dated December 5, 1810. Not used.

3. William Poel
          London, King's Hall, Covent Garden   December 10, 1912
   Enthoven Collection (Poel Collection)
   [Two books. Cassell edition, 1889, 3½ x 5½; blue cloth boards; title gilt up spine.]
   Lightly marked promptbooks. Cuts on full text. Names of some of the actors. Little stage business, few cues for effects.

4. The Players   New York, Moss's Broadway   June 6, 1932
   The Players: PB.39A
   [Three books. Typescript, 8½ x 11; green paper.]
   Promptbook of The Players' Eleventh Annual Classical Revival. Stage business, cues for effects.

5. [The Players]
   The Players: PB.39B
   [Forty-five booklets. Typescript, 8½ x 7¼; green paper.]
   Partbooks for 24 characters, mostly in duplicate.

[ACTOR LISTS FOR FOLLOWING BOOKS ARE GIVEN IN THIS ORDER: Pandarus, Troilus, Cressida.]

6. B. Iden Payne   Stratford-upon-Avon   April 24, 1936
   Shakespeare Centre Library: 71.21/1936TR
   [New Temple edition pasted in a workbook, 7¼ x 9; purple cloth boards and half black leather; title on cover and spine labels.]
   Cast includes Randle Ayrton, Donald Eccles, Pamela Brown.

Designed by Barbara Heseltine. Much stage business, maps, cues for effects.

7. Anthony Quayle   Stratford-upon-Avon   July 2, 1948
   Shakespeare Centre Library: O.S.71.21/1948T
   [New Temple edition pasted in a workbook, 8 x 11⅞; green boards and red cloth spine; title on spine label.]
   Cast includes Noel Willman, Paul Scofield, Heather Stannard. Designed by Motley. Much stage business, maps, cues for effects.

8. Glen Byam Shaw   Stratford-upon-Avon   July 13, 1954
   Shakespeare Centre Library: O.S.71.21/1954T
   [New Temple edition pasted in a workbook, 8 x 13; blue cloth board spring binder; title on spine label.]
   Cast includes Anthony Quayle, Laurence Harvey, Muriel Pavlow. Designed by Malcolm Pride. Stage business, maps, cues for effects. Production papers: scene plots, 19 maps on mimeographed groundplans.

9. Tyrone Guthrie   London, Old Vic   April 3, 1956
   Old Vic, Publicity Department
   [Temple edition pasted in a workbook, 8 x 10½; black ring binder.]
   Cast includes Paul Rogers, John Neville, Rosemary Harris. Designed by Frederick Crooke. Calls, some stage business, maps, cues for effects. Production papers: properties, flys, etc.

10. Jack Landau   Stratford, Connecticut   July 23, 1961
    Festival Theatre, Production Department
    [Mimeograph, 8½ x 11; black board ring binder.]
    Cast includes Hiram Sherman, Ted van Griethuysen, Carrie Nye. Designed by Robert O'Hearn and Motley. This book, signed by J. Bronson, is not marked.

Twelfth Night

1. Anonymous   1600's
   Folger: TN, Second Folio
   [Pages 255-275 from a Second Folio, 1632, 8⅝ x 12½; reddish marbled boards and half red leather gilt.]
   Seventeenth-century promptbook of unknown provenience. Cuts, calls, entrance symbols (horizontal line with vertical slashes), cues for effects.

2. Joseph Ashbury   Dublin, Smock Alley   1670's
   Folger: TN, Smock Alley
   [Pages 255-275 from a Third Folio, 1663, 8 x 12¼; red marbled boards and half brown leather gilt; title gilt up spine.]
   Promptbook. Cuts, scenic indications, calls, cues for effects. (See G. Blakemore Evans, *Shakespearean Prompt-Books*.)

3. Anonymous   Douai   1694
   Bibliothèque de Douai: MS.7.87
   [Manuscript, folios 1-31 of a volume, 6¾ x 8⅝; parchment.]
   Manuscript version used for amateur staging at Douai. Cuts and alterations, some stage business, cues for music. Dated June 13, 1694. (See G. Blakemore Evans, *Philological Quarterly*, XLI, 158-172.)

4. Anonymous   c.1790
   Library Company of Philadelphia: OEngShak.Log2063.0.2
   [J. Rivington edition, 1771(?), 3⅞ x 6½.]
   Promptbook of the late eighteenth century, the marginal notes badly cropped. Cuts, calls, some properties, cues for effects.

5. John Philip Kemble London, Covent Garden January 5, 1811
   Garrick Club
   [Kemble edition, 1810, 5 x 8¼; interleaves; blue cloth boards and brown leather spine; title gilt up spine.]
   Promptbook marked by Kemble. List of "Persons represented" (but not the cast), property lists, stage business, maps.

6. [Kemble]   January 7, 1818
   Folger: TN, 16
   [Kemble edition, 1810, 5 x 8¼; interleaves; brown leather; title gilt on red leather spine label, "TR/CG/P.B./T./12" stamped on spine.]

Promptbook originally marked by Kemble with additions by later hands. Characters listed with lengths for some of them (and someone has added the actors for 1818), calls, some properties, stage business, names of supers, maps, cues for effects, timings (2:45). Later belonged to Walter Lacy, "Professor of Elocution," with dates and addresses for 1877, 1881, 1884; and to Henry Irving.

7. Charles Kemble   London, Covent Garden   November 8, 1820
   Folger: TN, 17
   [Kemble edition, 1811, 5 x 8¼; interleaves watermarked 1818; brown marbled boards and brown leather spine; title and "TR/ CG/MB/T/12" gilt on spine.]
   Promptbook of Frederic Reynolds' operatic version. Much of the dialogue rewritten, a masque of Juno and Ceres and 8 songs inserted. Partial cast, some roles marked for lengths. Some grooves, calls, little stage business. Belonged to G. Martin.

8. William Farren   London, Covent Garden   November 8, 1820
   Folger: S.a.27
   [Manuscript watermarked 1818, 6⅛ x 7½; red marbled boards and half blue leather gilt; title gilt up spine.]
   Farren's 16-page partbook for Malvolio. Some stage business.

9. Jane Shirreff   London, Covent Garden   October 10, 1833
   Enthoven Collection
   [Acting edition, 4⅛ x 6¾; interleaves; white cardboard; title inked on cover.]
   Rehearsal copy of the operatic version checked for Viola. Cuts. Several songs added.

10. Elizabeth Vestris   London, Covent Garden   May 8, 1840
    Harvard Theatre Collection: TS.2678.50
    [Acting edition, 3¾ x 6, with Introduction from another acting edition; interleaves, 4½ x 7¼; tan paper under gray pamphlet boards and blue cloth spine.]
    Promptbook signed and dated by John Moore in 1840. Covent Garden cast. Traditional drinking songs given in full. Scenic indications, grooves, calls, much stage business, maps and sketches, cues for effects, timings. Much augmented with stage business, etc., from William Burton's production of March 29, 1852 (see

no. 17). Sketches of the garden scene are related to photographs of the Daly production of 1893. (See nos. 34-42.)

11. Samuel Phelps   London, Sadler's Wells   January 26, 1848
    Folger: TN, 20
    [Oxberry edition, 1821, $4\frac{1}{4}$ x 7; interleaves watermarked 1847; heavy brown paper and brown leather spine, unsewn; title inked on cover.]
    Promptbook marked by Phelps and Williams, the prompter. Many restorations; order of the opening scenes (reversed by Kemble) corrected. Scenic indications, grooves for first act, calls, some stage business, maps, cues for effects. Signature of Charles K. Elliston.

12. Anonymous   1850's
    New York Public Library: *NCP.342987
    [Modern Standard Drama, $4\frac{1}{4}$ x $7\frac{1}{2}$; blue interleaves; green and black marbled boards and black cloth spine; title inked on spine.]
    Lightly marked promptbook. Calls, cues for effects, timings (2:30).

13. Eliza M. A. Hamblin   c.1850
    Harvard Theatre Collection: uncatalogued
    [Cumberland edition, $3\frac{1}{2}$ x $5\frac{3}{4}$; interleaves, 4 x $6\frac{1}{4}$; green cloth boards; title gilt up spine.]
    Promptbook checked for Olivia, marked by J. B. Addis, the prompter. Grooves, calls, considerable stage business, maps, sketches, cues for effects.

14. Charles Kean   London, Princess's   September 28, 1850
    Folger: TN, 14
    [Kemble edition, 1811, $5\frac{1}{4}$ x $8\frac{1}{2}$; interleaves, $6\frac{3}{4}$ x $8\frac{1}{2}$; tan cloth boards and half brown leather; title gilt up spine, "Mr. Charles Kean/Prompt Copy" gilt on blue leather cover label.]
    Final or souvenir promptbook made in 1859 by T. W. Edmonds, the prompter. At the front a list of property manuscripts and chart of timings (2:20). Grooves, calls, some stage business, maps, cues for effects.

15. [Kean]
    Folger: TN, 25
    [Allison edition, New York, 1883, $4\frac{1}{4}$ x 6; green publisher's wrappers.]

"C Kean's bus." Promptbook record in the hand of Edwin Booth, who transcribed the cuts and markings he found in a promptbook "Cut & marked (in Cumberland) for Mr. Chas Kean by T. W. Edmonds, Prompter Royal Princess' Theatre 1857." The notations differ somewhat from those in the preceding book. Cuts on full text, grooves, calls, cues for effects, timings.

16. John B. Wright   Boston   1851
New York Public Library: *NCP.342953
[Modern Standard Drama, 4½ x 7⅝; gray interleaves; black and green marbled boards and black cloth spine.]
Roughly written promptbook. Some restorations, addition of traditional drinking songs. Rough sketch of garden scene. Some grooves, calls, stage business, cues for effects.

17. William E. Burton   New York, Burton's   March 29, 1852
Folger: TN, 5
[Modern Standard Drama, 4½ x 7½; interleaves; heavy brown paper and purple paper spine; title on cover and on spine label.]
Promptbook in the hand of John Moore. Traditional drinking songs inserted. At the front a list of property manuscripts and costume note for Viola-Sebastian. Grooves, calls, stage business, maps, cues for effects. (See no. 10.)

18. [Burton]
Folger: TN, 19
[Pages 249-328 from volume I of a *Works*, 6⅝ x 10½, with fragments of other editions inserted; interleaves, 6⅞ x 10⅞; heavy tan paper; title inked on cover.]
Very full promptbook written by John Moore, based mainly on the Burton production, with penciled cuts and additions from Adelaide Neilson's in 1878 (see no. 26). Order of opening scenes much altered. Texts of three drinking songs. Costume note. At the front plots of scenes with grooves, properties, Miss Neilson's order of scenes. Calls, copious stage business, maps, cues for effects. Enclosures: partbooks for Sir Andrew, "Roberto," Friar; property manuscript of Sir Andrew's challenge; fight routine; playbills for Covent Garden in 1840, Burton's in 1857, 1858, 1859; reviews of Robson and Crane in 1881, of Modjeska in 1882.

19. Thomas Barry   Boston, Boston Theatre   c.1854
Harvard Theatre Collection: uncatalogued

[Oxberry edition, 1821, 4⅛ x 6⅞; bound with *Measure for Measure* in brown boards and half brown leather; titles and "37-38" inked on cover labels.]

Promptbook marked by Charles Melville, the English prompter, and brought to Boston by Thomas Barry in 1854. Grooves, calls, cues for effects.

20. J. B. Buckstone   London, Haymarket   July 2, 1856
Folger: TN, 4
[Kemble edition, 1815, 4⅛ x 6⅞; interleaves; brown paper; title inked on cover.]
Promptbook made by George Hastings, the copyist. Cast for above date. Cuts, list of property manuscripts, grooves, calls, stage business, maps and sketches, cues for effects, timings (2:16). (See no. 24.)

21. [Buckstone]
Folger: TN, 6
[Kemble edition, 1815, 4⅛ x 6¾.]
W. H. Chippendale's rehearsal copy for Malvolio.

22. W. H. Sedley Smith   Boston   1859
Princeton University, Seymour Collection: TN, 2
[Oxberry edition, 1823, 3¾ x 5⅞; stiff cloth; title inked on cover.]
Rough but systematic promptbook. Cast for 1859 with Mrs. Barrow as Viola. Scenic indications, grooves, some stage business, maps, cues for effects, timings (2:15).

23. Mr. and Mrs. F. B. Conway
          Brooklyn, Academy of Music   April 23, 1864
New York Public Library: *NCP.285350
[Music-Publishing Company issue of Cumberland edition, 3½ x 5½; interleaves; red cloth boards; title gilt on spine.]
Promptbook of George Becks dated 1864. Some scenic indications, grooves, copious stage business especially for Malvolio and the comics, maps, cues for effects.

24. J. B. Buckstone   London, Haymarket   1867
Folger: TN, 3
[Lacy edition, 4 x 6⅞; interleaves; limp blue cloth boards; title gilt on cover.]
Neatly written promptbook often verbatim from Buckstone's

1856 book, notations underlined in red ink. Slight cuts and restorations. Grooves, calls, stage business, maps, cues for effects. Cue
for "Song introduced by Miss Robertson." (See no. 20.)

25. Augustin Daly   New York, Fifth Avenue   October 4, 1869
Folger: TN, 9
[French's Standard Drama, 4 x 7½; interleaves, 5⅞ x 7⅝; heavy
buff paper; title and Daly's name inked on cover.]
Promptbook of an early Daly production, much used (probably
also used as a preparation book for later productions), marked
by John Moore and others. Scenes reordered to accommodate
scenery. Restorations, some scenic indications, some stage business, maps, cues for effects. At the front call-lists. (See nos. 10,
34-42.)

26. Adelaide Neilson   London, Haymarket   February 2, 1878
Folger: TN, 18
[French issue of Lacy edition, 4⅛ x 7⅛; interleaves; stiff gray
paper and blue cloth spine; title printed on cover label.]
Promptbook as "arranged by Miss Neilson 2/78." At the front a
plot of scenes with grooves, 2 good groundplans, 2 ink-wash
drawings of "Garden Set" and "Staircase Set," list of supers. Play
begins with "Wreck Tableau," and scenes are reordered to accommodate scenery. Cuts and alterations, addition of traditional
drinking songs, calls, much stage business, maps, cues for effects,
timings.

27. William Seymour   1880
Princeton University, Seymour Collection: TN, 5
[Modern Standard Drama, 4⅜ x 7½; interleaves, 5 x 8; paper
wrapper; title pasted on cover.]
Carefully written promptbook signed by James Seymour and
William Seymour. The additional drinking songs added. Scenic
indications, grooves, considerable stage business, maps, cues for
effects.

28. Henry Irving   London, Lyceum   July 8, 1884
Folger: TN, 13
[Pages 351-450 from volume III of a *Works*, 4 x 6⅜; interleaves;
limp brown leather gilt; title gilt on spine and cover.]
Rehearsal copy. Cuts on full text. Partial cast, costume notes.
Malvolio lines marked for stresses, pauses, key words. Many de-
tails of stage business. Pencil sketch of garden scene.

29. [Irving]

Folger: TN, 15

[Irving edition, 1884, 5¼ x 8¼; red leather gilt; title gilt up spine.]

Preparation copy. Cuts, revision of scenery list, notes on music, some pencilings around Malvolio passages.

30. Julia Marlowe   New York, Star   December 17, 1887

Museum of the City of New York: 43.430.670

[Rolfe edition, 5 x 6⅞, tipped between leaves of a workbook, 6 x 8⅝; black cloth boards.]

Preparation copy made by Miss Marlowe probably before her association with Sothern. Stage business keyed to the text with numerals entered on interleaves. Opening scenes in Shakespearean order. (See nos. 58-70.)

31. George Becks   1890's

New York Public Library: *NCP.343034

[Music-Publishing Company issue of Cumberland edition, 3½ x 5½; interleaves; blue cloth boards; title gilt on spine.]

Promptbook record compiled by George Becks: "This is general version & as followed by Neilson—who ended it with a 'Measure' —followed by steps of the dance." Much stage business verbatim with Becks's Conway book of 1864 (see no. 23). At the back Miss Neilson's dance routine. (See no. 26.)

32. [Becks]

New York Public Library: *NCP.342990

[French's Standard Drama, 4½ x 7½; interleaves, 5 x 8; black and green boards and black cloth spine.]

Very full promptbook record compiled by George Becks, mostly drawn from tradition but partly original and provisional. Restorations, reordering of scenes to accommodate scenery, scenic indications, grooves, copious stage business especially for the low comics, maps and sketches, cues for effects. (See nos. 37, 38.)

33. [Becks]

New York Public Library: *NCP.172942

[Alden edition, 4 x 7; black and white boards.]

Rough preparation copy. Cuts on full text. Random notes on stage business, etc.

34. Augustin Daly   New York, Daly's   February 21, 1893
    Folger: TN, 29

    [Daly edition, 1893, 6⅞ x 11; interleaves; red cloth boards and
    half red leather gilt; title gilt on spine, Daly's name gilt on red
    leather cover label.]

    Handsomely developed promptbook given to Ada Rehan by Wil-
    liam Winter in 1903. According to a printed notation, it con-
    tains the text and stage business as arranged by Daly and John
    Moore. Many songs added, including the traditional drinking
    songs. Prison scene penciled out. Stage business, very carefully
    drawn maps, curtain calls, final dance, etc. Note from Ada Rehan
    to William Winter. Note of David Belasco commenting on the
    arrangement. (See nos. 10, 18, 25.)

35. [Daly]
    Folger: TN, 10

    [Daly edition, 1893, 5⅞ x 9½; interleaves; blue cloth boards.]
    William Winter's copy in which he penciled most of the essential
    matter from the preceding book. Comments on omission of prison
    scene. Note from Daly to Winter about Shakespeare repertory.

36. [Daly]
    Folger: TN, 11

    [Daly edition, 1893, 5⅝ x 8¾; interleaves; blue cloth boards;
    title gilt on cover.]

    Rehearsal copy checked for Fabian. Belonged to William Winter.
    A London review of April 19, 1894, celebrating Daly's hundredth
    performance. Notes on Daly and Rehan. Letter from Daly to
    Winter in 1892 paying for prefaces, praising Rehan, etc.

37. [Daly]
    New York Public Library: *NCP.342955

    [French issue of Lacy edition, 4 x 7½; interleaves, 4⅞ x 7⅞;
    black and green boards and black cloth spine.]

    George Becks's book, said on the flyleaf to be a record of Daly's
    production but if so a very incomplete one. Some stage business,
    etc.

38. [Daly]
    New York Public Library: *NCP.346534

    [Alden edition, 4 x 7; interleaves, 8 x 10; black and green boards.]
    George Becks's book, in the main a record of Daly's production

but with notes on others. Cuts on full text. Scenic indications, grooves, copious stage business, maps, cues for effects. Notes on opening scene at the sea; on omission of the mad scene; on Modjeska's practice of showing Malvolio imprisoned under the porch of the house; of Owen's, Compton's, Irving's way with Malvolio in prison. Publicity notices of Buckstone, Marie Wainwright. List of music from a Marlowe bill of 1887.

39. [Daly]

New York Public Library: 8-*NCP.42217B

[Various editions cut and rearranged and pasted in a workbook, 6½ x 8; red cloth boards; title gilt on spine.]

Fine souvenir promptbook of Daly's production made by William H. Young. At the front the cast for 1895-96; at the back a synopsis of scenes. Scenic indications, excellent sketches, stage business given briefly.

40. [Daly]

Folger: TN, 21

[French's Standard Drama pasted in a workbook, 5⅜ x 8½; black cloth boards and half black leather gilt; title gilt on cover.]

Ada Rehan's touring promptbook, made by William H. Young. Text much rearranged, scenic indications, stage business, maps, sketches (good drawing of the garden scene), cues for effects. Clipping of playbill of March 17, 1896.

41. [Daly]

New York Public Library: 8*T-*NCP+.686473

[Daly edition, 1893, mounted in an album, 12¼ x 16⅞; green, red, and blue marbled boards and half black leather gilt; title gilt on spine.]

Ada Rehan's souvenir album given her by Daly. The acting version, many old prints, some contemporary prints, playbills, 2 watercolor costume designs, reviews, a great many photographs of Miss Rehan and of the production.

42. [Daly]

Folger: Prints and Engravings

[Daly edition, 1893, mounted in albums (2 volumes), 12¼ x 16⅞; green and gold marbled boards and half brown leather gilt; old-spelling title gilt on spines.]

Souvenir album in 2 volumes containing the acting version. The first volume contains colored portraits of Ada Rehan, many old prints of past actors, scenes from the play, prints of old theatres, a Daly bill for 1893, 29 photographs of actors and 7 photographs of scenes from Daly's production, 13 plates (30 figures) of water-color costume designs. The second volume contains many old prints and bills, photographs of many modern actors associated with the play, several reviews of Daly's production, 11 photographs and 17 watercolors of Daly's production.

43. William Poel   London, Middle Temple   February 12, 1897
Enthoven Collection (Poel Collection)
[Cassell's National Library edition, 3¾ x 5⅝; tipped to stubs between leaves of a workbook, 5½ x 8½; blue cloth boards and half brown leather; title on cover label.]
Rough promptbook. Cuts on full text. Cast, calls, little stage business, maps.

44. F. R. Benson   London, Lyceum   March 22, 1900
Shakespeare Centre Library: 72.935BEN
[Favourite Classics edition pasted in a workbook, 8 x 10; blue boards; title on spine label.]
Rough promptbook, much used. Plots of properties, cast, supers. Stage business, cues for effects.

45. John T. Laphore   1901
New York Public Library: *NCP.47x1117
[French's Standard Drama, 4½ x 6⅞; interleaves; black cloth boards; title gilt up spine.]
Promptbook inscribed "Lelia Whiteside, which it is her book. . . . Through the Kindness of her friend John T. Laphore who has staged the play many hundreds of times." At the front plots of scenes and grooves, properties. Printed stage business underlined. Random notes, maps, cues for effects.

46. Herbert Beerbohm Tree   London, Her Majesty's   Feb. 5, 1901
Enthoven Collection: Tree, 138
[Temple edition pasted in a workbook, 7 x 9; red marbled boards and green cloth spine.]
Preparation book. Cuts through 4 acts (some suggested by Mr. Taber) but not the fifth. Much stage business as far as the letter scene.

47. [Tree]
Enthoven Collection: Tree, 138

[Temple edition pasted in a workbook, 6½ x 8⅛; red marbled boards and black cloth spine; title on cover label.]

Completed promptbook, done in red ink and pencil. Cast penciled in. New final song for Feste. Copious stage business (some of it typewritten and pasted in), maps, cues for effects.

48. [Tree]

Enthoven Collection: Tree, 138

[Temple edition pasted in a workbook, 6¼ x 7¾; white boards and green cloth spine; title on cover label.]

Completed and much used promptbook, signed by H. W. Varna, February, 1901, done in red ink with penciled additions. New final song for Feste. Printed cast. Copious stage business, maps, sketches, cues for effects.

49. [Tree]

Enthoven Collection: Tree, 138

[Two books. Favourite Classics edition, 1904, 3⅝ x 6; green cloth boards; title gilt up spine.]

Rehearsal copies for Sir Andrew and Orsino.

50. [Tree]

Folger: TN, 24

[Cassell's National Library edition, 1902, 3¾ x 5½.]

Rehearsal copy for Maria. Cuts, several bits of stage business.

51. [Tree]

Enthoven Collection: Tree, 136, 138

[Papers.]

Printed plots for properties, electrics, limes. Partbooks for Sir Toby and Valentine. Copies of new song for the last act, cast lists, dressing room assignments, etc.

52. [Tree]

Enthoven Collection: Tree, 144

[Notebook, 4⅝ x 7; black leather.]

Call-lists, etc., for American tour.

53. Fred Grove   London

Folger: TN, 12

[Shakespeare edition, 3¾ x 5¾; interleaves; green cloth boards; title gilt on red spine label.]

Rich accumulation of stage business especially for Sir Toby and the low comics.

54. Viola Allen   New York, Knickerbocker   February 8, 1904
   Folger: TN, 1
   [Shakespeare edition, 4⅛ x 6; paper.]
   Preparation copy. Cuts.

55. [Allen]
   Harvard Theatre Collection: uncatalogued
   [Shakespeare edition pasted in a workbook, 7⅜ x 9¼; black cloth boards and half red leather; in box of gray cloth boards and black leather spine; title gilt up spine.]
   Fine promptbook made by Frank Andrews, the stage manager. In an enclosed note he explains that Miss Allen studied prompt-books of Irving, Tree, and Daly, and mainly followed Irving in making up her version. He claims credit for arranging one of the street scenes. At the front a list of songs, a photograph of Miss Allen and James Young as the twins, notes on doubling, elaborate plots of scenes, properties, lights, music. Much stage business, maps, cues for effects, final pantomime. Penciled notations of later vintage.

56. [Allen]
   Folger: TN, 28
   [Typescript, 8 x 10½; black cloth boards and half red leather gilt.]
   Promptbook. Scenes reordered to accommodate scenery. Detailed scenic indications, excellent groundplans, much stage business, maps, cues for effects.

57. [Allen]
   New York Public Library: *NCP.349744B
   [Carbon typescript, 8 x 10½; brown cloth boards; title gilt on spine.]
   Unused copy of the acting version. Stage directions underlined in red. At the back a property plot nearly 5 feet long.

58. E. H. Sothern and Julia Marlowe
       New York, Knickerbocker   November 13, 1905
   Folger: TN, 36
   [Shakespeare edition pasted in a workbook, 8 x 10½; black cloth board and half red leather ring binder.]

Promptbook made up by Francis T. S. Powell, the stage manager, with the assistance of Frederick Kaufman. Lines marked for stresses by Miss Marlowe. At the front, 25 pages of plots of lights, properties. Very detailed stage business, maps and groundplans. "The text, arrangement of scenes, business of the actors and music cues are exactly as used in the presentation of the play." (See no. 30.)

59. [Sothern and Marlowe]
Folger: TN, 31, 32
[Two books. Typescript, 8¼ x 10¾; black cloth boards and half black leather.]
Promptbooks developed under the stage managership of Frederick Kaufman. At the front, plots of lights, properties, music. Groundplans very carefully drawn. Copious stage business, maps.

60. [Sothern and Marlowe]
Folger: TN, 33, 34
[Two books. Original and carbon typescript, 8½ x 11; brown paper.]
Fresh typing of the preceding book.

61. [Sothern and Marlowe]
The Players: TS.115
[Carbon typescript, 8½ x 11; brown paper.]
Probably a copy of the preceding book.

62. [Sothern and Marlowe]
New York Public Library: *NCP.51x304
[Carbon typescript, 8½ x 11; brown cloth boards; title gilt up spine.]
Probably a copy of the preceding book.

63. [Sothern and Marlowe]
New York Public Library: *NCP.276556B
[Carbon typescript, 8¼ x 11; red cloth boards; title gilt on spine.]
Another typing of the preceding book, much used in stage management by V. H. Collins. Many crudely penciled maps, notes on properties, etc.

64. [Sothern and Marlowe]
Museum of the City of New York: 43.430.671

[Carbon typescript, 8¼ x 10⅝; black cloth boards and half black leather.]

Promptbook of Mr. Tilden, used in stage management. Ground-plans and sketches showing position and focus of lighting instruments. Much stage business, maps, cues for effects, timings for several cities. Two "written letters."

65. [Sothern and Marlowe]

Princeton University, Seymour Collection

[Typescript in black and red, 8½ x 11; brown paper.]

Unused copy said to be a duplicate from the Museum of the City of New York.

66. [Sothern and Marlowe]

Folger: T.a.81, 82

[Notebook, 6⅝ x 8⅛; brown and red marbled boards and black cloth spine.]

"Sothern & Marlowe Co Elect Dept" by M. E. McGarry. Light plots for 5 Shakespeare productions, including 8 plots (sketches) for *Twelfth Night:* instruments, colors, maps, cues. With it a typed light plot mounted on cardboard for use at the controls.

67. [Sothern and Marlowe]

Joint University Libraries, Nashville

[Temple edition, 1904, 4 x 5⅛; red leather, worn; title gilt on spine.]

Promptbook record of the production made by Lark Taylor, the actor, on his own rehearsal copy. Cuts and rearrangements on full text, 5 groundplans, scenic indications, some stage business, cues for effects. Notes on the roles he played (Fabian, Toby, under-study Malvolio), a note on Kate Phillips, who played Maria in London, some rough costume sketches, autographs of the players.

68. [Sothern and Marlowe]

Folger: TN, 23

[Shakespeare edition pasted in a workbook, 6¾ x 8¼; green and white boards and cloth spine; title on cover label.]

Promptbook record of the production made by Lark Taylor. Cuts and additions (traditional drinking songs). Copious stage business, maps. Critical notes.

69. [Sothern and Marlowe]

W. A. Clark Library, Los Angeles

[Acting edition, 4¾ x 7⅛; interleaves; brown cloth boards; title gilt on spine.]

Souvenir promptbook made by Lark Taylor. Cast of 1906. Copious stage business, groundplans, cues for 'effects underlined as printed.

70. [Sothern and Marlowe]

Joint University Libraries, Nashville

[Sheets from a Shakespeare text pasted in a workbook, 4 x 6½; black imitation leather; circular insignia "JLT" pasted on cover; inscribed at the back "Mary Lee Taylor—Pat Mills—St. Louis— Cook Book."]

Arrangement of the play made by Lark Taylor for public reading. Some account of the Sothern and Marlowe production, some scenic indications, bridge passages.

71. Winthrop Ames   Boston, Castle Square   January 7, 1907

New York Public Library: 8*NCP+.42216B

[Temple edition cut and pasted in a workbook, 8¾ x 13; red cloth boards; title gilt up spine.]

Preparation copy. Cuts marked from French edition in brown, from Daly in blue, from Marlowe in red. Scenic notes, stage business, many maps. (See no. 78.)

72. [Ames]

New York Public Library: *NCP+.42214B

[Typescript, 7¾ x 13¾; green cloth boards; title inked on spine.]

Heavily marked and much used production book. Cast, lists of extras, synopsis of scenes, copious stage business, cues for effects. At the back, plots of lights, music, properties, costumes. Notes on text and interpretation taken from standard critics. Production notes derived especially from Irving and Sothern.

73. [Ames]

New York Public Library: *NCP+.42218B

[Typescripts, 7¾ x 6½; blue cloth boards; title gilt on spine.]

Eighteen partbooks and plots for lights, properties, costumes. Two different casts have used these.

74. Ernest B. Lawford

    Cambridge, Harvard University   June 3, 1908

Library of Congress, Batchelder Collection: 425

[French's Standard Drama, 4¾ x 7¼; lavender and green paper.]

Some notes made by Lawford in 1929 of his Malvolio business when playing with Maude Adams.

75. Margaret Anglin   Melbourne   October 28, 1908
New York Public Library: 8-*NCP.54x218

[Partial edition pasted in a workbook, 5⅞ x 9⅜; black cloth boards; title gilt up spine.]

Preparation copy. At the front, plots for properties, lights, music. Detailed stage business for 5 scattered scenes. At the back, 7 groundplans for *As You Like It*.

76. [Anglin]
New York Public Library: 8-*NCP.54x218

[Shakespeare edition cut and pasted in a workbook, 7¼ x 9½; black cloth boards; title gilt on spine.]

Preparation copy. Copious stage business, rough maps, cues for effects. At the front a plot of properties 3 feet long.

77. [Anglin]
New York Public Library: 8-*NCP.54x218

[Rolfe edition pasted in a workbook, 7¼ x 9½; black cloth boards; title gilt on spine.]

Fully developed promptbook. Cuts on full text. Contents much the same as in the preceding book but carefully organized and entered.

78. Winthrop Ames   New York, New Theatre   January 26, 1910
New York Public Library: *NCP+.42215B

[Typescript, 8½ x 13; green cloth boards; title inked on spine.]
Unused first copy of the final version of Ames's New York production. (See nos. 71-73.)

79. Miss A. E. F. Horniman Manchester, Gaiety December 23, 1911
British Drama League

[Temple edition, 1894, 4½ x 7; blue cloth boards; title gilt up spine.]

Rehearsal copy for Viola. Cuts on full text, names of actors, random stage business.

80. Harley Granville-Barker   London, Savoy   November 15, 1912
University of Michigan, Shakespeare Collection

[Favourite Classics edition, 1904, tipped between sheets of a workbook, 9⅞ x 12; red cloth boards; title gilt up spine.]

Full production book. Copious stage business, excellent maps and groundplans, cues for effects. At the front a program, plots of scenes, cloths, full sets, electrics, properties, and 10 large photographs of the sets. At the back the vocal music as published by French, and scores for incidental music. (This book or any part of it cannot be copied without the written permission of Mr. C. B. Purdom, 39 Woodland Rise, Welwyn Garden City, Hertfordshire, England.)

81. Henry Jewett   Boston, Boston Opera House   March 10, 1915
Folger: TN, 30
[Typescript, 8 x 10½; gray cardboard and green cloth spine.]
Much used promptbook. Scenes reordered to accommodate scenery. Scenic indications, much stage business, cues for effects.

82. Albert Lang   c.1920
Princeton University, Seymour Collection
[Acting edition pasted in a workbook, 7⅜ x 9⅜; red marbled boards and half black cloth; title pasted on cover.]
Excellent promptbook of an itinerant producer from 651 Sixth Avenue, New York. Groundplans, much stage business, many maps, cues for effects. Plots of properties, lights, and curtains, and music scores for several songs including "Under the Greenwood Tree" and "Full Fathom Five."

83. Lena Ashwell   Bath   1922
Birmingham, Shakespeare Memorial Library: 370/421205
[Cassell's National Library edition pasted in a workbook, 7 x 9; green marbled boards and black cloth spine; title gilt up spine.]
Promptbook of the Lena Ashwell Players. Cues for effects. At the back, a groundplan and 6 penciled sketches.

[ACTOR LISTS FOR FOLLOWING BOOKS ARE GIVEN IN THIS ORDER: Viola, Malvolio, Sir Toby.]

84. Isabel Jeans   London, Everyman   December 23, 1922
New York Public Library: *NCP.283817B
[Shakespeare edition pasted in a workbook, 8 x 10¼; black cloth boards; title gilt up spine.]
Cast includes Mary Barton, Herbert Waring, Frank Cellier. Miss Jeans played Olivia. Cuts on full text. Cast list. Copious stage business, maps and sketches, cues for effects.

85. Eva LeGallienne   New York, Civic Repertory   Dec. 21, 1926
Museum of the City of New York: 39.500.763
[Temple edition pasted in a workbook, 8½ x 11; black cloth board ring binder.]
Cast includes Eva LeGallienne, Sayre Crawley, Egon Brecher. Calls, little stage business, cues for effects.

86. Jane Cowl   New York, Maxine Elliott   October 15, 1930
New York Public Library: *NCP+.53x146
[Typescript, 8 x 11; brown cloth boards; title gilt up spine.]
Cast includes Jane Cowl, Leon Quartermaine, Walter Kingsford. Directed by Andrew Leigh. Designed by Raymond Sovey. The version said to be that of Granville-Barker, 1912 (see no. 80). Stage business, maps, cues for effects. Belonged to John Sola.

87. W. Bridges-Adams   Stratford-upon-Avon   April 25, 1932
Shakespeare Centre Library: 71.21/1932
[Temple edition pasted in a workbook, 8 x 10; blue cloth boards gilt; title on cover label.]
Cast includes Fabia Drake, Randle Ayrton, Roy Byford. Designed by George Sheringham. Traditional drinking songs. Stage business, cues for effects. The book had been used in 1929, 1930, and for American tours.

88. [Bridges-Adams]   April 17, 1934
Shakespeare Centre Library: 71.21/1934TW
[Temple edition pasted in a workbook, 7⅛ x 9; purple cloth boards and half black leather; title on cover and spine labels.]
Cast includes Dorothy Black, Baliol Holloway, Roy Byford. Designed by George Sheringham. Traditional drinking song. Much stage business, cues for effects.

89. Maude Adams   Ogunquit   July 16, 1934
Museum of the City of New York: 48.367.135
[Typescript, 8½ x 11; orange paper.]
Cast includes Marie Adels, Frederick Roland, C. Norman Hammond. Miss Adams played Maria. Rough and incomplete copy of a much altered version. Scores for songs.

90. F. Owen Chambers   Leamington Spa   1937
Shakespeare Centre Library: 72.935CHA

[Temple edition pasted in a workbook, 7½ x 9½; black cloth boards and half red cloth; title on cover and spine labels.]

Carefully made promptbook. Much stage business, good ground-plans.

91. Columbia Broadcasting System   August 30, 1937

    Folger: TN, Folio 1

[Mimeograph, 8½ x 11; decorated green paper folder; title on cover.]

Radio adaptation by Brewster Morgan. Cast includes Tallulah Bankhead, Cedric Hardwicke, Mark Smith. Unmarked.

92. Irene Hentschel   Stratford-upon-Avon   April 13, 1939

    Shakespeare Centre Library: 71.21/1939TW

[New Temple edition pasted in a workbook, 7 x 9; purple cloth boards and half black leather; title on cover and spine labels.]

Cast includes Joyce Bland, John Laurie, Jay Laurier. Designed by Motley. Traditional drinking song. Much stage business, groundplan. Letter from Alec Clunes explaining the fight routine.

93. Milton Rosmer   Stratford-upon-Avon   April 17, 1943

    Shakespeare Centre Library: 71.21/1943T

[Temple edition pasted in a workbook, 6¼ x 7¾; green boards and red leather spine; title on cover and spine labels.]

Cast includes Patricia Jessel, Abraham Sofaer, Geoffrey Wincott. Much stage business, some cues for effects.

94. Robert Atkins   Stratford-upon-Avon   April 6, 1945

    Shakespeare Centre Library: 71.21/1945T

[New Temple edition pasted in a workbook, 7⅛ x 9; purple cloth boards and half black leather; title on cover and spine labels.]

Cast includes Claire Luce, David Read, Robert Atkins. Designed by Danae Gaylen. Much stage business, cues for effects. The book had been used for B. Iden Payne's 1938 production, was erased and reused. Traditional drinking song included, probably for the earlier production.

95. Walter Hudd   Stratford-upon-Avon   April 23, 1947

    Shakespeare Centre Library: O.S.71.21/1947TW

[King's Treasuries of Literature edition pasted in a workbook, 8 x 12⅞; red cloth boards; title inked on spine.]

Cast includes Beatrix Lehman, Walter Hudd, John Blatchley.

Designed by Riette Sturge Moore. Begins with "Shadow Play." Much stage business, good groundplans, cues for effects.

96. John Gielgud   Stratford-upon-Avon   April 12, 1955

Shakespeare Centre Library: O.S.71.21/1955TW

[New Temple edition pasted in a workbook, 8 x 13; red cloth boards; title inked up spine.]

Cast includes Vivien Leigh, Laurence Olivier, Alan Webb. Designed by Malcolm Pride. Very much stage business, cues for effects.

97. Tyrone Guthrie   Stratford, Ontario   July 2, 1957

Festival Theatre, Library

[Two books. New Stratford Shakespeare pasted in workbooks, 8 x 12¾; black cloth boards and red cloth spine; title pasted on cover.]

Cast includes Siobhan McKenna, Douglas Rain, Douglas Campbell. Designed by Tanya Moiseiwitsch. The first book has much stage business, maps, cues for effects, timings, list of singers. The second has calls, cues for effects.

98. Peter Hall   Stratford-upon-Avon   April 22, 1958

Shakespeare Centre Library: O.S.71.21/1958T

[New Temple edition pasted in a workbook, 8 x 13; blue cloth board spring binder; title on spine label.]

Cast includes Dorothy Tutin, Mark Dignam, Patrick Wymark. Designed by Lila de Nobili. Very much stage business, 18 maps on mimeographed groundplans, cues for effects. Production papers. Book also used for Russian tour in 1958-59.

99. [Hall]   May 17, 1960

Shakespeare Centre Library: O.S. 71.21/1960THE

[Cambridge Pocket Shakespeare pasted in a workbook, 8 x 13; blue cloth board spring binder; title inked on spine.]

Revival of the 1958 production. Cast includes Dorothy Tutin, Eric Porter, Patrick Wymark. Designed by Lila de Nobili. Very much stage business newly recorded, cues for effects.

100. Jack Landau   Stratford, Connecticut   June 8, 1960

Festival Theatre, Production Department

[Two books. Mimeograph, 8½ x 11; interleaves; blue cloth board ring binders.]

Cast includes Katharine Hepburn, Richard Waring, Loring Smith. Designed by Rouben Ter-Arutunian. Both books have copious stage business typed on interleaves, maps, cues typed on text pages. Production papers include calls, mimeographed groundplans, understudy list, plots of properties, costumes, wigs.

101. Peter Hall   London, Aldwych   December 19, 1960
Shakespeare Centre Library: O.S.71.21/1960-61 Aldwych
[Same format as preceding Hall book but red binder.]
Revival of the preceding Hall production with some cast changes. Cues for effects. Production papers.

102. Other books of *Twelfth Night:*
Folger: TN, 2, W. L. Ayling; TN, 7, Ernest Clarke; TN, 8, Henrietta Crosman; TN, 22, Ogden Stevens; TN, 26, 27, 35, anonymous.
Historical and Philosophical Society of Ohio: 812.3/R283/203, Alvin Read.
Museum of the City of New York: 32.485.397A, J. H. Ring, Tremont, 1838.
New York Public Library: *NCP+.172667B, anonymous typescript.
Shakespeare Centre Library: 50.35(1879), C. E. Flower.

The Two Gentlemen of Verona

1. William Charles Macready

   London, Drury Lane   December 29, 1841

   Folger: Two Gent, 11

   [Pages 179-259 from volume I of an eighteenth-century *Works*, 4⅝ x 7⅝; interleaves; gray marbled boards and half brown leather; title stamped on spine.]

   Final or souvenir promptbook made for Macready by George Ellis, the prompter. Cuts on full text. Printed description of Drury Lane scenery. Grooves, calls, some stage business, maps, cues for effects, timings (2:06). At the front a note about the command performance for the King of Prussia on January 31, 1842.

2. [Macready]

   Folger: Two Gent, 12

   [Pages 1-80 (incomplete) from volume III of a *Works* (Steevens text), 5⅜ x 8⅝; gray interleaves, 7¼ x 9½; gray wrapper, unsewn.]

   Incomplete penciled copy of the preceding book. The stage business, though developed for Act I only, is given in greater detail, apparently in preparation for the following book.

3. Charles Kean   New York, Park   October 6, 1846

   Folger: Two Gent, 10

   [Pages 89-171 from volume I of a *Works*, 4¾ x 7⅝; interleaves, 6¼ x 8½; red, yellow, and blue marbled boards and half black leather gilt; title gilt on spine, "Charles Kean" gilt on black cover label.]

   Promptbook made for Charles Kean by George Ellis from Macready's book and dated December 31, 1845. Through Act I verbatim with the preceding book. Cuts, scenic indications, grooves, calls, stage business, maps, cues for effects. At the front 8 brown ink-wash drawings (6¾ x 5) of the scenes.

4. Henry Betty   c.1857

   Folger: Two Gent, 4

   [Pages 11-79 from volume I of Knight's Cabinet Edition, 3¼ x 5⅛; interleaves; gray boards and green cloth spine; title penciled on cover.]

   Lightly marked promptbook. Cuts, some grooves, calls, some stage business, cues for effects.

5. Samuel Phelps   London, Sadler's Wells   February 18, 1857

Folger: Two Gent, 13

[Pages 87-161 from volume I of a *Works*, 4⅜ x 7⅜; few inter-leaves; tan paper; title, etc., inked on cover.]

Lightly marked promptbook mainly in Phelps's hand. Cast, cuts, some grooves, calls, some stage business, cues for effects.

6. Owen Stanley Fawcett   1864-91

Folger: Two Gent, 6, 7, 8, 9

[Four books. Modern Standard Drama, 4½ x 7⅝; Cumberland, 3½ x 5¾; Modern Standard Drama, 4⅜ x 7; Oxberry, 4⅞ x 8½.]

The first is a rehearsal copy for Speed: cuts, addition of a passage for Launce, a plot of scenes, casts for Baltimore, April 23, 1864, and Washington, June, 1864. The second is dated October 13 and 14, 1879, from Ypsilanti and St. Louis; the third June 12, 1864, from Baltimore; the fourth December 5, 1891, from Oswes-try.

7. George Becks   1890's

Folger: Two Gent, 1

[Modern Standard Drama, 4⅝ x 7¼; interleaves; black cloth boards and black leather spine; title gilt up spine.]

An old promptbook augmented by Becks. Addition of the traditional (Kemble) scene for Launce, grooves, calls, some stage business, maps, cues for effects, score for a song called "Light o' Love" "recovered from a MS. by Sir John Hawkins." Becks's notes criticize the Kean (MSD) version, refer to Kemble's, and are generally provisional in tone.

8. [Becks]

Folger: Two Gent, 2

[Shakespeare edition pasted in a workbook, 5½ x 8¾; black cloth boards and black leather spine; title gilt up spine.]

Promptbook record or preparation copy more fully developed than the preceding book. Many references to the Kean and Kemble versions. Considerable stage business, cues for effects.

9. [Becks]

Folger: Two Gent, 3

[Cumberland edition, 3½ x 5⅝; interleaves; brown cloth boards and black leather spine; title gilt up spine.]

Promptbook. "This book was probably Peter Richings'." Calls,

cues for effects. Numerous textual notes probably entered by
Becks.

10. James Taylor

   Harvard Theatre Collection: uncatalogued

   [Pages 3-72 from volume I of *Comedies,* 6¼ x 9½; bound with
   Timon of Athens in marbled boards and black leather spine; title
   gilt on spine.]

   Partial transcription of an old promptbook, completed only into
   the third act. Cuts on full text, some scenic indications, grooves,
   stage business, cues for effects.

11. Augustin Daly   New York, Daly's   February 25, 1895

   Folger: Two Gent, 5

   [Double-column Shakespeare edition cut and pasted in a workbook, 7½ x 12⅜; red cloth boards and half red leather gilt; title
   gilt on spine, Daly's name gilt on cover label.]

   Uncompleted preparation copy. Cuts. Cast.

12. [Daly]

   New York Public Library: 8*T-*NCP+.686474

   [Daly edition, 1895, 5½ x 8⅝, mounted in an album, 12¼ x 16¾;
   blue, red, and green marbled boards and half red leather gilt;
   title gilt on spine.]

   Ada Rehan's souvenir album with the acting version, 2 large
   photographs of Miss Rehan, and 41 other photographs of actors
   in the play.

13. [Daly]

   Folger: Prints and Engravings

   [Daly edition mounted in an album, 12¼ x 16¾; red and green
   marbled boards and half brown leather gilt; title gilt on spine.]

   Souvenir album with the acting version, a large photograph of
   Ada Rehan, many old prints of actors, several old playbills, reviews of Daly's production, 46 photographs of the actors in the
   play.

14. William Poel London, Merchant Taylor's Hall Nov. 28, 1896

   Enthoven Collection (Poel Collection)

   [Cassell's National Library edition, 3⅝ x 5⅝, tipped to stubs
   between the leaves of a workbook, 4⅜ x 7; black imitation
   leather.]

Promptbook. Cuts on full text. Cast, some properties, maps, dressing room assignments.

[ACTOR LISTS FOR FOLLOWING BOOKS ARE GIVEN IN THIS ORDER: Valentine, Proteus, Julia, Sylvia, Launce.]

15. W. Bridges-Adams   Stratford-upon-Avon   April 15, 1925
Shakespeare Centre Library: 71.21/1925T
[Favourite Classics edition pasted in a workbook, 6¾ x 8⅞; blue marbled boards and blue cloth spine; title on cover and spine labels.]
Cast includes James Dale, Maurice Colbourne, Florence Saunders, Ruth Taylor, Randle Ayrton. Designed by Tom Heslewood. Little stage business, cues for effects.

16. B. Iden Payne   Stratford-upon-Avon   April 19, 1938
Shakespeare Centre Library: 71.21/1938TW
[Two books. Eversley edition pasted in a workbook, 7 x 9; purple cloth boards and black leather spine; title on cover and spine labels.]
Cast includes Gyles Isham, Francis James, Valerie Tudor, Peggy Livesay, Jay Laurier. Designed by J. Gower Parks. Some stage business, cues for effects. The second book is an unused transcription of the first.

17. Michael Langham   London, Old Vic   January 22, 1957
Old Vic, Publicity Department
[New Temple edition pasted in a workbook, 8 x 10½; black ring binder; title on cover and spine labels.]
Cast includes Richard Gale, Keith Michell, Barbara Jefford, Robert Helpmann. Designed by Tanya Moiseiwitsch. Cuts, calls, stage business, maps, cues for effects. Production papers: groundplans, properties, flys, time sheets, cast, etc.

18. [Langham]   London, Ontario   February 14, 1958
Festival Theatre, Library
[Two books. Penguin edition pasted in workbooks, 8 x 12¾; black cloth boards and half red cloth; title pasted on cover.]
Cast includes Eric House, Lloyd Bochner, Ann Morrish, Diana Maddox, Bruno Gerussi. Designed by Tanya Moiseiwitsch. The first book has copious stage business, cues for effects. The second has cues for effects and inserted cue sheets.

19. Peter Hall   Stratford-upon-Avon   April 5, 1960

    Shakespeare Centre Library: O.S.71.21/1960TWO

    [Cambridge Pocket Shakespeare pasted in a workbook, 8 x 13; red cloth board spring binder; title on spine label.]

    Cast includes Denholm Elliott, Derek Godfrey, Frances Cuka, Susan Maryott, Patrick Wymark. Designed by Renzo Mongiardino and Lila de Nobili. Much stage business, cues for effects. Production papers: cast, understudies, music cues. At the end an Elizabethan jig, "Singing Simpkin," which was not produced.

20. Other books of *The Two Gentlemen of Verona:*

    Brown University: Eng. P.17a, Asa Cushman.

    Essex Institute, Salem: 822.08/S24/29, John B. Adams, Boston Museum.

    Folger: Two Gent, 14, anonymous.

    Shakespeare Centre Library: 50.36(188–), Charles E. Flower.

The Winter's Tale

1. Anonymous   c.1640

   Biblioteca Universitaria, Padova

   [Pages 277-303 in an unbroken First Folio, 8½ x 12⅞; brown leather, newly bound.]

   Promptbook. Cuts, calls, one act warning, one music cue. (See G. Blakemore Evans, *Shakespearean Prompt-Books*.)

2. Joseph Ashbury   Dublin, Smock Alley   1670's

   Folger: Wint T, Smock Alley

   [Pages 277-303 from a Third Folio, 1663, 8 x 12½; maroon cloth boards and half brown leather gilt; title gilt up spine.]

   Preparation copy. Cuts in 3 acts and part of the fourth.

3. John Philip Kemble   London, Covent Garden   Nov. 11, 1807

   Garrick Club

   [Kemble edition, 1802, 4½ x 7⅜; interleaves; blue cloth boards and brown leather spine; title gilt up spine.]

   Promptbook marked by Kemble, checked for Leontes. Grooves, calls, some stage business, maps, cues for effects. A few later pencilings.

4. [Kemble]   November 28, 1811

   Garrick Club

   [Kemble edition, 1811, 5⅛ x 8¼; interleaves; blue cloth boards and brown leather spine; title gilt up spine.]

   Promptbook marked by Kemble, considerably more developed than the preceding book. List of supers including 84 figures. Some scenic indications. Grooves and sometimes the "cuts" in the grooves: "1 G. 2C." Calls, some stage business, careful maps, property lists, cues for effects.

5. [Kemble]   1811-37

   Shakespeare Centre Library: 50.37(1811)

   [Kemble edition, 1811, 5 x 8¼; interleaves; brown leather; title gilt on red leather spine label, "TR/CG/PB/W/14" stamped on spine.]

   Promptbook originally marked by Kemble with the matter of the preceding book (second Garrick Club book) plus timings (3:45). Later markings in pencil include cuts, a cast of December, 1827, timings of January 3, 1828 (2:40), May 22, 1837 (3:04), May 29, 1837 (3:02), etc. The 1837 markings appear to be by

John Willmott, the prompter, and mention Macready and some of his supporting actors. Belonged to William Creswick.

6. William Warren   Philadelphia

Library Company of Philadelphia: Oe2+.11606.D

[Inchbald edition, 4 x 6½; marbled boards and brown leather spine.]

Partbook for Antigonus. Cuts.

7. William B. Wood   Philadelphia   1813

Folger: Wint T, 22

[Barber edition, 1794, 4 x 6⅝; green and gray marbled boards and brown leather spine.]

Preparation copy. A few entrance marks and a cut.

8. James R. Anderson   London, Covent Garden   Sept. 30, 1837

Folger: Wint T, 2

[Inchbald edition, 3⅞ x 6½; brown paper.]

Anderson's partbook for Florizel and (understudy) Leontes, dated October 2, 1837. Some grooves, some stage business, rough maps.

9. William Charles Macready
            London, Covent Garden   September 30, 1837

Toronto Public Library: Taverner Collection

[Small cards and scraps of paper in a manila envelope.]

Spectator's notes on Macready's acting of Leontes, by J. W. Taverner, the elocutionist.

10. Samuel Phelps   London, Sadler's Wells   November 19, 1845

Folger: Wint T, 14

[Cumberland edition, 3¾ x 6; interleaves, 3⅞ x 6⅜; heavy gray paper.]

Promptbook dated for 12 seasons between 1845 and 1862, marked by Phelps and by Williams, the prompter. At the front 2 lists of supers (20 to 22 figures) and a list of property manuscripts; at the back a dance for 8 couples. Calls, grooves, some stage business, maps and sketches, cues for effects, timing (3:00).

11. Barry Sullivan   c.1852

Shakespeare Centre Library: 50.37(1797)

[Pages 459-565 from volume II of the Robinson *Works*, 1797, 6⅞ x 9½; interleaves; brown marbled boards and half brown leather; title gilt on black leather spine label, Sullivan's name as of the Haymarket gilt on cover label.]

Promptbook derived from the Oxberry acting edition, apparently marked by George Hastings. Probably not used. Cuts on full text. Calls, stage business, maps and sketches, cues for effects. Part of a set gathered by Sullivan when at the Haymarket in 1852.

12. John B. Wright   1852

Folger: Wint T, 19

[Pages 263-358 from a *Works,* 4¼ x 7.]

Lightly marked preparation copy, dated September, 1852. Cuts, some scenic indications and grooves, some stage business, cues for effects.

13. [Wright]

Folger: Wint T, 17

[Cumberland edition, 3¾ x 5⅞; interleaves; purple cloth boards and half red leather; title gilt up spine.]

Promptbook which Wright got "from Mrs. Archbold, Boston, 1853." George Becks notes in it that its stage directions are incorporated in the version Wright prepared for Spencer's Boston Theatre. Cuts and restorations, scenic indications, grooves, calls, stage business, maps and sketches, cues for effects.

14. John Moore   New York, Burton's   February 13, 1856

Folger: Wint T, 13

[Inchbald edition, 3¾ x 6⅛; interleaves; green marbled boards and half brown leather; "C/137" gilt on spine.]

Promptbook neatly marked by an earlier owner, with many additions by Moore. At the front a list of property manuscripts. Cuts and restorations, scenic indications, some grooves, calls, stage business, maps and sketches, cues for effects. Playbills for the above date.

15. [Moore]

Folger: Wint T, 11

[Pages 7-108 from volume III of a *Works,* 6¾ x 10¾; interleaves; brown paper; playbill clipping pasted on cover.]

Very full, much used promptbook done in various inks and pencil. Contains all the matter of the preceding book. Cast lists for Covent Garden in 1839, Marylebone in 1847, Chambers Street in

1851 and 1856. Cuts on full text. Scenic indications, grooves, calls, much stage business, maps, cues for effects. Extra matter includes a partbook for Old Shepherd; 2 systems of scenes and grooves; 5 sheets of calls and maps; an "Allegory of Four Seasons" for the Act IV chorus; a news account of Mary Anderson's opening at the Lyceum in 1887; a playbill for Burton's; a plan for a descent of Jupiter on a Republican eagle with an American flag in his hand and reference to "manifest destiny."

16. [Moore]

Folger: Wint T, 12

[Workbook, 6¾ x 10½; brown paper.]

Stage manager's working papers, etc., to accompany the preceding book. Very detailed lists of properties, scenery, costumes. A playbill, an advertising leaflet, and about 20 reviews of Burton's production. Reviews of Kean's London production; of Lawrence Barrett's 1871 production. A non-Shakespearean partbook.

17. [Moore]

Folger: T.b.2

[Notebook, 6⅛ x 10¼; blue boards and black cloth spine.]

Cues for the band for 48 plays including *Winter's Tale*.

18. Charles Kean   London, Princess's   April 28, 1856

Folger: Wint T, 7

[Pages 333-393 from volume II of a double-column illustrated *Works*, 6¾ x 9⅞; brown paper.]

Preparation copy on which George Ellis, the stage manager, noted that the cuts were made by J. W. Cole and the production notes by himself. Cole's marks include comments on earlier versions, especially Kemble's. Ellis corrected the cuts and restorations, and entered groove numbers and notes on effects.

19. [Kean]

Folger: Wint T, 10

[Shakespeare edition (Steevens text), 6 x 9¼; lavender interleaves watermarked 1855, 7⅞ x 9⅝; white cardboard.]

Workbook of George Ellis, the stage manager, done in pencil. Cuts on full text. List of 112 supers. Scenic indications, very much stage business, maps, notes on effects.

20. [Kean]

Enthoven Collection

[Bulmer Shakespeare Press edition, 8¾ x 12⅛; gray interleaves; gray cardboard spine, covers lost.]

Original promptbook marked in pencil but mostly redone in ink in the hand of T. W. Edmonds, the prompter; a few pencilings by George Ellis. Cuts on full text, copious stage business, maps, cues for effects, timings (3:12 to 3:30). Belonged to Mary Anderson, Sir Barry Jackson.

21. [Kean]

Folger: Wint T, 8

[Kean edition, 1856, 5⅛ x 8⅛; interleaves, 6¾ x 9; tan cloth boards and half brown leather; title gilt on spine, "Mr. Charles Kean/Prompt Copy" gilt on blue cover label.]

Final or souvenir promptbook made by T. W. Edmonds in 1859. Calls, much stage business, cues for effects, timings (3:30). Fine watercolor designs of 16 scenes.

22. [Kean]

Folger: Kean Costume Book, Prints and Engravings, 182

[Scrapbook, 14⅜ x 21¼; brown cloth boards and half brown leather; "Charles Kean's Scrap Book" gilt on spine and red leather cover label.]

Contains color prints of 6 scenes of the play, with figures, published by Joseph, Myers & Co.

23. [Kean]

Enthoven Collection: 94G27, plate 1768

[Scrapbook, 15¼ x 21⅜; blue cloth boards and half dark blue cloth; "Kean Theatrical Scenery" gilt up spine.]

Watercolor of the cave scene.

24. [Kean]

Enthoven Collection: Box DT.43

[Watercolors mounted on large display boards.]

Fine watercolor designs of 19 scenes and 11 plates of properties.

25. Anonymous   Boston, Boston Museum   1858

Princeton University, Seymour Collection: WT, 2

[Spencer's Boston Theatre, 4½ x 7½; interleaves; coarse cloth; title, date, and "Boston Museum" inked on cover.]

Lightly marked promptbook. Cuts, some stage business, maps, cues for effects.

26. Henry Jarrett   1875
   Princeton University, Seymour Collection: WT, 3
   [Spencer's Boston Theatre, 4½ x 7½; interleaves, 6 x 7¾; paper
   wrappers.]
   Promptbook. Scenic indications, grooves, calls, stage business,
   good maps and groundplans, cues for effects.

27. Charles Dillon   London, Drury Lane   September 28, 1878
   Folger: Wint T, 24
   [Kean edition, 1856, 5⅛ x 8⅛; publisher's wrappers.]
   Spectator's notes on the Dillon production. Playbill.

28. Mary Anderson   London, Lyceum   September 10, 1887
   Folger: Wint T, 3
   [Anderson edition, 1887, 5⅛ x 8⅛; interleaves; red marbled
   boards and half maroon leather; title gilt up spine.]
   Final or souvenir promptbook made by Napier Lothian, the stage
   manager. Cuts, copious stage business, maps, some cues for effects.
   Lists of supers, groundplan for opening, sketches of wreath designs, Shepherds' dance, stage dimensions of Lyceum, dimensions
   of scenic pieces, timings (2:08).

29. George Becks   1890's
   Folger: Wint T, 4
   [Spencer's Boston Theatre, 4⅜ x 7; interleaves; black and white
   boards and black leather spine; title gilt up spine.]
   Compilation of traditional stage business and effects by George
   Becks, using the edition prepared by John B. Wright (see no. 13).
   Becks augmented it "with additions from Wallack and Macready
   in red." Restorations, calls, much stage business, maps and
   sketches, cues for effects.

30. Charles B. Hanford   c.1900
   Folger: Wint T, 6, 5
   [Two books. Pocket Shakespeare edition pasted in a workbook,
   7½ x 9½; gray cloth boards and red cloth corners.]
   Promptbooks of a version in 6 acts. Detailed scenic indications,
   grooves, copious stage business, cues for spectacular effects, timings (2:15). Book no. 5, nearly identical to no. 6 but unused, contains pictures of Hanford and Marie Drofnah as Leontes
   and Hermione, and an envelope of fabric samples.

31. Frederick Warde　　　　　New York, Broadway　　　　　1904

Folger: Wint T, 22

[French's Standard Drama, 4⅜ x 7½; brown paper.]

Rehearsal copy for Leontes used by Warde in the touring production of Wagenhals and Kemper. Cuts and alterations, some stage business for Leontes. At the front the cast and synopsis of scenes clipped from a playbill.

32. Viola Allen　　New York, Knickerbocker　　December 26, 1904

New York Public Library:　8-*NCP.330694B

[Allen edition, 1905, 5 x 8⅜; interleaves; red cloth boards; title gilt on spine.]

Fine promptbook marked in the same hand as Miss Allen's *Cymbeline* (see CYM, 28). At the front plots of properties, hand properties, lights, music. Careful groundplans of all scenes, copious stage business, cues for effects, timings (2:50). At the back a detailed dance routine.

33. [Allen]

Folger: Wint T, 1

[Allen edition, 1905, 5½ x 8⅞; brown publisher's wrappers; title printed in white ink on cover.]

The acting version much cut and rearranged. Contains 4 photographs of Miss Allen as Hermione and Perdita. Program for June 3, 1905.

34. Herbert Beerbohm Tree

　　　　　　　　London, His Majesty's　　　September 1, 1906

Enthoven Collection:　Tree, 187

[Two books. Favourite Classics edition pasted in a workbook, 7 x 9; red marbled boards and red cloth spine; title on cover label. Second copy has purple cloth spine.]

Rehearsal promptbooks initialed by Cecil King. The first book has some stage business, cues for effects, timings. The second has few markings.

35. [Tree]

Enthoven Collection:　Tree, 187

[Favourite Classics edition pasted in a workbook, 7 x 9; red marbled boards and purple cloth spine.]

Final promptbook carefully done in black and red inks. Excellent groundplans for all scenes with names of scenic artists, other notes.

Copious stage business, cues for effects, timings. Cast and plots for electrics, limes, props are all at the front.

36. [Tree]

Enthoven Collection: Tree, 187

[Sixteen books and 15 booklets. Favourite Classics edition (13), green cloth boards; Stage Shakespeare (1), red cloth boards; Cassell's National Library (2), red cloth boards; typescripts, 8 x 7, in black paper covers.]

Rehearsal copies variously cut and marked with stage business. Fifteen typed partbooks.

37. [Tree]

Enthoven Collection: Tree, 192

[Photographs.]

Large photographs of the 10 sets.

38. [Tree]

Enthoven Collection: Tree, 187, 188

[Papers.]

Production papers: lists of characters, understudies, dressing room assignments; plots for limes, electrics, properties; Shepherds' dance; program.

39. Ellen Terry   London, His Majesty's   September 1, 1906
Smallhythe

[Temple edition, 1894, 3⅞ x 5; maroon limp leather; title gilt up spine.]

Rehearsal copy, cut and checked for Hermione. Little stage business.

40. E. H. Sothern and Julia Marlowe

Museum of the City of New York: 43.430.675

[Leontes scenes from Temple edition pasted in a workbook with Prospero scenes, 4 x 6⅛; black oilcloth.]

Partbook for Leontes, penciled for stresses and some stage business.

41. [Sothern and Marlowe]

Museum of the City of New York: 43.430.669

[Hermione and Perdita scenes from Temple edition pasted with Miranda scenes in a workbook, 4 x 6⅛; black oilcloth.]

Partbook for Hermione and Perdita. Few markings.

42. Winthrop Ames   New York, New Theatre   March 28, 1910

New York Public Library: *NCP+.42607B

[Temple edition pasted in a workbook, 8¼ x 11; red cloth boards; title gilt on spine.]

Preparation of the acting version by John Corbin. Comments by Ames. Typescript Introduction explains production style.

43. [Ames]

New York Public Library: *NCP+.42605B

[Carbon typescript, 8 x 13; blue cloth boards; title gilt on spine.]

Production book. Cuts on the typed text. Critical and interpretive notes from standard authorities. Dramatis Personae, time analysis of the action, character distribution chart, notes on sources, timing estimates, critical notes on various acting versions, productions, actors of the past.

44. [Ames]

New York Public Library: *NCP+.42606B

[Three books. Typescript and 2 carbons, 7½ x 11; bound together in blue cloth boards; title gilt up spine.]

Lightly marked copies of the acting version. Some stage business.

45. Lena Ashwell   London   1919-29

Birmingham, Shakespeare Memorial Library: 370/421206

[Temple edition pasted in a workbook, 7 x 9; tan marbled boards and black cloth spine; title gilt up spine.]

Promptbook of the Lena Ashwell Players. Groundplans, cues for effects.

46. Henry Jewett   Boston, Boston Repertory   1929

Folger: Wint T, 9

[Typescript, 8½ x 11; gray cardboard and green cloth spine.]

Much used promptbook. One typed and 2 penciled casts, costume plot, essay on the play. Calls, much stage business typed in red with additions typed and penciled, maps, cues for effects.

[ACTOR LISTS FOR FOLLOWING BOOKS ARE GIVEN IN THIS ORDER: Leontes, Hermione, Perdita.]

47. Frank Woolfe   Stratford-upon-Avon   July 11, 1932

Shakespeare Centre Library: 71.21/1932W

[Temple edition pasted in a workbook, 7⅜ x 9¼; black oilcloth; title on cover and spine labels.]

Cast includes Wilfrid Walter, Dorothy Massingham, Hilda Cox-head. Costumes designed by Eric Maxon. Stage business, maps, cues for effects. Formerly used for 1931 production.

48. B. Iden Payne   Stratford-upon-Avon   April 23, 1937
Shakespeare Centre Library: 71.21/1937W
[Eversley edition pasted in a workbook, 7 x 9; purple cloth boards and half black leather; title on cover and spine labels.]
Cast includes Baliol Holloway, Joyce Bland, Valerie Tudor. De-signed by Molly McArthur. Stage business, maps, cues for effects.

49. Dorothy Green   Stratford-upon-Avon   May 4, 1943
Shakespeare Centre Library: 71.21/1943W
[Eversley edition pasted in a workbook, 6¼ x 8; red boards and red cloth spine; title on cover and spine labels.]
Cast includes Abraham Sofaer, Anna Konstam, Christine Adrian. Designed by Charles Reading and Barbara Curtis. Some stage business, maps, cues for effects.

50. B. Iden Payne   New York, Cort   January 15, 1946
New York Public Library: *NCP.347022B, 57x10
[Two books. Typescript, 7¾ x 11; one in red cloth boards, one in black; titles gilt up spine.]
The version produced by Theatre Guild, Inc. Cast includes Henry Daniell, Jessie Royce Landis, Geraldine Strook. Designed by Stewart Chaney. At the front a synopsis of scenes and note on music; at the back a light plot and inventory of electrical equip-ment. Some stage business, cues for effects.

51. Anthony Quayle   Stratford-upon-Avon   June 4, 1948
Shakespeare Centre Library: O.S.71.21/1948W
[Shakespeare edition pasted in a workbook, 8 x 11⅞; green boards and red cloth spine; title on spine label.]
Cast includes Esmond Knight, Diana Wynyard, Claire Bloom. De-signed by Motley. Some stage business, maps, cues for effects. Pro-duction papers: cast, music score and cues, light plot, timings, etc.

52. Michael Benthall   London, Old Vic   November 1, 1955
Old Vic, Publicity Department
[New Temple edition pasted in a workbook, 8 x 10½; black ring binder; title on spine label.]

Cast includes Paul Rogers, Wendy Hiller, Zena Walker. Designed by Peter Rice. Stage business, maps, cues for effects. Production papers: cast, understudies, songs, properties, flys, etc.

53. John Houseman and Jack Landau
                Stratford, Connecticut   July 20, 1958
Festival Theatre, Production Department
[Three books. Mimeograph, 8½ x 11; one in stiff green paper, one in yellow cloth board ring binder, one in black board ring binder.]
Cast includes John Colicos, Nancy Wickwire, Inga Swenson. Designed by David Hays and Dorothy Jeakins. The first book, called "Original Blocking," has much stage business, maps. The second has stage business typed on facing pages, cues typed on text pages; production papers include 25 pages of ad libs for walk-ons, plots for machines and traps, flys, colonnades, scenery, wigs and beards, properties, sound. The third, called "Operating Script" has cues for effects.

54. [Houseman]
University of California, Los Angeles: Houseman Box 10
[Mimeograph, 8½ x 11; black cloth board ring binder.]
Rough production book. Cuts, some stage business, other working notes.

55. Douglas Campbell   Stratford, Ontario   July 21, 1958
Festival Theatre, Library
[Two books. Penguin edition pasted in workbooks, 7¾ x 13⅛; blue cloth boards bordered in red; title pasted on cover.]
Cast includes Christopher Plummer, Charmian King, Frances Hyland. Designed by Tanya Moiseiwitsch. The first book has copious stage business, maps on mimeographed groundplans, cues for effects. The second has calls.

56. Jack Landau   Stratford, Connecticut   April 25, 1960
Festival Theatre, Production Department
[Three books. Mimeograph, 8½ x 11; interleaves in first; one in black board ring binder, one in black leather ring book, one in blue cloth board ring binder.]
Cast includes Douglas Watson, Diana Douglas, Harriette Hartley. Designed by David Hays and Dorothy Jeakins. Revival of the 1958 production for the School Season, 1960, and for touring the

506 THE WINTER'S TALE

following winter. The first book has copious stage business penciled on interleaves, cues for effects; production papers include plots of scenery and machines and company lists. The second, called "Operating," for the tour, has cues for effects. The third, called "Operating," has copious stage business penciled on facing pages, cues for effects on text pages, and many production papers.

57. Peter Wood   Stratford-upon-Avon   August 30, 1960

Shakespeare Centre Library: O.S.71.21/1960W

[Cambridge Pocket Shakespeare pasted in a workbook, 8½ x 13; blue cloth board ring binder; title on spine label.]

Cast includes Eric Porter, Elizabeth Sellars, Susan Maryott. Designed by Jaques Noel. Very much stage business, cues for effects. Production papers: cast, 25 maps on mimeographed groundplans.

58. Other books of *The Winter's Tale:*

Boston Public Library: K.34.21, John Gilbert and Thomas Barry, cast for Philadelphia.

Folger: Wint T, 15, Thomas H. Lacy; Wint T, 18, 20, 21, 23, anonymous.

Mander and Mitchenson: J. G. Ward.

Museum of the City of New York: 32.485.442, J. H. Ring.

Addenda

JULIUS CAESAR

ad7. Anonymous   England   c.1815

Shakespeare Centre Library: 50.15(1812)

[Roach edition, c.1812, 3¾ x 6; two interleaves; marbled boards and half red leather gilt; title on spine.]

Promptbook. Cuts, some stage business, procession list, map for scene in Capitol, some cues for effects. Presented to the Birthplace Trust by J. O. Halliwell, 1864.

KING LEAR

ad18. Anonymous   England   1830's(?)

University of Illinois: x792.9/Sh15ki/no.5

[Kemble edition, 1815, 4¼ x 6⅞; red cloth boards; title gilt up spine.]

Crudely marked but much used promptbook, checked for Cornwall. Cuts, cues for effects. For the final scene "Cumberland's Edition is played instead of this"—i.e., the tragic ending. Partial manuscript cast includes Ryder as Burgundy, Barry as Albany, Bunn as Old Man.

THE MERCHANT OF VENICE

ad1. James Whitely   England   1750's(?)

Shakespeare Centre Library: 50.21(1701)

[Lintott edition of *The Jew of Venice*, 1701, 5½ x 7¾; blue cloth boards and half brown leather gilt; title gilt up spine.]

Used promptbook. Cuts, cues for effects. Manuscript cast list includes Mr. and Mrs. Whitely, Mr. and Mrs. Miller, Mr. and Mrs. Albany, etc. Presented to the Birthplace Trust by J. O. Halliwell, 1864.

ROMEO AND JULIET

ad11. Henry C. M. Dyer   England   1815

Shakespeare Centre Library: 50.29(1784)

[Lowndes edition (Garrick version), 1784, 4¼ x 7; 4 interleaves; marbled boards and half black leather gilt; title on red spine label.]

Much used promptbook. Cuts, calls, some stage business, cues for effects, funeral procession list. Dyer was a prompter. J. Booth's name appears at head of first scene. Wrongly noted on flyleaf as "D. Garrick's own copy."

Index

Abbey, E. (1852-1911), Am.-Eng. artist:
MV, 64

Abbott, Mrs., Am. actress, mid-19th c.:
TS, 12

Abingdon, William (1888-1959), Eng. actor:
HVIII, 63

Ackerman, P. Dodd, Am. designer, 20th c.:
MAC, 138; OTH, 106

Ackland, Joss, Eng. actor, 20th c.:
HV, 39; MWW, 88; TEM, 55

Adams, Edwin (1834-77), Am. actor:
HAM, 85; JC, 92; OTH, 54; RIII, 42, 54

Adams, John B., Am. actor at Boston Museum, mid-19th c.:
MA, 102; OTH, 119; R&J, 32; TG, 20

Adams, John Quincy (1767-1848), President of U.S.A.:
HAM, 26

Adams, Miriam (b. 1907), Eng. actress:
AYL, 92; MV, 119, 132; R&J, 89; TS, 61; TN, 74, 89

Adams, Miram (b. 1907), Eng. actress:
TEM, 46

Addams, A. A. (d. 1851), Am. actor:
HAM, 24

Addis, J. B., Am. prompter, mid-19th c.:
HAM, 24; MA, 10; TN, 13

Addison, Carlotta (1849-1912), Eng. actress:
R&J, 107

Adels, Marie, Am. actress, 20th c.:
TN, 89

Adolphus, John (1768-1845), Eng. writer:
KL, 4

Adrian, Christine, Eng. actress, 20th c.:
WT, 49

Adrian, Max (b. 1903), Eng. actor:
AYL, 109

Aicard, Jean (1848-1921), Fr. playwright:
OTH, 119

Aickin, Eleanor (1834-1914), actress:
R&J, 57

Aickin, J. (c.1739-1803), Eng. actor:
COR, 1

Albany, Mr. and Mrs., Eng. actors, 18th c.:
MV, ad1

Alexander, George (1858-1918), Eng. actor and manager:
AYL, 79

Alger, William R. (1822-1905), Am. writer:
KL, 72

Allen, Charles Leslie (1830-1917), Am. actor:
HAM, 179; MAC, 84

Allen, J. H., Eng. prompter with Irving at the Lyceum:
HAM, 90, 93

Allen, Mark:
MV, 11

Allen, Patrick, Eng. actor, 20th c.:
MV, 130

Allen, Viola (1869-1948), Am. actress:
AYL, 74, 85; CYM, 28-31; MAC, 84; TN, 54-57; WT, 32, 33

Allestree, Mary (d. 1912), Eng. actress:
HAM, 149

Alleyn, Miss, Eng. actress at Stratford in 1880's:
CYM, 21; LLL, 5; MM, 35

Alswang, Ralph (b. 1916), Am. designer:
KL, 110

Ambrose, John Thomas:
HAM, 179

Ames, Winthrop (1871-1937), Am. director:
A&C, 36, 37; AYL, 79-81; JC, 67-71; MV, 56, 101, 102, 117, 118; MWW, 65, 66; MA, 74-76; R&J, 64; TN, 71-73, 78; WT, 42-44

Anderson, J. L., Eng. prompter, early 19th c.:
JC, 7, 8

Neals:
AYL, 3
Needles, William, Can. actor, 20th
c.:
TS, 74
Negri, Richard, Eng. designer, 20th
c.:
AYL, 109
Neilson, Adelaide (1846-80), Eng. ac-
tress:
AYL, 72, 110; CYM, 20; MV, 132;
MA, 21; R&J, 22, 42, 43, 57; TS,
21; TN, 18, 26, 31
Neilson-Terry, Phyllis (b. 1892), Eng.
actress:
HVIII, 68; MAC, 141
Nesbitt, Cathleen (b. 1889), Eng. ac-
tress:
KL, 107
Ness, Annie:
KL, 28
Neu, Thea, Can. designer, 20th c.:
MND, 44
Neuffer, D.:
JC, 92
Neville, J.:
KJ, 65
Neville, John (b. 1925), Eng. actor:
AW, 15; AYL, 104; HIV2, 16; HV,
39; JC, 89; LLL, 13; MM, 34; RII,
43; T&C, 9
Newton, Miss:
CE, 28
Nicholls, Anthony, Eng. actor, 20th
c.:
COR, 36; MM, 33, 34; MV, 127
Nicholson, L. D.:
MV, 66
Nicolai, Otto (1810-49), Germ. com-
poser:
MWW, 89
Nimmo, A. W., Eng. prompter at
Edinburgh, early 19th c.:
HAM, 20; R&J, 16
Nisbett, Louisa (c.1812-58), Eng. ac-
tress:
AYL, 37; MA, 21
Noel, Jacques, Eng. designer, 20th
c.:
WT, 57

Noguchi, Isamu (b. 1904), Am. artist
and designer:
KL, 114
Norris, Herbert, Eng. designer, 20th
c.:
HV, 31, 32, 34; HVIII, 68, 69; RII,
40; RIII, 88
Northen, Michael, Eng. designer, 20th
c.:
HAM, 172; MAC, 146; MM, 25
Norton, John W., Am. actor, 19th c.:
MWW, 89; MA, 43, 102; OTH,
119
Novelli, Ermete (1851-1919), Ital. ac-
tor:
MV, 102; OTH, 119
Nye, Carrie, Can. actress, 20th c.:
T&C, 10

Ober, George A.:
HAM, 79
O'Brien, David (b. 1930), Eng. actor:
KL, 114; MND, 43; TEM, 50
O'Brien, John S., Am. actor, early
20th c.:
HAM, 154
O'Brien, Timothy, Eng. designer,
20th c.:
HIV1, 56
O'Day, Alice (d. 1937), Eng. actress:
COR, 29; R&J, 93
Oenslager, Donald (b. 1902), Am. de-
signer:
COR, 34
O'Hearn, Robert, Am. designer, 20th
c.:
AYL, 108; MAC, 149; T&C, 10
Olivier, Laurence (b. 1907), Eng. ac-
tor and director:
COR, 36; HV, 33; MAC, 147; TA,
1; TN, 96
O'Neill, Eliza (1792-1872), Eng. ac-
tress:
R&J, 23
O'Toole, Peter, Eng. actor, 20th c.:
MV, 130; TS, 79
Owen, W. F. (1844-1906), Eng. actor:
HIV1, 18, 42; MWW, 31, 32; TN,
38
Oxley, John H.:
HAM, 19

Trefusis, Irish actor, late 17th c.:
HAM, 1
Tudor, Valerie (b. 1910), Eng. actress:
HAM, 164; HV, 31; MWW, 79;
TG, 16; WT, 48
Turleigh, Veronica (b. 1903), Eng. actress:
LLL, 12
Tutin, Dorothy (b. 1930), Eng. actress:
HAM, 174; MV, 130; OTH, 118;
R&J, 102, 106; TN, 98, 99
Tyler, George (1867-1946), Am. producer:
MAC, 130, 133-136
Tyrrell, T. W.:
RIII, 92

Ure, Mary, Eng. actress, 20th c.:
OTH, 116

Valk, Frederick (d. 1956), Germ.-Eng. actor:
MV, 126
Valpy, Richard (1754-1836), Eng. schoolmaster:
MV, 83
Van Bridge, Tony, Can. actor, 20th c.:
MND, 47; MA, 99
Vance, C. W.:
RIII, 83
Vance, Dennis, Eng. director, 20th c.:
HIV1, 56
Vandenhoff, George (1813-85), Eng.-Am. actor and elocutionist:
HAM, 51
Vandenhoff, John (1790-1861), Eng. actor:
COR, 23; HAM, 37; MAC, 15
Vandenhoff, May (see Makeah, M. E. J. N.)
Van Fleet, Jo, Am. actress, 20th c.:
KL, 110
Van Griethuysen, Ted, Am. actor, 20th c.:
T&C, 10
Van Volkenburg, Ellen, Eng. director, 20th c.:
OTH, 104

Varna, H. W.:
TN, 48
Vercoe, Rosemary, Eng. designer, 20th c.:
MV, 131; TS, 71
Vestric, Elizabeth (1797-1856), Eng. actor and director:
CYM, 28
Vestris, Elizabeth (1797-1856), Eng. actress and manager:
LLL, 2; MWW, 13, 30, 31; MND, 10; TN, 10
Vezin, Hermann (1829-1910), Eng. actor:
AYL, 22; HAM, 30; JC, 15; KJ, 42; KL, 57, 78; MV, 18; MA, 18; OTH, 44; RIII, 47, 48; TS, 15
Vincent, Felix A.:
MAC, 150; MA, 102
Vincent, Leon John, Am. actor, 19th c.:
AYL, 110; HIV1, 57; HV, 27; JC, 38; OTH, 62
Vining, Fanny (see Davenport, Mrs. E. L.)
Vining, Frederick (1790-1871), Eng. actor:
MA, 12
Vining, George (1824-75), Eng. actor:
CE, 19
Vivian, Percival, Am. actor, 20th c.:
MV, 116
Voltz, Ed. Charles:
HAM, 98

Waas & Son:
MA, 80
Wagenhals, Lincoln (1869-1931), Am. manager:
WT, 31
Wainwright, Marie (1853-1923), Eng. actress:
TN, 38
Wainwright, W. L.:
HIV1, 5
Waldron, Mrs.:
KL, 73
Walker, Roben:
AYL, 3
Walker, Zena, Eng. actress, 20th c.: